Canada and the New World Economic Order:

Strategic Briefings for Canadian Enterprise

Second Edition

edited by

TOM WESSON
Schulich School of Business
York University

CAPTUS PRESS

Canada and the New World Economic Order:
Strategic Briefings for Canadian Enterprise, Second edition

Captus Press Inc.
York University Campus
4700 Keele Street
North York, Ontario
M3J 1P3 Canada

Phone: (416) 736–5537
Fax: (416) 736–5793
Email: Info@captus.com
Internet: http://www.captus.com

Canadian Cataloguing in Publication Data

Main entry under title:

Canada and the new world economic order: strategic briefings for Canadian enterprise

2nd ed.
Includes bibliographical references and index.
ISBN 1–55322–014–5

1. Industrial policy — Canada.   2. Canada — Foreign economic
relations.   3. Canada — Economic policy — 1991–   .*
4. Canada — Economic conditions — 1991–   .
I. Wesson, Thomas James.

HD3616.C33C33 2001   338.971   C00-933278-2

Canadä *We acknowledge the financial support of the Government of Canada through the Book Publishing Industry Development Program (BPIDP) for our publishing activities.*

0 9 8 7 6 5 4 3 2 1
Printed and bound in Canada

Table of Contents

Acknowledgements   v

Introduction   vii

SECTION 1 — ASSESSING CANADA'S ECONOMIC PERFORMANCE

Canada's Global Competitiveness
David Barrows and John A. Cotsomitis   3

Canada's Economy: Structure and Performance
Donald J.S. Brean   34

The Sectoral Structure of Canada's Economy
Tom Wesson   58

SME Entrepreneurship: A Comparative View
James H. Tiessen   81

SECTION 2 — CANADA IN A CHANGING WORLD

The New World Order: In a New Millennium
Ed Hooven   101

International Trade and Investments
David Barrows and John A. Cotsomitis   144

Globalization and Canadian Economic and Industrial
Strategy in the Twenty-First Century
James M. Gillies   178

iii

SECTION 3 — GOVERNMENT, SOCIETY AND ECONOMIC PERFORMANCE

The Changing Role of the Public Sector
David Barrows and Tom Wesson 205

The Socio-Political Environment: The Quest for Accommodation
John Saywell 229

The Effects of Changing Demographics: Marketing and Human Resource Trends
David K. Foot 259

SECTION 4 — THE INPUTS OF ECONOMIC ACTIVITY

Now More Than Ever: Why Unions Still Matter in the Twenty-First Century
Gil McGowan 281

An Overview of the Financial Services Industry
Peter A.T. Campbell and Tom Wesson 308

Reforming Canada's Financial Services Sector
Wendy Dobson 322

Technology and the New Economy: A Canadian Strategy
Charles J. McMillan and Eduardo M.V. Jasson 357

SECTION 5 — POTENTIAL RESPONSES TO A CHANGING WORLD

Global Showdown: The Future of Democracy in the Era of Economic Globalization
Maude Barlow 389

Canada's Prospects
John H.G. Crispo. 403

The Quagmire of Industrial Policy
H.T. Wilson. 413

Index **421**

About the Contributors **427**

Acknowledgements

Obviously, a book like this one is the result of the efforts of many people. I would like to thank the authors of the various articles for their hard work and patience in bringing out this edition. I would also like to thank my assistant at York, JoAnne Stein, for her help in completing the book.

Randy Hoffman and Pauline Lai of Captus Press have once again guided me through the process of putting the book together with the utmost patience. Pauline has been particularly cheerful and understanding throughout the numerous delays and setbacks involved in a work like this one.

This book would not exist without the work of Jerry Dermer, the editor of the Strategic Briefings series that preceded this volume. I hope this publication still reflects Jerry's basic vision for the project, and works towards his desire to create a generation of Canadian managers with a better understanding of the environment in which they operate than has historically been the case.

The book has also benefited greatly from the input of those who use the book teaching, especially those teaching MGMT 5250 and MGMT 1010 at the Schulich School of Business at York University. In particular, I would like to thank Dave Barrows for his indispensable help and advice.

Finally, I would like to thank my wife, Brenda, and my children, Amy and Andrew, for putting up with me when working on this book made me hard to put up with, and for helping me forget about the book when I needed to forget about it.

v

Introduction

A lot has changed in Canada and in the Canadian economy since the Strategic Briefings series that preceded this volume was first published in 1991. We have been through one of the deepest recessions since the end of World War II, and into a period of sustained economic growth the likes of which we have not seen in many years. Even our federal fiscal deficit is under control, and we are making some progress in paying down our debt. Most of the provinces have made as good, if not better, progress than the federal government in getting their fiscal houses in order.

Many of the topics covered in this book have moved from the headlines to the back burner as our economic performance has improved. We no longer are inundated with discussions of issues like Canada's competitiveness, our trade balance or the value of our dollar. There are no longer fears that the IMF may have to step in to save us. The 1994 *Wall Street Journal* editorial which compared us to a Third World nation now seems like ancient history.[1]

To some observers it may seem, therefore, that the urgency associated with the topics and issues that are examined in this book has lessened over the past few years. As a nation, we seem to have much less cause for the introspection and self-doubt that plagued us through the last recession. Thus, in some ways, the need for this book, which seemed so critical 10 years ago, may, at first, seem less pressing today.

However, while in the terms described above the crisis in our economy has passed, today, more than ever, it is essential for Canadian managers, and those outside of Canada who have substantial dealings with our country, to understand Canada and its economy in the context of the global political economy. The reasons such an understanding is now more important than ever have much more to do with long-term trends than with any cyclical fluctuations. Thus, our entry into an extended period of economic growth has given us room to breathe: Not licence to fall into complacency. Instead, it can be argued that a time of respite from financial pressures is the ideal time to deal proactively with endemic problems, re-examine Canada's place in the world and move to restructure domestic arrangements and international relationships. These activities first require well-informed decision makers.

Why must Canadian managers become more aware of Canada's place, and their firms' place, in the world economy? For Canadians, as for most of the rest of the world, there is the well-known litany of reasons. These include: exports making up an ever-increasing part of our GNP; a world economy which is becoming more integrated, with trade growth far exceeding economic growth; new competitors producing the same products we do, often more cheaply and with higher quality; and capital markets which are truly global, requiring Canadian firms to provide real returns comparable with those available in the world's strongest economies in order to attract the capital they need. We know these facts so well, they are becoming truisms. Nonetheless, they are all valid reasons Canadian managers must better understand both the world economy and Canada's place in it in the years to come. However, in Canada's case, there are additional reasons why the topics we deal with in this book are particularly important. Many of these reasons are unique to Canada.

First, Canadian managers must become more global in their outlook and understanding in order to reverse the effects of historic weaknesses in our management development. For many generations, few Canadian managers actively considered markets beyond Canada; or, possibly, Canada and the United States. For a number of reasons relating to the development of the Canadian economy, some dating back to our earliest days as colonies of the European powers, Canadian business has been narrowly focused in terms of the markets served and the products produced. Several articles in this book explore this theme in great detail.

Canadian managers, and Canadians in general, are often, sadly, unaware of our own place in the world. We are not just quieter versions of our American cousins. We have been shaped by a unique physical environment and a unique history. With these influences we have developed a unique social system, a unique labour relations system, a uniquely structured corporate sector, a unique financial system and a unique and independent set of relationships with the rest of the world. This book examines all of these aspects of Canada from a managerial perspective. We attempt to place the Canadian political economy of today in context both with respect to the rest of the world and with respect to our own history.

Canada is also different than many other nations in that we seem to have a fairly strong internal consensus that the role of business in our society goes beyond merely being guided through a series of transactions by the invisible hand of the marketplace. In a great number of ways, ranging from antitrust policy to science policy to regional development policies, governments in Canada act to redirect market forces to achieve societal goals. Canadians do not place their complete faith in the ability of market forces to optimally allocate resources in our society. Given this fact, it is essential that Canadian managers understand the other factors — social, political, cultural and so on — that are influencing their activities. This volume attempts to put Canadian business fully into its societal context, addressing the various influences on Canadian business.

Finally, Canadian business has a role to play in Canada's ongoing struggle to complete the task of nation building begun at Charlottetown in 1864. One of the suggested responses to the threat of Quebec separatism has been to outline for Québécois the benefits of remaining Canadian. While these benefits involve all aspects of modern life, a number of them are economic — from membership in such international organizations as the G7 and NAFTA, to the ability to trade on Canada's positive reputation in the rest of the world, to the benefits Quebec receives under our system of so-called "fiscal federalism." If Canadian managers are to play a positive role in either the sovereignty debate in Quebec or some future initiatives to renew our federal system, they will need to understand both what it means to be a Canadian firm in the international economy and what Canada's federal system does to support businesses domestically.

The Structure and Goals of the Book

This book is divided into five sections. Within each section the articles address related, but distinct, issues. The first section describes several aspects of Canada's economy and assesses its performance. In a sense, the articles in this section provide the foundation for much of the discussion that follows. They describe the economic problems which confront Canada, and begin to examine the causes for these problems. The later sections examine the causes of Canada's problems in greater detail, and move increasingly into suggesting solutions for at least some of these problems.

The second section of the book places Canada and its economy in the context of the so-called "New World Order" which has evolved since the end of World War II. The next section of the book looks at some of what could be called the "softer" aspects of Canadian society from a managerial perspective. Topics covered include Canadian social values and Canadian culture, and the changing role of government in our society. The penultimate section of the book looks at the Canadian markets for what can be thought of as the three inputs of a modern economy — labour, capital and technology. Finally, the book concludes with three very different views of what Canada should do in response to the changes that are taking place in our society and our environment. A brief introduction before each section describes the articles included in more detail.

The principal goal of this volume of readings is to inform Canadian managers about the context in which they work. Our goal is not just to describe this context, but also to communicate some appreciation for its complexities and for the interrelationships among the various elements of the Canadian business environment. Only by understanding these interrelationships can a manager begin to anticipate changes in his or her environment and play a positive role in assisting policy makers as they shape the economic environment faced by Canadian business.

Although the primary goal of the book is to be descriptive rather than prescriptive, many, if not all, of the authors include either implicit or explicit policy recommendations for Canadian governments stemming from their analysis of a particular aspect of our political economy. The prescriptive content of the articles tends to increase as one moves through the book. The final section is almost entirely prescriptive. There is a natural progression from the first section of the book, which describes our economic problems, to the final one, which presents three different recommended paths for us to follow in order to reduce our problems.

Finally, the reader should note that this book is intended to be the beginning of the reader's exploration of the issues discussed, not the end. To this end, the authors of the individual articles in this book come from both ends of the political spectrum and from various disciplines (including economics, sociology, law and history), and from the various sectors of our society (business, government, academia and special interest groups). We do not intend that the reader should take any of the authors' views of the issues as the definitive view. A reader who approached the book this way would soon become confused and frustrated. However, we hope that by presenting various viewpoints we are able to assist our readers to develop a sense of the factors which have shaped these diverse positions. Understanding what underlies the differences among various author's viewpoints is as important as understanding the differences themselves. We hope that this book continues the Canadian tradition of celebrating diversity.

It is not the intention of this book to answer all of the reader's questions. Rather, the book is intended to provoke as many questions as it answers, and to stimulate critical thinking on the part of our readers. We hope that after reading this book our readers will be able to ask more informed and insightful questions than they could before reading it. If we succeed in this, we will have helped our readers to become both better managers and better citizens.

NOTE

1. Michael R. Sesit and Suzanne McGee, "Long-suffering Canadian dollar slips to 8 ½-year low," Wall Street Journal (Eastern Edition), January 11, 1995, p. C1.

Assessing Canada's Economic Performance

The purpose of this section of the book is to provide the reader with a foundation for the later discussions. Before we discuss the context in which Canadian business operates and develop recommendations for Canadian businesses and governments to improve that context where possible and adjust to it where necessary, we must have some base line understanding of how Canadian firms and the Canadian economy as a whole are doing. This section provides that understanding, while also beginning to describe the structural context of Canadian business.

The first article in this section, "Canada's Global Competitiveness," by David Barrows and John Cotsomitis, asks two fundamental questions relating to one of the great buzzwords of the last decade — competitiveness. Most fundamentally, Barrows and Cotsomitis ask, "Just what do we mean by 'competitiveness,' and why does it matter?" They discuss the strengths of several definitions of competitiveness. They also discuss why we should care about Canada's competitiveness. In the course of their discussions they address the second major question: "How competitive is Canada?" These discussions move us a long way towards identifying the problems with Canada's economic performance at both the firm and national levels. Much of the rest of the book is aimed at identifying the causes of, and potential solutions to, these problems.

The second article in this section, "Canada's Economy: Structure and Performance" by Don Brean, describes Canada's economy in terms of numbers while providing the reader with a short primer in macroeconomic theory. The article covers complex issues in a way that is easily accessible and intuitive. Again, this article is part of the foundation for the rest of the book. It identifies the major macroeconomic issues facing Canada today and relates them to each other through the fundamentals of macroeconomics. A theme this discussion highlights, and which will come up again and again in the book, is that most economic policy decisions involve making trade-offs — there are no easy solutions to our problems.

The third article in this section, Tom Wesson's look at "The Sectoral Structure of Canada's Economy," describes Canada's changing economy, developing several themes. First, Canada's economy is increasingly service based. Second, a significant proportion of Canadian firms are controlled by foreigners. Third, economic power and wealth in Canada are highly concentrated in the hands of a relatively small number of individuals and corporations. Finally, governments in Canada play a very active role in the economy as both controlling and non-controlling owners of firms, although this role is diminishing. The article explores the causes and consequences of these trends and what, if anything, can or should be done to reverse them.

The final article in the section, "SME Entrepreneurship: A Comparative View" by Jim Tiessen, looks in more detail at one sector of the economy which is generally agreed to be increasing in importance — the entrepreneurial sector. The article looks at the size and performance of Canada's entrepreneurial sector, both in isolation and in comparison to other nations. In doing so, the chapter highlights some particular challenges facing Canadian entrepreneurs.

Canada's Global Competitiveness

David Barrows and John A. Cotsomitis

C anada's economic system is a market economy, encompassing the production, sales and distribution of goods and services based upon prices set in the marketplace. The marketplace establishes an economic framework within which firms compete on the basis of a number of factors: price, quality, delivery, after-sales service etc. Competitiveness is a measure of the ability to succeed in this context. This article presents several different approaches to measuring competitiveness, and analyzes many of the factors influencing its enhancement.

THE CONCEPT OF COMPETITIVENESS

The World Competitiveness Report, prepared by the Geneva-based World Economic Forum and the International Management Development Institute in Lausanne, defines competitiveness as "...the ability to design, produce and market goods and services, the price and non-price characteristics of which form a more attractive package than those of competitors."[1]

Global Competitiveness

Until relatively recently competitiveness could be viewed primarily from a domestic perspective, since the majority of firms competed only in a domestic marketplace. Manufactured goods tended to be large and bulky, making it difficult to conduct significant international trade. Of course, considerable international commerce did take place, but it was primarily in commodities — agricultural products and natural resources.

This is no longer the case. The nature of production and distribution in the world economy has changed dramatically in the past 50 years or so. The advent of technologies (such as microelectronics) and the introduction of new materials (such as plastics) resulted in the miniaturization of many goods, leading to the development of manufactured products that are much more easily transported. It is now possible — and indeed, common — to ship significant quantities of automobiles from Japan to North America, an undertaking that would have been unthinkable even 30 years ago. With technological break-throughs in communications and transportation, there has also been a signifi-cant increase in the exchange of tradeable services in a wide variety of fields, including construction, engineering, architecture, legal and accounting services and tourism.

As a result of the significant increase in international trade of manufac-tured goods and services, many economists and business strategists have con-cluded that competitiveness must now be defined in a broader, international, context. Competitors are no longer within the same community or nation state. Firms must think of competition as truly global in terms of both gaining export markets and defending against competitors in domestic markets.

Goals of Competitiveness

From a broader societal perspective, it is not useful to view global compet-itiveness as an end in itself. Rather, an internationally competitive economy is a means to an end — the requirement for enhanced social well-being. Wealth cre-ation is necessary in order to fund social services and produce a high and rising standard of living. It also appears to be a necessity for society to ultimately achieve its higher-order goals, including personal freedom, security and a better quality of life. Therefore, competitiveness must be viewed in a broader societal context that goes beyond materialism.

Competitiveness Through Productivity Enhancement

Some definitions of competitiveness are based upon driving down costs to the lowest common denominator by hollowing out corporations, outsourcing jobs, shifting operations to lower-cost locales and reducing the wages, benefits and social entitlements of workers. A more appropriate definition of competi-tiveness, however, involves increased productive capacity achieved by innovation, superior technology, continuous skill-enhancing training and a concern with social equity and environmental preservation. The latter approach can better lead to the creation of a value-increasing society.

THE KRUGMAN CRITIQUE

In a widely quoted article in *Foreign Affairs*, the prominent economist Paul Krugman argued that competitiveness is, at best, an essentially meaningless con-cept when applied to countries. At worst, it can lead to incorrect policy formu-lations such as protectionism. Krugman argued that unlike companies, countries do not face any bottom line. They do not compete with each other in any meaningful economic sense. Moreover, international trade is not a zero-sum game. All parties benefit from trade by specializing in those productive activi-ties where they are most efficient. If competitiveness does have any meaning whatsoever, "it is as a poetic way of saying productivity."[2]

Krugman does raise valid concerns. Yet, despite its actual and potential negatives, it would appear that the concept of competitiveness retains its validity when applied to national economies. As a recent article in *The Economist* notes, nations do compete, in that they choose policies to promote higher living standards. In addition, loss of competitiveness might, in the long run, restrict a nation's economic potential and render it vulnerable to the actions of other political regimes and international consortiums.

ECONOMIC GROWTH AND COMPETITIVENESS

The issue of economic growth is closely linked to the notion of competitiveness. Nearly all the present day literature on the subject emphasizes the importance of savings and investment, cost of capital and technological learning, factors which also play prominent roles in economic growth theory. Moreover, the renewed interest of the economics profession in long run income growth coincides with a growing concern among many economists, management academics and politicians about the competitiveness of the western industrialized economies. Both interests have a common origin — the well documented slowdown in economic progress in North America, Europe and Japan over the past few decades.

It is difficult to overstate the importance of economic growth. The wealth of the world's nations is largely linked to the long run growth rates of their respective economies. Understanding the various factors that promote, or conversely hinder, economic growth remains a key task of economics.

The vast literature on economic growth theory falls into three broad categories. The early post-World War II growth models, primarily associated with the work of Evsey Domar and Roy Harrod, emphasize the importance of savings and capital investment in stimulating economic growth. The basic assumption underlying these models is that an economy's output depends upon the underlying amount of capital investment, and that it is the savings of people and firms that make such investment feasible. An economy's output is linked to its stock of capital by a capital-output ratio which is constant.

This emphasis on savings and capital investment as the foundations of economic growth has a long tradition in economic theory. As a recent article in the *Journal of Economic Literature* points out, much of Adam Smith's famous treatise, *The Wealth of Nations*, is devoted to analyzing the forces that determine the rate of capital accumulation and to extolling practices that tend to increase it, mainly the frugality of the emerging bourgeoisie of the time.

The early growth models of Harrod and Domar tend to subsume other determinants of growth under the capital-output ratio, which, in turn, obscures differences in growth rates between countries. In response to these limitations, Robert Solow and Trevor Swan developed what has come to be known as the neoclassical model of economic growth. In this model, output grows in response to increases in inputs of capital and labour as well as the efficiency with which these inputs are used. The model assumes a perfectly competitive economy that obeys the law of diminishing marginal returns. Each addition of a unit of capital, given a fixed supply of labour, will generate a smaller yield than the one before it.

As a special report of *The Economist* notes, these assumptions give the neoclassical model two important attributes. As the stock of capital in an economy increases, growth will slow down and eventually come to a halt. Without continuous technological progress, the diminishing marginal productivity of capital will ultimately choke off economic growth. Second, poorer nations should grow more rapidly than advanced countries. Starting from a smaller capital base, they should garner higher yields from each new unit of investment.

While the neoclassical model of growth emphasizes the importance of technological progress to economic growth, it does not attempt to explain it. Rather, it treats technology as an exogenous variable, one which arises from outside the model. However, such an assumption is difficult to maintain. Technological knowledge accumulates for the same reason that capital stock does, because economic agents decide to invest resources in activities that are intended to make it grow.

In the mid-1980s, economists such as Robert Lucas and Paul Romer formulated a new model of economic growth which endogenizes technological progress (i.e., puts it explicitly in the model). New growth theory, as it is commonly referred to, emphasizes the importance of human capital, learning by doing and technological spillover effects in generating economic growth. As well, new growth theory postulates increasing returns to knowledge-based investment. That is, each additional dollar of capital invested in knowledge creation yields more than a previous dollar invested. Increasing returns can provide accelerated growth rates over the long term.

CANADA'S GLOBAL POSITION

Because international competitiveness is such an important condition for social and economic well-being, it is important to understand how the Canadian economy has performed relative to other countries.

Canada has been described as one of the best places in the world to live. Again in 2000, for the seventh consecutive year, in the United Nations' annual profile of human development, Canada attained the highest ranking in the world.

The United Nations index takes into account such factors as education, health care, life expectancy and infant mortality rates. Canada scored particularly well in the fields of education spending and low infant mortality rates. Yet many Canadians feel that our economy is "not competitive." In order to explore this paradox, we must look at how competitiveness is measured at a national level.

ASSESSING COMPETITIVENESS

In a world of rapid global change, any country can lose its position relatively quickly, with significant consequences for its economic well-being and subsequent societal development. There is no guarantee that any country's competitive position can be sustained and enhanced in the future. Therefore, it is important to examine the trends in a country's global competitiveness as well as its current position. Three different approaches to measuring competitiveness are presented: a factor model, which identifies critical success areas and compares the performance of different economies in each area; an assessment of trade performance, based on indicators of outputs and efforts at improving inputs; and an assessment of productivity using cost-based indicators. The three methods are not mutually exclusive; they present three different (but complementary) perspectives on the same phenomenon — Canada's global competitiveness.

FACTOR MODELS

The annual *World Competitiveness Report* is an example of a multiple-factor model, and is used to assess the global competitiveness of the countries of the Organization for Economic Cooperation and Development (OECD). Its eight factors are designed to integrate quantitative and qualitative data to develop a composite assessment of a country's competitive position. The total of a country's scores on each of these factors make up its ranking.

The *World Competitiveness Report* used to be published jointly by the World Economic Forum and the International Institute for Management Development (IMD), both of which are based in Switzerland. Partly as a result of differences over how to revise the competitiveness index of countries, the organizations have gone their separate ways and the IMD now publishes its own competitiveness report.

Figure 1 provides the IMD World Competitiveness Scoreboard as of April 2000. At that time, Canada ranked eleventh of the countries analyzed. If Singapore, Luxembourg and Iceland are excluded from the ranking, because of their status as small economies with narrow economic bases, then Canada ranks seventh in the world. Canada's ranking has been as follows:

Rank	Year
17	1993
20	1994
13	1995
12	1996
10	1997
10	1998
10	1999
11	2000

Figure 2 indicates the eight factors employed in the IMD analysis.

An analysis of each of these factors indicates that Canada has a number of strengths and weaknesses. In 2000, Canada achieved a relatively high ranking in the areas of infrastructure, people and management, while exhibiting weaknesses in the areas of internationalization, and science and technology.

Domestic Economic Strength

To capture domestic economic strength, the statistical analysis reviews countries' national income accounts and assesses growth in macroeconomic data

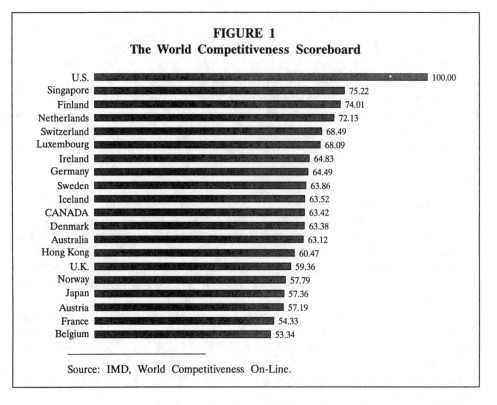

FIGURE 1
The World Competitiveness Scoreboard

U.S.	100.00
Singapore	75.22
Finland	74.01
Netherlands	72.13
Switzerland	68.49
Luxembourg	68.09
Ireland	64.83
Germany	64.49
Sweden	63.86
Iceland	63.52
CANADA	63.42
Denmark	63.38
Australia	63.12
Hong Kong	60.47
U.K.	59.36
Norway	57.79
Japan	57.36
Austria	57.19
France	54.33
Belgium	53.34

Source: IMD, World Competitiveness On-Line.

FIGURE 2
Factors of Competitiveness — Canada

	Ranking						
	1993	*1994*	*1995*	*1996*	*1997*	*1998*	*1999*
Domestic Economy	29	32	27	26	21	12	12
Internationalization	26	23	21	17	19	22	24
Government	28	29	23	10	9	7	12
Finance	11	13	13	13	10	12	11
Infrastructure	4	4	4	4	6	6	8
Management	24	26	20	16	10	11	8
Science & Technology	18	17	17	10	9	12	13
People	12	17	9	6	2	6	7

Source: IMD, Lausanne.

such as GDP. As well, it includes a review of performance in sectors such as manufacturing and services.

In the early to mid-1990s the Canadian economy performed significantly below its economic potential. High real rates of interest and relatively slow economic growth resulted in a Canadian unemployment rate which is almost double that of the United States. In the last three years the Canadian economy has rebounded and performed very well.

Internationalization

Internationalization attempts to measure the degree to which a country participates in international trade and investment. Quantitative data include indicators of the country's global share of goods and services markets, technology transfers and foreign direct investment (FDI).

Canada performs relatively poorly (24th) with respect to the internationalization rankings. One might find this surprising, given the fact that a large proportion of Canada's GNP is based upon international trade. However, a more detailed analysis of Canada's economic trading patterns indicates that a significant proportion of exports are "tied" or "managed" trade. That is, the trade occurs on an intracorporate basis rather than at "arm's length." A good example of this is production of automobiles in Canada for subsequent sale in the United States. That a great many automobiles move from Canada to the United States is reflected in Canada's export statistics. However, these are not really exports, but the movement of a final product as part of an integrated North American production system. There is no transaction involved in the sense of one company marketing a product to another firm or final consumer.

Similarly, much of Canada's export of natural-resource products occurs with little international marketing. Natural-resource products tend to be highly standardized commodities and are traded internationally on the basis of price. This requires relatively little international marketing expertise. As well, many of the normal international trade functions, such as after-market servicing, are not applicable to natural-resource products.

Government

Government actions are an important factor in determining a nation's international competitive position. The extent to which government policies are conducive to international competitiveness can have a great impact on a country's position, as can measures that affect the domestic competitive market, such as competition policy.

The IMD ranking of the government criterion for Canada indicates significant improvement over the period 1993 to 2000 (28th to 12th position). Much of this improvement is due to governments' (federal and provincial) ability to eliminate their annual budget deficits. As well, the socio-political instability with respect to Quebec sovereignty has receded as an issue, at least outside of Canada.

Canadian governments have also instituted policy and program reforms which are designed to lead to more adaptive and flexible labour and capital markets.

Finance

The performance of the financial markets is important insofar as they reflect the availability of capital and the diversity of capital markets. Canada continues to rank reasonably well on this measure: eleventh in 2000. Nonetheless, the Canadian banking system has exhibited a conservatism in terms of making funds available to small- and medium-size businesses.

Infrastructure

In the 2000 ratings Canada ranked eighth with respect to infrastructure. Infrastructure includes the telecommunication, natural resource and energy sectors and the ability of these sectors to provide a basis for economic growth and development. As well, Canada's natural-resource base has been a historic strength.

Canada has invested heavily in telecommunication and transportation networks and facilities, and as a result has been able to maintain relative cost competitiveness notwithstanding the extreme distances involved in the Canadian market and the harsh physical climate.

Management

The management factor attempts to evaluate a nation's entrepreneurial drive, customer orientation, product-service capability and business efficiency. Canada's rating in this category has shown significant improvement.

Canadian economic policy has historically been predicated on protecting the domestic market for manufactured and some agricultural products (for example, eggs and milk) and on opening markets for resource exports. It also relied upon high tariff barriers to prevent imports of finished manufactured products. This resulted in the development of a number of small, inefficient manufacturing facilities that were able to prosper in the domestic Canadian marketplace only as long as they had tariff protection from international competition.

In the wake of successive rounds of tariff reductions predicated by the General Agreement on Tariffs and Trade (GATT), the Canada–U.S. Free Trade Agreement (FTA) and the North American Free Trade Agreement (NAFTA), the Canadian marketplace has been subjected to greater international competition.

The improvement in Canada's ranking suggests that the recent restructuring of the economy may have contributed to enhanced managerial capability.

Science and Technology

This factor attempts to capture a nation's commitment to R&D activities, the creation of intellectual capital and the degree to which business and government cooperate in innovative activities. Canada has ranked poorly on this variable.

Canadian industry has historically relied upon a domestically protected market, the transfer of technology from abroad and abundant natural resources. For these reasons there has been relatively little emphasis placed on R&D and innovation.

However, in a changing world environment where comparative advantage can be created, it is critical that developed nations invest heavily in R&D and innovation. Canadian industry now appears to be undertaking these key investments.

People

The human-resource factor captures the educational, attitudinal and employment characteristics of a country's population.

Canada has made significant efforts at enhancing the quality of life of its population, through social-services spending and providing access to educational opportunities. Notwithstanding Canada's commitment to people-oriented activity, there are concerns that the money expended in this area does not result in maximum benefit. Canada continues to have a high rate of adult illiteracy. In the province of Ontario the dropout rate in the public secondary school system has averaged 30 per cent. Past competitiveness reports noted that the Canadian labour force appears to have reacted slowly to changing labour markets.

TRADE PERFORMANCE

Competitiveness in the Traded Sectors

In order to understand industrial competitiveness in a global economy, it is necessary to distinguish between traded and non-traded goods and services. For an entire economy to be successful, both the traded and non-traded sectors must be productive. However, productivity is most needed in traded goods and services — those products that enter the international marketplace either as exports or as import competition in the domestic market.

Figure 3 provides a framework for analyzing the traded-goods sector. This framework classifies traded manufacturing industries into the following three categories:

➤ resource-based businesses
➤ low-wage businesses
➤ high-wage businesses

Figure 3 also lists some means for acquiring competitive advantage, pointing out that each of these types of traded businesses competes on a different basis in the international marketplace. For all of these categories it is important that the costs of production, distribution, sales and service be competitive. For some high-wage businesses, such as high-technology enterprises and emerging industries, it is also possible to compete on a premium-price basis. A premium price must be justified by unique product characteristics such as product quality, distinction in service or brand name.

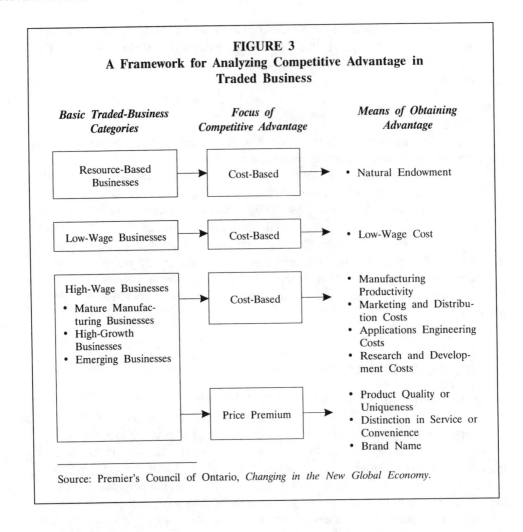

FIGURE 3
A Framework for Analyzing Competitive Advantage in Traded Business

Basic Traded-Business Categories	Focus of Competitive Advantage	Means of Obtaining Advantage
Resource-Based Businesses	Cost-Based	• Natural Endowment
Low-Wage Businesses	Cost-Based	• Low-Wage Cost
High-Wage Businesses • Mature Manufacturing Businesses • High-Growth Businesses • Emerging Businesses	Cost-Based	• Manufacturing Productivity • Marketing and Distribution Costs • Applications Engineering Costs • Research and Development Costs
	Price Premium	• Product Quality or Uniqueness • Distinction in Service or Convenience • Brand Name

Source: Premier's Council of Ontario, *Changing in the New Global Economy.*

Trade Indicators

International trade is critical to Canada's economic well-being. In 1998 exports accounted for 42.0 per cent of the Canadian GDP; this figure was only 11 per cent for Japan and 12 per cent for the United States.

Resource-Based Trade

The Canadian economy could experience difficulty in generating sufficient wealth to sustain Canadian society if it continues its heavy reliance on the export of unprocessed and semi-processed raw materials. As Figure 4 shows, in 1995 over 30 per cent of Canada's exports were unprocessed and semi-processed resource-based exports. For the United States in the same year the proportion was less than 20 per cent; for Germany it was less than 10 per cent; for Japan, less than 2 per cent.

Dependence on the export of resource-based products should not, in itself, be a cause for concern as long as the value for these products on world

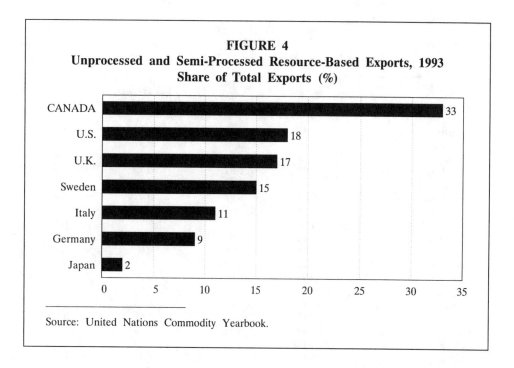

FIGURE 4
Unprocessed and Semi-Processed Resource-Based Exports, 1993
Share of Total Exports (%)

Source: United Nations Commodity Yearbook.

markets continues to rise. However, the commodity price index for Canadian products has shown a significant downward trend from its peak in 1973–74.

High-Technology Trade

Figure 5 indicates Canada's export/import ratio in high-technology products (such as aerospace, computers, electronic equipment, telecommunications, scientific instruments, machinery and chemical products) in comparison to other jurisdictions. The German and Japanese economies have attained a relatively high ratio of exports to imports of high-technology products. Canada lags behind most of the other developed nations in this area.

Part of the explanation for Canada's lack of export orientation in the high-technology sectors may have been the previously high tariff rates in Canada for imported products. For many years Canada had tariffs that were among the highest in the industrialized world. This, in combination with the branch-plant orientation of the Canadian economy, suggests that Canadian manufacturers have been more interested in serving the relatively highly protected domestic market than in aggressively pursuing export markets.

Geographical Distribution of Trade

An assessment of Canada's export activities indicates that the majority of products are sold in the U.S. market, and this proportion has been increasing. In 1960 approximately 56 per cent of total Canadian exports were sold to the United States; by 1999 this proportion had increased to 86 per cent.

ЪЪ

FIGURE 5
Export/Import Ratios by Industries in 1997

Industry	Aerospace	Electronic	Office Machinery and Computer	Drug
Australia	0.43	0.20	0.27	0.45
Austria	0.63	0.79	0.35	0.81
Belgium	0.72	0.93	0.71	1.40
CANADA	0.93	0.55	0.43	0.39
Czech Republic	1.79	0.32	0.24	0.28
Denmark	0.67	0.87	0.43	2.78
Finland	0.21	1.97	0.75	0.30
France	1.84	1.05	0.75	1.37
Germany	1.20	1.09	0.59	1.59
Greece	0.15	0.18	0.08	0.08
Hungary	0.77	0.77	1.35	0.80
Iceland	2.36	0.01	0.27	0.13
Ireland	0.71	2.00	1.66	3.23
Italy	1.15	0.61	0.56	0.97
Japan	0.41	2.45	1.69	0.48
Korea	0.43	1.58	1.74	0.38
Mexico	1.18	1.03	2.19	0.61
Netherlands	0.65	1.14	0.91	1.07
New Zealand	0.08	0.16	0.07	0.14
Norway	0.41	0.46	0.26	0.21
Poland	0.30	0.39	0.04	0.22
Portugal	0.40	0.61	0.13	0.24
Spain	0.74	0.55	0.39	0.56
Sweden	1.43	1.94	0.30	2.54
Switzerland	0.41	0.51	0.33	2.28
Turkey	0.15	0.23	0.03	0.13
U.K.	1.28	0.93	0.96	1.79
U.S.	2.74	0.80	0.60	0.94
Total OECD	1.42	1.06	0.79	1.14
North America	2.87	0.71	0.54	0.78
EU	1.25	0.98	0.39	2.16
Nordic countries	0.88	1.60	0.31	1.92

Source: OECD, Bilateral Trade database.

As was discussed earlier, a significant proportion of trade between Canada and the United States is "tied" trade — transactions that appear as exports in the trade statistics but are in reality intracorporate exchanges. In firms undertaking managed trade, the location of important functions such as technology development and implementation is determined mostly by strategic decisions made at foreign corporate head offices.

Recently, there has been significant growth in worldwide trade in services. This has led to the development of strategic alliances to build networks of

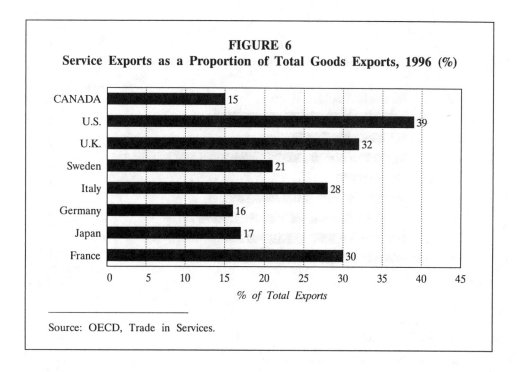

FIGURE 6
Service Exports as a Proportion of Total Goods Exports, 1996 (%)

% of Total Exports

Source: OECD, Trade in Services.

professional capability: for example, international business-network relationships now exist in management-consulting and accounting services.

An examination of Canada's export activities in the service sector suggests a relatively weak competitive position. Figure 6 indicates that service exports amounted to only 15 per cent of total goods exports from Canada in 1996, whereas they account for 39 per cent in the United States and over 32 per cent in the United Kingdom.

Canada is thus exposed to two forms of risk in its international trade. Exports are primarily focused on a single market — the United States — and on a relatively narrow range of products. Therefore, it is important that Canada remain cost competitive in the U.S. market.

Research and Development Indicators

In classical economic theory, trade advantages are assumed to be relatively fixed over time and dependent on stable comparative advantages. However, the performance of economies such as Japan's has persuaded some observers that international trade competitiveness can also be created by investing in what can be broadly defined as innovation. One major component of innovation is industrial R&D.

Canada invests a significantly lower proportion of domestic expenditures in R&D activities than most of its major competitors. Figure 7 indicates that Canadian gross domestic expenditures on R&D activities were approximately half of those in Sweden, the United States, Japan, Switzerland or Germany.

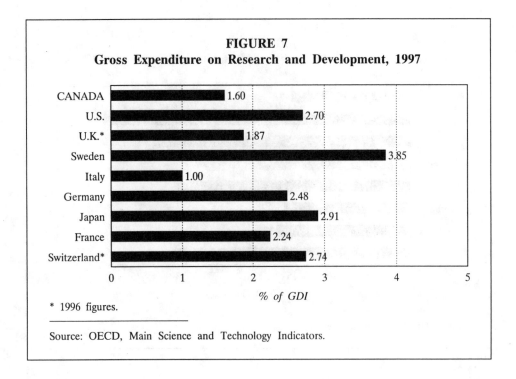

FIGURE 7
Gross Expenditure on Research and Development, 1997

Country	% of GDI
CANADA	1.60
U.S.	2.70
U.K.*	1.87
Sweden	3.85
Italy	1.00
Germany	2.48
Japan	2.91
France	2.24
Switzerland*	2.74

% of GDI

* 1996 figures.

Source: OECD, Main Science and Technology Indicators.

This relative lack of R&D expenditures may handicap Canadian industry in competing in premium-price products.

PRODUCTIVITY ASSESSMENT USING COST-BASED INDICATORS

Macro versus Micro Indicators

In the absence of specialized factors that would allow it to compete on a premium-price basis, Canadian industry must ensure that it is cost competitive in the international and domestic marketplaces. At the macro level, cost competitiveness is affected by exchange and interest rates, which are determined by national policies and global forces and hence beyond the influence of industries and firms. At the micro level of the firm and industry, wage rates and productivity determinants come into play. These include manufacturing scale, length of production runs, managerial effectiveness, implementation of new technology and the work effort of the average worker.

Ideally, macro- and micro-level cost competitiveness should be mutually reinforcing. If returns to the factors of production (land, capital and labour) reflect microproductivity performance, then governments can manage macroeconomic policy to achieve stability and long-term growth. However, it is difficult for individual firms and industries to attempt to offset poor macroeconomic policy by productivity improvements at the micro level.

Input Costs

Unit labour cost is a convenient summary measure. It is equal to the time required to produce a unit of output times hourly compensation, which is adjusted for the prevailing exchange rates.

Figure 8 indicates the nominal growth in unit labour costs in manufacturing for selected developed countries. Canadian labour costs are currently below those of Japan, Germany and the United States. However, the relative cost of capital in Canada has been high in comparison to other jurisdictions.

The cost of capital and labour could be offset, to some extent, by investment in new plant and equipment that would improve productivity. Economists have therefore attempted to measure competitiveness using the concept of productivity, which measures output per unit of input. Ideally, it should be an assessment of total-factor productivity, capturing all of the inputs in the production process: labour, land and capital, as well as such intangible factors as management quality, and relate these inputs to the amount of output produced.

The net result of the relatively high cost of capital has been pressure on Canadian industry to improve its productivity significantly in order to remain internationally competitive. However, Figure 9 indicates that Canadian productivity growth has been limited over the period 1993 to 1999.

Figure 10 indicates the 1993 to 1998 growth in Canadian unit labour cost and the long-term Canadian unit labour cost comparison with the United States. The data indicate that Canada has been unable to secure a unit labour cost advantage with respect to the United States because Canadian labour costs have risen faster and/or productivity growth has been slower. Canadian industries have retained cost competitiveness by means of the significant devaluation of the Canadian currency vis-à-vis the United States dollar, since the early 1990s.

THE PORTER MODEL

Professor Michael Porter made use of all three of these approaches (factor models, trade assessment and cost competitiveness) in formulating his competitiveness model.[3] The Porter model attempts to integrate the economic theories of trade and development with corporate strategic theories of creating and sustaining competitive advantage to yield another factor-type model. For Porter, the key question is why some firms in some nations achieve international success while others do not. By assessing the trade and unit cost performance of selected successful nations, he identified the most influential causes. It is Porter's belief that nations do not compete — rather, it is the firms within a country that must be competitive.

Porter also pays significant attention to the fact that industries tend to be geographically concentrated within nations. The United States has Hollywood and Silicon Valley. In Canada, four of our five major banks have their head offices at the intersection of Bay and King Streets in Toronto. The fifth is one block south. Porter suggests that in many cases the nation might be too large a unit of analysis for assessing competitiveness; however, for political and practical reasons (availability of data, etc.), it is the unit used by Porter and most others.

FIGURE 8
Unit Labour Costs in Manufacturing, U.S. Dollars, 14 Countries, 1950–1998
(Indexes: 1992 = 100)

Year	U.S.	CANADA*	Japan	Korea	Taiwan	Belgium	Denmark	France*	Former W. Germany	Italy	Netherlands	Norway	Sweden*	U.K.
1950	NA	22.4	NA	NA	NA	NA	9.6	18.4	9.5	14.7	12.7	7.8	10.7	10.0
1955	NA	28.7	12.7	NA	NA	NA	12.0	25.6	9.4	15.1	14.5	10.2	15.5	13.2
1960	NA	31.8	10.9	NA	NA	19.4	13.5	21.1	10.4	16.0	16.0	11.3	16.8	15.6
1965	NA	27.1	13.4	NA	NA	24.8	16.5	24.0	13.0	20.3	22.0	13.9	19.6	18.0
1970	NA	34.7	15.3	22.8	14.0	27.0	20.3	23.0	17.1	24.9	25.7	17.8	23.0	19.2
1975	NA	50.8	34.5	29.2	27.9	60.9	40.9	48.7	35.1	48.9	58.7	40.7	46.8	36.1
1980	77.2	65.4	51.3	61.9	42.0	88.3	58.9	76.7	59.6	63.3	82.3	63.9	69.6	77.8
1985	85.5	68.9	49.9	58.4	50.0	46.9	42.3	54.2	41.7	47.9	48.7	50.8	45.4	54.0
1990	92.8	97.2	83.1	94.9	88.2	89.5	91.3	94.1	87.3	93.8	88.9	95.0	90.8	92.5
1995	93.9	83.8	135.1	122.3	96.9	105.2	101.1	99.9	115.5	78.0	103.0	105.0	70.8	91.6
1998	93.4	80.8	93.1	60.0	74.3	83.8	84.7	80.2	89.1	89.1	82.0	99.9	65.2	105.2

NA: Not Available

Note: The data relate to employees (wage and salary earners) in Korea, Taiwan, Belgium, Denmark, and Italy, and to all employed persons (employees and self-employed workers) in the other countries.

* Compensation adjusted to include changes in employment taxes that are not compensation to employees but labour costs to employers.

Source: U.S. Department of Labor, Bureau of Labor Statistics, April 2000.

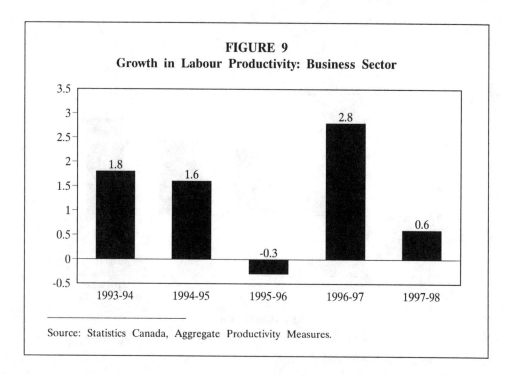

FIGURE 9
Growth in Labour Productivity: Business Sector

Source: Statistics Canada, Aggregate Productivity Measures.

Porter presents a four-factor, interactive model of competitiveness that he calls the "diamond." The four factors are assessed quantitatively and qualitatively, in a methodology similar to that used by *The World Competitiveness Report*. It is important to note, however, that this is not a fully determined model where the interaction of all of the variables has been specified by statistical methods. Nor has its predictive validity been determined. Rather, it is inductively derived, the outcome of a review of data and qualitative factors used to evaluate an industry's and, therefore, a country's competitive evolution and current position.

Porter's diamond is based on the hypothesis that the following four variables are the most significant:

➢ factor conditions
➢ demand conditions
➢ related and supporting industries
➢ firm strategy, structure and rivalry

Porter also includes two outside factors: chance and the impact of government.

Factor Conditions

Porter distinguishes between basic and advanced factors. Basic factors include human and physical capital, generally available knowledge, financial

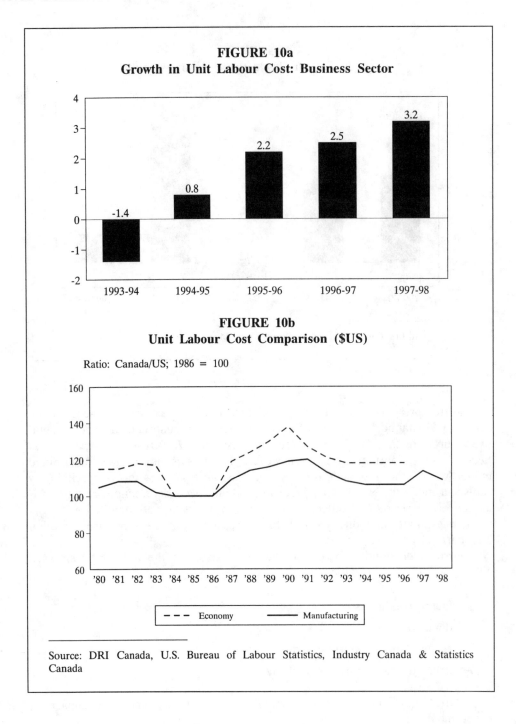

FIGURE 10a
Growth in Unit Labour Cost: Business Sector

FIGURE 10b
Unit Labour Cost Comparison ($US)

Ratio: Canada/US; 1986 = 100

Source: DRI Canada, U.S. Bureau of Labour Statistics, Industry Canada & Statistics Canada

investment capital and infrastructure. Basic factors are passive — they are undifferentiated base abilities available to most competitors. Advanced factors involve higher levels of knowledge and lend themselves more to building competitive advantage. For example, basic factors are involved in a fishing industry, but advanced factors are required for an industry based on marine biology.

Factors can also be generalized, as opposed to specialized. Porter compares developed economies, which all tend to have generalized factors such as highway systems and public education. Specialized factors involve upgrading personnel to higher-skilled activities — such as training not just electrical engineers but electro-optics specialists — and so lend themselves to developing distinctive competence.

Porter maintains that a reliance on general factors makes an economy vulnerable. Economic activity can be easily moved to another jurisdiction where either the cost of these general factors is lower or advanced factors are being used to create an advantage.

Demand Conditions

Market characteristics can be important — large markets, for example, provide the opportunity to develop economies of scale in production. However, Porter views scale economies as a static advantage, in as much as scale, in and of itself, does not necessarily lead to products of greater added value. In his opinion, quality of demand in the domestic market is a more important criterion for success. As nations create wealth, consumers become less price-sensitive and are more interested in quality products supported by higher levels of customer service. In marketing terms, higher value-added niches are created, and consumers are less interested in standardized, mass-produced products. As well, Porter believes that a large number of independent buyers leads to more intense pressures within the domestic marketplace and, therefore, to increased concern for the quality of the goods and services produced.

Porter is a firm believer in the importance of intense competition in the domestic market. His public policy recommendations are oriented towards enhancing domestic competitive pressures. This also leads to synergy with the other factors in the diamond, such as firm rivalry.

Related and Supporting Industries

Because modern industrial economies are complex and highly interrelated, industries require a network of supplier relationships in order to be successful. Porter explicitly recognizes the importance of developing effective supplier relations as one of the four principal factors in the diamond model. It is important to stress that Porter's concept of related and supporting industries is influenced by Japanese practice and represents a substantial change from past North American supplier-purchaser relationships. Porter envisions a working relationship that will help to create both advanced and specialized factor conditions. The net result would be an enhanced competitive base for all of the firms in an interrelated "cluster" of advanced economic activity.

Strategy — Structure — Rivalry

Porter suggests that no one managerial style is best. In Italy small- and medium-size family-owned firms have been successful. In Germany, the focus is on technical backgrounds and organizational hierarchies. Differences in managerial approach are dependent upon such factors as the training and orientation of leaders, group versus hierarchical styles, the relative importance a society places on individual responsibility and initiative, relationships with customers and the state of labour-management relations. He also suggests that different firm structures and management styles work best in different industries.

Porter stresses the importance of organizational goals. These goals may differ from country to country depending upon such factors as ownership structure, motivation of owners, debt structures and alternative forms of corporate governance.

The roles of banks and capital markets may differ as well. Porter argues that the United States has a greater focus on taking risks and restructuring mature sectors than many other developed countries. For example, the United States has developed capital market mechanisms that have created funding for new ventures and start-ups.

Porter stresses the importance of domestic rivalry in this component of the diamond to ensure the development of sophisticated and specialized factors of production. As well, domestic competition is based upon a "level playing field," and so normally must be construed as a fair test. On the other hand, foreign competition may be considered unfair because rules and regulations may differ from country to country.

Finally, Porter strongly opposes the creation of monopolies, cartels or national champions as an approach to succeed in international markets. In his opinion, a lack of domestic competition inhibits the development of world-class, internationally competitive firms.

The Roles of Government and Chance

Porter does not believe that government is integral to the diamond. Rather, its role is that of a facilitator, only influencing the factors in the diamond. For example, governments can provide assistance to firms by reducing pressures in the business environment that impede competitiveness. Alternatively, they can slow the process of adapting to competitiveness if they unduly protect industries from domestic and international pressures.

Porter acknowledges the role of chance in the development of competitive industrial structures. Wars, technological change and other factors can lead to the development of new, competitive industries. For example, many important synthetic materials, such as nylon, were developed during World War II when natural resources were unavailable for use in the military effort. An antitrust case in the United States led to the creation in Canada of Nortel Networks which has gone on to become one of Canada's major innovators.

Stages of National Competitive Development

Porter's analysis suggests that there are four stages through which a national economy evolves; the first three involve growth, and the fourth indicates decline.

The Factor-Driven Stage

In the first, or factor-driven stage, the nation competes on the basis of the basic factors of production, such as raw materials, climate and a pool of labour. These factors form the basis for a limited range of industries. At this stage of wealth creation, technology is transferred into the nation but is not created domestically. The factor-driven stage is highly sensitive to world business cycles, changes in exchange rates and international prices. Porter suggests that it is possible to sustain a high standard of living in the factor-driven stage but that it represents a poor basis for long-term growth.

The Investment-Driven Stage

In the second, investment-driven stage, the emphasis is on acquiring and improving upon foreign technology. This stage features investment in large modern facilities and the development of a pool of skilled workers, as well as the development of domestic rivalry and some focus on external markets.

The investment-driven stage also focuses on upgrading institutional structures such as educational and research institutions. However, competition in this stage is driven primarily by standardized production for a relatively unsophisticated home demand.

While a nation can experience rapid growth in the investment-driven stage, its economy can be vulnerable to increasing costs in the factors of production and to a continuing dependency on foreign technology. At this stage, government can play an important role in focusing on the creation of risk capital and promoting risk-taking and export activities.

The Innovation-Driven Stage

The third, innovation-driven, stage represents a significant advancement. Porter suggests that in this stage the nation reaps the benefits of the entire diamond with all of its interactions. For example, increasing consumer sophistication in local demand necessitates increased development in sophisticated industrial production. New entrants into the business community increase rivalry, and firms are forced to innovate further.

Clusters of related firms and industries both deepen, through the enhancement of supplier and related industries, and widen, through the development of new industrial activity. There is also a focus on innovation, particularly in the export of higher-value-added services such as engineering, law and advertising.

In the innovation-driven phase, government takes on a new role. There is less of a necessity for direct intervention by government, and it can now focus on creating the advanced and specialized factors of production that are required for a sophisticated market economy. As well, government can provide an environment that facilitates new-business start-ups, and increases rivalry in the domestic market.

The Wealth-Driven Stage

The final, wealth-driven, stage leads to decline. In this phase there is less rivalry within the domestic market, and labour-management relations become more adversarial as the key players in the economy attempt to preserve their existing positions.

Porter suggests that the wealth-driven stage leads to an increase in non-functional business activities such as mergers, acquisitions and takeovers by foreign firms. This non-functional activity leads ultimately to a decline in personal income, which erodes quality demand in the home market. At this stage, price becomes an important consideration, and the economy is no longer quality driven.

In the wealth-driven stage it is possible to attain a dual economy with pockets of wealth and some highly successful firms but a great deal of unemployment and a general sense of drift. The government may be forced to introduce taxes on wealth to pay for the sophisticated social services that were developed when the economy experienced sustained growth. These taxes further dampen the rewards to successful economic activity.

THE CASE OF CANADA

In a 1991 article Porter suggests that the Canadian economy is operating with an old and outdated model of economic development, and may be in the wealth-driven stage.[4] Figure 11 indicates Porter's views of the major systemic barriers to upgrading the Canadian economy. It may be argued that Canada has moved directly from the investment-driven to the wealth-driven stage without experiencing the innovation-driven stage. Activities are inward looking and based upon conservative business strategies. Canadian industries continue to rely on abundant basic factors of production, with little emphasis on upgrading and factor specializations.

In a more recent study, Martin and Porter reaffirm Porter's original critique of the Canadian economy.[5] They go on to assert that during the 1990s Canada chose the familiar and comfortable path of replication, benchmarking and operational improvement instead of embracing a culture of innovation, uniqueness and differentiation. As a result, impressive macroeconomic gains over this period have been offset by a decline in the sophistication of company operations and a slide in national competitiveness and relative prosperity. Martin and Porter argue that Canada must move to a more innovation-driven economy if it is to prosper in the twenty-first century.

According to Martin and Porter, the barriers impeding Canada's long-term industrial competitiveness are primarily attitudinal and behavioural. Canadian firms must decide to compete globally on the basis of innovative products and services in order to succeed. They must turn their backs on a competitive strategy of benchmarking against competitors and replicating their choices. Instead, they must adopt first-mover strategies of unique positioning that create tailored webs of activity which generate customer values distinct from those of competitors. Canadian governments as well must pursue bold and innovative strategies that foster a positive macroeconomic climate and create favourable microeconomic conditions for business.

Martin and Porter's premise is supported by Daniel Trefler's finding that Canada's productivity gap is a product innovation gap.[6] In other words, Canada's

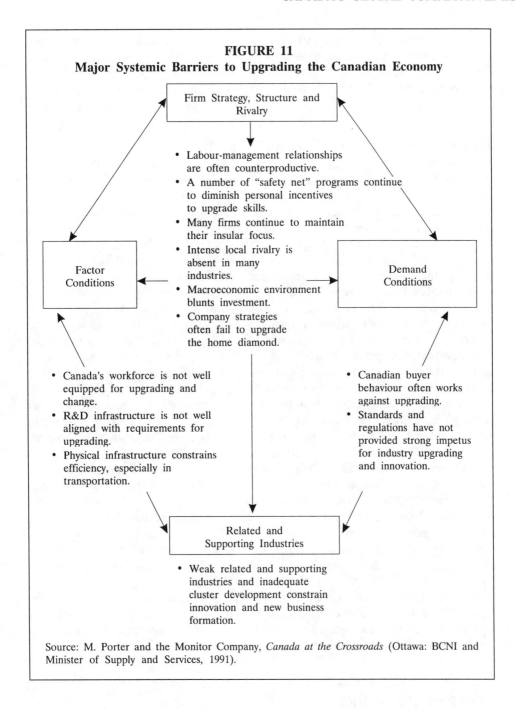

FIGURE 11
Major Systemic Barriers to Upgrading the Canadian Economy

Firm Strategy, Structure and Rivalry

• Labour-management relationships are often counterproductive.
• A number of "safety net" programs continue to diminish personal incentives to upgrade skills.
• Many firms continue to maintain their insular focus.
• Intense local rivalry is absent in many industries.
• Macroeconomic environment blunts investment.
• Company strategies often fail to upgrade the home diamond.

Factor Conditions

Demand Conditions

• Canada's workforce is not well equipped for upgrading and change.
• R&D infrastructure is not well aligned with requirements for upgrading.
• Physical infrastructure constrains efficiency, especially in transportation.

• Canadian buyer behaviour often works against upgrading.
• Standards and regulations have not provided strong impetus for industry upgrading and innovation.

Related and Supporting Industries

• Weak related and supporting industries and inadequate cluster development constrain innovation and new business formation.

Source: M. Porter and the Monitor Company, *Canada at the Crossroads* (Ottawa: BCNI and Minister of Supply and Services, 1991).

failure to introduce innovative products lies at the heart of its poor productivity performance. Also, Manuel Trajtenberg notes that Canada is far less innovative that the United States in leading-edge technologies such as computers and tele-communication equipment, and issues the warning that we may be missing the technology boat.[7]

An examination of these criticisms suggests that there is nothing inherently wrong with the Canadian economy that cannot be changed with the development of alternative attitudes and behaviour on the part of labour, management and government, leading to innovative higher-value-added activities.

THE PORTER MODEL IN PERSPECTIVE

Porter's framework for assessing the competitive advantage of nations functions more as a list of important topics for consideration than as a deterministic, causal model. Porter does not provide a series of equations that could be used to test his model or to forecast economic growth and development. So, the framework provides only a checklist of factors that, in some combination, are normally associated with economic growth.

It should also be noted that Porter focuses on the traded manufacturing sector of the economy. His analysis appears to assume that if the traded sector is internationally competitive, then the rest of the economy — the non-traded sectors — will also be. However, this assumption has not yet been proven. In fact, Porter's assessment of the Italian economy indicates that it has performed relatively well in selected traded sectors, notwithstanding inefficiencies in significant non-traded activities. It might be prudent to conclude that a highly competitive traded sector is a necessary, but not sufficient, condition for the achievement of overall national economic competitiveness.

Nor has it been established that the innovation-driven component of an economy is, in itself, sufficient to ensure national competitiveness. Productivity must increase in all sectors — the traded and non-traded, and also the government and other public-sector institutions such as education and health care.

In another study, D.J. Daly concluded that Porter underestimated the importance of exchange rates in determining an industry's world market share.[8] The Canadian Manufacturers' Association (CMA) also believes that the increase in the value of the Canadian dollar (which appreciated in value by 21 per cent against its U.S. counterpart over the period from 1986 to 1991) resulted in a loss of competitiveness for Canadian manufacturers. The CMA estimates that Canadian manufacturers' share of the domestic market fell from 73.2 per cent in 1980 to 40 per cent in 1996.[9]

To compete internationally industry must be cost-competitive as well as innovative. Competitive pressures ensure that a firm's comparative advantage can be quickly lost as competitors act to lower costs, compete on price and continue the innovation process.

OTHER APPROACHES

Attract Model

Developed by Kimon Valaskakis, the Attract Model is a modification of traditional economic growth models, as well as some elements of Porter's National Competitive Advantage framework. The model proposes to address the "new reality of the stateless corporation" (Valaskakis, 1993).[10] The premise is that a country has a set of competitive elements that combine to attract business to it. The elements identified by Valaskakis are:

> naturally induced competitive elements

> policy induced competitive advantages

> acquired competitive elements

> competitive handicaps induced by policy

> demand conditions

> supply conditions

This model emphasizes the advantages and disadvantages of direct government involvement in the economy.

An important observation by Valaskakis, and other leading business and economics leaders such as Ohmae and Drucker, is the importance of the Multinational Enterprises (MNEs) in Canada.[11, 12] His recommendation for a national strategy for Canada is based on the conclusion that corporations are becoming stateless. Unlike Porter's theory, this approach does not acknowledge that corporations have a genesis in a nurturing environment, or home base.

Technology Districts

Recent work by Michael Storper (1992) examines the relationships between "technology districts" and changes in the nature of international trade.[13] Storper analyzes trade data for specific products. This work indicates that international trade and competitiveness is experiencing changes which encourage trade specialization. Among the factors encouraging specialization are:

> dynamic technological learning in specific products (product-based, technological learning, or PBTL);

> production networks of related firms that can adapt and react to new technologies, facilitate PBTL and avoid "lock-in" to maturing technologies;

> "the existence of networks and the geographical agglomeration of important parts of the production systems" (Storper, 1991); and

> technological learning in a district that can result from the linkages between firms, and clusters of firms, in the district.

Storper argues that trade specialization is not the result of a static resource endowment but of a dynamic sharing of knowledge.

These observations on the notion of trade specialization are very similar to Porter's concept of "revealed competitive advantages." The theory is not intended to provide a framework for discovering which region will be most successful in a particular industry. However, it does indicate an increasing awareness of the relationship between regional growth and national competitiveness.

Storper's evidence of networks of firms engaged in mutually advantageous product-based technological learning (PBTL) is both remarkable and significant. Its implication — that firms benefit from being located close to similar organizations (even competitors!) is important and fully in line with Porter's conclusions.

Capital Skills Complementarity

The hypothesis of capital-skill complementarity (CSC) is relevant as an approach to competitive analysis, as it seeks to explain the relationship between physical capital and human capital. That is, "physical capital is more complementary to human capital (i.e., educated labour) than to raw labour (or less educated labour)" (Rice, 1989).[14] This approach attempts to explain the relationship between the distribution of manufacturing and the distribution of educated labour. It implies that manufacturing is centred more in areas with a higher concentration of educated labour than in areas where lower education levels are apparent.

It is interesting to speculate on the relatively recent ability to locate sophisticated manufacturing activities in newly developing economies. This may relate to a change in the nature of the manufacturing equipment, perhaps becoming easier to use, or improvement in the general level of education worldwide.

This approach attempts to predict movement of high quality labour to manufacturing-intensive geographic areas. It is not applicable to the overall economy, but provides insight into a critical issue (labour and capita affinity) affecting the competitiveness of specific geographic zones.

The Region State

As an approach to the issue of competitiveness, Ohmae's concept of the borderless world, where political borders are increasingly irrelevant, is perhaps the most radical. It is his view that the economy is interlinked and firms are not bound to nationality.

This concept relies on "natural economic zones" as the place where "the key ingredients for successful participation in the global economy are located."

The key ingredients that lead to a region state are: (1) population size and density (including education and consumption characteristics); and (2) infrastructure (including communication and transportation) to compete in global markets. The economic well-being of the inhabitants of the region-state is linked "with the global economy and not with their host nations." An observation made by Ohmae is that the region state has a consistent set of consumer interests which lead to service economies for firms competing in the zone.

The Multinational Enterprise (MNE) is a key driver of economies worldwide, since it can "migrate between countries." The fact that consumers "buy products based on their comparative value and not nationality" is the one fundamental basis for his argument on the disintegration of national boundaries.

Trade patterns seem to bear out Ohmae's insistence of the regionality of markets transcending political boundaries. An example of a natural trade zone is the Pacific Northwest (e.g., Seattle, the United States and Vancouver, Canada).

The arguments and data presented are essentially qualitative and are based on a presumption that markets are of foremost interest in the issue of competitiveness. Capital markets are increasingly mobile, so that assets are also tradeable. Thus, we witness the movement of production within key MNEs and not the emergence of new national firms jockeying for position within the world market.

There is little mention by Ohmae of what factors create the wealth necessary for an economic zone to begin, nor does he mention how to attract firms or to develop them. It is as though firms simply exist and draw competitive advantage wherever they can find it. While Ohmae's concept of natural economic zones provides insight into product marketing, many questions remain from a policy perspective. For example:

> If a region is not of sufficient size to be a natural economic zone, what can be done to become one?

> How do multinationals develop?

> What role do small- or medium-size national enterprises play in the region state?

> What is the role of services in the borderless economy?

With the development of the region state and the reduced relevance of national borders, the issue of competitiveness is also seemingly irrelevant. In his words, "a trade deficit is not the result of loss of competitiveness; it is the corporate decision to produce or procure elsewhere." Competitiveness of firms in a nation is no longer of concern; rather, attracting MNE's for specific activities within jurisdiction should be the concern for policy makers.

GENERALIZABLE FINDINGS

As a result of this literature review, there are a number of major implications.

Factors: Competitiveness theory is becoming more complex with respect to the number of factors that are considered. The *World Competitiveness Report* is drawn from perhaps the widest range of potential factors considered to be important in a nation's competitiveness. The diamond framework advanced by Porter is most successful at communicating the interaction and complexity of how factors affect the competitiveness of a nation. Virtually all of the factors considered in other approaches could easily be categorized into one of the four key determinants in the Porter model. Ohmae, of course, would not consider the competitiveness of a nation to be a relevant issue any longer.

Manufacturing Focus: Competitiveness analysis continues to focus on the manufacturing sector, assuming that manufacturing leads to growth in the economy. None of the models attempts to explain competitiveness and economic growth in the service sector economy. Some authors do try to tailor generic approaches to specific sectors, and Van Duren and Westgren attempt with the Canadian agriculture sector.[15] The service sector is dealt with in the regional development and urban planning models, but is assumed to grow as a result of overall industrial growth. Virtually all approaches acknowledge that the service sector is becoming more important in the global economy. In Canada, for example, approximately 70 per cent of GDP is in the service sector. While manufacturing is a key driver of the economy, its overall importance will continue to evolve.

Focus on the Firm: An increased focus is apparent on the role of individual firms as a key driver of a competitive and growing economy. Porter has written most succinctly that "firms, not nations, compete." Reviewers have credited Porter with almost single-handedly bridging the gap between international trade theory economics and firm level strategy. Porter, through *Competitive Advantage of Nations* and previous competitiveness work, has emphasized the importance of effective strategy, in comparison to traditional determinants of competitiveness such as labour, raw materials, capital, or land costs and other factors of production.

In theory, firms in a perfectly competitive environment are assumed to receive constant returns and zero profits. Krugman (1992) and McCulloch (1993)[16] suggest that, in practice, strategic behaviour provides increasing returns to firms engaged in research and development and those with oligopolistic control over markets. In the world context, the competitiveness of a nation's firms is dependent on the strategy (which leads to increasing returns) of the individual firms.

The Stateless Corporation: Two major schools of thought exist on the influence of MNEs on a nation's competitiveness and the world economy. One view, largely attributed to Ohmae, is that stateless corporations move throughout all countries in the world and transcend political boundaries. Little can be done but to attract these firms to a jurisdiction in order to employ its citizens. The other view, usually attributed to Porter, is that the "home base" of a corporation is critical in shaping a firm's competitive advantage and its capability of competing on a world scale.

Hu (1992) has investigated the current status of multinationals and their nationality.[17] He has concluded that even the largest MNEs are national companies with multinational operations. In essence, "the primary source of a company's international competitive advantage lies in its home nation; foreign sources of advantage can supplement national sources but cannot be sufficient as a substitute." While examples of corporations with directors and officers of different nationalities and which operate in many different countries can be found, only a few actually operate in a way that could be construed as stateless.

Policy development with respect to attracting MNEs is difficult, involving taxation, funding and other fiscal policy inducements. Governments may have to play a different role in the future, such as helping to manage the growth of corporations. Restructuring of MNEs will occur regardless of the effectiveness of management, and will affect local economies. Enderwick (1989) discusses the influence that local economic conditions have on restructuring.[18] Regardless of the economic conditions elsewhere, "the labour market is a critical locational influence and its operation has a major impact on the type of restructuring strategy likely to be implemented." The recent United Nations *World Investment Report* (1993) explores MNE activity in structural and strategic terms, concluding that increasingly complex forms of organization allow MNEs to integrate and coordinate across borders. Functional, product-specific and regional organizational structures may coexist within the same firm but be dispersed throughout the globe. Simple replication of firms within countries is no longer the norm for MNEs in entering specific geographic areas.

Location and Agglomeration: International economics and spatial economics appear to be converging on the issue of location and competitive advantage. Early literature on trade was based on examples of agricultural economics, which relied heavily on the factor endowments of geographic location. Capital skill complementarity postulates that location and economic developments are related, and a body of literature exists which attempts to explain these relationships. Krugman (1989), using an economic geography model, demonstrated that transportation costs lead to agglomeration, and how agglomeration leads to increasing returns for the firms in a region. Storper and Porter identify reasons why regional groups of companies are important because they lead to creation of sophisticated and specialized factors of production. Human capital, information and other factors move to clusters, further shifting the region's economy and competitiveness.

Innovation, Technology and Competitiveness: Economic theory is now attempting to capture and measure the influence of innovation and technology on competitiveness. Early macroeconomic models assume technology to be volatile, and thus some or all of the influence of technology is exogenous. As noted by Storper (1992), "conventional economic theory has had little success in defining what causes technological change." Schumpeter identified technological change and innovation, driven by entrepreneurial spirit, as a prerequisite for economic growth. Porter's work assumes innovation to be a key driver, but includes chance as a determinant, and thus allows for technological leaps. Storper's work on technology districts concludes that product-based technological learning is apparent in export specialized, subnational units. He advances a measure of the influence of technology on competitiveness as "economies of variety over time." (Storper 1991)

Capital-skill complementarity suggests that high quality labour and manufacturing investment go hand in hand. "Knowledge workers" and the knowledge they possess are "the primary resource for the economy overall." (Drucker 1992) The importance of human resources and knowledge capital as a source of competitive advantage for regions, nations and companies is one of the few issues that is consistently agreed upon in the literature.

In a related manner, Reich (1992) asserts that the most important issue in the broad arena of competitiveness is not which company from which country is most competitive, but that workers in a particular country continue to get better jobs.[19] The true goal of creating competitive companies, regardless of origin or nationality, is to provide good jobs for people in that country.

CONCLUSIONS AND IMPLICATIONS

Assessment of the various competitiveness and economic development approaches yields a number of conclusions on what has changed and what has remained constant in economic theory. As economists have struggled to explain the business activity of their time, the guideposts that allow them to assess why certain economic behaviours occur have remained very similar.

Institutional roles and activity continue to have a profound effect on the nature of business activity in nations and between nations. At any time the activity of government will be a key determinant in the economic growth and international competitiveness of a nation. The notion that government is most beneficial to business when it facilitates rather than intervenes has gained increasing support.

Factor inputs remain the key building block for economic growth and individual firm competitiveness. Some of the key factor inputs for firms and nations have changed, from land and raw materials to knowledge and technology. However, capital resources remains a critical determinant to the success of all economies and firms.

With respect to the future, the key issues that will need further research and demand greater understanding include the following:

➤ The role of the knowledge worker in the economic health and wealth generation of an economy. Given their potential importance, the knowledge worker could or should become a key focus of policy making. The increasing complexity of multinational firms and the emergence of virtual corporations decrease the importance of the firm as the economic unit. Researchers such as Drucker, and others in organizational behaviour, note that the team and the individual are becoming the basic economic unit. Reich argues that it is the individual jobs and the quality of jobs that matter. We have gone through a period of focus on the nation as the key economic unit in studying economic growth; then the firm, the multinational enterprises in particular; and perhaps the future will focus on the team or individual knowledge worker.

➤ While it is evident that technology often leads to competitiveness at the multinational level, the impact of technology at a small or medium enterprise level needs to be better understood. Some countries are using their base of existing small- and medium-size businesses to accelerate the economic growth and competitiveness of their economy through communications and other technology.

> On a much broader scale, the impact of the service and knowledge sectors on economic growth and wealth generation needs to be better understood. The manufacturing sector is no longer the sole engine of growth.

In summary, our theories of competitiveness and economic growth appear to be moving to a microeconomic focus. At present, the focus is on the firm, and specifically, the multinational enterprise. Competitiveness in future may be even more micro in nature, with an increasing focus on the team or individual knowledge worker.

NOTES

1. *The World Competitiveness Report*, World Economic Forum and IMD, 1997.
2. P. Krugman, "Competitiveness: A Dangerous Obsession," *Foreign Affairs*, March/April 1994.
3. M. Porter, *The Competitive Advantage of Nations* (New York: Free Press, 1990).
4. M. Porter and the Monitor Company, *Canada at the Crossroads* (Ottawa: Business Council on National Issues and Ministry of Supply and Services, 1991).
5. R. Martin and M. Porter, "Canadian Competitiveness: Nine Years after the Crossroads," Centre for the Study of Living Standards, Conference on the Canada–US Manufacturing Productivity Gap, January 21–22, 2000.
6. D. Trefler, "Does Canada Need a Productivity Budget?" *Policy Options*, July–August 1999.
7. M. Trajtenberg, "Is Canada Missing the Technology Boat?" Industry Canada, Discussion Paper No. 9, January 2000.
8. D.J. Daly, "Exchange Rates and Trade Flows: Recent Japanese Experience," unpublished paper (Toronto: Ontario Centre for International Business, 1992).
9. *Year-End Review and 1997 Economic Outlook* (Toronto: The Canadian Manufacturers' Association, 1996).
10. K. Valaskakis, "A Prescription for Canada Inc.," *The Globe and Mail*, 1993.
11. K. Ohmae, "Managing in a Borderless World," *Harvard Business Review*, May/June 1989.
12. P. Drucker, "The New Society of Organizations," *Harvard Business Review*, September/October 1992.
13. M. Storper, "The Limits to Globalization: Technology Districts and International Trade," *Economic Geography*, 1992.
14. R. Rice, "Capital Skill Complementarity and the Interregional Distribution of Human Capital in U.S. Manufacturing," *Regional Economics*, 1989.
15. M. Van Duren and R. Westgren, "Assessing the Competitiveness of Canada's Agrifood Industry," *Canadian Journal of Agricultural Economics*, 1991.
16. R. McCulloch, "The Optimality of Free Trade: Science or Religion," AEA Papers and Proceedings, May 1993.
17. Su Hu, "Global or Stateless Corporations are National Firms with International Operations," *California Management Review*, 1992.
18. P. Enderwick, "Multinational Corporate Restructuring and International Competitiveness," *California Management Review*, 1989.
19. R. Reich, "Towards a New Economic Development," *Industry Week*, 1992.

Canada's Economy:
Structure and Performance

Donald J.S. Brean

The following headlines appeared in the Canadian press in the past year:

➤ Forecast: Canada's Output Growth Remains Strong
➤ Unemployment Drops Below 7% for the First Time in 30 Years
➤ Huge Government Surplus Forecast: $120-Billion Over 5 Years
➤ Inflation Is Dead!
➤ Higher Interest Rates Threaten Construction Industry
➤ Capital Flows Out of Canada, Our Dollar Weakens
➤ Minister of Industry Says Exports Are the Key to Growth

The issues addressed in these headlines affect us all, whether directly or indirectly. They deal with employment, income, the cost of living, taxes, security and the economic well-being of Canadians in general. These issues are all within the realm of macroeconomics.

This article provides an overview of macroeconomics in the Canadian context. We identify the main questions addressed by macroeconomics. We examine the structure of the Canadian economy. We show how that structure lends itself to a set of accounts that depicts the Canadian economy as an interdependent set of markets, including the markets for:

➤ goods and services
➤ labour
➤ capital and credit

In addition, our overview of the Canadian economy explores the role of the government, the Bank of Canada and our important economic links with the rest of the world.

An important purpose of this article is to make sense of the contentious economic issues of the day. Economic growth, or the lack of it, unemployment, inflation, interest and exchange rates, foreign ownership, regional disparities, fiscal deficits and trade balances — these emerge as connected elements in a complex yet coherent framework that describes the Canadian economy.

Macroeconomics uses a jargon that can be forbidding to the uninitiated. We shall cut through the jargon to deal directly with the economic issues we read about in newspapers and that confront us in our daily lives.

THE STRUCTURE OF THE ECONOMY

Our focus — macroeconomics — ought to be distinguished from its counterpart, microeconomics. Microeconomics, sometimes referred to as price theory, is concerned with how individuals — as consumers and producers — make decisions in markets. For instance, microeconomics deals with why one chooses to work or not to work, or to go to fewer movies when theatre prices go up, or to buy more CDs when CD prices fall. Macroeconomics, on the other hand, is concerned primarily with aggregates — such as the total number of people employed (or unemployed) and the total amount of spending on goods and services.

Roughly speaking, macroeconomics is the sum of microeconomic activity. The macroeconomic framework helps to explain and predict the economic growth of the economy as a whole, the business cycle, employment, inflation, international trade and factors that determine the government deficit.

This first section presents a few fundamental concepts that are helpful in understanding the Canadian economy. We show how the "national accounts" depict the economy as a set of interdependent markets.

Dealing with Aggregates

Macroeconomics proceeds from the idea that an economy can be represented as a whole — an interrelated system — without accounting for the behaviour of individuals and firms within the system. There are significant reasons to work with aggregates. First, the behaviour of a large number of economic players can be described collectively. In the labour market, for example, no single individual sets the unemployment rate or the average wage. Nevertheless, it is useful to understand what determines the aggregate unemployment and average wage rate — and especially the relation between the two.

Second, stable relationships can be observed among aggregate variables, such as between income and spending, or between investment and the interest rate, or money and prices, or exports and the exchange rate. Stability in such relationships provides explanatory and predictive power — the basis of economic policy.

Third, many economic concepts are relevant only in the aggregate. A change in the overall level of prices, for example, is a different phenomenon from the change in the price of a loaf of bread, or an automobile, or a movie ticket. A change in the price of a specific good reflects a change in the supply of, or the demand for, that particular good. Such changes may arise from a change in income or tastes ("on the demand side"), or in production costs, technology or competition ("on the supply side"). On the other hand, changes in the overall price level — inflation — are largely determined by the rate at which the Bank of Canada supplies money and credit to the economy.

The Canadian economy represents a trillion dollars worth of activity. The trillion dollar figure includes the value of all goods and services produced in Canada in 2000, our Gross National Product. Canada's GNP amounts to more than $28,000 per person.

As a sum, GNP takes into account your income, your spending and, likewise, the incomes and spending of all Canadians. However, this sum hardly seems pertinent to many of the economic issues with which individual Canadians deal in day-to-day life. Gross National Product says nothing, for example, about the price of bread, rent controls, union negotiations or the closure of a plant in Barrie. Such issues are microeconomic.

The Four Sectors

Canada's economy has four major sectors: households, business, government and the foreign sector. Each plays a unique role in Canada's market economy.

The household sector provides labour. The 31-million people in Canada provide a labour force of approximately 16-million. In return for their labour, households earn income in the form of wages and salaries. Income is then either spent on the consumption of goods or services or it is saved. Savings are turned into investments, such as loans and share ownerships in business, for which households receive income in the form of interest and dividends.

The business sector uses productive capital assets (buildings, machinery and equipment), together with labour, to produce goods and services of value. The business sector pays wages, salaries and interest to households for the labour and capital used in production. In the final tally, business earns profit, which likewise flows to households in the form of dividends.

Governments are involved in the economy in many ways. They levy taxes on households and businesses, and use the resulting revenues to redistribute income, to provide services and to maintain social programs. In Canada, this sector is complicated by the fact that there are three levels of government (federal, provincial and municipal), each of which has some scope to raise taxes, provide services, redistribute income — and go into debt.

The foreign sector is not as precisely defined as are households, business and government because, in our open economy, each of the three primary sectors has foreign connections. For example, households buy imported goods and services; businesses export and import goods and services; and governments borrow abroad.

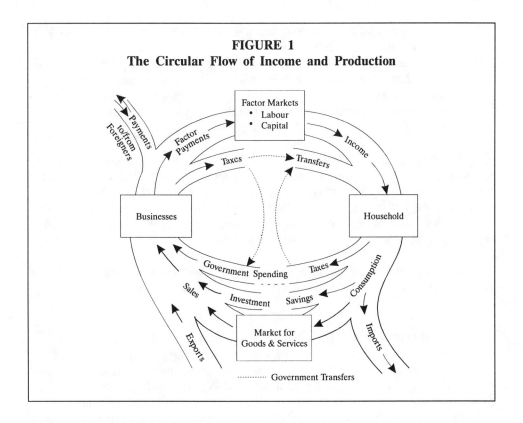

FIGURE 1
The Circular Flow of Income and Production

Macroeconomic Structure — The Markets

The circular flow model (Figure 1) is a simple representation of the inter-relations among the four sectors of the Canadian economy. Households provide labour, buy goods and services and generate savings. Businesses employ labour, produce goods and services and borrow funds.[1] The foreign sector puts in by buying exports and draws out by selling imports. Other foreign flows (such as loans and investments) can also be in either direction.

As we shall discuss later, the government plays a major role in spending, as well as in influencing savings and investment. The government is also responsible for redistributing income.

The system consists of three major markets — the market for goods (and services), the labour market and the capital market. A "market-clearing" price is determined in each market. The goods market generates commodity prices, while the labour market produces wage rates. Capital markets, where borrowing and lending occur, generate the interest rate, which is the "price" of money.

A market is said to "clear" when suppliers and demanders jointly agree to deliver and to purchase a specific amount of labour, goods or capital, as the case may be, with neither shortages nor excess production — that is, with supply equalling demand. A market that clears is said to be in balance or "equilibrium." Equilibrium occurs in domestic markets when:

1. in the labour market, unemployment is at a "natural" rate, and no one is out of work involuntarily;
2. in the goods and services market, inventories are not mounting or, conversely, there are neither queues nor empty shelves; and
3. in the capital market, savings equal investment. If Canadian savings exceed domestic investment, the interest rate will fall. If plans for investment exceed savings, the interest rate will rise.

The openness of the Canadian economy creates a fourth market: the market for foreign exchange. This market is linked to the international markets for goods and capital. The foreign-exchange rate is simply the Canadian dollar price of foreign currency, such as the U.S. dollar, as determined by the balance of trade and investment between Canada and the rest of the world. Equilibrium, then, in this market is reached when:

4. exports equal imports (and there are no international capital flows), or exports minus imports equals the net international capital flow.

Equilibrium, Disequilibrium and Sticky Prices

Price flexibility is crucial for continuous equilibrium in markets. The basic "laws of supply and demand" apply to macroeconomic markets as much as they do the micromarkets for specific commodities. Prices, if they are *flexible*, adjust to changes in supply or demand so as to restore market equilibrium.

Real-world influences sometimes interfere with this clearing process — there are factors that prevent prices from adjusting, or at any rate, adjusting quickly, to changes in demand or supply. The labour market, for example, may not clear because of long-term labour contracts, minimum-wage regulations and expectations that are slow to adjust. When a price is higher than its market-clearing value, the result is "excess supply." In the labour market, this would be manifested through unemployment.

A price that does not adjust downward to a market-clearing level is said to be "sticky." Sticky prices have considerable practical significance. For example, at the onset of an economic recession, such as we have not seen since 1992, a slowdown in growth triggers widespread cuts in production and a drop in demand for intermediate products and capital goods. Unemployment rises sharply. Both labour income and business profits fall. Negative effects such as these ripple through the economy more rapidly and with more damaging consequences if prices are inflexible rather than if they adjust smoothly and rapidly.

The greatest price flexibility is found in the capital market. Excess demand or supply of capital, associated with savings relative to investment, is rapidly accommodated by adjustments of the interest rate. This is, perhaps, to be expected, since the commodity traded in capital markets — money — moves very rapidly. Units of money are identical, and they bear no storage or transportation cost. Small differences in the price of money — the interest rate — are sufficient to draw a transaction from one financial competitor to another. Intense competition in capital markets means that interest rates adjust quickly. Indeed, they may change from minute to minute.

The Economy in Numbers

The national accounts provide the score card for macroeconomics. Important questions addressed empirically by the national accounts include:

➤ How large is the economy?
➤ What are the most important components in the economy?
➤ How fast is the economy growing?

The entries in the national accounts add up to the Gross National Product, the total value of all goods and services produced and sold in Canada in, say, a year. In 2000, for example, the GNP in Canada was approximately one trillion dollars. Between 1985 and 1990, the rate of real growth of GNP averaged 2.8 per cent per year. From 1990 to 1992, however, the Canadian economy hardly grew at all. The recession bottomed out in mid-1992, and strong economic growth occurred from then through 1996 to the present at an average annual rate of 4.7 per cent.

Our national accounts are set up in a way that is useful for understanding key issues in macroeconomics — just as financial statements provide a basis for understanding business performance.

The national accounts record GNP as the sum of *outputs* or, alternatively, as the sum of *inputs* in production. The two complementary views are similar to business accounting, wherein the firm may be described in terms of value of its output or, alternatively, by its inputs including costs of production plus profit.

The computation of GNP as the sum of outputs is referred to as the "expenditure basis" because the value of outputs is determined and recorded when expenditures are made. The major expenditure categories are:

1. consumption, primarily by households
2. investment, primarily by businesses
3. government expenditures on goods and services
4. net exports (exports minus imports)

Consumption, investment, government expenditures and (net) exports represent demands on the economy. The sum of the four is termed aggregate demand. In shorthand, aggregate demand or the expenditure composition of GNP is defined as:

$$Y = C + I + G + (X - M)$$

where:
$$
\begin{aligned}
Y &= \text{national income (expenditure basis)} \\
C &= \text{consumption} \\
I &= \text{investment} \\
G &= \text{government spending} \\
X &= \text{exports} \\
M &= \text{imports}
\end{aligned}
$$

Alternatively, GNP can be calculated on an "income basis" by summing all the earnings of all labour and capital. Wages, salaries, interest, corporate and

DONALD J.S. BREAN

FIGURE 2
National Accounts: Gross National Product
Expenditure-Based and Income-Based
1999, Current Prices
(millions of dollars)

Expenditure-Based			Per Cent of GDP
Household Expenditures		559	58
Goods	250		27
Services	301		31
Government Expenditures		200	21
Current	155		16
Capital Formation	45		5
Construction		96	10
Residential	49		4
Non-Residential	47		3
Machinery & Equipment		70	7
Net Exports		28	3
Exports	414		43
Imports	386		40
Gross Domestic Product		958	100
Net Payments of Investment Income to Non-Residents		27	3
Gross National Product		931	97
Income-Based			
Wages and Salaries		499	52
Corporate Profits		101	11
Interest		48	5
Net Farm Income		2	0
Unincorporated Business Income		60	6
Inventory Valuation Adjustment		−3	0
Total		715	75
Indirect Taxes		124	13
Capital Cost Allowances		120	13
Gross Domestic Product		958	100

Note: Income-Based GDP equals Expenditure-Based GNP minus Net Payments of Income to Non-Residents.

Source: *Bank of Canada Review*, August 2000, Table H1.

unincorporated business profits and rent are the main elements. Indirect taxes, such as sales and excise taxes, must be added back in because they are part of the market value of output diverted to government. The two ways are shown in Figure 2.

The National Accounts —
More Than Just Accounts

The disaggregation of the Canadian economy along lines of expenditure is especially useful for a number of reasons pertinent to our discussion of the structure of the economy. Above all, the expenditure basis of GNP identifies various demands on the economy which, while distinct, nevertheless jointly contribute to the level of national income and its growth.

Increases in consumption, investment, government spending or net exports all add to "aggregate demand." The wheels of Canadian industry must turn faster in order to meet an increase in demand. In addition, expansion means more wheels — investment — and more people employed. Sales rise, output increases, service industries serve more, and business profits go up, as does government revenue. Governments can spend more on economically productive investments, such as infrastructure, and less on welfare and income support. The general expansion of output and productive activity illustrates the virtuous circle of economic growth.

Alas, we also must realize that an economy can contract and enter a downward spiral. This was the Canadian experience in the 1990–91 period, which provides for us a convenient illustration of the behaviour of the business cycle.

By late 1991, the United States and Canada showed classic signs of being in the downward phase of a business cycle. U.S. retail sales fell 0.4 per cent in December 1991. Half of this was in the automobile sector, with dire consequences for Canada. Manufacturing output in both countries, slow to read the signs, rose despite slumping sales. New goods stayed on the shelves (or in the parking lot). Inventories, which had risen in October and November, continued to rise in December. By January 1992, the backlog of unfilled orders had shrunk considerably, and new orders were evaporating. Both the United States and Canada were producing in excess of sales. The two countries, being reciprocal markets, saw their bilateral trade diminish dramatically. Canadian exports fell by $178-billion in November 1991, while Canadian imports from the United States fell by $325-billion.

The economic malaise touched all sectors because they all are interdependent. Businesses closed, unemployment rose, the welfare system was strained and corporate tax revenues fell sharply.

By June of 1992, the Canadian economy showed signs of having bottomed out, and recovery was at hand. Housing starts were 30 per cent above the previous year, and retail and automobile sales jumped. Manufacturers' shipments were unchanged, but new orders were up 1.2 per cent, and inventories started to decline. Labour income was 3 per cent higher than a year earlier. Exports were up 11 per cent on the year, and imports rose 13 per cent. In retrospect, 1990 to 1992 illustrates a textbook case of the decline and bottoming out of a business cycle.

Bouncing off its 1992 low, the Canadian economy had impressive growth throughout 1993 and 1994. Among the important contributing factors, the strength of the U.S. economy pulled Canadian export volumes up to record levels. Indeed, most Canadian indicators were pointing up: employment, output, investment, and consumption as well as trade. Remarkably, inflation remained low — almost zero — a continuing effect of the rigidly tight monetary policy in place prior to the economic turnaround.

Comparing Canada with the World

Figures 3 and 4 compare the composition of aggregate demand in the industrial countries of the "Group of Seven" industrial nations. In Figure 3, GNP is reported on a relative scale; the largest economy, the United States, is equal to 100. Figure 4 reports recent growth rates of the main components of aggregate demand.

A striking macroeconomic point illustrated by these comparative data involves the United States vs. Japan. In recent years, Japan has had a relatively high rate of investment (and therefore a relatively high rate of savings), a trade surplus and low government spending. It has also demonstrated impressive economic growth, low interest rates, a strong currency and rapid technological development. The United States, on the other hand, shows fairly low investment and savings rates. Although investment has risen significantly in the United States over the last few years, high consumption, high government spending and a troublesome trade deficit persist. During the early 1990s, the United States saw its investment growth stagnate and its exchange rate deteriorate. In the last few years, however, investment in the United States has taken off, contributing significantly to the sustained boom which started in the mid-1990s.

FIGURE 3
Composition of Aggregate Demand
International Comparisons, 1998

	GNP	C	I	G	(X – M)
		as % of GNP			
U.S.	100	68	17	16	–1
Japan	52	60	29	10	1
Germany	26	58	21	20	1
France	18	61	18	20	1
U.K.	15	64	16	21	–1
Italy	15	61	22	16	1
CANADA	7	60	15	19	6

GNP = Gross National Product, Expenditure Basis
C = Consumption (Private plus Public)
I = Investment, Net
G = Government Expenditures
X – M = Exports minus Imports

FIGURE 4
Key Macroeconomic Variables: Growth Rates
International Comparisons
Average Annual Growth (%)
1988 to 1998 Constant Prices

	GNP	C	I	G	X	M
U.S.	2.5	2.0	4.4	0.5	8.7	7.3
Japan	4.2	2.3	1.5	1.9	5.2	4.7
Germany*	1.4	1.3	0.9	1.5	4.2	4.9
France	1.8	1.4	1.1	2.0	6.2	4.7
U.K.	1.9	2.0	2.1	1.0	5.5	5.0
Italy	1.5	1.5	1.2	0.4	5.9	5.0
CANADA	3.7	2.1	2.4	0.8	7.1	6.1

GNP = Gross National Product, Expenditure Basis
C = Consumption (Private plus Public)
I = Investment, Net
G = Government Expenditures
X = Exports
M = Imports

* 1991–1998 (post-reunification).

The Japan–U.S. comparison illustrates a number of points that are generally applicable in macroeconomics. First, since national savings and investment tend to be correlated, a "saving" nation is also an investing nation. Second, since investment is the foundation of efficient, competitive production, a "saving" nation is likely to be an exporting nation. Third, government expenditures that lead to government deficits are a drain on national savings. Similar but less striking comparisons can be drawn, for example, between Germany and the United Kingdom.

Canada, the smallest economy in the group, is distinct in having the lowest investment share in GNP as well as the highest net exports. In other respects, Canada occupies the international middle ground in virtually every category.

MORE ON ECONOMIC STRUCTURE
To understand how economic policy choices can affect how an economy performs, a little more discussion of the structure of macroeconomics is useful.

Injections and Leakages
Increases in consumption, investment, government spending and/or exports all impose "demand" on the productive capacity of the Canadian economy.

43

More consumer spending — for food, household appliances, root canals and so on — induces the businesses that produce such goods and services to expand. Likewise, an increase in investment in, say, residential construction or industrial machinery gives rise to increased demands for Canadian construction materials and industrial goods. Increased aggregate demand thus boosts employment or, if there is already full employment, puts upward pressure on wage rates.

The amount of real economic growth that results from an increase in demand depends on the supply side of the economy. If the economy has unused productive capacity, as would be the case at the low point of a business cycle, an increase in demand will lead to increased real output and a rise in real GNP. On the other hand, if the economy is already operating at full employment of people and industry, an increase in demand will probably be expressed in higher prices, higher interest rates, reduced exports and an increased inflow of both imports and foreign capital. Nominal GNP may rise, but real GNP will be unchanged.

Investment, government spending and exports are "injections" into the circular flow of expenditures and income between the household and business sectors. Injections augment the circular flow by increasing aggregate demand.

Taxes, savings and imports, on the other hand, ease the demand on domestic productive capacity. They are referred to as "leakages." Taxes draw spending power away from consumers, household savings come at the expense of spending and imports divert spending abroad. Taxes, savings and imports thus tend to dampen the economy by deflecting spending out of the circular flow.

The analogy of injections and leakages is useful for understanding the dynamics of the economy, as well as for illustrating the objectives and instruments of economic policy. For example, when the economy is operating at less than full employment, an injection (or the reduction of a leakage) will increase aggregate demand; hence, the appropriate policy prescription involves some combination of increased government spending, tax cuts or lower interest rates to induce investment.

On the other hand, when demand pressure on the economy is excessive, it will likely result in inflation if left unchecked. The pressure can be relieved by controlled leakages, including higher taxes, reduced government spending and/or removal of impediments to imports.

Government spending, especially transfers and public-sector investment, can thus be used to stabilize an otherwise cyclical pattern in the private sector. The idea that taxes and government spending can be used strategically to control aggregate demand and the rate of economic growth in a less-than-full-employment economy was first formalized in 1936 by John Maynard Keynes in *The General Theory of Employment, Interest and Money*. What has since come to be termed Keynesian macroeconomic policy calls for counter-cyclical government intervention. When the economy is in a downturn, tax cuts and more government spending can increase aggregate demand. On the other hand, when the economy begins to "overheat," tax increases and less government spending ("a fiscal surplus") dampen overall demand. This approach also uses investment to control economic stimulus. This may be done directly with public-sector investment, or indirectly by using interest rates to influence private investment.

An alternative, less direct approach to foster economic growth focuses on removing government restrictions on commerce, enhancing productivity, embracing new technology and keeping labour in check. If such "supply-side" policies are effective, they result in increased supply at the same or even lower prices; consumers will then buy more and GNP will increase.

The Multiplier

The next question concerns the extent to which a stimulus (injection) or leakage will cause national income to grow or shrink as a result.

To determine this, it is necessary to realize that when an individual's income goes up, only part of the increased income is likely to be spent on consumption. Some will be saved. Conversely, when income goes down, both consumer expenditures and savings go down. The individual's splitting of increased income between new spending and saving results in what are referred to, respectively, as the "marginal propensity to consume" (MPC) and the "marginal propensity to save" (MPS): MPC plus MPS must equal 1.

Imagine now that the Sultan of Brunei arrives in Canada with $1-million to buy Mountie hats and maple syrup. The sultan's spending immediately puts $1-million in the hands of Canadian hat and syrup producers. Assume that these people save 20 per cent of their windfall ($200,000), and that they spend 80 per cent ($800,000) on a variety of things, including their costs of operation. That $800,000 of spending takes us to a third round wherein $160,000 is saved and $640,000 is recycled as new expenditure. The fourth round sees $128,000 (0.20 times $640,000) saved and $512,000 spent. The ever-diminishing rounds of spending and re-spending triggered by the sultan's initial $1-million eventually reach a cumulative total of $5-million. As Figure 5 shows, that means a $5-million increase in national income. The 5:1 ratio is termed the "multiplier." The "multiplier" is simply 1/MPS.

The marginal propensity to consume is the key to a number of important relations in macroeconomics. First, in view of the circularity of the flow of income in a macroeconomy, the MPC describes the amount of spending and re-spending that results from a sequence in which one person's spending is another person's income. The multiplier effect explained above depends directly on the MPC (or inversely on the MPS). The higher the marginal propensity to consume, the greater the consumer spending and re-spending induced by an initial boost to aggregate demand.

Second, income that is not consumed is saved. What is saved is funnelled through financial intermediaries to business, which uses the funds for investment. That is why savings must equal investment, although this is strictly the case only in a closed economy.

The Paradox of Thrift

The third key point that derives from the marginal propensity to consume is the "paradox of thrift." Think of what would happen to the economy if

DONALD J.S. BREAN

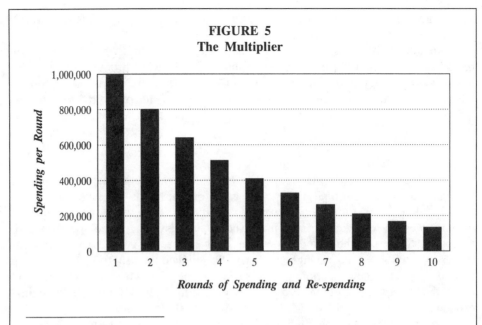

FIGURE 5
The Multiplier

Rounds of Spending and Re-spending

The multiplier determines the total amount of expenditure — involving rounds of spending and re-spending — that results from an initial (exogenous) expenditure increase. The value of the multiplier depends on the "marginal propensity to save."

The multiplier also runs in reverse. When expenditure is withdrawn from the economy, the multiplier explains the full extent of the resulting economic contraction.

suddenly all Canadians decided to spend a little less of their income and save a little more. Suppose that, instead of spending $90 out of every $100 of income and saving $10, everyone decides to spend $80 and save $20. What happens?

In theory, savings go up and so the business sector, with more funds to finance investment, invests more. The problem, however, is that if everyone saves more and spends less, the expenditure on goods and services will drop. Businesses will find that they cannot sell their wares. They certainly will not need to invest in order to expand production. Quite the contrary — they will probably contract, invest less and lay off workers. National income will fall, since fewer people will be employed. Eventually, as income falls, savings will also fall.

At the end of the day, though everyone will have tried to save more, everyone will have saved less. That is the paradox of thrift. But it is not so paradoxical when one realizes that one person's consumption supports another person's income. If that consumption subsides, production and income fall, and the whole economy declines.

The paradox of thrift arises out of the fact that a macroeconomy has crucially interdependent sectors — households and businesses in particular. It also demonstrates that the vibrancy of an economy depends on spending and production, both of which depend on consumer confidence.

MONEY, CREDIT AND MONETARY POLICY

This section examines the ways in which money — with its own special supply and demand — affects the economy. We focus largely on the interest rate and inflation, the factors most directly linked to monetary policy.

Money and Prices

Money is integral to macroeconomics. All commercial activity, investments, accounts and financial assets are measured in monetary terms. Every market transaction involves an exchange of money, in legal tender or its equivalent.

Goods and services have both *nominal* monetary values and *relative* real values that are determined in markets. For example, if a Coke costs $1 and a Big Mac costs $2, two Cokes equal one Big Mac. Those are relative values. The two nominal values ($1 and $2) reflect relative values (1:2).

The interest rate that one observes in the market, referred to as the "nominal" interest rate, has two distinct components. One part is the real interest rate, the other part represents inflation. No lender will lend money without taking into account an estimate of the erosion of the money's value through inflation while the loan is outstanding. Changes in the nominal interest rate, then, reflect changes in expectations of inflation. The real rate is equal to the nominal rate minus the inflation rate.

Money: Demand and Supply

There is both a demand for and a supply of money. The demand for money is derived from its use as a means of exchange. The amount of money needed for transactions varies directly with the level of economic activity — the more transactions, the greater the demand. The demand for money thus tends to rise and fall with the rise and fall of national income.

The supply of money is controlled by the central bank, The Bank of Canada. The Bank of Canada has several mechanisms at its disposal to control the money supply. First, it can simply print money and loan it to the federal government (by buying Government of Canada bonds) or a chartered bank. Similarly, it can create a deposit in the account of a chartered bank without actually producing any additional currency. The Bank of Canada influences the demand for loans from chartered banks by setting the rate it charges for these loans. This rate is called the bank rate. Decreasing the bank rate causes the chartered banks to borrow more from the Bank of Canada. The chartered banks then loan this money to businesses or consumers, thereby increasing the money supply. The Bank of Canada also uses the bank rate to signal its intentions regarding monetary policy. For example, lowering the bank rate indicates that the Bank of Canada is relatively unconcerned about inflation and is intending to stimulate the economy through expansionary monetary policy. The Bank of Canada is also directly involved in monetary transactions when it buys or sells government financial securities. When the bank sells such securities, it, in effect, "mops up" money that would otherwise have circulated in the economy. When the bank buys those securities, it puts money back into circulation.

Recall the earlier discussion of the income multiplier, which accounts for total spending and re-spending that results from an initial amount of spending. A similar phenomenon occurs on the monetary side of the economy. For example, when the Government of Canada funds part of its budget deficit by borrowing from the Bank of Canada, it will usually take the money it receives and deposit it in a bank. The bank receiving the Government's deposit will then lend most of the money to someone else. Banks always keep some of the deposits they receive on reserve, however, in case a depositor wants to make a withdrawal or in case they have some other need for funds. The lender who borrows money from the bank will also deposit the money so it can be reloaned, and so on. This process of borrowing, depositing and re-loaning will continue until the commercial banks involved hold reserves equals to the full amount of the original injection into the system. For example, if commercial banks typically hold 10 per cent of their deposit on reserve, then a purchase of $1-million in Government of Canada bonds by the Bank of Canada will lead to the creation of $10-million in new credit in the system.

Monetary Policy

By controlling the money supply and credit expansion, monetary policy influences the interest rate, the rate of inflation and, especially in Canada, the exchange rate. The need to hit three targets with one instrument — variations in money supply — makes monetary policy a tricky proposition. An increase in money supply or, more accurately, an increase in the rate of growth of money supply, tends to cause (1) a decrease in the interest rate; (2) an increase in prices (inflation); and (3) a depreciation (weakening) of the Canadian dollar.

Monetary Policy and the Interest Rate

The interest rate is the cost of money. When it goes up, businesses face higher costs for financing operations or purchasing buildings and equipment. Consumers are also discouraged from buying on credit. Thus, higher interest rates discourage both investment and consumption.

Investment and consumption underlie employment, economic growth and national income. When tight monetary policy makes credit more difficult to obtain, businesses and households respond by cutting capital expenditures, residential construction, inventory accumulation and indeed any expenditure based on credit. Tight monetary policy and higher interest rates thus dampen the economy.[2]

Timing is crucial in monetary policy. Just as horses trot on for a while after the reins have been tightened, a tighter monetary policy needs time to take effect. Likewise, it takes a while for economies to pick up speed after the reins have been loosened. Experience shows that it takes four to six quarters for monetary policy to take effect. Responsible monetary policy demands a steady hand on the rein.

In modern macroeconomic management, monetary policy has virtually completely replaced fiscal policy. Aggressive fiscal policy aimed at growth, especially via public-sector investment or tax-based redistribution to encourage consumer spending, has given way to a much greater concern for long-run stability achieved through sound monetary policy — where the targets are the interest rate, the exchange rates and inflation.

Monetary Policy and Inflation

Inflation is a general rise in all prices. It is usually measured by an index (such as the Consumers' or Producers' Price Index), using a constant basket of goods over time. If inflation is running at 10 per cent per year, a basket of goods that sells for $100 today will cost $110 this time next year.

Figure 6 illustrates the annual inflation rate in Canada for each of the past 20 years. The *cumulative* effect of these annual nominal price increases has pushed the price index (using a base of 100 for 1980) from 100 to 194. An income of $19,400 in 1999 thus had the same real spending power as an income of $10,000 in 1980.

The basic cause of inflation is excessive growth of the money supply. When the money supply grows at a faster rate than is required to accommodate real economic growth, the excess money growth lowers the value of outstanding money. For example, if real growth is 3 per cent per annum and money growth is 5 per cent, the expected inflation rate would be (5 – 3) or 2 per cent per year. Obviously, then, one method of controlling inflation is to control the money supply.

Growth in the Money Supply

Why does the money supply become "excessive" in the first place? There are at least two interdependent reasons. First, when the federal government incurs a deficit (that is, when federal spending exceeds tax revenue), that deficit is often financed in full or in part by monetary expansion. The Bank of Canada

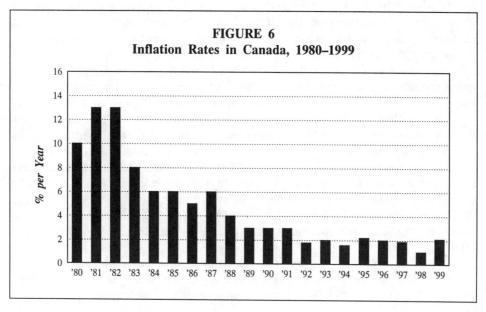

FIGURE 6
Inflation Rates in Canada, 1980–1999

creates new money to purchase new government bonds. Thus, an increase in the deficit may lead to monetary expansion and "monetization" of the debt.

The second reason why money growth may exceed real growth is more directly attributable to monetary policy aimed at economic growth. Expansionary monetary policy calls for an increase in money and credit in order to lower interest rates and thereby spur investment and consumption. But often the timing of the policy is wrong. If its effect on real interest rates is misjudged, or if investment and real expenditures do not respond to lower interest rates, expansionary monetary policy is largely inflationary.

The Battle against Inflation

Inflation is a destructive force. It weakens the integrity of the currency and causes hardship for those with fixed incomes; even those whose incomes are indexed or can be otherwise adjusted may experience lags before such adjustments take effect. Thus, inflation is inequitable: different segments of the population are affected differently.

By causing random changes in relative prices, inflation also reduces the information provided by prices, information that is crucial for consumers, employees and firms. This can lead to market inefficiency.

Inflation is particularly insidious in financial markets. Borrowers and lenders must anticipate and agree on future values of financial assets; otherwise, they will not borrow and lend. Inflation makes such predictions risky and thus discourages long-term finance. In Canada, the "long end" of the financial market virtually disappeared during the inflationary decade between 1975 and 1985.

Most industrial countries have experienced high and erratic inflation over the past 25 years, due largely to undisciplined monetary policy.[3] For the past 12 years in Canada, however, the Bank of Canada, with the endorsement of the Minister of Finance, has been firmly committed to the goal of low inflation and steady prices. In public statements, John Crow, the governor of the Bank of Canada until 1994, declared that if the pursuit of price stability compromises economic growth or the exchange rate, so be it. So steadfast was the governor, his policy came to be termed "the status Crow." But the policy has worked. In 1992, the Bank of Canada inflation rate fell below 6 per cent for the first time in more than 20 years, and by June 1992, inflation was 1.1 per cent, a 30-year low. Figure 6 shows that we continue to have low inflation in Canada.

Nevertheless, it is painful to squeeze inflation out of an economy. A decrease in inflation is not immediately matched by a decrease in interest rates and hence, investment and consumption continue to be discouraged. Fiscal policy must be tightened as well, to reduce aggregate demand. This means higher taxes and reduced government spending. In recent Canadian experience, such measures resulted in the unemployment rate rising as high as 11 per cent, which represented 1.5-million people out of work in 1992. Since then, with economic growth, the unemployment rate has fallen steadily to less than 7 per cent.

When an economy is suppressed to control inflation, some real output is inevitably lost in the process. This represents an economic cost in the battle against inflation. The made-in-Canada economic decline arrived earlier, and was both deeper and longer than the recession in other industrial countries. Estimates of the damage inflicted on Canada indicate that the economy did not resume its full output potential until late in the 1990s.

Nevertheless, the battle against inflation has been won. Canadian inflation has remained below 3 per cent per year for the past seven years. This price stability is reflected in low commercial interest rates.

Monetary Policy, International Capital Flows and the Exchange Rate

The effects of monetary policy are both weakened and enhanced by the fact that Canada is an "open" economy, with a very large foreign sector, a floating exchange rate and capital markets that are highly integrated with the rest of the world.

When Canadian capital requirements exceed the savings generated in Canada, the additional capital is imported. In other words, Canada borrows from abroad by selling Canadian securities to foreigners. Foreigners will buy Canadian securities when interest rates on them are at least as high as rates available in other countries.

Canadian interest rates, as we saw, are driven up by tight monetary policy. Therefore a tightening of monetary policy will raise Canadian interest rates and this, in turn, will attract foreign capital flows into Canada. This inflow offsets the effects sought by raising Canadian interest rates, and thus, to some extent, neutralizes domestic monetary policy.

Currency values are also affected. Before foreigners can buy Canadian securities, they must first buy Canadian dollars on the foreign-exchange market to pay for those securities. International "buy pressure" on the Canadian dollar drives up the exchange rate, and the Canadian dollar, being in demand, costs more. A Canadian dollar that is "higher" or more costly relative to other currencies makes imports less expensive for Canadians, and Canadian exports more expensive for foreign purchasers. In both respects, Canadian competitiveness is adversely affected.

The impact of monetary policy on inflation, interest rates and exchange rates is, then, complex. It is, perhaps, useful to give a point-by-point summary of economic developments in Canada since 1988, when the Bank of Canada embarked on a program of strict — some would say overly strict — monetary discipline.

➤ The growth of the money supply was sharply curtailed. In 1990, the amount of currency plus bank deposits in Canada actually decreased;

➤ Inflation dropped from 5 per cent in 1989 to less than 1.5 per cent in 1992;

➤ Short-term interest rates fell from 12 per cent in 1989 to 6 per cent in mid-1992;

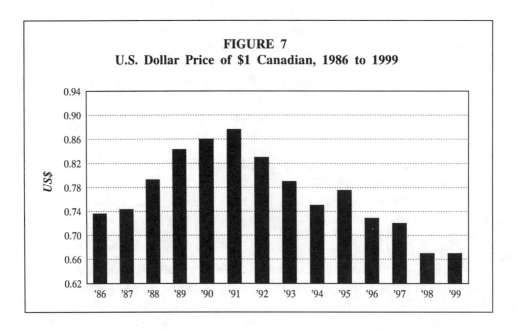

FIGURE 7
U.S. Dollar Price of $1 Canadian, 1986 to 1999

➢ The exchange rate rose from US$0.76 in 1987 to US$0.86 in 1992 (see Figure 7);

➢ In 1991, the Canadian balance of merchandise trade shifted from surplus to deficit. Both imports and exports fell, but exports fell more. The effect of the U.S. recession on Canadian exports was exacerbated by the high value of the Canadian dollar;

➢ Production and aggregate demand fell sharply in 1990. The Canadian economy entered a period of slow or no growth through to 1992;

➢ Unemployment rose from 7.8 per cent in 1988 to more than 11 per cent in 1992;

➢ High interest rates reduced domestic investment directly, and the high dollar compounded the adverse effects by rendering Canadian exports substantially more expensive in the United States, the largest market.

As outlined earlier, the tide began to turn by mid-1992. A strong U.S. recovery began to pull up the Canadian economy. Canadian exports, output, investment, employment and incomes all rebounded from the lows of 1992. The years 1993 and most of 1994 were buoyant and relatively prosperous times for Canadians.

Unfortunately, the bloom on the Canadian economic rose began to fade by late 1994. The seemingly unmanageable fiscal deficit (much of it owed to foreigners), together with the political uncertainty over the question of Quebec separation, added a huge risk premium to Canadian interest rates and dramatically weakened the Canadian dollar. By January 1995, the Canadian dollar sank to a nine-year low vis-à-vis the U.S. dollar, while real interest rates hovered in the 9 per cent range — the highest in the industrial world.

By 1997, the bugbear of inflation was gone. Equally important, *expectations* of inflation also faded. As a result, nominal *and* real interest rates fell. The Canadian economy steamed ahead at close to 4 per cent annual growth, driven largely by exports.

FISCAL POLICY AND THE NATIONAL DEBT

Every nation decides for itself the extent to which its government will be involved in the economy and the social system. The assignment of economic responsibilities between Canada's public and private sectors means, for example, that Canadians have socialized medicine, but not socialized dentistry; publicly funded elementary and secondary education, but only partially funded university education; private forestry companies paying fees to cut wood on Crown lands; and a military system that contracts out many services to the private sector.

While governments, like households, may conceivably spend less money than they take in, such has not been the recent experience, especially for Canada. The Canadian federal government incurred a deficit every year from 1975 to 1996. That deficit and especially its **cumulative** effect — its addition to national debt — has profound implications for our economic stability.

A deficit is simply the difference between a government's expenditures and its revenues. In fiscal year 1999, for example, federal government expenditures were $153-billion and revenues of $156-billion, a surplus of $3-billion. This may be compared to a $7-billion deficit in 1981. Figure 8 charts the course of the deficit from 1980 to 1999.

Canada currently has a national debt of approximately $560-billion, or $18,000 per person. In 1975, the government debt was approximately 20 per cent the size of the GDP. At present, the debt-to-GDP ratio is more than 60 per cent. Interest paid on the public debt has risen from 3.5 per cent of the GDP in 1975 to more than 9 per cent today. This is now the largest government expenditure after social welfare. It is larger than outlays on education or health. More than 35 per cent of federal government revenue is used to service the debt.

The strong, steady economic growth that Canada has enjoyed throughout the 1990s has had various positive and enriching effects, but perhaps none so dramatic as the change in the finances of the government sector — both the federal government and the provincial governments. At the start of the 1990s, the government had been running fiscal deficits (spending in excess of tax revenue) and financing this excessive spending by borrowing money. The government was deeply in debt, and getting even deeper so.

Things began to change by about 1994. Economic growth brought in increased tax revenue and provided a more favourable climate for cutting government spending. As a result, the deficit fell and the government's need for borrowing was reduced. By 1997, the government moved into fiscal surplus as tax revenue exceeded spending. By 2000 the surplus was impressively large and forecast to continue. The tide had turned. The weight of government borrowing and the economic dislocation that it causes was reversed. A burden on economic growth was gone.

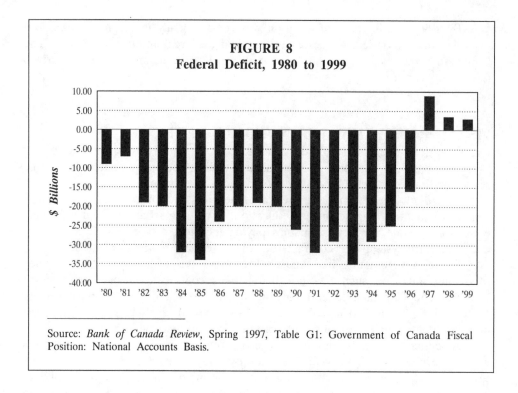

FIGURE 8
Federal Deficit, 1980 to 1999

Source: *Bank of Canada Review*, Spring 1997, Table G1: Government of Canada Fiscal Position: National Accounts Basis.

Deficits, Exchange Rates and Trade

To appreciate the complex relationships among the deficit and other variables, we must return to the national accounts. These relationships can be illustrated by extending the framework begun above:

(1) $\qquad Y \qquad = \quad C + I + G + (X - M)$

(2) $\qquad GNP \qquad = \quad Y + R$

(3) $\qquad GNP \qquad = \quad C + T + S$

(4) $\quad C + I + G + (X - M) + R \quad = \quad C + T + S$

(5) $\qquad (G - T) + (I - S) \quad = \quad (M - X) - R$

where:

Y	=	GDP (Gross Domestic Product)
C	=	Consumption
S	=	Savings
I	=	Investment
G	=	Government Expenditure
X	=	Exports
M	=	Imports
R	=	Foreign Investment Income
T	=	Tax Payments

Recall that GDP can be expressed in two ways: on an expenditures or income basis. Equation (1) states that GDP is the sum of consumption, investment, government expenditures and net exports. The difference between GDP and GNP (gross national product) is foreign investment income (denoted by R above). In terms of income uses, equation (3) indicates that Canadians use their income by consuming goods, paying taxes and/or saving. Equation (4) simply combines equations (1), (2) and (3). Rearranging terms, we obtain equation (5), which gives us the fundamental relationship between budget deficits, the investment/saving balance and the current account. That is:

$$\boxed{(G-T)} \quad + \quad \boxed{(I-S)} \quad = \quad \boxed{(M-X)-R}$$

Budget Deficit   Investment/Saving Balance   Current Account

If $G > T$ we have a budget deficit. Given a deficit, if either $I = S$ or $I > S$, it implies that $(M - X) - R > O$ (that is imports > exports + foreign investment income). Thus, a government budget deficit implies a current account deficit.

Canada's balance of payments is the consolidation of our economic transactions with the rest of the world. The balance of payments must "balance":

The balance of payments = current account + capital account = O

$$(6) \quad (X-M) + R + \Delta K \quad = \quad O$$

where: ΔK = capital flows

Rearranging terms, we have:

$$(7) \quad -(X - M + R) \quad = \quad \Delta K$$
$$(8) \quad (G - T) + (I - S) \quad = \quad \Delta K$$

In other words, when Canada spends more than it earns, the difference must be financed with capital inflows.

Canada's deficit was indeed financed to a large extent through imports of foreign capital. The Canadian government ran deficits in order to serve Canadians — providing a social safety net, addressing regional disparities and so on. But the gap between spending and government revenues was met by domestic and foreign borrowing, putting payment off until sometime in the future.

Deficit Reduction

Why then was it so difficult to reduce the government deficit? By the late 1980s, business leaders, economists and organized labour all agreed on one point — government spending, at all levels, must be brought into line.

Criticism — or defence — of fiscal deficits inevitably involves complex judgements about the economic and social value of government spending and the consequences of increasing revenue through taxation. Those who argue for lower government spending must identify social programs, government departments, services or transfers to be cut — health, education, defence, farm support, foreign aid etc. Those favouring deficit reduction via higher taxes — a much smaller group than those who support expenditure reduction — must identify additional sources of government revenue, such as higher personal income tax, higher corporate taxes or sales taxes (such as the GST). Such decisions on the level and structure of tax inevitably have implications for income distribution (who will pay the tax) as well as for economic growth (since taxation generally discourages both private investment and labour).

The way the deficit is financed has important economic consequences. The government can finance the deficit either by borrowing or by "printing money." Both methods affect the economy, but in significantly different ways. Government borrowing tends to raise interest rates and "crowd out" private investment by diverting private savings to public purposes. And since the debt must eventually be repaid, taxes will be higher at some point in the future.

On the other hand, when the government finances its deficit by "printing money" — which it does by selling bonds to its bank, the Bank of Canada — the result is inflationary. This is perhaps easiest to understand if we assume an initial position of zero deficit. The subsequent introduction of a fiscal deficit itself reflects an increase in government spending and thus, an increase in aggregate demand. Monetary expansion to finance the deficit then creates a "double-whammy" effect — it increases the money supply and the demand for goods and services.

In recent years, the policy of the Bank of Canada has been to steadfastly resist excessive growth in the money supply. Thus, recent government deficits were financed largely by increases in government borrowing. This, as we have seen, puts pressure on interest rates, which in turn crowds out private investment. The effect of tight monetary policy, in the face of expansionary fiscal policy, is a fall in inflation and nominal interest rates, yet a rise in real interest rates. Foreigners, assured that their investments will not be debased by inflation, are thus encouraged to lend to Canada, driving up the value of the dollar. The uniquely Canadian and very perplexing phenomenon in the mid-1990s was that a steadily increasing risk premium — due to the debt plus political uncertainty regarding Quebec — drove up real Canadian interest rates as the Canadian dollar weakened.

TOMORROW'S ECONOMY

This briefing opened with a series of newspaper headlines dealing with Canadian macroeconomic issues. The press points to a buoyant Canadian economy in short- to medium-term future. The current upbeat headlines disguise a painful preceding period of economic adjustment to lower fiscal deficits, tight money and economic difficulties that to some extent are rooted in our complex political make-up.

Although Canada's economic recovery is surprisingly strong, it is also perilous. New factors introduce new uncertainty to Canadian economic performance. For example, the U.S.–Canada Free Trade Agreement, later extended to include Mexico (NAFTA), has led to numerous Canadian plant closures amid general economic growth, as Canadian business faces increasing pressure to be internationally competitive. Also, as mentioned, any loss of credibility in control of government debt, or failure to resolve our political uncertainties, would have profound implications for Canadian interest rates — a factor which tends to dampen growth.

The Canadian economy is nevertheless fundamentally sound. Canada has an abundance of natural resources, a well-educated and flexible labour force and a dependable industrial infrastructure — including a world-leading position in resource technology, telecommunications and transportation. As we look ahead, the Canadian approach to economic policy — in monetary, fiscal and industrial dimensions — by dint of painful necessity, now appears to be more sensitive to consequences for economic growth than was perhaps the case in the past. Canada can be expected to weather the immediate difficulties, and to maintain our position as an economically strong and stable nation.

NOTES

1. Enquiring minds may be puzzled that there is no place for banks in the circular flow model. Important as they are in the economic system, banks are nevertheless not a sector unto themselves, but "intermediaries." Banks and other financial institutions are integral to the flow of savings to investment. More discussion of chartered banks, and the key economic role of the Bank of Canada, is provided later.

2. Bond prices and interest rates are closely — and *inversely* — related. A "discount" bond is a contract to borrow money now and repay it later. The amount borrowed is less than the amount repaid. The difference, the "discount," represents interest on the borrowed money. Say $90 is borrowed now with a promise to repay $100 one year from now. $100 is the "face value" of the bond; $90 is the price. The interest rate is (100 − 90)/90, or 11 per cent. If the Bank of Canada buys such bonds in sufficient volume, the price will move up from $90 to, say, $92. As a result, the interest rate will drop from 11 per cent to (100 − 92)/92, or 9 per cent.

3. It is perhaps interesting to note that over the long run, the federal government *must* run a cumulative deficit as the means to expand the money supply.

The Sectoral Structure of Canada's Economy

Tom Wesson

This article will provide an overview of the sectoral structure of Canada's economy. First, we will look at the evolution of Canada's economy from an agrarian to a manufacturing and finally to a service-based economy. Some of the consequences of our new reliance on services will also be discussed. The second part of the article will trace the development of Canada's corporate sector, which is unique in several ways. We will look at why our corporate sector developed in such an unusual way, and then at its consequences for Canada and Canadians, focusing on the effects of two key factors: the high degree of concentration of wealth and corporate power within Canada, and the high degree of foreign ownership of Canadian businesses.

THE SECTORAL COMPOSITION OF THE CANADIAN ECONOMY

Taken together, Figures 1 (1900–1960) and 2 (1961–2000) show how the sectoral composition of Canada's economy has changed dramatically over the course of the twentieth century.[1] Looking first at Figure 1, we can see that at the turn of the century, there was a degree of balance between employment in the primary sectors of the economy — agriculture, mining, logging, fishing, hunting and trapping — and the industrial and service sectors. Within the primary sector, employment was dominated by the agricultural sector. Employment in agriculture declined more or less steadily until World War II, at which point agriculture's share of Canadian employment began to drop rapidly. In fact, since World War II, the absolute number of Canadians employed in agriculture has been dropping. A trend that is closely related to the declining role of agriculture in Canadian employment has been the increasing urbanization of the Canadian population. More and more Canadians now live in cities, as people

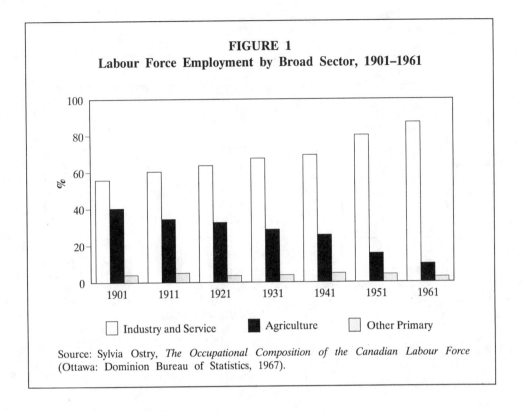

FIGURE 1
Labour Force Employment by Broad Sector, 1901–1961

Source: Sylvia Ostry, *The Occupational Composition of the Canadian Labour Force* (Ottawa: Dominion Bureau of Statistics, 1967).

leave rural areas in search of employment, and cities attract the lion's share of new immigrants.

The flip side of the decline in agricultural employment in Canada has been great increases in the share of Canadians employed in goods producing and service industries. Again, this change was most notable in the first 15 years or so immediately following World War II. While it continued through the 1960s, 1970s and 1980s (see Figure 2), it has slowed somewhat. What is a more significant trend in the later post-war period is the growth in service employment. While even in 1960, the majority of Canadian workers were employed in services, today the ratio of service to manufacturing employment is about twice what it was in 1960.

Economists have devoted much effort to explaining these shifts in employment, and have had some success to show for their efforts. First, the shift from agricultural employment can be attributed in large part to an increase in the productivity of agricultural labour: that is, it now takes far fewer agricultural workers to produce the same output. This fact is easily explained by the increasing sophistication and mechanization of agricultural production. Developments from the internal combustion-engine-powered tractor to synthetic hormones to boost milk production have all helped fewer agricultural workers to produce more output.

The shift from manufacturing to service employment is not as simple to explain as the shift from agricultural employment. Several explanations have

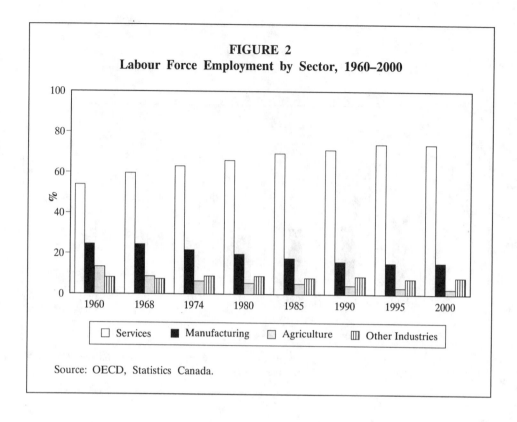

FIGURE 2
Labour Force Employment by Sector, 1960–2000

Source: OECD, Statistics Canada.

been put forth, and they all seem to have some validity, although none is significantly better than the others when tested statistically.[2] Furthermore, it is especially difficult to test these theories because, in general, available statistics concerning the service sector are much less detailed than those for the manufacturing sector.

One possibility is that the transformation of the Canadian economy into a service one rests, like the shift away from agriculture, on differing rates of productivity improvements. It is hypothesized that labour productivity growth in manufacturing has outpaced that in services, since many service functions (often very simple ones, like waiting tables, and very complex ones, like performing heart surgery) do not lend themselves well to mechanization. Thus, productivity growth in these areas is slow relative to manufacturing. The result of this difference in productivity growth rates is that more Canadians need to be employed in services in order to maintain the relative levels of service and manufacturing output.[3]

A second explanation for the shift towards services in the Canadian economy is a change in consumer demand from manufactured goods to services. The underlying assumption behind this argument is that as incomes rise, people spend more on services than on goods. In other words, it is thought that services tend to be considered luxuries compared to goods. Since, in general, the incomes of Canadians have been continually rising, this assumption implies that

Canadians' consumption of services relative to goods will also be rising. A related reason why Canadians' relative demand for goods and services may have shifted is the growth in households in which all adults are employed outside the home. This trend has been a boon to such "luxury" service industries as fast-food restaurants and housekeeping services.

Closely related to the hypothesis that consumers are demanding more services today than in the past is the hypothesis that other industries are demanding more services as inputs than in the past. For example, 30 years ago the information-systems consulting industry did not exist. Today, Canadian firms spend billions of dollars annually on this service. Even the demands for traditional services, such as transportation and logistics, may be increasing as Canadian firms expand the geographic scope of their markets and rationalize production among their plants.

A final reason given for the growth in services in the Canadian economy is the trend towards contracting out of services by manufacturing firms. For example, if a manufacturing firm contracts out the job of cleaning its facilities instead of maintaining its own cleaning staff, employment in the manufacturing sector is reduced while manufacturing in services increases. This change occurs without any change in the actual work performed. However, all estimates indicate that contracting out is a relatively small contributor to the growth in service employment in Canada.

Whatever their relative importance in transforming Canada into a service economy, the combined effect of these changes is clear: services are playing a far greater role in our economy than they have in the past. This change, in turn, is significant for several reasons. First, it means that to be successful in the future, Canadians will require different job skills than in the past. Furthermore, in a service economy, an individual's success is more dependent on his skill level than in manufacturing industries. High-productivity, and thus high-paying, occupations in the service sector are those which demand greater skill levels, while in manufacturing labour productivity is often a function of the capital employed. In services, it is the skills of the employee that most often determine her value to the firm. Obviously, this fact has implications for education and training which must be considered by workers, employers and governments alike.

The shift to a service economy has other implications for government policy as well. The mere fact that the data collected by governments on services are sparse and ill-conceived shows that governments typically focus on manufacturing industries in their economic policy discussions. Governments must realize that service industries have been a major driver of economic growth in Canada for several decades, and must adapt such aspects of economic policy as industrial, tax and regional policies to reflect this fact.

Now that we have some picture of the sectoral make-up of the Canadian economy, we will turn our attention to the economic actors who actually employ workers and produce output in these various sectors — firms. The rest of this article is devoted to describing what can loosely be called the Canadian corporate sector. Before we go into detail exploring the Canadian corporate sector, however, it is necessary to understand what is implied by the word "corporation" and what alternative forms of business organization exist.

THE MAKE-UP OF THE MODERN CORPORATION

The word "corporation" is derived from the Latin word *corpus*, meaning body. The essence of a modern corporation is that it is a separate legal body, or entity, distinct from its owners. This legal separation between the corporation and its owners leads, in turn, to the concept of limited liability. This means that any investor in a corporation is risking only the amount of his investment and is not liable for any losses of the corporation beyond this amount. In contrast, in an unincorporated business (known either as a sole proprietorship or a partnership, depending on the number of investors), the firm's owner/managers are fully liable for the firm's debts, up to the full amount of their ability to pay. Thus, for example, if a doctor loses a malpractice suit, not only must he use the assets associated with his practice to pay the settlement imposed, but he must also use his personal assets to whatever extent necessary. In contrast, while the asbestos-related lawsuits against the U.S. firm Johns Manville bankrupted the firm, its shareholders lost only the value of their investment, not their personal assets.

The fact that corporations are distinct legal entities has many benefits for them and their investors, as well as the economy as a whole. If corporations were not legally separate from their owners, there could be no capital markets as we know them. Investors would not put money in a business over which they had essentially no control if their entire worth could be put at risk by poor management decisions. Similarly, the process of trading shares in a corporation would be greatly complicated if every time the corporation's ownership changed, the underlying financial strength of the corporation changed. Furthermore, corporations have a continuity that other forms of business enterprise lack. The Hudson's Bay Company is over 330 years old and has evolved into a completely different organization than it was originally, with different ownership, goals, activities and so on; yet it has had a legal continuity over that period which has facilitated its various strategic changes. Finally, but perhaps most important, corporations are able to enter into contracts and other legal commitments independently of their owners. Imagine if all the workers, suppliers and customers of a large corporation like Bell Canada had to enter into contracts with the firm's individual shareholders! The specialization of labour and exploitation of scale economies which drove the Industrial Revolution in the late eighteenth and early nineteenth centuries, and the growth of the industrialized economies since then, would have been impossible without the corporation.

Of course, incorporation for a business owner is not without its costs, most of which are government imposed. As they do with most other legal entities under their jurisdiction, governments, at both the federal and provincial levels in Canada, tax and regulate corporations. Because of this, incorporation necessarily involves trade-offs which limit its desirability somewhat. However, it is important to note that the vast majority of economic activity in Canada involves corporations.

While corporations were an essential element in the industrialization of the world economy, their origins are actually much older. Similar forms of organization have been used since the late Middle Ages to raise money for such activities as trading, which require large investments up front. Initially, these organizations were created by royal charter to perform some particular function. For example, the Hudson Bay Company charter gave it the right to trade in all of the territory that drained into Hudson Bay. By 1700, English business people and lawyers had combined aspects of contract and trust law to develop the joint-stock company. Joint-stock companies were much like corporations in practice, except they lacked the benefit of limited liability. However, they had a great advantage over chartered companies, in that they could be created without a royal decree or an act of Parliament. By the early part of the nineteenth century, most jurisdictions had enacted legislation which enabled individuals to form corporations without legislative approval, providing certain legal conditions were met.

Only during the late nineteenth century, however, did the professionally managed corporation that we know today begin to evolve. As corporations became larger and involved in increasingly complex activities, their owners found it difficult to effectively manage the activities of these growing enterprises. It also became harder for a small number of owners to meet the equity capital needs of a large corporation as production technologies became more capital and scale intensive. Out of these increasing managerial and financial challenges, together with the expansion of the middle class with funds available to invest, grew the modern structure of the large corporation. Under this structure, the shareholders play no direct role in the operations of the corporation beyond electing a board of directors to represent their interests. The board of directors, in turn, hires a group of professional managers to run the corporation. Typically, some of these managers are also board members. These employee-directors are known as inside directors, while board members who are not employees of the corporation are called outside directors.

Among the duties required of directors under the Canadian Business Corporation Act is to "act honestly and in good faith with the view of the best interests of the corporation and ... [to] exercise the care, diligence and skill that a reasonably prudent person would exercise in comparable circumstances...."[4] A corporation's directors do not have the duty to act as the shareholders would like them to, but they do have a clear duty to act in the best interests of the corporation and, therefore, its shareholders. James Gillies has likened a board member to a member of Parliament, elected to represent shareholders' interests, but with their first responsibility being to do what they believe is in the best interest of the corporation.[5]

In recent years, there has been much criticism of the way boards of directors fulfil their fiduciary duty to the corporation and its shareholders. It has been argued, by such authors as Peter Drucker, Irving Olds (the former chairman of the board of U.S. Steel), and Harold Geneen (the former chairman of the board of AT&T), that in many corporations the board is essentially a ceremonial body.[6]

It is very difficult for boards to provide an effective check on management activities for several reasons. First, although board members are normally elected by the shareholders at the corporation's annual meeting, in most cases the meeting is poorly attended, and the election is largely ceremonial. Second, outside directors are essentially dependent on management for the information they use in decision making, while inside directors obviously cannot provide an effective check on their own activities. Finally, board members often feel an obligation, or at least a practical need, to concur with the views of those responsible for their election. As we will see, in Canada this is often a single large shareholder who controls the corporation. However, in the United States it is often the corporation's management which effectively elects the board, since shareholders often assign their proxies to management, giving it de facto control of the corporation without significant ownership.

In fact, today, boards of directors are coming under greater scrutiny, and are being forced to be more responsible to shareholders for several reasons. First, investors are becoming more sophisticated and more critical. As large institutional investors, like pension and mutual funds, expand their portfolios, they are becoming major shareholders of more and more corporations. Unlike large individual or corporate investors, these funds usually wish to play no role in the daily management of the firm's operations. They merely wish to have their interests — that is, the shareholders' interests — protected by an effective board of directors to which management is responsive. Because of their size and their ability to influence other investors, many pension funds are able to exert at least indirect influence over such large corporations as General Motors, IBM and Exxon. The rise of large institutional investors means that many of the largest corporations are forced to deal with shareholders whose economic clout is comparable to their own for the first time since corporations began to grow so large that no individual could reasonably hope to maintain a controlling interest in them.

Also forcing boards to be more responsive to shareholders is the fact that, to a great extent in the United States and to a lesser degree in Canada, board members are being held legally responsible for their actions and those of the corporation. Shareholders are suing board members who fail to carry out their fiduciary responsibility, while interested parties outside the corporation are suing board members when they feel they have been harmed by the corporation's activities. Shareholder suits have forced boards to look much more critically at the information provided to them by management, especially when issues are involved in which management might have a biased position, such as a takeover.

In many ways, suits by outsiders are the most threatening to boards of directors, since they can involve matters about which the board had essentially no knowledge. For example, an environmental group might sue the board of a corporation which pollutes a waterway, or the employees of a corporation may sue its board if the company pension fund is mismanaged. These third-party suits are evidence of a general feeling that, in fact, the board of a modern corporation should be responsible not just to the firm's shareholders, but to the other stakeholders of the firm as well. In many European countries this recognition has resulted in legislation which gives employees the right to representation on the board, while in the United States many states have passed legislation recognizing the general principle that boards should represent other stakeholders in addition to shareholders.

Finally, it is important to recognize another trend that affected both the role of boards of directors in the modern corporation and the entire way in which corporations are managed. During the 1980s there was an enormous boom in what has been called the market for corporate control, that is, in the market for takeovers, leveraged buyouts (LBOs) and other changes in corporations' ownership structure. Many of the takeovers and LBOs of the 1980s were aimed at breaking down the cosy relationship between the target corporations' management and their boards of directors. It was argued that because boards of directors were not forcing management to operate in the best interest of shareholders, there were profits to be made by taking over the corporation and replacing the existing management team with a new one which would act in the best interest of the shareholders. Often, the process was accomplished by buying a public corporation (that is, one whose shares trade on an established stock exchange) and converting it into a private corporation in which the shareholders took a direct role in its management. This phenomenon was so prevalent that Michael Jensen, a prominent author in the field, wrote of "The Eclipse of the Public Corporation."[7] While the public corporation will probably not be eclipsed any time soon, it is undoubtedly true that the takeover and LBO booms did serve to heighten boards' awareness of the need to maximize shareholder value.

Now that we understand what a corporation is, and something about how corporations are governed, we will now look at the development of Canada's unique corporate sector.

THE CORPORATE SECTOR IN CANADA

While Canadians often think that our corporate sector is largely similar in structure to that of the United States, the fact of the matter is there are profound and important differences between the two nations in the way in which businesses are organized, managed and operated. As Canadians, we have never fully trusted the market mechanism to allocate resources and rewards optimally, and therefore have not done as much as our continental neighbours either to encourage the growth of what has been called free enterprise, or to discourage conditions which inhibit its growth. The result has been the development of a uniquely Canadian corporate sector which, like many Canadian institutions, is a curious mix of contrasts and contradictions, growing out of a series of historical accidents, poorly coordinated government policies and politically, rather than economically, motivated policy decisions.

There are several key aspects to our corporate sector's uniqueness. The first is related to ownership and control. To a significant extent, Canadian corporations are controlled by foreigners. Furthermore, many Canadian-controlled corporations are controlled by a relatively small group of individuals and firms. Next, relating to the competitive environment faced by Canadian corporations is the fact that Canada often has a relatively small number of corporations in any particular industry. A final unique aspect of our corporate sector relates to the activities performed by Canadian corporations. To a far greater extent than is typical of a nation of Canada's level of wealth, Canadian corporations are involved in the extraction and processing of natural resources.

All of these aspects of Canada's corporate sector have a negative impact on our economic and political well-being. To a large extent, they developed out of a series of poorly planned and coordinated government policies, often brought about by the government of the day's unwillingness to make hard political choices (or by the unwillingness of the people of Canada to re-elect a government which makes such choices). We will now explore how these policies came about.

Canada, like most nations which began as colonies of the European powers, was initially seen as a source of raw materials for its colonizers, as well as a market for their finished products. This role for Canada is apparent in the early histories of such British-controlled Canadian firms as the Hudson Bay Company (founded in 1670), The General Mining Association Limited (1825) and the Canada Company (1826). As British-controlled firms in Canada grew, financial firms like the Bank of British North America (1836) and the Trust and Loan Company of Canada (1845) were set up by British investors to serve other British firms operating in Canada.

However, a major local spur to the industrialization of Canada came after the American Revolution, when thousands of United Empire Loyalists came to Nova Scotia, Quebec and Ontario from the United States. The Loyalists were mainly middle-class merchants and small businessmen who were opposed to the liberal ideals which motivated the American Revolution. They tended to be politically conservative, but did feel that the state should intervene to protect small businesses from competitive pressures. (This would prove to be a very persistent idea in Canadian politics and economics.) The Loyalists started myriad small industrial enterprises, especially in Ontario (particularly in the southwest) and Nova Scotia. However, the businesses founded by the Loyalists soon outgrew the financing available locally, and Canada began to rely on British financing not just for British firms operating in Canada, but for indigenous ones as well.

While historical circumstances favoured a Canadian corporate sector with a high degree of foreign investment and an ambivalent attitude towards competition, government policies, most notably the National Policy introduced by Sir John A. Macdonald's Conservative government in 1878, greatly accelerated these trends. The National Policy, arguably Canada's most important economic policy until the 1988 Free Trade Agreement with the United States, was designed to encourage investment and economic growth within Canada as well as build an east-west flow of goods to tie the country together economically. The policy had two simple components — high tariffs on manufactured goods and an open market for foreign investment. Under the National Policy, the average tariff on Canadian imports rose from 17.5 per cent to 25 per cent between 1878 and 1879.[8]

The tariff was seen as a means of encouraging the growth of manufacturing industries in Central Canada, allowing them to reach a scale that would enable them to compete internationally. The Conservatives were greatly helped in their efforts to sell the tariff to the electorate outside Central Canada by the fact that the economy had slumped badly under the Liberals in the five years preceding the 1878 election, and by the rejection of Canada–U.S. free trade by the U.S. Senate in 1873.

Those in Canada who might have opposed the tariff were also appeased in several ways. First, for the most part, the machinery needed by Canada's natural-resource industries was exempt from the tariff or charged relatively low rates of duty. Second, it was pointed out that the tariff and resulting east-west flow of goods would help make the Canadian Pacific Railway viable. Many Western Canadians were willing to make economic sacrifices in exchange for the railway, since it was seen as an essential means of solidifying Canada's claim to the Prairies in face of U.S. expansionist elements. Finally, Macdonald used what today would be called the "infant industry protection" argument to sell the tariff. He argued that by temporarily protecting Central Canada's young industries from competition from their larger and more fully developed U.S. counterparts, the tariff would give Canada's industries the opportunity to grow and become efficient. Then, the tariff could be removed and Canadians would have access to competitively priced Canadian-made manufactured goods as well as foreign goods and would have manufacturers who could compete internationally. As it turned out, this "temporary" protection lasted, at least in part, until 1988. (Figure 3 shows average Canadian tariffs for the period 1971–1985, while Figure 4 shows average Canadian tariffs on various categories of manufactured products for 1987.)

The second central element of Macdonald's National Policy was a wide open-investment policy. Macdonald described his feelings towards investment this way: "The bigger the capitalist and the more he has invested in the country, the better for the country."[9] The Conservatives felt that one of the factors constraining the Canadian economy was a lack of capital for growth, and hoped to attract both foreign and domestic investors to Canada's protected markets. Under this policy, foreign investment in Canada grew relatively slowly but steadily for about 30 years. Then, during the economic boom of 1908–1922, foreign investment in Canada boomed also. During this later period, however, an important change began to take place in the source and type of foreign investment in Canada. As previously mentioned, most of the early foreign investment in Canada was from Britain, and this was debt, not equity financing. During the early twentieth century, however, more and more of the foreign investment in Canada was equity investments by American firms and individuals. In 1900,

FIGURE 3
Canadian Tariff Rates, 1971–1985

Year	Nominal Tariffs on Imports	Nominal Tariffs on Dutiable Imports	Per Cent of Imports Not Dutiable
1971	7.1	15.4	54.0
1975	6.7	15.1	55.9
1980	5.4	13.8	60.6
1985	4.2	11.2	62.8

Source: The General Agreement on Tariffs and Trade, *Trade Policy Review: Canada* (Geneva: The General Agreement on Tariffs and Trade, 1990).

FIGURE 4
Canadian Tariff Rates, 1987

Product	Average Rate — Import Weighted	Average Rate — Production Weighted
Agriculture	2.8	3.0
Forestry	0.0	0.0
Fishing and Trapping	0.1	0.2
Mining	0.0	0.2
Manufacturing	4.6	5.4
Clothing	22.5	20.3
Tobacco	12.2	16.3
Furniture and Fixtures	18.3	12.5
Electrical Products	6.0	7.9
Metal Fabricating	7.8	7.5
Chemicals and Chemical Products	5.1	6.0
Food and Beverage	4.2	5.6
Machinery	3.1	4.9
Transportation Equipment	1.5	2.8
Petroleum and Coal Products	0.6	0.5
Total Average	4.3	4.6

Source: The General Agreement on Tariffs and Trade, *Trade Policy Review: Canada* (Geneva: The General Agreement on Tariffs and Trade, 1990).

14 per cent of the foreign investment in Canada was by Americans. By 1926, this figure was 53 per cent and by 1948, 74 per cent.[10]

To a large extent, these new equity investments were an unforeseen consequence of the National Policy, although in retrospect, they were a perfectly logical one. Since foreign firms importing goods into Canada were placed at a great disadvantage by the tariff, but were free to invest in Canada as they saw fit, more and more foreign firms invested in Canadian subsidiaries and/or bought existing Canadian firms in order to produce goods in Canada for the Canadian market. These branch plants typically produced a broad product range at a small scale and, therefore, never became the efficient manufacturers which the National Policy was supposed to foster. Because they were foreign owned, these firms had no incentive to improve their efficiency and compete internationally, since they would only be competing with their parents. Thus, one of the legacies of the National Policy was a branch-plant economy — a Canadian manufacturing sector which was a miniature replica of the U.S. manufacturing sector, producing goods for Canadian consumption at an inefficiently small scale.

In addition to encouraging a high level of foreign investment in Canadian manufacturing industries, the National Policy allowed foreigners continued open access to Canada's raw material resources. Macdonald's open policy towards investment allowed firms like the precursors of Inco and the Aluminum Company of America to invest in Canada to extract ore, and then to export the ore back to the United States for processing. Later, large American oil companies were responsible for the development of Western Canada's oil and gas reserves, and American firms opened up Labrador's iron reserves for development.

Often these foreign firms (usually American) were able to open up Canada's resource frontiers before Canadian firms because for them, their investments represented opportunities for vertical integration, while for potential Canadian investors, they did not. This meant that for the American investors, these resource developments had a certain market for their output and were, therefore, less risky than for potential Canadian investors. This pattern of foreign-owned firms exporting unprocessed natural resources meant that Canada never developed a strong presence in the production of either the manufactured goods which used our raw materials as inputs, or the machinery inputs required by our natural resource industries. Thus, the foreign investment encouraged by the National Policy permeated the Canadian economy.

A second major legacy of the National Policy is the concentration of ownership and market power among Canadian firms. The National Policy made Canadian industries very attractive places to compete. At the time that the National Policy was implemented, supporters of free trade referred to the tariff as the "mother of the trusts."[11] Foreign competition was reduced by the tariff, and domestic competition was often naturally limited by economies of scale and other economic factors. Canadian firms in many industries were, therefore, protected from competition to a large extent and were immensely profitable. Once established, many Canadian firms were able to grow to dominate their market using mostly internally generated funds, allowing the firms' founders and their descendants to retain tight control of their respective organizations. Thus, in industries such as brewing and many types of retailing, the number of major competitors dropped continuously, while the remaining firms stayed tightly controlled and very profitable. Concentration of sales within Canadian industries and concentration of wealth within Canada went hand in hand as family fortunes grew.

We will now look in more detail at the consequences of the two legacies of the National Policy: a high level of foreign ownership of Canadian corporations, and the concentration of wealth and market power within Canada.

Foreign Ownership in Canada

As shown in Figure 5, Canada has a high level of foreign ownership compared to other industrialized nations. Figure 6 shows the level of foreign control of Canadian corporations by industry. From Figure 6 we can see that while the foreign ownership of Canadian industries averages 22.6 per cent, very high by international standards, in some industries, particularly in manufacturing, the degree of foreign control of Canadian industries is much, much higher than this average.

What does a high level of foreign ownership mean for the Canadian economy? Macdonald and the Conservatives of his day clearly felt that foreign investment was preferable to no investment, and it is hard to argue with this proposition. Similarly, however, it is hard to argue with the proposition that Canadian ownership and control of corporations is preferable to foreign

69

FIGURE 5
Role of Foreign-Owned Firms in Economies of
Leading Industrial Nations, 1990

	Share of Foreign-Owned Firms' Sales (%)
U.S.	16
Japan	1**
France	28
Germany	18**
U.K.	20
CANADA	28*

* 1993; ** 1986

Source: E.M. Graham and P. Krugman, *Foreign Direct Investment in the United States* (Washington, DC: Institute for International Economics, 1994), p. 33; and Statistics Canada.

ownership and control. To understand more fully the costs of foreign ownership for the Canadian economy, we need to move beyond these simplistic propositions and look at what it means to the operations of a corporation for it to be foreign, rather than Canadian, controlled.

Typically, only about 10 per cent of a Canadian corporation's sales fall to the bottom line as after-tax profits. Clearly, for Canadian-owned corporations, these profits go to Canadians and contribute to the wealth and material well-being of Canadians, while the profits of foreign-owned firms do not. However, of much greater significance to the Canadian economy is what happens to the other 90 per cent of the cash the corporation generates through its sales. This money, the lion's share of the corporation's revenue, is spent by the corporation in performing all of the various activities required to design, produce and sell its product: research and development, production, distribution, marketing and so on. Assessing differences in how foreign- and Canadian-controlled firms spend this money is more complex than dealing with corporate profits, but is essential to understanding the effect of foreign ownership on Canada's economic well-being.

Some foreign-owned Canadian corporations design, manufacture and market products for a worldwide market. These firms are often described as having a "world product mandate" for a particular product. For example, ICI Explosives Canada is the worldwide headquarters of its parent's (Imperial Chemicals Industries of the United Kingdom) explosives business.[12] ICI Explosives Canada performs much of the strategic planning, research and development and marketing for its parent's worldwide explosives business. Similarly, although it is 98 per cent owned by the American firm United Technologies, Pratt and Whitney Canada has sole worldwide responsibility for its parent's small turbofan and turboprop airplane engine lines. Pratt and Whitney Canada exports more than 90 per cent of its annual production.

FIGURE 6
The Ownership Structure of Canadian Industries by Asset (%), 1997

		Canadian		
	Foreign	Total	Private	Gov't Bus. Enterprise
Food, Beverages & Tobacco	30.4	69.6	60.4	9.2
Wood and Paper	31.7	68.3	67.6	0.7
Energy	19.8	80.2	44.2	36.0
Chemicals, Chemical Products & Textiles	71.1	28.9	28.6	0.2
Metallic Minerals & Mineral Products	19.7	80.3	79.8	0.4
Machinery & Equipment (except Electrical)	43.7	56.3	56.3	0.0
Transportation Equipment	52.6	47.4	47.2	0.1
Electrical & Electronic Products	44.4	55.6	55.6	0.0
Construction & Real Estate	13.4	86.6	82.7	3.9
Transportation Services	4.7	95.3	67.8	27.5
Communications	10.2	89.8	83.6	6.2
Deposit-accepting Intermediaries	11.9	88.1	84.4	3.7
Insurers	32.6	67.4	64.2	3.3
Consumer & Business Financing	41.2	58.8	38.4	20.4
Other Services	16.1	83.9	80.0	3.9
Other Consumer Goods & Services	25.4	74.6	74.6	0.0
Total Non-financial Industries	26.7	73.3	62.6	10.7
Total Finance* & Insurance Industries	18.7	81.3	75.6	5.7
Total All Industries	22.6	77.4	69.2	8.1

* Excluding Investment & Holding Companies

Source: Corporations Returns Act: Foreign Control of the Canadian Economy, 1993–1997, May 2, 2000.

Unfortunately, however, examples like Pratt and Whitney and ICI Explosives are the exception and not the rule for foreign-owned companies in Canada. Many more, and more prominent, foreign firms — the multinational oil companies, the big three automakers and so on — have Canadian subsidiaries which produce products designed and engineered outside Canada, often using imported components.[13] These Canadian subsidiaries have been described as "truncated" corporations because they do not perform the full range of activities needed to bring a product to market — most notably strategic planning, research and development and product design.[14] These companies are the traditional branch plants which have been the focus of so much attention in Canada.

However, before we vilify foreign-owned firms for not performing a full range of activities in Canada, it is important to realize that the same complaint could be made about an increasing number of Canadian-owned firms. For example, before falling out of Canadian control as part of the Universal Studios-Vivendi merger, Seagram produced and blended whisky in Canada, but performed almost all other functions relating to its whisky business, including controlling the all-important marketing of its products, in its New York office. Similarly, Nortel Network's central office switch business is now centred in its U.S. subsidiary, based in North Carolina. Furthermore, many smaller Canadian firms perform little or no research and development and instead license or copy foreign products.

Based on our discussion so far, we can say that being foreign owned is neither a necessary nor a sufficient condition for a Canadian corporation to rely on affiliated foreign firms to perform key activities. However, there is significant evidence that, on the whole, foreign affiliates in Canada do tend to rely to a large degree on their parent, or other foreign firms, for important activities and inputs. In their study of 25 Canadian industries, Michael Porter and the Monitor Company found only a few examples of foreign-controlled Canadian corporations which autonomously managed a business unit with responsibilities beyond serving the Canadian market.[15]

Furthermore, foreign ownership is highest in Canadian industries where there are significant extra-plant economies of scale. That is, there is more foreign investment in industries where there are high, firm-level fixed costs, like research and development and advertising, which can be shared among several production plants. The accepted explanation for this finding is that foreign firms, coming mostly from nations with larger economies than Canada's, have a clear advantage over Canadian firms in these industries, since the foreign firms have more domestic output over which to spread their fixed costs before they consider undertaking foreign investment. The obvious implication of this is that these foreign firms invest in Canada on the assumption that those activities which provide for the extra-plant economies of scale will be centrally performed; that is, will be performed in the foreign firm's home nation and not in Canada.

This trend towards "truncated" Canadian subsidiaries seems to have accelerated in recent years. Under increasing pressure from Japanese and European competitors, U.S. firms are rationalizing their North American operations and are choosing to eliminate such activities as manufacturing, research and development, marketing and strategic planning from their Canadian operations. Media reports have focused on Canadian subsidiaries of U.S. multinationals being transformed into little more than sales offices, with all of their strategic decisions made by their parent, and all of their high value-added activities performed in the United States.[16]

The Concentration of Corporate Wealth and Power in Canada

The wealth of Canada has always been concentrated in the hands of a relatively small number of individuals and corporations. In 1914, the social critic Gustavus Myers contended in his *History of Canadian Wealth* that "fifty men controlled one-third of Canada's material wealth as expressed in railways, banks, factories, mines and other properties and resources."[17] This one-third figure is even more striking when one considers that about half that amount again was controlled by foreigners. Thus, the remaining 99.99 per cent plus of

Canada's population controlled only about 50 per cent of Canada's wealth. Perhaps most surprising, however, is the fact that, in her 1985 book *Who Owns Canada*, Diane Francis estimated that 32 families and five conglomerates owned about one-third of Canada's non-financial assets.[18] According to *Forbes Magazine*, Canada had 15 billionaires (measured in U.S. dollars) in the year 2000. This compares to 57 in the United States — a country with about 10 times Canada's population. These 15 families control over US$46.2-billion in assets (see Figure 7). Both the number of Canadian billionaires and the wealth they control have tripled over the last three years. Thus, the concentration of wealth in Canada which had appalled Myers at the time of the great trusts and robber barons in his native United States, and of similar concentrations of wealth in Europe, had changed little almost a century later.

It could be argued that this concentration of corporate wealth in Canada is merely the result of a healthy free-enterprise system. The story could go something like this: those corporations which are well managed, have competitive advantages over their rivals and are well positioned to exploit those advantages, are more profitable than their competitors and naturally grow larger and make their owners wealthier. However, there are several aspects of Canada's corporate sector which do not fit this model.

First, many of Canada's largest corporate empires are conglomerates. They do not participate in just one or a few related industries, where some competitive advantage relating to their core business or businesses could have allowed them to grow rapidly. Rather, these conglomerates participate in many, largely unrelated, industries. For example, Lord Kenneth Thomson controls businesses

FIGURE 7
Canada's Billionaires

	Wealth (US$ in billions)
Kenneth Thomson	16.1
Irving Family	4.1
Bombardier Family	3.8
Charles Bronfman	3.3
Jeffery Skoll	2.9
W. Galen Weston	2.4
David and Cliff Lede	2.1
Bernard (Barry Sherman)	1.9
James Pattison	1.9
Edward S. (Ted) Rogers	1.7
Ron Mannix	1.3
Wallace McCain	1.3
Charles Sirois	1.2
Harrison McCain	1.1
Israel Asper	1.1

Source: Forbes Magazine, July 3, 2000.

as diverse as *The Globe and Mail* newspaper, The Hudson Bay Company, Thomson Travel and several North Sea oilfields. Jim Pattison built his Pattison Group from a single car dealership in 1960 into a conglomerate which includes, among many other businesses, Canada's largest group of auto dealers, Canada's largest outdoor advertising sign company, a large manufacturer of canned seafood and the chain of Ripley's Believe It Or Not museums. It is hard to believe that any single competitive advantage has allowed such empires to grow.

It is natural to ask at this point why Canadian business is still dominated by conglomerates at a time when conglomerates have been out of favour in the United States for over 20 years. During their heyday in the 1960s, it was argued that a well-organized conglomerate operated an internal capital market which was more efficient than the external one. It was felt that a conglomerate could optimally reallocate assets among its constituent parts, while also offering its investors ready-made diversification, and bring a new external discipline to the corporations under its control. As the conglomerates began to perform poorly compared to their undiversified rivals, however, it became clear that most conglomerates merely added another layer of overhead for their subsidiaries to support, while bringing no real operating benefits. Internal capital markets proved less efficient than external ones, since many decisions were made by managers, not the suppliers of the capital. By the mid-1980s, new fortunes were being made breaking up the conglomerates, which had made their initial investors rich in the 1960s.

If the U.S. markets realized that conglomerates were the proverbial emperor's new clothes, why do conglomerates persist in playing such a key role in Canada? The simple reason is that most of them are not subject to market forces. They tend to participate in concentrated industries, where inefficiencies result in higher prices paid by consumers, not lower profits for firms. Furthermore, Canadian conglomerates are often tightly held; thus they are not regulated by the market for corporate control.

An example illustrates these points well. The Irving family of New Brunswick controls an empire of over 400 corporations, which all grew out of a single car dealership, founded in 1924, and a small lumber mill. From the car dealership, the family's patriarch, the late K.C. Irving, diversified, naturally enough into repairs and gasoline sales. After buying control of the family lumber mill after his father's death, Irving began to acquire timberland and build more mills. As his empire grew, Irving's interests expanded to include a construction company, which built his gas stations as well as houses, a shipbuilding company, fleets of barges and tankers, a truck-assembly operation and companies which used his paper and lumber products, including newspapers, hardware stores, building material firms and a pre-fabricated house company.

Irving was able to start or acquire all of these businesses because he had such a high degree of control of all of the markets in which he participated. Obviously, he could not assemble a truck for his own use as cheaply as Ford or General Motors, but this did not matter to him since he could pass the added costs on to those who purchased gasoline or hardware from his retail outlets. On the other hand, it made sense for him to invest in new businesses in New Brunswick rather than expanding his existing businesses outside the province because by doing so he increased, rather than lessened, his control over the markets in which he competed. For example, by investing in hardware stores to sell his lumber products and timberlands to supply his sawmills, he was able to build a full vertical monopoly over the entire chain of production. If, instead, he had tried to expand his lumber business into the rest of Canada, he would have exposed himself to competition, and possibly even retaliation in his own tightly controlled New Brunswick market. Similarly, other Canadian lumber firms, even if they could overcome Irving's monopoly of lumber-products distribution in New Brunswick, could only enter that market at their peril, knowing it would likely prompt harsh retaliation from Irving. Of course, Irving was protected from U.S. competition by Canada's tariff wall.

Further evidence of the lack of competition in the Canadian corporate sector is found by looking at the list of businesses in which the various Canadian conglomerates have interests. Many of them are in the same industries (e.g., Bell Canada Enterprises, Thompson, CanWest Global and Québecor, all in newspapers and television). In fact, many Canadian conglomerates even share interests in the same firms. For example, at the peak of the real estate market in the mid-1980s, not only did the Reichmanns have their Olympia and York real estate empire, but they also had significant holdings in their major Canadian competitors — Cadillac Fairview, Trizec and Bramalea.

However, perhaps the most damning indictment of the Canadian conglomerates is that many of them do not actually build businesses, but merely buy and sell existing businesses in ever more complicated financial transactions. While the Irvings, the McCains and even the Reichmanns are best known for businesses they created, many other Canadian conglomerates have made most, if not all, of their money merely buying and selling companies. Perhaps the best example of this is Conrad Black, who burst onto the world financial scene when, in 1978, at the age of 33, he convinced the widows of E.P. Taylor and Bud McDougald to sell him a controlling interest in the Argus Corporation, where Black's father had worked. Black raised the money for the purchase from friends and several banks. In the seven years following the Argus takeover, three of the firm's key components — Massey-Ferguson, Dominion Stores and Standard Broadcasting — were losing so much money that Black sold them. Still, although the companies he controlled did not always do well, Black and his partners did.

We need to be careful, however, not to blame people like Black for making money. We need to concern ourselves with the question of why it is so easy for so-called paper entrepreneurs to make money in Canada, while we seem to have so few people who are willing and able to build a business from the ground up.[19] While the American economy has been criticized on similar grounds, it is startling to see comparatively young and specialized companies like Intel, Microsoft and Hewlett-Packard at or near the top of *BusinessWeek's* list of the world's most valuable companies.[20] Canada simply does not seem capable of producing new corporate stars at the pace needed to maintain the vitality of our corporate sector.

Concentration in Canadian Industries

The concentration of sales in the hands of a relatively few firms in many Canadian industries is an issue that, in many ways, is related to the concentration of wealth in Canada. While Statistics Canada, in contrast to its American counterpart, does not collect industry-level concentration data, we can all list many examples of Canadian industries with only a few competitors in them. From beer (Molson and Labatt) to banks (the big five) to department stores (The Bay and Sears), Canadian business abounds with concentrated industries.

Concentration is an important issue because our entire economic system is predicated on the assumption that prices are set by competitive markets. If the law of supply and demand sets the prices for both buyers and sellers, then using the prices set in a free market to measure the value of a good or activity will allocate the economy's scarce resources efficiently. If an industry is too concentrated, however, then the firms in it begin to act as price setters, not price takers. In the extreme, of course, if the industry has only one member (or if its members are able to collude perfectly), then the firm has the absolute power to set its price. Such non-competitive behaviour has two consequences. First, it is obviously going to result in a higher price for the good, and transfer of wealth from the buyer to the seller in the industry. More subtly, however, it can be shown that there is also an overall loss of efficiency in the economy. The perfect allocation of resources achieved by the price mechanism in a competitive economy is distorted, and the economy as a whole is worse off.

Of course, no industry in the real world corresponds to the economists' notion of perfect competition. The policy maker's job becomes, therefore, to decide how far to allow industries to deviate from pure competition and what to do when an industry crosses that imaginary line. Canada and the United States provide an interesting contrast in their approach to this issue. Canada's competition policy does not treat industry concentration per se as undesirable, but rather it aims to prevent the abuse of the power enjoyed by firms with high market share. In contrast, in the United States, legislation has typically been built around the presumption that concentration will always lead to abuse of power and, therefore, is aimed at preventing concentration.

The makers of Canadian competition policy have traditionally justified their willingness to live with relatively high degrees of concentration in two ways. First, it is argued that because the Canadian economy is quite small, the country cannot support more than one or two competitors in many scale-intensive industries without a great loss of efficiency. Thus, concentration in Canadian industries, when it occurs without abuse of market power, might actually be a net benefit to the economy. Second, because the Canadian economy is relatively open, and is highly integrated with that of the United States, many analysts are not concerned about concentration in Canadian industries, since most of our firms face competition from abroad. In fact, a high degree of competition from the United States has actually prompted some analysts to advocate that concentration be encouraged in certain Canadian industries. For example, the federal government actively encouraged the merger of Air Canada and Canadian Airlines International. The government's lack of control over the eventual outcome of the airline consolidation illustrates the pitfalls of government policy aimed at controlling rather than preventing industry concentration.

The principles of competition policy in Canada have been articulated in a constantly evolving series of laws since 1889. In that year, Canada became the first Western industrialized nation to enact legislation aimed at preventing firms from entering into agreements to limit competition. Compared to the legislation soon enacted by other nations, however, Canada's policy was weak and ineffectual, and its enforcement was lax. Over the next century, Canadian competition law evolved, but never gained any real teeth. In fact, it became murkier as it became abundantly clear that Canadians were ambivalent towards competition. For example, the Dominion Trade and Industry Commission Act of 1935 set up a commission to enforce Canada's competition laws, while at the same time allowing businesses to collude when "wasteful" or "demoralizing" competition was occurring.

Canada's most recent pieces of competition legislation, the Competition Act and Competition Tribunal Act, both of 1986, are perhaps the clearest statements of competition policy in our history, and they are very lenient statements. For the first time, the Competition Act formally recognizes that efficiency gains can be used to justify a merger that otherwise would be prohibited because it would lead to a high level of concentration in an industry. Another pro-merger provision of the act allows firms to apply to the Director of the Competition Tribunal for pre-approval of a proposed merger. Pre-approval can significantly reduce the risks and uncertainty involved in entering into a merger and, thus, make it more attractive to the firms involved. Clearly, more than 110 years after our first anti-combines legislation was passed, Canada is still without a strong competition policy.

As a final note concerning competition policy, it is worth mentioning one of the key findings of Michael Porter's 10-nation study, *The Competitive Advantage of Nations*.[21] Porter found clearly and consistently that national industries which were successful internationally were characterized by intense domestic competition, and that concentrated industries were highly susceptible to entry by foreign competitors. Porter hypothesized that intense local competition forces firms to be innovative and provide high-quality products, while firms without strong local competitors have often been able to survive for long periods without offering good value to their customers.

CROWN CORPORATIONS

While the preceding discussion provides an understanding of the biggest segment of Canada's corporate sector, there is one more element which must be understood if one is to have a full picture of the sector. In 1997, 8.1 per cent of the corporate assets in Canada were controlled by government business enterprises — otherwise known as Crown corporations. As Figure 6 shows, these are spread across almost all industries. Not surprisingly, the greatest share of an industry held by Crown corporations is in energy, where the largest Crown corporation in Canada — Hydro-Québec — is found. Other industries with high government participation are transportation services (e.g.,

Via Rail) and consumer and business financing (Caisse de dépôt et placement, Canada Mortgage and Housing Corporation, Business Development Corporation etc.). By 1991, there were about 550 Crown corporations in Canada, with the federal government controlling a little more than a third of them, the Quebec government about a quarter and the rest of the provinces the remainder.

Crown corporations have been used by Canadian governments for a variety of purposes. They have been used:

> to provide services which a private corporation could not profitably provide but which the government feels are needed (e.g., the CBC, Canada Post);

> to provide services in industries which are natural monopolies (e.g., hydro utilities);

> to provide services which the government felt in some way reluctant to entrust to the private sector (e.g., the Royal Canadian Mint, Atomic Energy of Canada); and

> to bail out politically important private enterprises which have run into trouble (e.g., Canadair, Ontario Bus).

There is, of course, much debate over whether Canadian governments should be operating businesses in as many sectors of our economy as they do, but examining this issue in detail is beyond the scope of this article. What we can conclude here, however, is that the role of Crown corporations in Canada's economy demonstrates once again our ambivalence towards the process of free and open competition.

We should also note that Crown corporations have been a factor in the high degree of concentration in Canadian industries. The existence of a large competitor, funded from the nearly bottomless pockets of government, at the very least, acts as a deterrent to potential new entrants in a particular industry. In fact, in some cases, Crown corporations have actually been formed by amalgamating two or more competitors under the auspices of the Crown. For example, Via Rail combined the passenger services of CN and CP Rail to create a single national passenger rail system. Here again, we see government policies acting at cross purposes in shaping Canada's corporate sector. The government enacts anti-combines laws while, in effect, creating combines itself.

Lately, there has been some effort to lower the number of Crown corporations. The federal government has privatized some Crown corporations, including Air Canada and Petro Canada, as have the provinces. Even Ontario's NDP government privatized the Ontario Stadium Corporation (SkyDome). Since the Progressive Conservatives were elected in Ontario, there has been much talk of privatization (but little action). It is argued that privatization benefits the economy because it brings the discipline of the capital markets to the firms involved. In some cases the government makes money by privatization. Of course, because market discipline often means job reductions, employees frequently resist privatizations. Furthermore, just as it is difficult for politicians to resist creating Crown corporations, it is often not easy for them to sell one.

The Caisse de dépôt et placement du Québec

The Caisse de dépôt et placement du Québec (the Caisse) is one Crown corporation which is worth special mention. It is a unique institution founded in 1965 and now manages over $57-billion in assets. The Caisse manages the funds of the Quebec pension plan and several other Quebec institutions. In this role, its official mandate is to protect the interests of those investing money in the plan. It is prohibited by law from owning more than 30 per cent of the shares in any one company and was envisioned to be a more or less passive investor, as pension funds typically are. Checks were put in place to try to ensure that the Caisse did not become a policy instrument of the Quebec government.

It seems now, however, that the Caisse has moved beyond its mandate to some extent. Since the early 1980s it has provided funds to Hydro-Québec at less than market rates. It also appears that the Caisse, while keeping below its 30 per cent ownership ceiling, has been able to gain effective control of some of its investments and is using that control to ensure that the firms in question are acting in accordance with the policies of the provincial government. The Caisse defines its mission as "seek[ing] an optimal return on investment while [making a] contribution to the validity of the economy...."[22] If, as it appears, the Caisse has taken an active role in shaping the policies of at least some of the firms it has invested in and in the economy, it is one further example of a Canadian government not trusting the markets to allocate resources optimally.

CONCLUSION

The structure of Canada's corporate sector, and how that structure developed over time, provide fascinating insight into the evolution of Canada's national economic and political philosophies. We seem torn between a concept of economic collectivism in which national champions are expected to represent Canada to the world in various industries, while refraining from abusing their economic clout at home, and the strong belief in the power of free markets which spills over our southern border. Those who have been able to play the two concepts of the corporation's role in Canada's economy off against one another effectively have grown very rich doing so. People like Irving, Pattison and Black have been able to use free market mechanisms to build exceedingly strong pockets of economic power around themselves. What we must consider, however, is whether our attempts to reconcile these contradictory views of the corporation's role in our society have created a corporate sector which has served us well in the past, and will be able to serve us well in the future. And then, of course, if we decide that change is needed, we must decide how to implement it.

NOTES

1. Because they are based on data from different sources, the numbers in Figures 1 and 2 are not completely comparable. Together, however, they do show clear trends in the changing make-up of the Canadian economy.

2. The following paragraphs are based largely on The Economic Council of Canada, *Employment in the Service Economy* (Ottawa: The Minister of Supply and Services, 1991), where a more detailed discussion of the causes and consequences of Canada's shift to a service-based economy can be found.

3. In fact, the difference in productivity growth will also result in relative price shifts that will result, in turn, in shifts in relative consumption between goods and services. This effect will lessen the expected change in relative employment resulting from differences in productivity growth.

4. Canadian Business Corporation Act, RSC, 1985, c. c.42, sec. 102.

5. James Gillies, *Boardroom Renaissance: Power, Performance and Morality in the Modern Corporation* (Toronto: McGraw-Hill Ryerson, 1992).

6. Ibid.

7. Michael Jensen, "The Eclipse of the Public Corporation," *Harvard Business Review*, vol. 67, no. 5 (September–October 1989).

8. Kenneth McNaught, *The Penguin History of Canada* (Markham, ON: Penguin Books, 1988), p. 168.

9. Ibid., p. 166.

10. A.E. Safarian, *Foreign Ownership of Canadian Industry* (Toronto: The University of Toronto Press, 1973).

11. Michael Bliss, "The Yolk of The Trusts: A Comparison of Canada's Competitive Environment in 1889 and 1989," in R.S. Khemani and W.T. Stanbury, eds., *Historical Perspectives on Canadian Competition Policy* (Halifax, NS: The Institute for Research on Public Policy, 1991).

12. Michael Porter and the Monitor Company, *Canada at the Crossroads* (Ottawa: The Business Council on National Issues and the Minister of Supply and Services, 1991).

13. In the case of the auto industry, the Auto Pact affects U.S.-based firms' sourcing decisions for component parts and finished product, but does not alter the fact that all of the cars assembled in Canada are designed elsewhere.

14. John N.H. Britton, *The Weakest Link: A Technological Perspective on Canadian Industrial Underdevelopment* (Ottawa: The Science Council of Canada, 1978).

15. Michael Porter and the Monitor Company, *Canada at the Crossroads* (Ottawa: The Business Council on National Issues and the Minister of Supply and Services, 1991).

16. John Saunders, "Head Office Flexes Its Might," *The Globe And Mail*, January 18, 1994, p. 1.

17. Gustavus Myers, *A History of Canadian Wealth* (Chicago: Charles H. Kerr and Company, 1914), p. i.

18. Diane Francis, *Controlling Interest: Who Owns Canada* (Toronto: Scorpio Publishing Limited, 1986), pp. 4–5. Francis provides thumbnail histories of many Canadian business dynasties. These provided much of the detail presented throughout this section of the article.

19. The term "paper entrepreneur" is used by Francis.

20. "The BusinessWeek 1000," *BusinessWeek*, March 28, 1994, p. 63.

21. Michael Porter, *The Competitive Advantage of Nations* (New York: The Free Press, 1990).

22. See <www.lacaisse.com/welcome.html>.

SME Entrepreneurship:
A Comparative View

James H. Tiessen

INTRODUCTION

> The search for the source of dynamic entrepreneurial performance has much in common with hunting the Heffalump. The Heffalump is a rather large and very important animal. He has been hunted by many individuals using various ingenious trapping devices, but no one so far has succeeded in capturing him.
>
> Peter Kilby, 1971[1]

This quote, taken from the introductory chapter to a collection of essays on entrepreneurship aptly invokes A.A. Milne's Winnie-the-Pooh stories.[2] Despite growing agreement on how entrepreneurship is defined, understood, and most importantly, "captured," researchers and policy-makers around the world are continuing their hunt. This is because entrepreneurship contributes vitally to economic growth, innovation and flexibility.[3]

In this essay, as I seek the same quarry, I address five questions:

1. What is entrepreneurship?
2. Why is it important?
3. What factors are associated with entrepreneurship?
4. How do governments promote entrepreneurship?
5. What should policy-makers do?

I would like to thank Rein Peterson for introducing me to the study of entrepreneurship, Tom Wesson for encouraging me to write about it in this book and Jerry Dermer for letting me lecture on the environment of business at Schulich.

WHAT IS ENTREPRENEURSHIP?

The term "entrepreneurship" is derived from the word "entrepreneur," which is defined by *Webster's* as "one who organizes, owns, manages, and assumes the risk of a business."[4] This definition reflects the classic view of entrepreneurship, which focuses on individuals who start businesses. The original French expression, which first appeared in 1828, referred to the "manager or promoter of a theatrical institution."[5] Now, the word entrepreneurship is used much more generally to characterize innovative, opportunity-seeking management in organizations of any size.

I will, following the traditional use of the term, focus on small and medium enterprises (SMEs) and their founders. The definitions of "small" and "medium" differ by region. Here I adopt those used by the Organisation for Economic Cooperation and Development, which defines firms employing less than 100 employees as "small," those employing 100 to 499 "medium," and those employing more than 500 "large."

Entrepreneurs start businesses by generating variety and stretching resources.[6] The first process involves making what mid-twentieth century economist Joseph Schumpeter called "new combinations" — new goods, methods of production or service delivery, markets, supplies and/or types of management.[7] The second element of entrepreneurship is gaining access to the resources — especially capital — needed to capitalize on the innovation. Sometimes opportunities are created by large disruptions in markets, such as those initiated by technological revolutions. At other times they are gaps or niches spotted by alert and motivated individuals.

WHY IS ENTREPRENEURSHIP IMPORTANT?

Entrepreneurship, especially SME entrepreneurship, plays very important economic roles. Such enterprises account for a large proportion of national output and employment. Further, this sector, which is characterized by significant levels of business entry and exit, contributes to making economies flexible. Finally, SMEs are a key source of innovations.

Shares of Output and Employment

Small and medium enterprises account for a large part of the economies of all countries. The OECD data, shown in Figure 1, indicate that SMEs contribute from 23 per cent to 66 per cent of total GDP, and employ from 45 per cent to nearly 80 per cent of workers in developed countries, depending on the definition of SME used and the sectors counted. In most countries the share of GDP accounted for by SMEs is lower than its ratio of those employed. This is largely because SMEs tend to use relatively more labour and less capital machinery than larger firms, so they use labour less efficiently. Further, SMEs are by definition smaller, and typically participate in more competitive markets than their larger counterparts, and this reduces their ability to charge high prices, which would raise the value of output per person.

FIGURE 1
The Share of SMEs in National Economies

	Employment %	SMEs' contribution to GDP
Australia	45.0[1]	23.0[1]
Belgium	72.0	—
CANADA	60.0[2]	57.2[2]
Denmark	77.8	56.7
Finland	52.6	—
France	69.0	61.8[3]
Germany	65.7	34.9
Greece	73.8	27.1[4]
Ireland	85.6[1]	40.0
Italy	48.9[2]	40.5
Japan	73.8[2]	57.0[3]
Spain	63.7	64.3[5]
Sweden	56.0[6]	—
United Kingdom	67.2	30.3
United States	53.7	48.0

Notes: All data are for 1991, except for Spain, Canada and Ireland (1989), Denmark (1992), Germany, Greece and Italy (1988), Japan (1992) and France (1990). Definitions of SME vary. For most countries it is 500 employees or less (e.g., Canada, United States, Germany and France). In Italy SMEs are firms with less than 200 employees, and for Japan they employ 300 or less (50 or less in wholesale and retail).

1. Manufacturing only.
2. For Canada, per cent of private sector employment and GDP in 1993.
3. Per cent of value added.
4. Per cent of value added in manufacturing.
5. Per cent of sales.
6. Per cent of private sector employment in 1992.

Source: OECD, *Technology, Productivity and Job Creation, Vol. 2, Analytical Report* (Paris: OECD, 1996), p. 179.

As Figure 2 shows, levels of self-employment, a subset of entrepreneurship, vary greatly between developed countries. In the United States, self-employment accounted for only 8.4 per cent of workers in 1996. In Greece, however, nearly half of those employed work for themselves, and in Italy 30 per cent run their own businesses. However, as the same table shows, many of the self-employed in the latter two countries are farmers.

In Canada, Ireland, the United Kingdom and Sweden, unlike many other countries, the percentage of self-employed has been increasing. In Canada, self-employment grew about 4 per cent per year from 1990 to 1997. At first blush it would seem that high unemployment during this period forced people to start

JAMES H. TIESSEN

FIGURE 2
Self-employment by Country and Gender

	Self-employment as % of All Employment[1]		Agricultural Self-Employment as % of Total Self-employment[1]	Share of Women Employers & Persons Working on Own Account[2]
	1986	1996	1995	1996
Australia	16.8	15.1	20.1	32.8
Belgium	18.1	18.4	11.2	28.7
CANADA	9.7	11.3	19.5	41.6
Denmark	11.6	9.5	23.6	—
Finland	14.9	14.5	37.6	30.5
France	15.8	11.6	30.0	—
Germany	11.5	10.6	17.4	27.9
Greece	50.7	46.1	42.1	19.7
Ireland	13.5	18.2	44.3	—
Italy	29.9	28.9	16.4	23.7
Japan	24.9	17.7	27.3	32.2
Spain	30.0	25.0	24.3	27.7
Sweden	6.5	11.0	17.9	25.9
United Kingdom	11.5	13.6	8.3	30.6
United States	8.9	8.4	15.8	39.2

Sources:
1. David G. Blanchflower, *Self-Employment in OECD Countries*. Paper presented at the Canadian International Labor Network Conference, Burlington. Ontario, September 24–26, 1998. Available at <www.OECD.org>.
2. OECD, "OECD Conference on Women Entrepreneurs in SMEs: A Major Force in Innovation and Job Creation" (Paris: OECD, August 26, 1998). Online: <www.oecd.org/dsti/sti/industry/smes/prod/synth.htm> (viewed June 26, 2000). These numbers exclude the farm sector and family workers.

their own businesses. However, analysis over a longer period suggests that in Canada there has been a small but statistically significant *negative* link between the unemployment level and the tendency to work for oneself.[8] This suggests that, rather than being pushed into working for themselves, people are attracted by the opportunities that arise in good economic periods. Other explanations for the increase in self-employment include a more experienced and more educated work force, the increase in contracting out by larger firms, and the growth in immigration.

Figure 2 also indicates that overall, women tend to be less likely to start businesses or work for themselves than men. Again, there is considerable variation between countries. In the United States and Canada women make up about 40 per cent of business owners and self-employed. In both countries, along with the United Kingdom, Australia and Norway, the evidence is that women are accounting for growing shares of self-employment. In nations with more traditional cultures, such as Greece and Italy, a smaller share of women run businesses, and there is not a clear pattern of change. Most independently employed women in OECD countries work in the service sector, especially retail and personal services.[9] Only about 1 per cent are in manufacturing.

Politicians ensure they pay special attention to SME managers, at least during election campaigns. A key reason is that, as shown, SMEs and their employees make up a considerable voting block. As well, SME owners, such as auto and house insurance brokers, tend to contribute significant time and money to community life and grassroots politics.

Flexibility

Darwin's theory of evolution in the natural world, the "survival of the fittest," also describes the dynamism of the small business sector.[10] This sector is characterized by churning: the start-up and growth of ventures in thriving industries, and the exit of firms from industries in which there are fewer opportunities. Economies with significant independent small business sectors are therefore typically able to more readily adjust to changes in technology, society and other parts of the environment. These adjustments are invigorating for mobile individuals with suitable aptitudes; they can be traumatic for those less able to adapt.

Figure 3 shows how the revitalization process unfolds in several countries. Overall, these data show that from 9 per cent to 17 per cent of establishments were either opening or closing each year, while 85 per cent to 91 per cent continued operations. For all of the countries, except Finland, there was a net birth of firms in the time period studied. Overall, international research suggests that about 60 per cent to 70 per cent of firms survive for three years, and only about half are still in business after five years.[11] Studies in Europe and North America have shown that SMEs tend to create the most new jobs. Larger firms, in contrast, are more likely to reduce their workforces. That said, the higher rate of job losses among SMEs means this sector's contribution to *net* job gain is still disputed by researchers and lobbyists. Research has, though, shown that most startups rarely become large firms.[12] For example, a recent University of British Columbia study found that only 0.2 per cent of new firms had more than 100 employees 10 years after founding.[13]

Innovation

Management guru Charles Handy, in his 1999 speech to the International Labour Office Enterprise Forum, described our world as being full of "elephants," large corporations, and "fleas." He said:

> We need the elephants, they transfer technology, they take ideas and they develop them, they have resources, they can spend a lot of money developing ideas into products and spreading these products around.... Unfortunately, all the evidence proves that they are not very good at creating ideas.... However, evidence shows that the people who create ideas — whom I call fleas — are

FIGURE 3

The Evolution of Businesses — Percentage of Firms in Each Stage[1]

	New Establishments[2]	Closing Establishments	Continuing Establishments	Of Which Expanding[3]	Contracting	Unchanged	Net Birth
Denmark 1984–89	14.2	13.6	86.4	29.3	25.9	31.2	0.5
Finland 1986–91	11.2	9.8	90.2	29.9	60.3		1.4
France 1984–92	14.3	13.2	86.8				1.1
New Zealand 1987–92	13.7	14.5	85.5	19.4	21.9	44.2	-0.8
Sweden 1987–92	16.8	14.6	85.4	24.1	24.7	36.6	2.2
United States 1984–91	13.6	9.2	90.8	15.0	10.3	65.6	4.4

1. Definitions of establishments and sampling periods vary between countries.
2. This percentage refers to enterprises which opened during the year, so this column is not included as a share of the total in the other columns.
3. With respect to number of employees.

Source: OECD, *Fostering Entrepreneurship* (Paris: OECD, 1998), p. 43.

not accepted by elephants. They are a nuisance. The world depends on fleas for innovation and creativity. These are individuals outside; they are consultants, the small and medium enterprises; the subcontractors, the suppliers of the elephants."

Handy's analysis, while intuitively appealing, has only been partially confirmed by empirical research. Large firms overall do spend more on innovation than their smaller counterparts. This conclusion is supported by European studies which have found that the shares of financial and human resources devoted to R&D by SMEs is lower than their weight in the economy.[14] However, these findings are based on numbers that likely do not fully capture SME R&D activity. This is because surveys can more easily gather large business data; SME figures are more elusive.

SMEs have a *different*, rather than a *smaller* R&D role. Much SME innovation is market oriented. These "new combinations" are products and processes developed on the shop floor and through interactions with customers. A study on Japanese practices found that 52 per cent of SME innovations were made by the *firm owners*; in large firms 72 per cent of innovations were made by *R&D technicians*.[15] A U.S. study showing that the SME share of innovations exceeded their share of R&D expenditure suggests that though smaller firms spend less, they are more efficient innovators.[16]

The link between entrepreneurship and innovation is a virtuous one. U.S. research by Scott Shane of the Massachusetts Institute of Technology suggests that more businesses appear when technological change is greatest.[17] Further, the same study found that as more firms start up, more firms follow. This cycle, once initiated, leads to more new businesses and innovations.

WHAT FACTORS ARE ASSOCIATED WITH SME ENTREPRENEURSHIP?

Nations, and sub-groups within them, differ in terms of their proclivity to start and grow businesses. Further, the rates of entrepreneurship differ between periods of time. Both of these facts suggest that entrepreneurship is affected by environmental factors, especially culture and general economic conditions. Another factor linked to entrepreneurship is the availability of private and early equity capital. However, it is difficult to determine the direction of causality. That is, does capital availability lead to a vital entrepreneurial climate, or vice versa?

International Differences in Entrepreneurship

The 1999 Global Entrepreneurship Monitor[18] report on entrepreneurship in 10 countries showed a broad range of entrepreneurial orientations, as seen in Figure 4. In Canada, along with the United States and Israel, more than 5 per cent of the sample indicated they were actively "attempting to start a business." Italy and the United Kingdom were in the mid range, while the rate of entrepreneurship was rarer — 2 per cent or less — in Germany, Denmark, France, Japan and Finland.

JAMES H. TIESSEN

FIGURE 4
Percentage of Adult Population Actively Attempting to Start a Business

	Start-up Rate (%)
CANADA	6.8
Denmark	2.0
Finland	1.4
France	1.8
Germany	2.1
Israel	5.4
Italy	3.4
Japan	1.6
United Kingdom	3.3
United States	8.4

Source: Rein Peterson, *Global Economic Monitor*, p. 10. Based on a February to March 1999 telephone survey of more than 1,000 respondents per country.

The same study gathered further data to identify factors associated with these differences. Analysis showed strong links between socio-cultural norms and levels of start-up activity. A very telling finding was that in the United States, Canada, Denmark and France, more than 75 per cent of respondents agreed that starting a new business is "a respected occupation"; in Japan the number was less than 10 per cent. Other country characteristics tied to start-up rates were the levels of perceived business opportunities and entrepreneurial skills and education. It is notable that in-depth interviews with entrepreneurs and experts, conducted in conjunction with the same study, found that government programs were seen as having only limited influence on national propensities to found enterprises.

National variations in entrepreneurship suggest that cultural factors are at work. David McClelland's research program during the 1960s and 1970s highlighted the importance of levels of the need for achievement, the tendency of a person to take responsibility for setting and achieving goals.[19] Other values linked by academics to entrepreneurship include risk-taking propensity and the perception that one has significant control over events.[20] That said, anecdotal accounts of the links between culture and entrepreneurship have not been indisputably supported by empirical evidence. It could be that different cultural characteristics — such as individualism and collectivism — may affect the type of entrepreneurship pursued, rather than levels of its incidence.[21] For example, individualists may be better at generating new concepts. Collectivists, in contrast, may be more adept at building the networks needed acquire the resources to exploit these innovations.

88

Entrepreneurship is recognized as being vital for economic development. This helps explain how entrepreneurship rates can vary over time. For example, United Nations data on the proportion of SMEs to total employment in the manufacturing sectors in Asia during the 1960s to 1990s show that SME/total employment ratio tends to be high in early stages of development.[22] These SMEs are typically craft or agriculturally based, and not internationally competitive. At middle levels of development large firms, either domestic firms or foreign multinationals, employ a larger ratio of workers. Finally, in wealthier nations SMEs become more efficient and, often in tandem with multinationals, develop greater competitiveness. This pattern is apparent when we compare the economies of Asian nations. The less developed, notably Indonesia and the Philippines, have lacked dynamic SME sectors over the past 30 to 40 years, so their development has been arrested. In contrast, Japan and Taiwan have prospered. Now SMEs account for about one-third of Japan's and one-fifth of Taiwan's output respectively.

Availability of Capital

Most SMEs experience difficulty accessing the money needed to start and, especially, grow. A firm's capital needs and sources change with its stage of growth. Entrepreneurs begin with an initial stake, usually accumulated by tapping their own savings and those of family and friends. They subsequently try to augment this stake with bank loans. However, the optimistic visions of entrepreneurs are typically not shared by loan officers. Bank representatives claim that their job is to safeguard depositors' money; if savers wanted to invest in SMEs, they could choose to do so themselves. This situation leads to a debt financing gap for new businesses, especially for owners reluctant to share control with venture capital investors.

Should a new venture's success warrant growth, further capital injections may be sought in the form of venture capital: public or private equity. The terms public and private denote whether the investments are traded on public stock exchanges (like the Toronto Stock Exchange). Venture capitalists place bets on promising firms with the expectation that the payoffs from the 20 per cent or so that succeed deliver exceptional returns. In their early stages SMEs tend to seek private rather than public equity because it is less regulated and therefore incurs lower fees and other compliance costs. Private equity is mostly provided by wealthy individual "angel investors," who play an important role fostering new businesses. It is estimated that these angels account for about twice as much young business investment as formal venture capital funds.[23]

Raising public venture capital usually follows success in attracting private equity investment. In this phase firm owners, including angels and often employees, issue shares to buyers by making Initial Public Offerings, or IPOs. This is when early investors can realize the returns to their investments. Most countries have "junior" exchanges to enable this process. The U.S. National Association of Securities Dealers Automated Quotation System (NASDAQ) is the most famous, and no longer "junior," exchange of this type. The Canadian Venture Exchange (CDNX), formed through the November 1999 merger of the

Alberta and Vancouver stock exchanges, plays a similar role, though on a much smaller scale.

America's venture capital industry dwarfs that of its competitors. It was estimated that about US$50-billion was invested in venture-capital funds during 1999, up from only US$3-billion in 1990. In Canada the 1999 number was just under US$2-billion, which is significantly lower than the levels in the United Kingdom (US$12.5-billion), Continental Europe (US$16-billion, total of 17 countries in 1998), and Japan (US$5.7-billion)[24]. The success of the NASDAQ, which listed Microsoft, Dell and other new economy stars, has led to its establishment as an international brand, operating 24 hours a day. In the year 2000, NASDAQ established joint ventures with London's and Frankfurt's exchanges (Europe), Japan's Softbank and the government of Quebec.[25]

HOW DO GOVERNMENTS PROMOTE SME ENTREPRENEURSHIP?

All national governments and international economic organizations have small business development policies. Their approaches share the assumption of the liability of smallness. That is, small firms, when compared to large companies, face greater competition and have more financial, human and other resource constraints. Therefore, policy-makers seem to agree that SMEs deserve special treatment.

While, consistent with the principles of entrepreneurship, there is considerable policy experimentation, governments and organizations around the world take similar steps to encourage SMEs. Three broad, interrelated, types of policies used are:

1. lowering financial and administrative barriers to establishing and running small businesses
2. reducing taxes on SMEs and their founders, and
3. creating a culture of entrepreneurship.

The broad range of government activities represented by these policies has led to the establishment of specific bureaucratic structures to coordinated SME-related initiatives.

Lowering Financial and Administrative Barriers

Entrepreneurs are busy. Starting and running a business involves offering a service or product to a market, of course. In the early stages founders face considerable risks and difficulties raising capital, as mentioned above. On top of this, running a business involves a substantial administrative burden which competes for the limited time and resources of a small firm. This lack of resources can inhibit the number and success of startups.

As discussed above, new businesses have a precarious existence and high failure rates. This, along with the relatively small size of most small business loans, makes banks reluctant to lend to SMEs. Governments therefore establish programs, or even financial institutions, which facilitate lending to this sector. In France, the *Société Française de Garantie de financements des Petites et Moyennes Entreprises* (*SOFARIS*) guarantees up to 50 per cent of a general loan, and 70 per cent for startups.[26] In Japan, about 10 per cent of capital loaned to SMEs is financed through its three government sources.[27] The U.S. Small Business Administration (SBA) performs a similar role.

In Canada, the Small Business Loan Act offers a government guarantee of 85 per cent against possible losses on loans made through this program by banks. As well, Canada's Business Development Bank has a mandate to finance small and growing enterprises. Canada, like most countries, also promotes SME exports by offering insurance and financing at preferred rates for foreign sales. In Canada's case, the Export Development Corporation (EDC) has this mandate.

Governments also try to increase the survival chances of startups by establishing new business incubators. These institutions typically offer subsidized infrastructure support — office and/or shop facilities, limited staff support and business advice — which enable new firms to become established. The success of the Helsinki area's 17 incubators, for example, shows this approach can work. Since 1995, they have created 760 knowledge-based companies and 1,300 jobs.[28]

Israel's country-wide technological incubator program is a another good example of this approach. It was established in 1991 in order to facilitate the absorption of large numbers of highly educated immigrants from the former Soviet Union.[29] By January 2000, more than 300 projects had left the incubators and were continuing business, employing about 1,900, mostly professionals. Incubators are also promoted as economic development vehicles for LDCs by agencies such as the United Nations Development Program. They are viewed the same way by those who wish to revitalize the inner cities of developed countries, especially the United States.

The administrative barriers to entrepreneurship vary between countries. For example, in Italy it can take more than 10 steps and up to about four months to register an unlimited company, while this procedure takes only a day in Germany or Canada.[30] However, in Germany new businesses in trades designated as artisanal, such as baking or hairdressing, must be run by or employ people who hold prescribed apprenticeship certifications. In most countries, zoning laws and commercial laws, such as those governing hours of operation, may inhibit the opening and expanding of young firms.

The paperwork does not end once the business is established. Compliance government regulations, such as those related to employment and consumer protection, create further reporting demands. Collecting and submitting sales and value-added-taxes like the GST, in Canada's case for the federal and provincial governments, also can consume significant amounts of an entrepreneur's time.

The trend through the 1990s around the world was to deregulate the SME sector and work towards minimizing the paperwork burden. For example, governments are streamlining the business establishment processes by setting up "one-stop" centres so potential founders do not have to spend time negotiating with complex bureaucracies. On another front, approved opening hours in

Europe, especially Germany, are lengthening, which is increasing the opportunities for new retail businesses. In Canada, the federal and Atlantic province governments recently harmonized the collection of the GST and provincial sales taxes to make things easier for owner/managers.

Reducing SME Taxes

Another way to foster entrepreneurship is to increase the rewards to those who take the risks of starting, financing or operating new firms. This is achieved by introducing tax policies favouring these activities. Therefore small companies in most countries enjoy a lower income tax rate than their larger counterparts.

Both the definition of a "small" firm and the tax advantage gained vary by jurisdiction. In Ireland, for example, firms making £50,000 (Cdn$90,000) or less pay a standard rate of 25 per cent, compared with 32 per cent for firms with higher incomes. Brazil's basic corporate tax rate is 15 per cent for firms with taxable incomes under RS 240,000 (Cdn$195,000).[31] In Canada, businesses with incomes of $200,000 or less pay a combined federal and provincial rate of around 18–22 per cent, depending on the province. The rates for larger firms range from 43 to 46 per cent, though rates on larger manufacturing companies are somewhat smaller (27%–39%).

A policy tool which has more recently captured the attention of economists and lobbyists is lowering taxes on the capital gains made by investors in successful startups. The spectacular venture capital fueled new economy boom in the United States, as discussed briefly above, has converted many to this approach.

Proponents claim that lower capital gains taxes drive entrepreneurship two ways. First, increasing the after-tax returns to equity investments would increase the availability of capital for growing firms. Second, lower capital gains taxes allow employees of new firms to profit more from the share options they receive, often in lieu of salary, during the start-up phase. Both business founders, who may lack funds to pay salaries, and workers, who prize the upside associated with selling their options at considerable gain, may prefer this kind of compensation. Stock options are also used as payment for business services — consulting, accounting and legal — in a firm's cash-poor but idea-rich period.

The evidence suggests that low capital gains taxes may be a necessary, but not sufficient, means of fostering new businesses. The U.S. federal capital gains tax was recently lowered from 28 per cent to five different rates, of which the most general rate is 20 per cent, for assets held longer than one and a half years.[32] In comparison, Canada's joint federal–provincial rate is three-quarters the personal income tax rate, or 37.5 per cent at a marginal income tax rate of 50 per cent. However, many countries, such as New Zealand, Singapore, Hong Kong, Mexico and the Netherlands, have no capital gains taxes at all.

A Culture of Entrepreneurship

Most governments and non-governmental organizations (NGO's) implement education programs aimed at teaching SME management skills and, more generally, creating an entrepreneurial culture. This has also been the aim of Junior Achievement Inc., a non-profit NGO founded in the United States in 1919. Each year this organization serves about 1,000,000 potential entrepreneurs around the world.

Officials behind the European Commission's SME-and-craft sector development program recognize, as do policy analysts elsewhere, that education is a key part of an entrepreneurship strategy.[33] In Denmark, for example, over two years in the late 1990s from 30 to 40 per cent of students, from primary to post-secondary age, received entrepreneurship training. Teachers as well were trained in the subject. Canada's government, through the Atlantic Canada Opportunities Agency operated a similar program during the 1990s.

Similar programs exist at the post-secondary level. For example, the Leicestershire, United Kingdom, Centre for Enterprise offers exchange programs between business people and academics. The former bring their knowledge to the classroom, and the latter are challenged to test their knowhow in the field. The Netherlands' University of Twente TOP program provides student entrepreneurs with infrastructure, mentoring and zero interest loans. Throughout all its courses, the university encourages "experimentation with enterprising projects."[34]

Bureaucratic Structures

This range of policy issues — from consumer and corporate regulations to taxation, finance and education — means that most parts of government are involved to some degree in small business development. That said, SME policies are typically coordinated either by a specific department or by an agency or section housed in a larger economic development or industry department. America's Small Business Administration is an example of the former, while Japan's Small and Medium Enterprise Agency, part of the Ministry of International Trade and Industry (MITI), is an example of the latter. In Canada, small business development is primarily a mandate of Industry Canada. In these countries, the designated SME offices interact with SME lobby groups. In Canada, the main specialized organization of this type is the 98,000-member Canadian Federation of Independent Business.

WHAT SHOULD POLICY-MAKERS DO?

Though decades of research have shed light on the factors associated with entrepreneurship, governments have yet to find sure ways of promoting it. A key reason for this arises from the oxymoronic nature of the term "entrepreneurship policy." Entrepreneurship is not predictable. Cycles, culture, chance and perceptions play important roles. New opportunities appear to be most common in the wake of technological shifts, which can be initiated anywhere but soon spread — especially today — everywhere. Once entrepreneurial activity starts in a region or industry, entrepreneurship begets entrepreneurship. Successful new businesses attract venture capital, which generates high returns, which leads to more investor interest, which encourages more people to start more businesses and so on. Another problem facing policy makers is that the agents of this activity, entrepreneurs, can often be just as unpredictable. They also can be headstrong individualists.

The word "policy," in contrast, suggests planning and administration by bureaucrats. Governments move slowly as they try to serve many political interests, who must be treated (or be perceived to be treated) fairly. Bureaucracies, which need rigorous controls, typically cannot move quickly enough to address changes associated with entrepreneurship. How can they plan for innovations that are to come? Further, the civil servants implementing policies — or the academics advocating them — tend to possess a more cautious, security-oriented approach to their lives than the entrepreneurs they are trying to help. This is demonstrated by their career choices. Many entrepreneurs question whether civil servants (or academics) can truly understand the SME world.

Given the unpredictable nature of these circumstances it is therefore not surprising that those consulted for the *Global Economic Monitor* report suggested governments can do little to foster entrepreneurship. But, given the real and political importance of SMEs, they realize they must be seen as doing something. So governments develop the policies mentioned above, such as SME finance programs. However, support granted by governments may not be necessary, or appropriately targeted. For example, a study on Canada's Small Business Loan Act found that only 60 per cent of program recipients indicated that they would not have got a loan without the program.[35] The need to address political realities and to avoid failures affects the practices of the Export Development Corporation: which, as noted above, aims to support SME exports. In fact, while 88 per cent of the EDC's clients are SMEs, in 1999 about 600 large companies accounted for 85 per cent of the value of sales supported by the EDC.[36] These large corporations, including Bombardier and Nortel, really do not need the assistance; but they will export and are very likely to repay loans.

That said, governments should recognize and foster SMEs, which are important to their economies. A sensible approach would recognize this sector for what it is. Rather than becoming the world's next Microsoft or Intel, most SMEs will be medium- or low-tech companies, spread across the country; they go in and out of business and, if they survive, stay small. Such a view is not defeatist for two reasons. The first is that it recognizes two important roles of SMEs: making economies flexible and offering motivated individuals the chance to have control over their working lives. Second, this perspective reflects an understanding that all sectors and regions can benefit from entrepreneurship.

The implication is that the most effective SME policies are those which enable any type of start-up, anywhere. Two of the policies introduced above are most appropriate. The first are steps taken which make it easy to establish a small business. This includes reducing the paperwork burden (e.g., tax payments, payroll administration and licencing), though public safety and security should not be compromised. The other useful approach is to encourage entrepreneurship education and experience among young people. This lowers the actual and perceived barriers to founding companies. Useful learning can occur in high schools, post-secondary institutions and through community linkages. Student summer employment should be fostered by providing employers (especially SMEs) with incentives to participate in coop programs.

A realistic view of SMEs *does not* justify targeted tax breaks and subsidies, unless they are related to training or education. Financial incentives targeted to businesses based on size, sector or region distort the choices made by entrepreneurs and investors. New business founders should focus on their ideas, not the government support available. As well, these types of programs, by encouraging high levels of entry and excess competition in targeted areas or industries, may actually decrease, rather than increase, the likelihood of success.[37] In the long run, these kinds of policies can discourage the growth of viable new firms.

The strong fiscal situation of most OECD countries (in late 2000) means politicians now have room to lower the taxes paid by, and thereby increase the returns to, entrepreneurs. This is reasonable. But such policies should be viewed in light of their broader social implications. Taxes, after all, subsidize the upbringing, health care and education of the less well off. Government budget policies which lead to further reductions in support for the underprivileged could, by restricting their opportunities, shrink the pool of future entrepreneurs. This could also increase the size of an underclass that, in the absence of attractive choices, practices entrepreneurship in the criminal sector.

FINAL THOUGHTS ON THE "HEFFALUMP"

It is clear that nearly 30 years after Peter Kilby wrote the passage quoted at the outset, entrepreneurship still resembles a "Heffalump." We can see its footprints — dynamic economic growth and flexibility — as the source of dynamism in many countries, especially the United States in recent years. The plethora of policies throughout the world aimed at capturing this beast show it is still considered "large and very important." Therefore it is in the interest of all governments, and the citizens they represent, to create environments which enable innovation, business start-ups and growth. In the end, however, it is up to observant and dedicated individuals, not governments, to act, and hope that conditions are right.

NOTES

1. Peter Kilby, "Hunting the Heffalump" in Kilby, P. (ed.), *Entrepreneurship and Economic Development* (New York: Free Press, 1971), pp. 1–40.
2. A.A. Milne, *The World of Pooh* (Toronto: McClelland & Stewart Ltd., 1957).
3. Howard H. Stevenson & J. Carlos Jarillo, "A paradigm of entrepreneurship," *Strategic Management Journal*, 11: 17–27.
4. Phillip B. Gove (ed.), *Webster's Third New International Dictionary* (Springfield, MA: G. and C. Merriam Company, 1971), p. 759.
5. Robert K. Barnhardt (ed.), *The Barnhardt Dictionary of Etymology* (New York: H.W. Wilson Company, 1988), p. 324.
6. James H. Tiessen, "Individualism, collectivism and entrepreneurship: A framework for international comparative research," *Journal of Business Venturing*, 12(5): 367–84.
7. Joseph A. Schumpeter, *The Theory of Economic Development* (Boston, MA: Harvard University Press, 1961), p. 74.
8. Zhengxi Lin, Janice Yates and Garnett Picot, *Rising Self-Employment in the Midst of High Unemployment: An Empirical Analysis of Recent Developments in Canada*

Research Paper Series #133 (Ottawa: Statistics Canada, Analytical Studies Branch, March 1999).

9. OECD, "OECD Conference on Women Entrepreneurs in SMEs: A Major Force in Innovation and Job Creation" (Paris: OECD, August 26, 1998). Online: <www.oecd.org/dsti/sti/industry/smes/prod/synth.htm> (viewed June 26, 2000).

10. Howard Aldrich, *Organizations Evolving* (London: Sage, 1999), pp. 20–41.

11. OECD, *Fostering Entrepreneurship* (Paris: OECD, 1998), p. 44.

12. Rita Gunther McGrath, "Entrepreneurship, small firms and wealth creation: A framework using real options reasoning" in Andrew Pettigrew, Richard Whittington and Thomas Howard (eds.), *Handbook of Strategy* (Thousand Oaks, CA: Sage, forthcoming).

13. James Brander, Ken Hendricks, Raphael Amit and Diana Whistler, *The Engine of Growth Hypothesis: On the Relationship Between Firm Size and Employment Growth*. Working Paper, University of British Columbia, Vancouver, 1998.

14. OECD, *Technology, productivity and job creation* (Paris: OECD, 1996), pp. 186–87.

15. OECD, *Small and Medium-sized Transnational Corporations: Role, Impact and Policy Implications* (Paris: OECD, 1993), p. 19.

16. Ibid.

17. Scott Shane, "Explaining variation in rates of entrepreneurship in the United States: 1899–1988," *Journal of Management*, 22(5): 747–81. Shane defined the rate of entrepreneurship as the number of businesses/capita and technological change as the number of invention patents issued.

18. Rein Peterson, *Global Entrepreneurship Monitor, 1999 Canadian National Executive Report*, Schulich School of Business, York University, Toronto, 1999. The Global Entrepreneurship Monitor is a research consortium comprising Babson College and the London School of Business. Its 1999 survey was administered in Canada by Professor Rein Peterson of the Schulich School of Business at York University.

19. David C. McClelland, *The Achieving Society* (Van Nostrand, NJ: Princeton, 1961).

20. Robert H. Brockhaus, Sr., "The psychology of the entrepreneur" in C.A. Kent, D.L. Sexton, and K.H. Vesper (eds.), *Encyclopedia of Entrepreneurship* (Englewood Cliffs, NJ: Prentice-Hall, 1982), pp. 41–56.

21. Tiessen, see note 6.

22. United Nations Conference on Trade and Development, *Handbook on Foreign Direct Investment by Small and Medium Enterprises — Lessons from Asia* (New York and Geneva: United Nations, 1998).

23. *Economist*, "Money to Burn" (May 27, 2000), pp. 71–73.

24. These estimates were collected from the Canadian Venture Capital Association, the U.S. National Venture Capital Association, British Venture Capital Association and the European Venture Capital Association (17 countries). The Japan figure is from Bain & Company, as cited in "Business in Japan," *Economist*, November 27, 1999.

25. *Economist*, "The world in its hands" (May 6, 2000), p. 77.

26. *Fostering entrepreneurship*, p. 73.

27. OECD, *Globalisation and Small and Medium Enterprises (SMEs) Vol. 2 Country Studies* (Paris: OECD, 1997), p. 192.

28. Commission of the European Communities, *Report from the Commission to the Council, the European Parliament, the Economic and Social Committee and the Committee of the Regions on Concerted Action with the Member States in the Field of Enterprise Policy* (Brussels, Belgium: European Commission, September 9, 1999), p. 63.

29. Office of the Chief Scientist, *Technological Incubators in Israel* (Ministry of Industry and Trade, Tel Aviv, <www.incubators.org.il/program.htm>, Viewed June 20, 2000).

30. *Fostering Entrepreneurship*, pp. 54–55. The requirements in all countries are typically lowest for unlimited liability firms (sole proprietor), higher for limited liability companies, and highest for public firms, as mentioned above.

31. KPMG, *Country Tax Facts* (KPMG, <www.kpmg.net/library/country_tax_facts>, Viewed June 20, 2000). In the United States, the rate is 15 per cent for firms with US$50,000 or less income, rising to 25 per cent for $50,001 to $75,000, and 34 per cent for incomes greater than $75,000.

32. Jack M. Mintz and Thomas A. Wilson, "Capitalizing on Cuts to Capital Gains Taxes," *C.D. Howe Institute Commentary*, No. 137 (February 2000), p. 1.

33. *Report from the Commission to the Council, the European Parliament, the Economic and Social Committee and the Committee of the Regions on Concerted Action with the Member States in the Field of Enterprise Policy*.

34. Ibid. p. 48.

35. *Fostering Entrepreneurship*, p. 73.

36. Patricia Adams, "Secret of EDC's 'success': Taxpayer's money," *National Post* (May 25, 2000), p. C19.

37. McGrath, forthcoming, pp. 21–22.

Canada in a Changing World

There has been much made recently of the so-called New World Economic Order. This section explores the political and economic meaning of this phrase, as well as its implications for Canadian policy makers and managers.

The first article in the section, Ed Hooven's "The New World Order: In a New Millennium," focuses first on the making of this New World Order, starting in the period at the end of World War II when the Allied powers were trying to design transnational institutions which would facilitate the reconstruction of war-ravaged economies and help prevent a renewal of conflicts among nations. What is clear as Hooven traces the history of the economic institutions is that if there is a New World Order in place today, it is a constantly evolving one. Each new crisis in the world has inspired a new response from the world's leading nations, resulting in a continuous cycle of creation, change and destruction of the institutional arrangements among nations. The first section of Hooven's article is focused on supra-national institutions. While these institutions, to a large extent, are dominated by the United States, this dominance has been diminished recently. The European Union and Japan have risen to represent economic and political forces comparable although probably not yet equal to the United States. The remaining two sections in Hooven's article focus in turn on the development of the European Union and post-war Japan.

The section continues with David Barrows and John Cotsomitis's article, "International Trade and Investment." The glue that holds the New World Order together is the huge daily economic flow of goods, services, capital and labour, which tie nations together in a web of interdependence. Barrows and Cotsomitis explore the economic theory of international trade and how our changing understanding of this theory has influenced trade policy over the last 500 years. The authors also look at the essential role that trade plays in Canada's economy. From here they move on to discuss the international institutions which facilitate and manage world trade particularly the WTO and NAFTA. Finally, the article looks at the increasing importance of foreign direct investment (FDI) in the world economy and at the relationship between FDI and trade in the New World Order.

The final article in this section is "Globalization and Canadian Economic and Industrial Strategy in the Twenty-First Century," by James Gillies. In it, Gillies explores the consequences of the New World order and the globalized economy for Canada, particularly our ability to set our own national economic policy in light of the increased external pressures placed on our economy. He discusses why some analysts support the adoption of an industrial strategy for Canada and why some oppose it. Gillies then presents Canada's traditional industrial policy, as articulated in the staple thesis, and examines how changes in the world have rendered the staple thesis untenable as a policy. He argues that the rise of "transnational" corporations has contributed to the eclipse of the staple thesis as the underlying premise of Canadian economic policy. Finally, he looks at how we have attempted to develop a national consensus on policies to replace those based on the staple thesis, and what we need to do as a nation to finally succeed in redefining our economy for the twenty-first century.

The New World Order:
In a New Millennium

Ed Hooven

This article is organized into three parts. The first deals with the international arrangements (political, economic and military) that were constructed under U.S. leadership in the wake of World War II. The second part examines the evolution of the European Union (EU) and its efforts to create a single market. The third and final part looks at the evolution of contemporary Japan.

PART I: INTERNATIONAL ARRANGEMENTS

The Creation of the Post-World War II International System

The Early Post-war Years

As the defeat of the Axis powers approached, Allied policy makers drew upon the experiences of the inter-war years (1919–1939) and began to focus upon the nature of the post-war world. Most important, they wished to avoid the downward spiral into trade protectionism, economic warfare and military conflict characteristic of the previous decades.

The international structure that was created in the mid and late 1940s had, as its major goal, the creation of an open world trading system. Freer trade was seen as providing for a number of solutions to the problems faced by post-war policy makers: economically interdependent countries could not wage war against one another without experiencing significant economic dislocation (thus precluding future military conflict); the reintegration of Germany into a strong Europe would be made easier in the context of trade interdependence (this was the aim of the Treaty of Rome and its creation, the European Union); the United States was concerned about a return to depression-like conditions if trade protectionism recurred (the weakened condition of many

101

war-ravaged countries around the world made this an ever-present possibility); and the theory of comparative advantage suggested that all would eventually benefit from a free trade-oriented international economic environment.

To create an open-world economy, the allies negotiated an institutional framework they believed would accomplish their task. Although the political and economic aspects frequently overlap, it is possible nonetheless to focus separately on these two dimensions for analytic purposes.

The Political Dimension

The creation of the United Nations at the Dumbarton Oaks Conference in 1944 was very significant. Unlike its failed predecessor, the League of Nations, the UN included all of the most powerful nations, as well as many lesser powers. Its official mandate was to provide a mechanism to mediate conflicts. It was organized in a two-tiered fashion, with a general assembly for all members, and a security council with only five permanent members.[1] Each of these major powers had a veto over decisions reached by the UN; a provision that had been required to assure their participation.

Also politically important, given the rise of the USSR at the end of World War II, was the founding of a variety of military alliances aimed at containing Soviet power. The most important of these was the North Atlantic Treaty Organization (NATO). This defence pact, since it involved the permanent stationing of U.S. and Canadian troops in Europe, enabled German military power to be part of a pan-European force and, therefore, much less threatening to countries such as France, Holland and Denmark that had suffered defeat and occupation during the war. The final political development was the founding of the EU.[2] After several false starts, agreement was reached and the EU's founding document, the Treaty of Rome, was signed in 1957. Once again the issue of German power — in this case economic power — was involved. It was the aim of the EU to embed German economic power in a Europe-wide economic and political system. This would not only facilitate the rebuilding of Europe, but would also help avoid the problem of another European war via economic interdependence as discussed above.

The Economic Dimension

In 1944, as the end of the war approached, Allied policy makers met in Bretton Woods, New Hampshire to lay the basis for the post-war international financial system. Given the inter-war experience of the abandonment of the gold standard and rounds of competitive currency devaluation, the Bretton Woods delegates hoped to create a structure that was flexible, yet sturdy enough to withstand a variety of pressures. Broadly speaking, what was needed was a mechanism to relate currency values to one another in a predictable way. Such a mechanism would facilitate the growth of world trade and foreign investment; global interdependence would become a reality.

To achieve this goal, three sets of technical problems needed to be solved:[3] liquidity — an adequate, but not inflationary, supply of the currency upon which world trade would be based was needed; the ability to adjust to balance-of-payments disequilibria; and the maintenance of confidence in the currency around which world trade was to be based — as well as confidence in the relative value of currencies.

From the beginning, the Bretton Woods agreement was a compromise between, on the one hand, the demand by all nations for a considerable amount of national economic autonomy and, on the other hand, an attempt to limit the impact of domestic economic policies on the international order. This compromise would ultimately fail.

The Bretton Woods talks focused on the central role of the U.S. dollar ("liquidity") that had been fixed in value at $35 to an ounce of gold by President Roosevelt in 1933. By formal agreement, the other currencies were fixed in value relative to the U.S. dollar ("confidence"). The International Monetary Fund (IMF), created at Bretton Woods and funded by the rich countries, loaned money to countries experiencing balance-of-trade problems. In return, recipient countries were required to alter economic policies believed to be responsible for the trade deficit situation ("adjustment to balance-of-payments disequilibria").

A sister institution to the IMF (also created at Bretton Woods) was the World Bank, which was initially called the International Bank for Reconstruction and Development, and was at first mandated to aid in the reconstruction of war-ravaged Europe. Its role has evolved into one of providing long-term development loans to poorer nations. Projects have included transportation and communication networks, as well as hydroelectric and urban infrastructural improvements. The goal of the World Bank was, and is, to help developing countries modernize on the basis of free markets, while at the same time diminishing the appeal of socialism/communism.

The post-war planners aimed to create a powerful trade organization to monitor and control, to some extent, the trade policies of member nations, and to promote ever-freer trade via a series of negotiating "rounds." To be called the International Trade Organization, it proved to be too much of an encroachment on national sovereignty, and failed to enlist the support of enough countries to come into being. What is very important is that, instead, the idea of a series of rounds of trade negotiations lived on in the form of a treaty: the General Agreement on Tariffs and Trade (GATT). Beginning in 1948, the signatory countries began negotiating ever-lower barriers to trade. Focusing initially on tariff barriers, it moved on later to consider non-tariff impediments to trade.

Finally, under the Marshall Plan,[4] the United States made a series of grants available for the rebuilding of Europe. Under this arrangement $13-billion[5] was spent to ensure that political parties of the extreme left did not come to power and create a closed European economy.

The Unmaking of the Post-War World

The Russian-American Confrontation

In 1949 the first of a series of military alliances, aimed at what was now called the "containment" of communism, came into existence. The North Atlantic Treaty Organization (NATO) was created for two purposes: to provide

North American aid to Europe in the event of a Soviet invasion, and to over-ride European resistance to a reconstructed and potentially powerful Germany. The latter was to be achieved by integrating the German military contingent into a NATO force under U.S. command. Since NATO was obviously directed against the Soviets, and since loans under the Marshall Plan (also offered to Russia) required the adoption of free-market principles, the result was a deepening of the division of Europe into hostile camps.

To combat the threat of communism outside of Europe, the United States entered into a series of security agreements that were global in scope. By the 1960s these worldwide commitments led the United States into involvement in the Vietnam War. This was a particularly fateful development, since the cost of the war was not paid for by tax increases or other fiscally prudent approaches. Rather, given the war's political unpopularity, the U.S. government printed money to pay for it, and in so doing helped to undermine the international financial regime established at Bretton Woods. (This is discussed further below.) By the late 1960s the United States had about 1.8-million troops in 30 countries, was a member of four regional defence alliances (and was active in a fifth), was involved in 42 mutual defence treaties, belonged to 53 international organizations, and was providing military or economic aid to nearly 100 nations around the world.[6]

As the end of the millennium approached, the post-war system of military alliances aimed overwhelmingly at the Soviet Union, and the (now disbanded) Warsaw Pact were clearly poised for profound change. Having achieved its goal of containing communism and of contributing to its collapse, NATO struggled with radically changed circumstances. To cope with the new realities, and perhaps the most important geo-political event since the 1989 collapse of communism, it was proposed to enlarge NATO. However, merely adding new members paled in comparison with the larger contemporary challenge: giving the 16-member organization a new purpose. "Power projection," supporting Western foreign policy outside of the alliance's territory, will require a difficult-to-achieve consensus among countries without a history of such agreement. This newly evolving mandate appears to be much more contentious compared to its earlier goal of containing and defending against communism.

The new members (Hungary, the Czech Republic and Poland, who joined in March 1999) will not see nuclear weapons placed on their soil, nor will they see large garrisons to avoid giving the Russians offense. In other respects they will be full NATO members — with joint training, military exercises and the nuclear umbrella, which, with the new members, will extend organization's reach to Poland's eastern border!

Given the organization's new mandate of projecting power outside of Europe, NATO's scope will certainly be large, but not global: China will remain a joint U.S./Japanese responsibility; Latin America looks certain to remain more-or-less peaceful for the foreseeable future; and no one would consider an intervention on the Indian subcontinent. Nonetheless, a huge area remains: southwest Asia and much of Africa, with many decrepit authoritarian regimes, militant Islam, and 40 per cent of the EU's oil and 10 per cent of U.S.'s supplies.[7]

While NATO will seek to prevent the rise of new nuclear powers and keep an eye on Russia, it must continue to prepare for the dozen or so military interventions that will likely occupy the organization over the next 20 or 30 years, and it must forge a foreign policy consensus that currently does not exist. Given this lack of consensus, we may see, in the context of each new crisis, "coalitions of the willing" doing the heavy lifting; yet rules will be needed to set the threshold for the number of willing participants to make the operation a go. Important also will be the continuation of the European and American world views that have developed over the past 80 or so years. This potential problem has been in clear view in recent years, as seen by the fact that while missiles and oil problems threaten the EU, it was the Americans who showed the greatest willingness to militarily confront these difficulties in Libya in 1986 and Iraq in 1991.

The 1999 NATO intervention in Kosovo reinforced the view that the organization was still suffering from a lack of cohesion, in terms of both policy and its implementation: the war fighting plan (which involved largely high altitude bombing) seemed to be concerned more with minimizing NATO casualties than with completing the task in the most efficient and effective manner possible. President Clinton, speaking to U.S. troops in Macedonia after the war ended, gave a civil rights spin when he outlined the goal of the intervention:

> Never forget if we do this here ... we can then say to the people of the world, whether you live in Africa, or central Europe or any other place: If somebody comes after innocent civilians and tries to kill them en masse because of their race, their ethnic background or their religion, and it's within our power to stop it, we will stop it.[8]

It would seem, however, that Martin Luther King's vision of racial harmony and reconciliation is not a popular one in Kosovo: by early 2000 only about 25 per cent of the previous Serb population of 200,000 remained in that unfortunate land.[9] The Kosovo episode appears to be quickly becoming a costly and long-term commitment; one that re-emphasizes the need for greater clarity of both the goals and the methods employed by NATO. Interventions in the future will likely suffer similar problems without significant changes to the way NATO does business.

A key question for the future of NATO is that of responsibility. For example, during the Kosovo conflict U.S. intelligence located nearly all the bombing targets, the United States flew two-thirds of attack missions, and nearly all of the "smart" missiles were American. The U.S. General who led the NATO bombing campaign curtailed some missions because of the poor performance of aging European aircraft, and a lack of night-vision equipment, computerized weapons and advanced communications. While the Western European defence budget is some two-thirds that of the United States, due to inefficient procurement practices it results in only about 25 per cent the number of combat capable troops.[10] While it is certainly true that NATO has always been an organization in which the United States played the lead role, the events in Kosovo clearly indicate that the gap in military capabilities between Europe and America has widened.

Meanwhile, NATO (with the help of UN police) by late 2000 was trying to police an uneasy peace between the warring factions in Kosovo. Along with regular violent clashes between Serbs and Albanians were repeated escapes from NATO custody of accused war criminals.

On a perhaps lighter note, it is reassuring that amidst the chaos of war and its aftermath, some semblance of what passes for normalcy in the early twenty-first century has returned to the Balkans. Beekeepers in Macedonia have filed a claim with a special NATO commission (sensitively created for such occasions, one presumes) for $222,300. It seems that noise made by the NATO jets was "a terrible stress" for their bees, and production dropped by 70 per cent.[11] The complaint is being considered by NATO.

The Bretton Woods International Financial Regime

Bretton Woods, in an important sense, was based squarely upon a contradiction: the U.S. dollar fuelled international trade and therefore, as world trade expanded, the United States, like Britain before it, was required to run constant balance-of-payments deficits. This, in the long run, meant that confidence in the United States' ability to defend the dollar at $35 to the ounce of gold would eventually waiver.[12] The United States permitted the EU and Japan to discriminate against U.S. imports in order to strengthen their weak post-war economies, thereby generating chronic trade surpluses for themselves and deficits for the United States.[13]

By the 1960s, the United States was increasingly thought to be abusing its role as liquidity supplier, which perhaps was something of a surprise since the U.S. dollar was the world's reserve, transaction and intervention currency, freeing the United States from short- and medium-term concerns regarding its balance-of-payments.[14] It also could not devalue its dollar since this, it was feared, would lead to a repetition of the competitive devaluations characteristic of the inter-war years. The strength of the American economy, combined with the relatively small size of its import/export sector, diminished the threat of devaluation. But by the late 1960s and early 1970s, the outflow of dollars became a raging torrent. By mid-1971, international inflation levels were rising. It became increasingly clear that a devaluation of the U.S. dollar was inevitable.

In August 1971, against a backdrop of a vast outflow of gold from Fort Knox, President Nixon suspended the dollar's convertibility into gold.[15] Delivering a stern message to America's trading partners, he also put a surcharge on imports into the United States and, to fight inflation, put in place wage and price controls. Thus began the current floating exchange rate regime. The formal end of Bretton Woods was acknowledged during meetings held in Kingston, Jamaica, in 1976.

Domestic U.S. political and economic imperatives had overwhelmed Bretton Woods; yet a failure to establish a new international financial regime meant a loss of financial discipline and, consequently, a dramatic expansion of private, national and international debt. Nations proved unwilling to allow market forces to determine currency values completely, and frequently intervened. Perhaps even more significant, in the search for security and high returns, capital flows were becoming larger than trade flows: national currency values therefore became increasingly influenced by these capital flows. Macroeconomic policies, especially those in the United States, became important in determining international capital movements and, in turn, national currency values. These capital flows, given increasing worldwide integration of capital markets, significantly undermined domestic economic autonomy (e.g., interest rate policy).

A case-in-point occurred during the Reagan presidency: Mr. Reagan, riding the crest of a conservative resurgence, promised lower taxes and a strengthened military. Since Mr. Reagan's plans to cut non-defence spending (especially entitlement programs) were thwarted by the Democratic Party's control of Congress, a borrowing binge resulted that required high real interest rates. Under the post-Bretton Woods flexible exchange rate regime, this meant a vast inflow of funds into the United States. The consequent demand for U.S. dollars drove their value up some 60 per cent between 1980 and 1985, reducing U.S. exports and increasing imports. Protectionist sentiment surged, and concern mounted over the resultant trade imbalances.[16]

In the absence of other options, world leaders felt that the best way to cope with this situation was through international monetary policy coordination. In 1985, at meetings held at the Plaza Hotel in New York, the industrialized countries agreed to a coordinated sell-off of U.S. dollars held in their central banks in order to drive the value of the U.S. dollar downward. At the 1986 Tokyo Summit, the allies refused to relink their currencies to the dollar — as they feared a return of old problems. They did, however, create the G5 (United States, Japan, Great Britain, France and West Germany, later expanded to the G7 with Canada and Italy) to monitor the global economic situation, and to exert a kind of peer pressure on individual nations, and to encourage them to undertake necessary policy changes from time to time.

It is perhaps possible to conclude that, while the end of Bretton Woods and the move to flexible exchange rates seemed to have uncoupled national economies from each other to some extent, growing financial interdependence had, in effect, recoupled them. With large deficit-related financial flows continuing, further exchange-rate instabilities will certainly continue to plague the "non-system" of floating rates that has replaced Bretton Woods. The dramatic decline in the value of the U.S. dollar to new post-war lows against the German and Japanese currencies in 1994, followed by its more recent appreciation, is a case in point. In an effort to stabilize currency fluctuations a communiqué was issued following a meeting of the G7 finance ministers and central bank governors held in February 1997: satisfaction was expressed that "major misalignments in exchange markets" that occurred in April 1995 (when the U.S. dollar plunged to a post-war low of 97.7 yen) had been corrected. The U.S. dollar continued to climb in the late 90s and well into 2000. While the currencies of nearly all other countries have fallen, a combination of strong growth, low inflation, higher interest rates and a large foreign appetite for U.S. assets has seen the American currency rise to new heights. The Canadian dollar trading in the mid-60 cents range against the U.S. dollar, has been benefiting from some of the same (if more moderate) economic fundamentals as its American cousin.[17]

The major driving force behind the strong U.S. dollar would appear to be an incredible growth in non-farm productivity of over 5 per cent (which led in turn to a drop in unit labour costs over 1999–2000).[18] In a speech to the Economic Club of New York in early 2000, the Chairman of the U.S. Federal Reserve Alan Greenspan indicated that the ongoing information technology revolution (IT) is behind the phenomenal expansion in American productivity growth: more efficient capital reallocation made possible by an unbundling of capital market risks as a result of new financial products made feasible by advances in IT; the reduction in "inventory safety stocks" (e.g., "just-in-time inventory" management) and worker redundancies (given that managers now have greater knowledge of the state of the ongoing production process); and cheaper machinery as IT makes for much shorter lead times for machinery orders (with consequently less need to build more complex machines than currently necessary to meet all plausible future needs).[19] Mr. Greenspan continues to be concerned about the "wealth effect" of high equity values on consumer demand and the future potential for inflation.

With a spike in oil prices (and the potential for still higher prices courtesy of another crisis in the Middle East)[20] combined with falling stock markets (with the NASDAQ down 34 per cent and the Dow down 13 per cent from their highs),[21] Mr. Greenspan's concerns were given new life in October 2000. As the chief economist at Morgan Stanley Dean Witter put it, "I'm concerned that the unwinding of the wealth effect, coupled with higher energy prices, could pose some significant downside risk for spending going forward."[22] With the U.S. economic fundamentals remaining strong, there is debate about the possible impacts of these recent events on the future performance of the American economy.

The IMF

As discussed above, the World Bank and the International Monetary Fund were also part of the Bretton Woods formula. The IMF's mandate is to provide financial (and policy) aid on a temporary basis to countries that can be relied on to pay their loans back quickly. With the end of fixed exchange rates and the (not unrelated) upward ratcheting of inflation, the IMF faced new challenges. As oil prices rose throughout the 1970s, oil-importing countries began to run large balance-of-payment deficits. The IMF broadened its lending activities in response to these changing circumstances: In the 1970s it made money available to developing countries suffering from the "oil shock," and provided extended terms. This was in keeping with the IMF's traditional concern with balance of payments, but it represented a new policy direction as well.

With the end of the Bretton Woods fixed exchange rate regime, countries could finance their deficits on (expanding) international capital markets, and/or let their currencies depreciate. By the summer of 1982, the growth of developing-country debt had become a serious problem: Mexico threatened to default on its debts to foreign banks. The crisis was brought on by a rise in interest rates. The IMF extracted loans from frightened banks in Europe and North America, which resulted in even more debt, combined with increased commercial bank exposure. The strict terms accepted by recipient countries resulted in fewer imports and a consequent reduction in external deficits.

This episode, and the IMF's response, did conform to its original mandate: to protect the integrity of the global monetary system. In this period the Fund also began to worry about longer-term development issues. It should perhaps have been unsurprising that austerity measures imposed by the Fund were highly unpopular. "From 1986 onwards, the Fund was receiving more in debt service from the heavily indebted developing countries, than it was extending to them in new loans."[23]

Meanwhile, the World Bank evolved from its initial concern with rebuilding war-ravaged Europe (in which it was overshadowed by the Marshall Plan) to a focus on Third World development. In the 1950s it concentrated on improving public sector infrastructure (power stations, roads, communication networks, etc.). In the 1960s, it added farming, education, population control and urban development projects. In the 1970s, it began to realize that poorly conceived macroeconomic policies could negatively affect its development projects. The Bank therefore began making non-profit loans in aid of specific economic policy reforms, thus encroaching on IMF territory. This so-called "policy-based" lending exploded in the 1980s. Further complicating the Bank's role is the fact that, as the 1990s approached, resolving the developing-country debt problem was increasingly seen as a development issue, rather than one of liquidity.

The IMF and the World Bank in the 1990s looked out at a developing world that appears to be increasingly receptive to what *The Economist* called "Bank/Fund orthodoxy."[24] This included the following elements: non-inflationary macroeconomic policies (with modest deficits and a prudent monetary policy), more openness to trade and foreign investment, and greater reliance on market forces to allocate resources (especially in agriculture and industry).

The December 1994 Mexican financial crisis indicated, once again, the parlous state of developing country financial systems. Pessimists were even proclaiming the end of the "emerging-market era." The financial panic occurred after Mexico revealed that it was near default on its short-term borrowings; causing investors to yank out billions and precipitating a cash crunch. Moreover, non-bank private debt (primarily bonds) which lay behind the Mexican crisis is increasingly popular in the world's "emerging markets": In spite of Mexico, $23-billion in this type of debt went to developing countries in 1995. In fact, a total net $201-billion of private capital flowed into these countries in 1995 (up from $182-billion in 1994).[25]

This is disappointing to those who had hoped for far-reaching reform of the global financial system. The problem to be resolved is how to cope with the possibility of future financial disasters involving numerous bondholders. In the Mexican case, the IMF and the United States cobbled together a $40-billion line of credit; clearly, new mechanisms are required. Indeed, a May 1996 report by the G7 clearly states that a Mexican-style bailout will not be repeated; they want to leave future such events to (hopefully better prepared) private financial markets. The report rejected as impractical proposals to establish an international bankruptcy court; instead, it wants bond contracts to include specific clauses to reduce the ability of a minority of bondholders to delay or even to scupper a debt rescheduling program (most current contracts require unanimity). The report sees a continuing role for IMF intervention in return for the emplacement of proper "adjustment" policies, and wants the World Bank to be empowered to lend to countries prior to any agreement on rescheduling by bondholders.

In late 1996 the IMF announced that it had put together a deal to create safeguards to ensure that there is not a repeat of the Mexican imbroglio: plans were unveiled to reach a formal agreement with about 25 countries which would allow the IMF to borrow about $28-billion to lend if there is a run by private investors on a cash-strapped country. The proposed plan would seek a sharp increase in funds for member countries, provide better surveillance of problem countries, and establish standards for the reporting of financial data.

But critics of the IMF see little reason for optimism: "The IMF is an extremely mediocre institution ... [with a] very small staff ... [which lacks] technical training. There has been some improvement ... [but none] that should give ready comfort to markets," according to Harvard economist Jeffrey Sachs. Not only did the IMF fail to anticipate the Mexican meltdown, but it had no clear procedures to deal with the crisis once it had occurred. Until Mexico, standard IMF practice was to hector countries with large trade and government deficits — but only those countries who also owed the Fund for outstanding loans (which Mexico did not). Only in 1996 did the IMF place news-wire screens in its offices to monitor market developments.

Unfortunately, as the Fund seeks to expand its activities, its staffing levels (about 2600 employees) and its budget (about $400-billion) remain unchanged. Since the Mexican crisis, the Fund and others have become aware of the degree to which developing countries have become dependent on private capital. Speed is now more important than ever: In the past, when the world's major debtors were government organizations, the negotiators could, in a more or less leisurely fashion, hammer out new terms with lengthened repayment periods.

In August 2000, the IMF's new Managing Director (and former German Finance Minister), Horst Koehler, announced plans to move the organization back to its original mandate: preserving stability in world financial markets. The fund has been overstretched in the past and needs to refocus on providing the kind of advice that will help countries anticipate and avoid financial problems. Mr. Koehler referred approvingly to the recent economic success of its most important Asian clients, Thailand and South Korea. He believes that their success is the result of loans and open-market policies that were imposed by the IMF during the 1998 "Asian Flu" crisis. Critics of the IMF, however, charge that the organization's history of bailing out countries that follow foolish fiscal, monetary and economic policies has encouraged the kind of speculative investments that led to the financial meltdown.

Apparently responding to IMF critics, Mr. Koehler acknowledged that while the Fund has made mistakes, it cannot print money and must rely on contributions from its 182 members: "Creditors and borrowers must assume responsibility for the risks they take, and taxpayers' money will not be easily available to protect them from the consequences of bad judgement."[26] The new managing director would appear to be a much stronger proponent of open markets and trade compared to his French predecessor. He argues that for Europe to begin to experience some of the rapid growth characteristic of the

U.S. economy in recent years, it must adopt "more convincing structural reforms," including tax relief and labour deregulation. He believes that the World Bank should focus on dealing with developing country poverty via loans for structural reform and for the reduction of poverty. The IMF will retain a secondary role with respect to poverty reduction with concessional lending and with programs for debt relief.

Mr. Koehler, at the IMF/World Bank meetings held in Prague in late September 2000, criticized the slow pace at which the world's rich nations are opening their borders to trade by insisting that they "recognize that it is both in their own interest and in the interest of the global economy to take a strong lead in opening their markets."[27] He also indicated that the Fund would scale back some of its loan conditions and, in response to the concerns of the U.S. Treasury Secretary, agreed to limit the length and scope of some of its loans to encourage the more credit worthy developing countries (e.g., Argentina, the Philippines, etc.) to access private capital markets.

The World Bank

In June 1995 James Wolfensohn, amid much talk about the need to "manage change," became the new boss of the World Bank; it took him a mere few months before he spoke of the need to "change the way we do business." The Bank faces a fundamentally new challenge: it was created to funnel "development" money to Third World countries; yet that role is increasingly overshadowed by private capital flows. Much of this capital is coming from multinationals who are expanding their operations in the developing world, as well as from mutual funds and pension funds which see opportunities. All of this represents a big change since the early 1990s. Another big change is that 50 per cent of private capital is flowing into productive assets; in the 1970s and early 1980s, such flows were from banks to foreign governments to assist in the financing of budget and balance-of-payments deficits.

In a study published in 1996, the Bank examined the matter of privatization (which it had been involved with) in developing economies. The report's findings are not positive. For example, state-owned enterprises accounted for nearly as large a share of economic activity as 20 years ago. Privatization was concentrated in a few regions: 40 per cent of recent divestitures occurred in Eastern Europe and Central Asia, and 20 per cent in Latin America. The Bank study also referred to a number of "horror stories": 23 per cent of African workers are employed in state enterprises (vs. 2 per cent in Latin America and 3 per cent in Asia); in India, government-owned enterprises cost at least $35-billion, and much more in potential asset sales; Turkey spends six times that country's average income in annual per-job subsidies in a government-owned mine (where the working conditions are so bad that workers die, on average, 11 years prematurely compared to the national average); a Tanzanian shoe factory (built with Bank funds) never exceeded 4 per cent capacity, and closed in 1990; and the West African nation of Guinea liquidated assets (to meet timetables set out by the Bank) and in the process sold an entire coconut oil-producing plant for about 20 per cent of the value of its two generators alone!

The Bank's study concluded the following:

> ➤ foreign aid can actually hinder reform (tough decisions such as plant closures or wage freezes can be avoided);

> ➤ governments should cut soft credit to state enterprises and phase out subsidies; and

> ➤ generous buyouts should be offered to employees in failing government-owned businesses.

It would seem that, historically, successful reforms have capitalized on changes in government (e.g., Czechoslovakia in 1989); or crises (e.g., Ghana and Mexico in the 1980s).

Unlike the new head of the IMF, World Bank President James Wolfensohn, speaking at the Prague meetings in September 2000, appeared not to take those critics seriously who argue that the Bank has moved well beyond its original mandate: new programs are being developed to hedge the impact of high oil prices, limit global warming, and even search for an AIDS vaccine! At the same time there are signs of change in the direction of reform for the World Bank: Canada's Finance Minister Paul Martin recently called for an immediate moratorium on developing country debt repayment and an elimination of the Bank's requirement that relief be tied to economic reforms. Mr. Martin's proposals were rejected at the Prague meetings. Yet, given the fact that currently 10 of 37 eligible countries have been approved for relief and that 10 more could join that group by the end of 2000, it would seem that the conditions faced by recipient countries are not as onerous as critics charge.[28]

To the Bank's critics, the possible reduction in the conditions for loans is alarming. Critics are concerned that the market for private capital will pay less attention to what the Bank and Fund say regarding the credit worthiness of a country if investors believe that recipient countries are under less pressure to get their fiscal policies in order. Countries such as Argentina and Columbia struggle to meet targets for fiscal reform for loans they do not intend to use because of the credibility this gives them with private capital markets. It also clearly separates such countries from those that are run badly. For example, the conditions placed on Indonesia in the context of the 1998 "Asian Flu" included a 71 per cent increase in gasoline prices, among other conditions which led to an ouster of that countries' leader after 32 years in power.[29]

The General Agreement on Tariffs and Trade and World Trade Organization

The post-war evolution of the GATT falls into two broad phases: a quite successful period of mutual tariff and trade barrier reduction up until the mid-1970s, followed by a period of less successful efforts until recently. Its original 23 members have grown to over 100. Its early successes are reflected in the fact that the GATT was able to reduce the average tariff on manufactured goods from 40 per cent in 1947 to less than 10 per cent by the mid-1970s, and less than 5 per cent by 1990.[30] Between 1950 and 1975 the average growth in merchandise trade among industrial countries was 8 per cent, while GNP growth averaged 4 per cent,[31] resulting in world trade growth of 500 per cent, while global output grew by some 220 per cent.[32]

By the mid-1970s the post-war growth in world trade had begun to slow. The shift to floating exchange rates had created new uncertainties. Oil shocks led to balance-of-payments problems for oil-importing countries. Competition from Japan and the newly industrialized countries was reordering the international division of labour. The developing countries' share of world manufacturing had risen from 6.5 per cent in 1953 to 12 per cent by 1980.[33] The United States, in the same period, saw a surge in imports from 4.3 per cent of GNP in 1953 to 10.6 per cent by 1980.[34] At the same time, the U.S. share of world manufacturing declined from 50 per cent in 1945 to 31.5 per cent by 1980.[35] Additional problems slowing world trade were a rise in EU protectionism as Europe created a single market, as well as global "stagflation" (stagnant growth and inflation).

The year 1986 was a key point in the post-war evolution of the GATT. Spain and Portugal joined the EU and became members of its Common Agricultural Policy (CAP). They were then obliged, under the terms of the CAP, to buy a certain portion of their food imports from other EU members, which affected about a billion dollars of U.S. agricultural exports annually. This increased U.S. concern over agricultural protectionism in Europe fed into another key event in 1986: the beginning of the most recent round of negotiations under GATT, the Uruguay Round.

In April 1994, after years of difficult negotiation, the Uruguay Round was completed and the agreement was signed at a meeting in Marrakesh, Morocco. It is significant that the negotiations took place against a background of the slowest growth in world trade (+2.5 per cent for 1993) in a decade. The negotiations extended GATT coverage into the areas of agriculture, intellectual property and services. Agriculture, hitherto excluded from GATT (at U.S. insistence), proved to be the most intractable area under discussion, the major hurdle being the high level of EU subsidies. From an average producer subsidy (as a percentage of value) of 38 per cent (1979–1986) the EU level rose, with the inclusion of new agriculture-dependent members Spain and Portugal, to 46 per cent (1987–1992), and by 1993 had reached an incredible 50 per cent![36] This against the United States' more moderate levels of agricultural "assistance" (22 per cent — 1979–1986; 24 per cent — 1987–1992; and 33 per cent — 1993). The agreement calls for a conversion of all barriers to agricultural trade to monetary ones and a coordinated phase-out over the next few decades. Speed is not one of the virtues of this portion of the deal!

The Uruguay Round agreement extended, for the first time, GATT rules to international trade in services. Success in this area was deemed crucial, since services have grown to 20 per cent of world trade, worth approximately $1-trillion annually. Investment and competition policies remain outside the agreement, and labour and environmental standards were excluded as well — the latter two seen as potential trade barriers in disguise. The case for including investment and competition policies rested with the effects of globalization: firms are increasingly selling services through foreign subsidiaries which are disadvantaged in countries like Japan, where current rules seem to discriminate against foreign companies.

The agreement now also protects intellectual property (a big U.S. concern), and established the World Trade Organization (WTO), which officially opened for business on January 1, 1995 with a mandate to enforce rules and monitor international trade. By early 1997 it had grown to 128 members, with about 28 others (including Russia and China) wanting to join. Unfortunately, instead of the policy leadership that many had hoped for, the WTO has become renowned for dealing with relatively minor squabbles: Costa Rican underwear, a long-running battle over bananas, a U.S. ban on shrimp caught without "turtle-excluding" nets, gasoline emission standards, and vodka duties, among other potential threats to world peace. Given that the powers of the WTO are greater than GATT (binding decisions, for example) it would seem that often-voiced fears of the organization becoming a sort of "Gattzilla" were over-blown, to say the least.

In December 1996 WTO meetings were held in Singapore to assess the organization's first two years. The members met against the backdrop of dramatic global trade growth, with world trade in goods and services surpassing the $6-trillion level for the first time in 1995.[37] However, the growth of global trade, while still robust (+5 per cent in 1996), was slowing from the previous year's levels (+8 per cent in 1995).[38] Concerns were widely voiced that should the WTO continue to fail to provide leadership on a broader scale, it was likely that we would continue to see a patchwork (or, in current WTO argot, a "spaghetti bowl") of regional deals; and that could limit future WTO initiatives. A major concern is that non-signatories are being hurt by regional deals: NAFTA, for example, by giving preferential access to Mexico, has hurt some Caribbean countries.

In terms of the divide between the rich and poor countries, perhaps the most contentious issue at the Singapore meetings was the U.S. proposal (backed by Canada and France) to raise labour standards, eliminate "sweatshops," and stop perhaps 250-million children from working in developing countries. In response, the prime minister of Singapore stated that "low labour costs ... [and] labour standards should not be used as disguised protection[ism]...." Since the WTO operates on the basis of consensus (although an arbitration panel can issue binding decisions), agreement in these areas is likely to be elusive for the foreseeable future. Efforts at the meetings, for example, to come out with a statement on the subject of child labour resulted in an outpouring of vagueness.

The Singapore meeting's official agenda focused on three broad areas: ensuring that countries meet their commitments made during the Uruguay Round, such as dropping agricultural trade barriers starting in 1999, and furthering progress towards freer trade in services starting in 2000; drawing up the WTO's agenda for the immediate future in the areas of labour standards, competition (or anti-trust/anti-combines) policy, and environmental issues; and to deal with "broader political concerns," such as the apparent "resentment from developing countries ... [that] the agenda seems to be driven by the Western industrial nations," as then Canadian Trade Minister Art Eggleton put it.

In spite of all the difficulties facing the WTO, the Singapore meetings ended with the announcement of a major agreement on free trade in the area of information technology. Some 300 such products — from computers, telephones, and software to semiconductors — would enter, perhaps, 40 countries tariff-free by the year 2000. The savings to consumers are significant: Canada, for instance, would have saved about Cdn$63-million in tariffs in 1995 had the agreement been in place. The deal was seen as a big victory for the United States, which had 1995 infotech exports of over $90-billion; exports which have grown over 42 per cent in the last four years. At least 40 countries have either signed the agreement or have indicated that they intend to sign it. Together, these countries control 94 per cent of global trade in the area.[39] All 138 members will be able to sell such technologies in the markets of the signatory countries, and even non-members, such as China, will have such access.

According to one estimate, the pact covers more than $500-billion in trade and will eliminate more that $8-billion in duties when fully implemented. However, critics of the deal note that land and labour costs are more important to the industries involved than tariffs. Tariffs were already rather low: in the United States, around 2 per cent; about 15 per cent in Asia.[40]

The Ministerial Declaration which aimed to sum up the week's work indicated that the contentious issues of child labour, collective bargaining rights, workplace safety standards, and more were fobbed off into the lap of the International Labour Organization. The meetings ended in confusion with respect to the continuing ability of the United States to use its (ambiguously written and discriminatory) anti-dumping and other "trade remedy" rules.

The meetings also ended with concern being voiced over the fate of the world's poorest countries. The poorest 48 make up about 15 per cent of the world's population but a mere 0.4 per cent of world trade.[41] The United States and Canada, among others, opposed a unilateral opening of WTO markets to these nations. While some measure of responsibility for the desperate plight of these countries perhaps resides with the rich countries (who are delaying cuts to barriers in clothing, textiles, footwear and leather goods — which are important developing-country exports — until 2004–5), much of the blame must lie with the governments in the world's poorest nations. Bangladesh, for example, fills buildings with bureaucrats with titles such as the "Ministry of Jute" (the polyester of the nineteenth century) and the "Ministry of Appointments to Ministries." Bangladesh also recently had nearly $5-billion in "undisbursed" aid funds (i.e., international aid monies they had not figured out how to spend — yet).[42] At the same time, they lack a reliable phone system (theirs does not even publish a directory), and the amount of paperwork required for a business traveller to bring a laptop computer into the country is astounding.

Since the Singapore meetings, the question of China's proper role in world affairs continued to bedevil governments around the world. Questions about possible espionage in the United States and arms sales to rogue states were among the key issues of concern. In an apparent attempt to try to bring China into a more normal international role, and after 14 years of discussion the United States granted China permanent normal trade relations (PNTR) in September 2000. The granting of PNTR was part of an agreement to bring China into the WTO and was granted in return for significant tariff cuts and reductions in trade barriers. Unfortunately, two amendments to the PNTR agreement were defeated: a link between trade and human rights improvements; and another that sought to limit Chinese weapons sales. Interestingly, both Taiwan and Hong Kong supported the PNTR agreement, as they fear an isolated China would become an even greater threat to the region.

Yet, even after bilateral trade deals are in place between China and each WTO member, difficult, highly technical issues remain to be resolved before China joins the WTO. For example, the implementation of WTO rules on intellectual property, trade-related investment measures, technical barriers to trade, and how quotas will apply to goods imported into China all have to be resolved.

Indeed, these problems turned out to be serious. In late September 2000 talks appeared to be at an impasse. Geneva-based trade officials privately blamed the United States and the EU for rushing the process for political reasons: Instead of doing a detailed, technical analysis of existing Chinese trade legislation before negotiating bilateral agreements, the process was reversed. The Chinese, for their part, were upset by the stalemate.

Canada, meanwhile, faced a host of problems that involved the WTO. The 1965 U.S./Canada Auto Pact was of particular concern. The Pact was originally intended to deal with a large automobile trade imbalance between the two countries. The agreement had become increasingly irrelevant as a result of a low Canadian dollar, publicly funded medical care (a large benefits cost in the United States), and the North American Free Trade agreement (which altered many auto trade rules), the net effect of which was that many more cars were assembled in Canada than specified in the deal. Nonetheless, a 6.1 per cent import duty remained for all non-big three auto importers. Recent auto industry mergers, such as Daimler-Chrysler, made the matter one of concern for the EU and Japan.

Canada failed in its efforts to defend the Auto Pact before the WTO, and in the spring of 2000 was ordered to eliminate the deal. By late 2000, with the Canadian government failing to act within the normal 90-day time frame, the Japanese and EU governments were demanding an arbitrator be appointed to speed up the process. This foot-dragging was perhaps to be expected: the ties between the auto industry and the Liberal government in Ottawa are close. Ford, for example, hosted a fundraising dinner for the Liberal Party in 1999 and raised $1.05-million, while a similar event hosted by General Motors in 1997 raised $1.25-million.[43] In October 2000, in response to demands from the WTO, Canada agreed to implement the changes by February 2001 — after the November 2000 Federal election.

Another WTO-related problem for Canada is occurring against the backdrop of the failed effort to begin a full round of negotiations for agricultural tariff reductions at WTO meetings held in Seattle in late 1999, with negotiations continuing at the committee level until WTO trade ministers meet again some time in the second half of 2001 in Uruguay. The U.S. grain industry is again coming after the Canadian wheat board (an ongoing irritant between the two countries). President Clinton is seeking an 18-month investigation into the organization's secret pricing strategies.

The WTO, in late 2000, also ruled against Canada's patent protection laws. The WTO sided with the United States when it agreed that Canada's laws allow patents to expire too quickly and are therefore a violation of the 1994 Intellectual Property Agreement. Pharmaceuticals were of greatest concern in this connection. Specifically, Canada is being ordered to change laws that permit companies to make cheap, generic copies of drugs whose patents are about to expire and to begin stockpiling them six months before the patents expire. Drugs are the fastest growing cost to Canada's public health care system.

Another problem area is an effort by France to ban asbestos imports from Canada. The WTO agreed with France, which cited health concerns in support of its position. Since the Canadian and Quebec governments have pumped about $40-million in subsidies to the industry in recent years, the approximately 1600 employees face an uncertain future.[44] Other trade difficulties include a dispute over subsidies to the manufacturers of regional jets between Canada and Brazil. Both countries won judgements against the other's subsidies. Both sides appear to believe a settlement can be reached sometime in late 2000.

By the end of 2000, and in the wake of the Seattle WTO meetings, which were the scene of protesters' violence, Canada and the United States called for a more "open" WTO. The U.S. trade representative put it this way: "Given the increasing prominence trade agreements play in the global economy, it is critical that WTO members immediately improve their communications with the public."[45] Other countries have long insisted that this could mean that so-called "non-governmental organizations" (notoriously packed with activists who oppose open markets and freer trade) could further bog down an already cumbersome process.

Yet, in spite of all of its trade difficulties, Canada announced in September 2000 that it will be ready to begin talks on liberalizing trade in a host of areas from telecommunications to financial services. The government claims it will have its initial negotiating position on services in place by the end of the year; engineering services, telecommunications, the Internet, banking and accounting have been given top priority. Canada, according to government figures, is the world's twelfth largest exporter of services.[46] A new round of negotiations in the area of services was mandated in the 1995 General Agreement of Trade in services. The Seattle meetings were intended to start the process; the meetings failed in this objective.

The United Nations

As discussed earlier, the UN was created to help resolve differences between countries, and thereby to avoid warfare. Originally it was a body composed of about 50 countries, most of which were European and Latin American. Since most were allied with the United States, the United Nations in the early post-war years was a reliable supporter of American foreign policy goals. In the late 1950s and early 1960s the UN grew to include (eventually) well over 100 members. The new members, mostly African and Asian countries, broadened the institution's concerns to include issues of "underdevelopment" with a distinctly anti-Western flavour.

While the UN's success in the Gulf War appeared to indicate that it was capable of extraordinary responses in times of crisis, some believe that the organization deteriorated significantly under the controversial leadership of former Secretary-General Boutros Boutros-Ghali. Missions in Bosnia, Somalia and Rwanda were poorly organized, and lacked both goals and adequate UN commitment. The major lesson appears to be that such armed interventions require a huge force ready to kill and be killed, and prepared to stay for a very long time. Organizational problems seem to plague UN efforts. Examples include troops arriving at an airport before the trucks to transport them; problems between UN soldiers and relief workers; the breaching of the UN arms embargo in Bosnia (by Iran); and, perhaps most important, placing U.S. troops under UN command and then failing to reinforce them in a timely fashion, leading to news photos worldwide of a dead American soldier being dragged through Somali streets by an apparently joyous mob.

Ongoing American unhappiness with the structure and the functioning of the UN peaked in late 1996, with the veto by the United States of a second five-year term for Secretary-General Boutros Boutros-Ghali. The complaints by the United States included that the United States pays too much (25 per cent of operating and 31 per cent of peacekeeping costs); that staff cuts have been inadequate; that the inspector-general's office has not performed adequately; and the fact that the United States was excluded from the powerful 16-member budget committee for the first time (the United States owes $1.5-billion in back dues). With little leverage, the United States has chosen to withhold its payments to the UN to force change (this tactic worked in the past to keep the PLO from full UN membership). This action precipitated similar moves by other nations (currently all but 31 members are in financial arrears to the organization).

Under an arrangement worked out during the Cold War, each major area of the world (excepting Russia and North America) would take turns providing the UN with a general secretary. Boutros-Ghali, an Egyptian, had served one five-year term of the normal 10-year posting; another "African" was needed to replace him. The new American-approved secretary-general was installed in office in late December 1996: Kofi Annan, a 58-year-old Ghanaian, who was educated at MIT and has spent his professional life living in New York and working as a career civil servant. Mr. Annan earned praise from the United States for his astute handling of the handover to NATO of the UN responsibilities in Bosnia. Even after the change in UN leadership, however, the head of the Senate Foreign Relations Committee, Jesse Helms, indicated that he will set a series of reform "benchmarks" that must be met before the United States pays its UN debts.

Also perhaps of concern was Mr. Annan's appointment of Canadian Maurice Strong to a $1-a-year post as senior advisor in charge of redesigning the UN. Mr. Strong was head of the technically bankrupt government-owned electricity-producing Ontario Hydro. His stewardship was highly controversial: he spent millions of taxpayer dollars purchasing Central American rain forest (to help the earth "breathe") and to purchase a power generating station in Peru that had been frequently bombed by anti-government rebels.

Critics such as former British Foreign Secretary Douglas Hurd have contributed to the debate over UN reform while recognizing that the organization now has created a new mandate for itself: "A new concept of intervention for humanitarian purposes has been taking shape...." A concept that critics have labelled "gunboat liberalism!" Mr. Hurd suggests that the organization should be a bit more modest in the responsibilities it shoulders in the future: If troops are to be sent into situations where peace does not exist, and more than 10,000 troops are needed, NATO — or perhaps, in the future, the Organization of African Unity — should be delegated the task. In late 2000, while soldiers from six different countries and numerous rebel groups struggled for dominance in the Congo, the UN dithered in response. Richard Holbrooke, the American ambassador to the UN, warned that the Congo could be the organization's last chance to prove itself at peacekeeping. The UN's critics warn that the insertion of troops into such extreme circumstances could be catastrophic.

Still, Mr. Annan faces a daunting task in regaining the full support of the UN's members. For many critics, the UN is an expensive talk shop where dangerous left-wing ideas abound. At the UN-sponsored 1992 Rio Summit (chaired by Mr. Strong), for example, much such "wisdom" was in evidence: "States shall ... respect international law providing protection for the environment in times of armed conflict; [and] ... [the] transition to revital- ized growth with sustainability will necessitate the innovative formulation and use of pricing policies." Repeatedly used words and phrases included: "global imbalances in production and consumption"; "basic reduction in debt service charges"; and the necessity "to ensure substantial positive net resource flows to developing countries...."[47] To critics this sounds very much like a sophisticated panhandling scheme — now very much out of favour among many North Amer- ican voters.

A major new initiative for the UN occurred in July 1998 in Rome. The Rome Statute, which aims to set up a permanent International Criminal Court, was adopted by the UN. By September 2000 only 12 countries had ratified the agreement, with 60 needed by the end of 2000. Signatories agreed to prosecute those who commit genocide, crimes against humanity and war crimes. The United States and China have not endorsed the treaty. The pro- posed court would even have the power to prosecute for environmental damage that occurs during armed conflicts; it would also extend jurisdiction to the nationals of countries that do not sign and ratify the treaty. The UN has set up two war crimes courts so far: for the Balkans wars and for the genocide in Rwanda in 1994. With about 120,000 Hutu suspects being held in custody and about 750 annual prosecutions since 1996, the process promises to be a long one.[48]

As the UN stumbled through the end of the 1990s, hopes were high that meetings scheduled for September 2000 in New York City would pave the way for a renewed organization. Grandiosely entitled the Millennium Assembly, and held at reported costs somewhere between US$100 to US$250-million, the meetings provided still more ammunition for the UN's critics: The President of Iran (a well known sponsor of terrorism) pledged "to take concerted action against international terrorism"; Jiang Zemin, representing China, promised to "strive for ... civil, economic, social and cultural rights for all"; Fidel Castro urged "democratic and participatory governance based on the will of the peo- ple."[49] For an organization that claims not to want one-world government, the New York meetings made some ambitious plans for its future. The largest-ever gathering of world leaders debated whether the UN should control the earth's "renewable resources," establish a world-wide program for "gender equity," should have the power to "redistribute wealth and land," and if the UN should be able to compel international lenders to "cancel the debts of developing countries."[50] The meetings also featured sessions on the possible elimination of national armies, the creation of an international gun registry, and compulsory "peace education" for the world's students.

A draft declaration approved at the end of the three-day summit called for reducing by half the 20 per cent of the world's population that do not have access to safe drinking water; ensuring that all children complete primary school; reversing the spread of AIDS; and improving the living conditions for the 100-million people who live in slums.[51] All of which is to be completed within a 15 to 20 year time frame! Given the ideological cast it is clear that solutions to these problems are not seen as coming from free markets and free trade. Mr. Castro perhaps summed up the Zeitgeist of the meetings the best: "Three dozen nations are coming up with the same recipes that have made us poorer, more exploited and more dependent."[52]

An updated version of the agreement from the 1992 Rio Summit was discussed at the meeting. Entitled the Earth Charter, the document calls for the adoption of "sustainable development plans and regulations," and would require that countries "act with restraint and efficiency when using energy," and includes a statement that "all beings are interdependent."[53] Unfortunately, the summiteers failed to discuss recent developments in the theory of global warming upon which many of the UN's initiatives are based. In 1997, in a direct outgrowth of the Rio meetings, the Kyoto Protocol was signed by many UN members (including Canada); it calls for reducing CO_2 emissions to 95 per cent of their 1990 levels by 2012. In August 2000 James Hansen, one of the founding fathers of the global warming theory, published a peer-reviewed paper in which he radically challenged his own theory: "Our estimates of global climate forcings (i.e., imposed changes) indicate that it is the non-CO_2 greenhouse gases that have caused most observed global warming."[54] Mr. Hansen's change of heart threatened to throw the debate over climate change into further confusion.

Given Maurice Strong's role as a senior advisor to Mr. Annan (and also to the head of the World Bank), none of this environmental extremism should be surprising. Mr. Strong spelled out his environmental views in a recently published autobiography, *Where on Earth Are We Going?* In the book he states that he is opposed to "industrial capitalism," which "risks spiralling into class war"; and, "Ecological destruction is a sign of the imbalance in the way our industrial civilization sets it priorities and governs itself. There is an increasing dichotomy between industrial capitalism's victors and its victims."[55] Unfortunately, it appears that Mr. Strong's views and those of other important UN officials are closer to the radical anarchists that sought to halt the Seattle and other such meetings in Washington, D.C., and Prague than most voters realize.

Among the most contentious issues discussed at the meetings was the question of when "peacekeeping" troops should intervene in conflicts within countries. Both Russia and China appear to be unlikely to approve the sort of broad mandate for such interventions sought by countries such as Canada. This is a bit of problem for Canada, since it lacks the credibility that comes from regularly placing Canadian troops in combat situations. As an American commentator put it: "The one problem that I see is that except for larger missions,

Canada is not going to be doing the heavy lifting. It is very easy to write IOUs when someone else has to pay in blood."[56] A fact which is hardly surprising given the dismal state of the Canadian Forces.

Canada's Major-General Lewis MacKenzie recently expressed concern over the continuing decline in Canada' military capabilities. He said that we have only about 16,000 effective combat soldiers. Aside from large budget cuts to the Forces made by a Liberal government that seems reflexively anti-military, a 1989 "humans rights" tribunal mandated a target of 25 per cent women in combat positions. Despite expensive advertising campaigns and signing bonuses, low retention rates kept the number well below those ordered. Comments by the British Deputy Commander of Operations in Bosnia pulled no punches: The Canadian military has "surrendered any claim to be a war-fighting force" and "is now really just a peacekeeping force."[57] Canada's "peacekeeping" troops reached an all-time high in 1992–93, when about 4,500 troops were deployed abroad; by the end of 2000 that contribution had declined to about 2,500. Since Canada has recently joined a 5000-strong UN Standby High Readiness Brigade, it may not be long before we find out how well Canadian troops do in combat situations.

The UN continues to talk about the problem of its less than adequate ability to deploy military force. In August 2000 the Panel on UN Peace Operations submitted a report urging member states to make more troops and equipment available for peacekeeping. It also called for more specialized personnel and a 30- to 90-day rapid deployment capability. The report also warned the UN Secretariat that it "must not apply best-case planning assumptions to situations where the local actors have historically exhibited worst-case behaviour."[58] Given that this proposal will surely increase the US$2.2-billion being spent on peacekeeping, this can only increase U.S. unhappiness with its UN fees. Yet change is needed: currently the UN has only 32 officers at UN headquarters, who are responsible for 27,000 troops from 20 countries, who are involved in 14 peacekeeping operations, and just nine civilian police at headquarters, who direct over 8,600 civilian police deployed on UN missions.[59]

A host of other problems continue to challenge the UN. Thousands of UN staff members held "silent marches" in late 2000 to demand better protection for aid workers. Since 1992, 199 UN staffers have been killed in a number of countries. One mission was thrown into chaos when 25 per cent of the UN force in Sierra Leone departed unexpectedly in September 2000. The move occurred after months of bickering between the commanding officers of the Indian and Nigerian contingents. As he pulled out his troops the Indian general, in a confidential memo (quickly made public), accused the Nigerians of wanting to dominate the mission so they could continue to traffic in diamonds and drugs.

It is clear that the promises of reform made by Mr. Annan when he became the head of the UN remain unfulfilled. As a recently resigned senior member of the UN Commission for Human Rights stated: The UN has "an absurd and unaccountable system of abuse, embezzlement and ineptitude.... Of each dollar spent by the UN, only an infinitesimal amount gets anywhere near the project on the ground."[60] Former British Prime Minister Margaret Thatcher summed up the view of many of the UN's critics:

Today's international policy makers have succumbed to a liberal contagion whose most alarming symptom is to view any new and artificial structure as preferable to a traditional and tested one. So they forget that it was powerful nation states, drawing on national loyalties and national armies, which enforced UN Security Council Resolutions and defeated Iraq in 1991. Their short-term goal is to subordinate American and other national sovereignties to multilateral authorities; their long-term goal, one suspects, is to establish the UN as a kind of embryo world government.[61]

PART II: THE EUROPEAN UNION

The creation of a united Europe with 370-million people is among the most important changes occurring in the world today. This section will examine the creation, growth, development and the future of the EU.

Moving towards a Unified Europe

Post-war Efforts

In the late 1940s the United States, under the Marshall Plan, began funding a series of efforts to rebuild Europe and protect it from the politics of extremism. These objectives were ultimately realized in 1957 with the signing of the European Union's founding document, the Treaty of Rome. While all six original signatories (Belgium, France, Holland, Italy, Luxembourg and West Germany) shared an interest in the economic advantages of freer trade, other considerations were also important: France and Holland (both occupied by the Nazis during the war) wanted to control a possibly resurgent Germany by making it economically and politically interdependent with the rest of Europe; Germany wanted to calm its neighbours' fears and provide markets for its export industries; and Italy was concerned about strengthening its recently created democratic political institutions.

Organization

The current EU is made up of 15 countries, organized around four principal institutions:

⊕ THE EUROPEAN COMMISSION

Headed by a president, the Commission is the EU's executive body. It has two commissioners from each of the larger members and one from each of the remaining EU countries. All commissioners are nominated by their national governments for four-year terms. Most decisions are made on the basis of a simple majority vote. The Commission submits drafts for new policies, implements those already decided upon, and ensures that EU rules are applied in all member countries. It enforces EU treaties and responds to any violations by member states. The Commission is headquartered in Brussels, Belgium.

⊕ THE COUNCIL OF MINISTERS

Composed of 15 members (one from each EU country), the Council is the final EU decision-making body. Participants in council meetings change according to the issue at hand. For example, if the agenda deals with finance, the EU's 15 finance ministers will participate. Twice per year the Council meets at the senior level — that is, the heads of state and of government meet; these gatherings are known as EU Summits. Ministers have the delicate task of protecting the interests of their own countries, while framing agreements that promote EU goals. The Council's headquarters are also in Brussels.

⊕ THE EUROPEAN PARLIAMENT

The only directly elected EU body, the Parliament has approximately 600 members elected every five years by the voters in the 15 EU member countries. It examines draft legislation, questions the European Commission and the European Council on their conduct of EU affairs, and debates current issues. Most draft legislation cannot be adopted by the Council without the Parliament's approval. The annual budget requires the Parliament's agreement. Members are expected to form political groups (left, centre and right) rather than national groups. The Parliament meets in plenary session for one week each month in Strasbourg, France.

⊕ THE COURT OF JUSTICE

The Court's mandate is to interpret European Union law for members' national courts. It also rules on questions pertaining to EU treaties. Its rulings are binding. The Court is composed of 16 judges (one from each EU member, plus one other). The judges are appointed for six-year renewable terms by the Council of Ministers. The Court of Justice is located in Luxembourg.

Broadly speaking, the European Commission drafts new policy, which the European Council can approve into EU law only after agreement by the European Parliament. The Court of Justice ensures that EU law is upheld by member states.

Early EU Growth and Development

In its first decade the EU faced significant challenges. In 1958, for example, fully 21 per cent of its population was engaged in farming. Its service sector employed only 30 per cent of the population.[62] France in this period was experiencing an erosion of self-confidence associated with the loss of her colonies, and was therefore a less-than-cooperative EU member. France resisted the strong central executive desired by other members, blackballed Britain's 1963 application for membership, refused a proposed change to majority voting in 1965, and pulled out of NATO's peacetime command in 1966.

In spite of the single-nation veto, the Union was still able to move forward in the 1960s and beyond. In 1969 the membership agreed to regular consultation on foreign policy. In 1970 members voted to increase EU revenues; in 1973 Britain, Denmark and Ireland were admitted to membership; in 1975 regular summits began, and in 1979 an EU fixed exchange-rate mechanism (ERM) was created for all members except Britain. This ERM was, in effect, a Bretton Woods-style fixed exchange-rate system for Europe alone. The exchange-rate mechanism required governments to keep their currencies within a narrow band (2.25 per cent) relative to the other EU currencies. Thus, high inflation countries could not devalue their currencies to offset a lack of competitiveness. This arrangement tended to create a convergence of national inflation rates downwards, towards the traditionally low German inflation levels. Inflation rates within the EU fell from 12 per cent in 1979 to less than 3 per cent by the late 1980s.[63] Britain would join the ERM in 1990, after much resistance by then-Prime Minister Thatcher.

"Eurosclerosis" and the Single European Act

As new members entered the Union in the 1980s (Greece in 1981 and Spain and Portugal in 1986), fear of "Eurosclerosis" (rapidly rising labour costs and sluggish productivity growth) began to appear. This concern resulted in efforts to move the EU forward, and in December 1985, after much negotiation, the Single European Act was signed. It set a target date of 1992 for the creation of a truly integrated Europe. Majority voting finally became a reality in the Council of Ministers, except on the delicate matters of taxation, conditions of employment and labour mobility. An agreement was also reached on the principle of "mutual recognition" of members' commercial rules — that is, if a nation's regulations meet minimum EU standards, they must be accepted by member nations and cannot be used to inhibit trade among EU countries. Also agreed upon was the need to eliminate frontier controls, to provide more competitive tendering of public procurement contracts and to deregulate financial services.

Subsequent to the signing of the Single European Act, a significant growth in cross-border mergers and acquisitions began to occur as European businesses prepared for the approaching single market. The number of joint ventures by companies from different EU countries went from 16 in 1986–87 to 55 in 1989–90; mergers went from 88 to 257 in the same period.[64] At the same time, merger regulations were strictly enforced to avoid a lessening of competition. This resulted, for example, in the blocking of the sale of the Canadian aircraft company, De Havilland, to a French and Italian company that would have then controlled 67 per cent of the EU commuter aircraft market.[65]

The Treaty of Maastricht

The unfolding of events gave still further impetus to EU efforts in the direction of a single market, culminating in the signing of the Treaty of Maastricht in 1991. Hungary opened its border to Austria, and East Germans began fleeing in large numbers. In November 1989, the Berlin Wall was opened; the following March, East Germans voted for a non-communist government. In October 1990, East Germany was absorbed into West Germany. At the same time, communist governments elsewhere in Eastern Europe were crumbling. By early 1991, the communist bloc economic organization Comecon, as well as the Warsaw Pact, had collapsed.

For EU members this meant political and economic instability all along their eastern borders. It also meant that the possibility of a truly integrated Europe able to absorb imports (especially steel and textiles from these struggling economies) and to commit itself to aiding in the reconstruction of Eastern Europe was now more imperative than ever. However, the huge gap in standards of living meant the possibility of large numbers of refugees flooding westward, as well as the likelihood of ethnic conflict and instability among the fledgling Eastern European democracies. In April 1991, in response to these problems, the EU formally inaugurated the European Bank for Reconstruction and Development to help Eastern Europe privatize and modernize.

The uncontrolled change in the East merely added to the intra-European changes that were already heightening security concerns among members, as the political harmony between Germany and her EU partners, characteristic of the period from 1945 to 1990, began to wane, as old border disputes re-emerged, and Germany pre-emptively recognized various secessionist provinces in Eastern Europe. Of course, the absorption of East Germany meant an even larger Germany — 77-million people and 27 per cent of the EU's GDP. Germany's EU neighbours were therefore more worried about German strength, and desired even more rapid movement towards integration in order to further dilute German influence.

These additional economic, social and security concerns led to the signing of the Treaty of Maastricht in Holland in December 1991. This treaty is of such significance that it must be considered nearly as important as the Treaty of Rome. The Maastricht treaty focuses on economic and monetary, as well as political, union. Its aims include the creation of a single European currency, a common foreign and defence policy, a common EU citizenship and a stronger European Parliament.

As in the past, each country had its own special concerns that shaped the course of the pre-Maastricht negotiations. France got Germany to commit to a single currency and a common foreign and defence policy. (Germany, with its tradition of low inflation, was concerned that monetary union might weaken the EU's ability to keep inflation down.) At Maastricht, the negotiators acceded to German demands that the proposed new central bank be as independent from political interference as Germany's Bundesbank. Germany, also aware of the fears of neighbouring countries, wanted and got agreement to strengthen the European Parliament.

Negotiations at Maastricht were simplified by the fact that EU members increasingly have similar outlooks on the necessity of curbing inflation, eliminating supply-side rigidities and limiting public spending. The European Parliament can now veto EU countries' laws where they interfere with the single-market project (this includes laws on consumer protection, health, education, culture, environmental policy and more).

European Monetary Union (EMU)

Among the most significant steps taken at Maastricht was the agreement on eventual monetary union. A common, non-inflationary currency would be a huge advantage to an expanding Union. The Maastricht negotiations established rigorous criteria for a single currency. For example, as the target year of 1999 approached, countries wishing to sign on needed inflation rates no more than 1.5 per cent above the average of the three member countries with the lowest inflation. Also, long-term interest rates needed to be within 2 per cent of the three countries with the lowest average long-term rates. A country wishing to join in the single currency project was also required to have a national budget deficit of less than 3 per cent of its gross domestic product. However, at Maastricht it was agreed to permit discretion to play a role — that is, countries could still be allowed in even if they failed one or even two of the above conditions.

From an international financial standpoint, European Monetary Union was expected to accelerate the shift away from reliance on the U.S. dollar in its function as an international currency. However, the Euro's poor performance against the U.S. dollar to date has lessened this impact to a large extent.

After a two-year hiatus for the contentious Maastricht ratification process, debate resumed in 1994 on the future of the European Union. The narrowness of the passage of Maastricht in many countries (Denmark required two votes to ratify) seemed to suggest that the goals of deepened unification appear far too ambitious for now.

The divisions within the EU were quite apparent during the selection of a replacement for outgoing Commission President Delors. Mr. Delors, seen by his critics as overly ambitious in his goals for the EU, was nevertheless able to combine a clever mix of free-market and "socially responsible" policies to gain support from classically liberal (e.g., Britain) and interventionist (e.g., France) governments.

Problems remain in the EU's efforts to build a unified policy front. The largest member states have shown little interest in harmonizing tax rates or company law arrangements. Legislation meant to promote competition across the EU has had little impact on public sector purchasing; such non-domestic purchases by governments rose from 6 per cent in 1987 to only 10 per cent in 1994.[66] Additional difficulties include: tedious border checks remain something of a problem in certain cases; the fact that member states remain free to set their own (higher) environmental standards (e.g., Germany's law, which requires plastic products to be manufactured in ways compatible with its recycling program); slower growth in services trade due to a lack of tax harmonization; the absence of a single value-added tax, which means mountains of paperwork; and the absence of a European company statute, which means that companies cannot organize themselves as "Euro-companies" but must tailor their activities around 15 sets of company laws and pay taxes in 15 jurisdictions.

All of this manoeuvring towards greater levels of EU integration took place against a backdrop of a generally robust European economy. Euro-stock markets had been charging upwards for more than a year; record highs were reached (in January 1997) in many equity markets, backed by the combination of low inflation, EMU-inspired "easy" money, and expectations of continuing profitability and economic growth. As well, many European companies adopted the concept of "shareholder value," in which return to investors, rather than warm and fuzzy ideas such as company "stakeholders," is seen as paramount.

As European countries squeezed budgets to meet the Maastricht targets, tax "leakage" became a matter of growing concern, as citizens sought to avoid the crushingly high levels of taxation. As elsewhere, part of the problem was countries that function as "tax havens" (or is it heavens?). The United States and Canada, for example, have moved to limit the ability of various Caribbean countries to function as tax havens. A main target of the tax man,

Luxembourg (with only 400,000 people), has fully 25 per cent of its GDP produced by its horde of tax specialists, treasury officials and money managers.[67]

The problem of tax havens continued to plague EU and non-EU countries into the new millennium: The Organization of Economic Co-operation and Development (OECD) in June 2000 released a report with the title, "Towards Global Tax Co-operation," which criticized 47 countries for preferential tax regimes which are "potentially harmful" to the tax harvesting efforts of the rich countries. The report estimated that more than US$1-trillion is invested in off-shore funds whose number has increased more than 1,400 per cent since 1985.[68] The report singled out 35 jurisdictions that have been given until 2005 to get rid of their allegedly "harmful practices." The OECD's definition of tax haven is a jurisdiction that "imposes no more than nominal taxes; allows non-residents to escape taxation in their country of residence, and engages in harmful tax practices, characterized by either a refusal to exchange information, a 'lack of transparency' or a desire to attract 'business with no substantial activities.'"[69] Some problems just will not go away.

While the politicians argue the various EU-related issues, European business is evolving to deal with the new competitive pressures as well as the spectacular new opportunities. A major structural problem is the traditionally organized European firm: plants which serve mostly the host country and produce the firms' entire range of products, which are sold by the local sales force; plants which are typically small (except those in major markets); plant locations that have been either the result of historical accident, or chosen for proximity to (formerly) local markets; each company being run independently of similar operations in other countries, normally by a "country" manager; and product characteristics and packaging that are determined locally.

The new organizational "paradigm" moves away from a geographically based strategy to a product-based one. The changes are significant: fewer products are made in each plant, and are shipped more widely; with fewer products, each facility can pay more attention to product flows, better materials handling, and new work practices; and new equipment and plant redesign, as well as the ability to adopt the latest manufacturing initiatives (from just-in-time inventory control, lean production, time-based competition and total quality management to employee involvement initiatives). With a smaller number of products per plant and higher volumes, companies possess a heightened ability to develop new products and focus on more efficient purchasing practices, as well as on reducing inefficiencies via more focus on process engineering. With more local autonomy via decentralization, there is less need for complex systems of coordination and a consequent ability to "delayer" the levels of management. Productivity improvements are made possible by the centralization of marketing and sales. Some of the less obvious advantages of the new model include: simplification of each operation means a better understanding of costs, more experience in "cross cultural" management, and that capacity use is much improved (as less buffer capacity is needed compared to country-based plants). These changes are likely to continue for the foreseeable future, as lower trade barriers, improved and cheaper distribution, and cut-throat price competition drive the movement to pan-regional, even global, manufacturing.

The Launch of the Euro

The January 1999 launch of the euro was met with great fanfare and expectations. Unfortunately, the markets quickly lost faith in the EU's willingness to improve its competitiveness, and the new currency fell by more than 25 per cent from it initial value. Making virtue of necessity, and sounding a lot like Jean Chrétien, German Chancellor Schroeder claimed that the flagging euro was "more reason to be happy than concerned," since exports will benefit from the devaluation.[70] Policies such as the recent imposition of a 35-hour work week in France (to force companies to hire more employees), along with high taxes and a huge regulatory burden, continue to stifle Europe's economies. Large outflows of investment money has left Europe for the United States: In the first seven months of 2000, European acquisitions of U.S. companies totalled US$113-billion, almost twice the US$57-billion that went in the other direction.[71] Another indicator of the lack of confidence in European economies is the ratio of stock market capitalization to domestic output, which is 172 per cent in the United States, compared to only 63 per cent in Europe.[72] Even Europe's strongest economy, Germany, has double the rate of unemployment (9.4 per cent in September 2000); as well, it has a much lower adult labour force participation rate than the United States.[73] German economic growth has averaged a meagre 1.5 per cent over the past five years, and even the most optimistic analysts know that German productivity growth will never approach the 5.7 per cent that occurred in the United States in the second quarter of 2000.[74]

Britain, not a euro nation, is enjoying both a strong currency and rising exports (up 5 per cent in June 2000).[75] This is the result of reforms begun under Margaret Thatcher over 20 years ago. But some in Britain are worried that the euro may come into widespread use anyway: Toyota and Unilever have been encouraging their UK suppliers to bill them in euros, and the total volume of transactions has grown steadily through 1999 to about 200,000 per month.[76] Not only are some in Britain concerned about this "euro creep," but the introduction of euro notes and coins in 2002, along with the disappearance of the old Euro-zone currencies, could accelerate the process.

Meanwhile, plans to reduce Europe's crushing tax burden are beginning to germinate: beginning in 2001 Germany's top personal tax rate will drop from 53 per cent to 42 per cent, corporate taxes will drop from 56 per cent to 37 per cent, and capital gains taxes on equity cross-shareholding share sales will be eliminated. The government even detailed plans in October 2000 to sell up to 33 per cent of its postal service in what could be one of the largest equity offerings of the year. France followed suit with a much smaller package of tax cuts, although the socialist government could not stomach the reduction in taxes for big business.

For those (such as Lady Thatcher) who are worried that the EU is evolving into a "superstate" which increasingly meddles in the internal affairs of its members, the events in Austria in 1999/2000 should give pause. In October 1999 elections were held in Austria, and a new parliament with members from six parties was the result. The Social Democratic Party, which has dominated Austria for the last 30 years, received 33 per cent of the vote and the Freedom

Party received a surprising 27 per cent of the vote. A coalition government was formed that excluded the Social Democrats, and very quickly the EU indicated its disapproval of Austria and its new government and imposed sanctions by limiting political, military and cultural contacts. The leader of the Freedom Party, Joerg Haider, resigned in May 2000 after the other 14 EU countries hit Austria with diplomatic sanctions. Mr. Haider was accused of harboring pro-Nazi sympathies.

Mr. Haider's party ran in 1999 on a 20-point agenda which included cutting the national debt, cutting taxes, improving the business climate and ensuring that more of Austria's national prerogatives do not continue to move to Brussels. The Freedom Party also ran on a promise to "control" the high rate of immigration into Austria — a point which provoked much consternation among mostly left-wing governments in the EU. However, given that Austria has Europe's highest per-capita immigration levels, it is unsurprising that some would want those levels reduced. Calling people like these racists merely confirms that there is new a definition of racism in the era of political correctness: a racist is someone who disagrees with a liberal.

According to one commentator:

> The Austrian crisis is not just about a single personality or a voter rebellion against deeply entrenched socialism. It is really about a split within the EU between those countries that strongly favor a united Europe — like Belgium and France — and more hesitant countries like Sweden, Denmark, and now Austria. Pro-federalist EU states support the attacks on Austria's new government, while the EU's bullying frightens states that are pro-national sovereignty. The attacks on Austria could backfire to encourage a Europe-wide surge in anti-EU resentment, intensify nationalism, and expose as foolhardy the expansion of an unaccountable supra-federal European government.[77]

Even the well known Nazi hunter Simon Wiesenthal criticized the EU's sanctions against Austria: In a joint declaration with the president of the Austrian Jewish community, Mr. Wiesenthal said, "Austria is a stable and democratic country which belongs to the European family. Racism and persecution are part of its heritage, but there is also a long tradition of tolerance and openness."[78] It is clear that the events in Austria threaten the left-wing coalition of governments that dominate the EU: writing about the June 2000 meetings in Berlin which sought to bring together "progressive" governments from Europe and elsewhere, Tony Blair and Gerhard Schroeder (along with the leaders of the Netherlands and Sweden) stated, "The Berlin Communiqué brought together politicians of the centre-left to forge a new progressive agenda. Although our four countries are part of many historic networks, we are today also part of a bigger political family of renewed, modernized progressive politics."[79] Mr. Blair and Mr. Schroeder are proponents of the Left's new "Third Way" movement. Similar to Mr. Clinton's "New Democrats," those espousing this viewpoint claim to have abandoned the "old left's" disdain for balanced budgets and fiscal conservatism. Even the New Democratic Party in Canada had a brief flirtation with this new policy position. Critics charge that this conversion has more to do with focus groups and election results than a change in political philosophy.

In addition to throwing its weight around in the above areas, the EU in late 2000 was embroiled in disputes with the United States over mergers and trade. Two American senators criticized the EU competition watchdog for trying to block the acquisition of Sprint Corp. by WorldCom Inc. after similarly obstructing a planned joint venture between the UK's EMI Group PLC and Warner Music. The senators wrote, "We are troubled by the possibility that your analysis and outcomes have been influenced in part by pan-European protectionism rather than by sound competition policy."[80]

In the area of trade disputes, the long-running banana dispute between the EU and the United States dragged on in 2000. Canada, for its part, was part of the Cairns group of 18 medium-sized agricultural exporting countries which continues to press the EU and the United States to eliminate their agricultural export subsidies. Canada continues to refuse to acknowledge that its agricultural marketing boards (which limit supplies to artificially raise prices) were restraints on trade. Canadian wines are also a point of contention with the EU, which limits imports to Cdn$400,000 annually. Ice wine from Canada is banned altogether, based on its high sugar content. Wally Brandt, the head of Ontario's Liquor Control Board, which is the world's largest buyer of beverage alcohol, journeyed to Europe only to learn that Australia, Chile, and New Zealand (among others) faced no such quotas. After privately being reassured that the problem would be quickly dealt with, the EU official went into a meeting and "completely reversed his position publicly in front of his colleagues," said Mr. Brant.[81]

The image of the EU suffered another blow in August 2000 when British MPs issued a report documenting the failure of the EU to deliver disaster aid in a timely way. It seems that nearly two years after Hurricane Mitch wrought havoc in Central America, not a penny of the US$390-million promised by the EU had reached the disaster's victims. In fact, the researchers found that it takes an average of over fours years for the EU's aid to reach the needy; that it takes 40 separate signatures to change any development contract in the Third World; that it built a US$36-million hospital in Gaza that remains empty, as no one thought to budget for the necessary operating funds; and that EU's Kosovo reconstruction agency must conduct all of its business in all 11 EU languages, effectively paralyzing efforts to disburse approximately US$450-million in emergency aid.[82]

PART III: JAPAN

Post-war Japan: The Making of a "Miracle"

In 1945, Japan was a country in ruins. In August of that year food production was down 30 per cent from pre-war levels.[83] There was an acute housing shortage and, because its colonial empire had been lost, a scarcity of raw materials. Inflation became a significant problem — the Consumer Price Index rose some 8,000 per cent between 1945 and 1949.[84] By 1948, although food production had returned to pre-war levels, industrial production was still at only half the level of the mid-1930s. Frequent rioting by the unemployed, as well as bloody strikes, were the order of the day.

By 1945, Japanese business had become highly concentrated. For example, the four largest family-controlled businesses (*zaibatsu*) owned fully 50 per cent of Japanese finance, 32 per cent of heavy industry and 11 per cent of light industry.[85] As in Germany, these large companies had been closely associated with the policies of military aggression that had led to the war. The Allies laid plans to break up Japan's large companies, and in 1946 the U.S. occupying authorities set up the Holding Company Liquidation Commission for this purpose. As a result, some 83 holding companies and 57 *zaibatsu* families were forced to give up conglomerate ownerships.[86] In the late 1940s, as the Cold War heated up, the United States began to reassess the idea of deindustrializing Japan (and Germany as well). An economically strong Japan, it was believed, would be a more reliable ally in the Pacific region.

By the Korean War (1950–53), the policy of breaking up large concentrations of corporate power was abandoned; within a decade large-scale enterprises were again the dominant force in the economic life of Japan. In the process, the old system of family-run cartels had been replaced by a system of oligopolistic enterprises, operating in a reasonably competitive framework and run by a managerial elite. The American occupation imposed a constitutional monarchy on Japan in this period, and in September of 1951, at the San Francisco Peace Conference, a treaty was signed that provided for an end to the U.S. occupation.

The Korean War provided an enormous economic boost to post-war Japan. The Japanese "miracle" is properly seen as beginning in this period, prior to which some of Japan's top companies were in trouble. "Toyota was in danger of foundering when it was rescued by the first of the U.S. Defence Department's orders for its trucks; and much the same happened to other companies."[87]

The Role of the Ministry of International Trade and Industry

Japan approached the rebuilding of its post-war economy in a manner that defied conventional economic theory. Rather than focus exclusively on exploiting its vast resources of cheap labour, it increasingly emphasized capital intensive industrial development. This, in the long term, led to high demand, rapid technological change and quickly rising labour productivity. The Ministry of International Trade and Industry (MITI) was the government body directing this broad new policy. MITI, in this period and beyond, provided two types of basic economic planning for Japan: Keynesian fiscal and monetary policies to moderate the business cycle, and longer-term plans, which frequently involved the fundamental restructuring of sectors of the Japanese economy.

To develop these plans, MITI coordinated a set of communications channels that brought together labour, management and governmental organizations in a virtually continuous dialogue concerning the present and future directions of the Japanese economy. Under the broad direction of MITI, and through the use of incentives such as cheap loans, subsidies, accelerated depreciation allowances, research and development support and the like, the Japanese government sought to chart a course for their economy with an emphasis on the long term.

By the early 1950s, MITI had guided the Japanese economy away from its former emphasis on light industry (especially textiles) to a new focus on heavy industry. It used many tools to nudge the economy in the desired direction,[88] including:

> its control over foreign exchange
> low-cost loans from the Japan Development Bank
> tax and depreciation incentives
> withholding licences from less favoured firms

MITI's record is a mixed one. In 1955 and again in 1961, it tried and failed to consolidate Japan's car companies. It also discouraged Honda's entry into auto production! These failures reflect the fact that MITI almost never rules by fiat, but rather on the basis of consensus among those involved. By 1960, Japan's exports had reached pre-war levels. In 1964 Japan enjoyed its first post-war trade surplus. Between 1960 and 1973, Japan's exports increased sevenfold.[89] By the early 1960s, Japan had become a world leader in synthetic fibres, autos, petrochemicals, steel and electronic goods.

In 1970 MITI published a study entitled, "Vision for the Seventies," that emphasized the growing importance of knowledge-intensive industries — in particular, the computer industry. It came up with conditional loans to cover 50 per cent of the costs of developing computers. It set up the Very Large-Scale Integrated Circuit Research Association to pool the research effort. The public sector was required to purchase domestic computers, and many imports were banned. By 1981, Japan had become a net exporter of computers. Between 1978 and 1983, Japan's share of OECD computer exports went from 5.2 per cent to 18 per cent.[90] This heavy investment in computers led in turn to the development of industrial robots. MITI even arranged for rental programs and technical advice to help small companies begin to use the new robotic technology. By the 1980s, MITI had moved on to focus on "sunrise" and "sunset" industries.

It is clear that MITI has attempted to function as a kind of long-range strategist for the entire Japanese economy. As such, it often seeks to override short-run tendencies of the market. While there is dispute regarding the actual contribution of MITI to the Japanese post-war "miracle," it is difficult to argue with the numbers: Japan's GDP growth averaged 10.5 per cent per year from 1950 to the oil crisis of 1973. Even after the oil crisis, Japan's growth rates stayed at almost twice the levels of its competitors.[91] This latter achievement is not a small one, especially in light of the fact that Japan is dependent on imported oil for 99 per cent of its requirements.[92] In the course of this phenomenal post-war growth, Japanese companies challenged world industry leaders in sector after sector: Swiss watches, German optical products, British and U.S. motorcycles and, more recently, luxury automobiles.

Japanese Management and Lean Production

While MITI's role remains controversial, the Japanese style of management must be considered a major contributor to the post-war growth and development of its economy. Japanese management has been aptly described as paternalistic, with such features as lifetime employment, a company-centred social and recreational life, "quality circles" that relentlessly push towards higher levels of product quality, a seniority-grade wage system that provides for continuous pay increases based upon length of service, and a bonus payments system based on company profitability.

A number of innovations pioneered at Toyota, and now characteristic of other lean production facilities in Japan and elsewhere, are worthy of a brief mention. Just-in-time inventory, or *kanban*, eliminates the need for warehousing large numbers of parts and components. Instead, parts are delivered in a highly coordinated fashion "just in time," and sent straight to the assembly line. An additional benefit of *kanban* is that, since the parts being put into the cars are typically only a few hours old, if defects are found in them a large backlog of unusable parts or components is avoided.

Lean production is further characterized by production equipment designed to allow for rapid change-over to produce different products, as well as machinery able to deal with a great variety of products coming down the assembly line. The products themselves are designed to be highly "manufacturable" — that is, to be assembled easily. Product design is quicker and uses far fewer resources than in traditional Western-style production. In the mid-1980s, one analyst wrote that "Toyota needs half the time and effort required by a mass producer such as GM to design a new car."[93] Therefore changes in consumer demand could be responded to more quickly and with less expense.

Parts suppliers are also dealt with differently. Instead of the adversarial relationship traditionally characteristic of Western firms, a more cooperative, long-term alliance is established. This is combined with a degree of expertise and information sharing unheard of in the world of mass production. Japanese suppliers often acquire equity stakes in each other, with the lean producer sometimes acting as banker. Suppliers are organized into tiers so that entire components can be designed with a high degree of coordination and virtually flawless results.

Even the retail auto dealers are brought into a closer relationship with the company. A customer database is kept by each dealership, which enables orders to be sequenced in line with the companies' production scheduling. This arrangement is facilitated by the fact that Toyota, for example, can deliver a finished product within two to three weeks of a customer's order. Compare this to the typical mass-production car dealership, which usually carries a 60-day inventory. Lean producers, by contrast, normally have only a 21-day stock of cars in the entire system — most of which have been presold. Retail personnel are frequently seconded to product development teams to bring their close-to-market perspective to bear in the design process for a new product. It can work the other way, also: Production personnel may be assigned to the retail end of the business to sell cars in times of lagging demand.

133

A final aspect of the Japanese form of management is the organization of companies into horizontal groupings in disparate industries, such as the huge Mitsubishi conglomerate, or in vertical groupings focusing on a single industry, such as the Toyota, Nissan and Honda industrial groups. Called *keiretsu* in Japanese, these economic hierarchies are groups of companies tied together by a common industrial or financial interest and coordinated at the centre by a bank, trading company or manufacturer.

The *keiretsu* system is an expression of the fact that mutual obligation has traditionally been an important element of Japanese business relationships. It is also related to the fact that, historically, the Japanese have distrusted the stock market which they see as focusing on the short rather than the long term. *Keiretsu* are characterized by the cross-holding of one another's equities, with the result that the companies can act, in effect, as though they were privately held. This fact, combined with the role of the *keiretsu* leader as provider of capital to the group, enables *keiretsu* members to virtually ignore the stock market while paying little in the way of dividends. The predictable result is that hostile takeovers almost never occur. The advantages of this arrangement include the availability of inexpensive capital, rapid sourcing of funds in times of crisis, and timely intervention by the *keiretsu* when member firms are threatened with insolvency. Member firms are constantly monitored so that when problems appear action can be taken quickly. For example, when energy prices surged in 1973, the Mazda company was selling its cars with only one engine — its technically advanced, but fuel-hungry, Wankel rotary design. Aid came from the Sumitomo group, which controlled Mazda through equity cross-holdings. The old family management was replaced, money was forthcoming for new fuel-efficient piston engines and new car models, and the decision was made to copy the Toyota system of manufacturing.

Recent Economic Developments in Japan

To understand the current condition of the Japanese economy, it is necessary to go back to the early 1980s when U.S. President Ronald Reagan, newly installed in the White House, began to carry out his campaign pledge to "rearm" America. To accomplish his ambitious goals, which included a 600-ship navy, the U.S. government began to borrow significant amounts of money, much of it from outside the country — especially from Japan. High real interest rates were necessary to attract the vast sums required. The consequent demand for U.S. dollars on international currency markets drove the value of the dollar up some 60 per cent by early 1985.[94] This began to price U.S. exports out of world markets. At the same time, the lower yen meant a flood of Japanese imports into the United States. By 1985, the United States had a significant trade imbalance and protectionist sentiment began to rise. The U.S. Treasury Secretary James Baker argued that the Reagan government's policy of unconcern over the high dollar must change. He called together the finance ministers of the world's five richest countries (the G5) at New York's Plaza Hotel in September 1985, where an agreement known as The Plaza Accord was reached. It provided for a coordinated sell-off of U.S. dollars by the G7 central banks with the aim of bringing down the U.S. dollar. Although the dollar had begun to fall in value earlier in the year, and some (e.g., Milton Friedman) have argued that the dollar would have declined without G7 intervention, the goal of a lower dollar was nonetheless achieved.

As the yen rose in relation to the U.S. dollar, Japanese policy makers were confronted with a dilemma: "... how to maintain a high level of capital investment deemed critical to Japan's continuing economic success, when industrial profits, largely led by exports, were collapsing."[95] The Bank of Japan responded by increasing the growth of the money supply from 7.8 per cent to more than 10 per cent between 1984 and 1987. The discount rate was reduced from 5 per cent to a post-war low of 2.5 per cent. With these low interest rates, capital spending in Japan between 1984 and 1989 rose to an annual average of 10.4 per cent — more than double U.S. levels.[96]

By the end of the 1980s, capital spending rather than exports was the driving force in the Japanese economy. All the while inflation stayed low, and the high yen meant cheaper imports. Oil prices in this period came down from $27 to $13 per barrel, with each $1 reduction taking 0.5 per cent from the Japanese inflation rate. A flood of low-cost consumer items from South Korea and Taiwan also helped keep a lid on inflation. Inexpensive money fuelled a growth in equity values: the Nikkei average went from 9,000 in 1983 to 20,000 in 1987. Over the next two years, stock prices went even higher, to nearly double 1988 levels. Low interest rates, a strong economy and an enormous amount of excess cash spilled over into land prices as well. In Japan's three biggest metropolitan areas, land prices skyrocketed: increasing by 97 per cent between 1987 and 1989.

The changing role of Japan's banks in this period — towards a reduced involvement in corporate finance — was related to the speculation in real estate described above. Historically, Japanese corporations relied on banks for most of their financing; however, by 1988, Japanese corporations repaid more loans than they made.

But even this understates Japan's banks' involvement in real estate. Japan also has "non-bank banks" — unregulated, non-deposit-taking institutions that borrow from regular banks at wholesale and lend the money out at retail rates. By the late 1980s, 30,000 of these "banks," with assets of $400-billion, had up to 50 per cent of their loan portfolios in real estate. Public companies began offering convertible bonds at rates as low as 1.5 per cent, which, after currency swaps, often meant the effective cost of capital approached zero. "Japan's liquidity boom had reached a new stage: money for nothing."[97]

The Ministry of Finance gave further impetus to the speculative boom by allowing companies to begin reporting these profits in earnings statements. In 1987, one-half of corporate profits came from speculation. By 1989, the booming economy had about 30 per cent more available jobs than workers to take them.[98]

By the late 1980s, Japan had become the leading lender of international capital, holding 25 per cent of total loans from one country to another. This outflow of capital became so large that it began to overshadow Japan's current-account surplus, causing a fall in the value of the yen, while at the same time increasing the cost of imports and, therefore, causing inflation to build. Increasing oil prices in the late 1980s pushed in the same inflationary direction. By 1987, inflation had risen to 2.5 per cent, and the discount rate had risen from 3.25 per cent to 3.75 per cent — while GNP was expanding at an annual rate of nearly 7 per cent.[99] At the end of the decade, asset prices had become so inflated that investors began to search outside of Japan for more realistically priced investments.

In December 1989, under a new chairman, the Bank of Japan published a paper critical of previous monetary policy, stating that it was inflationary and encouraged speculation. The discount-rate was hiked from 3.75 per cent to 6 per cent in three steps over the next year. The Bank of Japan also instructed banks to reduce their real-estate exposure. The Nikkei average plunged by 48 per cent over the next nine months, while convertible bond rates went from 1.5 per cent to 5 per cent.[100] Banks were also under pressure from new international banking regulations, which required increased reserves. Since banks would no longer be able to count on constantly rising equity values to add to their capital, they were facing an uncertain future. To adjust to these new and still-evolving circumstances, banks have had to further reduce loans.

Towards the end of 1991, the slowing of the Japanese economy had produced some of the desired results. "For all its stern talk about inflation, the Bank of Japan is taking a decidedly easier monetary policy stance.... Inflation in assets and prices has, for the present, been squeezed out of the economy."[101] Further, it appeared that a solid foundation for renewed economic growth was in place: a stable yen, weak commodity prices, considerable pent-up demand for capital spending and a savings rate of some 15 per cent of disposable income.[102] Further, Japan's trade surplus had begun rising again. Yet, business confidence remained low and inventories, high and major Japanese corporations planned large cuts in capital investment. It had become obvious that a major recession was on the way.

By the fourth quarter of 1994, there were hopeful signs that the worst recession since the oil crisis of 1973 had begun to abate. However, the yen having risen to 100 to the U.S. dollar had an inevitable impact on manufacturing employment, which dipped 2 per cent by the fourth quarter of 1994. Japanese companies continued to shift employment overseas — provoking rioting in Korea, for example, in response to the December 1994 announcement that Nissan and Samsung would join forces in the production of automobiles. Nonetheless, manufacturing remained (at 26 per cent GDP) more important in Japan than in other rich countries.[103]

In spite of the overvalued yen, the stubbornly high current account surplus (3 per cent of GDP) remained a source of friction with Japan's trading partners — especially the United States. Japan's leaders have been ever more aware that, having become an international economic powerhouse, it is naive to expect continued large trade surpluses. In 1990, for example, the government relaxed restrictions on big retailers, and discount outlets have emerged which bypass Japan's expensive distribution system. They do this by selling imports bought through their own channels. Past practices were blamed by the OECD for driving up consumer prices in Japan to 80 per cent above the OECD average. Further changes in May 1994 made it easier to set up large stores and to keep them open longer hours. Anti-trust enforcement was also increased dramatically.

Indicative of the changing views in Japan relative to its trade surplus are statements by the then recently resigned (November 1994) chairman of Sony Corporation. Indeed, his changing views on the subject may mirror an ongoing shift within elite circles in Japan. In 1989 he co-authored a book (*A Japan That Can Say No*) which argued that his country should be much tougher in its dealings with the United States.[104] By 1992 he had begun writing articles distancing himself from that position and calling for a "remaking" of Japan in order to make it more typical of other rich countries — including a lessened trade imbalance. He even had his portion of the 1989 book removed from the English translation.

For its part, the United States' fears of the economic might of Japan were diminished. Various reasons could account for the unconcern in America: the rapid U.S. growth versus stagnation in Japan, the huge losses ($320-billion by one estimate) suffered by Japanese investors holding U.S. assets, the corruption scandals which resulted in frequent changes of government, and the 1993 apology by the prime minister for Japan's role in World War II.[105]

The recent U.S. shift of opinion vis-à-vis Japan is certainly related as well to American technological achievements: the Japanese electronics industry (with government encouragement) focused upon developing an analog technology for the emerging field of high-definition television — a U.S. firm has developed a digital version which is to become the world standard. The United States also took the lead in developing the advanced communications networks referred to popularly as the "information superhighway." Display screen technology is the only area in which the United States continues to lag.

Given that many aspects of Japanese life are currently in a state of flux, recent changes in Japanese politics should be unsurprising. Indeed, by the 1980s the Liberal Democratic Party (LDP), which had ruled Japan since 1955 (the end of U.S. occupation), had become extremely corrupt. Imagine, for example, the public outcry if one-third of the U.S. House or the Canadian Parliament were related by blood or marriage, as has been the case with the Japanese Diet. A constant stream of scandals, from political favours to bribes and improperly tendered public contracts, filled the press. The electoral system weighted rural votes up to three times more heavily than urban votes, and the absurdly high levels of protection given Japanese "farmers" (many of whom were part-time and harvested primarily the tax system) reflected this electoral imbalance.

By the late 1980s, the cost of being a member of the Diet was far greater than the members' official income. This latter fact was the result, in part, of a tradition of gift giving by Japanese politicians to important constituents at various ritual occasions. The value of the gifts (high by tradition) meant parliamentarians had to find outside sources of income; corruption seemed to be built into the system.

Pressures towards political reform came from the tendency of the political system to favour producers over consumers (e.g., agriculture and retailing), and from a growing public concern with political corruption. The latter gained its initial momentum from the 1988 Recruit stock-for-favours scandal, and has been fuelled since then by a seemingly endless flow of such stories in the press.

Beginning in 1991, attempts to reform Japan's political system were repeatedly derailed by Japan's old-line leaders. Public outrage led to an internal rebellion that shattered the LDP in 1993. This resulted in three prime ministers within one year. In 1993, the LDP was replaced by a coalition of reformists (including LDP members). Construction executives, who had provided funds to the LDP, were charged with criminal offences. Electoral reform was begun, and culminated in the passage of a sweeping electoral reform package in November 1994.

The government faces cash flow problems that result from Japan's aging population. The government currently uses post office deposits (a popular savings vehicle) and public pensions to fund subsidized housing and public works, but the growth of retirees will reduce the sums available for these purposes. To make matters worse, even if the age of retirement is raised from 60 to 65 (as is proposed), pension contributions will need to rise substantially.

In 1993 East Asian leaders issued the Bangkok Declaration on human rights. It claimed to identify an "Asian Way" of democracy which was collectivist, disciplined and harmonious. Today, however, the Asian values of conservatism and discipline are increasingly seen as impediments to innovation. In the past, Japan's economic successes have been based upon technologies and ideas borrowed from abroad and improved upon, but since the future appears to be in the creation of new technologies, creativity is now at a premium.

Lifetime employment may soon be a thing of the past. The growth of the white-collar workforce in recent years, when combined with slower growth, has resulted in few promotions. Heroes in the past, "salarymen" are currently depicted in the press and popular novels as snivelling bootlickers. Since Japanese white-collar workers are estimated to be only about two-thirds as productive as Americans, recent estimates place the number of redundant workers at one to two million.[106] Some firms, such as Nippon Steel, tried in the 1980s to diversify (e.g., mushroom farms and theme parks) to create jobs for these workers, and are now backing off as diversification created management problems.

Another aspect of Japanese success stories — low cost capital — is also fading. The aging of the population and increased consumption will significantly reduce the traditionally high savings rate (one-third GDP — twice U.S. and U.K. levels). Also, the traditional cross-holding of shares was based upon rapid growth in their value, and allowed very low dividends, as discussed above. But companies now need to refocus away from market share to the bottom line and, as elsewhere, be alert to the interests of shareholders.

Even Japan's tradition of an interventionist industrial policy is being questioned. A 1994 study sought correlations between the rate of growth in 13 industrial sectors and the amount of government assistance between 1955 and 1990. The correlations were negative — losers were being supported to a greater extent than successful industries.[107] The failure of the Japanese government's fifth generation computer project seemed to symbolize the probable end of massive government economic intervention. Indeed, only few years ago Japan appeared to be invincible. Its manufacturing companies had steamrollered their competitors in Europe and North America; they celebrated with an enormous spending spree, acquiring skyscrapers, movie studios and golf courses. In North America the left seized upon the apparent success of Japan's MITI and argued that the United States and Canada needed an "industrial strategy" structured along Japanese lines: with "enlightened" government intervention in the economy, consensual decision making, and lifetime employment.

Why has Japan ceased to be a role model for big-government aficionados? After a decade of recession it has become ever clearer that Japan's "crony capitalism," with its emphasis on the now discredited (at least in North America) Keynesian economic pump priming based on short-term tax cuts and large-scale public works, is in need of massive reform. Additional aspects of the Japanese system that have come under criticism include the cosy relationship between the government and the banks (which has led to billions in bad loans) and the need for sweeping deregulation to increase competition and efficiency.

Reflective of the ongoing failure of Japanese leadership to come to terms with the country's problems is the very high level of public debt. By the end of 2000 the Japanese government will owe the equivalent of 130 per cent of GDP (and 10 per cent of global GDP!), the highest level among industrial countries and twice the ratio of 1990.[108] The OECD predicts this could rise to 150% of GDP by 2004. Historically, few countries emerge from such a level of indebtedness without default, devaluation, high inflation or other such problems. Yet, amazingly, the yield 10-year bonds remained at a mere 1.85 per cent, which is indicative of the facts that Japan has the world's largest volume of private savings and that Japanese citizens remain confident in their government. Only 5 per cent of government bonds are held by foreigners.[109]

The peculiarity of the situation in Japan is revealed in the differing perspectives on the situation amongst the credit rating agencies. Moody's, for its part, in September 2000 downgraded Japan's rating to two notches below the top rating, putting it just ahead of Italy and on the same level as Portugal. Standard & Poor's, on the other hand, is keeping Japan's rating at AAA (the highest possible). Moody's concern is that the large pool of domestic savings could flee out of the country and precipitate a financial crisis. But, given that no other country has been in these circumstances, uncertainty is bound to continue.

There are some positive signs: "Industrial production, machinery orders, labour demand, corporate profits and wholesale prices are all the strongest in more than a decade."[110] The GDP is once again growing. Yet the hangover from the "bubble economy" of the 1980s remains. The growing number of bankrupt Japanese firms has left in its wake a mountain of total debt which hit a post-war high in 2000 and was up 21.4 per cent on a year-on-year basis in July 2000.[111] Among the casualties was the department store Sogo, which was the second largest insolvency in the post-war period. Also declaring bankruptcy was the largest life insurance company to fail since 1945. In this latter case, a 1998 deregulation of this sector had led to increasing competition.

In August 2000, the governor of the bank of Japan, Mr. Masaru Hayami, nudged rates up 0.25 per cent, the first rise in interest rates in 10 years. Since a new law means that Mr. Hayami is independent from political interference and cannot be fired until his term ends in March 2003, he has been able to resist entreaties from politicians that the Bank of Japan directly underwrite government bonds as well as raise interest rates in the face of political opposition.

Of concern to Mr. Hayami and others was the spike in oil prices that occurred in 2000. While the price increase itself was not expected to be a problem, should it fuel inflationary pressures that lead the U.S. Federal Reserve to push interest rates up, the entire region would plunge into recession.[112] The spectre of the July 1997 meltdown of the currencies and stock markets in Thailand, Malaysia, Indonesia, Singapore and the Philippines lingers in the background. The question of whether the United States would continue to permit Japan (and the EU and Canada) to use currency devaluation to mask flagging competitiveness is also a future threat.

At the beginning of the twenty-first century it appeared, once again, that the United States and its emphasis on more limited government, lower taxes and a relatively free private sector was ascendant. The much heralded Japanese model of capitalism, with its emphasis on personal relationships playing an important role in business and governmental decision-making (thus the "crony capitalism" moniker), and Keynesianism, was floundering. The Japanese and their government should take notice.

NOTES

1. The United States, Britain, France, Russia and China.
2. Initially, this new political entity was referred to as the "European Economic Community," and then the "European Community" and now the "European Union," with each new title intended to indicate a deepening level of integration.
3. Robert Gilpin, *The Political Economy of International Relations* (Princeton, NJ: Princeton University Press, 1987), pp. 118–19.
4. After U.S. Secretary of State George Marshall.
5. All dollar figures in U.S. currency unless otherwise noted.
6. Ronald Steel, *Pax American* (New York: Viking Press, 1967), p. 134.
7. *Report on Business Magazine*, January 1, 1997.
8. John C. Hulsman, "Kosovo: The Way Out of the Quagmire." The Heritage Foundation: <http://www.heritage.org/library/backgrounder/bg1349.html> (00-02-25).
9. Ibid.
10. Ibid.
11. *The National Post*, September 15, 2000.
12. This has been called the Triffin Dilemma; see Gilpin, *Political Economy*, pp. 134–35.
13. U.S. balance-of-payments difficulties placed European nations squarely on the horns of a dilemma: European central banks were flooded with U.S. dollars; had these "euro-dollars" been exchanged on currency markets on an ongoing basis, a devaluation of the U.S. dollar would have resulted — thereby ending Europe's cheap-currency advantage. However, as European leaders remarked at the time, this amounted to the export of inflation since, not being redeemable, many of these euro-dollars ended up being a part of the money supplies of the various EU countries. The existence of these large quantities of euro-dollars gave impetus for the creation of the borderless international financial system which has since evolved — among other things, allowing levels of governmental indebtedness previously thought unimaginable.
14. Large quantities of the U.S. currency were held in banking systems around the world for day-to-day activities, used for trade in countries lacking a sound currency and the like. This meant that a smaller proportion of the U.S. currency found its

way to currency markets, resulting in something of a free ride in the short and medium term.

15. Canada, trading mostly with the United States, allowed its currency to float against the U.S. dollar (and all other currencies) in 1950.

16. Canada responded by signing the Free Trade Agreement with the United States to avoid becoming vulnerable to the rising protectionist impulse.

17. *The National Post*, September 12, 2000.

18. *The National Post*, August 9, 2000.

19. Alan Greenspan, "The Technology Revolution" in *The National Post*, February 11, 2000.

20. President Clinton's end-of-term efforts to create a "legacy" meant that enormous pressure (the United States provides Israel with billions per year in aid) was placed by the U.S. administration on the Israeli government to negotiate what had never been considered before: the re-division of the city of Jerusalem. The unrealistic expectations thereby created led directly the violence that began in October 2000. Given that Mr. Clinton had loaned some of his top political operatives to help the Left win control of the Israeli government, it is likely that the U.S. president's long-term strategy involved influencing the electoral results in aid of his own political agenda.

21. *The Wall Street Journal*, October 16, 2000.

22. *The National Post*, October 14, 2000.

23. *The Economist*, December 10, 1991.

24. Ibid.

25. *The Economist*, May 18, 1996.

26. *The Washington Times*, August 14, 2000.

27. *The National Post*, September 27, 2000

28. *The National Post*, September 27, 2000.

29. *The National Post*, September 29, 2000.

30. *The Economist*, September 22, 1990.

31. Gilpin, *Political Economy*, 194.

32. *The Economist*, September 22, 1990.

33. Paul Kennedy, *The Rise and Fall of the Great Powers: Economic Change and Military Conflict from 1500 to 2000* (New York: Random House, 1987), p. 215.

34. Ibid., p. 194

35. Ibid., p. 423

36. *The Economist*, November 6, 1994.

37. *Toronto Star*, December 10, 1996.

38. *Globe and Mail*, January 10, 1997.

39. *Toronto Star*, December 14, 1996.

40. *Globe and Mail*, December 13, 1996.

41. *Toronto Star*, December 12, 1996.

42. P.J. O'Rourke, *All the Trouble in the World: The Lighter Side of Over Population, Famine, Plague, Ecological Disaster, Ethnic Hatred and Poverty* (Toronto: Random House, 1994), p. 47.

43. *The National Post*, August 12, 2000.

44. *The Toronto Star*, September 19, 2000.

45. *The National Post*, October 11, 2000.

46. *The National Post*, September 25, 2000.

47. O'Rourke, *All the Trouble*, 214–15.

48. *The Toronto Sun*, September 21, 2000.

49. *The National Post*, September 11, 2000.

50. *The National Post*, September 9, 2000.

51. *The National Post*, September 6, 2000.

52. *The National Post*, September 7, 2000.
53. *The National Post*, September 7, 2000.
54. *The National Post*, September 5, 2000. The Canadian government also ignored this dramatic development when it approved $500-million aimed at achieving one-third of the emissions-reduction targets it agreed to in 1997. The plan's key provision involves purchasing as much as 20 per cent of all federal electricity from "green" sources, including wind and solar power.
55. *The National Post*, October 11, 2000.
56. *The National Post*, September 7, 2000.
57. *The Toronto Sun*, September 19, 2000.
58. *The Washington Times*, National Weekly Edition, August 28/September 3, 2000.
59. *The Toronto Star*, August 24, 2000.
60. *The National Post*, September 5, 2000.
61. *Federalist Digest*, September 15, 2000. Online: <www.federalist.com>.
62. *The Economist*, November 16, 1991.
63. *The Economist*, November 30, 1991.
64. *The Economist*, October 7, 1991.
65. Ibid.
66. *The Financial Post*, November 2, 1996.
67. *The Globe & Mail*, February 2, 1997.
68. *The National Post*, August 22, 2000
69. Ibid.
70. *The National Post*, September 12, 2000.
71. *The National Post*, August 28, 2000.
72. Ibid.
73. *The National Post*, October 6, 2000.
74. *The National Post*, September 8, 2000.
75. *The National Post*, September 1, 2000
76. *The National Post*, August 22, 2000.
77. "European Union Swallows Camels And Chokes On Austrian Gnat," *Lieutenant Colonel Robert L. Maginnis* (U.S. Army, Ret.). Online: <www.frc.com>.
78. "Wiesenthal Opposes Austrian Sanctions," *European Foundation Intelligence Digest*, No. 90, March 10–23, 2000.
79. *The Toronto Star*, September 7, 2000.
80. *The Toronto Star*, October 10, 2000.
81. *The Toronto Sun*, October 22, 2000.
82. *The National Post*, August 8, 2000.
83. James Laxer, *Decline of the Superpowers: Winners and Losers in Today's Global Economy* (Toronto: Lorimer Publishing, 1987), p. 49.
84. Ibid., p. 50.
85. Ibid., p. 49.
86. Ibid., p. 51.
87. Kennedy, *Rise and Fall*, 417.
88. MITI was in control of Japan's meagre foreign-exchange earnings for much of the post-war period in order to allow for the importation of only the most necessary foreign products. It has since surrendered this control as the Japanese economy has grown stronger.
89. Kennedy, *Rise and Fall*, p. 418.
90. Laxer, *Decline*, p. 56.
91. Kennedy, *Rise and Fall*, p. 417.
92. Ibid., 461. Japan was able to reduce its dependence on oil by 25 per cent between 1977 and 1987.
93. Laxer, *Decline*, p. 64.

94. Gilpin, *Political Economy*, p. 56.
95. John J. Curren, "Japan Tries to Cool Money Mania," *Fortune*, January 28, 1991, 66.
96. Ibid., 67.
97. Ibid., 68.
98. Ibid., 68.
99. Ibid., 69.
100. Ibid., 69.
101. *Financial Post*, October 15, 1991.
102. Ibid.
103. *The Economist*, October 10, 1994.
104. *Toronto Star*, November 26, 1994.
105. *The Economist*, July 9, 1994.
106. Ibid.
107. Ibid.
108. *The National Post*, October 30, 2000.
109. Ibid.
110. *The National Post*, August 15, 2000.
111. Ibid.
112. The National Post, November 10, 2000.

International Trade and Investments

David Barrows and John A. Cotsomitis

This article presents some basic elements of the theory of international trade and investment, and fleshes them out with data to reveal Canada's position in the global scheme of things.

THE THEORY OF INTERNATIONAL TRADE

Peoples and nations trade to gain the mutual benefits of exchange. Trade allows one party to specialize in the production of certain goods and services. Such specialization brings the benefits of learning and also allows for economies of scale. Economies of scale occur when output expands by an amount significant enough to lower the unit costs of production and distribution.

Mercantilism

The development of nation states in Europe in the seventeenth and eighteenth centuries led to the establishment of an early form of trade theory called mercantilism. This approach to trade assumed that a nation state would attempt to maximize its exports to other nations (more "primitive" civilizations and, later, colonies) while limiting imports. The goals of trade were to maximize exports, to limit the importation of goods and services and to collect as much foreign revenue as possible. The overall objective was to transfer as much wealth (gold and silver) as possible to the emerging nation states. The assumption behind mercantilism is that trade is a zero-sum game — one party always wins and another party loses. Mercantilists assumed that there were no reciprocal benefits to international trade.

The theory of mercantilism is still popular even today. As practised by post-1945 Japan, it focused on rebuilding a war-ravaged economy by maximizing exports and restricting imports through a complex web of non-tariff barriers. Japan's success caused trade theorists to rethink conventional trade theory, leading to the proposal of what has become known as strategic trade theory.

Early economic theorists, however, demonstrated conclusively that mercantilist theory (and strategic trade theory) is fundamentally unsound. In the long run, an economy acquires and sustains wealth based upon its productive capacity. The short-term accumulation of international foreign exchange will dissipate quickly if a nation cannot maintain international competitiveness. As well, although a subset of nations can acquire a disproportionate share of wealth in this way, economic welfare in total falls well short of what could have been achieved under a free trading system. Therefore, to economists, the superior approach is always free trade.

The Ricardian Model

The origins of this theoretical belief lie with the work of two British economists: Adam Smith and David Ricardo. Smith advanced the theory of absolute advantage of nations, while Ricardo developed the complementary theory of comparative advantage of the factors of production. This theoretical approach is based upon the premise that nations will specialize in those areas that are best suited to their productive capabilities, and will then exchange with other nations.

In the Ricardian model, it can be shown that both parties gain from trade. By specializing in those areas within which they have a comparative advantage, nations can produce more goods and services than they could without exchange. The surplus production created can then be used to exchange with other nations for goods and services in which they have specialized.

The Ricardian model suggests that comparative advantage is based upon a nation's factor productivity. Ricardo's approach measured productivity in terms of one factor: labour. That is, while other factors of production, such as land, capital and management, contribute to productivity, these are embedded in the measurement of output per unit of labour. An examination of unit labour costs and trade data shows that the Ricardian model is a relatively good predictor of a country's capacity to produce goods and services and exchange them through international trade.

The Heckscher-Ohlin Model

In the early twentieth century, two Swedish economists, Eli Heckscher and Bertil Ohlin, suggested that comparative advantage may occur because of different resource endowments. The Heckscher-Ohlin theory assumed that all countries would have access to the same technology. Therefore, countries with an abundance of a specific factor of production would likely have a comparative advantage in those goods and services whose production involved the intensive use of that factor in the production process. In the case of Canada, Harold Innes suggested a staple theory of trade based upon the notion that Canada has a significant endowment of natural resources. Innes's theory was consistent in many respects with the Heckscher-Ohlin approach.

Dissatisfaction over the ability of the Heckscher-Ohlin model to adequately describe increased trade in manufactured products between developed countries following World War II led many economists to re-examine the determinants of trade. New approaches to trade were developed which broke with traditional theory by stressing the importance of technological change and economies of scale in explaining international exchange.

Technological Change

In the early sixties, Michael Posner first proposed technological innovation as a source of trade. Posner framed his Technology Gap theory of trade in terms of an absolute advantage held in one industry in one country in relation to the same industry in another country. In his model, a product or process innovation gives the innovating country both an absolute advantage and a monopoly in trade. However, this monopoly is only temporary. Firms in the other country, threatened by the introduction of the new product or process, will, after a period of time, begin to imitate it. Faced with this imitative behaviour, the innovating country must continue to generate new innovations in order to maintain its trade advantage.

Posner presented his model not as a general theory of trade, but as a complementary approach to explain the increasing importance of trade between countries with similar factor endowments. His model explicitly illustrates how a supply side influence — namely, temporary industry differences in technological knowledge — can stimulate trade.

A subsequent development to Posner's Technology Gap theory is Raymond Vernon's Product Life Cycle model, which focuses on the implications for trade of the various stages of development through which a product passes. Vernon argues that in the early stages of a product's life, development and production remain in the home market of the advanced country. This is due both to the existence in the advanced country of high-income consumers who rapidly accept or demand new products and to the existence of a large pool of skilled labour. As demand for the new product expands and some standardization takes place, it will begin to be exported from the advanced country where it was initially produced. It is only later still, as the product is fully standardized and the technological knowledge on which it is based becomes freely available, that factor price considerations predominate and production starts to move to lower-cost locations. In a final stage, production of the commodity will decline in the advanced country, and imports increase as low-wage countries begin to export part of their output.

Vernon developed his Product Life Cycle model with particular reference to the United States. However, over the past three decades U.S. income and relative wage differentials with both Western Europe and Japan have diminished significantly, suggesting that other countries are now major innovators and that the preferred location for the production and export of new products may be outside the United States. This process has lessened the predictive power of Vernon's model, as it is less able to describe the relationship of the U.S. economy to other industrialized countries. Nonetheless, the observed production and trade patterns of many products do seem to fit into a framework similar to that developed by Vernon.

Economies of Scale

During the 1980s, economists such as Paul Krugman at MIT developed a new view of international exchange in which economies of scale act as a determinant of trade. Since economies of scale are generally associated with imperfect competition in product markets, these models emphasize the relationship between trade and industrial organization.

Trade models based on economies of scale are particularly useful in depicting the portion of international trade that is not readily explained by the basic Heckscher-Ohlin model, such as trade between similar countries. This type of exchange cannot be easily described in terms of a comparative advantage arising from factor-endowment differences. However, the presence of economies of scale in such situations will incite countries to specialize and engage in trade with each other so as to gain the advantages of larger scale production. In general, the more similar countries are, the greater will be the volume of trade. The gains derived from this trade are over and above those obtained through traditional comparative advantage.

Economies of scale also provide a straightforward explanation of intra-industry trade. Faced with global competition, firms in developed countries manufacture only a few varieties of a product, since this enables them to maximize economies of scale and reduce unit costs. Each developed country then imports other varieties of the product from other industrialized nations.

The resulting pattern of intraindustry trade will, however, remain indeterminate. The issue of which country produces which goods is more likely to be resolved by unpredictable initial events and the accumulation of historical factors than by specific country attributes.

While models of trade based on economies of scale share many common assumptions and insights, they do not as yet constitute a general theory. To do so will require economists to agree on a comprehensive theory of imperfect competition. Despite the success of these models in establishing economies of scale as an independent source of trade, they remain complementary, in most respects, to the Heckscher-Ohlin theory.

Location Theory and Trade

Location theory deals with the location of production in space. In many respects, trade theory can be treated as a special case of location theory. Bertil Ohlin observed that instead of asking why specific countries exchange certain goods with one another, one could ask why production is divided between these countries in a certain way. In this perspective, geographic distance, borders and the actions of national governments can play an important role in determining the location of production and resultant trade patterns.

In recent years, Paul Krugman has been especially prominent among economists in stressing the need to incorporate the insights from location theory and economic geography into international economics. According to Krugman, trade between countries is driven as much by increasing returns to scale and externalities as it is by comparative advantage. Since these economies are most likely to be achieved at the regional level, Krugman argues that, in order to understand international trade, one must first comprehend the mechanisms that lead to local concentration of production. In a like manner, Michael Porter asserts that the spatial characteristics of industries in a national economy are a key factor in determining which of its domestic sectors will be competitive in the global economy. Porter discusses the geographic clustering of industries within nations. He points to many examples where strong national industries are highly concentrated within their home nations (e.g., the U.S. motion-picture industry in and around Los Angles, the German cutlery industry around Soligen and the Swiss chemical industry around Basel).

The Leontief Paradox

Following World War II, an economist at Harvard University, Wassily Leontief, attempted to test the Heckscher-Ohlin model for the United States. Using data for 1947, Leontief tested the distribution of U.S. exports and imports. The results were paradoxical: Leontief found that the United States was exporting labour-intensive goods and importing capital-intensive goods. The United States in 1947 was the pre-eminent manufacturing nation in the world. It was thought that U.S. production techniques were relatively capital-intensive and the United States had relatively high labour costs, so it was naturally assumed that the United States would export capital-intensive manu-factured products and import labour-intensive products.

Further research has continued to sustain the Leontief paradox for both the United States and other nations. In general, it would appear that, in its simplest version, the Heckscher-Ohlin model does a relatively poor job of explaining trade patterns in manufactured products. In particular, it fails to explain both the extensive volume of trade in manufactured products between industrialized countries and the prevalence in this trade of two-way exchanges of differentiated products, commonly referred to as intraindustry trade. To better explain comparative advantage and the export and import intensities of countries, the Heckscher-Ohlin model must be expanded to include other factors, such as human capital and technology.

Factor Price Equalization

A beneficial effect of free trade often associated with the Heckscher-Ohlin theory is factor-price equalization. International trade entails the export of products in which a country has a comparative advantage and the importation of other goods and services from countries with advantages in those products. Historical evidence suggests that, over time, the returns to the factors of pro-duction, in nations that exchange with each other, tend to equalize.

Countries can import goods and services featuring resources that they lack. The ability to import these goods (increased supply) tends to drive down the returns on those factors that are scarce in the importing nation. Simi-larly, returns are raised on abundant factors (increased demand) as the nation exports these products. This adjustment process leads to the returns on factors of production equalizing both within a jurisdiction and among trading nations.

In the case of Canada, this process would imply that the returns to labour (the relatively scarce factor of production) would fall relative to the other factors. However, trade theory posits that, in the longer term, all of Canada, including Canadian labour, would be better off economically as a result of trade. Therefore, while relative-factor prices equalize through trade, it is important to stress that, collectively, suppliers of all of the factors should be better off economically as a result of enhanced international trade.

Free-Trade Detractors

Despite economists' commitment to the principles of free trade, the theory has a number of detractors who are more sceptical about the actual realization of the prophesied benefits. Among the first to come to mind are labour leaders, since, through the immediate effects of wage adjustments, labour can clearly be a short-term loser from free trade. So too are industries and firms benefiting from protectionism, especially those lacking the wherewithal to compete: uneconomical farms, inefficient manufacturers and legislated services.

In light of the unfavourable consequences of free trade already experienced, even some economists are now rethinking what was heretofore unquestionable logic.

The highest profile among these sceptics belongs to economist Lester Thurow. In his book *Head to Head*, he takes a hard look at who loses in the adoption of free trade. Advocates have always acknowledged that adjustments will occur (the short-term pain for long-term gain argument), but have always tended to gloss over the adjustment period, preferring instead to look towards the longer term when total welfare will be increased. Theory states that gains will outstrip losses; winners are expected, somehow, to compensate losers.

Thurow argues that the winners never compensate the losers. Thus, although free trade may be an increasing-sum game, there are still significant losers who must be expected to oppose free trade. History recently has provided sufficient evidence to justify this scepticism. Workers who are displaced invariably do not find jobs of equivalent earnings, even if the jobs are equivalent. Many remain unemployed permanently. Regions that lose major industries, mines or farms never recover. New regions may prosper, but their development requires new investment in infrastructure; little salvage value can be realized from the old. So when all the costs are factored in — both measurable ones, especially unemployment compensation, and unmeasurable ones, such as rupturing social and historical ties — there is no guarantee that the nation is better off. What is needed, therefore, is a fuller accounting of the effects of this type of change. To free-trade sceptics, economic theory invokes too many restrictive assumptions which do not necessarily reflect reality. This challenge to free-trade orthodoxy has particular significance for Canada, which has experienced many negative shocks attributable to the Canada–U.S. Free-Trade Agreement and the North American Free Trade Agreement.

DAVID BARROWS AND JOHN A. COTSOMITIS

The Role of Multinational Enterprises

In *Beyond Free Trade* David Yoffie argues that multinational enterprises are of critical importance in determining patterns of the international trade and investment. He suggests that the standard theories of comparative advantage work well in describing behaviour in competitive markets, but not in a typical market in today's technology intensive economy. Yoffie argues that the theory of comparative advantage explained trade and investment patterns in the nineteenth century.

The modern world is dominated by a relatively small number of multinational enterprises. These large corporations are concerned with issues of international diversification, in order to reduce business, political and exchange-rate risks. Yoffie suggests that there are four factors which affect international trade and investment patterns, as follows:

➢ country advantages
➢ industry structure
➢ organization structure and strategy
➢ government policy

It is important to assess each of these proposed factors individually.

Country advantages are based on the standard economic theory of comparative advantage. They are key when industry structure is fragmented and there is intense competition in the market. Such a structure would include relatively few barriers to the entry of new firms into these industries. In this case there is relatively little opportunity for multinational enterprises to influence trade patterns.

Industrial structure assesses the role of oligopolistic industries. Competition in these industries is based on the global rivalry of these corporations. Barriers such as high capital costs, logistics, branding, etc. restrict entry into these industries. Industry advantage is now based upon economies of scale and scope. Firms in these industries behave strategically. For example, they may buy market share and be prepared to wait for profits for a relatively long period of time. It could be argued that this is the behaviour of a number of multinational firms in China.

Organizational structure and strategy refers to the roles of the senior management and Board of Directors of the Corporation. Is it important to the Corporation to have a presence in all of the major markets? How long is a Corporation prepared to cross-subsidize an emerging market with profits from a developed market? The behaviour of these multinational corporations can be determined, in part, by the degree of state ownership of these enterprises. Some state ownership might imply the Corporation will act in the interests of the home country.

Government can play a role in determining trade and investment patterns. Governments can influence the behaviour of multinational enterprises. There can be incentives for multinationals to establish in the country. Conversely, the host country could establish regulations to restrict the behaviour of multinational enterprises in those jurisdictions. Government can also assist local industries to compete with multinationals, based on the infant industry theory. Local government can also work with multinationals to ensure maximum learning, or spill-over effects for the domestic industries.

Finally, the theory suggests that there may be "corporate inertia." That is, having established a presence in a local market, the multinational enterprise may find it difficult to reduce or limit local activity.

Strategic Trade Theory

Although economists have generally agreed that the economic welfare of all nations increases through freer trade as a result of scale and specialization economies, theoreticians have always recognized that there are imperfections in the model. For example, the free-trade model does not fully reflect some situations, such as the development of infant industries and the role of externalities.

The infant-industry argument is based on the need to protect developing local industry from foreign competition until it matures. This period of time can be used to establish the domestic industry and allow it to reach sufficient levels of skill and expertise to be able to compete in the international marketplace.

Similarly, the free-trade model does not take into consideration all of the externalities (indirect benefits and costs) in the development of the national economy. For example, there are benefits to be gained through industry linkages among technology developers, component suppliers and end-product producers — linkages that take time to develop. Exposure to intense international competition may prevent these externalities from developing properly. Protection in the form of tariffs and other barriers are the means used to achieve the desired ends.

Notwithstanding the infant-industry and externalities arguments, most economists are of the opinion that freer trade, on its own merits, is beneficial and indispensable because it increases total welfare. However, there has recently emerged a new theory of strategic trade policy, which highlights strategies that benefit national as opposed to world welfare.

Strategic trade policy adopts a game-theory approach, focusing on a group of "players" to determine the optimal course of action for each to follow in order to capture economic surpluses (called rents) from international transactions. For example, there may be a mix of policies that could deter foreign firms from entering a profitable domestic market, thereby enhancing returns to the local firms. A country following this strategy becomes a "cash sanctuary" when it protects its firms, allowing them to build up sufficient capital to tackle foreign markets.

A strategic trade policy is built on minimizing the negative effects of free-trade competition. It focuses on acquiring competitive (as opposed to comparative) advantage by managing trade so as to acquire, and then enjoy, such benefits as learning curves and scale economies. Through intervention, it is argued that governments can encourage activities that generate positive externalities, thereby shifting profits from foreign to domestic firms. Governments can also induce domestic firms to undertake socially beneficial activities they would not under free-trade conditions.

Strategic trade policy is predicated on the notion that one player can capture the gains from trade as long as the other players or parties do not retaliate. If a miscalculation is made, then retaliation could harm all of the parties. In the pursuit of individual national self-interest, it is possible to initiate a trade war such as occurred in the 1930s.

Yet, despite the actual and potential negatives, it is possible to point to the benefits of following such strategies in selective instances. In addition to the Japanese success, there is the triumph of the European Airbus. The European Union (EU), disregarding scale-economy disadvantages, subsidized the development of a competitor to Boeing's commercial jet offerings to ensure that the EU was not left out of the large-scale passenger airplane market and to realize the infrastructural benefits that a high-technology, multi-tier industry brings. The action can also be explained in terms of infant industry protection. Since, at that time, airplanes were purchased primarily by governments for national airlines, subsidization was simplified. The Airbus turned out to be a solid product that has gone on to greater success.

It should also be noted that strategic trade theory can apply within a nation. The application of this theory could be used to explain the existence of interprovincial barriers to trade in Canada.

THE IMPORTANCE OF WORLD TRADE

World trade has grown significantly since World War II. Figure 1 indicates the volume of trade among the major trade areas in 1998. The data indicate that there are extensive trade flows among the major trading blocs. Figure 2 shows that the growth in world trade has exceeded the growth in real-world output for every period to 1999. This suggests that world trade in the post-war period has been one of the primary engines for international economic growth and development, and that any nation seeking growth must therefore be concerned with trade.

CANADA'S INTERNATIONAL TRADE

International trade has been very important for Canada because it has a small, open economy. Figure 3 indicates that trade accounts for a higher proportion of Canada's GNP than it does for many of the other developed countries of the world. For example, although Japan has achieved significant prominence in international trade since the end of World War II, the data indicate that world trade is nonetheless of relatively less importance to the Japanese economy than to the Canadian one.

In recent years, Canada has attained prominence in a selected number of high-tech areas. Figure 4 indicates high-technology export areas in which Canada has ranked among the top 10 developed nations. The data suggest that Canada is capable of competing successfully in selected high-technology market niches.

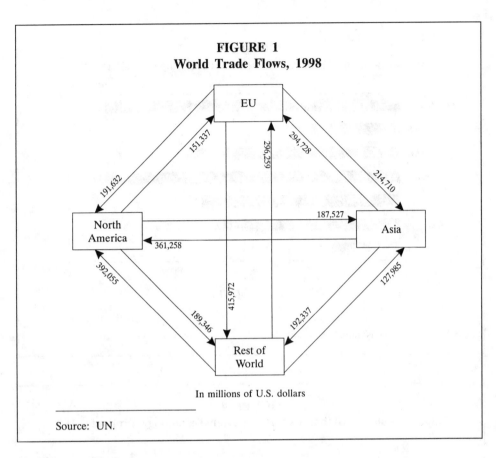

FIGURE 1
World Trade Flows, 1998

EU

151,337

296,259

294,728

191,632

214,710

North America

187,527

361,258

Asia

392,055

127,985

415,972

189,346

192,337

Rest of World

In millions of U.S. dollars

Source: UN.

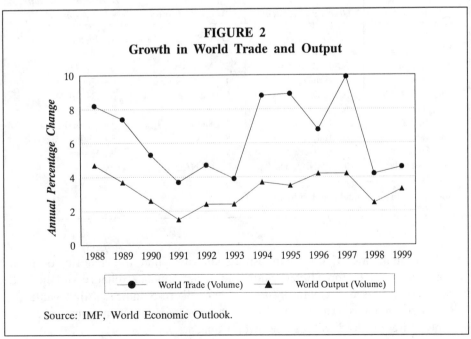

FIGURE 2
Growth in World Trade and Output

Annual Percentage Change

World Trade (Volume)   World Output (Volume)

Source: IMF, World Economic Outlook.

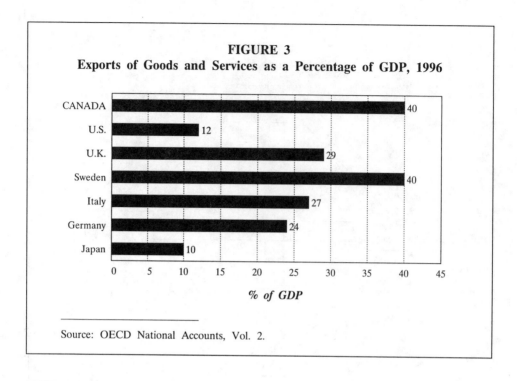

FIGURE 3
Exports of Goods and Services as a Percentage of GDP, 1996

Source: OECD National Accounts, Vol. 2.

FIGURE 4
Canada's Role in Global Exports of High-Technology Products, 1992

Aerospace	Organic Chemicals	Microelectronics	Telecommunications Equipment
1. U.S.	1. Germany	1. U.S.	1. Japan
2. France	2. U.S.	2. Japan	2. U.S.
3. Germany	3. Netherlands	3. Malaysia	3. Sweden
4. U.K.	4. France	4. South Korea	4. Germany
5. CANADA	5. U.K.	5. Germany	5. CANADA
6. Italy	6. Japan	6. Taiwan	6. Taiwan
7. Netherlands	7. Belgium	7. Singapore	7. South Korea
8. Japan	8. Italy	8. U.K.	8. Netherlands
9. Sweden	9. Switzerland	9. France	9. France
10. Switzerland	10. CANADA	10. CANADA	10. U.K.

Source: Statistics Canada and others.

An examination of Canadian exports indicates that the majority of products are exported to the United States. In fact, Canada's reliance on the U.S. market has increased dramatically since 1960. Figure 5 indicates that while the U.S. market remains critical for Canadian exporters, other nations have also become more involved with trade with Canada.

FIGURE 5
Top 30 Export Markets for Canada, 1999

Rank	Trading Partners	Canada Exports (Cdn$ '000)	% of Total
1.	U.S.	308,076,347	86.81
2.	Japan	8,393,246	2.36
3.	U.K.	4,793,623	1.35
4.	China, R. Rep.	2,656,319	0.75
5.	Germany	2,413,530	0.68
6.	S. Korea	1,984,402	0.56
7.	France	1,885,989	0.53
8.	Belgium	1,878,547	0.53
9.	Mexico	1,632,244	0.46
10.	Netherlands	1,555,848	0.44
11.	Italy	1,443,996	0.41
12.	Taiwan	1,142,577	0.32
13.	Hong Kong	1,096,066	0.31
14.	Brazil	1,037,795	0.29
15.	Australia	960,098	0.27
16.	Norway	736,193	0.21
17.	Spain	630,016	0.18
18.	Indonesia	544,874	0.15
19.	Iran, Isla. Rep.	539,275	0.15
20.	Venezuela	524,080	0.15
21.	Switzerland	484,966	0.14
22.	Algeria	479,096	0.13
23.	Malaysia	418,750	0.12
24.	India	418,438	0.12
25.	Ireland	409,758	0.12
26.	Cuba	395,980	0.11
27.	Sweden	392,579	0.11
28.	Singapore	368,900	0.10
29.	Chile	360,514	0.10
30.	Thailand	301,632	0.08
	Total Top 30 Export Markets	347,955,678	97.96
	Total Exports to the World	354,894,316	100.00

Notes: Data has been rounded.

Source: Statistics Canada.

A sector-by-sector assessment of Canadian manufactured exports indicates a strong focus on the automotive sector. Much of this trade is in reality intracorporate, or tied trade. That is, these transactions are based upon corporate decisions and do not reflect the traditional approach to export that would be involved in the development of an arm's-length transaction. For example, Canadian sales of new automobiles to the U.S. market are categorized as exports. However, these transactions occur as part of an integrated North American production system, and do not reflect true arm's-length export activity.

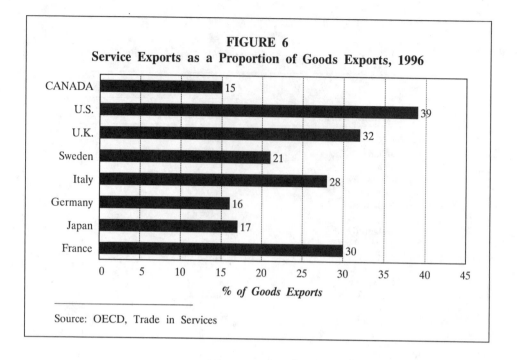

FIGURE 6
Service Exports as a Proportion of Goods Exports, 1996

Source: OECD, Trade in Services

While services account for approximately two-thirds of Canada's GDP, Canada has relatively low penetration of the world export market for services. Figure 6 indicates that Canada has one of the lowest ratios of service exports to goods exports among major developed economies.

The Alliance of Manufacturers and Exporters estimates that in 1980 approximately 73 per cent of all manufactured goods purchased in Canada were made in Canada. For 1996, the CMA estimate was 40 per cent. A proponent of free trade would say that this change reflects enhanced specialization — Canada focusing on those products in which it has the greatest comparative advantage. On the other hand, it could also suggest that Canadian manufacturers are experiencing greater competitive pressures in the domestic market.

Figure 7 shows the pattern of Canadian imports. An examination of these data indicates that the sources of Canadian imports are more diverse than the destinations of Canadian exports. The United States remains the largest supplier of Canadian imports. However, Japan, Mexico, China, the United Kingdom and other countries are assuming a greater role in exporting products to Canada.

THE INSTITUTIONAL FRAMEWORK
FOR WORLD TRADE

Throughout recorded history, people have engaged in the exchange of goods and services in order to improve their standard of living. During the early phases of the Industrial Revolution, many manufactured products were large,

FIGURE 7
Top 30 Countries Exporting to Canada, 1999

Rank	Trading Partners	Canada Imports (Cdn$ '000)	% of Total
1.	U.S.	215,425,696	67.29
2.	Japan	15,032,253	4.70
3.	Mexico	9,540,773	2.98
4.	China, P. Rep.	8,917,286	2.79
5.	U.K.	8,111,639	2.53
6.	Germany	6,946,739	2.17
7.	Canada	5,533,181	1.73
8.	France	5,311,189	1.66
9.	Taiwan	4,592,974	1.43
10.	Italy	3,597,046	1.12
11.	S. Korea	3,573,791	1.12
12.	Norway	2,547,557	0.80
13.	Malaysia	2,057,506	0.64
14.	Thailand	1,507,993	0.47
15.	Sweden	1,488,417	0.46
16.	Brazil	1,358,733	0.42
17.	Hong Kong	1,303,340	0.41
18.	Switzerland	1,265,299	0.40
19.	Singapore	1,252,370	0.39
20.	Netherlands	1,223,899	0.38
21.	Australia	1,215,261	0.38
22.	Ireland	1,137,653	0.36
23.	Philippines	1,044,016	0.33
24.	India	1,016,080	0.32
25.	Venezuela	1,013,659	0.32
26.	Belgium	931,863	0.29
27.	Indonesia	865,103	0.27
28.	Spain	854,553	0.27
29.	Algeria	653,655	0.20
30.	Austria	646,861	0.20
	Total Top 30 Suppliers	309,966,385	96.83
	Total Imports from the World	320,159,252	100.00

Notes: (1) Data has been rounded. (2) The Canadian import totals may include trans-shipments from one province to another through a foreign jurisdiction and are reported as imports from Canada.

Source: Statistics Canada.

bulky and heavy. This made it extremely difficult to transport these products over long distances; this low value-to-weight ratio restricted trade to a small number of manufactured products.

Since World War II there has been a significant increase in world trade in manufactured products. Much of this can be attributed to the nature of the products themselves, the technology of production and the product design. For example, the rise in microelectronics has resulted in the miniaturization of many important products, which has facilitated their transportation over long distances.

Most countries have understood the benefits of international trade. However, some have made periodic attempts to gain advantage by limiting imports in order to attempt to protect domestic markets. For example, during the depression of the 1930s, a number of countries attempted to maintain domestic economic activity (and jobs) through protectionist measures. These attempts proved singularly unsatisfactory, and resulted in declines in employment throughout the world.

In 1928, total world imports were estimated to be US$60-billion. After a series of protection measures and the results of the Great Depression, the value of world imports had fallen to US$25-billion by 1938. It became apparent that this decline in world imports adversely affected all of those countries that had attempted to maintain domestic economic activity by means of protectionist measures.

The World Trade Organization

At the end of World War II, the Western industrialized countries shared a strong desire to create institutions that would foster international trade. Many observers felt that the rampant protectionism and trade disputes of the 1920s and 1930s had contributed greatly to the tensions leading to war; as the United Nations and related agencies were being created, there was a call for an international trade organization. An agreement was eventually negotiated, fixing rules to govern international commerce and creating a mechanism for settling trade disputes. This agreement, the General Agreement on Tariffs and Trade (GATT), came into force in January 1948.

The principal objective of the GATT has been to reduce tariffs and thereby liberalize trade. The mechanism for doing this is to bring together negotiators from each member country to try to win concessions from each other in a large and lengthy negotiation. These "rounds," as they are called (named after either the people who initiated the round [Dillon, Kennedy] or the location in which the round was initiated [Tokyo]), can last several years, and normally result in an extensive package of tariff cuts and other agreements affecting all members. The most recent Uruguay Round, begun in 1987 and concluded in 1994 after seven years of negotiations, was global in every sense, involving more than 100 countries and covering every sector of world trade. It was one of the most ambitious rounds of multilateral-trade negotiations ever undertaken, achieving results not only in tariffs on manufactured products but also in the barriers erected against trade in services and agricultural products. It also secured the eventual integration of textiles and apparel into the GATT by eliminating the Multi Fibre Agreement over a 10-year period.

The status of the GATT had remained relatively ambiguous because of the failure of member states to establish an international trade organization. The creation of the World Trade Organization (WTO) under the Uruguay Round removed this ambiguity, and provided an institutional framework within which international trade can now take place.

The WTO is the embodiment of the Uruguay Round results, and the successor to the GATT. It is the platform on which trade relations among nations emerge through collective negotiation and debate. Its main roles are:

> administering and implementing the multilateral trade agreements which together make up the WTO;

> acting as a forum for multilateral trade negotiations;

> overseeing national trade policies; and

> cooperating with other international institutions involved in global economic policy making.

The WTO also provides security and predictability to the world trading system through its dispute-settlement system. If member states have a bilateral trade dispute they can, after consultations, request that a panel be formed to adjudicate the dispute. This adjudication process gives member states a forum within which to address issues of concern to them. It ensures that countries comply with the rules and procedures of the new dispute-settlement system and that trade wars do not erupt.

The WTO continues the practice of decision making by consensus which had evolved under the GATT. Where consensus cannot be reached, decisions are taken by a majority of votes cast on the basis of "one country, one vote." Figure 8 indicates a number of differences between the WTO decision-making process and that followed under the GATT.

The WTO, like GATT, is based upon three principles: reciprocity, non-discrimination and transparency.

Reciprocity means that an offer to lower a tariff barrier made by one country to another must be available to all countries. Negotiations on tariff reduction tend to follow a reciprocal process through a period of formal negotiations conducted under one of the rounds.

Non-discrimination among WTO nations means that the most-favoured nation principle is applied universally. That is, all of the countries in the WTO must be treated equally.

Transparency focuses on measurable barriers to trade, such as tariffs, to insure that all member countries can understand and assess the nature and extent of trade restrictions; WTO negotiations focus on binding tariffs to a specified schedule in order to insure that they are not raised in the future, even if a country encounters short-run difficulties in its domestic economy.

The workings of the WTO and its predecessor, the GATT, have become more complex with each round. The successive reductions in tariffs have led to a rise in non-tariff measures, such as quotas and voluntary restraint agreements, designed to protect domestic industries from foreign competition. Because these actions violate the principles of reciprocity, non-discrimination and transparency, a key result of the recent Uruguay Round negotiations has been to restrain the use of these measures. As well, the increase in

FIGURE 8
The WTO and GATT Decision-Making Process

Issue	WTO	GATT
Status	has legal personality	no legal personality, a multi-lateral treaty
Voting Rights	one country, one vote	one country, one vote
Decision Making	by consensus, if a consensus is lacking decision making by a majority vote of members	by consensus
Interpretation	¾ majority vote of members	majority of votes cast (by at least ½ of all members)
Amendments	⅔ majority vote of members	⅔ majority vote of members
Waiver of Obligations	¾ majority vote of members	⅔ of votes cast (by at least ½ of all members)
Non-compliance with Panel Decisions	complaining member may seek authority to retaliate	complaining member may seek authority to retaliate

Source: Office of the United States Trade Representative.

international transactions has resulted in the WTO addressing an array of new issues, such as the following:

➢ intellectual property rights, including patent and trademark protection
➢ trade barriers to services
➢ trade-related investment measures

While the original GATT did apply to agricultural trade, it contained many exemptions. For example, it allowed countries to use non-tariff barriers, such as quotas and subsidies. Over the succeeding years, agricultural trade became very distorted, especially with the use of export subsidies. As part of the Uruguay Round negotiations, the European Union, Japan, the United States and other major agricultural exporting nations such as Canada, Australia and Argentina agreed on a consistent set of rules to liberalize trade in agricultural products, and to reduce subsidies and protectionism. In the interest of transparency, nations also agreed to convert quotas on agricultural products to equivalent tariffs (e.g., Canada has replaced quotas on some dairy products with tariff on milk).

A great deal of time and energy was expended to complete the Uruguay Round of negotiations. Rather than attempt to initiate another round of comprehensive multilateral negotiations, member states undertook sectoral negotiations focused on the telecommunications industry. Negotiations on liberalization of trade in basic telecommunications were completed in early 1997. There were over 50 offers, covering 69 member states. Services covered included:

FIGURE 9
Tariff Duty Reductions, 1934–1994

GATT Conference	Average Cut in All Duties	Estimated Remaining Duties as a Proportion of 1930 Tariffs
Pre-GATT (1934–1947)	33.2%	66.8%
First Round (Geneva, 1947)	21.1	52.7
Second Round (Annecy, 1949)	1.9	51.7
Third Round (Torquay, 1950–1951)	3.0	50.1
Fourth Round (Geneva, 1955–1956)	3.5	48.9
Dillon Round (Geneva, 1961–1962)	2.4	47.7
Kennedy Round (Geneva, 1964–1967)	36.0	30.5
Tokyo Round (1974–1979)	29.6	21.2
Uruguay Round (1987–1994)	38.0	13.2

Source: Real Phillipe Lavergne, "The Political Economy of U.S. Tariffs" (PhD thesis, University of Toronto, 1981); reproduced in Robert E. Baldwin, "U.S. Trade Policy Since World War II," in R.E. Baldwin and A.O. Krueger, eds., *The Structure and Evolution of Recent U.S. Trade Policy* (Chicago: University of Chicago Press, 1984), 6; updated to include the Uruguay Round.

> voice
> switched data transmission
> telex, telegraph and facsimile
> mobile data
> paging
> satellite

The successful completion of the telecommunication agreement has stimulated additional sector negotiations; for example, in the agricultural and financial services areas.

In December 1999, trade ministers from some 134 countries met in Seattle to try to launch a new WTO round of multilateral trade talks. However, due to differences on a number of key issues, such as agricultural export subsidies, U.S. anti-dumping laws and North–South relations, trade ministers failed to reach a consensus and the talks were suspended. Progress on launching a new round was further hampered by wide-spread WTO protests led by diverse non-governmental and civil society parties, such as labour, environmental, academic and consumer groups, outside of the Conference. The Seattle protests reflected a growing public concern over the apparent lack of transparency and accountability associated with increased trade liberalization and globalization in general. At the present time, it is not known when the talks on a new WTO round will resume. However, when the talks do resume, the concerns of non-governmental and civil society groups will surely have to be taken into account, and a formal mechanism developed to enable them to provide their views to the negotiators.

Other Multilateral Groups

Canada is a member of many international groups, some with overlapping participants. None is more important than the G8, the eight largest industrial democracies: the United States, Japan, Germany, France, Britain, Italy, Russia and Canada. Heads of government of the eight meet annually in a summit to address an international agenda of issues and seek a broad consensus. Finance ministers meet more frequently to discuss fiscal and monetary policy.

A subset of the G8 is the Quadrilateral Trade Ministers' Group, which brings together, on a quarterly basis, the senior political officials responsible for trade in the United States, Japan, the European Community and Canada. This is a forum for addressing both multilateral trade issues, such as the progress of negotiations in the GATT Uruguay Round, and bilateral issues, such as trade disputes between Canada and Europe. As in the G8, the emphasis is on achieving consensus, on harmonizing policies and on bringing the power of governments to bear on trade disputes.

The Organization for Economic Co-operation and Development (OECD), with headquarters in Paris, monitors and reports on economic growth around the world and makes recommendations to governments on the management of their economies. The OECD also studies trade problems and offers its views on appropriate solutions.

One of the great engines of growth in the Third World is infrastructure. This term includes elements as simple as a narrow dirt road in the jungle that permits Peruvian banana growers to get their produce to a port before it ripens, and others as sophisticated as a hydroelectric power project in China to bring energy to a vast province. Projects of this kind are often financed by developing countries with the help of the World Bank in Washington, or of the regional development banks in Asia, Africa and Latin America. The European Bank for Reconstruction and Development was established in 1991 to assist the struggling economies of Central and Eastern Europe and the former Soviet Union.

Canada's own program of assistance to developing countries through the Canadian International Development Agency (CIDA) also provides a spin-off benefit to exporters. One of CIDA's objectives is to encourage the growth of small businesses and industry in poorer countries, and contracts are frequently awarded to Canadian companies to provide technical assistance as well as equipment.

TRADING BLOCS

Trading blocs are built up out of bilateral and multilateral relationships that discriminate against other countries. The foundation of the WTO is the mutual granting of most-favoured nation status among all the members, as discussed

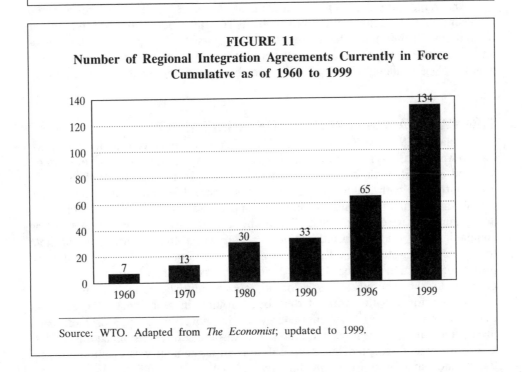

FIGURE 10
Examples of Existing International Trading Relationships

- Caribbean Community and Common Market (CARICOM)
- European Union (formerly European Community)
- Association of South East Asian Nations (ASEAN)
- Commonwealth of Independent States
- Mercosur (South America)
- South Asian Association for Regional Cooperation
- Australia and New Zealand
- North American Free Trade Agreement (NAFTA)
- Asia Pacific Economic Community (APEC)
- Free Trade Area of the Americas (FTAA)

FIGURE 11
**Number of Regional Integration Agreements Currently in Force
Cumulative as of 1960 to 1999**

Source: WTO. Adapted from *The Economist*; updated to 1999.

earlier. However, the WTO has provisions that allow for the creation of bilateral and multilateral relationships, and even regional trading blocs, if the overall effects are deemed to be trade enhancing. Figure 10 lists a number of existing regional trading blocs.

Regional trading blocs are predicated on using WTO codes and rules as the basis for international exchange, then establishing additional rules and regulations designed to enhance trade liberalization among the members of the bloc.

Most members of the WTO belong to a regional trading bloc. As Figure 11 indicates, no less than 134 free trade agreements or customs unions are currently in place. More than half of these have come into being since 1995. A number of analysts have identified the development of three major regional trading blocs, a configuration that has been called the triad. The triad appears to be developing around the NAFTA, the EU Treaty and a third building bloc that is forming based on the Japanese sphere of influence.

By drawing neighbours and allies closer together, regional trading blocs act as a credible second-best alternative to multilateral free trade and help to forestall a rise of protectionism. As well, regional free trade blocs can cover certain aspects of trade that the WTO does not, such as the financial services and investment provisions of the NAFTA. However, in recent years, recognized specialists in international trade, such as Jagdish Bhagwati, have raised concerns about the growing number of regional trading blocs. They argue that these trade arrangements are not free enough and can cause overall economic loses by diverting trade and investment away from other countries.

The rapid spread of regional trading blocs makes it all the more essential to insure that they not only conform to WTO rules but also reinforce rather than detract from multilateral free trade. The issue of regional trading blocs and their impact on the multilateral trading system is certain to be one of the major policy challenges facing WTO members over the next few years.

THE CANADA–U.S. FREE TRADE AGREEMENT

The Canada–U.S. Free Trade Agreement (FTA) was conceived, at least in part, to do what the GATT could not do at the time, namely provide a prompt, fair and efficient method of settling trade disputes. In the middle 1980s Canada was confronted with a growing list of cases where U.S. authorities had taken action discriminating against Canadian exports: softwood lumber, steel, hogs and many other of our most important exports were targeted. Exporting companies and trade associations were calling upon the government for help to protect their businesses from arbitrary and sometimes politically motivated protectionist actions in the United States. The government's response was to propose to the United States a broad, comprehensive trade agreement that would carry forward the work of the GATT rounds in reducing tariffs, establish rules in related areas such as energy trade, government procurement and investment, and, most important, create a dispute-settlement mechanism. The U.S. government accepted this proposal, and an agreement was eventually negotiated and came into force on January 1, 1989.

THE NORTH AMERICAN FREE TRADE
AGREEMENT

Soon after the implementation of the FTA, negotiators from the United States and Mexico began discussions on a bilateral free trade agreement. Canada requested to be included in the initiative, and on June 12, 1991 trade ministers from the three countries met to open formal negotiations for a North American Free Trade Agreement (NAFTA). Less than two years later, the three ministers met again in Washington to formalize the new trilateral free trade agreement.

The effect of the NAFTA, which came into force on January 1, 1994, extends the trade and investment enhancing provisions of the Canada–U.S. FTA to Mexico. It established one of the largest free trade areas in the world, with a combined annual trade and investment flow of over US$500-billion. For the first time, a developing country agreed to open up its economy to full competition with mature industrialized nations.

Figure 12 indicates relative sources of competitive advantage among Canada, the United States and Mexico as prepared by the staff of the Bank of Montreal at the time of the NAFTA negotiations. Analysis of this figure suggests that the United States probably held the strongest position going into the NAFTA agreement, followed closely by Canada. The Mexican position is weak in a number of key areas, such as availability and cost of capital, marketing expertise, productivity, technology and infrastructure. Therefore, NAFTA will likely result in significant and fairly rapid adjustments in Mexico as it seeks to improve its competitive advantage vis-à-vis its partners. However, the highly competitive position of Mexico with respect to wages is also likely to affect both the United States and Canada in selected manufactured products.

The NAFTA incorporates a number of elements originally found in the FTA that are designed to enhance commerce between Canada, the United States and Mexico. Some of its major provisions are discussed below.

FIGURE 12
Relative Sources of Competitive Advantage
Canada, U.S. and Mexico

Source	U.S.	Canada	Mexico
Availability/Cost of Capital	VS	M	VW
Government Regulation	VS	M	W
Labour/Management Relations	VS	M	M
Labour Skills	VS	VS	W
Macroeconomic/Fiscal Policy Setting	M	M	M
Marketing	VS	S	VW
Political Stability	VS	S	W
Product Quality/Design	VS	VS	VW
Productivity	VS	S	VW
Quality of Management	VS	VS	VW
Resource Endowment	M	VS	S
Tax Structure	VS	M	M
Technology	VS	S	VW
Transportation Infrastructure	VS	S	VW
Wages	W	VW	VS

VS — Very Strong; S — Strong; M — Medium; W — Weak; VW — Very Weak

Note: Assessments reflect qualitative judgements of the Bank of Montreal Economics Department.

Tariff Reduction

The NAFTA provides for the complete elimination of tariffs between Canada, Mexico and the United States by January 1, 2003. The Canada–U.S. tariff phase out follows the pre-existing FTA schedule. All tariffs between Canada and the United States were eliminated by January 1, 1998.

Rules of Origin

The rules of origin under the NAFTA specify that products which move duty-free between the two countries must meet certain minimum standards of North American content. They are designed to insure that products produced in third countries do not enter either Canada, Mexico or the United States and then move duty-free among the three jurisdictions.

The determination of a product's place of origin under these rules can be complex. The essential principle is that any material, parts and components purchased from third countries must be "substantially transformed" in North America — that is, sufficient North American value must be added to them — to move within North America duty-free.

Under the NAFTA, the FTA rules of origin were revised to include Mexico, and were clarified and made more precise. During the NAFTA negotiations, many North American automotive producers and unions expressed concerns with respect to the rules of origin as they apply to the automotive industry. In order to insure sufficient North American content in automotive products produced and sold in North America, the minimum content provision under the NAFTA was increased to 62.5 per cent for cars and light trucks and 60 per cent for other automotive goods, up from an average 50 per cent in the FTA. It should be noted that the 60 or 62.5 per cent North American content provision does not provide a Canadian content safeguard. That is, a product can enter Canada duty-free as long as it is produced within the North American free-trade area with the required North American percentage content. More stringent rules of origin were also established under the NAFTA for textile and apparel products. For apparel, the NAFTA rules of origin require that the yarns, as well as the fabric, in a garment be made in North America. For most yarns the new rules require that the fibres be sourced in North America. Figure 13 indicates a number of other important differences between the FTA and NAFTA.

Labour Mobility

Before the implementation of the FTA, Canadian personnel sometimes had difficulty gaining temporary entry into the United States in order to service customers. The FTA acknowledged this difficulty, and put new rules into place that appear to have made it significantly easier for Canadian business personnel to enter the United States temporarily for sales and servicing functions.

Dispute Resolution Mechanism

The FTA created a unique mechanism for the resolution of bilateral disputes regarding the provisions of the agreement based on a panel review

FIGURE 13
Differences between the FTA and the NAFTA

Issue	FTA	NAFTA
Rules of Origin	goods must originate or be substantially transformed in either the U.S. or Canada	rules of origin extended to include Mexico and made more precise; content provision for automotive goods increased to either 60% or 62.5%; stricter rules of origin for textiles and apparel
Services	incorporates disciplines on trade in service sectors	service sectors expanded to include land transport and specialty air services
Investment	investors from both countries to be treated equally	extends obligations and includes provisions for dispute settlement
Duty Drawback	expired in 1994	extended until 1996, replaced by a permanent program
Intellectual Property	no provisions for the protection of intellectual property rights	contains a comprehensive agreement on intellectual property rights
Dispute Settlement	panel review system set up for resolving bilateral trade disputes; panel system to be replaced by common set of rules	panel review system made permanent and expanded to include Mexico
Accession	no accession clause	includes accession clause
Labour and Investment	no provisions	side deals commit all three countries to enforce their domestic labour and environment laws

system. Under the NAFTA, this panel review system was made permanent and extended to include Mexico. The Canadian, Mexican and U.S. governments also preserved the option of bringing disputes between the parties to the WTO for dispute settlement.

It should be noted that the bilateral panels are not empowered to rule on the fairness or legitimacy of a nation's trade laws. They can only judge whether or not the government has followed all of the rules, regulations and procedures of the laws that they have put in place.

Liberalization of Investment

The NAFTA has provisions for liberalized investment in Canada, Mexico and the United States. This has resulted in the reduction of threshold limits and conditions for investment in particularly sensitive sectors of the economy.

FREE TRADE AREA OF THE AMERICAS

It is possible that the NAFTA could eventually form part of a hemispheric free-trade initiative that would include many, if not all, of the nations of the Western Hemisphere. The effort to unite the countries of the Western Hemisphere into a single free trade area was initiated at the First Summit of the Americas, held in Miami in 1994. The heads of state of 34 countries in the region agreed to establish a Free Trade Area of the Americas (FTAA) by 2005. Formal negotiations on an FTAA were launched in 1998 during the Second Summit of the Americas held in Santiago. If successful, they will open up a market of 800-million people with a combined GDP of US$10-trillion.

At the time of this writing, President Clinton's administration has been unable to obtain fast-track authority from the U.S. Congress in order to begin large scale hemispheric trade talks. The president has met opposition to his proposal from members of Congress who fear that an expanded NAFTA might result in job losses and diminished labour and environmental standards. A new public debate on the merits of a free-trade area of the Americas appears likely.

FOREIGN DIRECT INVESTMENT

An important factor in the increasing integration of the world economy since World War II has been the rapid growth in foreign direct investment. Foreign direct investment is commonly defined as an operating and controlling interest in a firm or industry by a non-national corporation or individual. In the United States, for example, foreign ownership of 10 per cent or more of a firm's outstanding stock is assumed to provide operating control of that enterprise.

No single theory can provide a complete explanation for the determinants of foreign direct investment, since the reasons for such activity are manifestly diverse. However, several major themes can be discerned. The industrial organization approach, based on pioneering work by Stephen Hymer, posits that foreign direct investment is largely the result of rent-seeking activities of multinational firms operating in imperfectly competitive markets. A firm which operates across national boundaries faces extra costs which domestic firms do not, such as dealing with different languages, cultures, technical standards and consumer differences. In order for such a firm to operate successfully in another country, it must possess certain internal, firm-specific, advantages which allow it to reap higher returns than rival domestic firms. These firm-specific advantages can take the form of product differentiation, economies of scale, superior technology or better management skills.

The cost of capital explanation of foreign direct investment focuses on imperfections in capital markets. According to this approach, foreign firms are no better at producing than domestic firms, and receive no extra returns. They simply apply a lower discount rate to expected cash flows. The impetus for foreign direct investment in the cost of capital approach is simply the search for the highest return to capital.

Rivalry among oligopolistic firms operating in the same industry, but not necessarily in the same country, can also drive foreign direct investment. Frederick Knickerbocker noted a "follow the leader" pattern in the investment

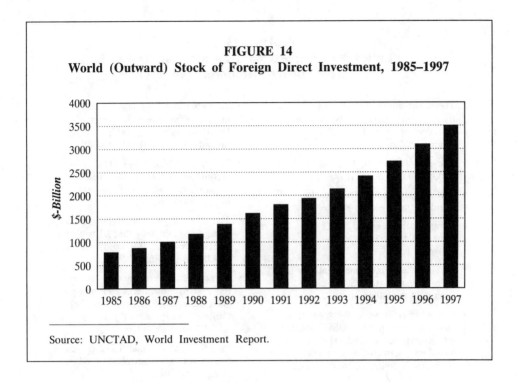

FIGURE 14
World (Outward) Stock of Foreign Direct Investment, 1985–1997

Source: UNCTAD, World Investment Report.

activities of oligopolistic firms. An initial investment in a foreign country by a leading oligopolistic firm will often induce a clustering of direct investment by other competitors. A similar process is posited in Vernon's product life-cycle theory, where domestic firms begin to invest abroad to maintain market share as foreign demand for the new product grows and standardization of production takes place.

Trends in Foreign Direct Investment

The past two decades have witnessed a dramatic increase in world foreign direct investment. As indicated in Figure 14, the world outward stock of foreign direct investment more than tripled to approximately US$3.5-trillion during the period from 1985 to 1997. As well, yearly growth in flows of foreign direct investment has followed an upward trend. It is estimated that between 1973 and 1997 the value of annual outward flows of FDI multiplied 26-fold, from US$25-billion to US$648-billion. In 1997 alone, the growth in outward flows of foreign direct investment was higher than that of exports of goods and services, world output and gross domestic capital formation.

This surge in foreign direct investment has, for the most part, been concentrated in triad regions centred around the United States, the European Union and Japan. In recent years, however, developing countries have become more important, both as host and home countries for foreign direct investment. At the same time, there has been a pronounced change in the composition

FIGURE 15
United Nations Facts on Transnationals and
Foreign Direct Investment, 1998

- There are about 60,000 parent transnational corporations (TNCs) that control more than 500,000 foreign affiliates.

- The global sales of TNCs amounted to US$7.0-trillion in 1997.

- TNCs control above one-quarter of world output.

- Intrafirm trade within TNCs is estimated to account for one-third of world trade.

- Foreign direct investment inflows in 1998 amounted to US$644-billion, up from US$460-billion in 1997.

- U.S. companies were the biggest foreign investors, putting US$133-billion into enterprises abroad. The United Kingdom, Germany, France and the Netherlands followed, in that order.

- The United States attracted the most foreign direct investment — US$193-billion in 1998. The U.K. ranked second with US$63-billion.

- The Triad (EU, Japan, U.S.) accounted for about 84% and 67% of worldwide FDI outflows and inflows in 1998.

- The 100 biggest TNCs (ranked by foreign assets) held US$2.1-trillion in assets abroad in 1997 and had sales of US$1.8-trillion.

- Three Canadian companies made the top 100 list: distillers/entertainment giant Seagram Co. Ltd. (23), Bell Canada Enterprises (49) and publisher Thompson Corp. (52).

- In 1992, Canada had 1,722 parent companies that controlled 4,562 foreign affiliates.

Source: United Nations, World Investment Report, 1999.

of foreign direct investment from the resource and manufacturing sectors to services and technology intensive production. Figure 15 summarizes a number of key facts on transnational corporations and foreign direct investment.

The rapid expansion in global foreign direct investment over the past two decades has been facilitated by a number of complementary and interrelated economic trends. Increased globalization has led to the integration of financial markets, making it easier than ever before for firms to invest in a foreign jurisdiction and to repatriate profits, dividends and capital. Strategic competition for world market share has become a key consideration in the locational decisions of firms. It has compelled firms to be present in those countries and regions of the world where economic growth is strongest. The skills and organizational requirements of the information and communication revolution, along with the need for firms to invest significantly in research and development, has resulted in the growth of corporate strategic alliances and investment activities to exploit synergies and to spread risk. Lastly, there has been a widespread removal of restrictions and barriers to the free flow of direct investment during this period, often as a result of the formation or strengthening of free-trade areas such as the European Union and the NAFTA.

Foreign Direct Investment and Trade

Traditionally, foreign direct investment and trade have been regarded as substitutes for one another, since direct investment was seen to be the result of trade barriers in host countries. However, with increased globalization and the rise in importance of multinational corporations, support has grown for the contrary view: That trade and investment are complements rather than supplements. The global strategies and activities of an increasing number of multinational companies can be expected to foster world trade, especially as a result of intrafirm trade between parent companies and their subsidiaries.

As a recent WTO report notes, in a progressively more integrated global economy, an export-oriented firm might well have to acquire facilities in other countries to remain competitive. This can include distribution networks, inventories and after-sales service. The result is likely to be not simply the maintenance of existing trade levels, but expanded trade. Foreign direct investment and trade also constitute a key component in the effort of many multinational firms to integrate their production processes on a world-wide basis in order to capture efficiencies of scale. By subdividing production into different stages and locating each stage in a country where that part of the production process can be done most efficiently, and then linking all the stages through trade, multinational firms can efficiently supply production and services to buyers across the world. The result of these trends is a much more complex and dynamic interrelationship between foreign direct investment and trade than traditionally was the case.

Interlinkages also occur between foreign direct investment and trade at the policy level. As an OECD study highlights, a positive relationship exists between foreign direct investment liberalization policies and trade performance. This relationship is, however, complex. It is determined by four sets of factors, each of which may or may not be related to the other:

➢ foreign direct investment policies
➢ foreign direct investment inflows
➢ export flows
➢ import flows

In order for a positive relationship to hold between the liberalization of foreign direct investment and trade flows, the liberalization policies must improve market access sufficiently so as to induce an expansion in investment inflows; the new direct investment must serve as a stimulus to economic growth; and the new economic activities must relate more to international trade than to the domestic sector.

At the same time, measures that liberalize trade may lead to increased foreign direct investment by enabling multinational corporations to set up production centres in low-cost areas, by permitting the creation of regional networks and by facilitating the integration of production on a global basis.

Foreign Direct Investment and Growth

Foreign direct investment plays a key role in promoting economic growth and progress, particularly with regard to developing countries. While small inflows of foreign direct investment are more symptoms than causes of under-development, it is hard to imagine how a meaningful improvement in the economic situation of the poorest countries can take place without increased foreign direct investment.

During the 1980s, economists such as Robert Lucas and Paul Romer formulated a new model of economic growth which emphasizes the importance of human capital, learning by doing and technological spillover effects in promoting economic development. New growth theory, as the model is commonly referred to, provides powerful support for the premise that foreign direct investment plays a vital role in fostering growth. Many of the factors that new growth theory identifies as key determinants of economic growth can be nurtured and promoted through inflows of foreign direct investment. In this connection, foreign direct investment is considered by many to be the main channel through which advanced technology is transferred to developing countries. In addition, foreign direct investment brings with it other, more intangible, resources, such as organizational, managerial and marketing skills. These resources then play a key role in restructuring and diversifying the economies of developing countries and making them more globally competitive.

A study released by the International Monetary Fund lends support to the premise that foreign direct investment can act as a powerful factor in promoting growth. The study examined the effect of flows of foreign direct investment on economic growth in developing countries over the past two decades. It found that foreign direct investment contributes to economic growth in developing countries in greater measure than does local investment. This higher marginal productivity of foreign direct investment is likely related to the combination of the technological and managerial skills of multinational corporations with domestic labour and inputs in the host country. The study also found that foreign direct investment increases the overall level of investment by attracting higher levels of domestic investment.

The growth-promoting potential of foreign direct investment requires a favourable policy climate. In the absence of such a climate, foreign direct investment may hinder rather than promote economic development. For example, governments may erect high tariff barriers to protect vulnerable or infant industries. This, in turn, may induce tariff-jumping foreign direct investment. Conversely, governments may offer subsidies to foreign investors to develop certain sectors of their economies which they deem to be of strategic importance. The result of such measures may be a flow of foreign direct investment that increases the rate of return of foreign firms but does little to promote, or even distorts, economic growth in the host country.

Multilateral Agreement on Investment

In 1995, industrial nations began negotiations on a Multinational Agreement on Investment (MAI) at the OECD. The purpose of the MAI was to consolidate in a single instrument what had already been achieved on investment rules and to provide a structured framework for further liberalization. In 1998, however, negotiations on the MAI were terminated without an agreement having been reached. Independent of the failure of negotiators to resolve outstanding issues in the MAI, the demise of the MAI was the result of the convergence of a number of political, social and policy trends not all of which had been foreseen when the negotiations started.

One such factor in the failure of the MAI was a change in the political climate during the course of the negotiations and the emergence of a public backlash against globalization and what was seen to be an opaque and non-accountable process. Another important reason was the activities of various non-governmental and civil society groups. Their innovative use of the Internet to rally public opinion against the MAI and influence elected officials brought a new dynamic to the negotiations. An additional difficulty was the absence of developing countries from the negotiating table. Their inability to make a direct input into the negotiations was all the more decisive, as the MAI was ultimately intended to be open to accession by all countries.

Despite the collapse of the MAI negotiations, international investment-related treaty activity has continued to be intense, mainly in the areas of investment protection and liberalization. At the bilateral level alone, the number of bilateral investment treaties reached 1,726 at the end of 1998, compared to 1,556 for 1997. At the time of this writing, there are some indications that the WTO might begin talks on establishing a multilateral framework of rules governing international investment. However, it is unlikely that these discussions would be either as extensive or controversial as the MAI negotiations.

Canada's Foreign Direct Investment Flows

Foreign direct investment in Canada has grown dramatically since the end of World War II, increasing more than 60-fold from $4-billion in 1950 to $240-billion in 1999. Direct investment into Canada tripled during the 1950s, and more than doubled in each of the following four decades. Correspondingly, the nature and extent of foreign ownership in Canada has become an ongoing policy issue. Concerns in the late 1960s over the extent of foreign control in the Canadian economy resulted in the creation of the Foreign Investment Review Agency (FIRA) in 1974 to screen foreign investment and to review foreign acquisitions of existing assets. This was followed in 1980 by the National Energy Programme (NEP), which monitored the extent of foreign ownership in the energy sector. As indicated in Figure 16, there followed a significant decline in foreign-controlled assets in Canada, from a peak of 36 per cent in 1971 to 20 per cent in 1988. In addition, foreign direct investment in Canada became more diversified. As Figure 17 shows, there was a significant growth in direct investment from countries other than the United States during the period 1985 to 1995.

During the 1980s, Canadian policy on foreign direct investment was substantially liberalized, partly as a result of the FTA and NAFTA. In 1985, FIRA was replaced by Investment Canada, which was set up with the mandate to promote foreign direct investment in Canada. Review of inward direct investment was substantially reduced and sectoral restrictions eased. Subsequently,

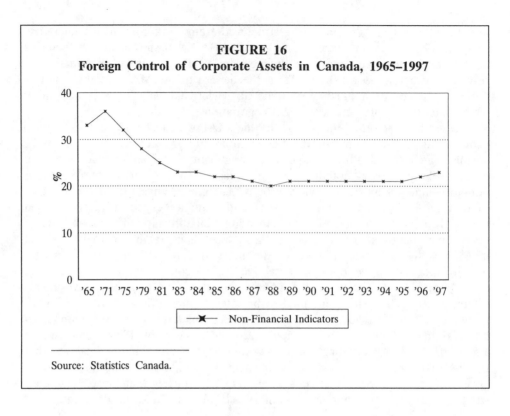

FIGURE 16
Foreign Control of Corporate Assets in Canada, 1965–1997

Source: Statistics Canada.

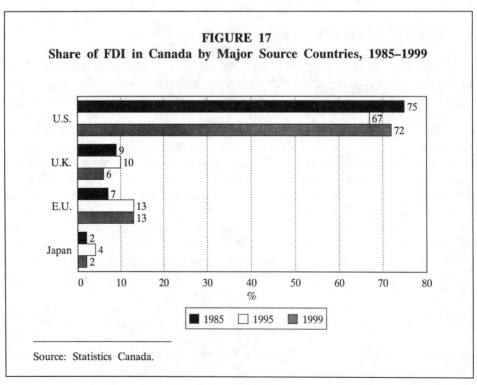

FIGURE 17
Share of FDI in Canada by Major Source Countries, 1985–1999

Source: Statistics Canada.

174

foreign ownership of Canadian assets rose throughout the 1990s to 23 per cent in 1997. At the same time, the United States reversed its previous decline as a source of FDI in Canada, raising its share of total FDI from 69% in 1995 to 72% in 1999. This gain in foreign control was widespread over most non-financial sectors.

Canadian direct investment abroad (CDIA) has also seen a significant evolution over the past two decades. It has more than quadrupled since the mid-1980s, from $57-billion in 1985 to $257-billion in 1999. Indeed, for the first time in Canada's history, the stock of CDIA surpassed inward FDI stock in 1996.

As Figure 18 indicates, the United States is the most-favoured location for Canadian direct investment abroad, accounting for 52 per cent of all CDIA in 1997. However, the U.S. share of CDIA has gradually fallen from its peak of 69 per cent in 1985. At the same time, Europe's share of CDIA has risen from 14 per cent in 1985 to 23 per cent in 1997. Most of this direct investment by Canadian firms has been in the manufacturing and finance sectors.

The rapid expansion in CDIA has brought Canadian direct investment assets and liabilities into a better balance. Canada is no longer primarily a recipient of foreign direct investment; it also acts as an important source of capital on the international scene.

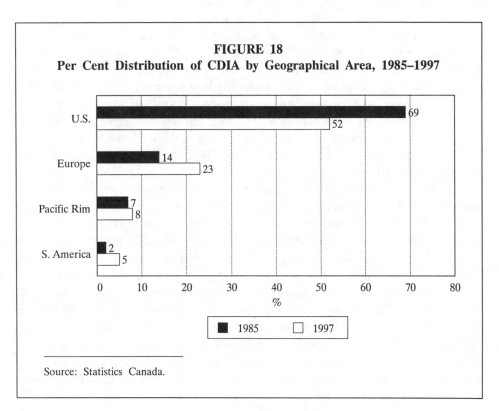

FIGURE 18
Per Cent Distribution of CDIA by Geographical Area, 1985–1997

Source: Statistics Canada.

CONCLUSIONS

International trade is based on comparative advantage. During most of the twentieth century, comparative advantage was created by capital, labour, natural resources and technology. Canada's comparative advantage was clearly in the production of natural resources.

However, once it became possible to transfer capital and technology almost instantaneously anywhere in the world, the underlying forces that create advantage changed. The merging of economic spaces as companies outsource increasing amounts of the production process has resulted in a kaleidoscopic form of comparative advantage, where small changes in cost result in sudden shifts in trading patterns.

The nature of the workforce, education, research and development and ability to adapt have, in turn, become important in driving trade. These new factors are largely determined by public policy. Public policy, not innate natural resources or historical characteristics, has become a modern cornerstone of advantage. Government action, not natural resources or capital, is the reason that 22-million Taiwanese export more to the United States than 60-million French, even though Taiwan is 10,000 kilometres away. Clearly, public policy and trade performance have become inseparable.

In fact, nearly everything that governments do can have an effect, positive or negative, on trade. In the context of international relations, most government actions are intended to help business, but some can also hinder. A too-restrictive policy on foreign investment in a sensitive sector can prevent Canadian companies from gaining access to the capital or technology they need to grow. Similarly, controls on exports of high-technology goods, or sanctions on trade with certain regimes, can be inhibiting factors, even though they may sometimes be justified. No government policy is created in a vacuum; it is the result of a play of interests, and business executives must understand the importance of putting forward their own concerns through their elected representatives and through their trade or industry associations. International business is a public-private partnership; like any partnership, it will only succeed if both partners put their best efforts into it.

In the 1990s, Third World countries, using modern technology, and operating within different political and social structures, are producing raw materials that are priced lower than those produced in Canada — and they are capturing market share from Canadian companies. Similarly, changes in the automobile industry have had a dramatic impact on Canada's capacity to compete effectively in the world market for cars. Yet Canada depends on these industries for its very economic survival. Obviously, there is a need for new policies appropriate to the new conditions that Canadian firms are certain to face. Protecting the status quo makes no sense; pretending that international markets have not changed is nonsense; attempting to retreat into some type of Fortress Canada is impossible; and stressing gaining access into new markets is meaningless, since most markets are already open. Canada needs a set of new, comprehensive strategies based on the new realities.

REFERENCES

Balasubramanyam, V.N., M. Salisu and David Sapsford, "Foreign Direct Investment and Growth in EP and IS Countries," *The Economic Journal*, 1996.

Borensztein, E., J. De Gregorio and L. Jong-Wha, *How Does Foreign Direct Investment Affect Economic Growth?* (Cambridge, MA: National Bureau of Economic Research, 1995).

The Economist, "World Trade," December 7, 1996.

————, "Balancing Act," January 4, 1997.

Feenscra, R.C., "Integration of Trade and Disintegration of Production in the Global Economy," *The Economic Journal, 1998.*

Krugman, P., *Geography and Trade* (Leuven University Press and MIT Press, 1991).

Krugman, P. and E. Graham, *Foreign Direct Investment in the United States* (Washington, D.C.: Institute for International Economics, 1995).

Martin, R. and P. Sunley, "Paul Krugman's Geographical Economics and Its Implications for Regional Development Theory: A Critical Assessment." *Economic Geography*, 1996.

Obstfeld, M., "The Global Capital Market: Benefactor or Menace?" *The Economic Journal*, 1998.

Organization for Economic Co-operation and Development, *Investment Liberalization and Trade Performance* (Paris: OECD, 1994).

Porter, Michael E. and the Monitor Company, *Canada at the Crossroads: The Reality of a New Competitive Environment* (Ottawa: Business Council on National Issues and Minister of Supply and Services Canada, 1991).

Statistics Canada, "Recent Trends in Canadian Direct Investment Abroad." *Canadian Economic Observer*, 1993.

Thurow, Lester, *Head to Head: The Coming Economic Battle Among Japan, Europe, and America* (New York: William Morrow, 1992).

United Nations, *World Investment Report: Transnational Corporations, Employment and the Workplace* (New York: United Nations, 1994).

————, *World Investment Report: Transnational Corporations and Competitiveness* (New York: United Nations, 1995).

————, *World Investment Report: Investment, Trade and International Policy Arrangements* (New York: United Nations, 1996).

————, *World Investment Report: Foreign Direct Investment and the Challenge of Development* (New York: United Nations, 1999).

WTO, *Trade and Foreign Direct Investment* (Geneva: World Trade Organization, 1996).

Yarbrough, Beth V. and Robert M. Yarbrough, *The World Economy: Trade and Finance*. 2d ed. (Hinsdale, IL: Dryden Press, 1991).

Yoffie, D.B., *Beyond Free Trade* (Boston, MA: HBS Press, 1993).

Globalization and Canadian Economic and Industrial Strategy in the Twenty-First Century

James M. Gillies

Whether we like it or not, indeed whether we want to believe it or not, one of the truly significant consequences of the development of a more or less free trade world has been the dramatic decline in the ability of individual nation states to determine their own economic well being through the implementation of traditional economic policies. For example, monetary policy in Canada is now, by and large, decided by international forces — when interest rates rise in the United States or Germany they rise in Canada, regardless of whether domestic economic conditions call for an increase in rates. And, while Canadian governments still have full jurisdiction over spending and taxing, there is no doubt that decisions with respect to fiscal matters are greatly influenced by the cost and availability of foreign capital. Monetary and fiscal policies can no longer be used to ensure full employment and price stability in as independent a fashion as was the case in the past. Moreover, as a result of participation in multinational and binational agreements, such as WTO or NAFTA, states have surrendered considerable sovereignty over many traditional industrial policy tools, such as tariffs and subsidies — which, heretofore, they have had unlimited freedom to use, as they saw fit, in the national interest.

Since Canada's economic prosperity is largely dependent on international trade, Canada's international industrial strategy, defined in the broadest sense, has, with some aberrations such as Macdonald's nineteenth century National Policy, been directed at gaining access for Canada's products into as many world markets as possible. In the 1930s, for example, the Canadian government

---

Based on an earlier article by James M. Gillies and Colin Dickinson.

hosted the Ottawa Conference on Imperial Preference, which was convened to increase free trade within the British Empire. Immediately after World War II Canada was a leading advocate of the formation of the International Trade Organization for the purpose of liberalizing trade. In the 1960s the Auto-Pact was passed by the federal government, and the ultimate culmination of the policy — freed trade with the United States — was achieved, when the North American Free Trade Agreement was signed in 1989.

At the same time, however, domestic industrial policy, since the first days of the nation, has been interventionist and protectionist. In order to induce Nova Scotia to join Confederation the new national government agreed to build a railroad linking it to central Canada. A few decades later the government of John A. Macdonald was involved in financing the CPR. In the 1930s the government of R.B. Bennett laid the foundation for the CBC, and Mackenzie King's government formed Air Canada. After World War II Quebec national-ized the power industry and created Quebec Power. In the 1970s the Liberal government of Prime Minister Pierre Trudeau enacted the National Energy Policy and passed the Foreign Investment Review Act; and on and on. Throughout the twentieth century practically every economic sector, from farm-ing to automobile production received a direct subsidy or some other form of government assistance. By the mid-1970s over 50 per cent of the gross national product flowed through government hands and, of the 10 largest corporations in the nation, five were owned by the government. In 1980 more than 700 Crown Corporations were involved in everything from selling liquor to produc-ing nuclear reactors, and every economic sector operated within the framework of literally thousands of regulations.

In almost every case, the reason advanced by governments, regardless of their political stripe, for intervening in the economy was that it was necessary to maintain the identity, indeed, the sovereignty of the nation. The fact is that it has not been easy to build and maintain an economic and culturally independent nation in the inhospitable northern half of the North American continent, next to a neighbour, regardless of how friendly, which buys more than 85 per cent of the nation's exports. The links between Canada and the United States are enormous; the north–south economic ties are very strong. It is not astonishing, therefore, that throughout the twentieth century, a major underlying purpose of Canada's domestic industrial strategy, for better or worse, was to maintain economic and cultural independence from the United States.

As a result of new international agreements governing trade, most of the domestic international policies followed by Canadian governments in the past are now prohibited. For this reason alone new industrial policies and strategies must be developed. But there is also another reason — one that is equally important — for a totally new assessment of Canada's economic programs. Dur-ing the last quarter of the twentieth century the Canadian economy operated well below its potential and, relative to many other nations, performed badly. In 1970 Canada's national debt approximated $15-billion, and there was almost no annual deficit in federal government financing. In 1998 the national debt exceeded $545-billion, the third highest in the world in per capita terms, and interest payments on the debt were more than $41.5-billion annually. Thirty years ago the Canadian dollar was one of the strongest currencies in the world — approximately on par with the United States dollar. A quarter of a century ago Canadians, along with the residents of the United States and Switzerland, were among the richest, in terms of per capita income, in the world. Since that time the real wealth and standard of living of Canadians, relative to citizens of many other countries, has continuously declined.

Consequently, even if it were not prevented by law from following many of the traditional strategies of the twentieth century, new and totally different policies from those of the past must be developed and implemented. If they are not, it is as certain as death and taxes that Canada's economic decline, relative to other countries, will continue and the standard of living of Canadians will, as it has over the past two decades, continue to fall. And among the most important of those new approaches must be a completely new industrial strategy based on the realities of the global market place of the twenty-first century.

THE ESSENTIAL FEATURES OF AN INDUSTRIAL STRATEGY

Every industrial country in the world, including Canada, has enacted hundreds of pieces of legislation that influence the manner in which business operates. Some, such as tariffs, excise taxes, quotas and subsidies, have a direct impact on business operations; others, like regional development programs, have a less direct impact but are no less important. The sum of all these measures, each of which is legislated for a particular (often political) reason, makes up the industrial policy of the government. Whether or not these policies add up to what can be considered a strategy, however, depends not on how many such programs there are, but on whether or not a country, through its government, has an economic goal (or goals) it is attempting to achieve (or as the Japanese call it, "some vision"), and the extent to which measures are put in place systematically to reach the goals.

A country does not have a productive industrial strategy simply because it has a host of regulations or laws influencing the way in which business operates. A sense of purpose and a defined objective must be present before a series of independent industrial programs add up to a coherent industrial strategy. The goals and means of industrial strategies may differ — indeed do differ — over time and among countries; but the single common denominator of them all remains the same: the implementation of policies that reinforce one another to achieve a predetermined national economic objective.

Clearly, it is impossible to generalize about the exact composition or nature of industrial strategies. They take their form from the needs of the time; they are always contingent. They are developed in relationship to what they are expected to achieve and, therefore, differ in "conception, content and form, reflecting changes in the development of an economy, its nature and historical circumstances, international conditions and its political and economic situation."[1]

Implicit in the formation of an industrial strategy is the expectation that it is possible to develop a comprehensive set of economic goals for a nation —

goals that are more than simply vague notions of the desirability of a high standard of living. For example, after World War II, the government of Japan realized that, given the lack of natural resources in the country, the road to prosperity for the Japanese was through programs designed to add high value to raw materials. It followed that the lower the price of these materials, which Japan had to import, the greater the opportunity for adding value. Consequently, a strategy of investing all foreign exchange in the development of resources throughout the world, with the objective of increasing supply and thereby lowering prices, was followed by the Japanese government. The results, in terms of stimulating growth and prosperity in the Japanese economy, were brilliant.

In the 1960s the government of France, as part of a national strategy, enacted policies that prohibited the sale of firms in certain industries to non-citizens. The reasoning behind the specific decision was as follows: the government developed a consensus that the national economic goal should be full employment; this goal, it was believed, could only be achieved by economic growth, and that growth could only come from the manufacturing sector increasing its level of exports. To increase exports, domestic industries had to adapt to new conditions, and that adaptation, it was hypothesized, would be easier to achieve in industries controlled by French citizens than by foreigners. It followed, therefore, that to carry out the strategy, the government should enact policies that prohibited the sale of firms in certain industries to non-citizens, and this is precisely what it did.

In post-World War II Austria, the strategy was to put in place policies that produced interest rates lower than those in West Germany. Many Third World countries' strategies have aimed at attracting capital to develop resources.

The nature of the goal is not important, although it must be sufficiently specific to be a guide for the implementation of relatively explicit action plans. Ensuring a high standard of living is much too general to be useful for operational purposes. However, a goal of the elimination of the deficit in the current account of the balance of payments — which would, in time, lead to a higher standard of living — could be useful, since it would be possible to design specific policies which would achieve the objective.

In short, the essential elements in an industrial strategy are a consensus on what a country wants to achieve in terms of economic performance, an understanding of the cohesive, non-conflicting policies that are necessary to achieve those goals, and the political capacity to put in place the policies necessary to meet them.

Obviously, the bottom line of any strategy and the policies enacted to implement it is to bring about change. It makes only good sense, therefore, to design and implement new policies and programs which bring about the transition of organizations and their resources from outmoded, inefficient uses to new ones, in as painless a way as possible. All programs and policies should include measures which assure that the costs of change are shared fairly. Otherwise, in a democracy the political support necessary to implement various policies necessary to bring about change cannot be attained without great difficulty.

In order to develop an effective industrial strategy in any country, at any time, the following elements are required:

> There must be a national consensus — various industrial sectors and geographic regions of the nation must agree on the general economic goals for the nation.

> There must be a trusting, working relationship between leaders in the private and public sectors.

> There must be a cadre of well-qualified public servants capable of preparing and implementing policies.

> There must be strong private sector support for the strategy.

> The people responsible for the implementation of the strategy must be involved in its preparation.

> Everyone must feel that there is an urgent need for a strategy.

In addition, from a substantive point of view, it is essential that:

> The costs of essential programs be distributed fairly.

> Private sector industries which perceive themselves to be politically and socially indispensable to the nation must be dissuaded from that point of view.

The industrial policies which are adopted to implement a strategy are usually most successful when:

> They are concentrated around selected industries.

> They are designed for industries where there are a few large firms.

> They have precise objectives.

> Their results are constantly monitored.

> There are systems in place for ending programs that do not work.

> There are plans in place to phase out programs once they have achieved their objectives.

While all these conditions for success are important, without question the most important one is the ability to gain consensus about the goals and objectives for the economy.

GAINING CONSENSUS THROUGH CONSULTATION

Despite the rejection of the Charlottetown Accord and the Meech Lake Agreement, seeking a consensus on policy is something that Canadians and their governments have always been more than willing to try to do; in fact, in many ways, consultation is Canada's national pastime. From 1867 to the present,

Canadians have continually come together officially to discuss everything from the trivial to the profound. An endless number of Royal Commissions, parliamentary committees, white papers, green papers, special commissions et al. have been employed to find out what Canadians feel about almost every question imaginable. No one should be astonished to learn that Canada's first Royal Commission was established in 1868. Indeed, there is so much consultation that offices have been established in the federal and some provincial governments simply to keep track of all the consulting that is going on.

Whether or not all this consultation has been worthwhile is open to debate. Clearly, some has been very useful, and has resulted in important legislation. For example, the report of the Royal Commission on Dominion Provincial Relations, better known as the Rowell-Sirois Report, issued in 1940, had an enormous impact on the restructuring of fiscal relationships in the nation; the 1985 Macdonald Report — the Royal Commission on the Economic Union and Development Prospects for Canada — had a significant impact in that it prepared Canadians to accept the bilateral trade treaty with the United States, signed in 1989. On the other hand, the Bryce Report, which emanated from the Royal Commission on Corporate Concentration, had little influence.

What has been true about consultation, in general, is equally true about specific consultation between and among business, government and labour. On balance it appears that, aside from significant exceptions, much of this consultation has been of relatively little importance when measured in terms of its impact on public policy. Some individual firms and industries have developed close relationships with their counterpart departments in government; trade associations, such as the Business Council on National Issues, the Canadian Chamber of Commerce and the Canadian Federation of Independent Business, meet, from time to time, with various cabinet ministers and other officials, but their influence on policy making is, at best, moderate. Despite universal condemnation by the Canadian business community, this is confirmed by the creation of the Canada Development Corporation, the Foreign Investment Review Agency, Petro-Canada, the National Energy Program and so on.

Moreover, in spite of all this consultation (or perhaps because of it), governments in Canada have never acquiesced in the idea that there should be a formal consultative relationship between government and business or among government, business and labour regarding major economic policies. Consultation has been constant, but it has always been on an ad hoc basis with selected groups. Often it has been used by governments when they are not sure what they should do about an issue. The easy answer is to appoint a Royal Commission. At other times, it has been used as a method of defusing an issue. Also, often, even when a government has shown a real interest in discovering a solution to a national issue, the results of the consultation have not been incorporated into the policies that eventually evolve. Nothing in Canada is comparable to the permanent consultative processes that are in place in Japan, Germany and many other countries. The concept of tripartitism — of labour, business and government meeting together to work out jointly acceptable policies — has never been part of the Canadian public policy-making process.

Nevertheless, from time to time, serious consultation has taken place and has succeeded. When the government launched its drive for a free-trade treaty with the United States, it knew that the negotiations would only succeed if they had strong business support. Consequently, the government organized a consultative mechanism consisting of a 38-member international Trade Advisory Committee (ITAC) and 15 Sectoral Advisory Groups on International Trade (SAGITs) for the dual purpose of keeping business on side — in favour of the treaty — and eliciting information which would be helpful in the negotiations. Originally, the government hoped that labour would participate with business representatives in the advisory groups, but the Canadian Labour Congress refused. While some labour organizations made small inputs in certain sectors, on balance, the labour role was insignificant.

The wisdom of developing the consultative mechanism from a political and implementation point of view was clearly demonstrated when the question of free trade became the central issue of the ensuing election in 1988. The Mulroney government benefited substantially from the very strong campaign waged by the business sector in favour of the treaty. There are many who believe that, without this support, the Progressive Conservatives could not have won the election, and therefore the bilateral trade treaty would not have been ratified. However, we should emphasize that the consultative mechanism had nothing to do with the original conception of the policy. Consultation was not a major factor in determining whether the Canadian government should pursue a strategy of gaining a free-trade treaty with the United States. They were by-products of the government's decision to do so.

In short, a brief review of the consultative process in Canada leads to the conclusion that, on specific issues and for technical matters, it is very important — and for political appearances, it may be crucial; but for determining broad goals and general policies for achieving them, it is not particularly useful.[2]

THE MAJOR OBJECTIONS TO INDUSTRIAL STRATEGIES

In spite of the success of some countries which have followed well-thought through policies, most notably Japan in the 1960s and 1970s, and the rapidly developing smaller economies in the Far East — Taiwan, South Korea and Singapore — there is still considerable scepticism among many economists, commentators and politicians about the efficacy of industrial strategies. Since there is nothing unreasonable about the concept, why is there resistance to formalizing a strategy? Why is there resistance to the idea of enacting industrial policies in a coordinated fashion to achieve some predetermined, agreed upon goals for the economy? To a large extent, this resistance is based on theory, ideology and pragmatism.

Perhaps the most important objection to formal industrial strategies is the perception that they cause an undue amount of inefficient interference in the economy by governments. The claim is made that "the invisible hand" of Adam Smith always leads to the most effective use of resources and that proclaimed strategies and policies interfere with the working of the market. Yet, there is no need, either in principle or in practice, for conflict between the development of strategies and the operation of a free market. Indeed, a major thrust of many well-designed strategies is to improve the allocation of resources through assuring the operation of the price system in a competitive marketplace.

The reality is that in most economies there are serious imperfections in many markets — indeed, economists such as John Kenneth Galbraith argue that imperfections dominate.[3] Certainly, in Canada, with its lack of strong antitrust laws and the enormous concentration of market power, the case can be made that imperfect markets outnumber perfect.

When markets do not allocate resources efficiently, policy makers have two choices. They can either enact measures to make the markets efficient, or they can do something to remedy the ill-effects of the imperfections. Needless to say, classical liberal economists favour the first approach. Such a resolution is appropriate if the sole goal of public policy is to maximize output. However, regardless of any theory, when the results of pure market allocation under conditions of perfect competition create perceived economic injustices, the very nature of the political process will ensure that governments will take some sort of action. Moreover, they usually do so without any analysis, let alone comprehension, of the costs and benefits associated with the intervention. Anyone who doubts this "need only think of the various ways in which governments intervene in the modern economy — from tariffs and other instruments of commercial policy, to purchasing and selling policies, to incentive policies in agriculture and natural resources, manufacturing, exports, etc...."[4]

The fact is, correctly or incorrectly, if there is no national consensus that the way in which the market is allocating resources is appropriate, there will be changes. Economic analysis which ignores the political aspects of its normative conclusions addresses only a small part of the issues involved in national economic policy making and is not particularly helpful to policy makers.[5]

In reality, developing and implementing policies within the framework of a comprehensive industrial strategy may lead to less government intervention rather than more. Indeed, the bottom line may well be that eliminating inefficiencies arising from random, politically inspired, excessive government intervention in the economy may be one of the most compelling reasons for developing a comprehensive national industrial strategy.

Another argument against devoting time and resources to the creation of an industrial strategy is the very pragmatic one that in a pluralistic democratic country it is simply impossible to do so. Indeed, it has been eloquently argued that the one thing that "government cannot do well at all is to make critical choices among particular firms, municipalities or regions, determining cold-bloodedly which shall prosper and which shall not. [Rather] a cardinal principle of ... government is never to be seen to do direct harm ... the formal and informal institutions of the political system are designed to hinder governments from making hard choices ... rewarding some and punishing others...."[6]

And yet for economic growth there must be, to use Schumpeter's felicitous phrase, "creative destruction" — the replacement of the old by the new. For the economic purist, this is achieved through the operation of the market. It is certainly something that many believe governments, designed as they are in a pluralistic democratic society to protect the status quo, cannot facilitate. Moreover, it is argued that it is unreasonable to expect anything else, and so trying to develop a consensus and a program for real change is a waste of time.

Whether or not this is true in any given case depends on both the nature of the political system and the extent to which change is needed.

Finally, more recently opponents of industrial strategies have argued that the globalization of markets makes the development of national strategies even more difficult. This is, of course, a reversal of the conventional thinking in the 1980s and the early 1990s, when it was contended that nations experiencing the strongest economic performance — countries such as Japan and Germany — did so because they had in place strategies based on recognition that international, not domestic, forces were driving economic activity. They made, as one authority stated, obtaining a "competitive position in the world economy the first priority in their policies — they have clearly recognized, as did the most successful multinational corporations — Toyota, Erickson, Mercedes-Benz — that economic dynamics have decisively shifted from the national to the world economy...."[7] The institutionalization of these international forces in treaties and agreements is making, according to some, the development of unique national industrial strategies, at least of the type based on national, inward-focused economic measures, such as industry- or firm-specific grants, impossible.

Proponents of the development of national industrial strategies are doing no more than searching for a process whereby the myriad of business policies which are deemed essential in a well-developed industrial economy are integrated to achieve a particular agreed-upon goal. Surely this is more sensible than having literally thousands of rules, regulations and laws developed independently, often with contradictory purposes, in an ad hoc fashion. If, and this is a big "if," an industrial strategy can assure a more efficient use of resources and a higher standard of living for more Canadians, it is only sensible to put one in place.

The fact is that throughout most of the twentieth century Canada did have a coherent economic strategy that resulted in the nation surviving and its citizens becoming among the richest in the world. As we enter the twenty-first century, the really significant question is not whether it is a good thing to have a strategy but whether it is possible for a small nation, such as Canada, to do so in a world with an almost fully developed global marketplace.

CANADA'S INDUSTRIAL STRATEGY, 1867–1980

From the days of the first explorers, Canada's wealth was — and, some would argue, still is — to a considerable extent, founded on fish, furs, forest products, agriculture, mines, natural gas and oil. Canada is currently the largest producer in the world of asbestos, nickel, zinc and potash; the second largest of gold and molybdenum; and the third largest of gypsum, platinum, copper, lead and iron ore. It is a leading producer of pulp and newsprint and other forest products and is self-sufficient in all types of energy, including gas and oil. All these products are produced for export, and the extent of world demand for them has always been a critical factor in determining Canada's growth and prosperity.

The original exploitation of these staples was largely financed, as is the case in any developing country, from abroad — first from Great Britain and other European countries, and then from the United States. By 1883, the latter had become, as it has remained, the largest market for Canadian goods, and starting in 1926 it became the source of most of the capital flowing in to develop the nation.

Given the enormous natural wealth of the nation and its fortuitous location, it is not surprising that over the years governments have fostered the unlimited development of resources and their by-products. Canada's comparative advantage in doing so was so self-evident that enacting a set of consistent economic policies — an industrial strategy — based on the exploitation of the natural wealth of the nation, seemed to be only logical.

The strategy required that:

> no measures be put in place that restricted the availability of foreign capital (or for that matter, domestic capital) for the development of natural resources;

> no tariffs be imposed that would increase the cost of producing commodities for export;

> all possible efforts be made to open foreign markets for Canadian natural resources and the products of natural resource industries;

> tax laws favour the development of resources; and,

> nothing be done that might result in any restriction of access to the United States' market for Canadian goods.

Building a consensus around this strategy was, for a number of reasons, relatively easy. First, it was given great credibility in the 1920s and 1930s by two eminent Canadian scholars — W.A. Macintosh of Queen's University and Harold Innis of the University of Toronto — who "separately and simultaneously worked out an explanatory framework for Canadian economic history."[8] They pointed out that Canada's economic development could all be explained by the overwhelming abundance in Canada of "staple products" which they defined as bulky, semi-processed, natural commodities with a high-weight-to-volume ratio, which were produced for export.

Second, the policies based on, and around, the "staple thesis" were supported because they were easily understood and appeared so logical. Finally, they were supported because the positive results of the strategy could not be denied. Through following these policies during the first three quarters of the twentieth century, Canada became one of the richest countries in the world.

In spite of the remarkable degree of agreement among all members of the academic, political, bureaucratic and business establishments, and the results of the policies based on the "staple thesis," there have, as is always the case, been some persistent critics of its use as the appropriate framework for the development of the nation's economic and industrial policies. The essence of these criticisms is that as a result of the policies:

1. Canada became a highly indebted country.
2. There was the development of a very high degree — the highest of any western industrialized country — of foreign ownership of many economic sectors.

3. There is very little competition in many segments of the domestic market.
4. Because of tariff protection and lack of competition, most domestic companies became very high cost producers of manufactured goods and of services.

While no Canadian government was ever ready to consider, let alone make, the radical policy changes inherent in abandoning the staple thesis, at the same time no government could ignore the increasing apprehension that was expressed about the degree of foreign ownership in the nation — a by-product, some argued, of the policies. Thus, at various times during the last half of the century, several studies were made on the impact of foreign investment, and guidelines were issued about good corporate citizenship for foreign investors. The Foreign Investment Review Act, which established a review mechanism to evaluate whether specific foreign investments were in the national interest, was passed, and in 1981 the government of Pierre Trudeau introduced legislation that directly regulated foreign controlled enterprises in the Canadian gas and oil industries.

None of these measures, however, really changed the thrust of Canadian economic policies. The "staple thesis" continued throughout most of the century as the framework within which major policy was constructed, and indeed the essential elements of the strategy were applied in the development of policies for sectors of the economy other than natural resources. The 1965 Auto Pact, which unified the North American automobile market, was a simple extension of the strategy, in the sense that it involved negotiating entry into foreign markets for Canadian goods, not blocking foreign investment and ownership, and working out difficulties with the United States. And the Auto Pact was a forerunner of the bilateral free trade treaty with the United States and NAFTA. From the Canadian point of view, these treaties were merely extensions of the policies which have always directed Canada's economic development.

THE 1990s: THE BEGINNING OF THE END OF AN ERA?

By the beginning of the 1990s, there was a marked change in perception about the appropriate role of the state in the economy, and with it a change in national economic policies. A variety of factors caused the change, but the most important was the fact that governments no longer were able to finance the various programs they had introduced during the 1960s, 1970s and 1980s. The introduction of a variety of social programs, a change in demographics and some slowdown in the rate of economic expansion, not only in Canada but throughout the world (Figure 1), meant that by the 1980s a progressively higher proportion of government expenditures, at both the federal and provincial levels, had to be financed through borrowing. Citizens and corporations had reached their highest level of tolerance for increased taxes. As a result, budget deficits became common, the national debt exploded in size, and taxes increased. In Canada, governments had to borrow abroad to finance consumption, and the per capita foreign debt of Canadians became the highest in the

FIGURE 1
Average Yearly Real GDP Growth (1990 prices), 1967–95 (%)

	1967–70	1971–75	1976–80	1981–85	1986–90	1991–95
CANADA	4.05	5.22	3.93	2.88	2.91	1.50
France	5.41	3.48	3.13	1.52	3.20	1.12
Germany[a]			0.98	1.17	3.36	1.43
Italy[b]	6.28	2.78	4.77	1.40	3.04	1.08
Japan[c]	11.37	4.42	4.59	3.73	4.48	2.64
U.K.	2.67	2.03	1.82	2.02	3.32	1.17
U.S.	2.33	4.20	3.22	2.53	2.64	2.26

[a] German 1976–80 figure based on only 1980 growth rate. 1990+ figures include GDR.
[b] Italian 1991–95 figure based on only 1991 and 1992 growth rates.
[c] Japanese 1991–95 figure based on only 1991 and 1992 growth rates.

Source: IMF, *International Financial Statistical Yearbook*, 1996.

FIGURE 2

Per-Capita Foreign Debt (in US$)			*Proportion of Foreign Debt to Total Debt (%)*
CANADA	1994	8,275.52	71.88
France	1995	206.41	1.79
Germany	1994	3,764.58	47.27
Japan	1990	70.72	0.49
U.K.	1992	910.63	17.14
U.S.	1994	2,642.36	19.44

Source: IMF, *International Financial Statistical Yearbook*, 1996.
Canada, "The Canadian Experience in Reducing Budget Deficits and Debt." Notes for an address by The Honourable Paul Martin, Minister of Finance, presented to the Federal Reserve Bank of Kansas City Symposium on Budget Deficits and Debt: Issues and Options, September 1, 1995.

world (Figure 2). Moreover, there was more and more evidence that governments, instead of being servants and benefactors for citizens, had become agents preventing change and hindering development, carrying out functions more for their own benefit than for citizens.

The growing support for "less government intervention" and "free market economics," particularly in the United Kingdom and the United States, spilled over into Canada, and in 1985 the historic trend towards more government intervention was rejected by Canadians when they elected a Progressive Conservative government with an overwhelming majority. The new government, at least in rhetoric, adopted a more laissez-faire attitude towards business than was historically the case in Canada; and the traditional Canadian social compact concept was as nearly rejected as it ever had been. Whether or not people were demanding less government is unclear, but there is no doubt that they were demanding more *efficient* government.

The industrial programs flowing from this ideology added up to a relatively coherent strategy designed to strengthen the operation of the free market in Canada. There was an acceleration of privatization of Crown corporations, and a removal of many regulations restricting private activity. The Foreign Investment Review Act was scrapped; the National Energy Policy was eviscerated. Moreover, in the ultimate expression of the policies flowing from the "staple theory," a free trade agreement was signed between Canada and the United States, an agreement which was later extended to include Mexico. Indeed, the basic positive policies flowing from the thesis — the encouragement of the importation of capital and a push for international free trade — dominated economic policy making in Canada during the late 1980s and the early 1990s.

As Prime Minster Mulroney enthusiastically proclaimed, Canada was "open for business," and being open for business meant free trade, less government intervention and more foreign investment.

One of the immediate consequences of the signing of the bilateral trade treaty was the repositioning of the Canadian tax system. For years, a sales tax was imposed on Canadian manufacturing activity, which placed many Canadian firms at a disadvantage compared with foreign producers. With free trade, it was imperative that such a tax be removed. Since the government either could not, or did not want to, give up the revenue generated from the tax, it was replaced by a new general consumption tax — the Goods and Services Tax (GST).

In addition, in order to comply with some of the provisions of the bilateral trade treaty, as well as with many of the sections of the General Agreement on Tariffs and Trade (GATT) to which it subscribed, Canada surrendered some of its sovereignty, particularly with respect to the right to offer subsidies and incentives to various sectors of the economy (especially through marketing boards), and of course had to agree to the elimination of most tariffs.

Consequently, by the mid-1990s, enacting policies from a strategy based on the "staple thesis" was either unnecessary or impossible. Interestingly, and somewhat paradoxically, the very success of the application of some of the policies inherent in the "staple thesis" caused the end of others. The introduction of free trade meant the end of tariff protection for most sectors of the Canadian economy and the illegality of special subsidies for Canadian industries — particularly agriculture. International treaties with respect to trade also brought into question the legality of Canadian governments subsidizing various industries through equalization payments to different geographic areas. In fact, almost all the policies for the protection of domestic production of goods and services, inherent within the staple thesis, became illegal.

Interestingly, the domestic industrial strategy policies of the twentieth century, to the extent that they were designed to keep control of the Canadian economy in Canadian hands, failed. Indeed, by the mid-1920s, when the United States became Canada's largest trading partner, more than 30 per cent of Canadian manufacturing had been acquired by American firms. Since then petroleum refining, production of chemicals, electrical machinery and automobiles, and much of retailing, as well as a host of other sectors, have become dominated by foreign ownership. In fact, by the end of the twentieth century, in spite of the policy of "defensive expansionism," the largest degree of foreign ownership in any western industrialized country was in Canada.

CLINGING TO THE PAST: ATTEMPTING NATIONAL INDUSTRIAL STRATEGY MAKING IN THE GLOBAL MARKET PLACE

By the mid-1990s, the conventional wisdom in Canada was that the nation's "continued prosperity is being threatened by a global economy where change is accelerating and competition is growing even fiercer."[9] It was argued that, compared with other industrial countries, Canada was already slipping, as indicated by the fact that:

➤ Our exports are losing market share.

➤ We are not attracting enough investment.

➤ We are not applying new technologies as well as our competitors.

➤ Not enough of our manufacturers offer innovative products backed by research and development.

➤ Too few of our companies provide training for their workers.

➤ We spend more per capita on education than other leading industrial nations, but the results are not what they should be.

➤ Too many young people are still not ready for school, and too many are leaving school ill-equipped for work.

➤ Too many adults are permanently sidelined for lack of skills.[10]

In order to begin to develop an action plan — strategies for dealing with these issues — the federal government invited 20 Canadians from various backgrounds to volunteer their time "to listen to what Canadians were saying, and — operating at arm's length from the federal government — to produce a plan of action to secure Canada's future economic and social well-being — a plan that all Canadians could support and help carry out."[11] The group, known as the Steering Group on Prosperity, held extensive hearings in every province and territory, meeting with a diversity of people and organizations in a variety of settings — round tables, workshops, focus groups.[12] It would be difficult to imagine a more extensive or thoroughly prepared consultative process.

The committee published its report in October 1992. It recommended, as a result of its consultations, a strategy for prosperity based on innovation, from which flowed a series of policies. Essentially, and not astonishingly, the report called for:

> ➢ disciplined fiscal policy
> ➢ fair and competitive tax systems
> ➢ leaner and more responsive governments
> ➢ a single Canadian market
> ➢ application of technology to facilitate investment and business financing
> ➢ better Canadian export performance
> ➢ better labour relations
> ➢ better programs to help workers adjust to change
> ➢ reorienting the educational and training system to achieve results
> ➢ the formation of a prosperity council to implement the recommendations

No one could quibble with the identification of problems and the recommendations for their solution. Moreover, the Steering Group on Prosperity made very specific recommendations as to who in society should deal with each problem, and furnished specific time lines as to when action should be taken.[13] Unfortunately, however, the committee's recommendations have been largely ignored. Clearly, its work was not used as a springboard for the launch of a serious undertaking on the development of a new, comprehensive industrial strategy.

MOVING INTO THE TWENTY-FIRST CENTURY

The Impact of the End of the Traditional Industrial Policies on Business

In response to globalization, Canadian policy makers had to make a choice. In face of worldwide pressures for the end of institutional barriers to trade, if Canada wanted our resources and their by-products, and other products such as automobiles, to have access to foreign markets, we had to give up protection for many segments of the Canadian economy. Given the importance of trade to Canada, the choice was relatively easy — we gave up protection, and the impact of this choice on Canadian businesses, which throughout their history have operated in the domestic, rather than the international, market has been enormous.

Technological changes in transportation and manufacturing in the last quarter of the twentieth century have made it possible for enterprises to produce and sell anywhere — and they do so where it is most profitable. As a result, with the end of tariff protection, no domestic market is excluded for long from competition, and so managers, whether they wish to or not, are being forced to operate their enterprises as efficiently as any in the world. Those who do not are being wiped out by the competition. There is no longer any place for the inefficient to hide.

It is almost a truism that strong market competition, and therefore great efficiency, has never been a dominant characteristic of many sectors of the Canadian economy. Indeed, the degree of concentration of market power in Canada is higher than in any other country for which there is comparable information. It has been estimated that in the mid-1980s four firms held more than 75 per cent of the market in areas such as tobacco, coal and coke, department stores, variety stores, air transportation, railways, pipelines, electric power, telephone, gas distribution, banks, consumer loan companies and other financial agencies. In certain activities, the concentration was even greater.[14]

Obviously, Canadian businesspeople would not have been able to develop such market power without the compliance of the federal government. While Canadian policy makers always fought for free trade in international markets for the products of the resource industries, the virtues of competition, which were seen to be so obvious in international markets, apparently were never assumed to be transferable to domestic.[15] It was, therefore, not only businessmen who preferred being protected from the forces of free markets; few, if any, governments, regardless of their political persuasion, totally embraced the idea that a goal of economic policy ought to be the pursuit of competitive markets. That such a philosophy should have prevailed, and to some extent still does, is not astonishing given the perilous state of the nation during most of its existence. The natural economic forces in the North American continent clearly run from the sparsely populated areas in the north to the concentrations of populations in the south, rather than east and west. Maintaining a country next to one 10 times larger has not been an easy task. Indeed, it may be, as it has been argued elsewhere in this chapter, that it could not have been done without positive intervention on the part of the state through creation of Crown corporations, massive government subsidies and other forms of government intervention — all of which usually made markets less competitive. In many ways Canada may be better defined through most of the twentieth century as a "public policy"[16] rather than a "free enterprise" nation.

Another major factor contributing to the high level of concentration of market power in Canada is the fact that various governments, in their efforts to secure rapid industrialization of the nation, placed few impediments in the way of foreign owners acquiring control of Canadian enterprise. As a result, by the mid-1920s foreign owners accounted for 30 per cent of all manufacturing in the country — most of it through wholly-owned subsidiaries. Once foreign firms gained dominance in the domestic market, it was almost impossible for local firms to replace them. As a result, Canadian interests lost out in petroleum refining, chemicals, electrical machinery, automobile manufacturing and many of the resource industries.[17]

A final factor contributing to the concentration of market power is the fact that Canada is a small country; consequently there have existed, and still do exist, close personal family and business relationships among a relatively small group of senior executives who own and operate Canadian enterprises. Various Canadian business historians have attributed much of the concentration of control and wealth to these connections among the executives of various types of enterprises — particularly between entrepreneurs and the executives of financial institutions. The high number of interlocking directorships — no CEO in Canada worthy of the position is without a bank directorship — supports this point of view. The reality is that there are relatively few business leaders in the nation — it is a closely knit community.

Regardless of the reasons, the fact remains that with the advent of globalization and free trade, few nations have had as many businesses in as many sectors that have had to adjust to completely new circumstances as Canada.

The Impact of the Rise of the Transnational Corporations

At the same time, as the opening up of worldwide markets created threats for many domestic Canadian firms, it also provided great opportunities. Corporations could now develop their strategies on a worldwide basis confident in the knowledge that national policies would have less and less effect on what they were able to do. As a result, great transnational firms were organized which operate with impunity throughout the world. These new transnationals are quite different from the multinational firms which dominated world trade in manufactured products for the past century.

As perhaps Canadians know better than anyone, historically, companies operating throughout the world normally did so by organizing subsidiaries in the countries within which they wished to produce and sell their products. They did so, often, not because of legal requirements, but rather because it was the most efficient way to operate a business. Even when technology made the interchange of information almost instantaneous, there were some advantages to having an organized physical presence in a local market: it led to a better understanding of local laws, customs and labour relations; and it probably made it easier to deal with government agencies and other institutions. Moreover, it occasionally made it easier to raise capital, and, under certain circumstances — for example, in Canada in the days of the Imperial Preference — a location in a particular nation state provided a base from which to penetrate other foreign markets.

While the exact nature of subsidiary companies varied, in most cases they were simply microcosms of the parent corporation. Most had a board of directors, a chief executive officer and the standard operating and staff structures. In many countries, shares were issued in the subsidiaries, so nationals could become shareholders; the parent, however, always retained the controlling interest. The degree of autonomy varied enormously from company to company, but by and large, the management of most major subsidiaries was focused on operating activities. Key strategic decisions with respect to the corporation were made at head office. Consequently, the board of directors and management of a subsidiary usually had little final control over such things as capital allocation, research and development, product introduction, advertising and other major strategic decisions.

Depending on the particular economic factors present in a country, a subsidiary might be given the mandate to produce all of one type of product for the world market, but in most cases, subsidiaries simply performed in the host market in the same manner as the parent did at home. Indeed, it was not unusual for major corporations to place individuals perceived to be candidates for general executive positions in the home office in subsidiary companies so that they could obtain experience in running all the facets of an organization in a smaller market. It is estimated that in 1995 there were about 50,000 subsidiaries, mostly of the great United States multinationals, operating throughout the world.[18]

With the advent of globalization, major corporations are no longer making strategies based on local markets; on the contrary, they are developing strategies totally *independent* of national boundaries. Transnational corporations are undertaking a number of structural initiatives to harness the opportunities presented by globalization: rationalizing their manufacturing processes along global lines; globalizing various functional responsibilities; globalizing company sourcing by centralizing all purchasing for the firm's global requirements; and, perhaps, most importantly, looking to a global rather than domestic or even multi-domestic markets for their products.[19]

Rationalizing Manufacturing can take on various forms. For example, rather than have plants in each of the corporation's markets produce a full line of products, the transnational corporation often has its national manufacturing plants produce only a single product for the whole global market. In this manner, the transnational corporation is able to offer a full line of products in each of its markets, yet at the same time reap significant economies of scale. Alternatively, the transnational corporation may take the rationalization of the manufacturing process a step further, having plants in different parts of the world produce different parts of the same product. For example, the transnational firm may decide to have standardized, labour-intensive components manufactured in lower-wage regions and complex, more skill-based parts manufactured in areas of the world where skilled labour is more abundant. In this way, the transnational firm is able to realize the required economies of scale *and* significant savings by reducing labour costs.

Globalizing functional responsibilities can also lead to cost savings. The transnational's finance department is one of the functions most amenable to globalization.[20] There are a number of reasons for this. For one, many of the world's financial markets are truly global. Significant deregulation of these markets in the past decade and a half has created an incredibly competitive environment where scale is the key to profitability. When transactions are often denominated in the trillions of dollars, it does not make sense for the national subsidiary of a major transnational corporation to go looking for financing in the tens of millions of dollars. On the other hand, by consolidating the financing needs of *each* of the transnational's various national branches into a figure in the hundreds of billions of dollars, the parent company can reap the full benefit of cost savings presented by the global financial market. Similarly, this consolidation of financing needs is essential to substantially improve the bargaining position of the transnational company.

Globalized company sourcing also benefits the transnational corporation through increased bargaining leverage. By centralizing all purchasing for the firm's global requirements, the transnational corporation is able to extract the best possible price for its various inputs, thereby realizing sizeable cost savings again. And while there are significant quantitative gains to be made through globalizing company sourcing (cost savings), there are also notable *qualitative* gains to made as well. Because the transnational corporation and its global suppliers become interdependent (because each is the other's biggest purchaser/ supplier), there are real benefits to coordinating their operations. For example, say a large chain of Canadian coffee shops enters into an agreement to purchase the majority of its coffee from a single South American supplier (thereby realizing significant cost savings). The chain might also decide that it would like to have an entirely new type of coffee to differentiate itself from its competitors. Accordingly, the company would work closely with its South American producer to develop this new bean. Because the coffee producer knows that it has a guaranteed market for this new product, it can go ahead with the research. Thus, global sourcing can lead to *qualitative* improvements for the transnational corporation by closer coordination of its operations with its suppliers and the removal of certain elements of risk on the part of the purchaser *and* the supplier (volatile swings in demand and price).

Global marketing of products is increasingly becoming the rule for many transnational corporations. Strategic imperatives of scale and scope demand that many Canadian companies expand their market beyond the Canadian border. This is particularly true in industries where technology is a key factor of the company's success. The development costs alone ensure that marketing only to the domestic market is simply not a profitable prospect. This is particularly true for Canadian companies, given Canada's relatively small market of 30 million consumers. Development costs in the billions of dollars by Bombardier on the design of an entirely new business jet or by Newbridge Networks on the design of new telephone switching technology require that these companies look to the world as their market. Of all the globalizing forces, the global marketing of products and the intense competition that it engenders are, by far, the farthest reaching. The simple fact — realized by more and more formerly domestic corporations — is that even if the firm chose to stay within its domestic borders, sooner or later its international competitors would come looking for it (enter its domestic market), and the firm would be forced to face them without the benefit of their international experience.

One of the major consequences of the change in transnational strategy — from a multi-domestic to a global strategy — is that the traditional subsidiary firm is no longer an essential element in their operations. It is no longer essential to build a completely integrated operation in a local market because, in a very real sense, there are no longer any local markets. There is now little need to have a fully developed enterprise in every country where there are operations. For example, at one time the shares of Canadian General Electric were traded on the Toronto Stock Exchange; there was a Canadian board of directors, a chief executive officer, and a number of mandates for the production of General Electric products for the entire world. Within the last few years, with a new global strategy, the General Electric Corporation has bought back all the shares from the public, disbanded the board of directors, eliminated the position of chief executive officer, and restructured the company, so that the head of each division producing for the world market reports to the appropriate officer at General Electric's head office in the United States.

While Canadian General Electric is a prominent example of the changes which globalization has brought about in the structure of foreign-owned firms operating in the Canadian economy, it is not an isolated one. A recent study of the subsidiaries of the largest 115 transnational corporations operating in Canada in 1995 indicates the decline in their Canadian character. In 1985, 68.6 per cent of these firms had no Canadian shareholders; a decade later 84 per cent of the top 115 had none. This indication of a decline of any Canadian ownership is supported by the fact that 32 of the 115 of the foreign-owned subsidiaries on the 1995 list "went through a corporate transformation — 16 were converted from public to private companies, six were dissolved, 11 were amalgamated with privately held companies and one was amalgamated with a public company."[21]

With the change in the structure of subsidiaries, particularly with the elimination of boards with local representation, it is reasonable to assume that the large transnational would begin to have more and more representation on their boards from the various countries within which they do business. The evidence does not indicate that this is happening. In 1994 over 80 per cent of all direct foreign investment was undertaken by the 100 largest transnational corporations. An analysis of their board structures indicates that by far the most important factor in determining the structure of the board is the location of the parent company. There is no correlation between the size of foreign sales or number of subsidiaries and the number of foreign directors. This generalization is true regardless of the industry or the country in which the transnational operates. Obviously, therefore, as transnationals reduce the number of their subsidiaries, they are not attempting to compensate for any loss that they deem this may bring to them by appointing more nationals from the countries in which they do business to the board of the parent.[22]

Does any of this matter? After all, three decades ago there was an enormous debate about the possible negative influence of subsidiaries in the nation, and now there is concern about their being removed. What is the issue? Some believe that none exists. It is argued that subsidiary boards in companies where there is a controlling foreign shareholder had little power, and so it only makes good sense in this new era of the transnational for these subsidiaries to be closed and Canadian boards abandoned. There is no reason, it is argued, to maintain such dysfunctional, expensive, unnecessary organizational structures in the globalized economy. With free trade, rapid movement of capital, and greater and quicker exchange of knowledge, local directors simply do not have even a marginal role to play.

On the other hand, a case can be made that transnational corporations and their subsidiaries are a dominant form of business structure in Canada. They play a major role in the economy. They are "major consumers of specialized services ... they are powerful participants in policy networks and public debates; they are benefactors or sponsors of artistic, educational, sporting and humanitarian organizations and events; they influence land markets, urban skylines; popular culture and attitudes of gender, race and class. Moreover, their executives and employees — in their personal capacities — are often an important clientele in specialized markets ... the restructuring of Canadian subsidiaries promises to dramatically weaken the market for legal services, deprive the arts and universities of much needed support, impoverish political discourse and exacerbate industrial conflict ... and (have) adverse effects on Canadian R&D, on higher education and skill training, on taxation, on urban development."[23]

The reality is that from the point of view of the large corporation, global-ization has led to a world without borders — the nation state really no longer matters. Because the nation state is not important, it follows that there is little need for full-blown foreign subsidiaries. Yet transnationals now play, and will continue to play, a major role in the Canadian economy, and what they do has, and will have, a major impact on the manner in which the economy of the nation evolves. So the question arises: Is it possible for a nation state to make economic policies for organizations that are not greatly influenced by the poli-cies of one national government?

ECONOMIC POLICY MAKING FOR THE TWENTY-FIRST CENTURY

During the past two decades, Canadian business has undergone enormous change. Firms in the natural-resource industries have experienced a new free-dom to enter markets throughout the world, while many domestically oriented organizations have faced unprecedented competition from foreign producers. Moreover, subsidiary firms that have traditionally dominated various sectors of the economy have been given new and different mandates, and have been restructured with a global, rather than a national, orientation. The goals of the basic policies flowing from the "staple thesis" have been achieved, are now impractical to implement or are contrary to international trade agreements. Obviously, the strategies of both business and government that were relevant for the twentieth century are not appropriate for the twenty-first.

While the engine of Canada's economic prosperity will continue to be international trade — albeit in a much freer marketplace — unlike in the past, Canadian domestic markets are being opened to competitors from all over the world. Consequently, the fundamental conditions for economic success, in the future, will be the capacity for producers of goods and services for all markets, domestic and international, to be able to compete effectively — to be as effi-cient as producers anywhere in the world.

Historically, competitive advantage in business, particularly international trade, was created by technology, capital and natural resources. However, in the twenty-first century, when it is possible to transfer capital and technology almost instantaneously to anywhere in the world, the underlying forces creating competitive advantages are different.

As a result, the priorities of government must change. No longer is it the responsibility of the public sector to produce goods and services directly, or to provide protection from competition, either domestic or international, for Canadian producers. Rather, what governments must do is simply to provide the framework of public policies necessary to ensure that Canadian firms can operate efficiently in a competitive world. And those policies will centre on providing the amenities for a high quality of life — health care, educational opportunities, public safety, competitive tax rates etc. None of these types of policies have a direct impact on the form and organization of businesses or the operation of the economy, but they all impact on how effective business can be. Such policies must now become the cornerstone of Canada's drive for competitive advantage.

Given this shift in emphasis in policy making, the dominant role which the federal government has played in creating economic policies should be reduced. It seems unlikely and, indeed, unnecessary for the federal government to undertake a mammoth consulting process to determine what the goals of the nation should be. Recent experience indicates that they have only modest success anyway. Moreover, many of the policies needed to assure competitiveness of Canadian businesses, at home and abroad, are in areas of responsibility of the provincial and municipal governments, not the federal. Such a change should not be difficult to make, given the fact that there is a movement to devolve more responsibilities to the provinces, and there appears to be a reaction against perceived excessive federal activities.

Similarly, the priorities of business leaders must change. Within the framework of social (not economic) policies, Canadian leaders must operate the most efficient business enterprises in the world. Whereas, in many respects, the economic success of Canada in the twentieth century was determined by policy makers and politicians, the success of Canada in the twenty-first century will be determined by business executives. And there is no reason why they should not be as successful as their predecessors in the public sector. After all, "they have access to capital at relatively competitive rates, the supply of professionally trained managers is increasing, the quality of the labour force is rising, governments are interfering in the domestic marketplace to a much lesser extent, and the demand for goods and services throughout the world is increasing dramatically."[24] In spite of all the changes of the last two decades, as Canadian business leaders prepare for the challenges of the twenty-first century, how much better could the business environment be?

It would be wrong to conclude that it is impossible, in a global world, for national governments and businesses to make policies which redound to the benefit of the nation and the businesses located within its boundaries. They can, but the policies, to be effective, must be quite different from those of the past. Priorities cannot be given to protecting sectors of the economy; they must encourage competition and innovation by providing a framework within which both will thrive.

Since economic changes, and economic goals, are seldom linear, it is impossible to predict what these changes may be. For example, in spite of the current extent of foreign ownership in the economy it does not, as the new century begins, appear to be a major concern of most Canadians. Indeed, it is difficult to believe that in the 1970s the political power of the nationalists at that time was such that the Trudeau governments enacted the Foreign Investment Review Act and the National Energy Policy. While supporters of the global economy and unfettered free markets currently overwhelmingly dominate public policy making and public opinion, there are already signs that this unquestioning support for freer international trade and markets may face a significant challenge early in the new century. Regardless, it is certain that if Canada is to fill its economic potential in the years ahead, leaders in both the private and public sectors must be receptive to new policies and adapt to them.

In the search for new strategies, one should never underestimate the importance of new ideas. As Keynes pointed out, there is nothing as powerful as an idea whose time has come. The seminal writings of Macintosh and Innis — their codification, simplification and popularization of the "staple thesis" — played an enormous part in creating solid support for the economic strategy of the twentieth century and the policies that flowed from it. Currently, there is widespread agreement about the influence of technological changes in transportation and communication and of the elimination of the many barriers to international trade on the national state and the business firm. What is badly needed is an analysis of the consequences of these changes for the entire Canadian economy, and of the types of policies that capitalize on the positive and most effectively mitigate against the negative impact of these changes. There is a basic need for an exposition of "the competitive thesis" and the strategy and policies which flow from it, in such a credible fashion that the leaders of all sectors of society — academic, business, political, labour and bureaucratic — will unite and support it. The nation needs another duo like Macintosh and Innis to create a strategy from which policies can be developed to assure prosperity for all Canadians during the new century.

NOTES

1. Hiroya Ueno, "Industrial Policy: Its Role and Its Limits." *Journal of Japanese Trade and Industry* (July–August 1983), as cited in Chalmers Johnson, ed., *The Industrial Policy Debate* (San Francisco: Institute for Contemporary Studies, 1984), p. 6.
2. For a complete discussion of the consultative process, see James Gillies, *Facing Reality: Consultation, Consensus and Making Economic Policy in the 21st Century* (Halifax: Institute for Research on Public Policy, 1986), esp. Chapter 8.
3. See John Kenneth Galbraith, *Economics and the Public Purpose* (Boston, MA: Houghton Mifflin, 1973), pp. 110–54.
4. Alfred Breton, *A Conceptual Basis for an Industrial Strategy* (Ottawa: Economic Council of Canada, 1974), pp. 11–32.
5. James Gillies, *Facing Reality: Consultation, Consensus and Making Economic Policy for the 21st Century* (Halifax, NS: Institute for Research on Public Policy, 1986), p. 33.
6. Charles L. Schultze, "Industrial Policy: A Dissent," *The Brookings Review* 2 (Fall, 1983), p. 9.
7. Peter F. Drucker, "The Changed World Economy," *Foreign Affairs* 64 (Spring, 1986), p. 791.

8. H.V. Nelles, "Looking Backwards: Interpreting Canadian Economic Development," in John Lennox, ed., *Se Connaître: Politics and Culture in Canada* (North York, ON: Robarts Centre for Canadian Studies, York University, 1985), p. 28.

9. *Inventing our Future: An Action Plan for Canada's Prosperity* (Ottawa: Steering Group on Prosperity, 1992), p. 1.

10. Ibid., p. 2.

11. Ibid., p. 1.

12. Ibid., pp. 66–71.

13. Ibid., p. 60.

14. R.S. Khemani, "The Dimensions of Corporate Concentration in Canada" in R.S. Khemani, D.M. Shapiro, and W.T. Stanbury, *Mergers, Corporate Concentration and Power in Canada* (Halifax, NS: The Institute for Research on Public Policy, 1988), p. 30.

15. See James Gillies, *Facing Reality: Consultation, Consensus and Making Economic Policy for the 21st Century* (Halifax, NS: The Institute for Research on Public Policy, 1986), esp. chapter 3.

16. Herschel Hardin, *A Nation Unaware: The Canadian Economic Culture* (Vancouver: J.J. Douglas, 1974).

17. B. Boothman, "The Dimensions of Canadian Big Business," paper delivered at the ASAC conference, Niagara Falls, 1991.

18. *International investment instruments: a compendium*, United Nations Conference on Trade and Development, Division on Transnational Corporations and Investment, 1996.

19. See, for example, J. D'Cruz, "Playing the Global Game: International Business Strategies," in *The New World Economic Order: Opportunities and Threats* (North York, ON: Captus Press, 1992), pp. 124–27.

20. Ibid., p. 124.

21. Harry W. Arthurs, "The Hollowing Out of the Canadian Corporation?" (Toronto: Osgoode Hall Law School, 1997). Unpublished manuscript, p. 7.

22. *Board Membership of Transnational Corporations* (Toronto: Schulich School of Business, York University, 1996). Unpublished manuscript.

23. Arthurs, op. cit., pp. 11–12.

24. James Gillies, "The Emerging Revolution in Canadian Business Leadership" in Gillies, ed., *Success: Canadian Leaders Prepare for the Next Century* (Toronto: Key Porter Books, 1996), p. 34.

Government, Society and Economic Performance

The previous section focused largely on the changing economic context in which Canadian firms find themselves operating today. This section focuses on the social and cultural context in which Canadian firms operate. The first article in the section, "The Changing Role of the Public Sector," by David Barrows and Tom Wesson, looks at the changing role of the public sector in modern society. The focus of the article is on examining our changing expectations of governments — starting with the explosion in government services, especially social services, in the 1960s through to the neo-conservative revival and the shrinking of governments in the 1990s. Many of the recent changes in the role which many Canadians (and others around the world) wish to see their governments play in society are driven by the pressures of globalization. In discussing the ability of governments to redefine their role in society in light of globalization, the authors look at the example of New Zealand, a nation which is often held up as an example of how nations can restructure their government and their entire economic system. As background for this discussion, the article also looks at the questions of why and how people first decided to come together to form broader societies. This leads to a discussion of the economic justifications for the creation of governments. The article also includes a brief appendix outlining the process of government decision making in Canada.

The second article in the section, "The Socio-Political Environment: The Quest for Accommodation," by John Saywell, looks at the politicalization of the Canadian economy and the fragmentation of Canadian society. The article covers an amazingly broad range of topics, including the constitutional debate and the meaning of federalism in Canada; Quebec separatism and language rights; the meaning of multiculturalism in Canada; and such socio-political issues as abortion and aboriginal rights. The main message of the article is that Canadian society is becoming increasingly complex and increasingly fragmented, and that our leaders seem to be poorly equipped to deal with these problems.

The final article in the section, David Foot's "The Effects of Changing Demographics: Marketing and Human Resource Trends," looks at Canadian society through a different lens: that of a demographer. Foot's analysis of Canada's population allows him not just to address who we are as people, but also to address who we are going to become as our population ages. This discussion leads Foot to draw many provocative conclusions for Canadian businesses based on the changes which will occur in their pools of prospective customers and employees.

The Changing Role of the Public Sector

David Barrows and Tom Wesson

The public sector has an enormous impact upon all Canadians. The purpose of this article is to review the historic role of the government in society and how this role has evolved with the development of the welfare state and the rise of neo-conservative ideas around the world. We will discuss why people come together and how societies have been organized. We will then talk about public economics and the economic rationale for government involvement in the marketplace. Next we will discuss the nature of the policy fields within which governments operate and the changing role of the state as internal and external forces have caused a reassessment of the historic role of government. We use New Zealand as an example of a nation which has re-engineered and redefined its approach to governmental structures. We conclude with a discussion of the need for accountability frameworks and potential future directions in public involvement in Canadian society. We also include an appendix which discusses the decision-making process in Canadian governments.

COMMUNITIES

People have always come together to organize themselves collectively. Historically, people have developed communities for purposes of defence, socialization and economic betterment and improvement. Many of the communities that have been established have been on the basis of religious, linguistic or racial characteristics.

The organization of government in small, homogeneous communities is an easier task than it is in today's complex, heterogeneous societies. Tribes tended to be composed of similar people usually, from extended families. The decision-making processes in these tribal communities tended to be, if not democratic, at least easily understood and accepted by the members of the community.

Early democracies also had decision-making structures which were much simpler than today's complex government structures. In ancient Athens, citizens congregated in the centre of the city and voted directly on the issues of the day. Later, the New England town hall decision-making processes were also highly democratic and retained a strong tribal quality. In the early New England colonies the members of the community would convene in the town hall, and collective community decisions were resolved at that time. Obviously, such decision-making processes were facilitated by the homogeneous nature of the community and by the capacity to fit all of the members of the community into a relatively confined space.

As societies became larger and more complex it was necessary to move to a representative form of governmental structure. Philosophically, the representative democratic model could be organized on either a liberal or conservative model. The traditional liberal model is perhaps best articulated by the economist Adam Smith, who talked about the invisible hand of the marketplace and the need for a limited involvement of government, particularly in economic matters. The conservative view is far more interventionist. Conservatives have an inherent mistrust in the market's ability to allocate resources optimally. This use of the term conservative should not be confused with its modern political meaning. In the sense used here, both Karl Marx, with his view that the means of production, at least initially, should be owned collectively by the state on behalf of all of the citizens of the community, and the mercantilist ideas of the colonial powers, would both be labelled conservatives.

These quite different approaches to government reflect both philosophical and practical considerations with respect to the optimal size of government and the roles and responsibilities that government should undertake.

PUBLIC ECONOMICS

As stated earlier, one reason for societies to organize collectively is for economic betterment. The branch of economics which deals with the economic actions of governments is called public economics. In addition to the philosophical approaches to the question of the optimal role for government to play in society, there are economic bases for the intervention of the state in the free market economy. The principles for state intervention are based upon the concept of market failure.

It is acknowledged by all economists that free and efficient markets may fail in a number of ways, including:

1. The failure of competition.
2. Public goods.
3. Externalities.
4. Incomplete markets.
5. Inefficient capital markets.
6. Information failure.
7. Macroeconomic disequilibrium.

A **failure of competition** is said to exist in an industry when there is a logical and inevitable movement to a concentration of power in the market's structure to the point that the market becomes an oligopoly or perhaps even a monopoly. The ability of private-sector actors to gain and exercise market power may result in non-optimal economic and social outcomes such as higher prices, lower levels of service or lower wages than would have been achieved in a purely competitive marketplace. One group of industries in which a competitive structure fails to sustain itself are the so-called natural monopolies. These industries are often characterized by high levels of fixed costs of market entry which make it almost impossible, and probably not socially optimal, for more than one firm to survive in the industry. Typical examples of such industries are electricity distribution, cable television and industries such as commercial aircraft manufacturing where there are economies of scale which are not exhausted at a production level sufficient to fulfil the entire demand of the market.

Public goods are goods which are either not supplied by the private sector or are supplied in quantities below their economically optimal level of output because it is difficult to exclude people from using, or taking advantage of, the good once it is supplied in any quantity. Thus, producers of the good have a difficult time capturing the economic value created by the good, and therefore underproduce. Obviously, this provides a powerful rationale for the delivery of public goods through collective, governmental processes. Examples of public goods include national defence, a whole range of areas of consumer and public protection such as marine safety and consumer goods, and environmental protection such as park land.

Externalities occur when third parties are affected by the actions of private sector actors. Free markets may experience both positive and negative externalities. Positive externalities are those which are beneficial to third parties, while negative externalities are those which are harmful to the welfare of third parties. Externalities result in non-optimal output decisions because the party making the decision does not consider the positive or negative value of the externality. The economists' classic example of positive externalities is that of the apiary and orchard located next to each other. When deciding how many bees to have, the bee-keeper does not consider the role played by his bees in pollinating the fruit blossoms in the orchard. Similarly, the farmer does not consider the role his fruit play in supplying nectar for the bees. Thus, with the bee-keeper and farmer each acting independently, their output decisions may be different than if they coordinated to maximize the value of their combined output.

More important examples include the positive externalities which occur through research and development and training and education undertaken by private-sector participants. Research often leads to discoveries which create value for third parties. For example, the total economic benefits of the invention of the transistor at Bell Laboratories in the 1950s have been enormous, but Bell Laboratories and its successor companies have not been able to capture anything close to the full value of this invention. Since the value of such positive externalities is not captured by the firm undertaking the research, it has been argued that there tends to be an under-investment in such areas of positive externality. Patent protection is granted in part to alleviate this problem. Similar under-investment can take place in the area of employee training.

Conversely, as individuals and collectively, we bear many negative externalities when the negative consequences of economic activities are not borne by the original parties to the transaction. A classic example is in the field of environmental pollution, where such pollution may impose significant third party costs which are not passed back to the polluter. Both positive and negative externalities are sometimes referred to as spillover effects.

Incomplete markets are markets which do not provide for a full range of products and services. Free markets may be incomplete from the perspective of social optimality. For example, some types of insurance, such as risk insurance required by farmers or flood insurance in flood-prone areas, may not be available through the private sector. Another possible example of incomplete markets is the poor record of banks in providing capital to minority-owned enterprises.

It has been argued that capital markets are particularly prone to being incomplete when they have difficulty assessing the risk involved in an investment. This is more likely when project returns are highly variable and are spread over long periods of time. If this is the case, capital markets will consistently under-invest in these types of projects and, therefore, there would be a need for government intervention. Capital markets may be incomplete in their ability to raise capital for projects such as the construction of hydro-electric generators or the development of oil off the coast of Newfoundland.

Information failures occur in many types of markets, particularly when there is asymmetry of knowledge between the buyer and the seller. A classic example of such a situation is in the market for used cars. In a used car purchase all of the information resides with the seller, and the buyer is at a significant disadvantage in the transaction. The seller knows about the car's past performance and how well it has been maintained, while the buyer can only guess at these things based on the car's outward appearance. Intuitively, it may seem that such an asymmetry can only work to the seller's advantage, and this is often the case. However, it may be that potential buyers perceive themselves to be at such a disadvantage in the market that they assume the worst about all of the products offered or that they choose not to participate in the market at all. In this case both the potential buyer and the seller may be harmed. The existence of information asymmetries in the used-car market helps to explain the old axiom that a new car loses 30 per cent of its value the minute it is driven off the lot. Many buyers would much rather buy a new car than a nearly new one and, therefore, the prices of nearly new cars are much lower than logic would dictate. Information asymmetries also help explain why many manufacturers (especially high-end ones) are now offering used-car warranties.

The inability of the potential buyer to secure adequate information may represent a need for consumer protection through industry regulation or self-regulation. Thus, the government makes sure that our banks are prudently managed and that airlines properly maintain their fleet. We also see organizations, such as the Canadian Marketers Association (formerly the Canadian Direct Marketers Association), which impose restrictions on their members, who join voluntarily in order to improve their credibility.

An extension of the idea of information failures is the concept of the "winner's curse," which applies to situations involving multiple bidders for a good of uncertain value. Bidding on oil-drilling rights is an excellent example to illustrate this concept.

No one knows for certain the amount of oil under a patch of ground until the site is actually drilled. However, one might expect the average of the estimates from all bidders would be closer to the true amount than any individual estimate. In a competitive bidding situation, if bidders for the drilling rights are willing to bid up to their estimate of the value of the rights (the net present value of the oil to be found at the site), the winner will be the bidder with the highest estimate. This estimate will clearly be above the average which, as we have already stated, is a better estimate than any single estimate. Thus, it is very likely that the purchaser will overpay for the rights.

Macroeconomic disequilibrium occurs regularly in our economy. The history of capitalist economies has been one of cyclical macroeconomic activity resulting in inflationary booms followed by recessionary busts of varying intensities. One of the potential roles for government is macroeconomic stabilization through the tax-and-expenditure system. We prefer smooth economic performance to the naturally occurring large swings caused by macroeconomic cycles. We are, in fact, willing to lower slightly our average income over the business cycle in order to reduce the variation in income we experience. As Figure 1 shows, over time, governments have become better at controlling the business cycle, especially since the end of World War II.

Given these economic rationales for government intervention in the economy, we will now look more closely at how governments intervene.

POLICY AREAS

It has been stated that governments are actively involved in primarily three major areas or policy fields — social, justice and economic. However, it is often not possible to make clear-cut distinctions among these areas. Is antitrust policy a justice policy or an economic one? Is employment insurance social or economic? We could pose an almost endless list of such questions. It may be clearer, therefore, to think of government's role in society in terms of the actions governments perform.

Clearly, one of the primary activities of government is to set the legal framework within which members of the community operate. Governments indicate what is acceptable and unacceptable behaviour and what are appropriate and inappropriate community standards. In this context, government establishes a whole host of laws, rules and regulations in a wide array of areas, from competition policy to immigration or criminal justice policy. Governments are also responsible for the production and distribution of goods and services in a wide range of areas such as health, education, national defence and infrastructure. Governments purchase large volumes of goods and services in order to operate their systems. Finally, governments tax and redistribute income and wealth in society in order to meet the broad-based objectives of the population.

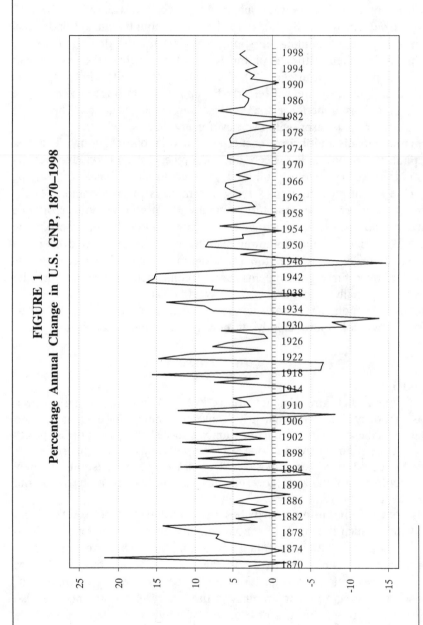

FIGURE 1

Percentage Annual Change in U.S. GNP, 1870–1998

Source: Robert J. Gordon, *The American Business Cycle: Continuity and Change*, Appendix B: Historical Data, Table 1, pp. 281–83. Chicago: University of Chicago Press, 1986; and US Department of Commerce, Bureau of Economic Analysis, Survey of Current Business, August 2000.

THE CHANGING ROLE OF GOVERNMENT

The policy goals of governments and their methods of achieving them are constantly evolving over time. Some have argued that a major shift in the role of government is currently taking place in Canada.

In earlier, simpler, times the role of government was fairly clear. Essentially, governments provided for infrastructure, defence and education. Social services, if any, were provided by religious organizations or through charities. Government activities were both very easy to see and very measurable. Roads were built or were not built. Wars were won or were not won. The educational system produced an acceptable number of competent and capable individuals or it did not. As modern life has become more complex, there has been an explosion in the roles and responsibilities of government. Governments are now actively involved in a wide variety of fields, from health care to transportation, to community and social services.

Perhaps the field of social services is the one in which we have seen the greatest increase in modern states' involvement in the day-to-day life of their citizens. Furthermore, it can also be argued that as governments have moved into areas that reflect human behaviour, their ability to influence events and our ability to measure the impacts of government have become more and more limited. As well, contradictions have emerged between an economically efficient state and one that provides the level of social services demanded by modern voters.

As the state has grown and become more involved in the lives of its citizens, economic efficiency has been only one of many criteria that have been used to evaluate the impact of government. Considerable emphasis is placed upon the equitable distribution of income and wealth and the provision of a strong social safety net. Similarly, the justice system is concerned with individual and collective rights and responsibilities based upon the legislation enacted by governments. This may or may not lead to an economically efficient justice system.

The peoples' view of the role of the state in the economy has been inconsistent. There has been an expectation that governments would be efficient and effective. However, for a long period of time governments were seen as a major source of employment opportunities, which could be created for supporters of the party in power. As well, government has been viewed by some analysts as an employer of last resort. That is, those who have been unable to secure alternative employment should, under this view, be able to find meaningful work in the public sector. It should be noted that this point of view still exists among many people in both the developed and the developing nations.

Growth in Government Expenditures

There have been a number of attempts to develop a theory to explain the growth in government expenditures. One of the earliest attempts was by Adolph Wagner. Wagner's Law suggests an elastic relationship between the growth in GDP and the rise in government spending. That is, an increase in GDP would produce a more than proportionate increase in government spending. Wagner

FIGURE 2
Government Expenditures as Percentage of Gross Domestic Product
for Selected Years 1926–2000

	Expenditures (% of GDP[a])
1926	15.7
1929	16.1
1933	27.4
1939	21.4
1944	20.5
1947	24.3
1950	21.3
1960	28.8
1970	34.1
1980	39.6
1985	46.0
1990	46.9
1995	46.3
2000	40.2

[a] Expressed as a percentage of gross national product up to the year 1947.

Source: Statistics Canada, *National Income and Expenditure Accounts, 1926 to 1974*, cat. 13–001; and Canada, Department of Finance, *Economic Reference Tables*, August 1966, cat. F1-26/1996E; and *Fiscal Reference Tables*, October 2000, cat. F1-26/2000E.

suggested that as income increases, citizens' demand for social goods and services would increase at a faster rate.

Data would suggest that this theory has a proven track record. Figure 2 shows an increase in government expenditures as a percentage of GDP in Canada over the last 70 years. Figure 3 indicates that this relationship is also true for many of the developed nations. However, the data indicate that the proportions are much lower in the United States. In fact, the Canadian statistics are more typical of a European country.

Figure 4 indicates that the largest increase in Canadian government expenditures has been in the form of transfer payments to individuals. The proportion of direct transfer payments to businesses is relatively small. Figure 5 shows that the majority of expenditures for fiscal year 1996–1997 for all levels of government are concentrated in the areas of health, social services and education. It should be noted that debt charges constituted the second-largest budgetary expenditure item in that year.

Beginning in the 1970s, Canadian governments experienced ongoing deficit financing. This was a new experience. There was no precedent for deficit financing in the absence of war or significant economic downturn. Budget deficits occurred during boom periods as well as during recession. Figure 6 shows that debt increased significantly as a percentage of GDP.

FIGURE 3
International Comparison of Total Government Expenditures as Percentage of Gross Domestic Product or Gross National Product for Selected Years 1970–1999[a]

	Percentage of GDP or GNP			
	1970	1980	1990	1999
CANADA	33.5	38.8	46.0	40.7
France	38.5	46.1	49.8	48.9
Germany	38.3	47.9	45.1	43.5
Italy	33.0	42.1	53.4	51.2
Japan	19.0	32.0	31.3	38.1
U.K.	36.7	43.0	39.9	39.3
U.S.	30.0	31.4	32.8	30.1

[a] Based on OECD data.

Source: Canada, Department of Finance, *Fiscal Reference Tables*, October 2000, cat. F1-26/2000E.

FIGURE 4
Shares of Government Expenditure by Economic Classification for Selected Years 1926–1999

	Goods and Services	Transfers to Persons	Transfers to Business	Gross Capital Formation	Interest on Public Debt	Other
			(percentage of total)			
1926	48.1	9.1	0.2	13.1	28.5	0.9
1939	47.0	18.8	1.4	12.3	22.8	0.6
1944	82.4	4.3	4.5	1.6	7.1	0.1
1950	47.3	25.1	1.8	12.1	13.3	0.4
1965	50.0	21.5	3.0	14.7	10.1	0.7
1975	48.6	24.9	6.9	9.2	9.6	0.9
1985	42.7	26.7	5.2	5.7	18.0	0.2
1995	40.6	31.1	2.7	4.8	20.5	0.4
1999	47.5	26.4	2.7	4.2	18.5	0.7

Source: Statistics Canada, *National and Expenditure Accounts, 1926–1974*, cat. 13–531; and Department of Finance, *Fiscal Reference Tables*, October 2000, cat. F1-26/2000E.

Figure 7 indicates that this growth in debt was not unique to Canada. However, the data show that Canadian debt, as a proportion of GDP, was much higher than the average for the G7 countries. This pattern of performance was not sustainable. It was necessary for Canadian governments to act aggressively to redress this very serious issue.

DAVID BARROWS AND TOM WESSON

FIGURE 5
Consolidated Government Expenditure Functions, 1996–97
(Financial Management System Basis)

Expenditure	Total ($ million)	Share Spent by	
		Federal Government	Provincial Territorial and Local Governments
		(percentage of total)	
General services	12,228	47.2	52.8
Protection of persons and property	28,465	55.9	44.1
Transportation and communications	17,657	18.1	81.9
Health	52,505	2.2	97.8
Social services	98,548	62.8	37.2
Education	54,255	6.1	93.9
Environment	8,456	14.8	85.2
Foreign affairs and international assistance	3,761	100.0	0.0
Recreation and culture	9,142	31.0	69.0
Resource conservation and industrial development	12,941	44.6	55.4
Debit charges	63,259	53.4	46.6
Other	10,033	45.0	55.0
Total	371,250	38.5	61.5

Note: Intergovernment transactions are eliminated. Transfers from one level of government to another are excluded from the expenditure of the paying government but are included in the expenditure of the receiving government. The shares therefore reflect those transactions occurring between level of government and the general public.

Source: Statistics Canada, *Public Sector Statistics*, cat. 213-XPB, April 2000.

FIGURE 6
Trends in Federal Public Debt, 1927–2001
($ million, and percentage of GDP)

Fiscal Year	Net Public Debt	Net Debt Percentage of GDP[a]
1926–27	2,348	45.6
1936–37	3,084	66.6
1946–47	12,669	106.6
1956–57	11,446	34.8
1966–67	17,707	27.5
1976–77	41,517	21.0
1986–87	273,323	54.1
1996–97	583,186	69.9
2000–01	576,824	56.9

[a] GDP for the corresponding calendar year.

Source: Canada, Department of Finance, *The Budget*, February 20, 1990 (Ottawa), p. 148; *Fiscal Reference Papers*. October 1997 (Ottawa), p. 23; and TD Economics, *Government Finance Tables*.

FIGURE 7
International Comparison of Government Net Debt[a] in
Selected Years 1980–1999 for G7 Countries

	Percentage of GDP				
	1980	*1985*	*1990*	*1995*	*1999*
CANADA	13.0	34.7	43.1	67.6	55.3
France	−3.3	10.8	16.3	36.0	43.0
Germany	9.3	19.2	20.7	42.1	47.0
Italy	53.0	80.0	84.4	108.7	104.4
Japan	16.4	25.9	10.6	13.0	37.7
U.K.	36.2	30.6	18.8	41.0	38.7
U.S.	21.6	32.2	38.5	59.3	49.7
G7 Average	20.5	31.6	32.1	50.2	50.2

[a] Total government net debt (all levels of government) national income and expenditure accounts basis.

Source: Canada, Department of Finance, *Fiscal Reference Tables*, October 2000 (Ottawa).

Government in Canada reduced expenditures. As a result, almost all of the governments in Canada now have balanced budgets or a surplus of revenue over expenditures. Nonetheless, there is still a large outstanding debt as a result of the period of deficit financing.

An important public policy issue is now the question of the proper use of the budget surplus. One estimate suggests that the federal government could have a budget surplus of $60-billion over a five-year period. The funding could be used for debt reduction, lowering taxes and/or new spending initiatives. Some studies suggest that higher personal and corporate taxes in Canada, with respect to the United States, have resulted in reduced Canadian competitiveness and have contributed to a "brain-drain" of managerial, scientific and professional workers from Canada.

During the period of rapid growth in governments, it was assumed by many analysts that the increase in the size of government would lead to a continuation of efficient, effective, measurable and beneficial government programs and services. However, this was not the case. The introduction of many programs and services was ill-conceived, and the ability to influence individuals and change human behaviour appears to be somewhat limited at best. As a result, there has been a rethinking of the beneficial effects of significant government intervention in areas which require massive behavioural change from both individuals and institutions.

In part, our evolving view of how big a role government should play in our lives has been moving in parallel to our perception of how governments make decisions. Figure 8 outlines three alternative models of government decision making. Clearly, very few Canadians today have the sort of faith in

FIGURE 8
Alternative Models of Government Decision-Making Process

RATIONAL	INCREMENTAL	PUBLIC CHOICE
A most desirable approach that assumes decisions are made with a comprehensive benefit-cost analysis of all alternatives available. *Pros* All alternatives are evaluated. *Cons* Analysis cannot be fully implemented because of the lack of full information and the required predictive capability.	An approach builds on past decisions and modifies policies and programs at the margin. *Pros* A pragmatic approach that recognizes conflicting goals, limited information and insufficient predictive capacity. *Cons* Slow in response to changes in the external environment.	This approach describes decisions as consequences of the relative power of the participants. It assumes all participants have their own self-interests and policies are vehicles for politicians to obtain political support. *Pros* Reflect real-world decision making. *Cons* Impossible to anticipate potential public-policy initiatives.

Source: Adapted from David Barrows and Sandra Morris, "Managing Public Policy Issues," Long Range Planning, Vol. 22 (December 1989).

our government which would be implied by a belief that governments made decisions rationally. Instead, we see government decision making as a combination of bureaucratic incrementalism and special interest politics. Thus, many of us are reluctant to hand over to the government any responsibilities beyond those which absolutely must be performed by a central authority.

E-GOVERNMENT

The electronic revolution is having a profound effect on government as well as on the private sector. E-government is an important component in government's attempt to enhance services to citizens. A recent study by the consulting firm Delloite Touche analyzed the concept of "consumer-centric" government. The study documents attempts by governments around the world to refocus activities on citizens as clients, or customers.

Delloite Touche suggests a six-stage approach to the development of E-government. In the first stage, Web pages are employed as an electronic encyclopedia. The objective is the provision of accurate and timely information which will allow citizens to conduct transactions with a government department or agency. In the second stage, citizens can execute single transaction on line.

The third stage will establish a single point of entry which facilitates multiple transactions. It is important to note that these transactions could be with the private as well as with the public sector. For example, the study discusses an Australian case where citizens can pay government utility bills, manage accounts and conduct stock market trades through a single entry point. The fourth phase will allow government to target the specific needs of citizens. This could greatly facilitate the provision of services targeted at the individual level. The fifth stage would permit the grouping of transactions. At this stage, the boundaries between government departments and agencies would no longer be relevant to the citizen/consumer. Now the focus would be on the transactions and the best grouping of activities from the perspective of the citizen. Finally, the sixth stage would have no gaps between the counter, the front office, and the processing centre, or the back office. In the final stage there would be seamless service delivery.

It should be noted that the technology in E-government could be utilized for other purposes. For example, it would be possible to contact polling or referendums on an ongoing basis. There is even the potential to return to the original Greek or New England town hall concept. Citizens would be able to voice interests and concerns, or even vote, on important issues in real time.

GLOBALIZATION

In addition to the inability to measure the effectiveness of many of the new areas of activity of government, there have been a number of other changes that have impacted government in the last 25 years. For the sake of simplicity we have categorized these changes under the broad heading of globalization.

In the economic sphere there is an increasing requirement to compete internationally. This process of the globalization of the production and distribution of goods and services has led to the need for competitive government structures that support the work of the private sector. There has been an impetus towards more efficient and effective government in order to enhance our nation's global competitiveness.

As a result of the emphasis on competitiveness in government, economic and management concepts have been introduced into the field of public administration. Concepts such as benefit-cost analysis, total quality management, customer service, team building, etc. have been taken from the private sector management literature and incorporated into the new public administration.

The utilization of information technologies has significantly facilitated the introduction of new management practices. The use of client-server technology has allowed for the more efficient collection and distribution of information and has permitted the re-engineering of many government processes and activities. For example, the province of Ontario has been able to re-engineer the new business registration process such that the time to register a new, unincorporated business has been reduced from as long as six weeks to 10 to 20 minutes. This registration process can be undertaken electronically at a distance from government offices.

The introduction of program management techniques, comprehensive audits and program evaluation have indicated that many programs do not work (such as regional economic development), and in some cases may actually make a situation worse (such as some forms of welfare assistance). These results of program evaluations and comprehensive audits are indeed quite startling and have caused many to question the advisability of programs and services that were based upon highly laudatory policy concepts but which were incapable of efficient and effective implementation. Since the productivity slowdown of the early 1970s there has been greater and greater pressure on governments to reduce expenditures, or at least the growth in expenditures, in order to respond to the new fiscal realities.

An overly simplistic view of the debate regarding the optimal size of the government is to state that liberals like big governments and conservatives prefer smaller governments. But of course, even phrases like liberal and conservative are highly ambiguous, and at best can only be applied in a relative sense. A politician who would be called conservative (or Conservative) in Canada would be too liberal on many issues to appeal to all but a few voters in the United States.

A more fundamental question than the *size* of the state is the *role* of the state in the twenty-first century. Certainly, with increasing globalization, the ability of the state to isolate a society from the international economic realities is limited at best. However, the nation state certainly can get its economic, social, political and justice policies wrong. In this case the nation state may well put its private sector at a competitive disadvantage and therefore contribute to slower economic growth. While this might suggest that the state must completely align itself with international pressures, this is not the case. The state has a number of options with respect to how it will organize production, distribution and income transfers within the context of global pressures that are impacting upon all jurisdictions. One nation which has been touted in recent years as a model for other nations to follow as they attempt to redefine the role of government in society is New Zealand. We will now look at the New Zealand model in more detail.

THE NEW ZEALAND MODEL

New Zealand is a small, developed nation. In 1938 the New Zealand gross domestic product per capita was approximately 92 per cent that of the United States. By 1988, New Zealand had failed to keep pace with growth in the rest of the developed world to the point that its gross domestic product per capita had fallen to only 50 per cent of that of the United States. Over this time, public sector and private sector debt increased such that by 1984 public and private sector debt amounted to 95 per cent of total gross domestic product. In fact, net public debt was over 30 per cent of gross domestic product, the current account deficit was 8.7 per cent of gross domestic product and the federal government fiscal debt was 6.5 per cent of gross domestic product by that year. New Zealand found itself in a crisis situation in which it was unable to meet its international obligations, and the situation was deemed to require immediate action.

The actions taken by the New Zealand government were both broad and deep.[1] They were intended to reduce the size of the government and to make public management in New Zealand more efficient and effective. Among the many changes made to reduce the role of the government in the economy were the elimination of government controls on interest rates, foreign exchange, prices, rents and wages; ending agricultural subsidies and export assistance; and removing protectionist measures, such as import licence requirements and tariffs. In order to improve public management, the government of New Zealand reformed the budget and tax systems; instituted measures to make public sector employment conditions on a par with those in the private sector; privatized many crown corporations and contracted-out many activities; and improved the government's information and accounting systems. Finally, in 1993 New Zealand announced its intention to implement proportional representation in the legislative branch of its government. Many of these reforms were announced in a flurry of activity during the period 1984 to 1986. In order to ease the transition these massive changes would cause, phase in periods of up to 10 years were used.

Figure 9 illustrates the configuration of the old state sectors in New Zealand. As can be seen, the lines of authority were from the minister through the control departments, which acted to control the activities of the organizations receiving funds through them, to the departments, which were large in scale and responsible for all programmatic activities. Figure 10 indicates the new model, where departments have shrunk in size and the control departments have been replaced by central agencies the role of which is expanded considerably. The central agencies now act to coordinate the activities of the various departments, Crown entities and state-owned enterprises.

Much of the actual delivery of government services in New Zealand today is undertaken by state-owned enterprises and Crown entities through a contracting-out mechanism designed to inject market forces into public sector delivery. Memoranda of understanding are developed which provide for hands-off day-to-day administration, allowing the service delivery agencies to bid on the provision of services and to respond to the impacts of market forces.

The economic renaissance of New Zealand has been well documented. Economic growth has increased, and the government fiscal situation has been significantly improved. There are, however, a number of concerns which have been expressed with respect to the New Zealand model. It is argued that there have been significant losers as a result of this transformation, and that those people have not been adequately compensated. From a public management perspective, it has also been argued that the creation of autonomous entities for the delivery of services has resulted in the creation of vertical silos, such that these agencies have little, if any, rationale for discussing mutually advantageous issues. To deliver public policy efficiently and effectively, it is necessary to address issues that cut across departments and agencies. For example, land use planning for municipalities must be correlated with activities taking place in agriculture, and must also reflect transportation and other infrastructure requirements. Such coordination, it has been argued, may be more difficult in

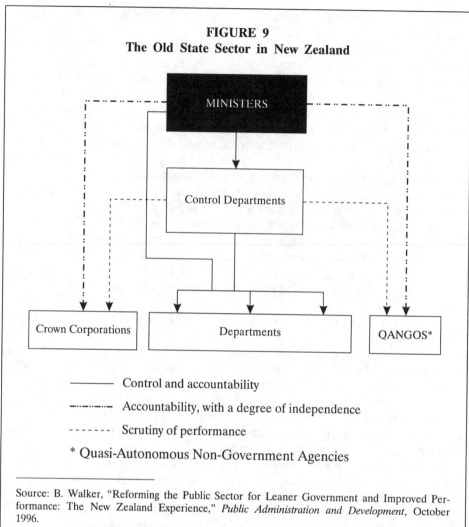

FIGURE 9
The Old State Sector in New Zealand

—————— Control and accountability

–··–··– Accountability, with a degree of independence

- - - - - - Scrutiny of performance

* Quasi-Autonomous Non-Government Agencies

Source: B. Walker, "Reforming the Public Sector for Leaner Government and Improved Performance: The New Zealand Experience," *Public Administration and Development*, October 1996.

an environment where services are provided by individual delivery agencies each of which works under the terms of a memorandum of understanding with respect to measurable activities in their specific area.

ACCOUNTABILITY FRAMEWORKS

The perceived success of the New Zealand model has led to work being undertaken with respect to more sophisticated and effective accountability frameworks. This is reflected in the movement towards performance management measurement and the implementation of performance audits and program evaluation methodologies.

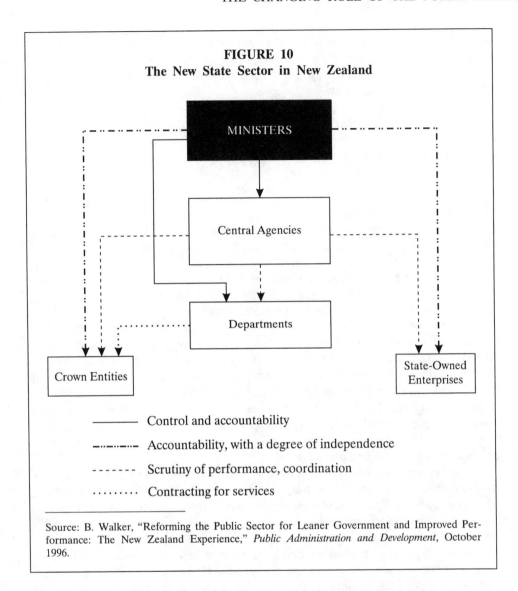

FIGURE 10
The New State Sector in New Zealand

MINISTERS

Central Agencies

Departments

Crown Entities

State-Owned
Enterprises

———— Control and accountability

—··——··—· Accountability, with a degree of independence

- - - - - - Scrutiny of performance, coordination

·········· Contracting for services

Source: B. Walker, "Reforming the Public Sector for Leaner Government and Improved Performance: The New Zealand Experience," *Public Administration and Development*, October 1996.

In a broader sense, it has evolved into a discussion aimed at redefining the roles and responsibilities of the state in modern society. The new view of public administration sees government as undertaking core businesses. These core businesses would include providing policy directives to service providers and providing those public goods which are naturally the sole purview of the state, such as defence.

There is a possibility of contracting-out literally all of the remaining activities to private sector delivery partners. There are a number of methodologies and approaches to contracting-out that include public-private sector partnerships and alternative service-delivery models. For example, in a recent paper Auld discusses the advantages of the privatization of Canadian universities or, if not the complete privatization of universities, then the injection of market mechanisms to make the university system more efficient, effective and responsive to the needs of the community.[2]

This view of contracting-out has led to the notion of the "contract state," in which there is diminished role for government as the provider of goods and services and more focus on government as a policy development agency, with service delivery through a more efficient and effective private sector.

FUTURE DIRECTIONS

The move to a contract state has been questioned by a number of policy analysts, who have pointed out that not all of the private sector is efficient and effective. At the same time, there is general public grumbling (if not actual outcry) over the profits made by Canadian banks. It is a fallacy to assume that for any and all goods and services, delivery through the private sector must be, by definition, better than delivery through public sector means.

A question that we have introduced in this article but, of course, have left unanswered is: What should we, as citizens, expect of our government? What should governments try to achieve on our behalf, and what tasks are best left unattempted? To many so called neo-conservatives the current backlash against government is a direct result of the failure of our governments' efforts to create what Pierre Trudeau referred to as a "just society." Others argue that while our governments' records are not perfect, their successes outweigh their failures, and that the failures are a result of poorly designed or executed programs, not of overly ambitious goals.

In a recent *Harvard Business Review* article Henry Mintzberg argues that "the object of democracy is a free people, not free institutions."[3] Mintzberg expresses concern that it is necessary to establish the right balance between public and private sector activities. He argues for the need for a proud, not an emasculated, government sector.

As we move into the twenty-first century, it is clear that governments must become more efficient, effective and responsive. However, that does not mean that government must disappear, to be replaced by a presumed efficient private sector. Rather, there is a need to find the right balance between the public and private sectors in the economy. The challenge will be to continually find the right mix with roles and responsibilities evolving over time. Philosophic approaches with respect to the role of the state will likely hinder, rather than help, in this assessment. It is argued that the role and responsibility of government will best be determined in a pragmatic sense that will reflect changing technologies and the expectations of society with respect to the roles and responsibilities that are to be played both by the public and the private sectors.

How we as a society define these roles, either explicitly or implicitly through our choice of government, will have a profound effect on Canadian society in the future. This effect will extend far beyond our economic and material well-being. How we define the role of government in our society will affect its very fabric — how rich and poor interact, how we care for our sick and elderly citizens, how we educate our children, and so on. The role chosen for government within Canada will also affect how we interact with other nations and what our role might be on the world stage. In fact, failure to develop some sort of national consensus on these issues may even contribute to the break-up of Canada, as various provinces and/or regions develop incompatible views of the role of government in Canadian society.

Throughout the world people are wrestling with the question of what role governments should play in modern societies. From the former Soviet Union and China to Ralph Klein's Alberta and Mike Harris' Ontario, there are profound changes occurring in the relationship between people and their governments. Where these changes will lead and, in fact, where they should lead are two of the great questions of our time.

APPENDIX: AN OVERVIEW OF GOVERNMENT DECISION MAKING IN CANADA

While it is clearly well beyond the scope of this article to enter into a discussion of any depth on the issue of how governments in Canada function, it is useful to quickly review a number of the key features of our system of government. If we are to discuss the role of government in Canada in any meaningful way, we must understand how governments in Canada perform their function and who in our society actually defines that at any given point in time.

The system of government we have in Canada is a parliamentary democracy. Alternatively, it can be labelled a constitutional monarchy. These phrases taken together describe the functioning of, and the relationship between, two of the three major branches of our government — the legislative branch and the executive branch. The third branch of our government, the judicial branch, is not a policy-making branch in the traditional sense, but rather interprets and enforces the policies made by the other branches (although, in some cases, the judicial branch does in some sense make policy by setting legal precedents with its decisions).

When we think of our government, we tend to think of aspects of the legislative branch — the House of Commons meeting in the Parliament Buildings in Ottawa, voting in elections, appealing to our local Member of Parliament on some matter of local interest and so on. The legislative branch of the government of Canada is comprised principally of two bodies — the House of Commons and the Senate. In theory, this is the branch of our government where ultimate power lies. The executive branch cannot do anything that the legislative branch has not empowered it to do, and the judicial branch exists only to enforce and interpret the decisions of the legislative branch. The two principal means by which the legislature empowers the executive branch are through enabling legislation and the approval of the expenditure budget.

However, as we shall see, in practice the executive branch has a great deal of influence over the legislature, especially in a majority government. The executive largely controls the agenda of the legislature and, given the strict adherence to party discipline which has traditionally marked Canadian politics, has a very strong say in the output of the legislative process.

A session of Parliament opens with the throne speech, delivered by the Governor-General but written by the governing party. In the throne speech the government outlines its legislative agenda for the session and generally sets the tone for the session. The other major cyclical event in Parliament's schedule is the annual budget speech, delivered by the Minister of Finance in February or March of each year. In the budget speech the government outlines its economic policies and outlook for the coming year,

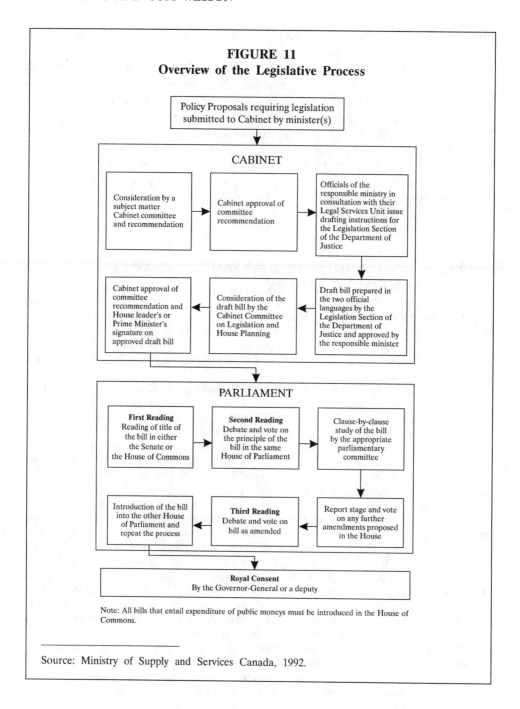

FIGURE 11
Overview of the Legislative Process

Policy Proposals requiring legislation submitted to Cabinet by minister(s)

CABINET

Consideration by a subject matter Cabinet committee and recommendation

Cabinet approval of committee recommendation

Officials of the responsible ministry in consultation with their Legal Services Unit issue drafting instructions for the Legislation Section of the Department of Justice

Cabinet approval of committee recommendation and House leader's or Prime Minister's signature on approved draft bill

Consideration of the draft bill by the Cabinet Committee on Legislation and House Planning

Draft bill prepared in the two official languages by the Legislation Section of the Department of Justice and approved by the responsible minister

PARLIAMENT

First Reading
Reading of title of the bill in either the Senate or the House of Commons

Second Reading
Debate and vote on the principle of the bill in the same House of Parliament

Clause-by-clause study of the bill by the appropriate parliamentary committee

Introduction of the bill into the other House of Parliament and repeat the process

Third Reading
Debate and vote on bill as amended

Report stage and vote on any further amendments proposed in the House

Royal Consent
By the Governor-General or a deputy

Note: All bills that entail expenditure of public moneys must be introduced in the House of Commons.

Source: Ministry of Supply and Services Canada, 1992.

and also, usually, provides budget and economic forecasts for the next three to five years.

Most pieces of legislation (called bills) in Canada originate in the House of Commons (see Figure 11 for an overview of the legislative process in Canada). Bills are usually introduced in the House by a member of Cabinet, although some bills are introduced by government backbenchers or the opposition, and bills which do not entail the expenditure of public funds can also originate in the Senate. Passage of a bill in the House of Commons requires that three votes be held. Each vote is called a reading. The first reading is merely designed to allow the Cabinet minister involved to introduce the bill to the House.

If the opposition wishes to defeat a bill, they will usually try to do so at the second reading. It is at this stage that major debate on the bill takes place. Occasionally, the opposition threatens to hold up a bill through the use of a filibuster — an extended debate on a bill — which can threaten both the government's credibility and its entire legislative agenda for the session. In the federal government, each opposition member is entitled to speak for 40 minutes during the debate on a particular piece of legislation, while in many provincial legislatures there is no limit at all. By threatening the government with a filibuster, the opposition can often force the government to amend or withdraw a piece of legislation.

When a bill passes its second reading it can be considered to have been approved in principle; it is then referred to a legislative committee which may recommend amendments to the bill based on its members' more detailed knowledge of the area the legislation covers. These amendments can either be accepted or rejected by the full House at the third reading. Sometimes, legislative committees hold extensive public hearings on bills, occasionally even travelling across the country to hold hearings. However, the effectiveness of the committee system is questionable, since bills have already been approved in principle when they reach committee. Moreover, membership by party on each committee, is roughly proportional to that of the House as a whole; it is difficult for opposition members to force the government members of a committee to accept amendments, especially in the case of a majority government.

After the legislative committee has finished its discussion on the bill, the bill goes to the House for the third and final reading, along with any amendments recommended. The third reading seldom produces serious debate, except possibly on amendments.

After approval by the House of Commons, a bill is passed on to the Senate — Canada's so-called "house of sober second thought." Senators are appointed by the Prime Minister, usually as a reward for faithful service to the party in power, and once appointed, they serve until age 75. After a change in government there is often a long delay before the Senate comes to reflect the views of the party in power. Because most Senators realize that the Senate lacks legitimacy as an institution, bills are rarely held up.

The final stage in approval of a piece of legislation is royal assent. A piece of legislation is not binding until it is signed by the Governor-General on the Queen's behalf. While this stage truly is a formality, it is important to note that the Governor-General does not sign a bill into law until formally asked to do so by the government. Thus, by delaying its request for royal assent, the government can effectively delay a piece of legislation.

In some cases the purpose of a bill is not to make a specific policy decision, but rather to pass the authority for making a particular policy decision on to a regulatory agency created specifically for that purpose. Regulatory agencies are ultimately responsible to a minister and to the legislature, but have a great deal of autonomy to make decisions within a basic policy framework provided by the legislature. Thus, for example, the Canadian Radio-television and Telecommunications Commission (CRTC) is responsible for setting rules and regulations governing the television industry in Canada within the framework of certain guidelines provided by the legislature (such as providing access to television programs for all Canadians and protecting our cultural sovereignty). It is also possible for Cabinet to overrule a regulatory agency, as it recently did to the CRTC in the controversial matter of direct broadcast satellite television.

As stated earlier, while the legislative branch of our government is powerful in theory, in practice it is actually the executive branch which controls the government. The executive branch consists of the Queen and her representative, the Governor-General, the Prime Minister, the Cabinet and the civil service.

The executive branch is generally controlled by the party which holds the most seats in the House of Commons. After a general election, the Governor-General asks the party which won the most seats to form a government. In cases where this party won more than half of the seats in the House, the government is called a majority government, and the party in power will have more or less complete control over the government. Where no party has a clear majority, however, and a minority government is formed, the government must ensure that all of the legislation it wishes to enact will be supported by at least some members of the opposition. Clearly, such governments are inherently less stable than majority governments, although there are those who argue that minority governments are often more democratic and can be more effective than majority governments.

As recent events have shown, it is definitely possible for a party to form a majority government without receiving the votes of a majority of Canadians. This sort of outcome is particularly likely to happen when there is fragmentation of the opposition parties. These outcomes occur because members of our House of Commons are elected based on what is known as a "first past the post" system. This simply means that each voter gets one vote, which counts solely towards the election of the local representatives, and whichever candidate in the local riding gets the most votes wins the seat outright. In other nations which use a proportional representation system, the seats in the legislature are distributed among the parties on the basis of the popular vote at the national level. There are also nations which use a hybrid system, where some legislators are chosen on a first past the post basis at the constituency level, while others in the same assembly are chosen based on the national popular vote.

Once asked to form a government by the Governor-General, the Prime Minister's first task is to select his or her Cabinet. The Cabinet is roughly analogous to the board of directors of a private sector corporation. Cabinet members are appointed by the Prime Minster, and continue to serve at his discretion. Cabinet members are most often members of the House of Commons, although occasionally the Prime Minister may choose to appoint a Senator or other non-member of the House. The Prime Minister also has full discretion over the size of the Cabinet. However, in appointing the Cabinet the Prime Minister must bear in mind several important conventions. For example, every province is usually represented in the Cabinet, and it is also necessary to strike a balance between anglophones and francophones and between men and women. As Canadian society becomes more fragmented, and Canadians identify themselves more and more with particular sub-groups within our society, the task of balancing the membership of Cabinet is becoming more difficult, and has contributed to its growing size in recent years.

To the outside world, the Cabinet functions as a single entity. All decisions made are by convention considered to be supported by the entire Cabinet. This, in turn, requires that the internal workings of Cabinet — its debates and discussions and so on — remain secret. A breach in either the convention of cabinet solidarity or of cabinet secrecy will almost certainly result in a minister being forced to resign from Cabinet.

In addition to meeting as whole, the Cabinet is subdivided into several committees, which look after broad policy areas, such as economic development, or specific tasks within the government, such as the Treasury Board, which is responsible for the preparation of the budget and overall management of the government and civil service.

Of course, in addition to being a member of the overall decision-making body of the government, each Cabinet minister is also generally responsible for the operations of one department within the government. As the political head of his or her department, a minister is responsible for dealing with questions and concerns about the department in the House. In this role, the minister is the only publicly accountable connection between the department and the people.

Within the department, the minister typically has a staff of political advisors whose role is to provide partisan political advice aimed at advancing the goals of both the governing party and the minister. It is important to note that these political advisors are not part of the formal hierarchy of the department.

The highest ranking civil servant in a typical government department is the deputy minister. This person reports directly to the minister and is responsible for the day-to-day management of the department. In private sector terms, it could be said that the role of the deputy minister is something like that of a chief operating officer, while the minister is more like a chief executive officer.

While it is impossible for such a high-ranking official to ignore politics, deputy ministers, and all of the civil servants who work under them, are supposed to be non-partisan. This is because Canada has what is known as a professional civil service. Civil servants in Canada are appointed and promoted on the basis of merit, not party affiliation. Thus, even as high-ranking an official as a deputy minister would be expected to serve governments from different parties with equal loyalty, diligence and enthusiasm. Our system is very different than that of the United States, where it is generally the case that several levels of management in each department are political appointees who will change as the administration changes.

A further important piece of the executive branch of our government is the so-called central agencies — the Prime Minister's Office (PMO), which is a highly partisan organization which exists to assist the Prime Minister; the Privy Council Office (PCO), which is a non-partisan organization which works for and advises the Cabinet; the Treasury Board; and the Department of Finance. The central agencies generally work to ensure that operating departments are working according to the policies and procedures imposed on them by the government and that the departments are accountable for their actions.

To conclude our brief discussion of government decision making in Canada, there are two important points which must be emphasized. First, there is at best a murky line of demarcation between the legislative and executive branches. Our constitution has none of the "checks and balances" which characterize the division of powers in the United States' constitution. In the United States there is a very clear separation between the powers of the President and those of Congress. Likewise, in the United States one cannot simultaneously be a member of both the executive and legislative branches of the government. This lack of such "checks and balances" in Canada has both advantages and disadvantages; however, its effect is clearly to make the Prime Minister, especially one with a majority in the House, a very powerful figure indeed.

A second point to remember is that while we have outlined our formal decision-making structure, there is a parallel system of special interest groups — paid lobbyists, industry associations and so on — trying to influence the decision making process. These groups and individuals use a wide range of techniques to try to influence policy on topics of interest to themselves, their members or their employers. Some argue that such attempts to influence public policy play an important positive role in a representative democracy such as ours, where decision makers are often separated from constituents both physically and metaphorically. Others argue that the system of interest group politics now in effect in Canada makes it impossible for those who most need the support of the system — those who lack resources and political power — to influence the system.

Whatever one's opinion is regarding the relative pros and cons of interest group politics, it is clearly the case that the influence of special interests over the decision-making process of Canadian governments is a fact of life which is not likely to change in the foreseeable future. For this reason, much of the focus of attention in interest group politics in the last few years has been on the issue of transparency — making sure that everyone understands who is working on which side of a particular issue and on whose behalf, and that there is some degree of equality in various interest groups' ability to access decision makers.

Looking briefly at special interest politics from the other side, that of the special interest group, we see that the most effective means by which to influence policy will depend on the decision-making model in use. Rational decision making can be influenced only by facts. Incremental decision making is best influenced by slow, steady pressure on the bureaucracy. Under public choice decision making, there are many tools at a special interest group's disposal, but all must be aimed at convincing individual politicians that agreeing to support the special interest group's position is in his or her best interest politically. This process may involve anything from the proverbial backroom meeting to television commercials aimed at increasing public visibility and sympathy for a cause.

Conclusion

This appendix has looked at how governments in Canada make decisions. It has focused on the formal process, while alluding to the informal process along the way. There has been much talk throughout our constitutional debates of changes that could or should be made in this decision-making process. However, we are still far from consensus on such proposals as the creation of a "Triple E" (elected, equal and effective) Senate, the introduction of some form of proportional representation into our electoral process and, in the extreme, the implementation of a republican form of government. Perhaps what is clear is that while our current system may not be perfect, no truly perfect system of government exists. What we are left with, as in so many facets of public administration, is a series of trade-offs, where our goal should be that we make well-informed choices and have some mechanism in place to revisit those choices as the needs of our society evolve. However, given our constant constitutional agony, we are clearly not at that point.

NOTES

1. For more detail on the reform process in New Zealand see L. Evans et al., "Economic Reform in New Zealand 1984–1995: The Pursuit of Efficiency," *Journal of Economic Literature* 34(4): 1856–902.
2. Douglas A.L. Auld, *Expanding horizons: privatizing universities* (Toronto: University of Toronto, Faculty of Management, Centre for Public Management, 1996).
3. Henry Mintzberg, "Managing Government, Governing Management," *The Harvard Business Review* 74(3): 83.

The Socio-Political Environment: The Quest for Accommodation

John Saywell

The politicians and the architects of Canadian public policy know only too well that Canada is a difficult country to govern. Indeed, despite our enormous success in achieving one of the highest standards of living in the world, it is, and always has been, difficult to make Canada work as a country. We have too much geography, and a history that has done as much to divide us as to unite us. The process of governing this country of diverse regions and peoples has been one of accommodating the diversity — of seeking strategies, policies and programs that can find and keep some form of unity — however precarious — across the broad face of the land. The objective of the state, particularly but not only the national state, has not been efficiency or rationality in the use of our physical and human resources, but the resolution of conflicts among regions or provinces, languages and cultures, economic interests and social classes, and, most recently, genders.

One problem is that it is difficult to find the pulse — or the reality — of either Canada or Canadians because, collectively, we are not certain who we are. Most of us have voted with our feet in choosing to remain, or become, Canadians; we prefer to be *here* rather than *there*, even if we are not sure where *here* is. Every Canadian ultimately makes his or her own identification with the country; for each, that *is* the Canadian identity. Our sense of being Canadian is filtered through the landscape that surrounds us, and the visual and emotional images evoked in each of us are as unique to the prairie farmer as to the logger in the rain forests of British Columbia. Our identity is filtered through ethnic backgrounds and the years, or generations, or even centuries we have spent in this new land. It is filtered through our sense of history, and the accomplishments of those who undertook the arduous task of building this country. Being Canadian is not to subscribe to some overarching national mythology, but rather arises from a private sense of belonging. Being Canadian is a reality, and those who try to define or measure it do so at their peril.

THE POLITICIZED ECONOMY

In the ideal (and unreal) world of the classical economist, a national economic strategy with global competitiveness as its objective would be based on efficiency, rational (market-driven) allocation of resources, due diligence in state support of winners and, perhaps, reduction of pain for losers. But these principles have never been the determinants of Canadian economic policy. And the economy, as it evolved, became hostage to too many fortunes to be easily transformed — or even marginally modified — by economists or other advocates of a market-driven economy. Not until the 1980s did a combination of globalization, the GATT, the Free Trade Agreement (FTA) and the ascendancy of privatization force a radical transformation of the Canadian economy. That transformation, however, is not being carried out as part of a national industrial strategy, but in response to the dictates of a global economy dominated by powerful trading blocs. Both the public and private sectors in Canada are reactive, not proactive. The role of government is not planning but damage control, and caring for the dead and the wounded with soaring unemployment insurance benefits and welfare payments.

Canadian nationalism was not the dynamic behind the creation of the state in 1867, but nation-making was the objective of the pragmatists who brought it into existence. Their goal was to create a political structure within which a national economy could develop, a structure strong enough to ensure the economic and political survival of the northern half of North America. Success demanded, so it seemed, an interventionist central government to offset the apparently predictable dictates of geography and the market. An open-door immigration and capital investment policy, more or less free land in the West for staple production, tariff protection to force import substitution, and a state-nourished integrated railway system were the components of the National Policy implemented in the decades after Confederation. The benefits were to be extensive growth in the GNP, economic integration and political survival; the costs, modern economists remind us, were economic inefficiency and a lower gross national income (GNI) per capita.

However hesitant its beginnings, by the 1920s the policy had achieved its objectives: the railways were built (and overbuilt); the West was oversettled; staple exports from the farms, the forests and the mines had mushroomed; and secondary manufacturing, much of it in American branch plants and services, had grown in Central Canada to serve a protected domestic market. But success created its own dialectic. Farmers' grievances against the perceived unequal incidence of the National Policy burst forth in a political revolt in 1921. Maritimers, left behind in the heady economic expansion, spoke sullenly of secession. The rise of new staples — mining and forestry — strengthened the economies of Ontario, Quebec and British Columbia, while the north-south flow of these new staples weakened the older east-west and transatlantic axis. The power of the provinces, enlarged by judicial review, was further enhanced, since many major new state functions that emerged, such as economic regulation, education, social services, highways and urbanization, fell within provincial jurisdiction.

The precarious equilibrium thus created broke down with the Depression of the 1930s. By the end of the 1920s all levels of government carried a heavy debt burden. The booming 1920s had been accompanied by enormous surplus capacity in such industries as automobiles and pulp and paper. A precipitous decline in exports, a drop in commodity prices — often to levels below the cost of production — and prairie drought shattered the economy. By 1933 the unemployment rate was 26 per cent, and 1.5-million people — one person in four in the cities — lived on relief. When the drought hit Saskatchewan, two-thirds of the population was dependent on government relief. Not only had the economy collapsed, so had the capacity of governments.

Even if they had had the will or the knowledge to act, Canada's governments could not have done so; they were paralyzed by the federal system. Responsibility for social distress lay with local and provincial governments. Many cities went bankrupt and could not even pay the interest on their debts. Before the worst was over the Prairie provinces were in default, and British Columbia had teetered on the brink. Direct taxes were levied, both federally and provincially, but the worst-hit provinces were the least able to raise revenues.

Although a central bank was established, it was not given a mandate to use monetary policy to combat the Depression. The courts had effectively denied Ottawa control over economic regulation, industrial relations and all trade but international trade; in 1937 federal legislation concerning unemployment insurance, marketing, wages and hours of work was ruled unconstitutional.

Faced with this complex crisis, Mackenzie King appointed a royal commission (Rowell-Sirois) to examine the interlocking economic and constitutional problems.[1] The report recommended a restructuring of revenues and responsibilities within the federation. Although the recommendations — such as total federal control over unemployment and the direct tax field — were not accepted, they were the beginning of what has been described as the second National Policy. Slowly implemented after World War II, this "New National Policy" — part political, part social and part economic — did much to reconstruct the Canadian state. It also initiated debates over public policy that are still with us today.

Put hopelessly simply, the "New National Policy" called for Canada to remain a capitalist federal state where the role of government was to encourage factor flows — investment, labour and technology — but to intervene to stabilize the economy, offset sharp differentials in regional income and protect Canadians against economic and social misfortune. Keynesian stabilization of fiscal and investment policy, equalization payments and regional development programs and a complex social security and welfare system all involved fundamental changes in the Canadian state system and the relationship between the state and the individual.

They also increased the burden the economy was to bear: in 1950, even with the heavy war debt, governments reaped only 20 per cent of the GNP; a generation later they took close to 50 per cent. Economics and politics became even more inseparable.

There had always been tension and conflict between Ottawa and the provinces as each pursued its perceived self-interest, dictated sometimes by conflicting economic interests, and at others by partisan political interests. But

implementing of the "New National Policy" brought the two levels of government into constant jurisdictional conflict over access to fields of taxation and
legislative and administrative power. No longer was there a clear distinction in
fact between the two levels of government. The buzzwords of the new era were
stabilization, equalization, regional development and shared cost programs.
Political scientists and politicians spoke of "cooperative federalism," but the
reality more often resembled a battlefield.

When Ottawa adopted Lord Keynes as its own in 1945 and explicitly committed the federal government to counter-cyclical fiscal and investment policies
to maintain a high and stable level of employment and income, the scenario
was predictable.[2] A successful counter-cyclical fiscal policy demanded a centralized and rationalized direct tax system in a state where both levels of government had constitutional access to all direct taxes, including all personal and
corporate income taxes.

Ottawa had taken over the taxes during the war, and in 1945 proposed to
"rent" them permanently in the interests of rationalization, efficiency, equity
and stabilization. Quebec refused the offer outright; Ontario was reluctant to
part with corporation taxes; and all the provinces demanded an ever-larger
share of the tax proceeds. As a result, federal–provincial fiscal relations
underwent a bewildering series of agreements — tax rentals, tax sharing, tax
abatements, and, finally, tax collection. This ad hoc process led to the many
different tax systems we have today. For all provinces except Quebec, Ottawa
collects the personal income tax at a standard rate, but each province adds its
own tax, in addition to that which it receives back from Ottawa. Quebec,
Ontario and Alberta, which together account for 75 per cent of corporate
income, all levy their own corporate income taxes. By 1992 there was talk of
ending tax collection and letting each province go its own way. Thus ended the
bold hope of the war years for a single, sensible, national tax system.

Keynesianism may have been dead, but the arguments for a rational tax
system were not. Separate tax systems only reinforce the sharp differences in
regional development and income. There are few industrialized countries where
regional diversity is so great and the unifying and equalizing forces so weak.
The 1940 Rowell-Sirois Commission recommended that, in return for the sur-
render of the direct tax field by the provinces, Ottawa should provide national
adjustment grants that would enable every province to provide an average level
of services with an average level of taxation.

The arguments in favour of this system were threefold: that direct taxes
were not levied where the income was earned; that a cost-benefit analysis of
Canada's economic policy showed it to favour Central Canada (although true
quantification was impossible, there was undeniably some truth in this asser-
tion); and that greater equality in the standard of living was essential to a common citizenship.

Despite these arguments, the principle of equalization payments was not
implemented until 1957 under Louis St. Laurent. Although the formula has
changed repeatedly since then, the policy has remained a part of Canada's
federal structure, and the principle was entrenched in Section 36 the 1982
Constitution:

> Parliament and the Government of Canada are committed to the principle of
> making equalization payments to ensure that provincial governments have suf-
> ficient revenues to provide reasonably comparable levels of public services at
> reasonably comparable levels of taxation.

In 1997–98 Ottawa transferred $8-billion in equalization payments to the poorer
provinces, with Ontario, Alberta and British Columbia paying the bill.

Described as "the glue that holds Confederation together," or "the lubri-
cant of the federal system," economists would argue that on the grounds of
economic efficiency, equalization is a dubious, if not a downright insane, policy.
By providing an artificially high standard of living (for example, in P.E.I., where
the province's revenue was 55 per cent of the national average before equalization, and 83 per cent after), the payments inhibit outward migration and other
factor flows from the poorer regions, and divert revenue from the richer areas
into less productive uses.[3]

The same argument has been made about the vast array of regional development programs financed by the central government in an attempt to remove
the cause of regional disparities. The government had always attempted to subsidize projects or sectors through bonuses, freight rates, tax benefits and other
measures, but it was only when John Diefenbaker arrived on the scene in 1957,
that the war on regional disparities really began.

Over the past 40 years there has been a bewildering variety of programs
(represented by a dazzling array of acronyms: ADA, ARDA, FRED, RDIA and
many more) reflecting various approaches and objectives. While these programs
were all based on some form of economic analysis, there has always been little
doubt that their implementation had a very strong political motivation. Critics
were quick to observe that as the threat of separatism grew in Quebec, so did
the amount of regional development assistance. By 1982 the entire province was
eligible for grants, and the province was spending 40 per cent of the total.[4]

Yet the billions of dollars spent to combat regional disparities in almost
all areas except southern Ontario, Alberta and British Columbia did little to
lessen the disparities, although this spending may have prevented the disparities from becoming worse. Whatever social or political merits the policy
had, economists argued that the cost of this artificially distorting resource
allocation is great because it delays necessary adjustment, reduces national
economic efficiency, and could in fact lead to greater disparities in the long
run. In recent years the programs have been reduced, and by 1995–96 the
federal government was spending $2.7-billion to encourage economic develop-
ment, largely in the Atlantic Provinces and Quebec, and to encourage economic
diversification in the West.

THE POLITICS OF THE PROTECTED SOCIETY

"At the most general level, capitalist economies and democratic politics are
rendered compatible by the welfare role of the state," declared the Royal Commission on the Economic Union and Development Prospects for Canada in
1985. It continued:

> There are debates at the margin. The particulars of how the state-welfare role should be handled in the interests of values pertaining to economic efficiency, to human dignity, and to evolving conceptions of equity, including the relationship among risk, innovation and reward, are always controversial.... [However] without the stabilizing integrating contribution of the welfare state, support for the relative autonomy of capitalist markets would crumble.[5]

The origins of the present-day welfare state — or the "protected society" as Tom Courchene more appropriately described it — can also be traced back to the Depression and World War II. The provinces (and their agents, the municipalities), within whose jurisdiction social policy fell, had already created a primitive, ad hoc security net: workmen's compensation; allowances for single mothers, the blind and other disadvantaged citizens; and assistance for the unemployed and unemployable. In 1927 the federal government agreed to help finance provincially administered old age pensions.

The Depression revealed the hopeless inadequacy of this security net. Ottawa's attempts to introduce unemployment insurance and national labour regulations were ruled unconstitutional by the courts. In the later 1930s and during the war, professionally trained bureaucrats in the federal civil service, supported by liberal-minded politicians, began to develop plans for a comprehensive social security system for the new and better post-war world. Threatened by the surging popularity of socialism, Mackenzie King was persuaded to move cautiously to the left as the war neared its end. The 1944 Speech from the Throne bluntly stated that the

> objective of our domestic policy is social security and human welfare ... plans for the establishment of a national minimum of social security and human welfare should be advanced as rapidly as possible. Such a national minimum contemplates useful employment for all who are willing to work; standards of nutrition and housing adequate to ensure the health of the whole population; and social insurance against privation resulting from unemployment, from accident, from the death of the breadwinner, from ill-health and from old age.

In the same session, Ottawa introduced family allowances as both an income security measure and a Keynesian stimulus to post-war consumer demand.

With the war over, the federal government put its "New National Policy" proposals before the provinces. It had no choice, because most of its proposals fell within provincial legislative jurisdiction. Unemployment insurance had been placed under Ottawa's control by a constitutional amendment in 1940; given that Ottawa has the power to make direct payments to individuals, family allowances did not require provincial legislation for their implementation. But the bulk of social security and welfare programs, including old age pensions, health insurance and welfare programs, fell within provincial jurisdiction.

Social security and welfare programs financed by the state are always controversial, since they create a division between left and right. In Canada, they also created a division between Ottawa and the provinces — sometimes a few provinces and sometimes many; often rich provinces like Ontario; and always Quebec, which consistently opposed any federal encroachment on its legislative or financial jurisdiction.

Gradually, however, through seemingly endless negotiations, conflict and compromise, the elements of the "New National Policy" were put in place between 1945 and 1968. In 1951, constitutional amendments permitted Ottawa to finance old age pensions out of taxation and, in 1964, to establish contributory old age pensions (CPP — Quebec established its own). But the other elements were achieved with the use of shared cost programs: hospital insurance (1957); welfare assistance (the Canada Assistance Plan, 1966), which incorporated existing and new assistance programs for the blind, the disabled, the unemployed without benefits, as well as child welfare and mothers' allowances; and medicare (1968). Ottawa offered to pay roughly half the cost of these programs if the provinces agreed to implement a scheme that met Ottawa's conditions. In the case of medicare, for example, the conditions were that the plan be comprehensive in scope, universal in coverage, accessible, portable and publicly administered. Since 1951, the federal government had also been assisting universities financially, and in 1966, it agreed to pay the provinces half the operating costs of universities without conditions.

Although there were warnings that the country was embarking on an income security system it might not be able to sustain, everything seemed possible in the heady decade of the 1960s. Not only were the above programs implemented, but the unemployment insurance scheme was so expanded as to become almost a guaranteed annual income; tax credits and deductions for old and young added to the cost through revenue forgone; in the public sector, where compensation was ultimately limited only by the ability of governments to tax, workers secured the right to bargain collectively and strike.

By the 1970s the illusions had gone. Faced with spiralling costs it could not control, the federal government put a lid on its spending, forcing the provinces either to control spending or pay a larger share. But costs continued to rise — health-care costs in particular, which became the largest single item of public expenditure. By 1994 transfer payments to the unemployed, the elderly, families and the ill amounted to 15 per cent of the GNP. With the population aging rapidly, the future looked bleak. Indeed, the cost of supporting the elderly scares many economists. By 1997–98 elderly benefits amounted to $22.3-billion, or over 20 per cent of federal government program spending, and would continue to increase.

By then it had become clear to most Canadians that public spending had gotten out of control. For over 20 years spending by the federal and provincial governments had far exceeded government revenue. By 1991 government deficits had passed $50-billion a year, and the direct debt of all government was over $550-billion. Despite attempts to cut spending, the direct debt had increased to $800-billion five years later — roughly $60,000 for every taxpayer. And as a percentage of GDP, the direct debt had risen from 35 per cent in 1980 to 99 per cent in 1996, and probably over 100 per cent in 1997.

However, while most Canadians believed that painful surgery was essential, few believed that they should suffer the pain. The view was widely held that Canada's acclaimed social security system could not be touched: what began as a program of social justice had become an untouchable entitlement — to unlimited health care, generous unemployment and welfare benefits, however economically unsound and susceptible to inventive manipulation, that did nothing to address the root causes of unemployment or poverty and for some were an inducement not to work.

But the pain had to be borne, and by the 1990s all governments were being forced to cut expenditures on social programs. In 1995 federal transfer payments for health, post-secondary education and welfare assistance (CAP) were consolidated under the Canada Health and Social Transfer, and the total payments were reduced by $6-billion (or more than a third) over a two-year period. Universal Family Allowance were replaced by an income-tested Child Tax Credit. The Unemployment Insurance program was tightened and coverage reduced. Led by Ontario and Alberta, the provinces made deep cuts in welfare assistance and other social programs.

By the late 1990s the immediate crisis was over. Spending cuts and, more important, increasingly buoyant tax revenues as the economy boomed enabled Ottawa and most provincial governments first to achieve a balanced budget, and some to have a surplus. But as the federal government anticipated a healthy surplus well into the twenty-first century, new conflicts emerged. In Ottawa the battle was joined among those who favoured debt reduction, tax reduction, and spending on new federal programs to build political capital. (With such new initiatives as the Canadian Foundation for Innovation and the Millennium Scholarship Fund, among others, the spenders seemed to be the early winners) At the same time the fight between Ottawa and the provinces was no longer over reductions but over the surplus. The provinces demanded the $4.2-billion that had been cut from health care and more, and Ontario and Alberta (and Quebec of course) wanted Ottawa to get out of the business of setting conditions or standards. Ottawa, on the other hand, wanted some form of a national report card monitoring each province's progress in improving the quality and efficiency of the health program. The reason was obvious: in 2000 it was clearer than ever — to the medical profession and the politicians — that the cost of medical care, as it currently existed and was predicted to increase, could not be sustained. The search for a solution was certain to be divisive.

The crisis of the 1990s had at least one positive result: a federal–provincial agreement on "A Framework to Improve the Social Union for Canadians." Initially the work of the provinces in response to the federal cuts, Ottawa finally joined the group, and the agreement was signed in 1999. Quebec had been part of the team, but in the end refused to sign because some of the provisions contradicted Quebec's determination to minimize or end a federal presence in areas of provincial jurisdiction. In brief, the agreement accepted the principle of using the federal spending power to fund social programs, but stated that it should "proceed in a cooperative manner," and there were to be no changes in funding without prior consultation. No new initiatives were to be launching without the agreement of a majority of the provinces, and there were provisions for partial opting out. And there was to be an accountability framework for such new initiatives — such as the report card the federal government was demanding for refunding health care — and procedures for dispute avoidance and resolution. If it worked, the Framework would mark a watershed in federal–provincial relations. The absence of Quebec was not necessarily a fatal flaw.

THE CHARTER OF RIGHTS AND FREEDOMS

The Charter of Rights and Freedoms in the 1982 Constitution is destined to be Pierre Trudeau's most lasting — perhaps his only lasting — legacy. For the first time, basic rights and freedoms were entrenched in the constitution; only with difficulty could they be overridden by any government. Before 1982, criminal law in Canada was whatever the federal government declared it to be, despite traditional assumptions about the right to counsel or the right to be presumed innocent until proven guilty. The Charter explicitly stated the rights and freedoms Canadians enjoy and endowed the courts with the power to police them. The only avenue by which the democratic process could prevail against the courts was the legal capacity of a government to invoke the "notwithstanding" clause in the Charter, openly declaring that a law was to operate **notwithstanding** the constitutional limitation.

The Charter was designed to provide a base for a common Canadianism, to serve as a unifying doctrine of rights. To some extent it has done so. But perhaps it has done more to divide us by introducing another element of conflict into Canadian society. As Alan Cairns put it, the Charter constitutionalized a profound social transformation:

> Various social transformations in the sixties and seventies that initially had no obvious connection to our constitutional agonies were pulled into the constitutional arena ... by the Charter project. The essence of the social change of the period is catapulted by the powerful phrase "coming out," initially employed by the gay community. The ambit of the phrase can appropriately be extended to include the coming out of women, of aboriginal peoples, of third force Canadians, of visible minorities, of linguistic minorities, and of the disabled. In each case, their coming out challenged the comfortable assurance by which yesterday's dominant élites and majorities had defined the boundaries of acceptable, normal behaviour, and had transmitted their definitive cures of who was significant and who was not.[6]

The Charter did not end questions about rights by entrenching them — or some of them; in fact, it was the beginning point of many new questions. What precisely did the rights in the Charter mean? Did "freedom of association" entrench the right to strike? Did the right to "life, liberty and security of the person" entrench the right of a mother to have an abortion or the right of a foetus to live? Did the right to equality mean the right of any group or person previously disadvantaged on grounds of race, colour or sex to see that inequality erased? What aboriginal rights did the Charter confirm? Did the instruction to the courts to interpret the Charter "in a manner consistent with the preservation and enhancement of the multicultural heritage of Canada" establish some kind of "multicultural rights"? And, more generally, if some rights were guaranteed, why not others? To some the missing right was the right to property; to others it was the right to economic and physical well-being.

The debate over rights changed the nature of the Canadian **community**. Canada became a society driven by the vocabulary of rights, not community. Most issues that reach the public policy agenda are capable of compromise, and politics, the art of the possible, is the art of compromise and consensus. But rights, once asserted, become absolutes, strongly and intractably held. It is hard to bargain over rights, or among them. Rights fragment society and paralyze politicians, for whom there is no correct choice other than personal conviction or party discipline. What Leslie Pal wrote of abortion might also be said with equal truth of other, less contentious, issues regarding rights: "To a government obsessed with the bottom line, with jobs and trade, with global competition and the budget, abortion policy is an unsavoury agenda item, something that wins no friends and makes many enemies."[7]

The words in the Charter mean nothing until the courts, particularly the Supreme Court of Canada, have given them meaning in the context of particular cases. The Court may follow a course of judicial activism, being very liberal in its reading of the scope of rights and freedoms, or it may follow a course of judicial restraint and be deferential to the legislation or the practices of state actors such as police and judges. Although opinions differ, my own view is that the Supreme Court has been highly protective — perhaps in some cases overly protective — of our legal rights. It has also been less than restrained in dealing with some equality issues, and has indeed made policy in the field of gay rights and same sex partners. For many special interest groups, the Charter and the Courts became the preferred, perhaps the only, means of securing change. A recent book described these groups as the "Court Party."[8] The most frequent to intervene in cases before the Supreme Court was The Women's Legal Education and Action Fund (LEAF).

Perhaps the most successful group in consistently defeating deliberate government policy has been the National Citizens' Coalition. Since the 1960s Canadian governments have attempted to control election expenditures by candidates and parties to assure a more level playing field. One method was to control expenditures by "third parties"; that is, organizations other than political parties themselves who had a particular interest in the outcome. In 1983 the NCC went to court in Alberta to charge that such provisions in a federal act violated the guarantee of "freedom of expression" on the Charter. A single judge in the Alberta Court of Queens Bench agreed. In effect, there was no law during the 1984 election, and there were no prosecutions of those who may have broken what had been the law. There was still no law in 1988, and millions were spent by third parties on both sides of the controversial free trade election. In 1993 a new law included a $1,000 third-party limit, but the Alberta courts threw that out as well. In May 2000 the federal government passed a new law limiting the total spending of each political interest group or individual to $150,000 across the country, with a maximum of $3,000 in any riding. The NCC went immediately into action, once again in Alberta, where the courts seemed sympathetic. At the time of writing, after apparently considering pre-empting an Alberta decision by referring the legislation to the Supreme Court of Canada, which would undoubtedly be more favourably disposed, the federal government intervened to defend the act in the Alberta court. An unfavourable decision would undoubtedly be appealed to the Supreme Court.

WOMEN'S RIGHTS: UNITY AND DIVISION

The modern movement for women's rights emerged as a political force in the late 1960s. Earlier movements had sought to establish the legal or political equality of women — as symbolized by the right to vote, or membership in the

Senate — and were, in part, based on the doctrine of moral superiority: the idea that a female presence in the political arena would bring the supposed virtues of maternal feminism to such issues as temperance and moral reform. The movement that began in the 1960s, by contrast, reflected the post-war emergence of women as part of the labour force. While only 16 per cent of workers were women in 1901, the figure had risen to 38 per cent by 1970. A decade later, it was 50 per cent — and 41 per cent of these women were principal wage earners who had never been, or were no longer, married.

At the same time, however, it was obvious that income in the labour force was segregated by gender — women earned, on the average, 60 per cent as much as men. Women not only predominated in occupations that tended to be lower paid, but were often paid less than male counterparts doing the same job — the doctrine of equal pay for equal work did not exist.

In the beginning, the demands were for equality of opportunity and affirmative action programs designed to achieve economic equality. But the issues changed during the seventies. The leaders of the movement became more strident, and raised such issues as the unequal power of women and the need for a feminist perspective on many public and private matters. The agenda no longer focused solely on economic equality, but encompassed a broad range of issues in which the private person was not seen as separate from the public or political one. The role of women in society, day care, single-parent social services, reproductive freedom, rape, wife and child abuse and pornography were all items on the new feminist agenda.

The appointment in 1970 of the Royal Commission on the Status of Women — which wrote a blueprint for social change on issues ranging from pay equity to abortion — led to the creation of the National Action Committee on the Status of Women to oversee the implementation of the commission's recommendations. A host of other organizations emerged over the course of the next two decades, representing woman professionals, women in sports, native women, black women, disabled women and others. Sometimes such groups pursued their own unique interests; at other times they acted in concert as a single feminist lobby group. And they had strong links to other, non-feminist, organizations in areas such as health, the family, religion, literacy advocacy, multiculturalism and labour. Other women's groups existed outside of, or even opposed to, the thrust of the mainline groups, such as those who opposed abortion, and some religious and professional women's organizations.

Women had become a powerful lobby group. Their concerted and persistent pressure led to the insertion into the Charter of Rights and Freedoms of Section 28, which states: "Notwithstanding anything in this Charter, the rights and freedoms referred to in it are guaranteed equally to male and female persons." The section was originally subject to the provisions of the "notwithstanding clause" (Section 33), but again formidable lobbying in the last stages of Charter fine-tuning led to this section being removed from the list of those that could be overridden.

With the Charter experience behind them, women became a far more powerful presence than ever before. On many issues, really all women were united: affirmative action, pay equity, wife and child abuse and the protection of victims of sexual abuse (as in the case of a law forbidding questions at trial concerning a defendant's previous sexual experience). But on some rights-related issues women were deeply divided. Such was the case with abortion.

Abortion is a lens through which we can watch the politics of social fragmentation and political paralysis. In most societies, abortion is, and has been, a contentious issue, because it involves profound questions of morality and conscience, usually in the context of legal and religious prohibitions. Until 1969, the Canadian Criminal Code stated that abortion was an offence punishable by life imprisonment (or two years if the convicted person was the mother), unless it had been deemed necessary in order to save the life of the mother. Despite a general trend in Western countries towards relaxing abortion laws after World War II, there was little organized pressure in Canada to liberalize the law — although there was pressure from lawyers and doctors to clarify it. Nevertheless, the Trudeau government modified the law. The new provisions did not actually "get the State out of the bedrooms of the nation," however; they left abortion as a crime punishable by life imprisonment, unless performed by a doctor in an accredited hospital, after a decision by a committee that continuation of the pregnancy "would or would be likely to endanger" the mother's "life or health" (Criminal Code, Section 251). The new law was only moderately less restrictive. Many hospitals (including all religious hospitals) did not establish such a committee, and many doctors remained reluctant to perform abortions because of moral or medical reasons, or because they feared the legal consequences, particularly through suits by third parties.

But the introduction of the new law served to mobilize opinion both for and against abortion liberalization. In particular, it brought Dr. Henry Morgentaler into the open as a determined advocate of an unrestricted right to abortion. Just as the stirrup revolutionized the history of medieval warfare, Morgentaler's adoption of the vacuum aspiration technique for abortion revolutionized the politics of abortion in Canada. Abortions could be performed quickly, cheaply and safely, in a doctor's office or a free-standing clinic.

Morgentaler established a clinic in Montreal in 1969 and was immediately arrested and charged. Although he admitted performing 5,000 abortions, a jury acquitted him in 1973. But the Quebec Court and the Supreme Court of Canada overturned the verdict, and Morgentaler was imprisoned. Upon his release he went before two more juries and was acquitted each time. In 1976, the government of Quebec simply decided not to prosecute him or any other doctors performing abortions. (This was possible since, while criminal law comes under federal jurisdiction, the administration of justice is in the hands of the provinces.) As pro-life forces mobilized to bring about more restrictive laws, Morgentaler allied himself with pro-choice activists and other organizations, to force the issue by publicly opening free-standing clinics in Toronto and Winnipeg. As predicted, with pro-choice and pro-life militants demonstrating on the streets in Toronto, the clinics were raided, and he and his associates were arrested. Again he was acquitted by a jury, and his case was appealed to the Supreme Court of Canada, which finally took on the task of determining the constitutionality of Section 251 of the Criminal Code.

Enter the Charter of Rights. Section 7 states: "Everyone has the right to life, liberty and security of the person and the right not to be deprived thereof except in accordance with the principles of fundamental justice." The questions before the Court were easy to frame, if difficult to answer: Did "security of the person" mean women had the right to terminate a pregnancy? Did a foetus enjoy the "right to life?"

Confronted with an issue of such complexity and a decision of such momentous and divisive consequences, a divided Court hedged. Two judges concluded that

> Forcing a woman, by threat of criminal sanction, to carry a foetus to term unless she meets certain criteria unrelated to her own priorities and aspirations, is a profound interference with a woman's body and thus a violation of security of the person.[9]

But rather than proceed with this substantive reasoning, the judges moved on to focus on process. Because Section 251 was not evenly applied in all hospitals and the criteria and process used were unclear, they concluded, its implementation violated Section 7. Although they stated that the foetus "may well be deserving of constitutional protection," they concluded that the current law was unfair and arbitrary, and could not, therefore, be sustained.

Two other judges concluded simply that the procedure in Section 251 could deny a woman access to medical services necessary to save her life. Only Madam Justice Wilson confronted the issue head-on and declared that women had a right to abortion, free of criminal sanction. But she did state that at some — indeterminate — point in the pregnancy the state could establish restrictive criteria enforced by sanctions.

Another two judges, in dissent, simply said that there was no evidence that the Charter intended to establish a right to abortion, and the court had no right to reject the deliberate will of Parliament.

With Section 251 struck down and Canada without a law on abortion, with doctors unclear about the law and provincial governments determining hospital policy, the ball was in the federal government's court. Although the government promised quick and decisive action, it could not carry the party caucus on any policy and after six months of agonizing deliberations decided on a "free vote" in the Commons. The proposal before the House endorsed the principle that in the early stages of pregnancy a doctor could perform an abortion if the "physical or mental well-being" of the woman was threatened, but in the later stages termination would only be allowed if two doctors concluded that continuation would "endanger the woman's life or seriously endanger her health." Leslie Pal summarized the result in the Commons in the summer of 1988 as follows:

> The Government's main resolution was defeated 147 votes to 76. An amendment which would have left the choice of abortion to the woman in the early stages and demanded only one doctor's opinion later was defeated 191 to 29. An amendment which would have left the decision entirely up to a woman and her doctor was defeated 198 to 20. An amendment which would have restricted abortion to the first 12 weeks of pregnancy was defeated 202 to 17. The most successful amendment — in that it was defeated by the narrowest margin — would have prohibited abortions except on the evidence of two doctors that the continuation of the pregnancy would endanger the woman's life. None of the 29 female MPs supported this proposal.[10]

The clear gender split on the last vote suggested to many pro-choice militants that men were still determined to control women's bodies. For months the government remained silent while pro-life activists took to the streets to close down abortion clinics and invite arrest for ignoring court injunctions. During the summer of 1989, the lives of Barbara Dodd and Chantal Daigle became front-page news as they successfully fought off anti-abortion injunctions secured by the natural fathers of the foetuses they carried. Finally, in the Daigle case, the Supreme Court ruled that a foetus was not a "legal person" in either the Charter or the Quebec Charter.

The Mulroney government then introduced a new abortion law, Bill C-43, which retained the criminality of abortion, but was less restrictive in principle than Section 251 — although the criteria for securing an abortion with medical approval remained deliberately vague and ambiguous. After heated debate, the bill passed the Commons (140 to 131) in May 1990. Not until January 1991 did the Senate turn its attention to the bill, where contradictory pressures from pro-choice groups, pro-life groups and the medical profession (which disliked the implicit "chill" factor in the ambiguous legislation) led to a 43–43 vote and the death of the bill.

As the country was once again without a federal law on the issue, the scene shifted to the provinces, which, since they were responsible for the delivery of medical services, could effectively take charge by permitting or prohibiting the licensing of clinics and the use of medicare fee schedules for abortions. It was not long before access to abortion was again before the courts. For over a decade a great deal of Canadian time and energy — on the part of politicians, interest groups, lawyers and judges — had been consumed by the question of abortion and rights, without reaching a final resolution. As far as abortion is concerned, politics seemed to be the art of the impossible.

The same threatened to be the case with assisted suicide. The Criminal Code makes it an offence to assist a person to commit suicide, even though suicide or attempted suicide is not itself a crime. Sue Rodriguez, terminally ill with amyotrophic lateral sclerosis (ALS), wanted a physician to assist her to die when she could no longer live with dignity, and challenged the law as a violation of her Charter rights under sections 7 and 15. Simply put, the question she asked was "Who owns my body?" In a 5 to 4 decision in 1993, the Supreme Court upheld the law, in effect implying that the state did. Despite the decision and the law, Rodriguez did secure a physician-assisted suicide in front of at least one witness, Svend Robinson, an NDP member of Parliament. The split decision and the widespread outpouring of support for Rodriguez — and the likely refusal of a jury to convict the culprit if he or she were ever arrested and charged — made it inevitable that the issue would join abortion as another divisive "right to life or death" issue on the public agenda.

THE ABORIGINAL "RIGHT" TO SELF-GOVERNMENT

In June 1990, Elijah Harper, the sole aboriginal member of the Manitoba legislature, prevented the Meech Lake Accord from coming to a vote in that province, thus effectively killing the agreement. Later that same summer, national and international television audiences watched incredulously as the Mohawks of

Kanesatake, in battle dress and carrying combat guns, fought the Quebec police and then the Canadian army to a standstill in support of their claims to contested land. For centuries, native people in Canada had their lives largely determined by the Europeans who controlled the Canadian state; now it seemed the future of that state would be decided in part by an agenda written by the aboriginal peoples. Speaking on behalf of these peoples, Harper gave a clear message that no new constitutional arrangement would be acceptable unless it recognized specific aboriginal rights. Foremost among those rights, it soon became clear, was the right to be recognized as a distinct society with the "inherent right to self-government" — whatever that might come to mean.

At issue was the place in our society of as many as a million Canadians who declared themselves to be of aboriginal origin. Of these more than half are registered or status Indians. Sixty per cent live on reserves and the remainder live in urban areas in southern Canada. There are also over 100,000 Indians — the number is not certain — who are not status Indians but are of aboriginal origin. The 150,000 Métis of mixed European and Indian ancestry are concentrated on the Prairies, while the 42,000 Inuit live in the north.

Dealing with aboriginal people has not been a Canadian success story. Since 1700, some 500 treaties had been signed with aboriginal peoples in which they usually ceded title to their land in return for reserves, the right to hunt and fish and annual payments. Between 1871 and 1921, as Western settlement proceeded, the new Canadian government, which was given jurisdiction over Indians and Indian lands, negotiated 11 treaties regarding vast stretches of land, including Northern Ontario, the Prairies, and parts of the Northwest Territories. But no land cession treaties were signed covering Northern Quebec, the Maritimes, most of British Columbia or much of the Arctic.

Historically, federal policy was made by the government without consultation and with little complaint. But by the 1950s, Indian organizations were becoming more active, demanding consultation and finding broad public support in their fight against poverty and general marginality. Only in 1960 did status Indians receive the right to vote. Although there were many new programs to assist Indians, none seemed to resolve the problems of poverty and marginality. Revising Indian policy in the late sixties, the federal government did consult with Indian leaders. But the new policy, when it emerged as part of Trudeau's "just society," did not recognize any special rights or historic land and treaty claims. Rather, in a 1969 statement on Indian policy, the government proposed to remove the "Indian problem" through assimilation. The policy was to rest

> upon the fundamental right of Indian people to full and equal participation in the cultural, social, economic and political life of Canada.... To argue against this right is to argue *for* discrimination, isolation and separation. No Canadian should be excluded from participation in community life, and none should expect to withdraw and still enjoy the benefits that flow to those who participate.

The government dismissed the principle of "aboriginal rights" with the argument that claims to land and associated rights were "so general and undefined that it is not realistic to think of them as specific claims capable of remedy." Termed cultural genocide by Indian leaders, this statement prompted a massive organization among aboriginal peoples. They wanted to retain their society and culture and negotiate new terms for their membership in the Canadian community. The force of the aboriginal opposition, combined with the support from the broader community, compelled the government to drop the proposal. Several court decisions also upheld the concept of an original title to the land and aboriginal rights that could be litigated.

In the face of these developments, the government had to begin to negotiate land claims and to consider seriously the broader question of aboriginal rights. By 1982 pressure had led to the inclusion of Section 25 of the Charter, which stated that nothing in the Charter limited any "rights or freedoms that pertain to the aboriginal peoples of Canada." Section 35 of the 1982 Constitution stated that the "existing aboriginal and treaty rights of the aboriginal peoples of Canada are hereby recognized and affirmed," and Section 37 committed the government to hold constitutional conferences to identify and define the rights to be included in a further revision to the Constitution.

Although a number of minor agreements were reached, three first ministers conferences over the subsequent four years failed to reach any agreement on what had become the central issue: the aboriginal right to self-government. In two 1990 decisions, the Supreme Court of Canada provided support for aboriginal claims. In one decision the court ruled that the Hurons outside Quebec City retained the right granted them in a 230-year-old treaty, to build campfires and cut trees in a provincial park. A week later, in *R. v. Sparrow*, the court acquitted an Indian who had fished with a drift net larger than regulations permitted, and made a strong statement that governments cannot limit aboriginal rights without consultation and agreement.

But as the deadline for the approval of the Meech Lake agreement loomed, there was no recognition of the historical and cultural distinctiveness of the aboriginal population, or their right to some form of self-government. Yet, if they were not distinct, who was? Elijah Harper spoke for the aboriginals when he refused to let Meech Lake pass until aboriginal rights had been recognized.

The aboriginal peoples' right to self-government became a critical issue in the new round of negotiations after the death of Meech Lake. The Charlottetown Accord in 1992 called for a constitutional amendment which recognized the right to self-government and aboriginal governments as one of the three levels of government with the right

> (a) to safeguard and develop their languages, cultures, economies, identities and traditions, and (b) to develop, maintain and strengthen their relationship with their lands, waters and environment; so as to determine and control their development as peoples according to their own values and priorities and ensure the integrity of their societies.

The principle of native peoples' inherent right to self-government, inherited from their self-governing ancestors, might be conceded. But there were too many questions left unanswered in the accompanying text. What did self-government mean: municipal government, something like provincial status, complete sovereignty within or without the Canadian state? What lands? What about urban communities? Who would pay and how much? Many Canadians, in areas of large aboriginal populations, were not prepared to gamble and voted against the accord. The vast majority of aboriginal peoples boycotted the referendum. With the defeat of the accord, the complex issues of land rights and self-government had to be resolved by negotiations between the First Nations and the provincial and federal governments and through concrete cases brought before the courts.

Over the next few years there were many agreements across Canada. Perhaps the most striking was the creation of Nunavut, which became a self-governing Inuit territory in 1999. Another was the agreement in 1996 of the federal and provincial governments with the Nisga'a of northern British Columbia to turn over 2,000 km² of land, pay $200-million over 20 years and allow the Nisga'a their own local government.

Meanwhile, in the best of Canadian traditions, a Royal Commission on Aboriginal Peoples, composed partly of aboriginals, had been at work. After five years of study, the Commission submitted a 3,537-page report in November 1996. The Commission recommended sweeping changes in every aspect of aboriginal life and their relations with governments. Nothing was overlooked: an apology for injustice, their House of First Peoples, settlement of land claims, self-determination, recognition of aboriginal law and customs, and a wide and expensive variety of programs to break the age-old condition of financial dependency. The report was enthusiastically received by aboriginal leaders, who warned: "This is no time to waffle. This is no time to be cute. This is your last chance." The federal government was less enthusiastic. The price tag was $30-billion over 15 years, and the provinces were concerned about expensive land-claim settlements. The Commission may have pointed the way, but the road to the future threatened to be rocky indeed.

On some routes, however, progress was remarkable. In the landmark decision of *Delgamuuk* v. *British Columbia* in 1997, the Supreme Court affirmed aboriginal rights in relation to land they had occupied long before the Europeans arrived and had not been ceded by formal treaties. Two years later, after 30 years of litigation, a most remarkable treaty was signed between the governments of Canada and British Columbia and the Nisga'a. The treaty gave the 5,500 Nisga'a, only 2,000 of whom lived in the Nass Valley in northern British Columbia, absolute ownership Of 1,991 km² of land, including all surface and subsurface resources, as well as fishing and hunting rights over a wider area. One central government and four village governments possessed wide powers of self-government in matters of culture, language, and family life, but the Charter of Rights and the Canadian Criminal Code remained in force. Many provincial and federal taxes would not apply. Finally the Nisga'a received $190-million in cash, most of it from the federal government. To the charge that the treaty was a form of cultural apartheid, a Nisga'a leader replied: "We are not negotiating our way out of Canada; we are negotiating our way back into Canada." But many non-native peoples opposed the agreement, for if all 50 treaties in British Columbia followed a similar pattern, there would be little land or resources left for the non-native population, and the social face of the province would be altered forever. There was almost an audible sigh of relief in July 2000 when the Squamish band accepted $92.5-million from Ottawa and gave up its claim to large tracts of land in Vancouver!

Far less controversial, but equally positive, was the federal government's relations with the Inuit. On 1 April 1999, a new Inuit territory was carved out of the Northwest Territories and came into existence as the largely self-governing territory of Nunavut, or "Our Land," with its capital of Iqaluit.

But on other routes the way ahead was rocky indeed. In 1990, Mohawk fought Quebec police and the military to a standstill until Ottawa agreed to buy land to be used for a golf course which the Mohawk regarded as sacred and turned it over to them. The Battle of Gustafson Lake in 1995 in British Columbia over the legal status of a sacred ceremonial site was the largest police and military action in provincial history, as about 20 armed native and non-native sundancers were surrounded by 400 RCMP officers. And in the summer of 2000 the Mi'kmaq of Burned Creek in New Brunswick were engaged in a confrontation with federal fishery officers when they defied regulations governing the lobster fishery, although they had been upheld by the Supreme Court. The wars were apparently far from over.

MULTICULTURALISM: MYTH OR REALITY?

As a historian, I have always been disturbed by the proud boast that Canada was not a "melting pot" like its southern neighbour, but a multicultural mosaic where new Canadians were not forced into the crucible of assimilation but encouraged to wear their ethnic or cultural origin on their sleeve. Through most of Canadian history — unless new arrivals wished to remain outside the mainstream of Canadian life — they had to assimilate, outwardly at least, to the language, behaviour and cultural norms of the host society. Indeed, since almost all Canadians were of European origin — 97 per cent as late at 1961 — the culture was simply not all that culturally diverse.

Canada has always been the destination of, and home to, a flow of people from other parts of the world. Some were pulled by the prospect of a better life; others were pushed by deprivation or persecution. But with some exceptions — notably Chinese, Japanese and Indian immigrants to the West coast — these immigrants were, through the 1950s, largely of European origin. Although the process of assimilation was sometimes slow and sometimes painful, over time the newcomers assimilated to the French or English culture in which they had settled. To some extent they preserved their cultural traditions and language, but in a couple of generations most had become Canadian, their national origin identifiable only by their last name and a few preserved cultural traditions. Canadians, it seemed, wanted it thus.

While Canada historically welcomed the "men in sheepskin coats," Canadian immigration policy was never an open-door policy that admitted all comers regardless of race or skin colour. Indeed, as late as 1947, Mackenzie King could state publicly that Canada did not "wish as a result of mass immigration, to make a fundamental alteration in the character of the Canadian population." At that time there were less than 100,000 Canadians, other than native people, whose origins were not British or European. Today, one Canadian in 10 belongs to a "visible minority" — a euphemism that seeks to avoid the words "race" and "colour." In Toronto, the ratio is almost one in three.

The change began in the 1960s, when Canadian immigration policy eliminated racial considerations as a criterion for entry. At that time 80 per cent of immigrants came from Europe; by the 1980s over 70 per cent were coming from Asia, Africa and Latin America. Of these, about 60 per cent were destined for the three largest cities: Toronto (35 per cent), Vancouver (11 per cent) or Montreal (14 per cent). The new, less restrictive immigration policy was not the only reason for the change, however. With the recovery of post-war Europe, emigrating to Canada was no longer as attractive as it had been.

Immigration policy was always contentious, with governments responding to pressure from a number of different constituencies. Usually cast in economic terms, the debate often centred on labour-force needs or the need to replenish an aging population with a younger element. But there was also the more generally humanitarian argument that it was Canada's duty to provide a home for the less fortunate of the world. Any attempt to tighten the criteria for entry, or to take a more hard-boiled approach towards refugees, aroused intense opposition from humanitarian civil libertarians and members of already established immigrant communities. Governments made adjustments in the policies every few years, but the general pattern of immigration of visible minorities remained constant throughout the 1970s and 1980s.

Most economists argue that the effects of immigration are beneficial, and a recent Economic Council of Canada study suggested cautiously that, although its net economic benefit to Canada was small, immigration was necessary to increase the population and the GNP. On the other hand, the study showed that, contrary to popular belief, nearly every immigrant paid for herself in scale economies and lighter tax burdens, with the possible exception of refugees, who cost the host society much more to process.

It was clear, however, that continuing the immigration pattern will continue to change the ethnic profile of the country and will test the tolerance level of already-settled communities, particularly if there is a sudden increase in the proportion of visible minority immigration or a deep economic recession with high unemployment.

The changes to immigration policy since 1960 wrought a profound change in the structure of Canadian society — and in the meaning of the word multiculturalism. Not only were the new immigrants "visible," but over 75 per cent of new immigrants were concentrated in five major urban centres, usually in compact communities that nourished their traditional cultures. It was not long before the contradictions in Canadian society began to appear. On the one hand was the rhetoric, fostered by the state, of respecting and nourishing multiculturalism; on the other was the inevitable real or perceived discrimination and racism.

The Trudeau government officially adopted multiculturalism as a policy in 1971, and appointed a minister responsible for its implementation the following year. Twenty-five years later, there is still controversy over the reasons behind the new policy. Some regard it as an attempt to appease the opponents of the policy of biculturalism and bilingualism; francophones certainly opposed it as somehow diminishing their unique position in Canada. Others scoffed that it was nothing but a cynical attempt to capture the "ethnic vote." Many others, however, believed that it was an appropriate response to the changing nature of

Canadian society; they watched to see if it would become something more than "folk dancing and feathers."

The verdict on the ultimate impact of multiculturalism has yet to be delivered. However, it was embedded in principle in Canadian policy when Section 27 of the Charter of Rights and Freedoms instructed the courts to interpret the Charter "in a manner consistent with the preservation and enhancement of the multicultural heritage of Canadians...."

By the 1980s, multiculturalism had been overtaken by the more sensitive and immediate issue of race relations. The increase in both the number and the concentration of visible minorities had led, inevitably, to racial discrimination. In the early 1980s race relations became a major component of the Ministry of Multiculturalism's jurisdiction with the establishment of its Race Relations Directorate. In 1988, when the Mulroney government gave multiculturalism legislative status with the passage of the Canadian Multicultural Act, this new mandate was made explicit. The act recognized "the diversity of Canadians as regards to race, national or ethnic origin, colour and religion as fundamental characteristics of Canadian society," and provided that the government should "assist ethno-cultural minority communities to conduct activities with a view to overcoming any discriminatory barriers and, in particular, discrimination based on race or national ethnic origin." The strategy to eliminate racial discrimination was to include, among other measures, public education, institutional change and support for community advocacy.

Promoting multiculturalism and countering racial discrimination are similar, but not identical, goals. Preserving Canada's multicultural heritage is not quite the same as abolishing discrimination in housing, investigating charges of police prejudice, or responding to a demand for differential university admission requirements or professional qualifications. What can we make of the 150,000 petitions to members of Parliament protesting the desire of the government to make the RCMP more representative of the community and, among other changes, allow Sikhs to wear turbans? Or of a best-selling pin that showed a white man dwarfed by a Sikh in a turban, a Chinese man, and a black man carrying a spear, with the words "Who's the minority in Canada?"[11]

By the early 1990s, many Canadians were becoming increasingly ambivalent about immigration policy and multiculturalism. A public opinion survey in the spring of 1994 revealed that although 73 per cent believed that "a mixture of different lifestyles and cultures makes Canada a more attractive place to live," most also believed that there were "too many immigrants," especially those of visible minorities. Six out of 10 agreed that "too many immigrants feel no obligation to adapt to Canadian values and way of life." (*Globe and Mail*, 11 March 1994). And another survey indicated that 72 per cent believed that "the long-standing image of Canada as a nation of communities, each ethnic and racial group preserving its own identity with the help of government policy, must give way to the U.S. style of cultural absorption." (*Globe and Mail*, 14 December 1993). The debate over immigration, multiculturalism and racism is now clearly on political agendas, and only realism, not rhetoric, will produce programs and policies that will lead to accommodation, not confrontation.

The same might be said for dealing with the refugee issue. By the mid-1980s Canada began to be swamped by thousands of people arriving who claimed to be refugees. Of the 18,000 claimants in 1986, an estimated two-thirds were not genuine refugees. Ever since 155 Tamils were picked up on lifeboats off Newfoundland in 1986, and 174 Sikhs waded ashore in Nova Scotia a year later yelling "refugees," successive governments have attempted to define a policy, and procedures were liberal and humane but could separate legitimate refugees from the more usual bogus claimants. Despite tightening and streamlining, Canada continued to admit more refugees per capita than any other country. In 1991 the Refugee Board granted refugee status to 64 per cent of those who applied. But later in the decade it became clear that many refugees were really the product of "human trafficking" on an enormous scale. In the summer of 1999, 600 Chinese migrants came by boat to the British Columbia coast who were alleged to have paid $30,000–$40,000 each to organized gangs of people smugglers. In January 2000 another group were found in a container ship in Vancouver.

Finally, in April 2000, the government announced sweeping changes to the Immigration Act. Admitting that the act was "tough," the minister responded to the usual criticism by interested groups that "closing the back door to those who would abuse the system will allow us to open the front door even wider, both to genuine refugees and to immigrants Canada will need to grow."

CANADA, QUEBEC AND THE CONSTITUTION

Since 1960, Canada has been convulsed by the question of constitutional reform. The problem has appeared in many forms, but the dynamic force behind the push for change has always been the demand from Quebec for a radical decentralization of the Canadian federal state. What began as an apparently simple request for more money and more power was soon cast in the rhetoric of "special status," "associate statehood," "distinct society" or "sovereignty-association" — each term carrying with it certain (usually unspecified) alterations to the constitution. The concrete matters debated during the sixties included an amending formula, patriation of the constitution, a new division of revenues and responsibilities, language and cultural rights, and reform of the institutions of the central government. By the 1970s the Western provinces had also become important participants in the debate, as they attempted to increase their clout at the political centre: most notably by demanding an "elected, equal and effective" Senate. By the 1990s Canada's aboriginal people had also become key players in the game; their primary demand was for self-government, whatever form that might take. But in 1992, the main topic in the debate that put the country at risk and preoccupied our governors was still the question of a new form of federalism or the independence of Quebec.

Historians, political scientists, sociologists and armchair experts have all attempted to explain "what happened with Quebec." None have had much success. For there **is** no simple explanation, other than the glib statement that the obsession of the Québécois (as they now call themselves) and of their political and religious leaders since the conquest in 1759 has been *la survivance*." Over the years this has meant a high birth rate (*"la revanche du berceau"*); political control of the territory of Quebec; the cementing of the French language, the Catholic religion and traditional rural, agrarian and familial values; and, after 1867, the protective shelter of a provincial government that controlled the social and cultural life of the Québécois and the institutions that enabled them to survive. But the twentieth-century forces of industrialization, urbanization and modernization weakened the cement within Quebec society, while the post-1945 expansion of the activities of the central government penetrated the walls of fortress Quebec.

The Quiet Revolution that began in 1960 was first and foremost a demand for modernization within Quebec. But it soon became a demand for a revolution in the relations between Quebec and the rest of Canada. The survival, that for two centuries had been a defensive obsession, now seemed to demand an offensive strategy. The state, which had for centuries been a somewhat passive participant in the struggle, replaced the church as an instrument to assure survival. This state was soon firmly in the hands of a new elite — of bureaucrats, academics, journalists, trade union leaders and upwardly mobile business leaders — that assumed all power within Quebec, and demanded either more power within the Canadian state system, or, if that proved to be impossible, independence.

Canadians outside Quebec responded with a mixture of sympathy, bewilderment, opposition and anger. The demand for more money and power was a familiar refrain in federal–provincial relations. Few objected to allowing Quebec (and other provinces if they wished, though none did) to "opt out" of national social security and welfare systems, provided it continued to provide the same services. Few objected to Ottawa sharing Canadian tax dollars more liberally with Quebec — and other provinces — although it threatened stabilization as well as equalization policies. Most objected to Quebec's claims to warrant its own foreign relations with French-speaking countries, but accepted the compromise of allowing Quebec to be represented as part of the Canadian delegation at meetings of La Francophonie. But most anglophones condemned the language policy of the Quebec government, and rejected the very idea of Quebec being recognized as a "distinct society" if that meant it had a status legally superior to that of other provinces.

A funny thing happened on the way to the new 1982 Constitution. The process had begun in 1968, largely as a response to nationalist pressures from Quebec for enlarged provincial powers. But under Pierre Trudeau, who had come to Ottawa in 1965 to fight nationalism in Quebec, and became prime minister three years later, the nature of the debate was slowly but surely transformed. Patriation of the 1867 Constitution — a statute of the British Parliament — was made to appear as a symbol of our nationhood. The debate over power-sharing was soon eclipsed by the discussion of a Charter of (individual and collective) Rights and Freedoms. The provincial premiers in Quebec and elsewhere, Trudeau argued, wanted to increase "their" power, while he was determined to increase the power of "the people."

The irony was that the conclusion of the 20-year debate over the demands of Quebec for a new constitution was the emergence of a new Constitution in 1982 that restricted, rather than expanded, Quebec's powers — this, despite Mr. Trudeau's promise of a "renewed federalism" when he appealed to the

Québécois to vote *non* in the 1980 referendum on independence. There was no redistribution of legislative powers; there was only a modest limitation of the federal government's power to offer the provinces new shared-cost programs in areas of provincial jurisdiction; and the new amending formula did not give Quebec a veto over constitutional change. In short, Quebec did not receive the special status it had demanded since 1960. In fact, the Charter of Rights and Freedoms restricted the power of Quebec, as it did that of every other government in Canada. The section on language entrenched official bilingualism at the centre and protected some anglophone educational rights in Quebec. The courts decided that the right to "freedom of expression" protected anglophones against some other sections of Bill 101, such as the prohibition against English in commercial advertising.

Recognizing these limits for what they were, the Parti Québécois government, led by René Lévesque, refused to endorse the new constitution — and so began the long journey to Meech Lake and beyond.

THE POLITICS OF LANGUAGE

Language, perhaps the most inflammatory of the issues that have bedevilled Canada over the last generation, was a crucial element in the debate over constitutional reform. Unlike the distribution of powers, which can seem arcane to the uninitiated, language is not just an issue, but a fundamental part of everyone's daily life. Language is part of our identity — we are, to a certain extent, what we speak. New Canadians urge their children to retain their mother tongue, for it is the key to retaining their cultural heritage. Conversely, language can be a barrier to complete assimilation by the host culture. The importance of language, as both a reality and a symbol, is readily understood by virtually anyone.

The critical importance of language to identity was best stated by Bernard Lee Whorf, the eminent linguist:

> And every language is a vast pattern system, different from others, in which are culturally ordained the forms and categories by which the personality not only communicates, but also analyzes nature, notices or neglects types of relationships and phenomena, channels his reasoning, and builds the house of his consciousness.[12]

René Lévesque, founder of the Parti Québécois, put it more bluntly:

> We are Québécois.... Being ourselves is essentially a matter of keeping and developing a personality that has survived for three-and-a half centuries. At the core of this personality is the fact that we speak French. Everything else depends on this one essential element and follows from it or leads infallibly back to it.[13]

Language has been a contentious issue throughout Canadian history; by the 1960s it was more contentious than ever — seemingly unsolvably so. The only language rights guaranteed in the 1867 Constitution were the rights of Canadians to speak English or French in the Parliament and courts of Canada and Quebec. Where more extensive language rights were protected by law (as in Manitoba) or existed in practice (as in Ontario), they were soon eroded by the sheer size of the anglophone majority.

By the 1960s most of Canada outside Quebec was unilingually anglophone; francophones who left Quebec had discovered that they had to learn the language of their new hosts to assimilate. Inside Quebec, most francophones were unilingual and few anglophones could function in French. On the whole, social class and language in Quebec were closely related: French was the language of the factory floor, and English of the boardroom. Upwardly mobile francophones had no choice but to become bilingual — and even then their chances of success seemed remote. In Ottawa, the language of work was basically English. It was a bad joke to note that French was the language of the elevator, and English of the executive offices.

To stem the tide of Quebec nationalism and separatism in the 1960s, Pierre Trudeau concluded that the federal government — in Ottawa and across the country — had to accommodate francophones as well as anglophones. If francophones could feel at home in the national capital and across the country, he reasoned, Québécois would be less interested in independence. The Official Languages Act of 1969 declared French and English to be the official languages of Canada "for all purposes of the Parliament and Government of Canada, and [to] possess and enjoy equality of status and equal rights as to their use in all the institutions of the Parliament and Government of Canada."

The civil service, at least in its upper echelons, was to be truly bilingual. Civil servants were packed off to language schools and rewarded for their bilingual proficiency; a language commissioner tracked the success of bilingualism in the civil service, Crown corporations and boards and agencies. Trudeau also embarked on a campaign to encourage the provinces to move towards bilingualism in their operations and to create or expand francophone schools.

Although it achieved limited success in Ottawa, Trudeau's policy aroused bitter opposition among anglophones who, not understanding the policy and believing that they had to become bilingual, protested that they would not have "French crammed down their throats." Meanwhile, this nationwide crusade for bilingualism did little — or nothing — to dampen the nationalist fires in Quebec. Indeed, if anything it fanned the flames.

In 1976, anglophone pilots and air traffic controllers went on strike, refusing to accept French as the language of communication over Quebec. The support for the strikers from anglophone Canada was strong, and included a measure of venom in its criticism of the bilingual policy. The federal government was forced to back down, but many Québécois went to the polls that November with buttons reading "Il y a du Français dans l'air" to cast their votes for the victorious Parti Québécois.

Language became even more important as other traditional elements of Québécois culture weakened. Quebec in the 1960s was becoming increasingly secular; the Church was losing its 200-year-old hold on society. There was less and less room for traditional rural, agrarian and familial values in an increasingly urban society.

Moreover, as the birth rate dropped from one of the highest in the industrialized world to one of the lowest, and immigrants to Quebec usually assimilated to English rather than French, demographic projections pointed to a declining francophone population in Quebec — to the point where it was conceivable that, in some distant future, the majority of Montrealers might be anglophones.

In the face of all this, members of the francophone elite that had gained power in 1960, whatever their political affiliations, were determined to be *"maîtres chez nous."* Their primary weapon was to be language: French would be the language of the province of Quebec at all levels, right up to, and including, the corporate boardrooms.

Introduced in stages, the largely unilingual language policy reached its fullest — to some, its most draconian form — in 1977 when the Parti Québécois introduced Bill 101. French became **the** official language: the government would operate in French; business and the professions would operate in French (Eaton's had to drop its apostrophe to provide a *visage française*!); all advertising would be in French; immigrant children would be educated in French — only the children of Quebec anglophones were to be excepted from the French-only education policy.

Bill 101 aroused intense opposition in anglophone Canada. The Supreme Court of Canada ruled that the provisions making French the only official language of government were unconstitutional, because they violated the guarantees of the 1867 Constitution. In 1988, the court further ruled that the French-only sign law violated the freedom-of-expression clause in the Charter of Rights. When Quebec used the Charter's "notwithstanding clause" to override the court decision, anglophone protests reached a hysterical pitch. Just as many Québécois had voted for the Péquistes over the language of the skies, many anglophones rejected the idea of a "distinct society" in the Meech Lake Accord after the crisis over the language of signs.

If left alone, Pierre Trudeau boasted, the new constitution he had fashioned in 1982 would have lasted a thousand years. But it could not be left alone because Quebec had refused to accept it as morally binding — regardless of its legal status — on the grounds that it had been passed without Quebec's consent. During the 1984 election campaign, Brian Mulroney had promised a policy of "national reconciliation" and to "bring Quebec back in" by renewing the process of constitutional reform. His overwhelming victory, followed by the defeat of the Parti Québécois in 1985, placed constitutional reform once again at the centre of the national agenda.

Although the immediate objective was to pacify Quebec, it was soon apparent that Mulroney had opened Pandora's box and released many voices and interests — women, aboriginals, minorities and majorities, regions and provinces — that demanded to be heard and recognized. Everyone, it seemed, had "rights" and unless **their** rights were entrenched in a new constitution, none would be. Those voices and interests killed the Meech Lake agreement in 1990 and, after two more years of agonizing, almost paralyzing, negotiations, still threatened, in the summer of 1992, to make any settlement impossible, regardless of the threat to the Canadian state as we know it.

Soon after their victory in 1985, the Quebec Liberals under Robert Bourassa set out their demands for a revised constitution. After months of negotiations, in 1987 the prime minister and all provincial premiers agreed at

Meech Lake, a federal government retreat in the Gatineau hills, to a set of constitutional amendments that satisfied Quebec. By far the most controversial was the recognition of Quebec as a "distinct society" and the affirmation of the responsibility of the government of Quebec to "preserve and promote" that distinct identity. At the same time, the existence of a French-speaking and an English-speaking Canada was stated to be "a fundamental characteristic of Canada." Other provisions permitted provinces to opt out of new shared-cost programs with fiscal compensation if the province undertook a comparable program, gave the provinces a voice in appointments to the Senate and the Supreme Court (as Quebec has demanded), expanded provincial powers over constitutional amendments and increased the power of Quebec (and of other provinces if they wished) over immigration and the integration of immigrants. The accord had to be approved by Parliament and all provincial legislatures by June 23, 1990.

On June 23, 1990, Meech Lake was dead. Technically, the accord died when, in Manitoba, MPP Elijah Harper, an aboriginal, refused on procedural grounds to let a vote be taken by a reluctant provincial government, and in Newfoundland, a new government, opposed to the accord, did not give its assent. But more generally, Meech failed because it had aroused intense opposition among many groups within Canadian society. While many argued that the accord would fatally weaken the central government, most of the opposition focused on the "distinct-society" and "fundamental-characteristic" clauses. Why should Quebec be regarded as a distinct society with enhanced powers? Would distinct-society status override the Charter? If Quebec was distinct, why not aboriginals, whose demands for self-government had not been accepted? If Quebec had special status, why not all the provinces? Where did the fundamental characteristic of biculturalism leave cultural minorities? Women asked — largely outside Quebec — whether the distinct-society clause would undermine the equality rights in the Charter and whether the limits on new shared-costs programs would prevent new programs such as day care.

Put most broadly, Meech Lake failed because it represented an elite consensus that did not exist in a political community too fragmented by the clamour of language, culture, region and rights.

With Quebec planning a referendum on its future in 1992, and refusing to enter into more negotiations until the other governments had firm proposals on the table, the process began all over again. This was not to be another "Quebec round," but a "Canada round" in which tens of thousands of Canadians were given the opportunity to present their views and demands. What had emerged in the Charlottetown Accord in the fall of 1993 was an elaborate set of proposals which went far beyond those in Meech. The ingredients in Meech, including the controversial distinct society clause, were still there. But there were strong statements concerning the aboriginal right to self-government, and gender, racial and ethnic equality. Advocates of a Triple-E Senate won the day, as did the supporters of a social charter which committed governments to maintain high levels of health care, public education, social services and environmental protection, as well as guarantees of the right to collective bargaining. Governments were also committed to strengthening the Canadian economic union with policies that would reduce the barriers to interprovincial trade, maintain full employment, ensure all Canadians a "reasonable standard of living," and ensure "sustainable and equitable development." The federal government also agreed to withdraw from the fields of tourism, housing, urban affairs, forestry, mining and recreation. Culture was also recognized as an area of exclusive provincial jurisdiction, but Ottawa retained its control over national cultural institutions and agencies. No group secured everything it wanted, but there was something for everyone, except the federal government — unless it was peace at any price.

Although the accord was accepted, often reluctantly, by every government, 54.4 per cent of the Canadian people voted NO in an October 26, 1992 referendum after an emotional and bitter campaign. The vote was overwhelmingly NO in Quebec and the four Western provinces, and narrowly NO in Nova Scotia. The three other Atlantic provinces voted strongly YES and Ontario went YES by a few thousand votes. While it is difficult to generalize, it would appear that those who voted YES believed that the proposals represented a reasonable set of compromises to resolve the constitutional impasse. On the other hand, there was no agreement among those who championed the NO cause. Women and aboriginal peoples voted NO because they did not get enough. Quebec separatists and nationalists voted NO because it offered too little, while sentiment in the West — led by the Reform Party — clearly believed it offered Quebec too much. The vote was indeed a crude calculation of profit and loss, whether selfish or principled. Whatever the reasons, the defeat of the accord did not blaze a trail towards the future, but left Canada deep in a seemingly impenetrable constitutional swamp.

The federal election of October 1993 confirmed the deep divisions within the country. After eight years in office, the Conservative Party was annihilated. The Liberals won all but one seat in Ontario, swept the Maritimes, and won seats in every province to win a comfortable majority. But in Quebec, the separatist Bloc Québécois, formed three years earlier in response to the defeat of Meech, won 54 of the 75 seats to form the official Opposition. The Reform Party, the six-year-old vehicle for the expression of Western discontent and anti-Quebec and other nativist sentiments, swept British Columbia and Alberta, and ran second in Saskatchewan, Manitoba and even Ontario. When Parliament opened in January 1994, Jean Chrétien faced Lucien Bouchard's Bloc Québécois, which wanted out, and Preston Manning's Reform Party, which was not prepared to make any concessions to keep them in.

The picture became bleaker in the fall of 1994, when the Parti Québécois, led by Jacques Parizeau, defeated the provincial Liberals, although there was some comfort in the fact that although the PQ won 77 seats and the Liberals 47, the PQ secured only 44.7 per cent of the popular vote and the Liberals 44.3. As promised during the campaign, the PQ held another referendum in 1995. Although some polls predicted a YES victory, when the 4.6-million votes were counted, 49.7 per cent of Québécois had voted NO, and 48.5 per cent YES: A margin of 53,498 votes.

There was relief, but little joy, in the rest of the country. It was clear that a majority of French Canadians had voted YES, but had been defeated by the anglophones and other minorities who make up 18 per cent of the population. Soon after the referendum Parizeau resigned and was replaced by the charismatic Lucien Bouchard, who had taken charge of the YES campaign. For the moment, Bouchard declared that the economy was his first priority, but sooner or later there would be another referendum and, sooner rather than later, he promised Québécois, "we will have our country."

But inside and outside Quebec there was an angry insistence that the territorial boundaries of that new country would have to reflect the wishes of the people: anglophones, minorities (even the francophone minority who opposed independence), and aboriginals (who had voted overwhelmingly in their own referendum against separation). And in learned conferences across the country, academics continued to debate the future of that other new nation they variously called ROC or CWOQ — the Rest of Canada or Canada without Quebec.

As the academics brooded, Ottawa moved ahead with its own agenda, described as Plan A — the carrot, and Plan B — the legal and constitutional stick. The first stage in Plan A was to honour Prime Minister Chrétien's promises during the referendum campaign. As promised, a week after the referendum the House of Commons passed a resolution stating that "Quebec is a distinct society within Canada," its distinctiveness including "its French-speaking majority, unique culture and civil law tradition," and encouraging all governments "to take notice of this recognition and be guided in their conduct accordingly." (Following the dictates of their consciences or their constituents, the best the provincial premiers could do in their Calgary Declaration in 1997 was to recognize the "unique character" of Quebec, but combine that statement of motherhood with the uncompromising principle of the equality of the provinces, appropriately described by Jeffrey Simpson of the *Globe and Mail* as merely "the latest in a series of concocted political attempts to square constitutional circles.") In 1996 the government passed the *Constitutional Veto Act*, a self-denying ordinance that prevented the federal government from approving any constitutional amendment that did not have the consent of Quebec, Ontario, British Columbia, and two of both the Atlantic and Prairie provinces with 50 per cent of the regional population, thus giving Alberta a veto as well. There was little enthusiasm in Quebec and little opposition in the rest of Canada for these conciliatory efforts that, of course, were not entrenched in the constitution.

Plan B involved putting a case before the Supreme Court to determine whether Quebec had the right to unilaterally declare its independence. Québécois objected that the question was not one of law but of democratic politics, and the government refused to argue in court. In an enlightened and sensitive opinion, a unanimous Court observed that the question involved the democratic rights of all Canadians, not just those in Quebec, the rule of law, and the order and stability of the country. But it also concluded that in the end the question was political:

> The Constitution vouchsafes order and stability, and accordingly secession of a province 'under the constitution' could not be achieved unilaterally, that is, without principled negotiation with other participants in Confederation within the existing constitutional framework....
>
> The negotiation process would require the reconciliation of various rights and obligations between two legitimate majorities, namely, the majority of the population of Quebec, and that of Canada as a whole....

> The task of the Court has been to clarify the legal framework within which political decisions are to be taken 'under the Constitution' and not to usurp the prerogatives of the political forces that operate within that framework.... However, it will be for the political actors to determine what constitutes 'a clear majority on a clear question' in circumstances under which a future referendum vote may be taken. Equally, in the event of a demonstrated majority support for Quebec secession, the content and process of the negotiations will be for the political actors to settle. The reconciliation of the various legitimate constitutional interests is necessarily committed to the political rather than the judicial realm precisely because that reconciliation can only be achieved through the give and take of political negotiations....[14]

By 2000 the political actors had defined their position. Ottawa declared in the *Clarity Act* that the House of Commons in a resolution would decide whether the question asked, which could not envision any continued association with Canada, was clear. The Commons also would determine whether the results represented a "clear expression of a will by a clear majority" to separate, but did not state what level of support was necessary. Finally, the Act indicated that negotiations must include all the provincial governments and perhaps other actors as well — conceivably the aboriginal peoples and the anglophone minority. Quebec responded with its own legislation, which stated that it alone would determine "the nature, scope and mode of exercise of its right to self-determination," and that 50 per cent plus one was enough for a referendum victory.

With support for separatism falling, but with that future an acceptable — if not, at the moment, the preferred — option for a majority of francophones, we wait for Premier Bouchard or his successor(s) to decide that the time has come, as he said, "to have a winning referendum."

THE WAY AHEAD

With Quebec at rest, a trillion-dollar economy, budget surpluses, and peace and prosperity (for most), perhaps only an historian could see shadows in the sunlight. There is little doubt that the momentum today in the field of federal–provincial relations, which determines so much in the area of public policy, is towards devolution or decentralization. The buzz-words of the movement are disentanglement, clarity, transparency, accountability in budgeting and delivery, comparative advantage, non-hierarchical relations, and subsidiarity in program delivery. Whatever the semantic description, the direction is clear but the destination is uncertain. If it appears that the destination is a return to the pre-1945 classical federalism, with minor modifications (which seems the choice of Ontario and Alberta as well as the Canadian Alliance), any consensus will soon disappear. The "Canada that has not" will be joined by those who believe that without a strong federal presence Canada will become a community of communities with an uncertain future. It is all very well for Thomas Courchene, that most passionate and persistent advocate of decentralization, to argue that Ontario is not a province but a regional nation-state and should act like one. That may be a recipe not just for decentralization but for dissolution. At a time when globalization undermines national sovereignties, economies and corporations, and when the international exports (largely to the United States) of all Canadian provinces other than Nova Scotia and Prince Edward Island were much greater than to the rest of Canada, when Canadian cultural space is monopolized by foreign, largely American, produced culture, one wonders whether a Canadian passport would be the glue that holds the nation together. If history be the guide, "executive provincialism" may be a problem, not a panacea.

NOTES

1. Royal Commission on Dominion-Provincial Relations, *Report* (Ottawa: King's Printer, 1940), 3 vols.
2. See the *White Paper on Employment and Income* (Ottawa: King's Printer, 1945). A useful survey of post-war federal–provincial relations is Garth Stevenson, *Unfulfilled Union: Canadian Federalism and National Unity* (Toronto: Gage, 1989).
3. By the late 1990s federal cash transfers through equalization and the Canada Heath and Social Transfer provided between 35 and 40 per cent of the revenues of the four Atlantic provinces.
4. Even after the federal government's program spending cuts in 1995, Quebec continued to receive about half the net benefit arising from major programs providing interregional distribution — including equalization and unemployment insurance, which since the 1970s had an interregional distribution from the five provinces west of Ottawa to the five east of it.
5. Royal Commission on the Economic Union and Development Prospects for Canada, *Report* (Ottawa: Ministry of Supply and Services, 1985), vol. 1, p. 46.
6. "Constitutional Minoritarianism in Canada," in R.L. Watts and D.M. Brown, eds., *Canada: The State of the Federation 1990* (Kingston, ON: Institute of Intergovernmental Relations, Queen's University, 1990), p. 75.
7. "How Ottawa Dithers: The Conservatives and Abortion Policy," in Frances Abele, ed., *How Ottawa Spends: The Politics of Fragmentation* (Ottawa: Carleton University Press, 1991), p. 270. *How Ottawa Spends* appears annually and provides an excellent survey of a wide range of public-policy issues.
8. F.L. Morton and Rainer Knopff, *The Charter Revolution and the Court Party* (Peterborough: Broadview Press, 2000).
9. *R. v. Morgentaler*, [1988] 2 S.C.R.
10. "How Ottawa Dithers: The Conservatives and Abortion Policy," in Frances Abele, ed., *How Ottawa Spends: The Politics of Fragmentation* (Ottawa: Carleton University Press, 1991), p. 285.
11. David Stasiulis, "Symbolic Representation and the Numbers Game: Tory Policies on 'Race' and Visible Minorities," in Frances Abele, ed., *How Ottawa Spends*, p. 251.
12. Cited in William Coleman, *The Independence Movement in Quebec 1945–1980* (Toronto, 1984), p. 183.
13. Ibid., p. 185.
14. *Reference re Secession of Quebec* [1998] 2 S.C.R. 217 at 220–22.

The Effects of Changing Demographics: Marketing and Human Resource Trends

David K. Foot

INTRODUCTION

Demographic trends in general, and population aging in particular, are important issues affecting the external environment of all organizations in North America and elsewhere, whether they be in the private or public sectors. As a discipline, demographics can be described as the "scientific study of human populations." Hence, demographics is about people — both as customers or clients and employees. Therefore, demographic trends have important implications for both the marketing and personnel functions in any organization.

This article explores the interrelationships between demographic trends, marketing and human resource planning, with particular emphasis on the future trends in North America and especially Canada. The analysis highlights the importance of the post-war baby-boom generation in influencing the external environment within which organizations have operated, and must continue to operate. Since individual organizations have almost no influence on demographic variables such as births, deaths, immigration and so on, demographic trends are truly external to the organization. It is not possible to use organizational decisions to internalize or modify these trends. They are inherently part of the external environment that must be monitored for the organization to be successful.

Interesting implications emerge from these observations. First, since people — and hence demographics — are the crucial element in both marketing and human resource planning, these two functions should be closely linked in any organization. Yet for many organizations it is often difficult to conceive of two more disparate areas, both physically and conceptually. An implicit message of this article is the need for a closer linkage between marketing and personnel functions.

Second, demographics is concerned with longer-term trends. In Canada annual population growth is around 1 per cent. Thus, incremental changes to the population are small compared to the total. This means that demographic shifts occur slowly and hence are easy to ignore — especially for those organizations with predominantly short-term goals, such as surviving to the next payroll, interest payment or the annual general meeting! Moreover, management styles and practices in North America have tended to reward and reinforce predominantly short-term goals. Salary and bonus packages tied to current (one-year-term or less) performances are one example. Consequently, demographic trends have tended to be ignored in corporate decision making.

Third, and perhaps a corollary to the short-term orientation in the corporate sector, has been the perceived need to be "more competitive." This goal tends to be associated with corporate downsizing (or "right-sizing") which so often resulted in the devolution of corporate functions to the front line. Emphasis is placed on moving these functions and their employees "closer to the customer" to make them "more accountable." While there may be undisputed benefits to this management practice, it does effectively downplay corporate functions such as strategic planning. Under this management style, trends that affect product performance are emphasized, and environmental monitoring tends to be product or niche-market oriented. To answer the bigger questions like "which markets should we be in and why?" requires not only a longer-term perspective but also a much broader, or corporate, perspective. Since demographic trends are probably more relevant to these types of corporate questions, these trends have tended to be ignored or to only receive "lip service" in the streamlined corporations of the past decade.

There is evidence that the tide may be changing again. Futurists such as John Naisbitt and Faith Popcorn re-emerged in the early 1990s with best-selling visions of future trends.[1] The short-term, predominantly inward-looking management style that dominated the 1980s was gradually replaced by a more longer-term, outward-looking style in the 1990s. In this emerging management style, corporate functions such as environmental monitoring and strategic planning take on more dominant roles.

It is within these various management styles and practices that demographic trends are positioned, interpreted and used. The management priorities of the 1980s, which focused primarily on short-term, product-oriented goals, resulted in the relative neglect of demographic trends in corporate decision making. In the 1990s, longer-term, corporate-oriented goals gave greater emphasis to the role of demographic trends in corporate decision making. Hopefully, this trend will continue in the new millennium.

This article provides two illustrations of the use of demographic trends in organizational decision making. After a necessarily cursory review of demographic trends in Canada, it examines the impact of demographic trends in marketing (people as customers or clients) and human resource planning (people as employees). While the focus is on the emerging trends of today and beyond, historical evidence is presented to provide the longer-term perspective so crucial to understanding and using demographic trends appropriately in the modern organization.

HISTORICAL DEMOGRAPHIC TRENDS: A REVIEW

Sources of Demographic Data

In Canada, the sources of major demographic data are the decennial censuses (1871–1941) and the quinquennial censuses (1951–1996) currently conducted mid-year by the federal statistical gathering agency Statistics Canada. The censuses provide details not only on the number of people but also on a variety of characteristics such as age, gender, location, marital status, ethnicity and so on. Additional information on related topics, such as labour-force status and housing, are also gathered at the same time. Thus the results of a census provide a snapshot of the Canadian population.

To fill in between the census years, Statistics Canada gathers additional data from a variety of other sources. Vital statistics on births, deaths, immigration, marriages and so on are collected from appropriate administrative registry authorities, while sample surveys are used to collect information in other areas (for example, the Labour Force Survey). In this way, consistent time series can be constructed to monitor the changes over time in the Canadian demographic, economic and social landscape. In many cases, the censuses provide useful periodic information that serves as a benchmark for these ongoing surveys.

Before reviewing historical Canadian census data, it is useful to be acquainted with the basic population identity that underlies these data and the future projections based on them. At any point in time (t), a country's population (P) is the population at a previous time period (t–1) plus births (B) minus deaths (D), plus immigration (I) minus emigration (E) over the intervening time period. (Births minus deaths is called the net natural change, while immigration minus emigration is called net immigration.) This means that the change in population (ΔP) can be expressed as the following identity:

$$\Delta P \equiv P_t - P_{t-1} \equiv B - D + I - E$$

Or

$$P_t \equiv P_{t-1} + B - D + I - E$$

In Canada, data on births, deaths and immigration are collected from appropriate administrative sources, but since it is not necessary to get permission to leave the country (that is, exit visas are not required) or to inform the authorities when doing so, there is no administrative source for emigration data. Consequently these data must be estimated, and the census provides an important benchmark for such estimates. In essence, the above identity is reversed to read

$$E \equiv B - D + I - \Delta P$$

to obtain estimates of emigration. These "residual" estimates of emigration ensure that the population identity is satisfied empirically.

For sub-national divisions within a country, such as provinces, the population identity must be modified to include movements of people within a country. Conceptually, this can be accomplished by defining $(I - E)$ to include all net immigrants to the population, both international and intranational. The census is also useful in identifying intranational movements of persons both between provinces and within provinces.

Results of Recent Censuses

Figure 1 displays the results from the 1971 and 1981 censuses in Canada to provide a historical perspective. This figure is called a "population pyramid." It shows the number of persons in each age-gender group for each census year.

A number of features of the Canadian population are apparent from Figure 1. Consider first the pyramid for 1971. Perhaps the most notable feature is that by 1971 the base of the pyramid had collapsed — there were fewer one-year-olds than 10-year-olds in the population. This reflects the declining numbers of births during the 1960s after the commercial introduction of the birth-control pill and as women entered the paid labour force. As a result, the increasing numbers of births that followed World War II came to an end, creating what is commonly referred to as the "baby-boom" and "baby-bust" generations.[2] From the 1971 population pyramid, the baby-boom generation in Canada can be conveniently defined as ranging from ages 5 to 24 years — that is, those born over the period from 1947 to 1966.

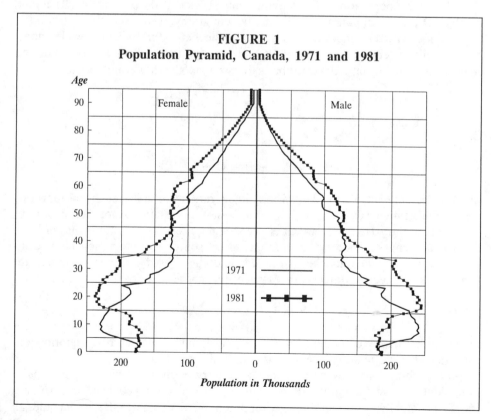

FIGURE 1
Population Pyramid, Canada, 1971 and 1981

To assess the extent of the baby-bust, it is necessary to move forward to the 1981 population pyramid. In so doing, note that the 1981 pyramid looks like the 1971 pyramid moved up ten years. Not surprisingly, ten years later people are ten years older! (This represents one of the truisms of demographics — indeed of life in general, since we prefer not to contemplate the alternative!) Yet, while individuals may get a year older each year, this is not true for a group of individuals, such as a country. This difference is primarily attributable to net immigration, which augments the population in certain age groups. The very young and the elderly tend not to migrate as much as those of working age and especially not as much as those in their early working years. Consequently, countries with large immigrant populations, such as Canada, the United States and Australia, will not age at the same pace as those with populations born solely within the country. While perhaps obvious in retrospect, this is one of those demographic "facts" that is not always easy to comprehend.

Turning to the 1981 population pyramid, note that those in the baby-boom generation are aged 15 to 34 years. There are more than 400,000 people in each single-year cohort. The baby-bust generation is under 15 years. Other parts of the population pyramid are also of interest. The indentation around age 65 years represents the impact of World War I when fertility dropped in Canada. Then "the boys" came home — the Roaring Twenties were obviously good times — and the number of births increased. This was followed by the Depression years of the 1930s and, once again, fertility and the number of births declined. Those born between 1930 and 1939 were aged 42 to 51 years in 1981 and these were not large cohorts. Because of this relatively long period of low fertility, further postponement of childbearing did not take place during World War II. In fact, births started to rise over the war years, although the substantial increase was delayed until the advent of the post-war baby boom.

While every year these generations have become one year older, a new anticipated phenomenon emerged in the 1980s. This is apparent from the 1991 population pyramid (Figure 2), which suggests that the base of the population pyramid has been expanding slightly. After a period of decline, the youngest age groups started to grow again in the 1980s. This phenomenon is not attributable to a rise in fertility. Rather, it occurred because over the 1980s the massive baby-boom generation entered the prime childbearing period of the mid-twenties to mid-thirties. Even though, on average, baby boomers continued to have somewhat fewer children, over the 1980s there were so many of them having children that the numbers of births increased. This generation — the children of the baby boomers — is often called the "baby-boom echo" generation.[3] Just how long this trend can be expected to continue is a topic for debate and will be examined in the projections outlined in the next section. However, it is probably useful to note that, by 1991, early baby boomers were in their forties and even those peak boomers, born in 1960, were 31. Consequently, this massive generation was entering the ages when infertility starts to increase and it becomes increasingly difficult to bear children. For this reason, most population projections anticipated a decline in births sometime in the 1990s, thus signalling the end of the echo generation. The issue will be more fully outlined in the next section.

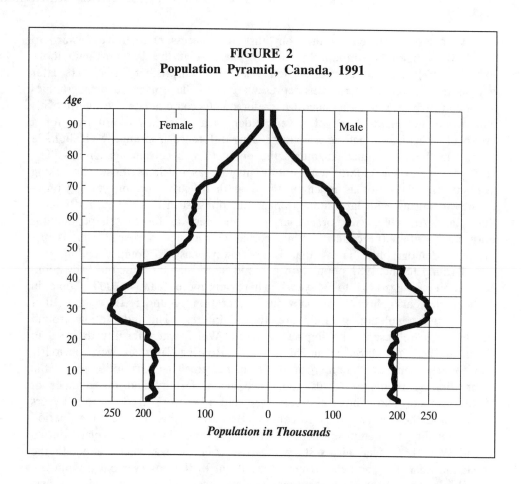

FIGURE 2
Population Pyramid, Canada, 1991

As postscripts, it should be noted that initial census results were adjusted for an estimated undercount — an adjustment that was larger in 1991 than in past censuses — and that the decision to now include "non-permanent" residents (primarily immigrant refugee claimants currently in Canada awaiting decisions on their applications) in the population count, both increased the population from initial estimates. The 1991 Canadian population was 28.1-million, well above the previous estimate of 27.0-million. Moreover, as might be expected, these non-permanent residents are concentrated in the younger age groups, particularly those in the 15 to 34 age group. Historical data consistent with this new definition are available back to 1971 (Figure 3), resulting in modest changes to population numbers and the implied growth rates.

Figure 3 summarizes these historical data. By 1991 in Canada:

➤ the relatively large group born prior to World War I were aged 76 years and over;

➤ the small group born during World War I were aged 72 to 75 years;

FIGURE 3
Population by Age, Canada 1971–1991 (millions)

Age Group (years)	1971	1981	1991
0 to 14	6.444	5.543	5.819
15 to 24	4.163	4.879	4.035
25 to 34	2.999	4.353	5.127
35 to 44	2.579	3.050	4.483
45 to 54	2.322	2.518	3.014
55 to 64	1.754	2.178	2.429
65 to 74	1.090	1.488	1.919
75 and over	0.675	0.891	1.292
Total	22.026	24.900	28.118

Source: Statistics Canada, Catalogue No. 91–537

➢ the relatively large group born during the "Roaring Twenties" were largely in the early retirement ages of 62 to 71 years;

➢ the small group born over the Depression years of the 1930s were aged 52 to 61 years;

➢ the World War II babies were aged 45 to 51 years;

➢ the massive, 9.6-million-strong post-war baby-boom generation was aged 25 to 44 years;

➢ the subsequent smaller baby-bust generation was aged 12 to 24 years;

➢ the relatively larger baby-boom echo generation consisted of pre-teens; and

➢ population estimates by Statistics Canada indicate that the Canadian population reached 30-million in 1996, by which time all of these groups had aged another five years.

These historical demographic facts have had important implications for the development of the Canadian marketplace both in terms of outputs (products and services) and inputs (labour). Both the marketing and personnel functions of all Canadian organizations have experienced the impacts of these demographic changes. But perhaps more importantly, with the absorption of the massive baby-boom generation into the Canadian labour force over the 1960s and 1970s completed, new trends emerged over the 1980s. Population aging has had an important impact on the marketplace as both the consumer and the worker have become noticeably older — a trend that can be expected to continue. In this sense, the trends of the 1980s became the watershed between the rapid-growth, youth-oriented decades of the 1960s and 1970s and the new slow-growth, older external environment of today.

But, perhaps most important of all, these are not unanticipated or unpredictable trends. The basic demographic truism that as individuals "every year we get one year older" provides an unassailable foundation on which to build a vision of the future of the Canadian marketplace and labour force. As the 1980s so clearly signalled, any Canadian organization that ignores these emerging demographic trends is likely to be ultimately destined to be at the "back of the pack" — if not at the "bottom of the harbour." After a cursory review of the population projection methodology, the following two sections provide a guide to a future, based on these historic demographic developments.

POPULATION PROJECTIONS

Population projections are based on the previous population identity and on the demographic truism outlined above. By making assumptions regarding the components of population growth, usually based on historical data, future populations can be projected. This is called the cohort component method, because it examines each of the components of population growth on a cohort (age) basis. By choosing different assumptions, alternative population projections are derived. This is the projection method employed by Statistics Canada.

In this approach, assumptions regarding fertility focus on the total fertility rate, a convenient statistical construct that provides an age-independent measure of fertility for an entire population at a point in time. Since each couple needs two children to replace themselves, a minimum replacement fertility level of 2 is established. However, since some members of the population cannot, or choose not to, have children, the replacement fertility rate for a population is slightly higher — around 2.1 children per woman. Canadian fertility peaked at almost 4 children per woman in 1960 at the height of the baby boom and thereafter declined dramatically to under 2 children per woman by the 1970s. Currently, the total fertility rate is around 1.7 children per woman, a figure used by Statistics Canada in its current "medium" population projection. This assumption determines the total number of births in each year.

Similarly, the number of deaths is determined by another convenient statistical construct called life expectancy at birth, which provides an age-independent measure of mortality for an entire population at a point in time. Life expectancy has been rising in Canada from around 60 and 62 years for males and females respectively in the 1920s, to 75 and 81 years respectively by 1991. In the projections of Statistics Canada, these increases continue, although at reduced rates — to 78.5 and 84 years respectively by 2016 in their "medium" projection.

Perhaps the most controversial and important assumption concerns immigration. The average annual level of immigration to Canada over the 1960s to 1980s (1960–89) was approximately 135,600 persons a year. Then, in the 1990s, annual immigration levels consistently exceeded 200,000 persons, a figure that had only previously been exceeded in 1967 and 1974. Without exploring the reasons for this dramatic change in policy, it is important to note that these higher immigration levels are incorporated into the latest population projections from Statistics Canada; the "medium" population projection uses an annual intake of 250,000 persons, considerably higher than their previous assumptions of 140,000 and 200,000 persons a year and higher than the approximately 200,000 persons a year that were being admitted by the mid-1990s.

Finally, Statistics Canada assumes an emigration rate for Canada of 50,000 people per year. This is consistent with historical data, derived by the residual identity method noted above.

These assumptions result in a net immigration that approximately equals the current net natural increase in the population; that is, the difference between immigration (250,000) and emigration (50,000), approximately matches the difference between births (400,000) and deaths (200,000). Moreover, in future years, births are projected to decline and deaths to increase, resulting in the assumed net immigration becoming the more important component of population increase. This underscores the importance of the immigration assumption in the population projections.

PEOPLE AS CUSTOMERS:
THE MARKETING IMPLICATIONS

There are many theories and approaches to marketing. A common theme that runs through almost all of these marketing concepts, whether they are broadly based or more narrowly focused on niche markets, is the need to know and understand your customer. Often psychographic information is assembled to provide suitable definitions of customers, but there are numerous other approaches to this problem as well.[4]

A useful and simple categorization of marketing is to view it as either volume-oriented or growth-oriented. Although these are not necessarily mutually exclusive categories, they require somewhat different strategies. Volume-oriented marketing usually implies mass-marketing in a mature market that is focused on small margins and large turnover. On the other hand, growth-oriented marketing usually focuses on new-product markets, where the competition may not yet be established, and so the margins can be higher on a smaller turnover, but with significant potential for enlarging the turnover. Demographic trends can be an important input into both volume- and growth-oriented marketing strategies.

Marketing is often seen as proactive — advertising, promotions, sponsorships and so on, are used to convince the customer to purchase the product or service. In the first instance, it is concerned with convincing the customer of the need for the item being offered. In the second instance, it is concerned with convincing the customer that, given this need, one particular brand or organization will best satisfy that need. The focus is often on recruiting new customers; although, organizations are increasingly directing marketing programs towards retaining existing customers. Nonetheless, marketing is often conceived as creating or changing customer preferences.

In many regards, this proactive approach to marketing can be a bit like "hitting your head against a brick wall so that it feels good when you stop!" Surely, it is not cost-effective to go to all the effort and expense of creating or changing a market in which customers often already have well-defined preferences. By using a life-cycle approach to demographic trends, it is possible

267

to identify existing requirements and to concentrate marketing strategies on satisfying them.

Since product or service development is not an "overnight" achievement, many organizations need to take a long-term view of the marketplace. In this long-term realm, marketing can afford to be — and may have to be — more reactive than proactive, since customers' needs and wants change over their lifetimes. A life-cycle approach to marketing is particularly attractive in a marketplace in which the age structure of the customer base is undergoing significant changes.[5] Once again, it requires a longer-term, more reactive approach to marketing than has traditionally permeated the discipline.

Figures 1, 2 and 3 provide information on the customer base in Canada. The most populous age cohorts in Canada are the baby boomers, so this is where volume marketing can best be directed. Members of this generation were children in the 1960s, youths in the 1970s and young adults in the 1980s. Those born at the peak of the baby boom in 1960 were 11 in 1971 and 21 in 1981. This helps to explain the young and active orientation of many marketing strategies in past decades. Baby foods gave way to sports products and services, and dynamic downtowns offering active events and nightclubs flourished in this era.

By 1991 the peak boomers were aged 31 — getting attached, if not married, and moving to their own abodes in the suburbs. Sports facilities were gradually replaced by fitness facilities, and baby foods and toys regained their importance as these boomers began raising families. Housing demand gradually moved from rental to ownership, minivan sales leaped and gardening began to appear as an important leisure activity.

Where are the volume markets of the future? Because of the shape and distribution of the baby-boom generation, the Canadian population profile provides a unique opportunity to examine the volume markets by looking at the growth markets of a decade before. The 20-year boom period has a skewed distribution with a peak (or mode) well to the left of centre; that is, the baby boom peaked 15 years after it began, and ended five years following the peak. The first decade of boomers, therefore, provides a leading signal for where the larger, second decade of boomers will be a decade later.

Figure 4 outlines the decadal growth rates by age over the period 1971–2011.[6] The most rapidly growing market in Canada in the 1960s was the youth market (15 to 24 years). By the 1970s (1971–81), they had become young adults (25 to 34 years); over the 1980s (1981–91), they matured into 35 to 44 year olds. Not surprisingly, in the 1990s the most rapidly **growing** marketplace was populated by customers aged 45 to 54 years, while the biggest **volume** marketplace was the second-half boomers, who are ten years younger. In the first decade of the new millennium, the most rapidly growing marketplace will be customers in their early-retirement ages (55 to 64 years), with the biggest volume marketplace, once again, ten years younger. It does not require a crystal ball to develop this vision of the future marketplace, since every year people **will** get one year older (although an increasing number will be confronted by the unattractive alternative).

Given this information, it should not be surprising that the rental housing market boomed in the late 1970s, since it is dominated by 25- to 34-year-olds,

FIGURE 4
Canadian Population Growth by Age, 1971–2011 (%)

Age Group (years)	1971–1981	1981–1991	1991–2001*	2001–2011*
0 to 14	−14.0	5.0	5.4	−0.5
15 to 24	17.2	−17.3	5.1	8.3
25 to 34	45.1	17.8	−11.4	5.8
35 to 44	18.3	47.0	21.3	−8.3
45 to 54	8.4	19.7	50.6	21.7
55 to 64	24.2	11.5	21.6	49.9
65 to 74	36.5	28.9	13.7	23.2
75 and over	32.0	45.0	43.1	24.0
Total	13.1	12.9	13.4	11.1

* Statistics Canada, Catalogue No. 91-520 (1994), "Medium" Projection (No. 2)

Source: Figure 3 and Statistics Canada, Catalogue No. 91-520 (1994).

or that the owner-occupied housing market boomed in the late 1980s, since in Canada, the age of the first-time house buyer tends to be in the early- to mid-thirties. What is next? We could see a growth of demand in cottage country, as some of the boomers seek recreation properties. The remainder will probably be renovating the city and suburban homes to accommodate their predominantly teenage families. However, in the rental market, vacancy rates are likely to continue to remain high and with the consequent lower rents, apartment buildings will no longer provide a good investment. The rental housing market, however, will likely begin to improve in the next decade as the baby-boom echo generation starts leaving home to move into their first apartments.

Given the unique Canadian demographic profile, the example of the housing market illustrates the way that a combination of life-cycle and demographic information can be used to identify growth, mature and declining markets in the Canadian marketplace. Moreover, this is likely to provide a very solid foundation, since the aging trend is both well established and inevitable. Yet it is only a foundation. Other factors, such as economic cycles and changing consumer preferences, must also be monitored and included in a complete analysis. But to focus on these factors to the exclusion of demographic trends, is to build longer-term analysis of the external environment on a cracked foundation. In general, these other factors either determine the variations around the demographic life-cycle, or modify it slightly. They seldom reverse a trend established by the combination of life-cycle and demographic information. For example, the declining standard of living experienced in the early 1990s might mean that consumers were not able to afford a recreation property. Such economic conditions might modify the housing trends mentioned above, but they are unlikely to reverse them.

DAVID K. FOOT

Figure 4 also contains additional useful information. The baby-boom echo generation is projected to be largely a phenomenon of the 1980s and early 1990s. Births peaked in Canada in 1990 and continued to decline over the remainder of the 1990s, resulting in less growth in the young people's market by the end of the 1990s and, especially, in the first decade of this century. The declining youth market of the 1980s was a growth market in the 1990s as the echo generation reaches its youth. Markets for products and services oriented to young adults (25 to 34 years) — such as rental housing, sports and life insurance — declined throughout the 1990s. Youth market growth is projected to continue through this decade as a result of above-average immigration levels. The declining group today is the 35- to 44-year-old market.

Perhaps even more surprising in an aging population, the growth of the seniors' market slowed down in the 1990s, especially the "young seniors'" market (aged 65 to 74 years). Why? Because those entering this market in the 1990s were mostly born during the Depression of the 1930s when birth rates declined. However, although the young seniors' market was slower-growing in the 1990s, it is a relatively affluent market. Not only are young seniors at a point in their lives when their net worth is the highest, those born in the 1930s are also the richest group in Canada as a result of having relatively little competition from within their age group. On average, having four children per family increased the value of many of their investments (e.g., houses, stocks etc.). They provide a low-volume, high-margin, niche market. One cannot help but question the appropriateness, from society's standpoint, of continuing senior-citizen discounts for this new group of relatively affluent young seniors.

Note, however, that the growth of the "senior seniors'" market (75 years and over) continued unabated through the 1990s and beyond. It is growing at over three times the rate of the young seniors' market, and is second only to the boomers in growth, as it was in the 1980s. This helps to explain the rapid growth in pharmaceutical products aimed at this group, and increasing concerns over the viability of health-care plans, both public and private.

Appropriate health care and housing for senior citizen was a rapid-growth market in the 1990s. Out-of-hospital delivery of health care to nursing homes, or other, more innovative housing options, is likely to be in increased demand. But while this may be a high-growth market, it is not necessarily one in which high margins can predominate. For one thing, much of this activity is being offered through the public sector in Canada, which often limits the size of margins. For another, many of these seniors are women (since their life expectancy is six years longer than for men), many of whom did not have their own careers or who were married to men whose pensions, if they had them, were not automatically transferrable. Consequently, seniors' market is likely to bifurcate into a much more slowly growing "rich young seniors'" and a rapidly growing, dominantly female "poor senior seniors'" market. Private and public policies for seniors in general, should be adjusted to reflect this changing seniors' marketplace.

This section has barely scratched the surface of the potential contribution of demographics to marketing priorities and policies. It has outlined how the use of life-cycle information, for which age is the suitable proxy, can be combined with population projections, developed on the basis of historical trends, to provide a vision of future market conditions in Canada. Growth, mature and declining markets are all part of the future marketing landscape, and each in its own way offers marketing opportunities and challenges for all organizations.

PEOPLE AS EMPLOYEES:
THE HUMAN RESOURCE IMPLICATIONS

Another area in any organization directly affected by demographic trends is personnel. The traditional approach to personnel management focuses on recruitment, selection and training. Recently, corporate downsizing made out-placement increasingly important. Just as environmental factors influence an organization's structure, conduct and performance, they also influence these human resource functions.[7] So, not surprisingly, if demographics is one of the most important environmental factors, it influences not only human resource planning, but also an organization's structure and conduct.

This section investigates the impacts of changing demographics not only on personnel policies, but also on the structure and conduct — or culture — of organizations. This analysis involves a combination of personnel management with organization behaviour, all viewed through the eyes of a demographer. This is because organizational behaviour and personnel management are uniquely intertwined and both are being driven into new directions by changing demographics. From this point of view, personnel management is no longer purely individually based, but becomes an essential part of the strategic planning of any organization. Hence, it can be more accurately referred to as human resource management — a description that will be used throughout the remainder of this section.

With the first baby boomers entering the Canadian labour market in the 1960s and the bulk of them entering in the 1970s, labour-force growth in Canada exceeded that of all other developed Western countries, and youth employment soared to record levels by the early 1980s. Over the course of that decade, as the first boomers entered their forties, and the bulk of them entered their thirties, there appeared to be an abundance of qualified candidates for middle-level positions in most organizations. Moreover, a shortage of entry-level workers emerged, and youth unemployment rates declined noticeably as the smaller generation of the busters entered the labour market. Consequently, labour-force growth dropped to one-half the previous rates over the 1980s. Organizations that maintained traditional hierarchical structures were faced simultaneously with a surplus of qualified candidates for middle-level positions and an emerging shortage of candidates for starting-level positions. The traditional functions of personnel management were thrown into increasing chaos as these labour market characteristics emerged in the 1980s. It became increasingly clear that problems initially dismissed as being attributable to "unrealistic expectations" of employees, had, in fact, a much more fundamental basis for their expression.

Keyfitz was the first to anticipate the problem. In 1973 he noted the direct relationship between population growth and promotional prospects, and concluded that decreased population growth associated with declining fertility, must inevitably lead to delayed promotion in organizational hierarchies.[8] Ten years later, Cantrell and Clark extended the idea to labour-force growth in the United States, and still later Denton and Spencer applied the analysis to the Canadian labour force.[9] The overwhelming conclusion from this research is that, to the extent that age matters in promotion, the baby-boom generation suffers a disadvantage as a result of its large size.

The impacts of these demographic trends on human resource management in specific organizations has also been recognized. Morgan documents the problem of blocked career paths in the federal public service in Canada.[10] Bardwick refers to these promotional blockages as "the plateauing trap." She emphasizes the impersonality of environmental factors, especially demographics, and the consequent frustration for the individual employee — often compounded by the employer's failure to fully realize, and honestly address, an employee's long-term prospects. Declining morale, increased psychological stress, absenteeism and decreased productivity are all likely outcomes of this phenomenon.[11]

Implicit in these analyses are the dual assumptions of linear career paths and pyramidal organizational hierarchies. Driver argues that these two concepts are linked.[12] The linear career path, which has been the most prevalent one for most employees, is characterized by continued mobility up the hierarchy towards the top of the organization. Achievement and power are the motives, promotion and recognition the rewards. In this world, promotional blockages are very threatening. These career paths are best fostered in tall pyramidal organizational structures with many occupational or employment levels. The culture in such organizations focuses on salary and bonuses, evaluation of performance potential and training for the next level.

Driver suggests that those born in the small generation of the 1930s experienced high demand and mobility as a result of their small numbers and the post-war economic recovery and, hence, have developed a strong commitment to the linear path. Their career paths provided the role model for the career expectations of the boomers. Since those born in the 1930s moved through to the top levels of organizations by the 1980s, it is not surprising that the most common organizational structure in the post-war period in North America became the tall pyramid.[13]

Increasingly, the baby boomers found the linear career focus to be at odds with reality, as they experienced promotional blockages. Bardwick noted that while plateauing was inevitable for most employees, it was occurring sooner for the boomers due to their large numbers and to organizational restructuring that eliminated middle-management positions.[14] Driver contended that a "linear career crisis" had emerged as the boomers' expectations clashed with reality.[15]

This problem can be readily envisaged by noting that the baby-boom generation has almost a rectangular shape in the population profile and that, as it aged in the labour force over the 1980s, managers in hierarchical organizations were faced with attempting to promote a rectangle up in the organizational triangle — an impossible task. Boomers were working ever-longer hours in an attempt to distinguish themselves as worthy of the limited number of available promotions. This is why the average work week lengthened during the 1980s, and the increased leisure time promised in the 1970s did not materialize.

Moreover, population aging resulted in increasing scarcity of candidates for entry-level positions as the baby-bust generation entered the labour market in the 1980s. Consequently, two types of mismatches between the triangular organizational hierarchy and the barrel-shaped labour force in Canada simultaneously emerged in the 1980s — too few younger employees and too many middle-level employees. Foot and Venne have estimated that the closest fit between the labour force and a representative organizational hierarchy occurred in the late 1970s and that, over the course of the 1980s, a mismatching problem emerged that reversed the trend of the previous two decades when the baby boomers entered the labour force. Moreover, from a demographical perspective, this trend of increasing mismatching can be expected to continue into the future unless corrective action is taken.[16]

Corrective action can be located both within individual organizations and within society at large. An economic environment that encourages appropriate organizational change will likely impose less pressure on individuals and society to take the necessary corrective actions, than an economic environment that impedes organizational change. Consequently, in the booming 1980s, corrective action was gradually taking place in many forward-looking organizations. However, the recession of the early 1990s impeded this initial progress, and more of the adjustment appears to have fallen on individuals, and, increasingly, on societal mores, laws and policies. The underlying trends are still the same — their manifestation takes different forms in different settings. The concern of this article is with organizational change, but the section concludes with a few observations on complementary corrective actions outside the individual organization.

To understand what that corrective action for the individual organization might be, Foot and Venne employ Driver's idea that individual career-path and organizational-structure concepts are linked. Figure 5 summarizes these linkages. Four general career paths and their characteristics are identified and linked to four organizational structures and cultures. The following provides a brief summary of these linkages.

The first two career paths are the most familiar. The steady-state career represents a lifelong career path where an employee is committed to an occupation for life (for example, a minister of religion or a professor). Since there are many employees at the same level, the associated organizational structure is almost flat (that is, rectangular). The accompanying culture emphasizes tenure, seniority and fringe benefits. The linear career is perhaps the most pervasive in North America. Here, the employee seeks upward movement towards the top of a tall, increasingly narrow, pyramid structure with numerous salary levels. Changes in occupation are infrequent, the most common being from a line occupation (such as an engineer or accountant) to a managerial one. Promotions and accompanying salary increases and bonuses are the main measures of career success.

The next two career paths may be less familiar. The spiral career, which combines mainly lateral moves with a few vertical moves, is associated with a moderate number of changes in occupation over a lifetime. The supporting organizational structure is a flat pyramid with a few, broad salary levels. Here the emphasis is on occupational flexibility with opportunities for lifelong re-

FIGURE 5
Career Paths and Associated Characteristics

Career Path	Direction of Job Movement	Number of Occupations	Organizational Structure	Reward Systems
Steady State	None	One	Rectangle	Tenure, Fringe Benefits
Linear	Upward	Two	Tall Pyramid	Promotion, Power
Spiral	Lateral/ Upward	Five (?)	Flat Pyramid	Re-education, Retraining
Transitory	Lateral	Many	Temporary Teams	Variety, Time Off

Source: D.K. Foot and R.A. Venne, "Population, Pyramids and Promotional Prospects," *Canadian Public Policy* 16(4): 387–98.

education and retraining. Last, the transitory career is characterized by frequent occupational change and lateral mobility. The associated organizational structure consists of temporary teams, such as a management consulting team or a royal commission; the organizational culture revolves around variety and possible breaks between assignments.

While the steady-state and transitory career paths are likely to remain applicable to certain organizational environments, such as the church and management consulting respectively, population aging will intensify the movement from tall organizational structures and linear career paths, to flattened organizational structures and spiral career paths.

The Foot and Venne findings provide dramatic verification of Driver's contention that "organizations are geared to reinforce precisely the wrong career concept — the linear concept."[17] While it is likely that some organizations will continue to maintain structures and cultures that foster the linear career path, many linear-oriented organizations have adapted to this new reality by flattening their pyramidal organizational structures. One motivation for this may be the desire to reduce the importance of promotions, by reducing the number of hierarchical levels.[18] When there are fewer levels, less upward movement is possible, and much of the employee's attention is directed laterally rather than vertically. In other words, employees are encouraged to move from the linear career path towards the spiral and transitory career path. Technological change, retrenchment during recessions and increased global competition are other reasons often cited for corporate flattening and eliminating middle management. These all serve to intensify the process.

The emergence of the spiral career path in North America, where the pressures from the baby-boom generation are the most intense, encourage the view of education as a lifelong process and the emergence of the "generalist"

or flexible employee. The multi-skilled employee with a solid training in basic skills and a variety of experiences who can be flexible and move laterally into new positions, is likely to be the most challenged and productive. Lateral swaps or exchanges are likely to become much more common. For example, three employees plateaued as directors of marketing, communications and human resources, might well be rotated to provide new challenges for each of them. Lateral moves can be a solution both to an individual employee's plateauing problem, and to the entire cohort of employees at that particular organizational level.

The "sensible" employer must recognize these employee contributions and reward the employee appropriately, even though no promotion to the next hierarchical level has taken place. In other words, employers who wish to keep their potentially plateaued employees challenged and productive must make sure that lateral, as well as vertical, moves are reflected in the financial rewards of the employees. With fewer levels in the hierarchy, each level will carry a much broader compensation range.

Both employers and employees have to make other changes as well. Employers will likely have to provide more information and support services to assist employees in establishing career "paths" (as distinct from career "ladders") as they adapt to the new work environment. In addition, it becomes increasingly necessary for employers to provide more training and education to help employees prepare for the occupational changes associated with lateral moves. For their part, employees will find it advantageous to encourage and use these services, rather than to resist their introduction. On the human resource planning side, far more attention will need to be paid to programs designed to encourage lateral movement. Information bases must be expanded to include data on employees' other skills and interests; policies to encourage the use of educational and training opportunities outside of the employee's current responsibilities will need to be developed; exchange programs must be designed so that employees are encouraged to seek out other employees and positions that may be of interest for lateral moves; and salary structures, that position employees in the organization hierarchy, may have to be abandoned, because an employee who has been rewarded for three lateral moves, may well have a slightly higher salary than the "boss" who may be in the higher-level position as a result of one vertical move.

Other changes within organizations are likely to be more subtle. Success in the workplace is likely to be redefined to include the variety of positions held, as well as their level in the organizational hierarchy. Reducing hierarchical levels may reduce formality, make leaders more accessible, improve communication and information flows, and lead to a more participatory style of management. Emphasis will need to be on the opportunities for increasingly independent and challenging work. Embracing challenge and mastering it needs to be rewarded. Extended study leaves or sabbaticals may become necessary to achieve these goals, as may employee access to improved health and recreation facilities.

This is only a representative, and by no means exhaustive, list of the changes that are required. Note that these changes that emphasize flexibility apply equally well to the transitory (or non-traditional) worker who emerged as an important force in the workplace of the 1990s. The key item is the likely transformation of the workplace in North America, from tall hierarchies and linear career paths, to flatter hierarchies, spiral and transitory career paths. This transformation needs to be accompanied by a much greater emphasis within organizations on human resource management issues, than has been the case in the past.

Finally, changes are also likely outside the individual organizations. Several public-policy issues dealing with the baby boom in the labour force need to be addressed. For example, to facilitate the need for continued re-education and training, it may be increasingly necessary for educational institutions, especially post-secondary ones, to offer timely and relevant courses. These may need to be scheduled at times that do not conflict with work (for example, evenings or weekends) or redesigned into compact, modular courses that can be completed during short periods (such as one to three weeks). Teaching methods must be modified; older students often have different expectations and different learning skills than younger students. Not only do they have more life experiences to draw on, they are also more likely to place a higher value on their time — especially if the workload continues to pile up back at the office. In addition, since employers may pay the fees for these students, educational institutions will be provided with an opportunity to broaden and increase their funding bases. The possible effects of the myriad on all educational policies deserve careful consideration and cannot be adequately explored here.

In the case study of the federal public sector, Morgan recommends early retirement as one measure to ease the career blockage problem.[19] Early retirement incentives and flexible retirement policies, such as easing employees into retirement by allowing them to become part-time mentors or consultants, are becoming more common. Bardwick refers to the latter as "transitional retirement" policies, and recommends that these part-time employees receive a proportional fraction of their salary and benefits.[20] Of course, the removal of mandatory retirement provisions and the introduction of various flexible retirement policies, such as have been introduced into the U.S. pension policy and the Canada/Quebec Pension Plan, could work in the opposite direction by allowing employees to remain longer in the senior levels of organizational hierarchies. However, Foot and Gibson note that this may be very appropriate in a slower growing workforce where, increasingly, the retraining of existing older workers is likely to provide one source of labour-force renewal.[21]

Changing demographics are inevitably driving these workplace changes, whether they are taking place within organizations or outside. If individual organizations cannot, or do not, adapt to the more flexible workplace, society will bear the brunt of this adaptation. In North America in the 1990s, many individuals found it necessary to retrain on their own, either in traditional educational institutions or elsewhere. Impediments to lateral moves between organizations must be reduced, once again raising the need for universally portable pensions, or some other innovative solution to this problem. Lateral mobility between occupations can be increased by simultaneously holding more than one part-time position in different organizations, perhaps in quite different sectors of the economy. This requires rethinking the traditional "job" as a full-time commitment to one occupation, if not one organization, with all the flexible pension, taxation and social service contribution arrangements that this requires. Increasingly, workplace flexibility is the key issue emerging from these longer-term trends, and people, whether as employees, employers or voters, will find it necessary to develop strategies and policies to facilitate these inevitable work-place trends.

CONCLUSIONS

Demographic trends, and population aging in particular, have been, perhaps, the most neglected environmental trends affecting all management in all organizations in Canada and elsewhere. People are both customers and employ-ees, so demographic trends have important implications for both the marketing and human resource planning functions in any organization. The Canadian demographic profile is dominated by the massive baby-boom generation, born between 1947 and 1966. This generation has had an enormous impact on all organizations, as it has aged over the post-war period, and these impacts can be expected to continue. Marketing will be increasingly dominated by products and services offered to those in the middle age, although other market seg-ments, such as seniors and teenagers will also offer challenging opportunities. Demographic trends are also cementing the unique relationship between chang-ing organizational structures and human resource planning policies. The simul-taneous emergence of plateauing and recruiting problems (in a non-recessionary environment) leads to the flattening of organizational hierarchies, and the move from linear to spiral and transitory career paths. The age of flexibility and the "generalist" has arrived and organizations must pay increasing attention (and money) to re-education and retraining, if they are to successfully adapt to the new organizational alignments. A strong emphasis on human resource planning, carefully integrated into other corporate functions, such as marketing, is needed to accommodate the inevitable aging of the Canadian labour force. Finally, it is important that public policies, such as education, retirement, pension and other workplace policies, be consistent with the changes taking place as a result of these predictable demographic developments.

NOTES

1. J. Naisbitt and P. Auburden, *Megatrends 2000: Ten New Directions for the 1990s.* (New York: Avon Books, 1990); F. Popcorn, *The Popcorn Report: Faith Popcorn on the Future of Your Company, Your World, Your Life.* (New York: Doubleday, 1991).
2. D.K. Foot and D. Stoffman, *Boom, Bust & Echo: How to Profit from the Coming Demographic Shift* (Toronto: Macfarlane, Walter and Ross, 1996).
3. Ibid.
4. D.R. Lehmann and R.S. Winer, *Analysis for Marketing Planning* (Plano: Business Publications Inc., 1988).
5. D.J. Luck and O.C. Ferrell, *Marketing Strategy and Plans*, 2nd edition (Englewood Cliffs, N.J.: Prentice-Hall Inc., 1985).
6. See also Foot and Stoffman, *Boom, Bust & Echo*, chapter 4.
7. W.L. French, *Human Resources Management* (Boston: Houghton Mifflin Co., 1986).

8. N. Keyfitz, "Individual Mobility in a Stationary Population," *Population Studies*, 27(2): 335–52.

9. R.S. Cantrell and R.L. Clark, "Individual Mobility, Population Growth and Labour Force Participation," *Demography*, 19(2): 245–63; F. Denton and B. Spencer, *Age Structure and Rate of Promotion in the Canadian Working Population*, QSEP Research Report No. 210 (Hamilton: McMaster University Faculty of Social Services, 1987).

10. N. Morgan, *Implosion: An Analysis of the Growth of Federal Public Service in Canada (1945–1985)* (Ottawa: Institute for Research on Public Policy, 1985).

11. J. Bardwick, *The Plateauing Trap* (New York: Amacom, 1986).

12. M.J. Driver, "Demographic and Societal Factors Affecting the Linear Career Crisis," *Canadian Journal of Administrative Studies*, 2(2): 245–63.

13. Ibid.

14. Bardwick, *The Plateauing Trap*.

15. Driver, "Linear Career Crisis."

16. D.K. Foot and R.A. Venne, "Population, Pyramids and Promotional Prospects," *Canadian Public Policy*, 16: 4, 397–98.

17. Ibid.; Driver, "Linear Career Crisis."

18. Bardwick, *The Plateauing Trap*.

19. Morgan, *Implosion*.

20. Bardwick, *The Plateauing Trap*.

21. D.K. Foot and K.J. Gibson, "Population Aging in the Canadian Labour Force: Changes and Challenges," *Journal of Canadian Studies*, 28(1): 59–74.

SECTION 4

The Inputs of
Economic Activity

Traditional economic models of production and international trade included two inputs — labour and capital. More recent models have included technology as an input to the production process, first with the endowment of technology being exogenous (outside of the model) and later with technological change endogenized (that is, determined by the actions of participants in the model). This section of the book looks at the markets for each of these three inputs of production — labour, capital and technology — in Canada.

The first article in this section is Gil McGowan's "Now More Than Ever: Why Unions Still Matter in the Twenty-First Century." This article looks at the role played by trade unions in the development of Canadian society, and looks forward to suggest what role unions can play in the future of the Canadian economy.

The second and the third articles in this section look at the capital market and the financial services industry in Canada. The first article, based on an earlier work by Peter Campbell and updated by Tom Wesson for this volume, acts a primer, discussing the role and importance of capital markets and something of the history of financial services regulation in Canada. The second of these two articles, by Wendy Dobson, provides a critical assessment of the federal government's proposed reforms to this regulation. In assessing the proposed legislation (which died as the order paper with the November 2000 election), Professor Dobson provides her own recommendations as to how best to reform the Canadian financial services sector to improve the efficiency of our capital markets.

The final article in this section, "Technology and the New Economy: A Canadian Strategy," by Charles McMillan and Eduardo M.V. Jasson, does not look at a market in the usual sense. Most technology is not purchased on a traditional market; it is either "produced" and "consumed" within a single firm, or produced by someone who does not have the means to capture the value of what is produced through a market mechanism (such as a university professor, indiscriminately publishing research findings in hope of being granted tenure). Of course, the production of technology is also atypical in that the output of a given amount of input into the production function is somewhat unpredictable. That is, the success of individual R&D projects varies greatly. The article discusses the factors which influence the demand for, and production of, technology in Canada. The authors conclude that Canada is importing far more technology than we should. They suggest ways in which we can increase both our inputs into the production of technology (i.e., our R&D spending) and the value produced by a given amount of spending.

Now More Than Ever: Why Unions Still Matter in the Twenty-First Century

Gil McGowan

THE UNION CENTURY

The twentieth century was a time of tremendous change, advancement and struggle. Over the past one hundred years, we saw the introduction of inventions that have changed the way we live — things like the telephone, the airplane, the television and the computer. The twentieth century was also a time of incredible political turmoil, social change and economic growth. Wars and political upheaval changed borders and toppled governments; mass social movements ended racial segregation in the United States and Apartheid in South Africa; and leaders like Martin Luther King Jr., Mahatma Gandhi, Adolf Hitler and Josef Stalin alternately inspired and horrified us.

At the same time, the twentieth century was a time of incredible prosperity in most western industrial countries. The wealth amassed in places like the United States, Canada, Germany and France is unrivalled in human history. At the beginning of the century, small local or regional companies produced only a narrow range of goods. Today, massive multinational firms mass-produce an almost unimaginable variety of consumer items — everything from automobiles and home computers to toothbrushes and toasters.

With all the dramatic changes happening on the scientific, political and economic stages, it's easy to overlook one of the other amazing revolutions that took place during the twentieth century — and that's the revolution that transformed the lives of working people.

This is an edited version of *Now More Than Ever: An examination of the challenges and opportunities facing Alberta unions in the 21st century* (Calgary, AB: Alberta Federation of Labour). Reproduced with permission.

In the years following the end of World War II, workers in western industrial nations like Canada experienced a dramatic jump in their standard of living. Part of the credit for this change can be given to the tremendous economic boom that followed the end of the war. But there had been booms before — booms that had not improved the lives of working people.

What made the post-war situation different? Why did the boom of the 1940s and 1950s so dramatically improve the lives of working people when earlier booms had not? The answer is simple — trade unions. For the first time in history, workers living in western industrial countries had effective worker organizations to speak on their behalf. They also finally had governments that recognized the right of workers to bargain collectively.

Thanks in large part to the efforts of unions, millions of working people in Canada, the United States and across Europe were, for the first time, brought into the middle class. Average incomes soared as workers were finally given a fairer share of the wealth they helped to create.

But unions did not just influence wages. Many of the things that Canadians take for granted today were only won after hard-fought campaigns by working people and their unions. For example, at the beginning of the last century, things like a legislated eight-hour day and a regular five-day work week were distant dreams for most workers. There were also no such things as workplace health and safety regulations, minimum wages, unemployment insurance, paid vacations, or pension plans. All these things have now become commonplace — thanks to the work of unions.

In addition to improving conditions in the workplace, unions have also used their influence to make possible changes in the broader Canadian society. For example, unions in the Southern Alberta coal fields were the first to establish hospitals and health care plans for working people — plans which would later be copied by the CCF government in Saskatchewan to form the basis of Medicare.

Given the profound and positive impact that unions have had on the society and the economies of the western world, it can be argued that the twentieth century was not just the century of invention or the century of industry — it was also the union century.

Will Our Future Be as Bright as Our Past?

Clearly, unions in Canada and around the world have a rich and proud history. But, as we stand on the threshold of a new century and a new millennium, the question remains: do they have a future?

For union members and supporters of the labour movement, a number of troubling trends have developed over the past 15 or 20 years that raise serious concerns about the viability of trade unions. Most alarming is the drop in unionization rates around the world. According to a report prepared by the International Labour Organization, a branch of the United Nations, the number of union members in many countries has stagnated — even while the labour force grows. The result is that the percentage of the workforce that is unionized is dropping in many countries. For example, between 1985 and 1995, unionization rates in the United Kingdom dropped from 46 per cent to 33 per

---

FIGURE 1
A Proud History

Over the past one hundred years, unions have won victories that changed the way Canadians live and work. Among other things, unions played an important role in bringing the following things to Canada:

- the eight-hour day
- workplace health and safety laws
- unemployment insurance
- pensions
- a middle-class standard of living

- the five-day work week
- medicare
- paid vacations
- the minimum wage

---

cent; in Germany they dropped from 35 to 29 per cent; and in New Zealand they fell from 54 per cent to 24 per cent.

In many of these countries, the sting of declining membership is lessened somewhat by the fact that large numbers of non-union workers are also covered by union contracts. In Germany, for example, only 29 per cent of working people belong to unions, but almost 90 per cent are covered by union-negotiated contracts. But even in these cases declines in membership are a serious concern, because with fewer dues paying members unions are robbed of the resources they need to function effectively (see Figure 2).

Looking at the international figures, it's clear one of the most dramatic changes in union membership rates has occurred in the United States. Forty years ago the American labour force was one of the more highly unionized in the world — especially in the key area of manufacturing. In fact, in its heyday, the American labour movement was so influential that presidents — both Democrat and Republican — consulted with union leaders on a regular basis.

But that's all a thing of the past. Union density in the United States has declined from a peak of more than 35 per cent of private sector labour force in 1954 to less than 10 per cent today. Now the American labour central, the AFL-CIO, has been reduced to little more than an interest group, albeit a relatively well-funded one. The situation has become so bad that labour leaders were not even able to convince Democratic Vice-President Al Gore to speak publicly in support of collective bargaining at a recent AFL-CIO convention.

The American experience is particularly alarming for Canadian unions for several reasons. First, the American and Canadian economies are more closely linked than those of any other two countries in the world — as a result, things that happen there have significant impact here. Second, the laws governing collective bargaining and the operation of unions in the two countries are — at least on the surface — quite similar. Unlike Europe, where most agreements are negotiated on a national or industry-wide basis, negotiations in Canada and the United States are much more decentralized. Some unions in the two countries do negotiate national agreements with large corporations. But in

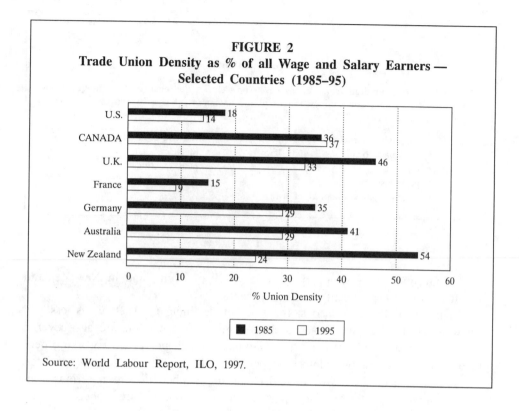

FIGURE 2
Trade Union Density as % of all Wage and Salary Earners —
Selected Countries (1985–95)

% Union Density

■ 1985 □ 1995

Source: World Labour Report, ILO, 1997.

general, collective bargaining in both Canada and the United States takes place between individual unions and individual employers.

Given that Canadian unions operate in similar economic, legal and social environments, it's not surprising that some people are worried that Canadian unions may follow their American cousins down the road to irrelevance.

What the Union Movement's Critics Say

Of course, many people have been predicting the demise of unions in Canada and around the world for years. Even during the immediate post-War years, when unions were helping to increase the living standards for millions of workers, the labour movement had no shortage of critics.

The difference now is that the critics seem to be getting the upper hand. Public and political attacks on unions increased in the 1970s — when unions and union wages were blamed by many for high rates of inflation, even though the problem was clearly related more closely to things like the oil crisis, spiralling military spending and the decision by governments around to the world to abandon fixed exchange rates.

More recently, critics of the labour movement have been arguing that the new "global economy" will make unions obsolete. They say the new economy is generating so much wealth and creating so many well-paid jobs in areas like the high-technology sector that workers no longer need the kind of protection that unions provide. They also argue that the continued existence of unions actually hurts workers by undermining the ability of Canadian firms to compete with firms from other countries.

Now More Than Ever

So, are the critics right? Do unions still have a legitimate role to play in the Canadian economy, or are they relics of the past? Do Canadian workers still want unions? Do they still need unions? Do unions in Canada still "deliver the goods" for their members? Despite all the negative talk about unions, the truth is that working people, both in Canada and around the world, still want and need unions. In fact, it can be argued that in the new "global" workplace, unions are more important than ever.

DO WORKERS STILL WANT UNIONS?

Looking at the international scene — and particularly the experience in the United States — one could easily come to the conclusion that unions are on their way out. But the truth is that unions in Canada are relatively strong.

One of the ways to demonstrate the strength of the labour movement in Canada is to look at overall membership trends — assuming that if workers no longer wanted unions, membership would be declining. It's also useful to look at the attitudes of non-union workers. Given the chance, would they join a union? In this section, we do both of these things. In the end, it will become clear that — despite all the anti-union talk coming from business, government and media circles — many Canadian workers still want unions.

Unions in Canada are not the dying organizations that they are in some other countries. In fact, the trajectory of membership in Canada over the past 30 years has been almost entirely opposite that in places like the United States. While membership south of the border declined steadily throughout the 1970s, 1980s and 1990s, the number of union members in Canada increased.

At the national level, about one in three Canadian workers currently belongs to a union. The rate of union membership is even higher among certain groups of workers and within certain industries. For example, more than seven out of 10 Canadians working in the public sector belong to unions. Unionization rates are also high among older workers (45–55) and among

---

FIGURE 3
Union Membership in Canada (1967–97)

1967	2 million
1977	2.8 million
1987	3.6 million
1997	3.5 million

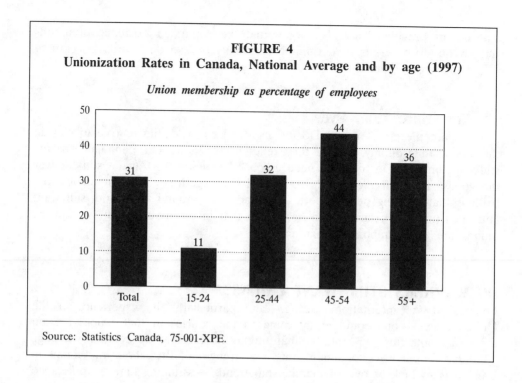

FIGURE 4
Unionization Rates in Canada, National Average and by age (1997)

Union membership as percentage of employees

Source: Statistics Canada, 75-001-XPE.

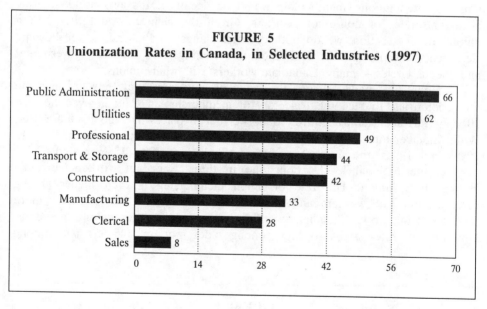

FIGURE 5
Unionization Rates in Canada, in Selected Industries (1997)

people working in industries like utilities, transportation and communications, and in blue-collar occupations like construction and manufacturing.

Perhaps surprisingly, one of the categories of workers with the highest rate of unionization is the group that Statistics Canada describes as "white collar professional." This group, which includes a variety of professional workers, such as nurses and teachers, boasts a national unionization rate of 49 per cent.

Another finding that may surprise some people has to do with education. In today's workforce, union members are actually more likely to have post-secondary education than non-union workers. Fifty-eight per cent of union members in Canada have a post-secondary certificate or a university degree, as compared to only 48 per cent for the overall population. Based on this information, its clear that the old myth that union members are low-skilled and lack flexibility is just that — a myth. The truth seems to be just the opposite: union members in Canada are better educated and more flexible.

Historically, the Canadian union movement grew most dramatically between 1940 and 1956. During this period membership almost quadrupled. After 1956, union membership increased more slowly — only slightly outpacing the overall growth in the workforce. Even so, in the past 30 years the total number of union members in Canada has almost doubled — from about 2-million in the 1950s to more than 3.5-million today. But because the growth in union membership has roughly paralleled the overall growth in the labour force, the union "density" rate has remained in the 30 to 35 per cent range. This is lower than the unionization rate in some northern European countries (i.e., Sweden, Finland, Norway, Denmark and Belgium), but substantially higher than in places like the United States, Japan and even Britain.

Of course, not all the statistics are so rosy. Today, unionization rates in the private sector are much lower than they are in the public sector. In 1998 only about one in five Canadians working in the private sector belonged to a union. Unionization rates are also significantly lower among young workers (15–

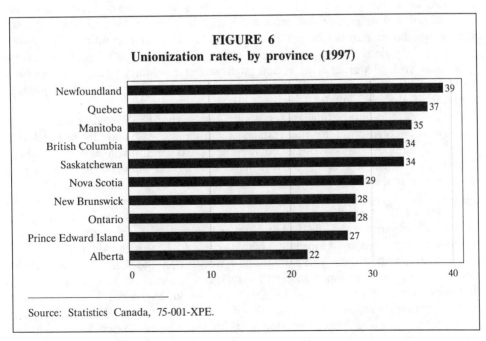

FIGURE 6
Unionization rates, by province (1997)

Province	Rate
Newfoundland	39
Quebec	37
Manitoba	35
British Columbia	34
Saskatchewan	34
Nova Scotia	29
New Brunswick	28
Ontario	28
Prince Edward Island	27
Alberta	22

Source: Statistics Canada, 75-001-XPE.

24), among part-time and temporary workers, and among employees of small firms. In fact, only 12 per cent of Canadians working in firms with fewer than 20 employees are unionized. This is a particularly serious problem because these firms currently employ about 35 per cent of the workforce.

The overall numbers on union membership also mask some significant changes in the composition of the union movement that have taken place over the past 30 years. As mentioned, public sector unions now represent a much greater portion of the overall labour movement today than they did in the past. Women also have been playing a much more prominent role in the Canadian union movement. As the number of women active in the labour force increased over the past 30 years, so did the number of women union members. Women now make up 45 per cent of all union members — up from about 20 per cent in 1967. This "gender re-alignment" has significantly changed the face of unions around the country.

"Latent" Unionism

In addition to the thousands of Canadians who already belong to unions, research conducted over the past 10 or 15 years clearly suggests that many more Canadians would join unions if given the opportunity. This is what University of Alberta sociologist Graham Lowe has described as "latent" unionism. In surveys conducted in the 1980s, Lowe and fellow University of Alberta sociologist Harvey Krahn surveyed the attitude of non-union workers towards union membership in Canada's most notoriously anti-union province, Alberta. Their results were surprising. They found that about 35 per cent of non-union workers in Edmonton would like to join a union.

Obviously, many things have changed since the 1980s — but apparently the opinions of workers about unions have not. In a much more recent survey of high school and university graduates conducted in 1996, Lowe and Krahn found that a significant number of young Albertans working in non-union jobs would like to join unions. More specifically, about 32 per cent of recent university graduates and 30 per cent of recent high school graduates who were working in non-union settings at the time of the survey said they would support joining a union if the opportunity presented itself.

One of the interesting things about Lowe and Krahn's findings is how closely they correspond to the results of earlier surveys and, in fact, to the results of similar surveys conducted in other parts of Canada and the United States. Ever since the 1960s, surveys have shown that between 30 and 40 per cent of non-union workers in both Canada and the United States would like to join unions.

One of the largest and most recent American surveys on worker interest in unions was conducted in 1994 by Richard Freeman, a prominent economics professor from Harvard University. Like Lowe and Krahn in Alberta, Freeman found that about one in three non-union workers in the United States would like to belong to a union. Among the workers who said they would not join a union, Freeman found a large number who would like some kind of worker representation in their workplace. Based on these findings, Freeman argued that there is a large "representation gap" in the United States. He concluded

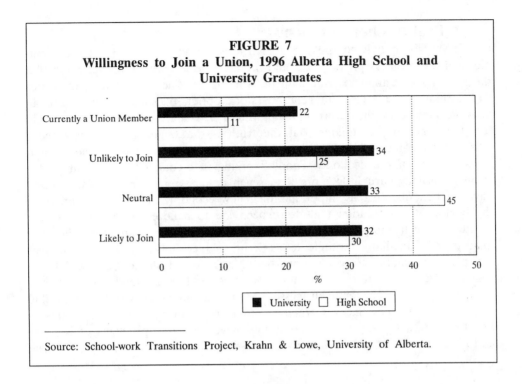

FIGURE 7
Willingness to Join a Union, 1996 Alberta High School and University Graduates

Source: School-work Transitions Project, Krahn & Lowe, University of Alberta.

that there are millions of Americans who want some kind of representation in the workplace, but who have not been able to get it.

Clearly, these studies have important implications for unions in Alberta, Canada and across North America. Even in the hostile climate of the "dog-eat-dog" 1990s, it appears that millions of unorganized workers were still open to the idea of joining unions. The research also suggests that the number would be even higher if workers could somehow be reassured that they would not be punished or disciplined for supporting a union.

DO WORKERS STILL NEED UNIONS?

One of the arguments often put forward by critics of the labour movement is that unions have outlived their usefulness. According to this line of reasoning, unions may have served a purpose in the first part of the century when wages were low, workplace conditions were poor and benefits almost unheard of. But these critics say the situation for working people has improved radically. Wages are better, health and safety regulations have been put into place and there are all sorts of mechanisms to protect the interests of unemployed, elderly and sick or injured workers (e.g., Employment Insurance, the Canada Pension Plan, workers' compensation). Given all the advances that have been made over the years, critics of the labour movement argue that workers no longer really need unions. In effect, they claim that all the battles in the workplace have been won.

But how true is the claim that things have never been better for working people? How true is it that workers no longer need unions?

A Reality Check on Jobs

If you listen only to spokespeople from government, the business community and the business press, you would probably be left with the impression that the majority of Canadians will soon be working for "new economy" companies and earning fat salaries with generous stock option packages. If this were an accurate picture of the future of employment in Canada, fewer workers would feel the need to join unions. But the truth is that many of the "high tech" jobs being created are no more rewarding or secure than jobs in more traditional sectors of the economy. People working in e-commerce call centres, for example, usually earn little more than seven dollars per hour — and they often have no benefits. Just as important, the "new economy" has not, so far, been the engine of job creation that we've been led to believe. Despite all the talk about high-tech industries and e-commerce, the fact remains that the vast majority of Canadians continue to work in "old economy" jobs. In fact, over the past 10 years, the two sectors that have created the most new jobs in Canada are retail trade, and food services and accommodations — hardly cutting edge, new economy businesses. Many Canadians also continue to find employment in areas like construction and manufacturing. Given this reality — and the fact that many new economy jobs have the same problems of low pay and poor benefits as old economy jobs — it is clear that unions still have a role to play.

Wages and Income

Another way to demonstrate that Canadian workers still need unions is to look at the share of overall wealth being returned to working people in the form of wages and salaries. In an economy that has been growing as rapidly as Canada's, you would expect to see a significant increase in the income being earned by workers. Unfortunately, this has not been the case. In fact, wages for most Canadians have declined or stayed stagnant for most of the past 15 years. There is also evidence of growing inequality between different groups of workers, and persistent inequality between male and female workers.

Figures from Statistics Canada tell a depressing story.

Real personal disposable (after-tax) income per person in Canada fell by an average of 0.33 per cent per year in the 1990s, down from average annual **increases** of 1.1 per cent in the 1980s, 3.0 per cent in the 1970s and 3.9 per cent in the 1960s. Thus, in 1999, real disposable income per Canadian was 3.3 per cent lower than it was in 1989.

There has been no increase in more than 20 years in the real annual earnings of Canadian men working on a full-time, full-year basis. In 1997, such men earned an average of $42,626, compared to an average of $42,635 in 1975 (both figures are in constant 1987 dollars).

Between 1981 and 1995, only the top 10 per cent of male earners experienced any increase at all in their real annual earnings (up 6.2 per cent over the entire period). The real annual earnings of the bottom 90 per cent of men fell, and fell the most for lower earners, with real annual earnings of the bottom 10 per cent of men falling by 31.7 per cent.

Between 1989 and 1997, the average "market" income of Canadian families from wages, salaries, self-employment earnings, and investments (adjusted for inflation) fell from $53,937 to $50,672, and average family income after taxes and government transfers fell by 5.6 per cent, from $48,311 to $45,605. Poorer families experienced the most serious decline in both market and after tax/transfer incomes. These incomes for the least well-off 40 per cent of families with children fell by 12 per cent over the period.

Over the past two or three years, the average wage situation for working Canadians has improved slightly. But workers — especially those lower down the income ladder — are making substantially less than they did a decade earlier. The most troubling aspect of this whole situation is that these long-term trends towards wage stagnation and erosion are happening at the same time that the Canadian economy is expanding.

After looking at the trends in wages and income, it's clear that the benefits of economic growth are not being shared by all working Canadians. Given this situation, it's also clear that unions still have a role to play. Unions have a proven track record of improving wage levels and reducing income inequality — exactly what workers in Canada need today.

Work Arrangements

At the same time that wages have been undermined in Canada, other major changes have been occurring in the workplace — changes which also prove that working people need more protection, not less. The most important changes include the following:

Two-income Families

One of the most obvious changes in the workplace of the 1990s has been the rise of the two-income family. Over the past 15 or 20 years, the number of two-income families has sky-rocketed.

Today, about two-thirds of mothers with young children are in the workforce, compared to about one-third in the 1970s. This change has put tremendous strain on workers as they desperately try to juggle their responsibilities at work and at home. Many workers say they would like to have the option to stay home or work fewer hours, but they cannot because of inflexible employers or because they cannot afford to give up the income.

Part-time and Temporary Work

Another trend that has characterized the 1990s in Canada is the increase in part-time and temporary work. In 1997, 19 per cent of all workers in the country had part-time hours, up dramatically from 12.5 per cent in 1976. Part-time jobs are also being created at a much faster rate than full-time jobs.

At the same time, the number of Canadians holding temporary or non-permanent jobs has also increased. In 1997, 11 per cent of Canadian employees worked in non-permanent jobs — up from slightly more than 8 per cent in the '80s. Aside from the inherent insecurity of part-time and temporary employment, these kinds of jobs have many other problems. Most important, they

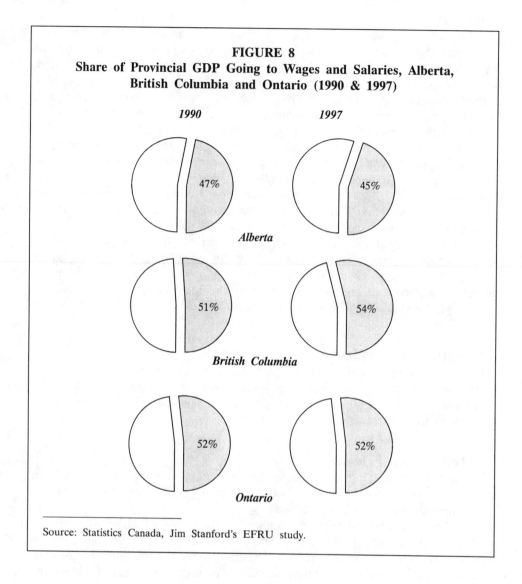

FIGURE 8
Share of Provincial GDP Going to Wages and Salaries, Alberta,
British Columbia and Ontario (1990 & 1997)

1990   *1997*

47%   45%

Alberta

51%   54%

British Columbia

52%   52%

Ontario

Source: Statistics Canada, Jim Stanford's EFRU study.

tend to pay much less than full-time, permanent jobs. Part-time and temporary workers are also much less likely to have pension plans, supplementary health plans or dental care plans.

Self-employment

In addition to the trend towards part-time and temporary jobs, more Canadians have either chosen, or been forced, to work for themselves. Between 1989 and 1997, self-employment accounted for 80 per cent of the overall increase in employment. In fact, over that period, the number of full-time employees actually declined slightly — gains in employment came almost exclusively from increases in part-time and self-employment.

As is the case with part-time and temporary employment, self-employment often means increased hardship for workers. On average, self-employed people in Canada earn only 60 per cent of the income earned by full-time employees. Self-employed workers also rarely have access to pension plans or supplementary health and dental benefits.

Polarization of Work Hours

Finally, one of the most dramatic recent changes in work arrangements in Canada has to do with hours of work. There has been a significant decline in the proportion of the workforce working "normal" 9 to 5 hours. In 1976, nearly 50 per cent of working Canadians had a "normal" workweek of 35 to 40 hours.

By 1997, only about 40 per cent fit into this category. Today about 30 per cent of Canadian workers put in more than 40 hours a week, and a roughly equal number put in less than 35 hours. The result is that the Canadian workforce is becoming more polarized — some people are working much more than they used to, and others are working much less.

Clearly, all these trends are having a profound impact on working people. They also have significant implications for unions. Clearly, too, there is a role for unions to play doing things like negotiating benefits for part-timers and restrictions on over-time work, and easing the strain on stressed-out two-income families.

One More Reason for Unions — Protection from "Bad Bosses"

In addition to wages benefits and work arrangements, there is another reason why Canadian workers still need unions — the treatment they receive in the workplace. The unfortunate truth is that many employers still do not pay their employees on time. Many do not pay for overtime hours worked or treat their employees fairly when it comes to things like time off, shift assignments or vacations. There are also many employers who regularly harass their workers, fire them on whim, or force them to do the work of three or four people.

The problem is particularly serious with small businesses and businesses in the service sector — especially restaurants and retail outlets. And the workers who are most likely to be cheated or unfairly treated are young workers, low-skilled workers and recent immigrants.

All these groups are easy targets for unscrupulous employers because they tend not to know much about their rights in the workplace — and even if they do, they often lack the confidence to stand up for themselves. As a result, the number of formal complaints filed with provincial authorities is probably just the tip of the iceberg. For every worker who complains, there are probably 10 or 20 more who keep quiet to avoid antagonizing "the boss," or who simply quit in hope of finding a more honest employer.

The problems experienced by vulnerable workers working in non-union jobs are compounded by the lack of protection they receive from the government. All provinces have an employment standards code, a law that sets out minimum standards for non-union workplaces. The problem is that these codes are often not enforced vigorously.

Most provincial governments do not conduct random checks of non-union businesses to ensure they're complying with the law. They do not investigate complaints unless they come from a specific employee. And even though most provincial codes allow for substantial fines for employers who mistreat their workers, these kinds of penalties are almost never levied.

Even in cases where complaints are filed and formal investigations are launched, the employer usually gets away with a slap on the wrist and a "stern talking to." It's not surprising, then, to learn that many unscrupulous employers who have had employment standards complaints filed against them do not change they way they treat their employees.

Unions — More Than Ever

So do workers in Canada still need unions? Many people in government and the business community would have us believe that the "new economy" is meeting the needs of all, or at least most, working Canadians. But this is clearly not the case. Despite the good economic times we are currently enjoying, many Canadian workers are still struggling. In fact, for many Canadians the 1990s were a time of declining wages and living standards, increased work load and work-related stress, precarious employment, and continued insecurity.

In this brave new "global" world, most workers clearly can still benefit from the kind of strong representation and protection that unions can provide. Far from being relics of the past, there is still a need for unions; maybe now more than ever.

DOES IT STILL PAY TO BE A UNION MEMBER?

Everybody knows that unionized workers get paid more on average than non-unionized workers. Most people also know that union members tend to get better benefits, pensions and vacations. But just how big is the union wage "premium"? How significant are the other advantages enjoyed by unionized workers?

For workers who are dissatisfied with their current conditions of employment or who are considering joining a union, these are extremely important questions. They want to know how union membership can improve their work lives. Most important, they want to know if unions in Canada can still "deliver the goods."

The short answer to this question is, yes — Canadian unions still have an exceptional track record when it comes to improving wages and conditions for their members. In this section, we take a closer look at some of the advantages of union membership. More specifically, we will look at things like wages, pensions, benefits and job security. In the end, it will become clear that it still makes sense to belong to a union — whether you work in a factory or behind a desk in a downtown office tower.

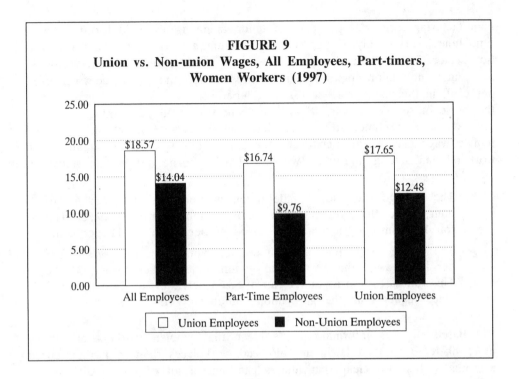

FIGURE 9
Union vs. Non-union Wages, All Employees, Part-timers, Women Workers (1997)

Wages and Income

One of the most obvious benefits of union membership is higher pay. In Canada in 1998, the average non-union worker earned $14.04 per hour, while the average union worker earned $18.57 per hour. In other words, the average union member makes 32 per cent more than the average non-union worker. This is a huge difference. It means that for every two dollars earned by non-union workers, union workers earn three.

The difference in pay is even more dramatic for part-time workers. On average, non-union part-timers make $9.76 per hour, while unionized part-time workers earn an average of $16.74. That translates into a union wage advantage of $6.98 per hour, or 72 per cent.

Of course, the difference in union-versus-non-union pay rates varies from industry to industry. In some cases, unions have been able to negotiate pay rates that are more than double the rates paid to non-union workers in the same sector. In other industries, the union and non-union wage rates are much closer. But in almost all cases, union members get paid more than non-union workers doing comparable jobs.

In addition to improving the base wages of all workers, unions have an important impact on wages earned by women and on the wages earned by people working over-time hours.

Union members are much more likely to receive premium pay for their over-time work than non-union workers (53 per cent versus 41 per cent). In some industries, the gap is even more considerable. For example, in the manufacturing sector, 94 per cent of union members are paid for their over-time hours, versus only 53 per cent for non-union workers; in the transportation sector, 74 per cent of unionized workers receive premium pay, versus 37 per cent of non-union employees; in business services, it's 61 per cent versus 32 per cent; in the health care sector it's 53 per cent versus 25 per cent; and in the personal services sector, it's 74 per cent versus 53 per cent.

At the same time, unions also have an important impact on the male-female wage gap. More specifically, the gap is much narrower among union workers than among non-union workers. This is borne out by the statistics:

> The average wage for female union members in 1998 was $17.65 hour, while the average male union member earned $19.62. This translates into a "gender gap" of $1.97 per hour, or 11 per cent.

> The average wage for female non-union workers in 1998 was $12.48 per hour, while the average non-union male worker earned $16.11. This translates into a gender gap of $3.63 per hour, or 29 per cent — much higher than the gap among union workers.

Based on this information, it's clear that women workers are much more likely to be paid fairly in unionized workplaces than in non-unionized workplaces. It's also clear that unions can take a lot of the credit for the overall narrowing of the "gender gap" over the past 30 years.

Critics of the labour movement say that all of these figures relating to the union wage advantage are misleading. They point out that unions tend to represent workers that would have higher wages, whether they belonged to unions or not: people like teachers and nurses, skilled tradesmen, and older workers with more experience.

This is true — up to a point. It's also true that unions have a bigger presence in industries like manufacturing, utilities and public administration. These industries tend to pay their workers more, whether they are union or non-union.

But even when these high-wage industries are factored out, union members still tend to get paid more than non-union members. Literally hundreds of researchers in Canada and the United States have examined the issue of union wage premiums. Many of these researchers adjusted their studies to compensate for the greater skill and training of union members, and they still found that union members get paid between 15 and 20 per cent more.

There is also evidence that the union wage advantage can even indirectly improve the earning of many non-union workers. This happens when certain employers pay wages at or near the union rate in order to discourage their employees from joining a union.

So, despite all the arguments from anti-union critics, the bottom line is that unionized workers earn more than non-union workers doing comparable jobs, whether those workers are employed in manufacturing, retail, or just about any sector of the economy you can think of. Clearly, it still pays to be a union member.

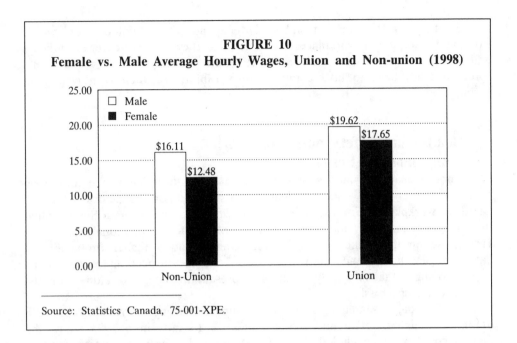

FIGURE 10
Female vs. Male Average Hourly Wages, Union and Non-union (1998)

Source: Statistics Canada, 75-001-XPE.

Pensions and Benefits

In addition to getting paid more, union members also tend to have better pensions and other benefits than non-union workers. In fact, the difference in access to these kinds of job-related entitlements is dramatic. A survey recently completed by Statistics Canada shows that more than 82 per cent of the Canadians employed in unionized workplaces have pensions of one kind or another. On the other hand, only 33 per cent of people working in non-union workplaces have them.

The link between union membership and access to pensions is even clearer when we look at the national figures on pension participation. In provinces where unionization rates are higher than the national average — like Quebec, British Columbia, Saskatchewan and Manitoba — between 40 and 50 per cent of wage and salary earners have pensions. But in provinces where the unioniza-tion rate is lower, the proportion of workers with pensions is also lower. For example, in Alberta, which has the lowest level of unionization, a lower propor-tion of workers have pensions than workers in any other province. Only 36 per cent of the wage and salary earning Albertans have registered pension plans — and the vast majority of these people are union members.

But pensions are not the only area where there is a clear union advantage. Union members are also much more likely to have other so-called "non-wage benefits." For example, 77 per cent of union members have dental plan cover-age, versus 42 per cent of non-union workers; 77 per cent of union workers are entitled to paid sick days, versus only 45 per cent of non-union workers; and 60 per cent of union workers have four or more weeks of paid holidays each year, versus only 30 per cent of non-union workers.

So it's clear that union members have an advantage. Not only do people working in non-union workplaces get paid less, they also have fewer holidays and sick days; they have to dig into their own pockets for things like dental care; and they have to take complete responsibility for their own retirement savings.

Health and Safety and Worker's Compensation Benefits

Another major advantage of union membership has to do with on-the-job health and safety. The evidence clearly shows that unions make for safer and healthier workplaces. For example, a 1991 study in the United States found that unions dramatically increased enforcement of the Occupational Safety and Health Act in the manufacturing sector. Unions had a higher probability of having regular health and safety inspections, and the inspections tended to be more probing — thanks largely to union representatives tagging along with the government inspectors.

In Canada, researchers have also found a strong correlation between unions and higher health and safety standards. In fact, in a 1993 study, the federal government concluded that union-sponsored health and safety committees have a "significant impact in reducing injury rates." More recently, a study

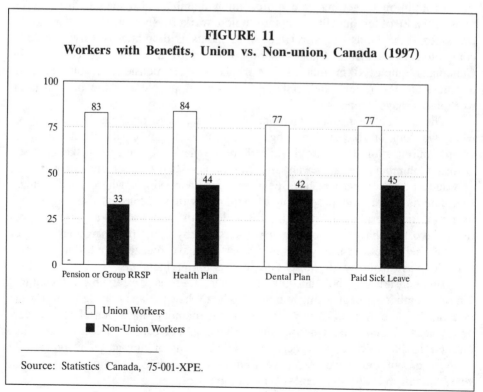

FIGURE 11
Workers with Benefits, Union vs. Non-union, Canada (1997)

Source: Statistics Canada, 75-001-XPE.

done for the Ontario Workplace Health and Safety Agency in 1996 found that 79 per cent of unionized workplaces reported high compliance with health and safety legislation, while only 54 per cent of non-union workplaces reported such compliance.

When it comes to health and safety standards, the big difference between union and non-union workplaces is that in the union environment workers feel empowered to bring forward their concerns. They know that the union will take their concerns and suggestions seriously and take action on them. Unions also provide workers with a clear mechanism for dealing with health and safety concerns and they ensure than workers have the support of trained union health and safety staff.

In cases where workers do get injured on the job or develop work-related illnesses, it's also advantageous to be a union member. Studies in Canada and the United States show that union members are more likely to receive Worker's Compensation Board (WCB) benefits when they are injured on the job than are non-union workers. This is attributed to the fact that union members can go to their union representative for help navigating the WCB's bureaucratic maze; non-union workers are on their own.

Job Security

As a result of the recession of the early '90s, one of the biggest worries for most Canadian workers is job security. Polls show that even today, more than four years after most observers declared the recession over, a significant number of workers still worry that their jobs may be eliminated.

Obviously, these concerns are shared by all workers — union and non-union. But statistics suggest that jobs in unionized workplaces tend to be more secure than those in non-union workplaces. At the national level, slightly more than 50 per cent of unionized workers have held their jobs for nine or more years, versus only 21 per cent of non-union workers. That's not to say that union workers never lose their jobs. Clearly, they do — just look at the experience of public sector workers over the past few years and the experience of workers in the manufacturing sector earlier in the 1990s. But the statistics suggest that workers in unionized workplaces do tend to hold on to their jobs longer than in non-union workplaces.

But the union advantage in this regard goes further than just job retention. In cases where jobs are lost or eliminated, it's clear that union members are much more likely than non-union workers to get some kind of severance package. Many unions have also been successful in negotiating contracts that require employers to give six to 12 months notice of any mass lay-offs. This gives the union more time to help members upgrade their skills and search for new jobs. In fact, unions often bargain for employer-funded training, so that workers facing lay-offs have the skills and flexibility they need to find new jobs quickly. So not only do union members tend to hold on to their jobs longer — they also tend to have a softer landing when they are laid off.

Complaints and Grievances

Another important benefit that union members enjoy is the grievance procedure. This refers to the process for handling the disputes and complaints that often develop between employees and employers.

In a non-union workplace, workers are usually at the mercy of "the boss." If an employee has a complaint related to the workplace, he or she can attempt to talk to a manager about it. But the manager does not have to do anything. The manager might act on the complaint, ignore it or even punish the employee for raising the issue — it all depends on the nature of the complaint, the company's labour-management philosophy, or even the manager's mood on that particular day.

In a unionized workplace, on the other hand, grievances and complaints are handled in an entirely different manner. Unlike the non-union environment where the workers are basically subject to the whims of management, workers in unionized firms have a clear set of rights — relating to things like hours of work, vacation, sick day, over-time pay etc. — which are outlined in detail in their collective agreements. If the employer breaches provisions of the collective agreement — for example, if he or she fires a worker without just cause, or if an employee is being harassed in some way on the job — then the worker can take defensive action through the established grievance procedure.

This might involve the union simply lodging a formal grievance with the employer. Or it might require a trip to a professional labour arbitrator, or even an appearance before the provincial Labour Relations Board.

When it comes to grievance and complaints, the most important point is that employees in unionized workplaces are not alone — they have the strength and resources of the union behind them. In non-union workplaces, on the other hand, individual employees are alone against the entire company. In many cases, the only real choice that non-union employees have when they feel wronged is to keep their mouth shut or quit. Neither of these options is particularly desirable — so you can see why many union members see the grievance procedure as the most important benefit of belonging to a union.

Collective Agreements vs. Employment Standards Act

Of course, some people will argue that non-union workers do have protection under the law. This is true — to a degree. In every Canadian province there is a law that spells out minimum standards for non-union workplaces. Usually that piece of legislation is called an Employment Standards Code.

Among other things, these provincial codes set the minimum wage; determine the maximum number of hours people can be asked to work before they become eligible for overtime; and outline the days throughout the year that have been designated as statutory holidays.

But there are three major problems with most provincial employment standard codes. First, they outline minimum standards — and the key word is "minimum." The standards set out in union collective agreements are almost always vastly superior. In fact, by law unions cannot bargain for anything less than the minimum standards set out under the applicable provincial code. So union contracts are, by definition, equal or superior to these codes.

Second, the codes are as notable for what they do not cover as for what they do. For example, most provincial codes make no mention of harassment or health and safety. They do not provide for paid sick days, bereavement leave or any number of special provisions commonly found in union-negotiated collective agreements.

Finally, the biggest problem with the Employment Standards Code is that enforcement of the codes is typically complaint driven. The government only steps in to investigate an employer or worksite if it receives a formal complaint from an individual worker. This is problematic because — as we have seen — workers are often intimidated by their employers. They hesitate to complain for fear of punishment or dismissal. Given this situation, it's not surprising that workers in unionized workplaces are much more likely to come forward with their complaints. They know that the union is behind them, and they know that the union will protect them from punitive actions by the employer.

Unions Deliver the Goods

So does it still pay to be a union member? Clearly, it does. Union members enjoy better wages, better benefits and increased job security. But the biggest benefit is the strength that comes from solidarity. Unlike non-union workers, unionized workers are not alone when they have grievances; they're not alone when they file WCB claims; and they're not alone when they raise health and safety concerns. This is the most basic lesson of the labour movement — that workers are stronger when they face management shoulder to shoulder than when they stand alone.

UNIONS AND THE ECONOMY

Another argument that is often used against unions is that they are bad for the economy. According to this point of view, unions "distort" the labour market by driving wages and benefits up to unreasonably high levels. This, in turn, is said to reduce the productivity and profitability of firms.

This argument has been around for years, but it is being raised with increasing frequency in relation to the new "global economy." Many business owners say that unions rob them of the "flexibility" they need to compete with companies from other countries: especially low-wage countries like Vietnam, Indonesia and, increasingly, China.

Unions, for their part, have never denied that their goal is to raise wages above the level that would prevail if workers did not have the right to bargain collectively. Union leaders and activists have always wanted to win the best possible deal for their members — and that means higher wages and better benefits.

On the surface, this may seem like an intractable problem — if employers get their way the workers suffer, and if the workers and the unions that represent them get their way business suffers. However, in many ways this is a false

301

conflict. According to research that has been done over the past 15 or 20 years, unionization can be a win-win situation for workers and employers. More specifically, the research suggests that unions can actually improve labour-management relations, enhance productivity and improve profitability over the long term.

In this section, we will take a closer look at unions and the economy. In particular, we will examine the impact of unions on the productivity and profitability of firms. Far from hurting the economy, we will show that unions can actually improve things — for workers, owners and investors alike.

Unions and Productivity

Much has been written about productivity in Canada lately — almost all of it negative. According to members of the Canadian Alliance Party and spokespeople from conservative think tanks like the Fraser and C.D. Howe Institutes, Canadian companies and Canadian workers are not producing goods and services as efficiently as they should.

They point to figures from the OECD showing that Canada has fallen behind the United States and other countries when it comes to productivity. They say this is a serious problem because it reduces the competitiveness of Canadian firms and forces down the standard of living for all Canadians.

There is some debate about just how bad the situation is. For example, recent figures from Statistics Canada actually show that over the past 10 years, productivity in Canada has been increasing at a faster rate than in the United States.

Despite this debate over the rate of productivity growth, the evidence does seem to support the notion that in absolute terms, productivity is lower in most Canadian industries than in comparable industries in the United States and other countries. The question then is why and what can be done about it.

FIGURE 12
Total Factor Productivity Growth and Union Density, Various Service Industries (1992–95)

Industries	Union Density (1997)	Productivity Growth (1992–1995)
Business Services	7.9	−15.6
Hotels and Restaurants	8.2	4.2
Finance	9.4	−0.8
Retail	11.0	−0.2
Transport and Storage	44.1	6.8
Utilities	62.1	9.7
Wholesale	11.9	−0.6

Source: HRDC Applied Research Branch, Statistics Canada, 71-005-XPB and 71-005-XPE.

Not surprisingly, conservative observers like Canadian Alliance MPs have their preferred villains. Most often, they say that taxes and regulations are causing the problem. But they also say the problem is at least partially caused by unions. They argue that workers are being paid too much based upon their output. The arguments about tax and regulation fall outside of the scope of this report. But we will take a closer look at the effect of unions on productivity.

The conservative argument is based on the old stereotype that unionized employees are lazy employees — that they work slowly, take long breaks and refuse to do work that is not "in the contract." The problem with this view is that is completely inaccurate — plain and simple. Far from acting as a drag on productivity, research conducted over the past 15 years shows that unions actually enhance it.

In an authoritative study of unions and the economy published 10 years ago, Harvard economist Richard Freeman concluded that unions increase productivity by improving morale and reducing staff turn-over. Other researchers have looked at the effects of unions on the performance of firms in particular sectors of the economy. For example, one researcher studied union and non-union paper mills in the United States, and determined that the non-union mills had significantly lower levels of productivity.

Closer to home, research has shown that unionized firms in Canada also tend to be more productive. For example, the applied research branch of the federal Human Resources department recently completed a study of productivity in various service industries. The effect of unions on productivity was not the main focus of the study, but it turned out that the industries with the best productivity performance over the study period were also the ones with the highest levels of union membership (see Figure 12). The industry that performed best was the utilities industry — with an increase in total factor productivity of 9.7 per cent over four years. Nation-wide, 62 per cent of people working for utilities are unionized. On the other hand, the industry that performed worst in the study — businesses services, which recorded a drop in productivity of 15.6 per cent over the study period — was also the industry with the lowest unionization rate.

Further support for the notion that unions can enhance productivity comes from the OECD. Its studies show that high productivity rates are not restricted to the anti-union USA, as some conservative observers would have us believe. In fact, labour productivity is also high in Belgium, Finland, the Netherlands and Sweden — all countries with high rates of unionization.

So how is it that unions increase productivity? The answer lies in the feeling of empowerment that comes with union membership. Unions give members a voice in what goes on their workplace which they would not have if there was no union. As a result, union members are more likely to be happy in their work. They are also more likely to speak their minds about how work processes could be changed or improved. And they are more likely to stay on the job for long periods. This all makes for a happy, motivated, self-confident and experienced workforce — exactly the kind of workforce that most employers want.

Interestingly, having a union seems to be particularly good for companies that are introducing new technologies or experimenting with different work practices. Unionized workers are more secure, and therefore more likely than non-unionized workers to request information and openly give their opinions and suggestions without the same fear of reprisal or arbitrary treatment. In the long run, this smooths the way for more effective workplace change.

Of course, encouraging union membership is not, by itself, going to solve Canada's productivity problem. According to many academics and researchers, the real key to enhanced productivity is to encourage more corporate investment in training, technology and research and development. Increased public spending on infrastructure, research and education are also part of the solution. However, blaming unions and workers for what are essentially the failings of management and government is not going to fix the problem. In fact, based on the evidence regarding unions and productivity, more anti-union rhetoric will probably only make a bad situation worse.

Unions and Profitability

Of course, there is a price to be paid for having a union in your business. If a company is paying more money out in the form of wages and benefits, there will obviously be less left over at the end of the day to pay dividends to investors; at least, in the short term.

But in the long run, the economic benefits of having a union far outweigh the short-term drawbacks. As we have already seen, in many cases unions actually enhance the productivity of firms by improving morale, encouraging participation and guaranteeing a more loyal and experienced workforce. All of these things enhance the competitiveness of a business and, as a result, improve its long-term profitability. The lesson from this observation is clear — paying a union wage should be seen as an investment, not a cost.

There is abundant evidence right here in Canada to show that unionized firms can also be very profitable. In fact, some of our nation's most prominent and profitable companies are unionized. For example, Suncor, one of the two big oil sands companies operating in Northern Alberta, is heavily unionized. But the relatively high cost of union labour has not stopped the company from turning huge profits each year. In fact, Suncor is doing so well that it recently announced a $2.5-billion expansion to its Fort McMurray operation. In 1996 and 1997, Suncor reported net earnings of $187-million and $223-million. In 1998 the company racked up net earnings of $188-million, even though the price for crude oil fell by more than 30 per cent.

But Suncor is not alone. Other well-known Canadian companies with large union workforces include: Bell Canada, Bombardier, Telus, Safeway, Imperial Oil and Petro-Canada and, of course, the Big Three automakers — General Motors, Ford and DaimlerChrysler. In all these cases, the companies have been able to maintain high levels of profit while at the same time paying their workers more than their non-union competitors.

The conclusion that should be drawn from these examples is clear: by paying their workers more and providing them with better benefits and enhanced job security, firms may sacrifice some short-term profits — but they make a number of important long-term gains, including better labour-management relations, improved productivity and more stable long-term profits. It's a win-win situation for both workers and employers.

CONCLUSIONS

Looking back on the past 100 years, it's clear that unions have played a central role in shaping Canada. Thanks to the hard work of union members and activists, Canadians now enjoy one of the highest standards of living in the world. But unions are not only important for what they accomplished in the past. In today's world of globalization, de-regulation and government cutbacks, unions are more important than ever.

Some of its critics claim that the labour movement is a spent force. They say that unions are obsolete relics of a bygone era. But the labour movement has been declared dead before. In fact, during the 1930s many critics argued that unions were destined for irrelevance. However, just a few years later, the labour movement in Canada and the United States experienced its most dramatic period of growth and vitality.

Whether or not the union movement surprises its critics in the twenty-first century as much as it did during the twentieth century remains to be seen. It all depends on decisions that union leaders and members make over the next few years. If unions are able to develop new plans for organizing the unorganized, and new strategies for addressing the evolving needs of workers, then their future will be bright. Far from fading into the pages of history, the twenty-first century may be the time for unions to reassert their central place in Canadian society.

BIBLIOGRAPHY

Alberta Economic Development, *Monthly Economic Review*, February and March 1999.

Alberta Labour Relations Board, *Annual Reports*, various years.

Alberta Labour, *Albertans: A Statistical Profile* (Alberta Labour Information Service, January 1999).

———, *Bargaining Update*, 11(1).

Bernard, Elaine, "Why unions matter," *Uncommon Sense*, March 1998.

Bethcherman, G. and R. Chaykowski, *The Changing Workplace: Challenges for Public Policy* (Applied Research Branch, HRDC, September 1996).

British Columbia Labour Relations Board, *Annual Reports*, various years.

Canadian Labour Congress, *Workplace Health and Safety Fact Sheet*, October 1997.

Chaykowski, R.P. and G.A. Slotsve, "Union wage premiums and union density in Canada and the United States," *Canadian Business Economics* (Spring 1996): 46–59.

Dinardo, J. and T. Lemieux, "Diverging male wage inequality in the United States and Canada," *Industrial and Labour Relations Review*, 50(4): 629–51.

Freeman, R.B. and D. Card, *Small Differences that Matter: Labour Markets and Income Maintenance in Canada and the United States*, NBER Comparative Labour Markets Series (Chicago: University of Chicago Press, 1993).

Freeman, R.B. and J.L. Medoff, *What do Unions do?* (New York: Basic Books Inc., 1984).

Freeman, Richard, "The future for unions in decentralized collective bargaining systems," *British Journal of Industrial Relations* (December 1995): 519–36.

Fuller, Tom, *Some Observations on the Economic Ramifications of Right-to-Work Legislation in Alberta* (Alberta Union of Provincial Employees, Fall 1996).

Hirsch, Barry, "Workers' Compensation recipiency in union and non-union workplaces," *Industrial and Labour Relations Review*, 50(2): 213–35.

HRDC Applied Research Branch, "Can organizational change resolve the productivity paradox?" *Applied Research Bulletin*, 4(2): 15–18.

Human Resources Development Canada (HRDC), *Alberta Wage Survey 1996–97*.

Hyman, Richard, "National industrial relations systems and transnational challenges: an essay in review." Working paper, Industrial Relations Research Unit, University of Warwick (U.K.), 1999.

———, "An emerging Agenda for trade unions?" Working paper, Industrial Relations Research Unit, University of Warwick (U.K.), 1999.

Ichniowski, Casey, "The effects of grievance activity on productivity," *Industrial and Labour Relations Review*, 40(1): 75–91.

International Labour Organization, *World Labour Report, 1997–98* (Geneva: United Nations, 1997).

Johnston, Paul, *Success While Others Fail: Social Movement Unionism and the Public Workplace* (Ithaca, New York: ILR Press, 1995).

Kuhn, Peter, "Unions and the economy," *Canadian Journal of Economics*, 31(5): 1033–56.

Lowe, G. and H. Krahn, *Public Attitudes Towards Unions: Some Canadian Evidence*, Population Research Laboratory, University of Alberta, 1983.

———, *Recent Trends in Public Support for Unions*, Population Research Laboratory, University of Alberta, 1988.

Lowe, Graham, "The Future of Work: Implications for Unions," revised version of the Fourteenth Sefton Memorial Lecture. Presented at Wordsworth College, University of Toronto, March 27, 1996.

McGowan, Gil, *Crumbs from the Table: Re-evaluating the so-called "Alberta Advantage"* (Alberta Federation of Labour, March 1997).

———, *Missing Out on the Boom?: A Report Card on Jobs, Wages and Economic Security in Alberta* (Alberta Federation of Labour, May 1998).

Morton, Desmond, *Working People: A History of the Canadian Labour Movement* (Toronto: Summerhill Press, 1990).

Ontario Labour Relations Board, *Annual Reports*, various years.

Pilat, Dirk, "What drives productivity growth?" *The OECD Observer*, OECD, No. 213 (August/September 1998): 12–15.

Rothstein, Richard, "Union strength in the United States: Lessons from the UPS strike," *International Labour Review*, 136(4).

Stanford, Jim, *Economic Freedom for the Rest of Us* (Ottawa: Canadian Centre for Policy Alternatives, 1999).

Statistics Canada, "A new perspective on wages," *Labour Force Update*, 71-005-XPB, Summer 1998.

———, "A statistical portrait of the trade union movement," *Perspectives on Labour and Income*, 75-001-XPE, Winter 1998.

———, "An overview of the 1997 labour market," *Labour Force Update*, 71-005-XPB, Winter 1998.

———, "An overview of the 1998 labour market," *Labour Force Update*, 71-005-XPB, Winter 1999.

———, "Canada–US Labour Market Comparison," *Labour Force Update*, 71-005-XPB, Autumn 1998.

———, "Non-permanent paid work," *Perspectives on Labour and Income*, 75-001-XPE, Autumn 1997.

———, "The rise of unionization among women," *Perspectives on Labour and Income*, 75-001-XPE, Winter 1998.

———, "The self-employed," *Labour Force Update*, 71-005-XPB, Autumn 1997.

———, "Unionized Workers," *Perspectives on Labour and Income*, 75-001-XPE, Spring 1996.

————, "Working overtime in today's labour market," *Perspectives on Labour and Income*, 75-001-XPE, Winter 1997.

————, "Youths and the labour market," *Labour Force Update*, 71-005-XPB, Spring 1997.

————, *Canada's Retirement Income Programs: A Statistical Overview*, 74-507-XPB, 1996.

————, *Employment, Earnings and Hours*, 72-002-XPB, monthly.

————, *Historical Labour Force Statistics*, 71-201-XPB, 1998.

————, *Pension Plans in Canada*, 74-401-XPB, January 1996

Voos, P.B. and L. Mishel, *Unions and Economic Competitiveness* (New York: M.E. Sharpe Inc., 1992).

An Overview of the Financial Services Industry

Peter A.T. Campbell and Tom Wesson

The financial services industry performs three basic economic functions. First, it provides the payments mechanism for the economy. By interfacing between buyers and sellers of real goods and services, the industry lubricates and depersonalizes economic transactions. The most primitive payment mechanism is a barter system. At the other extreme, it is a sophisticated system of electronic funds transfer. The financial services industry is an integral part of the electronic highway.

Second, the industry facilitates the saving and investment process, providing a link between those with excess funds and those who have a need for funds. By creating acceptable substitutes for legal tender, the industry provides a mechanism for converting savings into bricks, mortar, processes, distribution systems, etc. This is referred to as the capital formation process.

Third, the financial services industry provides the pricing mechanism for capital — both existing and newly created financial assets. This pricing mechanism allocates capital based on relative rates of return, subject to certain other factors such as risk, liquidity and time horizon.

Figure 1 provides a snapshot of the size of the financial services industry by institution type for 1997.

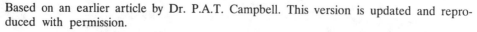

Based on an earlier article by Dr. P.A.T. Campbell. This version is updated and reproduced with permission.

FIGURE 1
Financial Services Industry Overview, 1997

	No. of Companies	Total Assets ($ millions)	Capital ($ millions)	Total Revenue ($ millions)	Net Income ($ millions)	No. of Employees
Banks including subsidiaries	55	1,322,085	54,699	42,124	7,954	219,977
Canadian	11	1,229,884	49,767	39,629	7,550	211,398
Foreign	44	92,221	4,932	2,484	404	8,579
Credit Unions and caisses populaires	2,315	121,100	6,825	5,905	567	61,600
Life Insurance	121	279,774	28,002	59,726	2,771	50,770
Federal	26	13,920	n/a	n/a	n/a	n/a
Provincial	73	283,159	n/a	n/a	n/a	35,000
Mutual Funds	216	53,014	15,513	19,110	1,866	37,055
Property & Casualty Insurance	2	13,920	n/a	337	92	3,361
Provincial government-owned banks	187	158,200	3,526	8,478	759	32,900
Securities Dealers including bank subsidiaries	23	52,178	2,418	2,353	78	22,900
Trust Companies excluding bank subsidiaries						

n/a Not available

Source: Department of Finance Canada, *Reforming Canada's Financial Services Sector: A Framework for the Future*, June 25, 1999, cat. F2-136/1999E.

FUNDAMENTAL CONCEPTS AND CHARACTERISTICS

Some Basic Concepts

Before embarking on any general discussion of the financial services industry, a brief discussion of a few of the concepts according to which industry functions is in order.

First of all, the financial services industry functions according to a unique concept of time. Essentially, all values are present values. Yields in the fixed income markets, price-to-earnings ratios in equity markets, capitalization rates in real estate and rates of return on real investment projects are all valued on a "time-now" basis.

The concept of the franchise is also very important to constituent parts of the Canadian financial industry. A franchise holds forth the promise of delivering excellence on a consistent basis — colloquially, this is known as the "confidence factor." If a financial organization does not enjoy the confidence of the public, either because it is not well known or because of its performance, then the survival of that organization is threatened.

Industry Characteristics

The financial services industry is both dynamically innovative and imitative. At its core are highly skilled, computer-oriented knowledge workers. They work as a close-knit entrepreneurial cluster, concentrated in few financial centres around the world. From these clusters emerge a never-ending stream of financial innovations: new twists on old financing instruments, or even entirely new instruments. These new products are then immediately replicated by competing entrepreneurial clusters. What was new yesterday becomes common practice today.

Because the industry is computer dominated, there is a constant need to convert procedures and instruments into simplified, almost commodity-like products. The driving force is cost reduction. Once systems are in place, their costs "flatten out"; marginal costs can often be eliminated. The difference between processing a $10 transaction and a $10-billion one for example, is negligible.

The industry is risk-oriented. There are six basic kinds of risk that need to be understood in this context. Credit risk relates to the borrower's ability to pay back. Market risk involves the improvement or depreciation in the value of existing assets as a result of market forces. Liquidity risk relates to the ready disposability, or marketability, of existing assets. Solvency risk relates to the equity base of an organization and its ability to meet commitments. Systemic risk relates to the confidence factor in the financial system or in a sub-group within it. If confidence evaporates, then the ability to perform the economic function disappears as well.

The risk of certain types of securities, particularly the solvency or default risk of debt instruments, is assessed by for profit firms called rating services. There are two Canadian and two dominant American rating services active in Canada: Dominion Bond Rating Service Ltd., Toronto; Canadian Bond Rating Service Inc. of Montreal; Standard & Poor's Corp. of New York; and Moody's Investor Services Inc., also of New York. Until recently, the Canadian rating services focused on Canadian ratings, and the U.S. services focused on U.S. dollar issues of Canadian debt. The U.S. services now also rate Canadian debt and preferred shares, and have established themselves in Canada.

The financial services industry is borderless. Innovations such as currency swaps and the multi-jurisdictional financing prospectuses make national borders irrelevant. Thus, the industry is at once both globalized and globally interdependent.

The industry is highly mobile. Because of its global reach and emphasis on modern telecommunications, capital can easily seek out the most attractive investment opportunities anywhere in the world. At the same time, entrepreneurs and the knowledge workers on whom the industry depends themselves become very mobile.

The industry is highly volatile. The compression of time brought on by globalization and modern telecommunications means that all participants who matter are aware of the same events simultaneously. Collective response to these events generates high volatility in asset prices.

Financial Intermediation

A debt obligation incurred in an economic transaction can be discharged directly by proffering the appropriate amount of legal tender. Obviously, however, when substantial sums are involved, more practical alternatives are needed. The financial services industry intermediates between transaction parties by creating acceptable substitutes for legal tender — the process of financial intermediation. There are seven main types, which are discussed below.

Payments intermediation has come to be identified with deposit-taking institutions, who confer the ability to transfer ownership of deposits through checking. Banks, trust companies, caisses populaires, credit unions and cash management accounts of securities dealers perform the payments intermediation function. These institutions perform this function so effectively that legal tender is of steadily decreasing importance as a medium of exchange.

Denomination intermediation refers to the process of gathering liabilities in small lots from the general public and acquiring assets in large pieces. Almost all intermediaries offer liabilities in small denominations, but deal in wholesale or large denominations in the financial markets. In effect, the efficiency of the intermediary process enables primary securities from large borrowers to be broken into small lots.

Default risk intermediation enables the intermediary to create assets for sale to the public with lower overall default risk than the individual assets which underline them. The public, in effect, has an indirect claim on a portion of a portfolio. This provides diversification for the public. Mutual funds are the most aggressive marketers of this form of intermediation, but diversification is a feature of all well-run financial intermediaries.

Maturity risk intermediation refers to the preference of the majority of savers to have access to their monies on demand or short notice, while the majority of borrowers prefer longer time horizons for their liabilities. Once again, the financial intermediary interposes its credit rating between these differing lender and borrower time preferences. By relying on its fund-gathering efficiency, the intermediary bears the risk of the time differential. All deposit-taking institutions engage in this form of intermediation.

Credit-rating intermediation relates to the perception that a financial institution has superior credit-rating strength. The institution can then interpose its credit rating between primary savers and those borrowers who have a lesser credit rating than the institution itself. The institution matches the maturity or duration of its liabilities with those of its assets. Because of its superior credit rating, the cost of its liabilities is less than the return on its assets. The difference becomes profit for the institution. Most deposit-gathering institutions engage in this form of intermediation, as do pension funds and insurance companies.

Capital-value intermediation focuses on the stability of liability value in the face of volatility of asset values. Institutions that engage in this kind of intermediation offer diversification and professional management to minimize risk and thus enhance the capital value stability of their liabilities. Mutual funds are dominant in this field.

Liquidity-risk intermediation relies on the marketability of the underlying security in asset portfolios. The security for bank loans, for example, is often property or equipment, which are not easily disposable in most market settings. The bank interposes its efficiency in fund-gathering between the demand nature of its liabilities and the non-liquid nature of its assets.

Price Formation

The core of the price formation process is dominated by securities dealers. Dealers buy and sell securities on behalf of clients and for their own account. The two traditional forms of market structure are over-the-counter and auction.

Over-the-counter markets involve dealers in their offices communicating with clients and competitors by telephone or electronically. The money, bond and foreign exchange markets are the principal illustrations of this market form.

An auction market is located in a specific place where dealers meet face to face or, increasingly, electronically and bid for securities. Most stock exchanges have taken this format.

Rapid advances in telecommunications technology are tending to blur the distinction between auction and over-the-counter markets. All market forms are rapidly adopting screen-trading techniques. Bids and offers are recorded systematically in video-based communication networks; and business is initiated on the basis of information received via the telecommunications network.

Today, securities markets are run on a 24-hour basis. As normal business hours come to a close in one time zone, the firm's securities position, or "book," is sometimes passed on to an affiliate in another time zone, usually in a different country. After Canadian markets go to bed, Asian markets are becoming active in Hong Kong and Tokyo. When Tokyo is winding down, Europe is opening. North American markets open when Europe is past mid-day. Firms' positions get passed around the world during the relevant working time zones. Markets are literally never closed, and are always being materially influenced by events around the globe.

The entire term structure of interest rates in readily marketable debt instruments is determined by this never-closing electronic price formation process. This price structure serves as a price leader for less marketable forms of securities, such as the mortgage and loan portfolios of major lending institutions. It is through actions taken to influence the structure of the Canadian interest rates that Canada's central bank, the Bank of Canada, transmits its monetary policy.

A shorthand form of viewing the price structure in financial markets is known as the yield curve. The government bond market has maturities ranging from a few days, in the case of maturing issues, to about 30 years. If you plot the yields on these maturities on a graph, with the vertical axis representing yield and the horizontal axis representing remaining term to maturity, the pattern that emerges is known as the yield curve. This pattern is used as a proxy for the price formation process in the entire capital market.

The government bond market is viewed as being a sufficient proxy, since the credit of the federal government is considered the prime credit in the system. Because the federal government has the sovereign right to print legal tender, it is not possible for the government to fail to meet a maturing obligation in its own currency.

The value of all other credits in the system is based on a spread above the government credit. These spreads are determined by the relative credit-worthiness of the borrowing entities, and are examined and recorded publicly by credit-rating agencies. These spreads from the government credit narrow and widen as the fortunes of the entities improve or deteriorate over time. Because these relative credit spreads relate to Government of Canada yields, movements in government yields are automatically transmitted to non-government yields, reinforcing the usefulness of the proxy value of the government market.

Values in the stock market are determined by myriad microeconomic factors. Unlike bonds, stocks have no maturity. Historically, equities have yielded in the vicinity of 12 per cent, assuming that all dividends are reinvested and that a representative basket of companies is reflected in the sample. In effect, this 12 per cent return becomes a benchmark yield for the latest maturity item in the yield curve.

The disciplines of economics and finance contain many theories to explain both the shape of the yield curve and its height. Among the more prominent of these are the loanable funds (supply and demand) theory, the real interest rate theory, the liquidity preference theory, market segmentation and expectations theory. Each of these theories provides a partial explanation of what goes on in the real world.

The yield curve is a convenient way of describing price transmission effects among both market-determined and administered prices, or between the two, within a capital market — or between two different national capital markets.

For transactions between national capital markets, the foreign exchange market becomes an important vehicle for transmitting price influences. Cross-border financial transactions are served by an efficient foreign-exchange market that has market depth in both spot (now) and forward (future) contracts. The existence of this foreign exchange market is prerequisite to an integrated global financial sector.

FINANCIAL INSTRUMENTS

Intermediation opportunities and pricing mechanisms shape and value many financial instruments. Financial markets involve three basic kinds of instruments for transferring purchasing power: debt, equity and foreign exchange. Debt instruments are promises to pay. Equity instruments represent ownership. Foreign exchange facilitates cross-border economic activity by transferring purchasing power from one currency to another.

Innovation in the financial services industry creates a wide variety of financing forms within each of these instrument groups. There are also hybrid forms that span groups, and synthetic instruments (called derivative securities) based on widely recognized industry benchmarks such as stock indexes.

FINANCIAL INSTITUTIONS

Institutions structure financial dealings in any society. There are three sets of financial institutions that play prominent roles in the financial services industry: public institutions, private-sector organizations and various associations representing segments of the financial sector.

Public Institutions

The principal public institutions affecting the financial services industry in Canada are the Bank of Canada, the Bank for International Settlements (BIS), the International Monetary Fund (IMF) and the World Bank. Additional special-function organizations play important roles in their fields: the Canada Mortgage and Housing Corporation (CMHC) provides guarantees and credit in the housing field; the Farm Credit Corporation (FCC) supports the agricultural industry; the Export Development Corporation (EDC) provides guarantees and credits in the export field; and the Business Development Corporation (BDC) provides assistance to small and medium-size businesses.

The Bank of Canada is the source of legal tender in the system and provides ultimate liquidity as the lender of last resort to the banks. The BIS, located in Basel, Switzerland, was originally established to manage war reparations payments following World War I. It has evolved into a truly international regulatory agency focusing on the capital adequacy of banks that operate internationally.

Private Sector Organizations

Financial institutions in the private sector are divided into those that are balance-sheet-dominated and those that are service-function dominant. The first group includes deposit-taking institutions, insurance companies, pension funds and mutual funds. Service-function-dominant organizations include actuarial advisors, financial planners, financial holding companies, investment counsellors, merchant banks, securities dealers and venture-capital companies.

Industry Associations

Each major financial-service-industry subgroup has established an industry association or organization. The purpose of these associations is to develop educational programs for industry members; to set standards for business conduct; to serve as a lobby group to further the collective interests of its members; and, in some cases, to regulate member activities.

THE STRUCTURE OF THE INDUSTRY

The organization of the financial services industry has always been shaped by regulation. In general, the object of regulation has been to achieve allocation, operational and social efficiency. Allocation efficiency involves allocating financial resources to the areas of highest expected economic rate of return. Operational efficiency means delivering financial services at the lowest possible cost. Social efficiency refers to maintaining the confidence factor in the system, ensuring competition and maximizing the industry's accessibility to the general public.

A number of other, more specific, objectives have always influenced the formulation of public policy. Consumer protection through full, true and plain disclosure of all material facts has been the watchword of provincial securities commissions. To enhance the smooth functioning of the payments mechanism and provide an effective milieu through which monetary policy can be implemented, is also important to many. Ensuring the stability of financial institutions, while at the same time fostering active competition among them, is regarded as a high priority. Concern over undue concentration of economic power is never far from political attention. Additional social goals, such as fostering housing or supporting the farming industry, often intrude into the regulatory debate.

Regulation in Canada is further complicated by the fact that some areas fall under federal jurisdiction, others are a provincial responsibility and still others are matters of overlapping responsibility between federal and provincial jurisdictions.

The Four-Pillar System

Until the middle of the 1980s, the modern Canadian regulatory system was known as the four-pillar system. The "four pillars" of the financial services industry were as follows: the banks, whose primary responsibility it was to administer the payments mechanism; the trust companies, whose primary responsibility was the fiduciary business — the discretionary management of other people's money; the insurance industry, whose business was the protection of life, health and property; and the security dealers, who performed both the underwriting function — marrying up primary savers with borrowers — and the market-making function in outstanding financial claims. Banks were the exclusive preserve of federal regulation, and security dealers were provincial. Trust and insurance companies could be either provincial or federal, depending on how they were incorporated.

Regulation of the four-pillar system was designed to foster competition within each pillar, but not among them. At the same time, there was a very strong bias against foreign ownership and control where it did not previously exist.

The separation of the pillars resulted from a blend of three forces. Separation meant a minimum of conflict of interest. At the same time, undue concentration of economic power was limited. Separation was also a function of effective lobbying by the three non-bank pillars. The bias against foreign ownership was both a function of the notion of nationalistic preservation of key industries and the product of effective lobbying.

The four-pillar system was in place for roughly 25 years. Through the 1980s, however, events and public debate successfully challenged the validity of the system. By the early 1990s, it had been swept aside and broadly based new legislation had been set in place to regulate the financial industry.

The Transformation of the Four-Pillar System

Many themes dominated public debate about financial services in the 1980s. Some were related to weaknesses in the four-pillar system itself, some to the political clout of those demanding change, and some to the revolution in telecommunications technology.

The four-pillar system did not adjust adequately to the development of new centres of power in the financial system. These included pension funds, investment counsellors, mutual funds and financial planners. These subgroups thrived almost without reference to the system. At the same time, the role of trust companies changed dramatically. Initially, their fiduciary business drove their fortunes. Later, their deposit-taking business came to dominate. In effect, the trust-company industry became just as expert in administering the payments mechanism efficiently as the banks.

Finally, through a process known as "securitization," the securities dealers began to strip away the prime assets of the banks, forcing them to move down-market into lesser credits to survive. Securitization is the process of converting non-marketable financial assets into marketable assets or securities. Banks, for example, had viewed providing working capital lines of credit to strong corporations as one of their prime functions. Security dealers created markets for commercial paper — promissory notes of prime corporations — which became a perfect substitute for working capital loans at the banks. European bond markets developed a taste for high-quality corporate debt. Security dealers met this demand by encouraging corporations to finance directly in these public markets. This reduced the need for corporate term-loan facilities at the Canadian banks, by creating asset-backed securities (financial assets backed by other securities) to finance the mortgage portfolios and receivables of finance companies. The rigidities of the four-pillar system made it impossible for the banks to compete directly with the securities dealers to get their prime business back. Something had to give.

The New Regulatory Environment

As in all policy discussions, the financial-industry regulation issues debated during the 1980s were always couched in terms of the national interest. Only by accident did the furtherance of a position happen to also advance the interests of the specific industry, subgroup or corporation supporting it. Principal among the issues discussed were the level playing-field concept, globalization, foreign ownership, commercial links, concentration and competition.

The concept of a level playing-field means organizations performing similar functions should be playing by the same set of rules. The banks argued effectively in favour of such a system. It was noted, for example, that the trust companies, through their deposit-taking operations, competed directly with the banks in administering the payments mechanism, but the banks were prohibited from operating in the fiduciary business. The securities dealers were securitizing the banks' prime assets, but the banks could not compete in the securities field in order to retain their clients' business. Through margin- and cash-management accounts, the dealers were, in effect, invading the personal loan and payment roles of the banks. The savings component of life-insurance policies competed with the deposit business of the banks. In order for the playing field to be level, the banks felt they should have direct access to the other pillars.

The globalization of the financial industry meant that Canadian financial organizations were faced with tough foreign competition in every sphere of activity. In order to compete effectively on the international stage, it was argued that fewer, more powerful, financial organizations would be necessary in order to withstand foreign encroachments within Canada, and enable Canadians to compete effectively abroad. The four-pillar system was viewed as fragmenting the Canadian financial industry, leaving it vulnerable to globalized competitive pressures.

Commercial links were another issue. The term refers to the commingling of ownership of financial organizations and commercial companies. Historically, commercial links were viewed as bad, because they could lead to abusive self-dealing, particularly if the commercial corporation was in trouble. Initially, the debate favoured the abolition of commercial links. By the mid-1980s, however, the federal government had reversed its position on this issue.

This change of heart turned on two sets of events. First, Quebec regulators were in favour of holding companies that combined strong commercial companies with financial services firms. This was part of Quebec's corporatist élan. The federal government was extremely reluctant to take on Quebec in this issue, given the fragility of Quebec's position in Confederation at the time. Second, through the financial holding company technique, a number of major corporate groupings had already been formed with a strong flavour of commercial linkage.

The four-pillar system crumbled in 1986, when ownership of securities dealers was thrown open. By the end of 1991, legislation was in place, for promulgation in the middle of the following year, that would re-regulate the rest of the financial system.

The new system of regulation was presented as having a consumer focus. By eliminating the four pillars, competition would be enhanced. Greater competition meant that financial services would be delivered to consumers at lower cost. Consumer protection would be strengthened by the establishment of a new federal regulatory agency — the Office of the Superintendent of Financial Institutions (OSFI). Measures were included to encourage widely held ownership of financial organizations. And the federal government made harmonization of regulation between the federal regulatory agency and its provincial counterparts an essential objective.

The key change between the new system and the four-pillar system was dropping the restrictions on ownership of more than one pillar by one firm. Cross-pillar diversification was now allowed.

The potential for conflicts of interest arising from commercial links was dealt with by banning non-arm's length transactions, establishing conduct review committees for permitted transactions and requiring that certain transactions obtain prior approval from the OSFI.

Two peculiarities remain. Banks are not permitted in the auto-leasing business, nor are they able to sell insurance through their branch systems. These anomalies are a tribute to the grass-roots political clout of automobile dealers and independent insurance agents across the nation.

The collapse of the commercial real-estate market from 1990 on fed into a serious deterioration of asset values in the portfolios of all financial intermediaries. What began as serious defaults in the development industry — Campeau Corporation, Olympia & York — quickly spread to financial intermediaries in the trust company field — Standard Trust, Central Trust, First City Trust; and in the insurance field — Les Coopérants and Sovereign Life.

The sorting-out of other intermediaries, weakened by deterioration in the real-estate-asset class, provided strong organizations with remarkable opportunities for cherry picking and accelerating growth of the strong at the expense of the weak. In the insurance field, Great West Life picked up Confederation Life, and North American Life picked up First City Trust. The Royal Bank acquired Royal Trust. The Bank of Nova Scotia acquired Montreal Trust, and the Toronto Dominion Bank absorbed Central Trust.

The impact of re-regulation of the financial-services industry was swift and brutal. The upshot was a concentration of economic power in the hands of the Canadian banks as they became owners and marketers of the full range of financial services.

SAFETY NETS

In many respects, the real test of the viability of a financial system is how it performs when the chips are down, particularly during a prolonged recession or when the system goes into shock for some reason. When a specific financial institution gets into trouble from time to time, only that institution must go under, not the whole class of organizations. When the confidence factor evaporates for a particular institution, leading to its demise, then how the financial system limits damage to only that organization, isolating it from the system as a whole, is a critical test of the system.

Each recession, each external shock and each realignment of global economic power teaches the financial sector more about how to deal with such events, while at the same time preserving and improving the performance of the industry's essential functions. In the face of such adversity, the Canadian financial sector has developed five clear safety nets: a central bank sensitive to systemic issues, deposit insurance, protection for securities investors, insurance within the insurance industry itself, and regulatory intervention. Each of these is discussed in turn below. It should be noted, however, that the system is constantly in flux; any analysis of these safety nets is therefore a shot at a moving target.

The Central Bank

The ethos of central banking has historically been acting as a lender of last resort to the banking system. Traditionally, banking systems based on a fractional reserve system have been subject to periodic crises of confidence — known as runs on the banks — where depositors want instant conversion of their deposits to legal tender. So long as the central bank has the authority to create legal tender and is willing to provide unlimited amounts to a bank experiencing a deposit run, then the central bank is said to be performing the lender-of-last-resort function.

In a financial system that is highly integrated, where prices are very sensitive to changes in the yield curve, the central bank's lender-of-last-resort function gets extended throughout the financial sector at a time of crisis or shock, merely by operating as the liquidity base of the banking system. When a central bank operates in this manner, it is said to be providing systemic relief, unrelated to whatever the prevailing monetary policy of the day might happen to be. When confidence in global equity markets evaporated in October 1987, leading to massive price changes and gaps in market continuity, Canada's central bank moved very quickly to liquify the base of the financial sector so as to provide a cushion to the system. Short-term interest rates fell sharply, confidence returned, equity markets stabilized and the Bank of Canada went back to whatever it was doing before. Its swift and decisive action provided systemic relief to the entire financial sector.

Deposit Insurance

Deposit insurance in Canada is provided and funded by all deposit-taking institutions, and is administered by the Canada Deposit Insurance Corporation (CDIC). The genesis of deposit insurance is the grass-roots political idea that the "little guy" should be protected from big financial interests. The present ceiling in deposit insurance is nominally $60,000 per account.

The economic impact of deposit insurance has a somewhat perverse aspect, known as the "moral hazard" problem. In effect, deposit insurance nationalizes the liability side of the deposit-taking institutions, but is silent on the prudent use of deposits by those institutions. The higher the insurance limit, the more open to abuse the system becomes. A depositor who is protected by insurance, for example, is indifferent to the quality of the institution to which she lends. Thus, relative price becomes the only guideline. Weak financial organizations that offer deposit insurance need only pitch their interest rates slightly above the prevailing market in order to attract funds. In effect, the existence of deposit insurance presupposes a strong regulatory presence. The higher the deposit-insurance ceiling, the greater the need for effective surveillance by regulatory authorities.

In the early 1980s in the United States, the insurable deposit ceiling was raised to $100,000, while the prevailing legislative ethic was for less regulation. The combination attracted a plethora of unscrupulous buccaneers, who hid behind the insurance ceiling on the liability side of their operation and committed grand larceny on the asset side. What has come to be known as the bailout of the savings and loan industry is estimated to have cost U.S. taxpayers $500-billion.

The CDIC can be said to have a split personality. Regulatory authority is vested in the OSFI, in the case of federal organizations, and in various provincial ministries, in the case of provincially incorporated ones; the insurance function is a separate entity. The CDIC thus has responsibility but no authority.

This separation of authority and responsibility is a faulty principle. If the regulatory authority is not responsible for paying the damage if things go wrong, then there is no sense of an urgent need to make certain things go right. At the same time, without a sense of urgency, regulators tend to overlook the needs of uninsured creditors and contributors of capital. Given deposit insurance, the regulators should only need to focus their attention on the other elements of the balance sheet.

Protection for Securities Investors

The Canadian Investor Protection Fund (CIPF) provides insurance against losses incurred against funds and securities left in safekeeping with securities dealers. The insurance limit is $500,000, which some firms increase by way of additional private insurance to more than $1-million. The CIPF provides industry surveillance and undertakes executive action, when necessary, under the authority of its board of directors, which includes both industry and public representation.

Insurance for the Insurers

The insurance industry provides consumer protection through two compensation entities — one for life and health insurance companies, and one for fire and casualty — which are together known colloquially as CompCorp. The insurance limit is $60,000.

Regulatory Agencies

The final safety net consists of the enabling legislation governing each financial organization and the power provided to the regulators under these acts. If the regulators are alert and do their jobs well, then their surveillance activities serve as an early warning system within the financial sector. Arrayed against their efforts, however, are powerful legal and accounting brains acting on behalf of financial entities, attempting to minimize the discretion of the regulators. On balance, this creative tension is a positive force.

CONCLUSION: THE CURRENT ENVIRONMENT

Financial historians will surely forever mark 1992 as a watershed in the evolution of the Canadian financial services industry. The promulgation in mid-year of sweeping financial reform legislation in Canada will be the focus of attention, as will the adoption of common capital adequacy standards among the international banks under the aegis of the BIS.

Had the Minister of Finance allowed the proposed mergers of four of Canada's five largest banks into two, 1998 may have proven to be another watershed year. As it is, however, we are left waiting to see what policy changes the federal government will enact and what their effect will be. The following chapter, by Wendy Dobson, deals explicitly with this question. Meanwhile, other factors are pushing the Canadian financial services industry in new directions. The Internet and other new technologies have the potential to radically transform how financial institutions compete and interact with their customers. New forms of competition — from super-specialized service providers, to financial supermarkets, to banks based in supermarkets — are pushing boundaries both within the financial services industry and between it and the rest of the economy. There is no doubt that the period of transformation in this most important of all Canadian industries is far from over.

Reforming Canada's Financial Services Sector

Wendy Dobson

The financial services policy framework paper, Reforming Canada's Financial Services Sector — A Framework for the Future (Canada, 1999), which Finance Minister Paul Martin released on June 25, 1999, concerns one of a growing list of public policy areas where governments are trying to tread an uneasy path between the pressures of globalization and the backlash of domestic interests.

Technological advances have recast how financial services are provided, forcing firms into markets and institutional arrangements that span many countries and time zones, resulting in fierce competition, requiring huge investments, and changing the business profiles of traditional producers. At the same time, customers have become more sophisticated and demanding. One consequence is tension between producers and the public, which wants high-quality, state-of-the-art services and accountability.

In the late 1990s, the financial services sector was in the forefront of the emerging, globalized, knowledge-based economy. Few industries experienced more dynamic change in the previous three decades than the sector's traditional industries: banking, insurance, and securities. Rapid innovation and advances in telecommunications and computer technology facilitated the moving of money into a global activity, one that crosses borders at ever-faster rates and in ever-greater volumes. New financial services also proliferated, with additional competitors, such as asset- and wealth-management companies, credit card suppliers, and securities analysts, challenging traditional services providers and accelerating the rate of change.

This is an edited version of "Prisoners of the Past in a Fast-Forward World: Canada's Policy Framework for the Financial Services Sector," *C.D. Howe Institute Commentary* 132 (Toronto: C.D. Howe Institute, 1999). Reproduced with permission.

The regulation of financial sector activities and institutions is still the domain of national authorities,[1] but increasingly regulators are scrambling to catch up with the pressures of globalization. Some governments stand back and accept the consequences of market forces. Others attempt to restrain them by erecting barriers to internationalization in the form of taxes, regulations, and added oversight. Still others facilitate the adjustment process by reducing past regulations on ownership, operations, foreign entry, and key prices such as interest rates.

It was against this background, of increasingly global and fast-moving competition in financial services colliding with national regulatory objectives, that the Department of Finance released its policy framework paper (the Paper). In preparing it, Ottawa commissioned several task forces, most notably the Task Force on the Future of the Canadian Financial Services Sector (the MacKay Task Force)[2] and the Payments System Advisory Committee, which reviewed access to and governance of the payments system. In addition, two parliamentary committees, the House of Commons Standing Committee on Finance and the Senate Standing Committee on Banking, Trade and Commerce, carried out public hearings and issued their own reports and recommendations. The national Liberal Party caucus also sponsored a task force, which published its own report.

Ideally, a financial sector policy framework should have several objectives: to promote a well-functioning financial system to meet the country's overall economic objectives; to improve the efficiency and soundness of the financial system; to safeguard the public in its dealings with the financial system; and to promote the adequacy of the financial system to meet the current and prospective needs of lenders, issuers, and borrowers in efficient, flexible, nondiscriminatory, and creative ways. Such goals are reflected in the Paper's stated objectives, which are to:

- promote an efficient and flexible financial services sector;
- promote choice and low-cost services to consumers;
- ensure equitable consumer access to quality services; and
- improve the regulatory environment.

While these objectives are commendable at the general level at which they are set, the particular measures through which the government aims to promote them deserve critical examination. Given the breadth of the issues at stake, they reflect to a remarkable degree the government's preoccupation with public attitudes and the public's intense criticism of the choice and access provided to small business and retail users by Canada's large banks.

The purpose of this chapter is to use the Paper as a lens through which we can evaluate the regulation and performance of Canada's financial services industry. We will evaluate the Paper in terms of its own objectives and examine how it positions the Canadian financial services sector for the long term and, therefore, how it could influence Canada's worrisome productivity performance. Are the goals the right ones? Are the government's chosen instruments the best ones to achieve these goals? What would be the likely impact of this framework in the long term?

In the next section, I assess the globalization pressures on the sector. In the third section, I discuss the Canadian public's backlash against banks in historical context. In the fourth section, I identify the Paper's seven main reform proposals and evaluate them on the basis of its own objectives. In the fifth section, I assess the Paper's overall implications, and in the sixth section I recommend modifications that should be reflected in the enabling legislation and the rules and regulations governing the Paper's implementation. A brief conclusion ends the chapter.

The theme throughout is that government and Canada's large financial institutions are prisoners of negative public attitudes and a backlash. In emphasizing "the consumer" (who is nowhere defined), the government seems to have lost sight of the big picture — of a policy framework to ensure that the financial system efficiently serves both users and producers of financial services.

This is not to say that Ottawa should ignore consumer concerns or that it has ignored efficiency. Both goals are valid; the problems lie in the means chosen to pursue them.

My argument is that the interests of *all* users of the financial system — which include small and medium-sized businesses, large corporations, and governments, as well as households — are best served when it is highly efficient and well functioning (see Figure 1). By putting Canada's low-cost producers

---

FIGURE 1
How the Financial Services Sector Is Different

A well-functioning financial sector plays a major role in the complex machine that is the modern economy. It is a source of growth, providing a wide range of services that assist capital accumulation through pooling funds and evaluating and managing risk. It contributes to productivity growth by channelling funds into innovative activities. Along the way, it provides the economy with new skills and knowledge.

Traditionally, several factors in this special sector — the fiduciary nature of many of its financial activities, its important role in the implementation of monetary policy, the existence of market failures such as information asymmetries, and its proneness to crisis — have provided rationales for regulation by governments.

In other words, national financial sectors are not the same as other industries. Even steel firms or airlines may, unless the government regards them as strategic, be allowed to go bankrupt or be taken over by foreign entrants if they fail to adjust to stiffened competition or technological change. But financial firms — particularly banks — often get more care. Unlike all but the largest firms in other industries, a bank that fails can have a significant impact on the rest of the economy. When depositors lose confidence, this loss can spread to other banks, leading to a run on the entire banking system. The consequences may be felt throughout the economy and spill over into the political realm.

In efforts to head off such crises, governments have traditionally entered into quid pro quo arrangements with banks. Governments provide them with an implicit safety net, in the form of an unstated promise by the central bank or public treasury, or an explicit one in the form of a public deposit insurance fund. In return, the banks submit to closer government oversight and regulation of their activities than is usual for a private sector industry.

Many governments also insist on domestic ownership and control of the largest banks.

---

in chains, the government, with its ill-advised adversarial approach, will not achieve their redemption, and its policy framework will be unsustainable in the face of inexorable market forces and technological innovation. Canada's long-term economic prospects could be harmed as a result.

THE RAPIDLY CHANGING INTERNATIONAL ENVIRONMENT

The international environment for financial institutions is being reshaped by three major forces: rapid technological innovation, globalization, and industry consolidation. The governments of most countries of the Organisation for Economic Co-operation and Development (OECD) have recognized these forces and have modified their policy environments to ensure that their financial institutions are able to anticipate and respond adequately to these changes.

Technological Innovation

Driving the wave of technological innovation is the revolution in information and communications technology (ICT), which is widening the choice of services, instruments, and institutions available to users of financial services and enhancing the ability of services providers to manage risk and to meet their customers' financing needs at home and abroad.

The ICT revolution has reduced the costs of the basic technologies used by financial services. An illustration is the drop in computer time required to value a complex financial instrument, such as a call option. In 1987, this task took 5.000 seconds of computer time, on average, in U.S. financial institutions; by 1997, the same task took 0.006 seconds (BIS, 1998).

A combination of ICT-based numerical tools and advances in portfolio theory underlies new products, such as derivatives and securitized assets (assets bundled into marketable securities), which have changed the traditional business of financial intermediation associated with banks. More recently, the Internet is altering how financial business is being conducted. For example, it is shifting power from bank managers to customers, who are increasingly likely to shop around for financial products, such as mortgages, because they can now easily be compared and purchased online.

To capture and sustain the advantages of the ICT revolution, financial services providers must purchase or develop ever-newer equipment, which is proving enormously expensive. These costs can be recouped only if they are spread over large numbers of users. Financial services providers also respond by increasing their spending on "brand" advertising to differentiate their products in the eyes of potential customers.

Thus, one of the criteria for evaluating domestic financial policy is whether it assists or inhibits financial institutions in their efforts to move towards and remain near the rapidly shifting technological frontiers and to differentiate their products. Policies that raise production costs or inhibit the scale over which technology costs can be amortized will hinder technological development by such institutions.

WENDY DOBSON

Globalization

The second fast-forward trend is globalization, which is reflected in the rise of cross-border capital flows and financial transactions and in foreign firms' entry into domestic markets. Consider some of the volumes of interinstitutional and international financial flows in 1997, reported by the Bank for International Settlements (BIS) and the International Monetary Fund (IMF, 1998):

> Cross-border transactions in Canadian bonds and equities grew to 358 per cent of gross domestic product (GDP) in 1997, a more than fourfold increase from 65 per cent in 1990 (the comparable U.S. numbers were 213 and 89 per cent, respectively).

> Outstanding international debt securities worldwide were US$3.6-trillion in March 1998, an increase of 80 per cent from the 1993 total of US$2-trillion.

> Nonresident holdings of Canadian public debt were 23 per cent of GDP in 1997, more than double the 1983 share, which was 11 per cent.

> In 1995, world exports of goods and services totalled about US$6-trillion, while **daily** turnover in foreign exchange markets was more than US$1-trillion, a sixfold increase since 1986.

These statistics illustrate in dramatic fashion the rising volume of international financial activity, particularly in foreign exchange and securities issues, which far exceed international trade and lending.

Yet these figures provide only a partial indication of the scale of international financial activities. An important aspect of international trade stems from the commercial presence of firms in countries other than their home country. Stocks of foreign direct investment (FDI), which are necessary for commercial presence, have grown dramatically, mainly among industrialized countries. By 1997, for example, total FDI flows were US$400-billion, twice the volume of 1990 and seven times that of 1980 (UNCTAD, 1998: 8).

These statistics imply increasing globalization of financial markets and a steady growth in international financial integration; but these processes are far from complete. As Feldstein and Horioka (1980) famously document, domestic savings rates are closely correlated with national investment rates, a finding that implies that capital flows are not tightly integrated across borders. Helliwell and McKitrick (1998) confirm those results from OECD data more than a decade later. Thus, the potential for further development of international financial activities may be great.

The range of such activities has widened dramatically with disintermediation (the provision of financial products that directly link investors and borrowers and replace borrowing and lending through banks) and securitization, reflecting increasing sophistication on the part of financial institutions in mobilizing the economy's resources and securing linkages between lenders and borrowers.

Consolidation

Intensifying competition among major services providers in the maturing OECD financial markets has created pressures to reduce costs and differentiate products. Excess capacity has appeared, spurring a wave of consolidation through cross-market mergers in Europe and North America (and more recently in Japan).

This wave of consolidation is the third striking feature of the international financial landscape. Merging partners have numerous motivations: to seek size in order to compete in the global environment; to capture economies of scale in ITC spending, asset-management, and global custody services; to diversify the financial services available under one institutional roof for one-stop shopping; to mitigate risk by diversifying instruments across geography, product lines, and industries; to respond to fierce competitive pressures to reduce costs by reducing excess capacity in a country or a region; and to respond, particularly in Europe, to the perception that the single-currency area requires a new breed of regional bank that can compete both within the European Union (EU) and against the U.S. giants.

By 1998, the world's two largest banks measured by assets were German and Swiss (see Figure 2). The next two largest were in the United States, followed by banks in Japan, the Netherlands, the United Kingdom, Switzerland, and France. Ranked by capital base, other banks appear: Credit Agricole Group (France), Chase Manhattan (United States), and the Industrial and Commercial Bank of China.

On the market capitalization measure, which indicates the value investors place on institutions and their strategies, many of these largest banks move well down the ranking, and others appear. Those banks most highly valued in the market include Lloyds TSB (United Kingdom), Nationsbank (United States), HSBC Holdings (United Kingdom), ING Groep (Netherlands), and Wells Fargo (United States). (For ease of reference, Figure 3 sets out the world's top five insurers and securities firms.)

The list of recent bank mergers[3] in Figure 4 illustrates how widespread is this trend. The top 10 merger partners are spread across the OECD countries, with three in the United States, two in Germany, and one each in the United Kingdom, France, Switzerland, Spain, and the Netherlands.

What is significant about this list is the way it reveals that most mergers have been among banks in the same home country. Some institutions have successfully executed cross-pillar mergers, such as the 1997 transaction between Credit Suisse Group and the Winterthur Group and the 1998 Citicorp-Travelers union, but these have been within-country combinations.[4] Very few of the largest have been across borders, and those that have been tend to be in Europe (such as ING-Barings in 1995) or have been executed with some difficulty (perhaps indicated by Deutsche Bank's relatively low position on the market capitalization list). Only the very largest institutions are becoming truly global and truly full-service (Citigroup and HSBC Holdings are the only banks that provide retail banking services in a large number of countries, for example).

The four Canadian banks that wanted to merge into two banks in 1998 rank far down the global lists, with capital and assets less than half of those

FIGURE 2
The World's Largest Banks, year-end 1998/99 ((US$ billions)

Ranked by Capital		Ranked by Assets		Ranked by Market Capitalization[a]	
1 Citigroup (US)	41.9	1 Deutsche Bank	732.5	1 Lloyds TSB	60.2,
2 BankAmerica Corp (US)	36.9	2 UBS	685.9	2 Nations Bank	51.4
3 HSBC Holdings (UK)	29.4	3 Citigroup	668.6	3 HSBC Holdings	48.4
4 Crédit Agricole Groupe (France)	25.9	4 BankAmerica Corp	617.7	4 Citicorp	42.0
5 Chase Manhattan Corp. (US)	24.1	5 Bank of Tokyo-Mitsubishi	598.7	5 ING Groep	41.7
6 Industrial & Commercial Bank of China (China)	22.2	6 ABN AMRO Bank	504.1	6 UBS	41.3
7 Bank of Tokyo-Mitsubishi (Japan)	22.1	7 HSBC Holdings	484.7	7 BankAmerica Corp.	41.2
8 UBS (Switzerland)	20.5	8 Crédit Suisse Group	474.0	8 Chase Manhattan Corp.	36.8
9 Sakura Bank (Japan)	19.9	9 Crédit Agricole Groupe	457.0	9 Bank of Tokyo-Mitsubishi	30.4
10 Bank One Corp. (US)	19.7	10 Société Générale	447.5	10 Wells Fargo	30.2
11 Fuji Bank (Japan)	19.6	11 Sumitomo Bank	439.7	11 Banc One Corp.	29.9
12 Deutsche Bank (Germany)	18.7	12 Dresdner Bank	427.3	12 Fortis	29.5
13 Sanwa Bank (Japan)	17.7	13 Sanwa Bank	418.4	13 Crédit Suisse Group	29.1
14 Crédit Suisse Group (Switzerland)	17.6	14 Westdeutsche Landes bank Girozentrale	408.4	14 Deutsche Bank	27.8
15 ABN AMRO Bank (Netherlands)	17.5	15 Norinchukin Bank	407.6	15 US Bancorp	26.3
16 Dai-Ichi Kangyo Bank (Japan)	17.2	16 Dai-Ichi Kangyo Bank	396.7	16 Barclays Bank	24.2
17 Sumitomo Bank (Japan)	16.2	17 Industrial & Commercial Bank of China	391.2	17 ABN AMRO Bank	23.9
18 Bank of China (China)	14.7	18 Sakura Bank	389.4	18 National Westminster Bank	22.6
19 Robobank Nederland (Netherlands)	14.7	19 Commerzbank	381.4	19 Sumitomo Bank	22.1
20 Industrial Bank of Japan (Japan)	14.5	20 Banque Nationale de Paris	379.0	20 Banco Bilbao Vizcaya	21.5
21 First Union Corp. (US)	13.6	21 Industrial Bank of Japan	370.4		
22 Barclays Bank (UK)	13.5	22 Chase Manhattan Corp.	365.9		
23 National Westminster Bank (UK)	13.4	23 Fuji Bank	358.2		
24 Tokai Bank (Japan)	13.3	24 Barclays Bank	353.4		
25 Dresdner Bank (Germany)	13.0	25 HypoVereinsbank	337.2		

Canadian banks, for reference		
Royal Bank of Canada	7.5	171.0
CIBC	7.3	175.3
Bank of Nova Scotia	7.0	151.4
Bank of Montreal	6.6	144.3
Toronto-Dominion Bank	4.9	111.4

[a] Pre-merger market capitalizations, where relevant.

Sources: *The Banker* 1999; *Financial Times of London* 1999.

FIGURE 3

The World's Largest Securities Firms and Insurers, 1998 (US$ millions)

Rank	Company (Country)	Assets	Net Income
	The Top Five Securities Firms		
1	Merrill Lynch (United States)	212,091	1,259
2	Morgan Stanley Dean Witter (United States)	168,682	3,276
3	Lehman Brothers Holdings (United States)	95,168	736
4	Crédit Suisse First Boston (Switzerland/United States)	212,923	−154
5	Salomon Smith Barney Holdings (United States)	123,818	818
	The Top Five Insurers		
1	AXA Group (France)	449,556	52,683
2	Allianz Group (Germany)	401,406	46,805
3	Nippon Life (Japan)	374,801	51,128
4	Zenkyoren & Prefectural Insurance Federations (Japan)	297,477	46,154
5	Dai-Ichi Mutual Life (Japan)	261,164	35,030

Note: Statistics are for fiscal year 1998.

Source: *Wall Street Journal* 1999.

---

institutions at the bottom of the top-25 lists. If the proposed mergers had gone through, however, the new banks would have ranked close to the top 10 in combined capital and assets.

THE DOMESTIC BACKLASH

Overall, banks offer two main kinds of banking services: wholesale banking, which includes equity financing, cash management, and financial risk management, as well as bank loans to large corporate customers; and retail banking, which supplies savings deposits and loans and an increasingly diversified set of investment and insurance services to households and small businesses.

Many retail banking customers charge, rightly or wrongly, that banks have become too powerful, largely ignoring these customers' interests in recent years. This backlash became a major political issue in Canada during the 1998 debate about two major bank mergers that were proposed before the completion of a review process leading to the new policy framework. The debate revealed widespread skepticism about the benefits Canadians believed they would realize from the banks' consolidating their domestic operations to give them the scale and efficiencies they deemed necessary to compete internationally.

A Look Back

Customer concerns about the inadequacies of the services provided by the major financial institutions, specifically the banks, were a major theme running through many of the submissions from households and small businesses to the

FIGURE 4
Major Mergers and Acquisitions in Financial Services, by Country, as of June 1999 (US$ billions)

		Global Ranking[a]	Capital	Assets
United States				
Citicorp Travelers }	Citigroup	1	41.9	668.6
Bank America Nations Bank Barnett Banks }	Bank America Corp.	2	36.9	617.7
Banc One First Chicago NBD }	Banc One Corp.	10	19.7	261.5
First Union Signet Core States }		21	13.6	237.4
Wells Fargo Norwest Corp.		30	12.4	202.5
Fleet Financial Bank Boston		50 80	7.4 5.0	104.6 73.5
United Kingdom				
HSBC Holding PLC Republic New York		3 110	29.4 3.4	484.7 50.4
France				
Crédit Agricole Banque Indosuez }	Crédit Agricole groupe	4	25.9	457.0
BNP Paribas		27 40	12.8 9.9	379.0 309.4
Switzerland				
UBS SBC }	UBS	8	20.5	685.9
Germany				
Deutsche Bank Bankers Trust		12 74	18.7 5.4	732.5 133.1
Bayerische Vereins Bayerische Hypo }	Hypovereins Bank	32	11.9	337.2
Netherlands				
ING Bank BBL }	ING Groep	26	13.0	326.8
Generale Bank ASLK-CGER Fortis Bank Netherland }	Fortis Bank	41	9.9	323.6
Spain				
Banco Santander Banco Central Hispano		37 98	10.7 4.3	180.8 95.7
Italy				
Credito Italiano Coriverona Banca CRT Cossomorca }	Unicredito	45	8.4	171.7
Canada, for reference				
Royal Bank of Canada		49	7.5	171.0
Bank of Montreal		58	6.6	144.3
CIBC		52	7.3	175.3
Toronto-Dominion Bank		84	4.9	111.4

[a] For 1998/99, by capital.

Source: *The Banker* 1999.

MacKay Task Force and the parliamentary hearings. Such statements built on the general dislike that people in most countries feel towards their bankers and on the findings of a series of Canadian reviews sponsored in 1994 by members of Parliament and by government committees.

These reviews aired the concerns of many, particularly small and medium-sized businesses, who felt they had been unfairly treated during the 1991–92 recession. An economic downturn usually produces an increase in nonperforming loans in bank portfolios, but the concentrations of bad assets, particularly in Ontario, and the way they were handled created difficulties for many who took their concerns to their elected representatives. When the Liberals came to power in 1994, they were determined to ensure these concerns were addressed in the political arena.

Analytically, there are two issues. First, many people are convinced that they need more institutions from which to obtain loans. Such concerns imply the possibility of market failure because of undue concentration in the industry, as well as widespread perception that the Canadian banking system is uncompetitive and unresponsive to the desire that financial products and services be affordable and accessible to all.

The second issue is the frequent perception that the banks have failed in a social role. Indeed, they are subject to high expectations that they will provide community leadership and support that are reflective of their economic importance and the favoured position they are seen to receive through such policies as the limits on foreign ownership, their exclusive access to the payments system, and the safety net of the deposit insurance system.

These concerns imply two basic questions for policy. First, as the MacKay report pointed out, policymakers must determine whether legitimate, creditworthy demands are going unmet, creating market gaps. Second, should Canada's banks be regarded as utilities — that is, as natural monopolies that provide essential services to which people are entitled and that are entitled to a riskless, regulated rate of return? Empirical studies provide inconclusive results to answer the first question. Looking around the world to answer the second question, it is noteworthy that the only banks that might be considered utilities are state-owned ones, and they are shrinking in number as they either fail because of inadequate risk evaluation and management or are sold off in privatization programs.

Demand and Supply

The tensions in the Canadian marketplace are perhaps inevitable because of factors on both the demand and supply sides. On the demand side, customers are increasingly sophisticated and discriminating. They demand choice, quality, and low cost from their services providers, as well as transparency in the terms, conditions, and risks of financial products. They expect effective redress if they believe they are being unfairly treated.

An added concern feeds the backlash against globalization. Many individuals fear that, when market forces are allowed to operate freely, "ordinary" people are the losers. The two sets of banks that were proposing to consolidate their businesses were seen as seeking to further restrict the choices available to small depositors and borrowers. (Because the issue is less of a concern to larger businesses, to which deep and liquid capital markets give access to a range of financing options wider than bank borrowing, they were notably silent in the 1998 debate.)

On the supply side, consolidation has been under way for the past two decades as financial institutions have responded to intensifying competition by reducing costs and seeking economies of scale. The MacKay Task Force and the Senate Committee both tackled the charges of undue concentration, but failed to settle the issue. The task force compared the banking concentration ratio in Canada with that in other smaller economies whose financial sectors we tend to use for comparison. Canada's five large banks controlled 81 per cent of domestic banking assets in 1997, a slightly larger share than that of comparable institutions in the Netherlands, Australia, and Switzerland, which stood at 75, 69, and 66 per cent, respectively (Canada, 1998b, 150). Anecdotal evidence in both reports implies that other OECD countries have a significant second tier of smaller financial institutions that take deposits and make loans to households and small businesses, providing the latter with more choice.

Such statistics are notoriously difficult to compare because of the large differences in financial structures and in the business strategies of financial institutions. In some OECD countries, state-owned or state-controlled savings institutions play prominent roles. Because these institutions serve certain social objectives, the rate of return is not as important as in private sector institutions, which means the playing field is not a level one. Germany still has a system of state-owned banks; other countries, such as Japan, rely heavily on a savings system based on the post office. Switzerland has a system of small cantonal and regional savings banks. The Netherlands has Rabobank Nederland, a large private cooperative banking institution dating back to 1900 that provides almost all agricultural credit and nearly half of the small and medium enterprise (SME) business (Canada, 1998c: 121).

Figure 5 shows the cross-national comparison of the distribution of financial assets across institutions, and also indicates bank concentration in Canada. But the banks' share of total financial assets in Canada, relative to the situation in other countries, reflects the facts that by 1996 Canadian banks had developed business strategies that took them into most segments of the financial industry and that Canada, unlike continental Europe, had developed corporate securities markets.

Repositioning

In responding to the international and technological forces of change, Canada's financial sector has reshaped itself in two ways. First, traditional firms have gotten more and more into each other's businesses of deposit taking and lending, insurance, trust, and securities activities. Competition has increased as the various types of institutions offer increasingly identical products.

As might be expected, the second trend is one in which other players specialize in particular products and services and innovate in how these are marketed and distributed. Canadian firms have responded both by repositioning themselves to compete across the spectrum of distribution channels and

FIGURE 5
Financial System Structures, Selected OECD Countries, 1996

	Australia		Canada		Netherlands		Switzerland		United Kingdom	
	Number	Share[a]	Number	Share[a]	Number	Share[a]	Number	Share[a]	Number	Share[a]
Commercial banks	32	43.6	11	47.0	84	47.0	935	58.0	135	23.0
Foreign-owned banks	18	2.8	50	3.4	b	b	291	8.0	333	30.0
Other banking institutions	0	0	3	5.4	14	12.0	1,150	30.0	b	b
Mortgage credit institutions	25	1.2	0	5.2	3	0.7	b	b	na	8.4
Finance companies	103	4.3	0	1.6	b	b	b	b	na	2.1
Other credit institutions	1,760	9.9	na	11.3	b	b	962	3.5	na	1.7
Insurance companies	165	17.6	na	7.8	7	13.0	b	b	na	15.4
Pension funds and foundations	139,000	14.6	7,000	16.6	98	26.5	b	b	na	15.3
Other insurance institutions	669	6.3	na	1.7	9	0.4	b	b	na	3.6

Notes: Shares may not add to 100 due to rounding; na = data not available.

[a] Percentage of total financial assets.

[b] No data provided for the category.

Source: OECD, unpublished data.

products and by refocusing and specializing. The large full-service banks face new players, often foreign firms, offering traditional and new products through the mail and through telephone-based and electronic distribution channels, which are lower cost and more convenient than traditional branch and agency networks.

This repositioning means that the banks' large share of assets reflects a wide range of products, but also that the asset share measures provide no indication of the range of institutions competing to supply the same products, particularly basic products such as savings deposits and loans. Almost all of the institutions listed in Figure 5 now vie with other types of firms for households' retail savings, mutual fund deposits, investment services, and loans.

In Canada, these competitors include banks' securities arms[5] and their trust arms, both of which supply wealth-management services. They include small, independent investment dealers and specialized financing companies, as well as insurers who also supply wealth-management services. Banks, however, have been heavily restricted in their insurance offerings and are barred from retailing insurance and providing auto leasing services in their branches.

More precise indicators of the competitiveness of Canadian banks include service charges and the spread between loan rates and deposit rates. The most recent evidence indicates that service charges (measured as a share of total deposits) were 80 per cent of those in the United States in 1992 and dropped to 50 per cent in 1997; in other words, Canadian bank service charges have been declining relative to those in the United States. Spreads were remarkably stable in Canada between 1978 and 1997; at about 2 per cent, they were among the lowest in the Group of Seven (G7) major industrialized countries (Smith, 1998). Spread comparisons can be misleading, however, since it is difficult to control for risk. In Canada–U.S. comparisons, for example, it is possible that U.S. banks are willing to price for risk, whereas Canadian banks may simply deny the credit.

Summary

The backlash against the banks is a complex issue based on popular dislike of banks — a sentiment found in most countries — and a perception that full-service banks' retail operations have not been as customer-oriented as many Canadians think they should be. Objective indicators of competitiveness in the industry do not indicate market failure or the existence of widespread credit market gaps. Thus, policy must carefully weigh the impact of the turbulent forces of international competition and technological change that the institutions face against measures that would respond to domestic complaints.

THE POLICY PAPER: AN EVALUATION

In this section, I evaluate the seven major reform proposals in the Finance Department's policy framework paper, grouping them by its stated objectives.[6] Each proposal is introduced with a short description of its background, followed by consideration of its advantages and possible disadvantages.

Promotion of Greater Efficiency and Flexibility

The primary thrust of three of the Paper's proposals — easing ownership restrictions, permitting banks to have holding companies, and permitting bank mergers (subject to a review process) — is to increase the efficiency, competitiveness, and flexibility of the financial sector.

Changing the 10 Per Cent Ownership Rule

At present, ownership policy varies between the banks and other federally regulated financial institutions. Banks must be widely held: specifically, no individual, domestic or foreign, is permitted to own more than 10 per cent of any class of shares. The Paper proposes easing these restrictions by raising the single-owner limit on voting shares to 20 per cent of banks and demutualized insurers whose equity is more than $5-billion. It would also allow a 30 per cent limit on the nonvoting shares of these institutions, subject to a "fit and proper" test to ensure that these larger shareholders are "not a source of weakness to the regulated institutions" (Canada, 1999: 3) and to "impose some degree of Canadian perspective at the governance level" (Canada, 1998b: 177–78).

The reasons for the old policy were to ensure wide ownership of banks, whether the bulk of the shares were held by foreigners or not, and also to make more effective a series of other restrictions, such as those ensuring that financial and commercial activity were separated (to reduce the associated risks of self-dealing that would undermine safety and soundness).

Now, the MacKay report argues, as the pillars separating banks, securities, trust, and insurance companies are eliminated, common ownership rules should be created. The 10 per cent restriction, it notes, is outdated in a world where institutional consolidation is increasingly commonplace and transactions occur through pooling of interest and share exchanges. The 10 per cent rule also constrains the potential for new entrants. Easing the ownership restrictions would increase the attractiveness of Canadian banks as joint-venture partners. And since no discretionary approval seems to be required from a regulatory agency or from the minister of finance, the stage would be set for market-based transactions.

The proposal has certain disadvantages and uncertainties. First, the Paper does not define the application of the "fit and proper test," leaving open the possibility that it would involve administrative discretion that is open to political pressures. Second, the permitted increase in the concentration of ownership could affect the governance of the major financial institutions.

Most notably, the stage would be set for an increase in foreign control of these institutions, which would imply greater weight on innovation and competitiveness. But would such shareholders accept pricing and productivity-augmenting strategies that would be acceptable to the same Canadian consumers who have been so critical of the banks up to now?

At present, aggregate foreign ownership of the large banks runs as high as 35 per cent in the case of the National Bank and 24 per cent of the Royal Bank (Canada, 1998a: 78), but this ownership is widely held. The Paper's proposal would make possible single ownership of 20 per cent of a bank's shares and prevent individuals or groups acting together to achieve greater control.

Ideally, best-practice corporate governance requires that directors take account of the interests of all shareholders, not any one in particular. In practice, however, it is difficult to ignore the views of a strong director, particularly if he or she represents a major shareholder.

Permitting Regulated Holding Company Structures

Financial services firms in the United States, the United Kingdom, and other industrialized countries are currently allowed to form holding companies (which allow firms to spin off from the bank itself into subsidiaries such activities as credit cards and other nonbanking activities). Canada has not had such provisions.

Now the Paper proposes permission to organize holding companies that could invest in five main areas:

> ➢ regulated financial institutions (banks, trust, and insurance companies)

> ➢ financial services providers (of credit cards and of loans to small businesses and consumers)

> ➢ financial agents and advisors, such as investment counsellors and payroll services providers

> ➢ complementary services, such as Interac and armoured car activities; and

> ➢ other activities, such as information and real property brokerage services

For banks, the holding company structure would be incorporated under the Bank Act. Oversight of the holding company and its entities would be consolidated, consistent with the Bank for International Settlement's "Core Principles for Effective Banking Supervision," released in 1997.[7] The proposed 20 and 30 per cent ownership rules would apply. So would the prohibition on commercial activities that now applies to banks.

This proposal has the potential to increase the efficiency of the large financial institutions by allowing them to restructure in ways that would open new possibilities for economies of scale and scope, for capital raising, and for strategic alliances. Banks and demutualized insurance companies would be able to move activities now undertaken in-house (and therefore subject to the banking or insurance regulatory regime) or in subsidiaries into affiliates that would be subject to varying degrees of regulation depending on the activity. Thus, for example, a bank, an insurance company, a mutual fund company, and a credit card company could work together within the new corporate group.

The acid test for this proposal would be whether the banks and insurance companies saw and acted on its advantages. The Paper does not provide the information necessary for such key business decisions, and it should be clearly spelled out in the legislation. For example, what investments would actually be permitted, and how would they be regulated? Would holding companies be allowed to invest in auto leasing? Would the large insurance companies be subject to market conditions after the grace period of three years permitted following their demutualization, or would they continue to be protected from market forces? What would be the rules for allocating capital to various businesses in a holding company? What would be the related-party rules? Where exactly would lighter regulation be permitted? And what would be the taxation rules?

From a broad prudential perspective, one concern is that of keeping failure in one part of the enterprise from spreading more widely: for example, into the deposit-taking (and therefore insured) part of the enterprise. From a narrower perspective, it would be necessary to ensure that holding companies did not become vehicles for reducing or avoiding taxation, regulatory requirements, or capital requirements.

Defining the Merger Review Process for Large Banks

Canada's longstanding rule that "big shall not buy big" has ruled out mergers among its largest financial institutions. The Paper proposes to end this prohibition by creating a process under which mergers would be extensively reviewed to ensure that they were in the best interests of the institutions, Canadians, and the Canadian economy.

In particular, the government proposes to establish a formal and transparent review process for the large banks (those with equity exceeding $5-billion). Three criteria would apply. Mergers could not unduly concentrate economic power, significantly reduce competition, or reduce flexibility to address prudential concerns.

Merger proposals would have to include a public interest impact assessment (PIIA) presenting the costs and benefits of the change, including the impact on sources of financing for households and small and medium-sized businesses, the implications for branch closings and service delivery, and the effects on international competitiveness, employment, and technology. The PIIA would be examined by the House of Commons Finance Committee, which would also conduct public hearings. At the same time, the Competition Bureau and the Office of the Superintendent of Financial Institutions (OSFI) would conduct their usual reviews and be authorized to negotiate any requited remedies. The final authority on the mergers would rest with the minister of finance, who would have legislative authority to enforce remedies or other undertakings given by the merger partners.

At first glance, this proposal may appear to be a significant new departure, but a closer look suggests it is less than meets the eye. While the Paper would end the explicit prohibition and it defines the merger review process, that process is onerous and unrealistic enough to make it exceedingly unlikely that the large banks would subject themselves to it. Yet the definition is intended to create some certainty for potential merger partners, and the process that is set out is an elaboration of what was required of the four banks proposing to merge in 1998. They failed to meet what are essentially the same criteria, so the only reason to expect a different outcome in future would be the different application of those criteria.

The criteria themselves are unclear, since they lack a definition of "economic power."

The Paper's proposed elaborated process also has significant potential disadvantages. It would be discriminatory. Huge mergers, such as those between TransCanada PipeLines and Nova in 1998 and Macmillan Bloedel and Weyerhaeuser Canada in 1999, received Competition Bureau and other regulatory review in the public interest, but they were not subjected to public hearings.

Moreover, the proposal is highly politicized. Public concerns were clearly uppermost in the minds of the Paper's drafters. From the perspective of merger proponents, the process would impose major costs and increase uncertainties about the eventual outcome of a business decision. And that process apparently would be open ended, rather than subject to defined time constraints.

For all these reasons, the proposed process would likely act as a significant deterrent to the economic rationalization of Canada's large banks and their adaptation to rapidly changing international market conditions.

Increased Focus On Consumer Interests

Two of the Paper's proposals aim to enhance choice and low-cost services for consumers by encouraging new entrants to the financial services sector, by increasing the types of institutions that have access to the payments system, and by expanding the financial cooperative sector, which includes *caisses populaires* and credit unions. Another provision of the Paper seeks to protect consumers by denying the banks permission to offer auto leasing and insurance services through their branches.

Before exploring these portions of the Paper, I must point out that it contains no definition of the consumer. The idiosyncratic and shifting implicit definition used in the Paper seems designed more to support the prejudices of the large banks' critics than as a basis for sound policy. For the purposes of this chapter, I assume that the intent of the term is to identify users of retail financial services, such as households and small businesses.

Encouraging New Entrants to the Financial Services Market

To promote competition in the domestic market, the Paper encourages new entrants, mainly smaller institutions, by offering liberalized ownership rules and reduced minimum capital requirements for new financial institutions, as well as permission for foreign banks to compete in the domestic market through branches, rather than solely through subsidiaries.

The Second Tier. To nurture a cadre of small financial institutions, the government proposes ownership rules for three size classifications of banks — small, medium, and large. Small banks would be institutions with equity of less than $1-billion. They could be wholly owned by a single shareholder, including a commercial enterprise. Medium-sized banks would be institutions with equity of $1-billion to $5-billion. They could be closely held, but would be required to have a 35 per cent float of voting shares. Large banks would be those with capital in excess of $5-billion. They would be subject to the 20 and 30 per cent ownership rules.

These measures are an attempt to respond to concerns expressed by the MacKay report that Canada does not have a well-developed second tier of financial institutions that are smaller in size and able to compete with large banks in regional or local markets. As the Paper says, only two new Schedule I banks have been established in Canada since 1987. The foreign banks active in Canada are engaged primarily in wholesale banking business, and trust companies mainly serve special purposes and local areas. (The country also has 2,200 individual credit unions and communities that respond to community and employee needs. An effort is under way, encouraged by the federal government, to overcome the fragmentation of the credit union system.)

The Paper fails to note that a number of the second-tier institutions in Canada have either failed during economic crises in earlier years or have been acquired by larger, more efficient institutions. It also omits the fact that those OECD countries with sizable second tiers of smaller financial institutions created them many years ago. The writers implicitly assume that, since 207 new banks appeared in the United States in 1997 alone, Canada should pursue a similar system. What is not stated is that while many new institutions do appear in the U.S. market, many fail. Indeed, the U.S. system is moving away from small, inefficient, local institutions. Canadian history is dotted with the failure of small, inefficient, high-risk community or regional institutions, such as the failed Canadian Commercial Bank, the Northland, the Continental, the Mercantile, and the Bank of British Columbia.

The Paper's proposal for small and medium-sized categories is designed to encourage start-up institutions, and the objective of increasing competition is an important one. The question is whether the instruments chosen are appropriate. It is not clear that new institutions would be established. The Canadian market is already a mature one, with intense competition among the large institutions seeking to enlarge their market shares in retail banking. Thus, the impact of new entrants in the near to medium interim would likely be marginal. In addition, the risk of such institutions would be high, and their rates of return could be low. A glance at recent annual reports of the Canada Deposit Insurance Corporation (CDIC), which give the return on assets by institutional category, shows that the average return on assets for the smaller institutions is often close to zero.

The possibility of more higher-cost, low-return small institutions raises two questions: How quickly would the authorities be prepared to move to close such institutions if they were failing? Would the federal government restrain itself from bailing out troubled institutions that might have been encouraged by its own policy changes?

If the authorities failed to act promptly and on stringent soundness criteria, they would contribute to moral hazard (taking more risks on expectation of a public bailout than if there were no such recourse). While the thrust of recent administrative reviews of the financial system has pushed towards prompt action to wind up weak institutions, the politicized environment of the past few years does not provide confidence that such decisions would, in practice, be free of political pressures. A small bank's getting into trouble would be unlikely

WENDY DOBSON

to pose a systemic threat, but financial markets tend to view such events negatively, with fallout for all domestic institutions.

Foreign Banks. The Paper also formally proposes to allow foreign banks to compete in the domestic market through branches rather than through subsidiaries. The power of the branches would be limited to the wholesale market, a market that is already globalized and one in which users already have substantial access to offshore facilities.

Thus, this proposal likely would not affect competition in the retail market. Perhaps foreign banks should be allowed into that market. The problem with such a scheme is that of access to the payments system and deposit insurance. Who would bear the risk of a U.S. bank that operated in Canada? If it failed, would its depositors be compensated by Canadian or U.S. authorities? In the EU, the single passport for financial services relies on the principle of home-country control and regulation of financial institutions — a German bank operating in the Netherlands has access to the payments system set up under the European Monetary Union and is regulated by German authorities.

If these problems could be solved in the Canadian case, foreign branching in the retail sector could increase domestic competition, enhance innovation, and use less risky institutions as the instrument to achieve this objective.

Broadening Access to the Canadian Payments Association

The Paper recommends giving life insurance companies, investment dealers, and money-market mutual funds access to Canada's payments system. This proposal is another significant one for reforming the domestic competitive environment to benefit users of Canada's financial services.

The Canadian Payments Association (CPA) was created in the 1980s as a network to facilitate financial transactions to pay for goods, services, and assets. Payment can take a number of forms, including currency, cheques, debit and credit cards, and, increasingly, electronic means such as stored-value cards. To play the intermediary role of collecting payments to settle obligations, an institution must be a member of the CPA, which operates two national clearing and settlement systems.

Membership in the CPA is now limited to deposit-taking institutions that are regulated by the federal and provincial governments, but since 1996 an advisory committee, appointed by the federal government, has reviewed the structure and operation of the system. On the basis of that report, the government has concluded that it would be safe to broaden access to the system to increase the competitive advantage of financial institutions other than banks, such as the life insurance companies, securities dealers, and money-market mutual funds. Competition in core banking activities would be promoted as life insurance companies, for example, gained an opportunity to capture a portion of their annual $35-billion payout to their clients through deposits that could be transferred with a negotiable order vehicle such as a cheque.

This proposal raises two concerns. The first is that, while new entrants would be welcome, it is not clear what impact they would have on the safety and soundness of the entire system. Second, the minister of finance would decide which products or services would be admitted to the payments system. This provision would mean that the minister, through effective control over the rules of the payments association, would also be able to control access to its services. This discretionary authority would require clear criteria for entry and fairness and transparency in its application.

Denying the Banks' Request to Offer Leasing and Insurance

The banks had asked that they be given additional business powers to offer leasing and insurance services through their branches. The Paper refuses this request. Although a significant decision, it is tucked away in the Paper's list of reforms to empower and protect consumers. An announcement that has significant implications for the objectives of promoting efficiency in the financial services sector and of ensuring choice and low-cost services to consumers, it states:

> the government agrees with the House of Commons Standing Committee on Finance that these regimes [measures to foster competition and promote consumers' interests] should be given time to work before any changes can be considered in bank business powers in the areas of car leasing and insurance networking. (Canada, 1999)

The MacKay Task Force had argued the advantages to consumers of a fully open and competitive trading and investment environment for Canada's financial services sector. After completing a cross-national study, it concluded that introducing competition into the insurance market would reduce costs, particularly to low-income Canadians, and expand the size of the market, and that "consumers, not the regulatory framework, should determine how insurance is purchased" (Canada, 1998c: 98). It also found that the combined share of banks and auto manufacturers in the United States is about 80 per cent. The latter's share alone in Canada is 80 per cent, a very high degree of concentration.

The task force recommended that all federally incorporated deposit-taking institutions should be allowed to retail insurance and offer auto leasing services in their branches. It recognized a concern that allowing banks to sell insurance might provide them with too much consumer information and thereby reduce competition. But its research showed no evidence that markets in Europe have been seriously disrupted by the practice of banks' underwriting and distributing insurance products. Indeed, there is some (admittedly not strong) evidence, the task force noted, that the lower costs and higher productivity achieved through bank distribution have led to overall expansion of the market.

Similarly, the task force research indicated that banks in most developed countries are allowed to engage in automobile leasing; Canada is the only outlier. In effect, Canadians depend on foreign providers for this service. Recognizing that this high degree of concentration would require time for the players to adjust to added competition, the task force recommended a transition period ending on January 1, 2002.

The Senate Banking Committee agreed with the MacKay Task Force's recommendations, with some qualifications (that life insurance be opened only in three years and that property and casualty insurance not be opened). The House Finance Committee recommendation of "no for now" prevailed, however.

The federal government refused the task force and Senate Banking Committee recommendations because of the power of the auto and insurance distribution lobbies. The decision was also closely linked to the popular concern about tied selling that surfaced in the public debate and hearings. Opponents expressed concern that the result would be more opportunities for such alleged abuse (although the only evidence is anecdotal).

The government's decision is a glaring flaw in the Paper. In refusing the average Canadian greater competition in these two product areas, it is sending the negative and contradictory message that, even though its stated objective is to help the consumer, its action is anti-consumer by protecting inefficient distributors of financial products. The lapse reverberates in the concerns I have expressed about the payments system.

Consumer Access

One of the Paper's major proposals and several of its lesser ones aim at the goal of ensuring consumer access.

Creating a Financial Consumer Agency

The major proposal here is to create a new financial consumer agency (FCA), which would improve oversight and consumer awareness to ensure that "the rights of consumers as a group are respected" (Canada, 1999). This agency would, most significantly, report to the minister of finance and enforce the consumer-oriented provisions of federal financial institution statutes. Thus, it would take some of the current OSFI mandate.

Associated with this proposal are a number of others. One would require banks to issue annual public accountability statements. Another would promote transparency and disclosure by financial institutions; yet another would respond to concerns about consumer privacy.

Given the major emphasis on consumer interests in the task force reports on which the Paper is based, it is not surprising to see proposals for additional regulatory and review agencies. The FCA would not improve overall economic welfare, but it would provide some benefit to consumers — and some added expenses. Its establishment would involve significant costs, most of which apparently would be paid by the banks. Once established, such an agency would have to find things to do, and the costs, both direct and involved in compliance, would surely escalate through time. Eventually these costs would be passed on to consumers, a factor that does not seem to have been taken into account in formulating the proposal.

A second concern is that the price ceilings the FCA might be empowered to impose could well turn into price floors — the agency might implicitly condone collusion.

The third issue, as already stated, is that all these proposals to protect and empower the consumer nowhere define the consumer. Is it, as this chapter assumes, users of retail financial services? Surely the interests of other users, such as small and medium-sized businesses, large corporations, and even governments, deserve consideration?

A fourth issue is that the FCA would represent an extra layer of regulation and oversight in the Canadian system, an addition to the OSFI, the CDIC, the Department of Finance, Industry Canada (which is concerned about privacy and small business), and the more than 70 provincial regulatory agencies. This proliferation of oversight in Canada contrasts sharply with the trend in, for example, the United Kingdom, where various agencies are being replaced by a single supervisory agency.

The Paper also proposes establishment of an independent Canadian financial services ombudsman (CFSO) to handle individual consumer complaints and report annually to the minister of finance. Funding would come from memberships; the banks would be required to join, and all Canadian financial institutions could do so. This independent ombudsman would replace or augment the Canadian Bankers' Association (CBA) ombudsman. In effect, the government is seeking to replace the CBA's self-regulation approach and to require the banks to fund the alternative — one more cost imposed. Whether the anticipated benefits in dispute resolution would materialize remains to be seen.

Other Reform Proposals

The Paper contains a number of other proposals, some more sensible than others.

Credit Unions and Cooperative Banks. Two related proposals seek to strengthen and encourage competition among retail institutions that are now small and essentially local. One of these proposals is to establish a national service entity for credit unions, which are now fragmented outside Quebec, where the Mouvement Desjardins has become a full-service financial conglomerate with a strong base built on local *caisses* (Canada, 1998c: 111). A similar proposal is to establish a framework for cooperative banks so that they could operate on a national basis, along the lines of Rabobank Nederlands, a Dutch private cooperative bank.

These measures are sensible and potentially significant, and they should be pursued. Rabobank's long history does, however, limit its relevance to what might be feasible in a modern, mature financial market.

Capital Taxation. The Paper also contains a promise to reexamine, with the provinces, capital taxation policy to see whether an alternative revenue-raising measure can be identified. This commitment to find a tax that does not place large Canadian-owned banks at a competitive disadvantage relative to their nonregulated and foreign competitors, as the capital tax does, is long overdue in a world of mobile capital.

Public Accountability Statements.   Other measures in the Paper reflect the recommendations of the MacKay Task Force. One would require banks to prepare annual public accountability statements. This measure would be discriminatory in that it would apply only to financial institutions with more than $1-billion in equity. Institutions of not-insignificant size that, for example, securitize credit card and other receivables would not be required to issue such statements. Surely this measure, given its policy justification, should apply to all organizations. (The Paper contains an extensive list of contributions to society that institutions are implicitly required to make.)

Coercive Tied Selling.   A second proposal aims to prevent coercive tied selling. This proposal responds to anecdotal evidence, as indicated earlier, which applies only to banks rather than to all financial institutions.

Statistical Reporting.   A third proposal would require better statistics on SME business financing. This measure would also be potentially discriminatory in that Schedule I banks account for half of SME debt financing. Would the institutions that supply the other 50 per cent also be required to submit such detailed reports?

It is also worth noting that each of these measures would have to be paid for. In the end, the added costs would be handed on to customers.

Standard Low-Cost Accounts.   One measure, to ensure access to a standard low-cost account, addresses a reasonable issue in an unnecessarily interventionist manner. Ottawa's goal is to ensure that all Canadians can obtain basic banking services, but the Paper provides specifics even on pricing and the number of transactions that should be available.

Many Canadians agree with the general thrust of such a proposal. But it is another matter for the government to design how such access should be provided. If there is a market to be served, the banks should be required to design a basic package that they can provide at reasonable cost. They should then be allowed to find the lowest-cost way of meeting the requirement.

Determining the pricing and contents of such a package through the regulatory framework would be a misuse of that framework and likely would be counterproductive. With no incentive to innovate, the account would be more expensive than necessary. And without clearly specified eligibility requirements (presumably to embrace those on welfare or disability benefits), there would be room for substantial abuse, something the government probably does not intend.

Regulatory Improvements

The thrust of the Paper's fourth objective is to make regulatory improvements. The focus is on prudential regulation and measures to enable the CDIC and the OSFI to respond to the evolution of the financial services industry.

The MacKay Task Force had recommended merging the CDIC with analogous institutions in the life insurance industry (the Canadian Life and Health Insurance Compensation Corporation, also known as CompCorp). The House

Committee accepted the idea with the proviso that it first be studied in more detail, but the Senate Banking Committee rejected the proposal, and the Department of Finance followed suit.

The MacKay Task Force's recommendation rested on the assumption that Ottawa's guarantee for deposits via the CDIC influences the competitive playing field between deposits and similar instruments supplied by insurance companies, such as short-term deferred annuities. One of the reasons for rejecting the proposal is that the CDIC and CompCorp insure different instruments. Only bank deposits pose systemic risk. Extending the government's financial commitments to insurance products would increase those commitments enormously and violate the systemic risk principle of such insurance. (Moreover, life insurance companies can gain access to CDIC's guarantee by setting up subsidiaries.)

The public debate also produced proposals to merge the OSFI and the CDIC, an argument the government rejected. But the Paper says that the way CDIC standards are administered would be streamlined, and the OSFI would be given additional supervisory powers to deal with the potential for increased risk associated with the additional competition the government seeks to introduce into the system. It would have added powers to discipline or remove directors of financial institutions who misbehave, to deal with related-party transactions, and to impose administrative money penalties for noncompliance with undertakings or violations of legislation and regulations.

IMPLICATIONS OF THE REFORM PROPOSALS

Canadians should expect that a major policy paper of this kind would promote a well-functioning financial system that advances the country's economic objectives, strengthens the efficiency and soundness of the financial system, safeguards the public in its dealings with that system, and ensures the system's adequacy to meet current and prospective needs of producers and users in efficient, flexible, nondiscriminatory, and creative ways. In this section, I discuss some of the Paper's main implications in the light of these criteria for good policy.

More Players

One of the Paper's main thrusts is to promote domestic competition by widening entry to the payments system and by encouraging more small players, including small, wholly foreign-owned banks: Which, presumably, the government hopes would provide Canadians with what they say they want — a wide range of deposit and lending services and credit availability to small businesses.

It is unlikely, however, that these services would be forthcoming from any institutions but the existing full-service players. In 1998, a widely cited foretaste of the future was Wells Fargo's provision of small business credit by mail; by late 1999, Wells Fargo had turned its sights elsewhere.

Encouraging smaller players is worth the try, but past experience with them in the Canadian market does not give much hope for the future. They have tended to be higher-cost, low-return players, insufficiently diversified in their asset base or inadequately managed to thrive.

Some of the potential foreign players could be expected to aim at the wealth-management sector of the market — which is not what policy intends. Others could be expected to service the retail market (which might include big retailers, such as Sears and Canadian Tire). But would they be willing to make the huge investments necessary to provide any but the most basic banking services?

The Issue of Scale

The Paper sidesteps the option of promoting an efficient, high-quality financial sector based on a small number of low-cost players that are allowed to achieve scale through mergers. Encouraging more small players implicitly assumes that they can operate successfully without seeking the economies of scale.

The issue of scale is worth examining in a little detail now that much of the smoke created by the 1998 bank merger proposals has cleared. Going forward, Canadians will still have to face the issue of the large banks in the mature Canadian market seeking to increase efficiency and to grow through domestic mergers. Policymakers ask why they cannot grow through cross-border mergers so that the issue of domestic concentration would not arise. The other option to achieve scale, it should be noted, is to undertake cross-pillar mergers.

Case Studies

Case studies in the MacKay report review the policy rationales for allowing consolidation in the United States (which is not really comparable to Canada because of its market size and its history as one of the world's most fragmented financial markets) and in Australia, the Netherlands, and Switzerland. In the three latter cases, governments decided to allow financial institutions to merge in order to achieve the critical mass deemed necessary to compete in the global marketplace (although the Australian government decided that its four major banks may not undertake mergers until certain credit availability criteria in the small business sector are met). Canada's policy framework rejects this strategy, though not the goal.

Academic Literature

The academic literature on scale is dominated by studies of U.S. institutions, mostly banks. Some studies on Japanese and European banks are available, but there are very few cross-border studies, and almost no international comparisons.

The U.S. studies generally indicate that cost savings on the order of roughly 20 per cent can be achieved through rationalization of operations and through greater managerial efficiency. But such studies are complicated by other evidence that diseconomies of scale set in when very large institutions merge; this evidence is backed up by qualitative judgments that, as size increases, more decisions (such as those on lending) are made by rules than by solution-oriented management judgments.

Where the literature is particularly weak is on the qualitative economies of scale, particularly in banking. Practitioners argue that the size of a bank's balance sheet influences the risks it can take, its brand, its reputation, and, linked to all of these, its access to low-cost capital from international sources. Those internationally recognized banks that are well up the list in Figures 2 and 4 tend to do business with other large, well-known institutions, which gain access to lower-cost capital and are able to participate in large, profitable syndicated financial transactions. In addition, the capital costs of leading banks are now huge because of the costs of technology, human capital, and advertising required to establish brand-name recognition.

If left to themselves, banks tend to grow rather than strip themselves down to leaner, more focused entities. This tendency may have a lot to do with their cost structures, which are very difficult to document and study in a systematic way.

As Figure 4 indicates, most of the largest bank mergers in the 1990s have been domestic mergers — that is, between banks (rather than cross-pillar) in the same country. Few are cross-border outside Europe.

There is, of course, no clear rule about success, since the perceived (and realized) benefits of mergers depend on managerial abilities to realize potential synergies and economies of scale after the fact. But the literature captures many of the potential benefits of domestic mergers: cost reduction; increased efficiency; new economies of scale in spending on technology, asset management, and custodial functions;[8] and the larger balance sheets and lower costs of capital necessary to retain domestic customers in wholesale banking (which foreign entrants are most likely to try to woo away). The social costs of consolidation are equally well known: increased concentration, reduced customer choice, job losses, and branch closures.

The Canadian Situation

Canadian banks could increase their scale by seeking cross-border mergers with (or acquisitions of) smaller U.S. banks, which would bring access to foreign knowhow, capital, and technology; help to retain Canadian wholesale customers who would otherwise go abroad; and presumably preserve choice, jobs, and branches in the retail operations in Canada.

The costs and risks of cross-border mergers are, however, considerable. Finding the right partner is difficult, and executing the merger of different cultures and institutions that have been regulated differently is a major challenge.

Several Canadian banks have acquired small U.S. banks over the years, but it is difficult to find a partner with which a pooling of interests and a share exchange are possible. For historical reasons, the U.S. banking system is uniquely fragmented, with many small banks focused on very localized business. The five largest Canadian banks are national full-service institutions, but they have smaller balance sheets and market capitalizations than the largest U.S. banks with similar businesses (about half the capital and assets of those at the bottom of the top 25 in Figure 2). The weak Canadian dollar is an additional obstacle at present.

These are some of the reasons Canadian banks argue they need to grow at home in order to internationalize.

An alternative exists. When the proposed mergers were denied in 1998, several banks changed their business plans so as to direct available finance to their successful lines of business and starve the unsuccessful ones. Over time, market forces will bring about greater specialization among the five large banks. (Differentiation is already apparent in their international operations.) More lively competition will appear in the Canadian marketplace as banks move away from their historical goal of being identical full-service players. The process will likely be slow.

One way to accelerate it would be to allow domestic mergers with the *quid pro quo* that the new partners aim to split themselves into more focused companies representing their major lines of business; for example, a merged entity could essentially divide itself into a corporate bank, a wealth-management institution, and a retail-only bank, each competing actively in the home market. While the merged entities of Figure 4 show no signs of stripping themselves down in this way, that is no reason Canadian banks could not change the rules of the game, to use strategic management parlance.

The Paper effectively continues to deny Canadian banks the option of domestic mergers. This approach denies them their preferred means to grow (with the exception of carrying out cross-pillar mergers and acquisitions, such as that of Canada Trust by the Toronto-Dominion Bank in 1999) unless they sell themselves to widely held financial institutions that are foreign owned (presumably by Americans). The possibility is quite real, therefore, that Canadian banks will become foreign controlled, or they will simply become minor-league players with relatively high production costs, a high cost of capital, and technology that is not state of the art.

Refusing domestic mergers hinders technological innovation, which requires scale for spreading costs. This proposition has been the subject of debate, it should be noted, with some arguing that banks can achieve their technology goals by buying new technologies off the shelf — that is, by outsourcing. This may be true for small and medium-sized institutions, but it is a management, not a policy, decision.

Foreign Ownership

Any discussion of scale among Canadian banks implies the issue of foreign ownership, since one strategic policy option, nowhere discussed, would have been to allow domestic mergers and to offset the impact on concentration of supply by allowing greater market access for foreign services providers as other countries, such as the Netherlands, have done. It is worthwhile to consider the case for and against foreign ownership as a way of promoting greater efficiency and flexibility in the financial services sector.

The economic benefits of foreign participation in a domestic financial system are well known. Foreign services providers, first and foremost, enhance domestic competition. They also bring knowledge of the latest products and risk-management techniques; they upgrade the skills of the people they employ; they often provide high-quality financial services at lower cost; and they diversify a country's financial system, both in terms of the choice of products and the way they are delivered to users of their services and in terms of ownership of and access to the resources of the foreign owners.

The costs or risks of greater foreign ownership (or, conversely, the case for Canadian control) are more qualitative. The MacKay report provided a thoughtful examination of Canadian control of the industry. It observed that, when firms are Canadian controlled, key strategic decisions are more likely to be made from a Canadian perspective, that the key head office jobs are more likely to be based in the country, and that the country benefits from the tax revenues generated by the industry. But it also points out:

> No single argument is sufficiently persuasive to justify retaining Canadian control as a public policy objective. Rather it is the weight of argument which leads the Task Force to conclude that it is not appropriate to abandon such a policy. (Canada, 1998b: 173)

The government's proposals call for "enhancing the international competitiveness of the sector in light of the globalization of financial services, while at the same time maintaining strong, vibrant domestic financial institutions" (Canada, 1999). If the government had been serious and thorough in weighing the costs and benefits, it would have given more weight to allowing larger, more globally competitive Canadian institutions, while opening up to more foreign competition. In sidestepping this option, the government is subjecting Canadians to a very real danger that the competitive players at home will be rendered less competitive by the overall approach in the Paper and fall further behind in terms of global best practice and efficient supply of services.

Discrimination and Higher-Cost Services

One of the Paper's internal contradictions is that it is discriminatory, something a major policy paper of this kind should not be. It professes to serve consumer interests, while it would deny the banks permission to offer auto leasing and insurance in their branches. It would leave consumers with higher-cost distribution systems — which, in the case of auto leasing, are owned by foreigners and in insurance are supplied by inefficient producers.

The Paper would also increase the regulatory burden on successful low-cost producers while constraining their options to enhance their competitiveness and productivity. The regulatory burden would grow in several ways. First, the added regulatory overlay of the FCA and the new accountability mechanisms would apply to banks but not to nonbanks. Why should new entrants choose to be banks?

Second, in a number of instances the government has chosen intervention and regulation over market forces to achieve many of its consumer objectives. The proposed FCA, CFSO, and public accountability statements are all designed to ensure that banks are more responsive to communities and customers, but these interventions would themselves increase the incentives to close marginal branches as quickly as possible.

Third, both the new ownership rules and the holding company structure are considered to be second-best alternatives to mergers, or banks would have chosen them before now.

Fourth, the Paper proposes new sources of administrative discretion and potential political pressure that could erode system soundness. Ministerial discretion would extend to new areas, such as membership in the payments system, and areas that seem to be open to political pressure, such as winding up failing institutions.

Focus on the Consumer

The Paper's emphasis on the consumer forces financial institutions to reevaluate their customer services models, which is a healthy, if not widely welcomed, focus. Consumers stand to gain from the added choice if new institutions are established; they stand to gain from better quality service resulting from innovations introduced because of added competition and new entrants with new models and new ideas; and they stand to gain from lower costs.

Consumers also appear to gain in that it is ostensibly their interests that the FCA would advance. But the Paper indicates that producers would cover the costs of the agency, which means that consumers ultimately would pay. They would also lose from the Paper's intention of confining them to inefficient distributors of auto leasing and insurance products.

Long-Term Growth

The Paper's authors have not considered the overall impact of its measures on the economy's long-term growth and efficiency. A well-developed financial services industry is a source of long-term growth in an economy. Financial services contribute to growth because these institutions have the skills to pool the capital of savers, the skills and resources to manage the risks presented by borrowers and other users, and the know-how to ensure that capital is used efficiently. These are the institutions that facilitate innovation and entrepreneurship by making capital available, appropriately priced for the risks, to unproven new enterprises. The information and communications technology revolution is also revolutionizing the ability of banks and other financial institutions to manage risk in ways that would have been impossible even five years ago and enabling them to serve small businesses more effectively.

Canada's big banks and insurance companies also contribute to the long-term growth of the knowledge-based economy because they are, above all, knowledge-based businesses. They employ large numbers of people and equip them with sophisticated skills in decision making, electronic applications, and risk management. Many of these individuals move on to start up their own businesses or to work in other sectors of the economy.

Summary

Taken together, some of the Paper's key decisions (on ownership, holding companies, and access to the payments system) would allow the large financial institutions to innovate, although much is still to be defined in legislation and regulations. These measures, particularly wider access to the payments system, would increase competition.

But many of the recommended measures, such as effectively denying banks domestic mergers and business powers and adding to the regulatory burden, would have a negative impact on competition and efficiency. They may enjoy short-term public popularity, but they would condemn both producers and users of financial services to long-term servitude.

RECOMMENDATIONS

The foregoing are significant issues that Canadians' elected representatives should take seriously in debating the Paper and its implementing legislation. A high-cost, over-regulated financial sector will not be a vibrant source of productivity growth and employment for the next generation of Canadians. The onus lies on government and the financial institutions to make alterations in the framework document and the industry.

With these concerns in mind, I offer eight recommendations for changes that should be considered in going forward.

1. **The objective of policy should be to improve the quality and efficiency of financial services, not to increase the number of players.**

The Paper is ambivalent about allowing a competitive marketplace. It puts existing, relatively low-cost producers (the large banks) in straitjackets with respect to how they carry on their business. It does not envision the use of competition in an optimal fashion. It counts on new entrants to increase competition and create a second tier of smaller financial institutions.

Whether the hope of encouraging new entrants to a mature market is realistic remains to be seen. Some view the effort as worthwhile and unlikely to run serious risks. Yet there are risks.

New entrants are unlikely to offer what Canadians say they want: a wide range of services and credit supply to small business. These will be provided only by current full-service players. In addition, financial history is replete with examples of small financial institutions' being wiped out because they lacked the diversified assets, geographic base, and management skills necessary to manage the risks of economic downturns and other adversities.

2. **The federal government should move to depoliticize the policy environment.**

A troubling feature of the Paper is the highly charged and politicized atmosphere in which it was written. One of the outcomes is its discriminatory elements. Ministerial discretion replaces competitive market outcomes. It lacks well-thought-out definitions of the consumer and what that consumer's interests are. It favours nonbanks over banks in the business powers decisions; it gives insurance companies access to the payments system but denies banks a *quid pro quo*.

The Paper is also interventionist, proposing increased ministerial and administrative discretion in several ways. Large bank mergers would ultimately be decided by the minister of finance. Standard bank accounts would be designed administratively, rather than by the banks. The minister would decide who gains access to the payment system and how products are distributed, rather than leaving it to the market.

3. The merger review process should be more realistic.

The available international research is ambiguous as to whether banks continue to be efficient beyond a certain size. Whatever the research says, in the end it is the banks that must compete in the international marketplace, and it is they, not policymakers, who should decide their business strategies.

The federal government must ultimately decide if proposed mergers serve the public interest, but its recent actions have been inconsistent. In 1998, the minister of finance refused to allow two proposed mergers, arguing that reducing the number of large banks from five to three would undermine the safety and soundness of the banking system, reduce competition, concentrate business credit decision making, and restrict Canadians' choice. Yet in 1999, the acquisition of Canada Trust by the Toronto-Dominion Bank was perceived to serve the public interest[9] by leaving the number of banks intact and avoiding the other negative impacts.

Going forward, Canadians must decide whether they want the federal government to chain the large financial institutions to the domestic market or allow them to become more competitive forces in the international marketplace.

4. Canadians should address the foreign ownership issue.

Going forward, if the federal government is serious about its intention to enhance the international competitiveness of the financial services sector in the light of its globalization, foreign ownership should be seriously analyzed and debated. The Paper proposes to redefine widely held ownership to allow for more cross-border transactions, other than mergers, and it encourages foreign institutions to enter the second tier. These proposals are insufficient to offset the risks of the Canadian financial sector's falling behind in terms of global best practice and efficiency.

The government will have to try harder to face up to the challenges and opportunities of globalization. This issue will not go away. Besides talking about competitiveness in international markets, Ottawa would better serve the public interest and awareness by examining alternative models for the Canadian financial system to ensure the country's main institutions are world class.

5. Administrative and regulatory layers should be reduced and consolidated, not increased.

Given the major political emphasis on consumer interests in the task force reports on which the Paper is based, it is not surprising to see it recommending establishment of an additional regulatory and review agency to focus on those interests. But creating such an agency, reporting to the minister of finance, would involve significant costs, which the banks would have to pay. Those costs, which would surely rise over time, would be passed on to the consumer, a factor the proposal's writers seem to have ignored.

6. Rules on ownership and holding companies should be spelled out more completely.

The new flexibilities that may be provided to banks to organize their businesses could be a major change from the status quo. But a number of questions arise.

What would be the "fit and proper" test to ensure the soundness and integrity of the 20 per cent share owners? It is difficult to envisage a truly foolproof one. Would it be the only test applied to approve share acquisitions? How would the government prevent share owners from acting together? Would the 20 per cent rule be a realistic response to the consolidation of the international financial industry? It is difficult to see this rule holding for long, since the impact of 20 per cent ownership on control can be the same as 30 or 40 per cent.

Similarly, the holding company proposal needs to spell out in more detail the implied supervision. How much would regulatory constraints be reduced on nonbank businesses? Would capital requirements be reduced for lower-risk businesses? Of even greater significance would be the rules to be drafted to implement this proposal. In what range of financial activities would banks be allowed to invest? What limits would be set on minority interests in investments? What would be the rules on related parties or on taxation?

7. The regulatory framework requires further improvement.

One issue in the proposed revision to the regulatory framework relates to institutional mandates. The MacKay Task Force thought the OSFI should take on consumer protection and the responsibility for balancing competition and innovation with safety and soundness. Both the House Committee and the Senate Banking Committee argued that the OSFI should continue to focus on safety and soundness. The Paper proposes the latter course, assigning consumer protection to the FCA and redress to the new ombudsman. The new agency would be given enforcement responsibilities currently carried out by the OSFI, making it an additional regulatory body.

Widespread support for a consumer watch-dog seems to exist, but it relates to the interests of households and small businesses that use retail financial services. Why should such a group have regulatory responsibilities? It should play the desired consumer advocacy role and be funded by those interests, not the financial institutions. Instead of proliferating regulatory agencies and the regulatory burden, Canada should be consolidating them.

A second issue relates to decisions on membership in, and therefore access to, the payments system. The government should reconsider whether it is giving the correct signal by giving such decisions to the Department of Finance, rather than to the OSFI or the Bank of Canada. I believe the latter course would be more advisable.

Finally, the tone in the financial regulatory environment needs to become less adversarial. Industry representatives and regulators need to work together to promote efficiency and safeguard the public.

8. The banks should respond to consumer criticisms as a strategic priority.

Both the banks and the government are imprisoned in an unsatisfactory status quo, despite all the reports and hearings. The Paper's message to the banks is, we will keep you in chains by constraining your business options and increasing your domestic competitors until you become more responsive to Canadian consumers (presumably households and small businesses). The effect of these policy restrictions is to constrain Canada's low-cost producers and increase the uncertainty they face.

One way out of this contradiction lies in the hands of the banks. The intensity of consumer and political sentiment suggests more than hostility. It signals a pent-up demand for a more responsive service model of retail banking for which people might be willing to pay. Banks may have a strategic opportunity in responding to this demand. At any rate, they face a constraint until they respond.

Surely it is possible for Canadian financial institutions to be both customer responsive and profitable, as Canada Trust has demonstrated. Canadians are likely to respond to such innovations. They have been among the world's fastest adopters of financial innovations, such as automated teller machines and debit cards, which can substantially enhance customer convenience and choice and solve the public policy constraints by providing access to remote users and underserved markets through telephone- and electronic-based services (Canada, 1998a: 15).

CONCLUSION

The contradictions in the federal government's framework paper on financial services policy that this chapter has outlined must be resolved sooner or later. The potentially significant proposals for holding companies can increase organizational flexibility for the large financial institutions and open new strategic possibilities. New players and expanded access to the payments system will increase domestic competition. But the impact will be offset by the possibility that more players will likely be high cost, by the chains placed on the large banks, and by the added regulatory burden. These contradictions make the proposed solution unstable for the Canadian financial services sector over the long term, and an uncertain stepping stone to the future.

Some people argue that the Paper represents the best set of compromises possible in the adversarial environment in which it was prepared. The public and private sector players bear some responsibility for the environment and for the decisions. But all Canadians will pay the price for the contradictions in the long term.

Does any of this matter? Will the threats and opportunities from rapid integration of capital markets, the Internet, and other technological change provide Canada's financial sector with the incentives and the means around the obstacles created by a policy framework seen as increasingly irrelevant? This possibility exists.

More likely, however, market forces will send both the customers and producers of financial services offshore. Restrictions on economies of scale and scope raise transaction costs. Customers seeking to reduce those costs will use the Internet and integrated capital markets to move their business to lower-cost, more innovative, better-connected offshore providers. Canadian financial firms will follow them.

Cross-border value chains are currently most visible in the goods-producing sectors, such as electronics and automobiles. What is less well recognized is that the financial sector has been ahead in arranging cross-border operations. In the goods value chains, production and marketing segments are located at sites around the world that are the most economically attractive. Since these segments are linked electronically, costs and taxes in one location can be avoided by moving activities to other locations. If Canada fails to be a low-cost producer of financial services, then customers, producers, and some of the best jobs will move out of the country.

The federal government has pressed its political points, and now has the responsibility to depoliticize the policy environment. It should focus more on the overall national interest, which urgently includes the competitiveness of Canada's financial services sector, not just encouraging more high-cost players in retail services. The political chances of such changes could improve significantly if the banks responded both to the depth of the dissatisfaction lying behind the political criticism and to the strategic opportunity in retail banking implied by the demand for realistically priced, customer-oriented services.

The financial services industry is rapidly consolidating, whether Canadians like it or not. Political leaders cannot both wring their hands about Canada's faltering productivity performance and wash their hands of efficiency concerns in one of the country's most significant sectors. If policy continues to shrink from this challenge, the financial services sector, which has been a Canadian strength, will become an also-ran in the world economy. The less-mobile among the Paper's much-mentioned Canadian consumers will be the losers.

NOTES

1. In Canada, a shared federal–provincial jurisdiction exists in the financial services sector.
2. The MacKay Task Force report will also serve as the basis of the next round of legislative and regulatory revisions governing the sector, which are scheduled for no later than 2002.
3. This list excludes two major mergers: one, announced in August 1999, that will combine three large Japanese banks, Dai-Ichi Kangyo Bank, Fuji Bank, and the Industrial Bank of Japan; and another, announced in October 1999, that will combine two more: Sumitomo and Sakura Banks.
4. More such cross-pillar mergers can be expected in the U.S. market as banks and insurance and securities firms try to survive in an industry increasingly dominated by a few large companies. The Financial Services Modernization Act of 1999, which took effect in early November 1999, eliminated restrictions on financial

services, dating back to the so-called Glass-Steagall Act, adopted in 1933, that had prevented banking, insurance, and securities firms from entering each other's businesses.

5. After banks were permitted to purchase or develop investments dealers in the early 1990s.

6. The Paper also contains several formalizations of intent, such as demutualizing large insurance companies and allowing foreign banks to set up branches in Canada. These are not dealt with at any length in this chapter because the policy changes are already being implemented.

7. These core principles include guidelines for best practices in banking supervision.

8. Indeed, Canadian banks have moved in recent years to merge their back office functions, such as cheque processing, in order to capture the large economies of scale available in such transactions.

9. Though still subject to review by the Competition Bureau, the OSFI, and the minister of finance.

REFERENCES

Bank for International Settlements (BIS). 1998. "Implications of Structural Change for the Nature of Systemic Risk." Report of a task force established by the Euro-currency Standing Committee of G-10 central banks. Basel. Word-processed.

The Banker 1999. "The Top 1000 World Banks." London: FT Publications. July.

Canada. 1998a. Task Force on the Future of the Canadian Financial Services Sector. Change, Challenge and Opportunity: Report of the Task Force. Chair of the task force was Harold MacKay. Ottawa: Department of Finance.

———. 1998b. Task Force on the Future of the Canadian Financial Services Sector. "Competition, Competitiveness and the Public Interest." Background Paper 1. Ottawa: Department of Finance.

———. 1998c. Task Force on the Future of the Canadian Financial Services Sector. "Organizational Flexibility for Financial Institutions: A Framework to Enhance Competition." Background Paper 2. Ottawa: Department of Finance.

———. 1999. Department of Finance. Reforming Canada's Financial Services Sector— A Framework for the Future. Ottawa. Available from Internet website: www.fin.gc.ca/finserve/docs/finserv1e.html.

International Monetary Fund (IMF). 1998. International Capital Markets: Developments, Prospects and Key Policy Issues. Washington, DC: IMF.

Feldstein, Martin, and C. Horioka. 1980. "Domestic Saving and International Capital Flows." Economic Journal 90: 314–29.

Financial Times of London. 1999. "FT 500 Annual Review, 1999." January 28.

Helliwell, John F., and Ross McKitrick. 1998. "Comparing Capital Mobility across Provincial and National Borders." NBER Working Paper 6624. Cambridge, MA: National Bureau of Economic Research.

Smith, R. Todd. 1999. "Money in the Bank: Comparing Bank Profits in Canada and Abroad." C.D. Howe Institute Commentary 124. May.

United Nations Committee on Trade and Development (UNCTAD). 1998. World Investment Report. Geneva: United Nations.

Wall Street Journal. 1999. "World business." September 27.

Technology and the New Economy: A Canadian Strategy

Charles J. McMillan and
Eduardo M.V. Jasson

In a world of global competition, technology has become the engine driving wealth creation. Indeed, it has been estimated that Silicon Valley alone produced in a single decade the largest legally produced increase in wealth in economic history — a staggering $500-billion.[1]

Canada's fundamental challenge is not to shift from a resource- to a knowledge-based economy — that process is well underway; but to become a world leader in the new economy based on knowledge and information. To many people, this transformation implies abandoning raw materials and primary industry — trading coal, oil and gas, aluminum, nickel, copper, gold, fisheries, agriculture, hydro, uranium etc. — for the new world of high technology — electronics, computers, aerospace and advanced information systems. In truth, nothing could be more unrealistic.

Canada's economic future is predicated on the very foundations of its economic history — its natural and human resources, and its infrastructure (transportation and communications), developed to commercialize them. Public opinion tends to revolve around several false contrasts:

➢ raw materials versus human resources

➢ low technology versus high technology

➢ domestic economy versus export economy

➢ primary resources versus manufacturing

➢ manufacturing versus service economy

➢ old economy versus new economy

Evidence from international trade statistics and from company data clearly reveal that much of the concern about these issues is seriously misplaced.[2]

Canada's problem is not its dependence on raw materials, but something much more fundamental. It is the dependence on undifferentiated commodities, which are sold purely on the basis of price. For too long, Canada has been locked out of the high-value-added sectors of raw materials, where technology, marketing prowess, quality and labour skills combine in an organizational package to produce real wealth. This pattern of investment, management and strategy, implicit or otherwise, has left the vast bulk of Canada's resource firms still in their historic roles as hewers of wood and drawers of water. Here is a telling example of Canada's weakness: In Canada's largest export sector, forest products, there is not a single Canadian firm among the world's top 10.

The real debate must, therefore, centre on the difference between low- and high-value-added goods, low and high export intensity, and competitive and uncompetitive sectors and products in the international economy. At the root of all these issues is the question of technology — the new key to wealth creation.

Technology — The Key

Why are science and technology so important in the modern industrial economy? Traditional economics has placed technology in a black box or treated it as a residual, with the major emphasis on the mix of labour and capital inputs. In the past two decades, however, as entire industries have shifted to new "knowledge inputs," the role of technology has been identified as the leading indicator of growth and the ratio of exports over imports. For example, in a study of some 22 nations in the Organization for Economic Cooperation and Development (OECD), Dosi et al.[3] found that between 1963 and 1977, technological innovation, measured by patent grants received by national firms in the United States, was the leading determinant of whether exports exceeded imports in a national industry. Company and industry case studies clearly point out the effects of innovation: a complex, highly dynamic shift in superiority, among firms, industries and countries, away from the United States, as witnessed by Japanese automobiles or European radial tires and aerospace products. These shifts raise serious questions about Canada's ability to compete against aggressive foreign rivals.

International comparisons expose Canada's weak position in science and technology measured by a range of indicators. For instance, in each of the number of domestic patents granted to residents per 100,000 population, the number of patents filed within the country, and the number of scientists and engineers per 1,000 people in the labour force, Canada has one of the lowest ratings among industrialized nations. More tellingly, Canada's weak performance in research and development (R&D) directly relates to its future trade patterns. Compared to its global competitors, Canadian private firms rank last in company-funded R&D; only a tiny fraction undertake any R&D at all. Of the leading industrialized countries, Canada's position is least favourable, especially compared with the United States and Japan. Yet those two countries are Canada's most important trading partners, together accounting for almost 90 per cent of Canada's trade.

Canada has experienced an increasingly negative trade balance in R&D-intensive industries. In 1980 the deficit was $4.6-billion, rising to $7.1-billion in 1987, $12-billion by 1991 and continuing to rise throughout the 1990s. Moreover, none of Canada's science-intensive sectors are in the traditional resource industries, where Canada supposedly has an international comparative advantage. The danger is that Canada will be caught in the middle, between the growth sectors represented by high-technology trade fostered by the United States and Japan, and the low-cost sectors, increasingly dominated by Asia, where labour costs and engineering applications are key to competitive success.

Why does Canada trail so badly in science-and-technology-related competitiveness? Canada is not a poor country. It has a rich tradition of invention and discovery, from telephones to jet engines, kerosene lamps to insulin.[4] Canada spends an enormous amount of money on education; indeed, it spends considerably more per capita on it than most other advanced countries. And as an immigrant nation, Canada, like the United States, is a net recipient of a hugely rich stock of human capital from other countries, especially of talented professionals and well-educated entrepreneurs.

Three observations help answer the question why Canada lags in technological innovation. First, Canada is not well organized for science and technology coordination. Federal efforts are widely dispersed; central agencies compete for resources regardless of either achievement or effort, and key instruments of science policy are saddled with ambiguous mandates. Second, Canada's federal system, in which education is a provincial responsibility and economic policy is a mixed federal–provincial mandate, creates a natural tendency towards program duplication, budgetary paralysis and policy ambiguity. Politicians and bureaucrats alike find this situation more comfortable than one of strategic focus, policy coordination and results-oriented implementation. And third, until recently, science and technology policy has not been a central part of the national agenda of the federal or provincial governments, the private sector, or the banking and venture capital sector.

The reality is that Canada lacks the dynamic "critical mass" in industry, academe or government to be a significant global player in the R&D game. Facing that reality requires a strategy, a commitment and resources (including people, money and specialized talent). Canada does not lack any of the specific elements, but strategy and commitment remain in short supply.

This article examines three issues that are critical to developing the needed policies:

➤ the organization of Canadian science and technology
➤ linkages between education and the economy
➤ government leadership, and the building of capital markets for technology companies

Before discussing these issues, the next section provides an overview of the new economics of science-based innovation.

THE ECONOMICS OF SCIENCE-BASED INNOVATION

Although its theoretical constructs may be remote to most people, the products of science-based innovation — from pharmaceuticals to computers, advanced materials in ski equipment, to electronics in home stereos — illustrate what is clear from empirical evidence: consumer value and quality are ever improving. Underneath this simplistic observation are some profound realities about the nature of innovation in the economic system and the role of knowledge creation and competitive advantage in firms, industries and nations. What is behind this new way of looking at economics and competitive advantage?

The classical theory of factor endowments as the centrepiece for international comparative advantage has been challenged. Classical economics focuses on the three factors of production: land (God-given), labour (skilled and unskilled) and capital (physical as well as technological). Some countries have comparative abundance in land and natural resources (Australia, Canada, Saudi Arabia, Argentina, the United States and Russia, to cite obvious examples). But contrast their economic performance with that of resource-poor countries like Germany, Japan or Switzerland. Clearly, other factors are at work.

Anecdotal evidence and case studies of companies and industries all point to the link between technological innovation and industrial growth. Unfortunately, theorizing and theory development in this area — in economics, business strategy and management — is still in its infancy and lacks an empirical base. A possible reason is that technological innovation occurs in a wide variety of forms: changes to products and processes, major and minor breakthroughs, linkages between public policies and industry activity and the like. Intellectual discovery sets in motion fundamental changes, causing the knowledge base of a company, an industry sector or an entire economy to be revolutionized by technological changes. Witness the impact of the Industrial Revolution on a single sector: shipping. Technology radically changed the nature of construction materials and methods of propulsion from sail and wooden ships, to coal and iron ones, and now to oil, nuclear power, and steel ships. Today the microchip is going through similar development, albeit at a much faster pace.

Labour, or more generally, human capital (workers and managers), has also made a significant difference, as contrasts between otherwise comparable countries readily show: consider Britain and Japan, or even Korea and Argentina. This view coincides with a classic study by Nobel economist Wassily Leontief, who discovered in the early 1950s that, contrary to expectations that American export success would lie in capital-intensive goods, U.S. trade surpluses existed in sectors with labour-intensive products.[5] One explanation is in the skill requirements of the production process.

There is no question that there is a need for additional qualitative and quantitative assessments to explain precisely how technological change impacts on economic outcomes. What is undeniable, however, is that in the last 25 years, the determinants of industrial success and wealth creation have altered as economies changed their competitive abilities. The primary reason for these changes has been the development of knowledge and intellectual capital.

Largely as a result of the staggering research budgets in the United States, but also in Europe, Japan and elsewhere, there has been a quantum leap in new knowledge (including underlying theories, engineering and commercial applications) in three generic technologies: biotechnology, electronics and advanced materials. In these fields, technological frontiers have moved dramatically into new theoretical directions, to be sure, but especially into new commercial applications.

In too many areas, Canada's industrial structure is increasingly dependent on low-value-added, price-sensitive commodities, while technology-intensive products increasingly dominate Canada's imports. Although the new strategic technologies all affect Canada's primary sector, too little use has been made of them by Canadian companies. Foreign companies often take the lead even in sectors like pulp and paper, where Canada should be a leader.

Consider the case of Japanese investment in Canada's resource sector. The Japanese are heavy investors in Canadian raw materials — forest products and coal in Alberta and British Columbia, aluminum in Quebec and hydrocarbons in the Arctic. They have also made major purchases of farmland, wineries and specialized fisheries in the United States. However, Japanese companies also conduct major research efforts at home, especially projects in aquaculture, superconductivity, ocean research, deep-water robotics, new ceramics, high-quality crystals and high-performance ocean chemicals. Japan's vision is in the potential for transforming resources into new products. The production of higher-value-added products is at the heart of a knowledge economy.

From a worldwide competitive perspective, these trends represent dramatic, new and challenging implications. Innovations are occurring both in products (such as semiconductors) and in production processes (such as electric arc mini-mills in the steel industry, or digital and fibre-optic technology in telecommunications). New technologies are evident in products as common as tennis rackets, the pill or satellite television. Winning and losing firms vary in size, industry structure, management, government support and innovative entrepreneurship. Consider some examples: U.S. tire makers against Bridgestone of Japan or Michelin of France; Caterpillar against Japan's Komatsu in earth-moving equipment; Detroit's "Big Three" against Japan's car sector; America's fast food giants (McDonald's, Pizza Hut etc.) against Europe's traditional food sector, Wal-Mart and Price Club against traditional retailers. No industry is immune; no country can escape the global impact of new knowledge, changed production processes and new skills. This is Schumpeter's classic process of creative destruction at work.

Clearly both the level and composition of R&D expenditures do count, a point that is especially relevant in assessing U.S.–Japan rivalry, since Japan's research does not have anything equivalent to the military focus of the United States. Moreover, there are additional factors that economists are now only starting to recognize. What are these factors?[6]

First, technology and knowledge are central to the economic growth process, in workers as well as managers. Second, knowledge inputs can lead to a growth spiral where new knowledge creation leads to new investment, which leads to new knowledge. A corollary is that, once ahead, a firm or country can stay ahead of rivals. Third, despite classical economic theory, inputs to production do not produce a fixed rate of return to scale. Rising inputs often lead to increasing returns, despite cuts in prices or rising outputs.

In this non-linear world, these factors lead corporate strategists to focus on being first to market with technologies, and relentlessly pursuing improved production processes in order to maximize returns. Compared to traditional resource-based industries such as mining, forestry and fisheries, the new knowledge-based sectors have developed a qualitatively different industry logic, where the process of knowledge creation and knowledge commercialization are inextricably combined in production and organizational methods. In this game, commercial and engineering concerns — production cycle times, resource use (minimization of waste) and consumer needs — require continual organizational innovation. In short, the new economics means new management strategies, corporate skills and organization forms, a point as true for government as for private firms.[7]

CANADIAN ORGANIZATION FOR SCIENCE AND TECHNOLOGY

Canada produces, at best, 3 per cent of the world's stock of scientific knowledge, relying on the world community for the 97 per cent sourced externally. Yet Canada's basic science organization and policy apparatus are oriented as if Canada were a major science creator, rather than importer.

Canada's science infrastructure — key institutions, scientific personnel and modus operandi — is almost an exact transfer of the British model.[8] Canada's Royal Society, established in 1882, is a direct copy of the British model of bringing scientists into a united stream of study and exploration towards national efforts. The formation of a national government in 1867 led to the establishment of such institutions as The Dominion Experimental Farms System (1886) and, later, the Biological Board of Canada (1912) and the Honorary Advisory Councils on Scientific and Industrial Research (1916).

One of the most important advances in scientific institution-building was the establishment of the National Research Council (NRC). Set up originally as part of the network of laboratories of the Advisory Council on Scientific and Industrial Research, it then became the basis of all federal government pure and applied research activity. Indeed, for 60 years the NRC has been a link between the scientific community and the application of science to industry. However, in its evolution the NRC became the basis of important spin-off creations, including the Defense Research Board (1947), Atomic Energy of Canada (1952), the Medical Research Council (1960) and, more recently, the Natural Science and Engineering Research Council (1978).

The structure of the National Research Council and the role of the funding councils point to a central dilemma facing government-sponsored, science-based innovation in Canada: is the mandate to support primarily basic research, to assist industry in applied, commercially driven research, or to do a mixture of both?[9] Despite the success of the much-lauded Industrial Research Assistance Program (IRAP) which focuses on direct technological improvements to industry performance, historically NRC activity has concentrated on purely

FIGURE 1
Annual Gross Domestic Expenditure on R&D as a Percentage of GDP

	1981		1991		1997	
Rank	Countries	%	Countries	%	Countries	%
1	United Kingdom	2.4	Sweden	2.9	Switzerland	3.9
2	United States	2.4	United States	2.8	Japan	2.9
3	Sweden	2.3	Japan	2.8	Korea	2.9
4	Switzerland	2.2	Germany	2.6	Finland	2.8
5	Japan	2.1	France	2.4	United States	2.7
6	France	2.0	Netherlands	2.1	Germany	2.3
7	Netherlands	1.9	United Kingdom	2.1	France	2.2
8	CANADA	1.2	Finland	2.1	Denmark	2.0
9	Finland	1.2	Czech Republic	2.0	United Kingdom	1.9
10	Denmark	1.2	Korea	1.9	CANADA	1.6
11	Denmark	1.1	Norway	1.7	Iceland	1.6
12	Austria	1.0	Belgium	1.6	Austria	1.5
13	Iceland	0.6	CANADA	1.5	Italy	1.1

Source: OECD, MSTI database, April 1999, on STI scoreboard of indicators — Recent trends in total R&D efforts.

scientific research. Typical of most government-department labs, NRC research activity has not been driven by industry and commercial applications, and has not been targeted to potential commercial clients. This pattern of development neglected the vital relationship between research institutions and industry, thereby inhibiting scientific tools and resources from contributing to Canada's commercial innovative capacity. The result is that, over all, Canada's post-war record in basic science is weak, and its comparative performance in technological innovation is weaker still.

International comparative data reveal just how much Canada trails other nations in terms of R&D spending — a key measure of innovation capacity. In 1997, Canada ranked 10th in R&D spending as a percentage of GDP (see Figure 1). Of the world's 200 top private-sector firms in terms of R&D spending, only one — Bell Canada — is Canadian. Indeed, Canada's industry base in science and technology is exceedingly small. In 1991, only 0.4 per cent of Canadian firms engaged in R&D; of these 3,566 firms, 25 accounted for 48 per cent of spending. Although more recent figures are not available, there is no reason to expect significant changes to have occurred. Total commitment to R&D expenditures (as a percentage of GNP) has improved marginally from 1.4 per cent in 1987 to 1.6 per cent in 1997.

In 1998, Canada's public-sector research funding accounted for over one third of the $13.9-billion total national spending on R&D (see Figure 2). The federal government directly funds $3.00-billion, the provinces $703-million, and

FIGURE 2
R&D Spending in Canada by Sector Performing and Funding R&D

Sector	1986 Performing $ in Mil.	%	1986 Funding $ in Mil.	%	1998 Performing $ in Mil.	%	1998 Funding $ in Mil.	%
Federal Government	1,407.0	18.9	2,368.0	31.7	1,593.0	11.5	2,994.0	21.6
Provincial Governments	217.0	2.9	470.0	6.3	181.0	1.3	703.0	5.1
Provincial Research Organizations		0.0	0.0	0.0	82.0	0.6	0.0	0.0
Business Enterprises	4,022.0	53.9	3,090.0	41.4	8,882.0	63.9	6,864.0	49.4
Higher Education	1,753.0	23.5	828.0	11.1	2,995.0	21.6	1,024.0	7.4
Private Non-Profit Organizations	61.0	0.8	142.0	1.9	160.0	1.2	450.0	3.2
Foreign		0.0	562.0	7.5	0.0	0.0	1,858.0	13.4
Total	7,460.0	100.0	7,460.0	100.0	13,893.0	100.0	13,893.0	100.0

Source: Statistics Canada, *Total Spending on Research and Development in Canada*, 1986 to 1997, and Provinces 1986 to 1995, Catalogue 88-001-xpb, Vol. 21, No. 8; Statistics Canada, *Total Spending on Research and Development in Canada*, on Estimates of Canadian Research and Development Expenditures (GERD), Canada, 1987 to 1998, and By Provinces 1987 to 1996, Catalogue 88-006-xpb, No. 11.

the higher-education sector funds some $1.02-billion independently of government contributions. The 1997–98 federal scientific activities report issued by Statistics Canada breaks down federal spending on science-based activities into 60 per cent in-house, 17 per cent to educational institutions, 15 per cent to industry, and the balance to foreign and other recipients.

Analysis of R&D spending is complicated in Canada by the fact that the source of funding, be it the federal government, a provincial government, industry or a foreign firm, is often different from the agency doing the spending — a government in-house agency, a university, industry etc. The data are further muddled by imprecise provincial reporting and inconsistent classifications. These difficulties are compounded when attempts are made to secure disaggregated international comparative data.

Yet Canadian industry's position in science and technology, whether measured by domestic patents, by scientists and engineers in the labour force, or by sectors with a positive trade balance, is weak. The low level of private sector R&D expenditures tells much of the story. Within corporate Canada, only Nortel Networks, which is increasingly run from the United States, has a big R&D budget comparable to those of large European, American and Japanese spenders. There is simply no large sector of the Canadian economy — for example, mining in advanced materials, food or agribusiness in biotechnology — to provide an engine of development equivalent to the pharmaceutical industry in Switzerland or the electronics sector in Japan.

Foreign ownership plays a role in reducing Canadian R&D spending as illustrated by the automobile sector in Ontario. But foreign ownership is as much a symptom as a cause. Although as a general rule, Canadian-owned firms spend more on research and development than foreign-owned firms operating in Canada, their actual expenditure levels, compared to their U.S. or Japanese counterparts, are still very low.[10]

Clearly, spending on research and development per se is not a panacea. Other factors are at work. For one, Canada has an anemic record in applying existing technology for competitive gain. For six advanced manufacturing technologies — computer-aided design, NC-CNC machines, program controllers, inter-company links, LAN for technical data, and LAN for factory use — Canadian usage is not only significantly less than American firms, the gap in technology application is the greatest among small firms, i.e., those with fewer than 500 employees. This is, in part, a reflection of how few engineers and scientists occupy prominent executive positions in Canadian firms; it is also a result of the low priority given to on-the-job training. Over half of Canada's spending on research goes outside the commercial market for tradable goods and services.

Canada, like all other developed nations, must import technology as part of the global marketplace. The problem is that other countries do it more effectively. As Japanese government support for R&D demonstrates, it is not the amounts governments spend — 80 per cent of Japanese spending in science and technology comes from the private sector — but what they spend it on which is important. What counts is the commercial leverage that can be gained by rapidly diffusing research output, or by developing commercial prototypes for new products, identifying new markets, or both.

In the past, commercial success did not depend on scientific output; German chemistry, British engineering and American electronics all preceded codification of scientific analysis and theory development. In certain areas, that remains true today. But in all the new technologies — biotechnology, advanced materials, electronics and their applications — real progress comes from the long-term work of basic science and the desire to move the technological frontier forward. But this is not a short-term process, nor a field where gains are likely without a highly educated management cadre and a well-trained workforce. According to Statistics Canada's first-ever Survey of Intellectual Property Commercialization, Canada's 12 largest universities account for 77 per cent of new invention reports, 68 per cent of new patent applications, and 74 per cent of active licenses.

Historically weak linkages between Canadian universities and the private sector compound our problems. Few Canadian universities enjoy the level of funding, either for research or overhead support, that their U.S. counterparts do; further, interprovincial rivalries, excessive duplication and lack of institutional specialization have decreased the potential for large concentrations of scientific talent, as well as for budget levels comparable to their counterparts in other countries. Canadian universities as a general rule lack the private sector linkages and industrial spin-offs of their U.S. counterparts, although this situation is changing, if slowly. The Universities of British Columbia, Waterloo, Toronto, Alberta and Guelph are all beginning to realize the benefits of linkages they have forged with the private sector.

Emphasizing Commercialization

In applying technology, a country's engineering infrastructure — software and hardware, people and machines, as well as the facilities for their interaction — can be more important than the technological idea itself, or even how it is marketed. It is a balance of strategic functions and their integration that leads to commercial success in science-based innovation, not emphasis on any one area. Indeed, this latter point explains why being on the technological frontier of scientific work does not, in itself, bring commercial success.

The need for commercialization accentuates the importance of the innovation cycle. The conventional view of science-policy analysis is science innovation as a chain of separate but distinct activities forming the basis of a dynamic innovation cycle.[11] The chain starts with basic research for new knowledge, and proceeds through a sequence of activities from the general to the specific, from the basic and non-proprietary, to the applied and proprietary. The next stages involve specific management functions linking the early stages to downstream areas such as engineering, tooling, production and marketing.

This conventional perspective applies to the vast majority of science-based innovations, although in many instances it has been significantly accelerated. Many product cycles are becoming shorter and shorter, and management is placing a premium on reducing them even more. Some of the Japanese-inspired innovations in the automobile industry (in inventory management, quality, quick-die change, and plant layout) are the most notable examples of reducing the time cycle. These new corporate capabilities also reflect another fact:

imitators can often learn from, and even surpass, product leads of innovating firms. The American economist, Edward Mansfield, estimates that companies can, on average, imitate a new product in only two-thirds the time and cost of the pioneering one.[12] Nonetheless, the chain from basic research to commercial applications can still be as long as 10 years or more, a requirement which dictates a strategic blend of patient capital, constant effort and a supportive research culture.

A second consideration is the multiplier effect of breakthrough research. In some areas, such as superconductivity, biotechnology and advanced materials, the cost of doing research is so astronomically high, and the impact of breakthroughs so pervasive, that the traditional innovation cycle may not hold. For instance, the changes introduced by the microchip, first developed in the Bell labs in the early 1950s, were so dramatic that the commercial opportunities flowed not from the royalties of the discovery, but from the multitude of applications inherent in the technology. Hence, commercial innovation became the key, rather than technological research per se. A parallel example in industry today is the advances in digital technology and its marriage to wireless transmission.

The third important factor in commercializing innovation is that the requirements for successful innovation do not apply equally across technologies or products. In electronics, for instance, the real cost is not labour, but research and technical equipment. In steel, the significant costs are in advanced capital equipment. In automobiles, labour costs are below 15 per cent of total costs and falling. This suggests that "process technology" — how something is made — can be as important as what is made. Japan's enormous emphasis on process technology is what has led to better strategies for commercial use of breakthrough scientific knowledge.

New Role for Policy

Every advanced industrial society has had a public policy vehicle to promote technological development, both direct or indirect, publicly owned or publicly regulated. Americans continuously point to the monolith of "Japan Inc.," and to the pervasive powers of its Ministry of International Trade and Industry (MITI), ignoring all the while, the fundamental pluralism of modern Japan. To be sure, the Japanese have their own vast web of industrial networks, public-private vehicles such as MITI, NTT, Technopolis Centres and strategic grants to support science and technology strategies into the next century.[13] In the United States, military spending, defence procurement, medical research funding, space development, agricultural support systems, and a huge complex of government-business-university spending take a central role in supporting American technological development. There are now similar networks in Europe — in space, computers, biotechnology and aerospace, to name a few sectors.

The question for Canada is simple: what master instruments does Canada have to reshape its science and technology organization to meet the needs identified, given that defence research is practically non-existent?

367

The weakness of the industrial base for R&D in Canada is compounded by political pressures to dispense scarce research funds across the country. This dispersion approach has inhibited the development of both a critical mass of research talent (universities, research centres or companies) and a degree of specialization in universities or research laboratories that fosters world-scale talent, research and focus. (Canada's National Research Council has won one Nobel Prize in a generation; Germany's equivalent has won 23.)

Geography and politics, in other words, play a big role in science and technology in Canada. The cards are rarely on the table. True, federal and provincial governments have taken steps to overcome political parochialism, but their approach remains worrisome.

Is the answer long-term, national mega-projects involving public and private sector collaboration, such as developing the Arctic? Is it a twenty-first century national telecommunications network or government infrastructure in electronic transportation control systems? Or is it an international initiative in biotechnology fields, such as preventive medicine, AIDS or population aging? Japan has its fifth-generation computer thrust; Europe was successful in developing the Airbus; the United States has NASA. Such mission activity is a big-country game, risky and limiting in its deep, but narrowly focused, allocation of resources. Canada does not have infinite research resources, nor has it the talent base to compete against other nations across the board. Specialization and focus — on an appropriate scale — are key.

Canada's response is hampered as much by structural problems as by money. Bear in mind that there is a difference between who funds research and who spends the money. Recall that Canada's public sector research funding accounts for about one-third of total national spending on R&D. From a competitive perspective, Canada devotes too much of this to non-commercial sectors that involve no linkage to tradeable goods or services. These sectors are also largely outside the mainstream of international scientific research and the professional mechanisms for publications and peer review, and thus independent of both scientific and commercial accountability.

Clearly, in all sectors of the economy, Canada needs improvement in adopting and applying technology, regardless of its source. In relative terms, Canada's record in the commercialization end of the innovation cycle is weak. From a perspective of economic growth, it is not theoretical knowledge alone that drives industrial innovation, but the capacity to develop industrial applications. Even the United States, despite its national excellence in higher education and postgraduate research, has trailed Japan's enormous resources for process technology and first-to-market innovation skills.

Recent changes at the federal level have started to realign budget allocations in Canada, particularly in such flagship institutions as the National Research Council.[14] The NRC is in the process of shifting its focus from its scientific origins to the industrial community, and serving as a bridge between basic and generic research, undertaken in concert with the universities and technological applications in the commercial world. Unfortunately, strategic assessments of research work undertaken in line departments — federally and provincially — are substantially underdeveloped, despite the unusually large proportion of funds devoted to government labs. Here again, the challenge is to develop better linkages to commercialize products and services in the global marketplace. Fortunately, Canada's leading universities have acted by establishing commercialization and IP (Intellectual Property) mechanisms.

Ironically, Canada's record in scientific research by university researchers stands up well by international criteria (see Figures 3 and 4). Yet there are many barriers to further progress, including aging plant and equipment, low levels of current funding, a lack of openness to commercialization and a complete reliance on peer review for judging performance. These institutional barriers now combine with two other problems in Canada: demographics and education-funding levels. The average age of Canadian research scientists in both universities and government labs is climbing steadily. At the NRC the average age is about 49, compared to 28 at Bell Northern Laboratories. Per-capita spending on higher education trails that in the United States by a growing margin; the gap is particularly noteworthy in science and engineering, precisely the areas where fundamental research is most likely to lead to subsequent commercial production.

EDUCATION AND THE ECONOMY

Some 200 years ago Adam Smith wrote, "the wealth of a nation depends upon two inherent determinants: first, the fraction of population gainfully employed and second, the skill, dexterity and judgement by which labour is generally applied." Smith foresaw the central role of education and training in an advanced economy.

Education in advanced industrial countries is big business, accounting for perhaps 10 per cent of employment in the United States. The OECD member nations spend over $1-trillion annually on education, which is increasingly seen as the basis of lifetime learning and the key to the continuous development of specific skills and credentials necessary for an advanced economy. Indeed, the evidence clearly shows that the basic "mismatch" between demand and supply for specialized skills is increasingly exacerbated in all Western countries — a sign of serious imperfections in the labour market. Countries like Britain, Canada and France, despite significant unemployment, rely on immigration to supply workers with particular job skills. In the United States, the Carnegie Foundation estimates that more than one million new teachers will be needed over the next several years — over 300,000 in mathematics and science alone — a figure larger than the entire education teaching force in 1991. In Japan, the Council of Science and Technology estimates a shortage of one million computer programmers and systems engineers, despite the fact that 40 out of every 1,000 Japanese students are studying engineering, compared to seven out of every 1,000 American students.

The relationship between education and a society's industrial performance has long been a preoccupation of social scientists in general, and economists in particular, and the abundant literature on the subject has owed much to the theoretical contributions of Canadian economists, notably the late Harry Johnson.[15] Much of this theoretical and empirical work has focused on two basic linkages: between the levels of educational attainment on the one hand, and

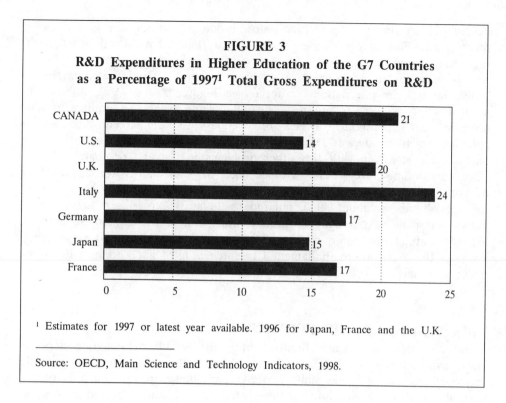

FIGURE 3

R&D Expenditures in Higher Education of the G7 Countries as a Percentage of 1997[1] Total Gross Expenditures on R&D

[1] Estimates for 1997 or latest year available. 1996 for Japan, France and the U.K.

Source: OECD, Main Science and Technology Indicators, 1998.

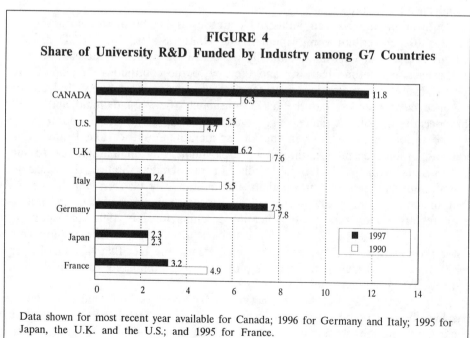

FIGURE 4

Share of University R&D Funded by Industry among G7 Countries

Data shown for most recent year available for Canada; 1996 for Germany and Italy; 1995 for Japan, the U.K. and the U.S.; and 1995 for France.

Source: Statistics Canada; National Science Board; Science & Engineering Indicators — 1998

earnings and career performance in the economy on the other. Clearly, for the individual and for society at large, there are major social benefits to be had from public expenditure on education, both in terms of a future flow of educational pay-offs through salary and earnings (where society reaps rewards or returns through taxation on earnings) and through society-wide benefits, such as having a more literate workforce, specialized skills and mobility in the job market. All Western countries — especially Canada, the United States, Sweden, Japan and France — have increased their public-education spending greatly since the 1960s. Yet many education systems are in peril. Even the very largest, the U.S. system, is recognized as being in trouble. Literacy and dropout levels, school-leaving rates, student truancy — all the basic indicators — are raising the spectre of educational stagnation. The U.S. Education Secretary, Lauro Cavosoz, summarized the situation in that country as follows: "The good news is that the schools are not worse. The bad news is that we are not making progress."[16] President Bill Clinton's 1997 state-of-the union speech, deploring America's low ratings in math and science tests as a barometer "that reflects the world class standards our children must meet for the new era" illustrates U.S. attention to basic education improvements. Education reform even became an issue in the 2000 presidential elections.

Increasingly, the focus on the education system, particularly in light of detailed comparisons between the U.S. and Canadian systems and that of the Japanese, brings forward a basic conclusion. In North America, the emphasis is on the "E-E" relationship: that between education (and all its forms, programs, institutions and curriculum) and the economy. The Japanese emphasis is on the "F-E-E" relationship: among family, education and economy. In Japan, where education and learning are social obsessions, the starting point is the family unit and, in particular, the role of the mother as a special link between student and the school.

Illiteracy

Illiteracy is a particularly important concern. Canada has been slow to face up to the crisis that low literacy attainments imposes on an advanced economy.[17] The challenge of literacy is related to education and training and also to learning skills. It is the capacity of an individual to cope, through reading and writing, with the changes in an information-based economy, including the skills needed to operate well in the home or at work. Studies in the United States suggest that illiteracy there is at the same level — that is, 60-million adult Americans, one-quarter of the population, are unable to adequately function.

Obviously, no single factor can explain Canada's illiteracy problem. Domestic studies and international reports all agree on the evidence of its effects in at least the following two areas:

> The fastest growing jobs in the economy are those that have the highest skills levels in basic mathematics and language capabilities.

> Literacy skills are directly related to a country's productivity and international competitiveness. Illiteracy levels have been shown to correlate closely with levels of poverty, crime and other social problems in local communities.

There is a pervasive presumption that the problem of illiteracy can be solved in the schools, or somehow by the education system, generally. However, studies in both the United States and Japan provide ample evidence that this presumption is false. Literacy must be tackled in the home, the family and the community. Fortunately, there is a growing awareness in Canada of the problems of illiteracy, and a host of voluntary organizations have sprung up to cope with the ongoing challenges. More significantly, the efforts of groups such as ABC Canada, a private-sector foundation promoting literacy, have active support from business and labour alike.

Educational Performance — Cost Relations

Recent U.S. experience in education has raised serious doubts about existing education policy. Not only is a huge percentage of the U.S. population functionally illiterate, but there are growing bottlenecks in the labour market owing to skilled labour shortages. Yet U.S. spending on education is enormous, and the heterogeneity of schools, the quality of the elite schools, the spending on research, the richness of diversity, all reflect well on U.S. education vis-à-vis the Canadian and European systems.

The unease within American education has never been greater as evidenced by President Clinton's initiative.[18] Even academics openly question the payoff of such enormous spending. The interest in the "expenditure-performance" relationship — from grade schools to business schools — has never been higher. Indeed, academic research on the factors underlying education performance show some remarkable challenges to orthodox policy conclusions. Spending more does not necessarily pay off. Moreover, Canada and the United States have school systems with far fewer days spent in school than under most other systems — about 180 days per year, compared to about 240 in Japan, 235 in Germany, 222 in Taiwan and Korea and 190 in England and Scotland.

Nowhere is the evidence of unease more obvious — because of the abundance of comparative data — than in scholastic performance in America's public schools. The standard measure of educational performance — imperfect and incomplete though it may be — is The International Maths and Science study (TIMSS). Of the 41 nations participating in the study, Singapore scored highest in both math and science, almost twice the level of lowest ranked South Africa, but also well ahead of such big education spenders as Canada (eighteenth) and the United States — twenty-eighth in math, and seventeenth in science (see Figure 5). Such ratings are obviously controversial, and national interest groups — teachers and education bureaucrats — find all kinds of reasons to criticize them.[19]

The International Association for the Evaluation of Educational Achievement reports that the average Japanese student outscored the top 5 per cent of U.S. students enrolled in college-prep mathematics courses. In chemistry and

FIGURE 5
13-year-olds' average score in TIMSS* (Int average=500)

Rank	Country	Math	Country	Science
1	Singapore	643	Singapore	607
2	South Korea	607	Czech Republic	574
3	Japan	605	Japan	571
4	Hong Kong	588	South Korea	565
5	Belgium	565	Bulgaria	565
6	Czech Republic	564	Netherlands	560
7	Slovakia	547	Slovenia	560
8	Switzerland	545	Austria	558
9	Netherlands	541	Hungary	554
10	Slovenia	541	England	552
11	Bulgaria	540	Belgium (F+)	550
12	Austria	530	Australia	545
13	France	538	Slovakia	544
14	Hungary	537	Russia	538
15	Russia	535	Ireland	538
16	Australia	530	Sweden	535
17	Ireland	527	United States	534
18	CANADA	527	CANADA	531
19	Belgium (W±)	526	Germany	531
20	Thailand	522	Norway	527
21	Israel	522	Thailand	525
22	Sweden	519	New Zealand	525
23	Germany	509	Israel	524
24	New Zealand	508	Hong Kong	522
25	England	506	Switzerland	522
26	Norway	503	Scotland	517
27	Denmark	502	Spain	517
28	United States	500	France	498
29	Scotland	498	Greece	497
30	Latvia	493	Iceland	494
31	Spain	487	Romania	486
32	Iceland	487	Latvia	485
33	Greece	484	Portugal	480
34	Romania	482	Denmark	478
35	Lithuania	477	Lithuania	476
36	Cyprus	474	Belgium (W±)	471
37	Portugal	454	Iran	470
38	Iran	428	Cyprus	463
39	Kuwait	392	Kuwait	430
40	Columbia	385	Columbia	411
41	South Africa	354	South Africa	326

+ Flanders; ± Wallonia
* Third International Maths and Science Study

Source: TIMSS

physics, advanced science students in U.S. high schools performed worse than their counterparts in almost all countries studied. In biology, they ranked dead last, behind such nations as Singapore and Thailand.

Other Challenges

Other problems cannot be overlooked. Consider the case of computers in U.S. and Canadian universities. There is a huge disparity in both the number of computer systems, and their value, on leading U.S. campuses compared to Canadian ones. Indeed, the University of Texas, the leading U.S. school, has more invested in its computer base than all of the top 10 Canadian schools combined! Moreover, U.S. schools have a higher percentage of mainframe and minicomputers, while Canada relies on a higher level of personal computers (55 per cent).

In Canada and the United States, the high-school dropout rate is extraordinarily high — as much as one-third of the total, and even more in certain provinces and among certain groups. High-school dropout rates signal a future problem in the labour market, where low skills begin the cycle of dependency on low-skill jobs and vulnerability to technological change. In the end, the unemployed increasingly face the prospect of being unemployable.

Spending priorities are also coming into question. Canada spends about $50-billion per year on education — $45-billion for formal education and $5-billion for adult training. Big firms undertake the largest proportion of adult training. Yet Canada's overall spending on adult education is only a fraction of other industrialized countries: total share of GDP in industrial training is 0.3 per cent, half that of the United States. Japan spends five times more than Canada on adult training, and Germany spends eight times more.

GOVERNMENT LEADERSHIP

A historic weakness in Canadian science policy has been the absence of a clear structure and of government leadership in promoting science-based innovation in industry, coordinating government-funded science, and developing a science culture in Canada. Unfortunately, Canada has no institutional base that can undertake long-term science policy and research. The Science Council of Canada, set up in the 1970s, served as a public-sector think-tank, but its influence rarely matched its promise, and it was abolished in 1992. The U.S. Congress has a highly influential American Office of Technology, Japan has its Science and Technology Agency and has launched a new initiative, the National Institute of Science and Technology Policy. Among Canadian universities, there is no equivalent, for example, of the Science Policy Research Unit at Britain's Sussex University. Science policy making has been dispersed, and instruments of science development have been given ambiguous mandates. In the competitive world of today, where technology is the key to shaping international competitive advantage, some priority-setting mechanisms must be established at the national level.

Canada has only recently raised the priority of its science and technology policy agenda. Although many think-tank groups — the Economic Council of Canada, the Science Council, the C.D. Howe Institute, The Hudson Institute and some business advisory groups — have attempted to promote the role of science and technology in Canadian public policy, but over the past two decades their actual impact on policy has been minimal. In recent years, however, the federal government has heightened the profile of science policy. There have been three thrusts to this: reorganizing the federal government departments involved, establishing science and technology advisory councils, and facilitating research consortia and strategic alliances.

Industry Canada

A major starting point for new initiatives came in the 1986 federal Throne Speech, which established a new government department: Industry Science and Technology Canada (ISTC). It was formally legislated and approved in Parliament, and given a clear mandate to:

> ➤ elevate science and technology to the top of the government's agenda
> ➤ encourage a commitment to international competitiveness and excellence
> ➤ create new attitudes towards commercially exploitable science and technology
> ➤ promote a technologically sophisticated industrial base
> ➤ coordinate policies and programs among industry, the science community and the government

Some outsiders saw ISTC as a Canadian-style equivalent of Japan's MITI. Clearly, this was not the case — Ottawa combines the "trade" function of government within the Department of External Affairs, with technology and industry operating as a separate departmental mandate. Over 20 years or more, the responsibilities of ISTC have been the subject of extensive bureaucratic review and reorganization. The labels attached to successive organizations — DREE, DRIE, MOSST, ISTC, and now, simply, Industry Canada — represent a depressing litany of attempts to balance the outward-looking supportive functions needed for growth in the sunrise sectors of the economy, with the politically expedient focus of job protection, government bailouts and subsidy support for sunset sectors. Moreover, Industry Canada also operates with a mandate to promote regional development, with all the attendant biases to support uncompetitive enterprises and direct scarce financial resources to sectors without a strong technological future.

What is clear from the operating structure at Japan's MITI, and increasingly from other jurisdictions, such as Britain's Department of Trade and Industry, or France's Centre Français de Commerce Extérieur, is that the key building blocks for Industry Canada must be strong sector-by-sector analysis, possibly modelled on the 15 Sectoral Advisory Groups for International Trade (SAGITs) first instituted in 1986 for the U.S.–Canada free trade talks.

Under this approach, public- and private-sector groups can work together to build the statistical analyses, data bases, assessments of comparative industrial structure, technological forecasting and various other tools that can serve as the basic input necessary to build a supportive climate for private-sector development and growth. The emphasis must be on continuous benchmarking, i.e., on international comparative performance, especially in the vital areas of productivity, technology innovation and export competitiveness.

Advisory Councils

Complementing these developments is a more dramatic, influential and long-term trend, namely the advent of science advisory councils reporting directly to political leaders. This idea was opposed by the senior echelons of the federal bureaucracy — a tell-tale sign of the traditional low priority given to science and technology in Ottawa, a preference for non-intervention in the economy and a concern over possible subsequent spending requests. The genesis of this lay in the creation of the National Advisory Board of Science and Technology (NABST) by Primer Minister Mulroney in 1986.

The formation of external advisory boards and the new ministerial initiatives at the centre of the science policy process have also extended to Canada's provincial governments. While Quebec had a science advisory board dating back a generation, Ontario was the first province to establish one with a major political leader in the chair, as in Japan. The initiative, known as the Premier's Council on Science and Technology, was announced in the April 22, 1986 Throne Speech as being designed "to steer Ontario into the forefront of economic leadership and technological innovation." Since 1986, every province has set up its own equivalent advisory council, each with a specific mandate to deal with public policy issues and develop science and technology plans, in both the short and long terms; and while their influence has waned, many public and private-sector policy changes grew out of the work of these councils.

Research Consortia

To compete in a global economy with rapidly changing technology, Canada needs to husband scarce resources and avoid wasteful duplication. Canada's companies are mostly too small to undertake generic research on their own. Few industrial research labs in Canada are of sufficient scale and quality to follow, let alone lead, global technological trends. The only viable alternative is research consortia — what some call strategic alliances — to drive the technology-commercialization cycle.

Industry Canada is the natural vehicle for initiating and funding a series of strategic technology alliances involving Canadian industry and universities. Funds could be reallocated from in-house government programs to non-government researchers committed to the types of investigations needed. Agreements have already been arranged in such areas as plastics and information technology, but the approach can be extended to robotics and artificial intelligence,

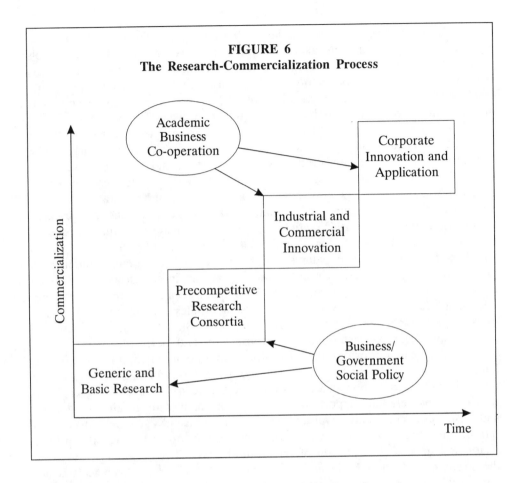

FIGURE 6
The Research-Commercialization Process

aquaculture, advanced materials, biotechnology and flexible manufacturing, to cite obvious examples. Agreements such as the one reached with the Canadian Plastics Institute are serving as prototypes for a number of other sectors — for research, training and technology diffusion.

Many areas of leverage are available. Consider Figure 6, which depicts the research-commercialization process. At the lower left is the generic and basic research block. This is where a country's basic technological infrastructure feeds into its industrial infrastructure. Support for basic research leads to precompetitive, non-proprietary research. At this stage, the aim is to support strategic technologies — those that are key to a wide band of industries and products — such as semiconductors. Physical infrastructure is important, but so too are the tools that build science infrastructure, such as access to advanced computer technology, journals and technical data, measuring and control instruments, and the like. For instance, the Japanese government translates over 20,000 technical journals and makes them available to Japanese and foreigners alike. The U.S. Congress was an early supporter of the Internet because it linked U.S. universities and research labs both domestically and internationally.

Alliances can play a key role here. Research consortia are neither novel nor confined to big markets like the United States or Japan. Denmark pools resources for export and technology studies, translation, industry fairs and overseas promotion of export sectors such as furniture. In Germany, the textile machinery association develops collective strategies for advertising, overseas markets, links to trade schools and research with technical institutes.

The Japanese are the leaders in research and technology consortia, yet even American companies now look with favour on this approach.[20] The Reagan and Thatcher administrations were supportive, and U.S. antitrust obstacles to industry consortia have been lowered by new congressional initiatives. Electronics and computers have been at the vanguard of the strategic-alliance approach. The first major U.S. initiative was the Semiconductor Research Cooperative, founded in 1982, with 35 sponsoring companies. It funds research, acts as a clearing house for technical literature, provides a first right to members for copyright and patents and funds up to 300 research students on priority projects. Equivalent consortia have sprung up in chemicals (the Council for Chemical Research, sponsored by 43 companies and 142 universities) and television (the Center for Advanced Television Studies, sponsored by four networks, five TV manufacturers and MIT). Detroit's Big Three have 12 research consortia working on such areas as electric cars and parts recycling.

Basic research provides the ideas for corporate research. In between are long-term applied research and specialized short-term applied research. The research-commercialization process (shown in Figure 6) is an evolving chain in which the institutional support for the research changes over time. In generic and basic research, funding typically involves close business-government collaboration, often with the government taking the lead in order to lever the private sector and to assume a portion of the front-end risk. This, of course, has been the strength of Japan's MITI and its Science and Technology Agency. It is not the level of funding per se that is important, but the speed of developing research consortia and the commitment to long-term horizons — of, say, 10 years or more. At the other end of the chain is the more applied side, where the key is closer business-university links, particularly for highly skilled personnel and mobility of personnel between companies and academic settings.

These efforts have two key goals: to bridge the gaps in the research-commercialization process and to build up a critical mass of first-rate personnel. They are succeeding, particularly in Japan, but also in the United States. Despite the perception that it is the Japanese who are most comfortable with the research consortia approach, it is the United States that has been the most aggressive in promoting research consortia, especially those involving companies and universities. Europe has a mixed record.

Canada has experimented with several large initiatives in research consortia, organized both provincially (most notably in Ontario) and federally.

Other federal initiatives — in copyright and patent legislation and support for science and engineering scholarships — reinforce the commitment to commercial R&D. But are they enough when other nations are devoting ever more resources to promote their knowledge-based industries? More radical proposals, such as privatizing governmental laboratories or fully deregulating university graduate programs, are not yet on the national science and technology policy agenda. Serious moves been made towards using the tax system to promote equity infusions into technology-intensive innovations, especially in small companies. However, the Chrétien government have made science and technology policy a highlight of their election platforms and budgets.

TECHNOLOGY AND FINANCIAL MARKETS

In recent years, the biggest shift in the growth of technology companies has been the availability of equity capital to finance start-ups. Technology companies, it must be remembered, have the unique characteristic that their main asset is intangible — the process of discovering, developing and nurturing intellectual capital across the technology cycle.

Traditionally, intellectual capital has been immensely more difficult to finance in Canada than the United States, mainly because the only real source of corporate financing was the banks. Canada's banks, nurtured in a highly protected regulatory environment, simply lend money on real assets (e.g., equipment, building and property), at a discount on receivables, or on whatever personal loan guarantees they could extract from entrepreneurs.

In the United States, by contrast, venture capital for intellectual capital has skyrocketed. The banking system is local or regional. Venture capital companies flourish. The NASDAQ Stock Exchange creates vehicles to finance intellectual capital. And then there is America's entrepreneurial and low tax culture, featuring mobility of labour, tolerance of failure, and easy mix of academic scientists, entrepreneurs, bankers, and financial engineers.

Canada's strides towards building an intellectual capital sector derive from several converging events. First, governments — led by Quebec but now supported by Alberta, BC and Ontario — have created a tax environment and public markets to make it easier to foster technology-intensive firms in public vehicles. Ottawa has responded as well, introducing tax measures to create various labour funds to channel equity capital into technology start-ups. Second, the banks themselves, largely in monopolistic control of the pool of Canadian savings (e.g., RRSP accounts and mutual funds), have themselves created technology equity pools to invest in technology start-ups. And third, because the chartered banks also own most of the investment banks, there has been a new appreciation of the advantages of high-technology start-ups — in underwriting fees, brokerage warrants, and instant wealth creation in a portfolio of investments where a few winners exceed financing a lot of losing investments (see Figure 7).

Related to these issues, of course, is the startling success of U.S. firms in the software and computer sectors, a field so overwhelmingly dominated by the Americans that foreigners drool with envy. Consider the simple reality: three companies that did not even exist 25 years ago — Microsoft, Netscape, and Oracle — have larger market capitalizations than GM, Ford or Chrysler. A 16-year old high-school drop-out might seem to many to be a family tragedy. A 16-year old whiz-kid writing a software program from a home computer may end up putting his entire family into a new condominium in Hawaii, thanks to a low salary and a few options in a take off company.

FIGURE 7
Canadian Venture Capital Investment by Location (1999)

Location	Financing #	Financing %	Investments #	Investments %	Amounts $ in Mil.	Amounts %
Alberta	75	8	176	12	250	9
Atlantic Canada	28	3	61	4	129	5
British Columbia	11	1	21	1	21	1
Manitoba	29	3	42	3	46	2
Ontario	258	26	480	32	1,257	46
Quebec	465	47	673	44	727	27
Saskatchewan	25	3	50	3	61	2
Foreign Countries	98	10	10	1	231	8
Total	989	100	1,513	100	2,722	100

Source: Macdonald & Associates Limited.

The incredible success of U.S. high technology companies has opened up a new debate about how to foster such ventures. Michael Porter has popularized the notion of industry clusters. Clusters are in fact an old concept, dating in history from the European city states and artistic centres like Florence under the patronage of wealthy rulers — from kings to the Papacy.

The great British economist, Alfred Marshall, identified the concept of clusters in the 1890s, explaining, for instance, how Sheffield, centred around the major Yorkshire coalfields, spawned steel making and specialized offshoots like cutlery. Today, cities are the natural clusters, building on a mix of institutions — universities, banks, consultants, research firms, suppliers and demanding customers. The real issues relate to the informal ideas, rumours, attitudes and knowledge, plus the intense sense of corporate rivalry, tolerance of mistakes, and desire to succeed in the entrepreneurial class and labour pool. As Marshall put it, in Sheffield steel-making was "in the air."

All countries experience the cluster characteristic — the United States' Silicon Valley is perhaps the best-known (or Hollywood in entertainment production). But think of Japan's Nagoya-Hamamatsu region in cars/electronics, or the City of London in finance, or in Paris or Milan fashion. In Canada, Ottawa's Nepean region has created a high-technology cluster, in part built around the prodigious success of Bell Northern Labs and numerous corporate spin-offs (see Figure 8).

THE CHALLENGE

Canada faces key challenges at both the national and the industry/firm level.

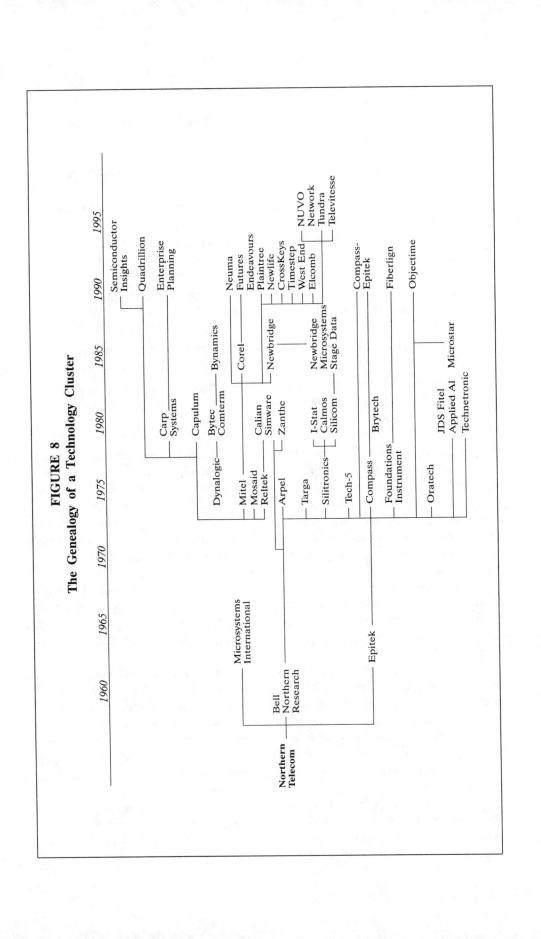

FIGURE 8

The Genealogy of a Technology Cluster

CHARLES J. McMILLAN AND EDUARDO M.V. JASSON

For the Nation

At the national level, addressing the following issues over the next few years is particularly important:

> - a corporate culture that is woefully weak in the areas of technological innovation and worker training
> - a labour-management climate that pays only lip-service to technological change and to science policy in general
> - a university system too often disdainful of commercial and private-sector linkages, precisely at a time when public spending on university education is well below comparable U.S. levels
> - a federal bureaucracy seized with fear over the embarrassment of the 1980s scientific research tax credit (SRTC) fiasco and the recent Human Resources and Development Canada (HRDC) scandal
> - a tax regime more accommodating to the real-estate industry than to knowledge-based research talent and innovative small companies
> - a political culture not yet grasping the implications of the knowledge economy — particularly the need for critical mass and world standards of evaluation

Another relative weakness of Canada's industrial structure can be succinctly summarized: the ratio of business start-ups to failures is too low. Too few start-ups are spin-offs from universities, large firms or research centres. Too few small firms emerge as medium-sized firms. Too few medium-sized firms become large companies, with appropriate strengths in finance, production, management and technology. Mitel, Corel, Spar Aerospace and De Havilland are all examples of companies that stumbled dramatically, underscoring the management pitfalls along the growth curve.

Our problems appear almost insurmountable. From where will innovation come? With a few notable exceptions, the truly innovative ideas do not flow from large resource companies, or from the foreign-owned sector (much of it under competitive pressure from Japan and Asia), or from universities and government laboratories.

From where will the required investment come? Funding inadequacies cannot be blamed on inadequate R&D tax incentives. It is widely believed, especially in the federal Department of Finance, that by all measures of tax credits, Canada is second to none in the world. Recent studies show that the issues are more complex: macroeconomic considerations, such as price stability and productivity, must be related to the capacity of the economy to produce the investment, and the capacity of the financial system to direct the funds towards growth enterprises developing science-based innovations.

Will Canada ever have a coherent strategy? There is no broad-based consensus underlying an industrial strategy, however defined. There is not even a general belief that realistic levels of resources must be devoted to developing one over the next five to 10 years.

For Industries and Firms

Canada is among the worst-performing nations in terms of a number of indicators of the technological intensity of industry: in the number and level of applications in information and computer technology; in the adoption of new methods of production, such as computer-assisted design and manufacturing (CAD/CAM) and robotics; and in the use of various modes of "mechatronics." These measures are all indicative of a lack of Canadian commitment to process technology — the special skills and engineering applications transforming the production process to increase flexibility and reduce cycle times. Other measures of technological sophistication include how closely the production process is being linked to the firm's strategic requirements, how many workers are skilled, how outward-looking is management and whether or not state-of-the-art capital equipment and production processes are being used. By most such measures, either on the input or output side, Canada is a serious laggard country.

New ways of thinking about individual organizations are required. In fact, the traditional stand-alone company research laboratory operating on "technology-driven" principles may well be obsolete, even in the United States and Japan. The alternative is a "business-driven" approach to research laboratories. As Drucker notes:

> The research lab may become a free-standing business, doing research work on contract for a multitude of industrial clients. Each client would then need a "technology manager" rather than a "research director" — someone who can develop business objectives based on the potential of technology and technology strategies based on business and market objectives, and who then defines and buys the technical work needed to produce the business results.[21]

The point is that science-based innovation requires different management strategies from those practised by Canada's traditional resource companies. Linkages with universities, strategic alliances for markets, venture capital for funding and public policy support for market entry and trade are central concerns. The style of management and the corporate values are outward oriented and growth demanding. Disruptive technologies and organizational methods are ever more threatening. The Internet challenge beckons as well. Few Canadian firms have the tools needed to meet these challenges.

CONCLUSIONS

The new game of science-based innovation represents a qualitative change in the ground rules of international competition. In many ways, it is a game of "chicken" economics — the basic decision is to play or not to play. It is like riding a roller coaster — once you have started, it is impossible to exit gracefully. It is a game of fierce stakes, of huge payoffs for winners and huge losses for losers — a game akin to Japan's sumo wrestling.

Science-based innovation, while still confined to only a few industrial sectors, turns the traditional wealth-creation theory on its ear. Firms on the leading edge of the technology frontier are not price takers; they are price setters (and temporary monopolists, because of superior technology). Returns to scale are not constant. They can be infinite, since the marginal cost of repro-ducing knowledge is theoretically zero. Imitators and followers are at a real dis-advantage; to fall behind may imply staying behind. Product innovation is closely linked to process innovation. The question of what to produce is linked to that of how to produce it. And finally, the complex interactions of customers, market rivalry and educational resources centre on the need for constant and relentless change, including cost-cutting innovation and technological upgrading.

In this sense, science-based innovation has become a never-ending match of wits, much like a championship game of contract bridge. There are three identifiable variables. The first, akin to the perspective of classical economics (land, labour, capital), is the lay of the cards. The players can only play the cards in their hand — in this sense, governments and industries are at the mercy of uncontrolled market forces and national resource endowments.

To this orthodox perspective is added the second tier of the bridge anal-ogy: how players play the cards. Here, strategy, cunning and guile all play a role (surrogates for international trade policy, political pressure groups and management processes and capabilities). But that relates to the third tier: how the competition plays the game — in the context of the cards played, of the competition's guile and strategy, and also of self-interest.

In a knowledge-based economy, it is the production of ideas that pro-pels growth. While the role of the private sector is important, so too, is that of government, not only through direct funding, but also through indirect aid, such as tax and research support, and incentives for university-industry cooperation. This approach amounts to what has been called an industrial strategy. It implies a model of an economy that is a far cry from the invisible hand of Adam Smith, or the laws of comparative advantage: it is a strategy for creating competitive advantage.

Technology-intensive exports are the key to economic growth; that is why trade in knowledge-intensive industries is so critical. Performance in trade reflects the effectiveness of a wide range of policies that form the basis for the new economics of wealth creation, and most of the countries of the developed and undeveloped world recognize it. This is the context that will determine Canada's future.

What matters is not only how Canadians play, but also how others play. That's one reason why *Business Week* in the United States and Britain's Department of Industry both produce an annual R&D scoreboard. Most Cana-dians (and governments) still believe a science and technology culture comes from public policy and government-spending programs. In fact, all the evidence from the world's technologically most advanced industries indicates that the key imperatives involve a judicious mixture of technologically literate employees, relentless adaptation to competitive forces in unfettered markets, and manage-rial and financial strategies that mix long- and short-time horizons.

Only slowly has science and technology moved to the centre of Canada's public-policy agenda. International competitiveness and prosperity issues are clearly driving the need for a fundamental rethinking of Canada's responses to develop science manpower, set science and technology priorities, allocate funds, assess the relative merits of competing institutions, and determine the role of the public and private sectors. Fortunately, the debate has moved beyond pointing fingers at past failures or inadequacies. Recent reports by the Conference Board of Canada, Industry Canada, the E-Business Roundtable, and Canada's provincial science advisory boards and industry associations have provided new impetus for a more coherent approach. Important federal programs have changed the national policy mix and improved the science-and-technology climate. New federal initiatives (2000 university chairs, R&D funding of science councils), new approaches to intellectual property (an updated patent policy, plant breeder's rights and software and book copyright), the Centres of Excellence programs, a national program for science and engineering scholarships, and tax incentives for business-university linkages, all add up to a very new approach to science policy.

For Canada, the familiar obstacles remain — low managerial recognition of the issues, interprovincial trade barriers and private sector inertia — in the resource sector, in manufacturing and in banking. Canada's resource sector, our traditional cash cow, has never been more challenged: the East-coast fisheries are all but bankrupt; more than a third of Canada's pulp and paper plants are almost 50 years old and technologically obsolete; rents from mining and some farm staples are at historic lows in real terms. Even the industrial base of Canada's heartland — automobiles and steel — is severely challenged as new global competition, especially from Japan and Asia, alters these capital- and technology-intensive sectors.

Whether Canada's public- and private-sector leaders are willing to seize the fundamental need to make science and technology a national priority remains an open question. The 1989 conference of Canada's science advisory committees produced an important document, *The Halifax Declaration: A Call to Action*. It expressed the sense of urgency and the need for action this way:

> No one seriously doubts the essential message. Canada is not maintaining its position. Canada is, in fact, slipping. No political rhetoric can disguise this fundamental reality.
>
> The strong consensus of the Halifax Forum was to adopt a real target, to accept a figure as a national goal, where all Canadian partners can and must play. A 2.5 per cent of GNP expenditure, achievable by the end of the century, would not be a federal target, a provincial wish or an industry approach. It would be a national target, involving real commitment, applicable to public and private sectors as well as to the Federal Government and to each Province.

Clearly, this target of 2.5 per cent of GNP was not met by the end of the century. Canada still lacks the kind of national commitment to R&D called for in the *Halifax Declaration*. We need such a national commitment now more than ever if we are to start moving in the right direction and catching up with our trading partners and competitors, rather than constantly losing ground.

NOTES

1. *The Economist*, "World Education League: Who's Top," 29 March 1997, pp. 21–23.
2. See the Annual Report, Catalogue 88-201, "Science and Technology Indicators," published by Statistics Canada. Obtaining reliable, consistent comparable R&D

data remains difficult, especially for up-to-date information. The situation in Canada is not helped by cutbacks to budgets for the Science and Technology Section of Statistics Canada, which will reduce the information available, and slow down the timing of publications. See also the annual reports from the Paris-based OECD.

3. G. Dosi et al., *The Economics of Technical Change and International Trade* (London: Harvester Wheatsheaf, 1990).

4. J.J. Brown, *Ideas in Exile* (Toronto: Penguin, 1965).

5. Wassily Leontief, "Domestic Production and Foreign Trade: The American Capital Position Reconsidered," *Proceedings of the American Philosophical Society* 97 (September 1953): 332–49.

6. *Technology and the Economy: The Key Relationships* (Paris: OECD, 1992). For a precise summary, see "Economic Growth: Explaining the Mystery," *The Economist*, 4 January 1992, pp. 15–18; and "Innovation: The Machinery of Growth," *The Economist*, 11 January 1992, pp. 17–19.

7. Charles J. McMillan, "Japan's Contribution to Management Development," *Business and the Contemporary World*, 4 (Winter 1992): 21–33; Kenichi Ohmae, *The Invisible Continent* (New York: HarperCollins, 2000).

8. M. Thistle, *The Inner Ring: The Early History of the National Research Council* (Toronto: University of Toronto Press, 1966).

9. Premier's Council on Science and Technology, *Competing in the New Global Economy* (Toronto: Queen's Printer, 1988). See also *Adjusting to Win*, chapter 4.

10. National Research Council, *A Practical Perspective* (Ottawa: Ministry of Supply and Services, 1987).

11. Raymond Vernon, "International Investment and International Trade in the Product Cycle," *Quarterly Journal of Economics* (May 1966): 190–207. See also Michael L. Dertorizon et al., *Made in America: Regaining the Productive Edge* (Cambridge, MA: MIT Press, 1989), p. 40.

12. Edward Mansfield, *R&D and Innovation: Some Empirical Findings* (Chicago: University of Chicago Press, 1984).

13. Sheridan Tatsuno, *The Technopolis Strategy* (New York: Prentice-Hall, 1986); Daniel I. Okimoto, "Regime Characteristics of Japanese Industrial Policy," in *Japan's High Technology Industries*, edited by Hugh Patrick and Larry Meissner (Seattle: University of Washington Press, 1986), pp. 41–42; Charles J. McMillan, *The Japanese Industrial System* (New York: de Gruyter, 1989), chapter 5.

14. *Revitalizing Science and Technology in the Government of Canada* (Ottawa: Supply and Services Canada, 1990).

15. Harry G. Johnson, *The Canadian Quandary* (Toronto: McGraw-Hill, 1963); for a thorough overview of the literature, see M. Blaug, ed., *Economics of Education*, Vols. 1 and 2 (Middlesex, U.K.: Penguin, 1969); Gary Becker, *Human Capital* (Chicago: University of Chicago, 1975).

16. Lawrence A. Uzzell, "Education Reform Fails the Test," *Wall Street Journal*, 10 May 1989.

17. See "Review of Education and Training," *Quarterly Labour Market and Productivity Review* (Spring 1989): 19–29.

18. Allan Bloom, *The Closing of the American Mind* (New York: Simon and Schuster, 1987); David Harmin, *Illiteracy* (New York: Columbia University Teacher's College, 1986); Jack E. Bowsher, *Educating America* (New York: Wiley, 1988).

19. Ibid.

20. See "Industrial Policy" *Business Week*, 6 April 1992, 70–76.

21. Peter Drucker, "Best R&D is Business-Driven," *Wall Street Journal*, February 10, 1988, p. 18.

Potential Responses to a Changing World

The final section of the book contains three very disparate views on how Canada should respond to the problems and issues raised in the preceding articles. Maude Barlow, in her article, "Global Showdown: The Future of Democracy in the Era of Economic Globalization," looks at the dark side of globalization, and provides some suggestions as to how concerned Canadians can avoid what Barlow sees as the negative consequences of the New World Economic order. In sharp contrast, John Crispo's look at "Canada's Prospects" says that Canada will have a bright future if we can embrace the New World Order and abandon many antiquated aspects of our economic and social policy. In many instances, Crispo advocates abandoning the very aspects of Canada's political economy which Barlow sets out to preserve at almost any cost. Finally, Tom Wilson, in his article "The Quagmire of Industrial Policy," instead of casting what could be seen as a deciding vote on these issues, confounds the discussion further. He argues, in effect, that Barlow and Crispo are both looking at the wrong unit of analysis. Wilson contends that a nation like Canada is simply too large and diverse to have a single set of economic policies. Wilson argues instead that individual provinces or regions in Canada should have the autonomy to set their own economic policies.

As stated in the introduction to this book, it is not our expectation that the reader would accept in its entirety any of these three views of how Canada should deal with the changes that have taken place in the environment in which our economy operates. What we do hope, however, is that reader is now better equipped to assess critically these diverse alternatives, to understand the assumptions upon which they are built, and to develop his or her own view of what path Canada should follow.

Global Showdown: The Future of Democracy in the Era of Economic Globalization

Maude Barlow

The Battle of Seattle

December 3, 1999 was not Charlene Barshefsky's best day. The U.S. Trade Representative was chairing the World Trade Organization's "Millennium Round" — a global meeting of 134 countries that she and WTO Director General Mike Moore had promised would launch the institution into the new century with a hugely expanded mandate. But things were not going well. Outside, many thousands of protesters trained in non-violent civil disobedience had brought the city of Seattle to a halt. Pepper spray and tear gas turned day into night in the downtown core, and dozens of helicopters hovered menacingly overhead. Police in full riot-gear engaged in hand to hand combat with black-clad youth; 600 were arrested.

Inside the Seattle Convention Center, the developing country delegates were furious at the high-handed treatment they were getting from the powerful countries of the North. Buoyed by the support from the streets, they banded together to demand a democratic process inside the meetings. The result was paralysis. Charlene Barshefsky, who had not slept more than an hour or two a night for close to a week, had lost what little capacity she has for subtlety. She had allowed this limited attempt at democracy, she declared, by inviting developing countries to participate. But the process had not worked to her satisfaction, she told an international press conference; she was now forced to exercise her authority and unilaterally impose her agenda on the meeting.

"Friendly" countries of the North and South were put into "Green Room" sessions with dissenting developing country delegates, where, seated in air-less rooms and not given coffee or even water to drink, they were badgered one or two at a time. Third World delegates were palpably furious. One stomped out into the hall, muttering that this was a "hell of a way to run the world."

Late that evening, Barshefsky received a call from a stern President Clinton. The meeting had become an international embarrassment. Three thousand journalists from all over the world were there to cover the liberalization of global trade and to sing the praises of the American economic miracle. Instead, they sent home stories about protesters, endangered sea turtles, sweat shops, child poverty, the plight of Third World farmers and demands for the democratization of the WTO. Clinton ordered his Trade Rep to close the mess down.

The news spread through the Convention Center and out onto the streets like an electric current. Protest organizer Lori Wallach of the U.S. group Public Citizen summed up the mood of the crowd: "The supposedly unstoppable force of economic globalization met the truly unstoppable force of democracy. The world will never be the same again."

The Birth of a Movement

The protest in Seattle was not a spontaneous event. An international coalition of environmental, public advocacy, cultural, human rights, public sector and labour organizations had worked for over a year to prepare for it and had drafted a civil society declaration on the WTO that was ratified by 2,000 organizations internationally. After intense negotiations, they agreed upon a common civil society demand going into Seattle best summed up by the slogan: "No New Round — Turnaround."

On the eve of the WTO meeting, the International Forum on Globalization held a "Teach-In" at the Seattle Benoroya Symphony Hall to a sold-out crowd of close to 3,000. Over 60 experts on economic globalization and the WTO presented information, analysis and strategy to a highly motivated, super-charged audience. Canadian groups were very involved from the beginning. Public meetings on the WTO were held across Canada, culminating in a Teach-In in Vancouver attended by 1,200 people. Thousands of Canadians joined the protests in Seattle.

As the world knows, this scene of protest was just the first of many: the World Bank meetings in Washington and Prague, the Organization of American States meeting in Windsor, Ontario, the Republican and Democratic conventions in the United States; the Olympics in Sydney, Australia. Similar protests have taken place in the Third World as well, although not well reported by the Western press. While the groups have a wide variety of concerns and refuse to be shunted into a structure or confined to one political camp, they have in common a deep and abiding criticism of economic globalization as it is unfolding in the world today.

For a growing number of people, particularly young people, governments around the world have become captive to global corporate forces that increasingly dictate all policy — economic, social and environmental. They fear that social programs and cultural diversity are under assault from the forces of privatization. They believe that international trade agreements like the WTO and NAFTA serve the transnational corporate sector almost exclusively, as do the major global financial institutions of our time — the World Bank and the International Monetary Fund. They watch with dismay as transnational corporations take control of the world's food supply, and more recently turn their attention to the world's water.

For many millions of people worldwide, politicians, political parties and elections have become irrelevant. Recent reports show that an unprecedented number of young Canadians, for instance, choose not to vote. This does not mean that they are uninterested in politics or their democratic rights, however. In fact, many are intensely involved in challenging the status quo, from the ideology they embrace to the lifestyles they choose. For them, a whole new form of political protest has to be developed, and they are creating it as they go. Most important for them is the need to directly confront these global institutions and the transnational corporations controlling them. They are practising what Indian scientist and activist Vandana Shiva calls "the politics of the new millennium" — the rise of civil society politics.

The Multilateral Agreement on Investment

Seattle was not their first success. The first successful global citizens' action was the defeat in 1998 of the MAI — the Multilateral Agreement on Investment. The MAI was a proposed global investment treaty, written by the International Chamber of Commerce and near ratification in 1997 by the OECD in Paris, when civil society groups in Canada got a hold of the draft text and leaked it to the world.

Essentially, under the MAI, governments would have agreed to give up all rights to set conditions on foreign investment, exposing their social programs, cultural protections and natural resources to global competitive forces. It contained a beefed-up version of NAFTA's Chapter 11, whereby corporations have the right to sue the government of another country if it introduces any legislation, even for environmental, conservation or health reasons, that could cost them lost future profits. All government "reservations" were to be subject to a "roll-back" clause; the clear intent of the MAI was the eventual elimination of government protections for any sector in which foreign investors might take an interest.

The civil society reaction was swift and highly organized; so much so that the government of France, which was the first to pull out of the MAI talks, issued a statement congratulating the international citizens' movement for the quality of its work. In fact, said the Cabinet report, the research, publications and arguments of this global alliance were so superior to what their own trade bureaucrats had produced, the French government ended up convinced that the activists were right and their own experts were wrong!

This campaign was successful for several reasons. First, the MAI was so outrageously undemocratic, that it half destroyed itself. Many non-trade politicians had never heard of it and were very uncomfortable defending it. Second, the groups brilliantly employed the Internet, sharing information, education tools, slogans and strategies around the world in seconds. These were groups that had been fighting the World Bank or trade agreements like the

GATT and NAFTA in their own countries and who had learned many skills to share with their international partners.

Most important, however, was the movement's political approach. Instead of assuming governments were potential allies, they agreed that governments were part of the problem. Instead of the traditional methods of lobbying and trying to influence their governments, they set out to form a powerful movement with its own power base, its own research capacity, its own demands and its own political analysis. In other words, this movement would form a power block of citizens and civil society groups that would rival the power block now established by transnational corporations and the global institutions that serve them.

What Kind of Globalization?

The power of this new movement is attracting a lot of attention from those who monitor shifting political trends. Professor Lestor Salamon of Johns Hopkins University is a leading expert on voluntary organizations and is engaged in a 40-country study of not-for-profit organizations. He reports that civil society groups are growing at such breathtaking speed, they are altering forever the political and economic landscape worldwide. He believes that this change is on a par with the rise of the nation state in the last part of the nineteenth century in importance, and notes that if all the resources of non-profit groups were amalgamated into a single country, it would form the eighth largest economy in the world.

Many in the media have tried to cast this as a clash of values between Luddites afraid of progress, on the one hand, and greedy business forces unconcerned about issues of human rights and the environment on the other. But it is not helpful to cast these as two totally competing ideologies. There are those in government and the business community who are genuinely trying to hear the concerns of civil society being voiced on the streets; conversely, civil society groups are filled with smart people keen to help build different institutions based on a more humane model.

Globalization of some kind is here to stay. The questions for us as we enter a new millennium are about what kind of globalization we are building and what it means for ordinary citizens in Canada and around the world. We will be judged in future times by what we have done with the great wealth and endless opportunities afforded us. The legitimacy of our economic system must be judged by the quality of life afforded the many, not by the licence provided the few. What are we doing to contribute to a balanced society in which the many benefit for the greater good of the whole?

Two Canadas

There is, indeed, much to celebrate. We seem in Canada, finally, to have left the recession of the last decade behind. Unemployment is finally being tamed, as is the debt. Canada has a burgeoning high tech industry, and our performers and artists are second to none in the world. In fact, Canadians in every walk of life are involved as leaders in international ventures, be they business, political, or humanitarian. Consumers finally seem to have some extra spending money again, and housing sales are up everywhere.

In the last decade, the number of millionaires in Canada has tripled. Corporate salaries have been growing at an average of about 15 per cent a year since 1995. In 1999, compensation for the top 100 CEOs in Canada grew by 112 per cent — regardless of whether their companies' profits rose or fell.

But there is another story. We are creating an entrenched underclass. Canada has the dubious honour of having the highest rise in child poverty in the industrialized world in the last decade — 60 per cent and counting. In Ontario, the number of poor children has grown by 116 per cent since 1989, the number of children in working poor families is up 103 per cent, and there has been an increase in the number of children living in unaffordable housing of 123 per cent. We have, in our own society, a real Third World; poverty has reached such proportions that we now have economic apartheid in our midst. People living in poverty live so differently from other Canadians that, in essence, they come from another country.

Ordinary workers are being hit from everywhere. In the same years that corporate salaries have skyrocketed, workers' wages rose just 2 per cent, less than the rate of inflation. Many Canadians are employed in the "precarious" workforce — part time or self employed, with no security, pensions, or benefits. A New York times cartoon said it best. A worker is being interviewed about the amazing number of jobs being churned out by the robust American economy. "Yes," he says, "it's great there are so many jobs available. I myself have three of them."

Workers have also been hurt by the dramatic drop in Employment Insurance (EI) benefits. Cuts of about $7-billion a year to the unemployed have been used to help eliminate the federal deficit. As a result, only one third of unemployed workers now receive EI benefits they have paid for, compared to almost 80 per cent in 1989. As well, federal funding of health care was slashed by $35-billion in the last decade and is only very slowly being restored in incremental stages. As well, the Canada Assistance Plan, which guaranteed every Canadian a dignified level of social assistance, was cancelled in the 1995 budget. In fact, spending on social programs, as a percentage of total federal government spending, is back to 1949 levels. The cuts to social programs and EI have been so deep that Standard and Poor says that the myth of a "kinder Canada" must be put to rest. For the first time last year, says the New York-based bond rating firm, Canada spent less on its elderly and unemployed than did the United States.

The cuts to EI and social programs have, not surprisingly, hit the poor far harder than the rest of Canadians. A new study by Stats Canada researchers John Myles and Garnett Picot shows that low-income families with children were able to stay afloat before these cuts; now they are drowning. But it is not just the already-poor who are affected. Study after study confirms that average Canadians are worse off than they were 10 years ago, and a new study from the Vanier Institute for the Family reports that Canadian families are currently facing the worst debt wall since the 1930s.

A Hardening Society

Canadians are reacting to these facts and this kind of attitude by retreating into themselves. In their annual survey of Canadians, the polling firm Environics has been mapping the Canadian mood for 17 years. In its 1999 year-end survey, Environics reported some very distressing long term trends. Canadians are experiencing a growing sense of insecurity, aimlessness, personal and social disengagement and a decline in vitality. In fact, the authors warn, for many Canadians, particularly young Canadians, this disengagement is expressed in a sense of growing nihilism. Middle aged people are pondering the legacy they are leaving their children, which they identify as a growing gap between rich and poor, rapidly increasing child poverty and environmental degradation.

The respondents are clear about the reasons for this new pessimism: a shredded social security network; technological advances that create inequality of job opportunity; and a system that does not work for ordinary workers, but rather for a small corporate elite best personified by the power and privilege of bankers. The report explains that, "These days, we worry less about unlikely threats like random murderers, and more about the very real threat of becoming dinner in a dog-eat-dog society."

It is hard to get excited by reduced government debts when people feel that the debt has simply been transferred to them personally. Many Canadians remember that it was the business press and corporate leaders who demanded that Canada reduce its debt or risk becoming a Third World country. The result, Canadians told Environics, is that in 2000 it is no longer Canada that is poor — it is Canadians. "Over all," says the study, "Canadians believe that in recent years Canada and its corporations have been doing well, but Canadians have not, and this discrepancy is taking a heavy psychological toll."

As a result, Canadians are becoming less "Canadian." They are becoming less interested in democracy and politics. Say the authors: "At one time Canadians felt they had power as citizens — one person, one vote. Now they feel that what little power they have is as consumers — one dollar, one vote." Fewer Canadians would now try to put themselves in other people's shoes or to understand where they are coming from. Growing numbers of Canadians say they would participate in the black market to avoid taxes and feel little compunction about ripping off the governments and corporations they see as ripping them off on a daily basis. Canadians are not opposed to paying taxes, they told the pollsters, but feel that the rich do not pay their fair share, so why should they?

This poll reflects the discomfort that many Canadians feel as we lose our historic social commitment to one another to "share for survival." Canada has adopted economic globalization on its terms, and Canadians are reflecting back the values of economic globalization in polls like this.

The Global Economy

In the new global economy, everything is for sale, even those areas once considered sacred, like air and water, health and education, genetic codes and seeds, heritage and culture. Increasingly, these services and resources are controlled by a handful of transnational corporations operating outside of any national or international law. The top 200 global corporations are now so big, their combined sales surpass the combined economies of 182 countries, and they have almost twice the economic clout of the poorest four-fifths of humanity. Of the 100 largest economies in the world, 52 are now transnational corporations. Wal-Mart is bigger than 161 countries. Mitsubishi is larger than Indonesia. Ford is bigger than South Africa. The new merged Time Warner-America Online colossus will have a market value greater than the economy of Australia.

A striking feature of economic globalization is the creation of a global monoculture. Around the world, North American corporate culture is destroying local tradition, knowledge, skills, artisans and values. Rich local culture is being replaced by a consumer culture at warp speed. A recent GenerAsians survey asked 5,700 Asia-Pacific young people to name their favourite food and drink. Their answers:

Australia:	McDonald's, Coca-Cola
China:	McDonald's, Coca-Cola
Hong Kong:	McDonald's, Coca-Cola
Indonesia:	McDonald's, Coca-Cola
Japan:	McDonald's, Coca-Cola
Malaysia:	KFC, Coca-Cola
Singapore:	McDonald's, Coca-Cola
Taiwan:	McDonald's, Coca-Cola
Thailand:	KFC, Pepsi

Another striking feature of economic globalization is the creation of dramatic inequality; an entrenched underclass is being created between regions and within every society in the world. The 225 richest individuals have a combined wealth equal to the annual income of half of humanity. The three richest people in the world have assets that exceed the combined gross domestic product of 48 countries. Eighty countries have lower per capita incomes today than they did a decade or more ago, and 200-million more people this year are living in absolute poverty (on less than $1 a day) than in 1987.

There is also a growing knowledge gap. The United States has more computers than the rest of the world combined. Everywhere, Internet access divides educated from illiterate, men from women, rich from poor, young from old and urban from rural. English is used in 80 per cent of websites, yet fewer than one in 10 people worldwide speaks the language.

Good Jobs, Bad Jobs

Millions of workers are losing out in a global economy that disrupts traditional economies and weakens the ability of their governments to assist them. They are left to fend for themselves in failed states against destitution, famine and plagues. They are forced to migrate, offer their labour at wages below subsistence, sacrifice their children and sell off their natural environment and personal health. Twenty-seven million of them work in the 850 Free Trade Zones around the world, soulless industrial parks where environmental, health, safety and labour standards are rare to non-existent, and workers who organize for a union often are blacklisted or worse.

A new global royalty now centrally plans the market, destroying lives and nature in its wake. Says writer and former World Bank official David Korten, "The world is now ruled by a global financial casino staffed by faceless bankers and hedge-fund speculators who move more than two trillion dollars around the world daily in search of quick profits and safe havens, sending exchange rates and stock markets into wild gyrations wholly unrelated to any underlying economic reality. With abandon they make and break national economies, buy and sell corporations and hold politicians hostage to their interests."

As even the World Bank admits, the deregulated economy has created a "boom and bust" financial crisis of increasing depth and regularity. All too often speculators are bailed out while workers are not. Education and health budgets are slashed to pay off debts. Children are taken from school. Millions lose their jobs. Real wages fall sharply. Mexican workers have lost 25 per cent of their purchasing power since NAFTA was signed in 1994, but Mexico created its first billionaires in those same years. The very remedies that the International Monetary Fund prescribes to nations in crisis — austerity, cutbacks to social programs, export-oriented farming — ensure that workers, domestic producers, and peasants pay for a crisis they did not create.

Even in the rich North, there is a Third World. In the United States, wage inequality has hit levels not witnessed since the Gilded Age of the 1890s, with the average CEO now earning 416 times more than the average worker. Wealth is gushing up to the top, and real poverty continues to rise, in spite of unprecedented wealth creation. North American workers are forced to accept lower wages and less secure working conditions or risk losing their jobs to non-unionized locations in other countries. Because of the relentless downward pressure on them, workers in the First World and Third World alike often cannot buy the products they produce. Last year, Nike payed more money to Michael Jordan to shill for the company than to all its Indonesian production workers combined.

The World Trade Organization

This is what exploded in the streets of Seattle. Many thousands came out to protest an international institution that would advance this system of entrenched inequality. The WTO protects corporations, not workers. Time Warner can sue China to block bootlegging of compact discs, but nobody can do anything about human rights abuses in China, the lack of a right to organize or the absence of minimum wage laws in that country, because to do so would constitute a barrier to trade.

The WTO has the power, and it has used it, to decide that environmental, health and safety laws and labour standards are barriers to trade that must be taken down. The state of Massachusetts was ordered by the WTO to stop prohibiting government contracts with companies doing business with Burma's infamous dictators. North American farmers cannot use pesticides like DDT, but they cannot keep products grown in other countries that use DDT and near-slave labour out of their markets.

The WTO and Food

The World Trade Organization has claimed intellectual property rights to the world's genetic heritage, and huge transnational agrifood corporations have redefined the role of agriculture. Where once it was about providing food for people, its purpose now is to provide profits for food corporations. In a stunningly short time, these corporate giants have decided that all the world's food is ripe for genetic engineering, and that the rules of international trade will discipline any government or society that rebels.

Farming, and the community way of life it has sustained, is becoming dominated at warp speed by a handful of transnational corporations working with governments to render farmers dependent on them for everything from their seeds to their fertilizers, pesticides and herbicides. Farmers around the world have become indentured slaves to companies like Monsanto, caught in an endless cycle of debt to corporations with no conscience and no soul.

The WTO and Water

Similarly, the private sector has recently identified water as the last great untapped natural resource to be exploited for profit. Giant transnational water, food, energy and shipping corporations are moving in to take control of the delivery of water services and kick-start the trade in "blue gold." Their goal is to render water a private commodity, sold and traded on the open market, and guaranteed to the use of private capital through global trade and investment agreements.

Water is already defined as a tradeable commodity in both NAFTA and the WTO; once the tap is turned on, it cannot be turned off without violating corporate rights established in these agreements. The WTO contains a provision prohibiting the use of export controls for any purpose, and NAFTA contains a clause giving corporations the right to sue for lost future profits if any government tries. Water services are also slated to become a commodity in the General Agreement on Trade in Services (GATS) — the services agreement of the WTO — under a new category called "Environmental Services." Once water is privatized, commodified and put on the open market for sale, it will not go to those who need it, but to those corporations, free trade zones and wealthy parts of the world able to afford it.

The WTO and Social Security

Another area of the commons ripe for commercial exploitation is social security. Services is the fastest growing sector in international trade, and of all services, health and education are shaping up to be potentially the most lucrative of all. Global expenditures on education now exceed $2-trillion, and global expenditures on health care exceed $3.5-trillion. Public education and health care have been targeted by predatory and powerful entrepreneurial transnational corporations who are aiming at nothing less than the complete dismantling of public education and health care systems by subjecting them to the rules of international competition and the discipline of the WTO.

Many countries have long ago privatized many of these services, forced by the IMF through structural adjustment programs. In order to be eligible for debt relief, dozens of developing countries were forced to abandon public social programs, allowing for-profit foreign corporations to come in and sell their health and education "products" to "consumers" who can afford them. Other countries, notably Europe and Canada, still have these services planted in the public sector and delivered on a universal basis. But the assault is on.

For the first time, all WTO countries have committed themselves to negotiating all services, including social security in the newly launched GATS negotiations. This would mean that, over time, for-profit transnational health, education, child and elder care corporations could be given the right to "establish a commercial presence" anywhere in the world and compete for public funding in these areas. Already, over 40 countries, including all of Europe, have listed education with the GATS, opening up their public education sectors to foreign based corporate competition, and almost 100 countries have done the same in health care.

The WTO and Culture

Yet another area of the commons is under assault by the WTO. Current WTO trade law basically subjects culture to all the disciplines of the agreement, including national treatment, most favoured nation and the prohibition against quantitative restrictions. There have been seven complaints concerning culture at the WTO since its inception; of those resolved, all have had the effect of limiting the right of a state to protect their cultural industries. The most significant was a 1997 ruling in which the United States successfully forced Canada to abandon protections of its magazine industry, even though American magazines make up 85 per cent of all magazines available at Canadian newsstands. U.S. Trade Representative Charlene Barshefsky said the decision would serve as a useful weapon against Canada's and other countries' protections of their film, books and broadcasting industries.

The United States is taking such a hard line because any exemption for Canada will set a negative precedent for other countries, especially in the developing world, where cultural protection is just emerging as an issue. The failed WTO Seattle talks do not mean the problems for the cultural community are over. In the ongoing talks under the GATS and TRIPs (Agreement on Trade-Related Aspects of Intellectual Property Rights), the telecommunications sector, including the Internet and Digital, broadcasting, patents, trademarks, and copyright law, are all on the table.

A System out of Balance

Simply put, economic globalization is not working for either the majority of the world's workers or for nature. Even President Bill Clinton, a big booster of globalization, has said that if the global market is to survive, it must start benefiting working families. In its 1999 Annual Human Development Report, the United Nations declared that global inequality had reached "grotesque proportions" and warned of a coming backlash if it is not dealt with. It also warned of a skewed value system. "Cosmetic drugs and slow-ripening tomatoes come higher on the list than a vaccine against malaria or drought-resistant crops for marginal land."

The UN warns that many transnational corporations have escaped nation-state law and no international governance, except global trade agreements, has grown up to replace now defunct domestic rules. Global conflict will almost certainly occur — "trade wars promoting national and corporate interests, uncontrolled financial volatility setting off civic conflicts, untamed global crime infecting safe neighbourhoods and criminalizing politics, business and the police." These are strong words from a moderate organization. So are these: "Ultimately, people and nations will reject global integration and global interdependence if they do not gain from it and if it increases their vulnerability. Pressure will mount to retreat to isolationism in economic policy, culture and in political priorities." The danger of not finding international solutions to the growing backlash is the potential development of more closed, xenophobic, even racist societies unwilling to cooperate on the burning issues of our day.

The UN has a number of recommendations. It says the world economy must balance concern for profit with concern for people disenfranchised by the global economy in all international institutions dealing with these issues, enforce a code of conduct on transnational corporations, support the development of technologies for the poor, and build in safeguards against the financial casino that has devastated so many millions of workers around the world.

We need to question the current economy that exists to empower the few at the expense of the many. The economy should serve people and community, and capital must be more locally rooted. The global economy should be reoriented from one of short-term speculation to one of long-term investment in the real economy that produces goods and jobs, not debt, and one that creates stability. Corporations should be held accountable for their behaviour, and all businesses should be required to pay their fair share of taxes, obey the law, and serve the needs of people and community by contributing to locally and nationally determined sustainable human development strategies.

Towards a New International Trading System

It is past time for a new international trading system based on the foundations of democracy, sustainability, diversity and development. We need a "Citizens' Agenda" as the beginning of a new democratic debate about the future of the earth and the future of its people and the next crucial step in the creation of a new international citizens' politics. To accomplish this, it is essential to radically cut down on the power of the WTO itself and reduce it to simply another institution in a pluralistic world trading system with multiple systems of government.

No new issues, especially investment, must be allowed into future WTO negotiations. The ability of WTO trade rules to overturn nation-state laws and practices that protect the environment, health, development and human rights must be eliminated, as must its current ability to override the Precautionary Principle in Multilateral Environmental Agreements (MEAs). Local, national and international environmental and social laws must be protected from unfair

challenges by ensuring that all relevant dispute fora are required to give a presumption of validity to national and local laws and policies and allow civil society groups to present before these dispute panels.

It is also necessary to create balance by giving more power to other, competing international bodies. To give crucial balance to the current power of the
WTO, we must create enforcement measurements in MEAs and other international agreements on social, labour and human rights, and remove the WTO
supremacy clauses contained in MEAs where they currently exist.

Further, as evidenced in Seattle, the world of international trade can no
longer be the exclusive domain of sheltered elites, trade bureaucrats and corporate power brokers. It must become accountable to legislatures, and all their
sectoral concerns, in every country around the world, and WTO negotiated
positions must come back for Parliamentary scrutiny and ratification.

To Protect the Commons

Trade is as old as humanity; fair trade rules can be a positive development if done with respect for other aspects of life. But in recent years, the
imperatives of economic globalization and international trade have overtaken
every other sphere of life. The World Bank turns commons into commodities,
and the WTO uses its massive power to enforce free trade rules on behalf of
commodity corporations.

Biodiversity, seeds, air and water are the bases of life, of the integrity of
ecosystems and of sustenance for human communities. Democracy, social
security and cultural diversity are the bases of human rights. As recognized by
the United Nations Universal Declaration of Human Rights, every person on
the planet has inherited the rights of "citizenship," including access to health
care, education, housing, meaningful work with fair wages, and human dignity.

We have an obligation to defend the integrity of biodiversity and its
components, as well the fundamental human rights of every person on the
planet. We must halt and reverse the commodification and privatization of the
commons, which is undermining the ecological survival of all species and the
basic needs of peoples everywhere.

To do so, it is time to determine which goods, services and sectors should
be subject to (fair) trade rules and which should not. Generally speaking, there
is a need to make a distinction between goods and services that are not part
of the commons, and those areas of life that define the commons. The list falls
into four broad categories. The examples are meant to be illustrative, and not
inclusive.

1. *Not to be traded because they are pernicious to the environment or public
   health, safety and welfare.* This list would include some goods that are currently traded and some that are not. It could include toxic waste, endangered species, nuclear technology and waste, armaments, and Genetically
   Modified Organisms. Trade institutions like the WTO could not use their
   power to overturn international agreements that limit or forbid the trade
   in these areas.

2. *Not to be commodified or traded for commercial profit because they are nec-essary for human and ecological survival.* This list would encompass the fundamental building blocks of life that are necessary for human and ecological survival. Air, genes and water belong to the earth and to all species; no one has a right to appropriate them or profit from them. All must be declared a public trust to be protected by all levels of govern-ment and communities everywhere, for all time.

3. *Not to be patented because they are the common inheritance of humanity.* This list would include those areas of life that might be traded under fair trade rules or are currently traded in traditional communities, but that must not be patented for private corporate use. It would include life-forms that are traded, such as seeds, plants and animals, and some that should not be traded or patented, such as genes and the human genome. It would also include patented drugs, such as generic AIDS drugs, that are sold and traded, but must not be patented for profit.

4. *Not to be subject to free trade rules and current international trade institu-tions like the WTO because they are the common public rights of all peoples.* This list includes those areas of the commons that are fundamental to self-reliance of communities and self-determination of peoples. In some cases, such as agriculture, citizens and their governments would likely encourage trade in these sectors. However, they would always retain the right to set fair trade conditions in order to maintain domestic control of the sector.

In other cases, such as health care, governments might declare these areas public rights and off limit to privatization altogether. In any case, no interna-tional trade agreement based on the current notion of free trade would have the right to overrule the democratically determined definitions in any of these sectors. They would include: food and agriculture, natural resources (except air and water), culture and heritage, health and education, and welfare and social security.

The time has come for this debate. When the world trading system was established after World War II, it was never envisaged that the very rights set out in the United Nations Universal Declaration of Human Rights would be one day privatized, commodified and put on the open market for sale to the highest bidder. Let us render unto Caesar that which is Caesar's. Let us take back under public, civil society control, that which is sacred to life on earth.

Conclusion

This must be the new face of globalization: international cooperation. While national and local governments must still have the right to provide public services, promote cultural diversity, and protect local food security and natural resources, increasingly we need to work together across boundaries to build a different world economy. We need a binding international legal framework for the conduct of transnational corporations to require financial transparency, stem capital flight, abolish offshore tax havens, tax financial speculation and make polluters pay for their crimes. International cooperation is needed for species, wilderness, water and air quality protection. It is also needed to start down the long, hard journey to end child labour and establish the right of every person on earth to dignified, decently paid employment.

Canadians, and peoples around the world, have the right to productive and fulfilling employment, to food, shelter, education, pensions, unemployment insurance, health care, universally accessible public services; to a safe and clean environment — food, water, and air; to the safekeeping of our wilderness spaces; and to develop and celebrate our diverse cultures and freely communicate our distinct experiences.

Canada's Prospects

John H.G. Crispo

T he twentieth century was supposed to be Canada's century but it did not quite work out that way. Although we have done well relative to most of the rest of the world, we have failed to live up to our potential. With everything Canadians have going for them, the challenge is to make sure that the twenty-first century is indeed ours.

Canada is the most blessed country on the face of the earth. We have plenty of clean air and water. We have bountiful land, space and resources. We have comparatively good communications and transportation systems.

On the social side, we have reasonably sound education, health care and social security systems. We are also a very civil and democratic society. One recent U.S. speaker referred to Canadians as "unarmed Americans with medicare." That certainly says a lot about us.

Finally, we have ready and secure access to the single wealthiest market on the globe. This is provided under the Canada–United States Free Trade Agreement (FTA) and its successor the North American Free Trade Agreement (NAFTA), and is reinforced by our mutual participation in the World Trade Organization (WTO).

With all these tremendous advantages, a natural question to ask is: why did the twentieth century not turn out to be our century? I wish I knew the answer, but I do not. Partially, I think, it is because of a lack of appreciation for what we've got and a tendency to take it all for granted. Added to this, over the past quarter of a century, has been our unforgivable propensity to be totally irresponsible on the fiscal front. We have been so selfish and short-sighted that we have allowed our politicians to bribe us first with our own money, then with that of our children and grandchildren, thereby running up massive deficits and debts and mortgaging the future of every young Canadian.

As if this is not enough of an indictment of our failures and shortcomings, I will cite two other contributing and mutually incompatible complexes at the end of this essay. If these complexes cannot be overcome, and fortunately there are signs that they can be, then my hopeful forecast for the future will have to be watered down considerably.

Before I get to the optimistic side of my overall outlook, I have to deal with three negative concerns — our constitutional debacle; a federal government that probably cannot be ousted, no matter how much it does wrong; and a potential inter-generational clash between a "more" and a "less" generations. After reviewing these problems, I will examine the economic outlook, and particularly our improving competitiveness, which is by far the brightest spot on our horizon, perhaps bright enough to offset the negative considerations just cited.

Let me briefly explain why these three negative concerns are so important even in solely economic terms. The greatest enemy of capital and investment and, therefore, economic and social progress is instability and uncertainty, things which have afflicted this country for some time now and are manifest in at least two of these three issues. These negative factors are hindering our ability to attract the investment needed to make our economy prosper.

Canada's Constitutional Crisis

It is hard to know where to begin when discussing Canada's constitutional difficulties, since they seem to have been with us forever, and seem as if they will last forever, as well. It fades in and out of the headlines, but is with us. However, if Quebec should decide to separate from the ROC — the rest of Canada — it will have such a profound effect on the future of the country that one has to begin with this very real risk.

I love this country so much, and so want Quebec to remain a part of it, that I have no problem whatsoever in recognizing that it does constitute a distinct society within our midst. First and foremost, this is so because it is the only province which represents the homeland of one of our two — or three, depending on whether one includes aboriginals — founding peoples. Not surprisingly, therefore, it has its own majority culture and language, its own civil code, its own pension plan, and other attributes of a different, but not special, society. The ROC has yet to recognize this basic fact of history.

What we are dealing with in Quebec is a form of tribalism which is increasing around the world. Whether in Yugoslavia, Rwanda, Russia, or wherever, ethnic, linguistic, nationalistic and religious groups are asserting their distinctiveness, either within or without existing national boundary lines.

If the ROC cannot accept this global phenomenon, and at least offer Quebec the gesture and symbolism of constitutional distinct society recognition, then I am afraid we will drive the province out of Confederation. Not because Québécois are not better off in Canada — after all, it is this country, as a whole, which has protected their culture and language from a flood of American homogenizing influences — but because of the emotional and irrational feelings which can so easily be aroused around the forces of tribalism.

Because the risk of Quebec separation remains so great, the ROC should take four steps before the next referendum campaign officially begins. Ottawa has already taken the first of these with the so-called "Clarity Bill." This bill clearly spells out the conditions under which the results of a vote for separation will be accepted as legitimate. These considerations include a fair campaign, a clear question and, obviously, a fair ballot and a clear majority.

The ROC should also agree on what it is prepared to offer Québécois, and particularly *Québécois*, so they will want to stay in Canada. I'm not at all sure distinct society status will be enough any more, but the ROC is not even in a position to offer this, despite the fact that most of our political leaders more or less conceded it in the last desperate moments prior to the 1995 referendum.

Even Prime Minister Jean Chrétien reversed his long-standing opposition to this concept in the dying moments of the campaign for the hearts and minds of Québécois. Yet all he has been able to deliver since then is a resolution of Parliament to this effect, something which falls far short of the constitutional amendment which is required.

However, if the ROC is to put its best foot forward before the next referendum, we must include such an amendment in the package we offer to Quebec, as difficult as this seems at this time. Quebec should also be offered a veto over matters pertaining to its culture and language so long as it respects our Charter of Rights. There should also be some more devolution of powers to the provinces — as in the case of retraining and skills upgrading — but only if it is offset by some centralization of powers in other areas, such as is long overdue in the field of securities regulations.

The third step the ROC should take, through Ottawa, is to tell Québécois what its conditions will be on the issues which will have to be resolved if Quebec decides to go its own way. Some of these conditions are fairly simple and straightforward, while others are anything but.

Among the former are the questions of currency and passports. As for currency, there is no way the ROC can stop a separate Quebec from using the Canadian dollar if that is its idea of sovereignty. As for passports, I hope English Canadians are big enough to allow those Québécois who are prepared to swear dual allegiance to retain their Canadian passports. After all, many of these people have fought hard to keep this country together.

Turning to two of the tougher issues: these are the questions of Quebec's membership in NAFTA, and of its territorial integrity. On the first, an independent Quebec is probably going to have far more trouble with the U.S. Congress than it is with either the ROC or Mexico if it wants to become a separate party to NAFTA.

As for its territorial integrity, Quebec's most serious problem is with the Cree and Inuit who occupy the northern part of the province, which was not part of Quebec when Canada was established. At the very least, I would insist that Quebec prove to the World Court that it is entitled to those lands if it chooses to separate.

The fourth responsibility the ROC should assume is that of examining its own prospects if Quebec does leave. I do not think these prospects are very good, if for no other reason than the fact that we will become a kind of East and West Pakistan if Quebec decides to split us asunder.

Worse than that is the fact that Ontario would end up with a majority of the votes in a Canada without Quebec. That is not going to sit well in the West, not to mention Atlantic Canada, and would require some delicate realigning and re-balancing to have any chance of proving acceptable.

JOHN H.G. CRISPO

When I speak in British Columbia, I invariably tell the audience that if Quebec pulls out, they should too. I say this because I believe British Columbia is the only province that could go it alone if it wanted to. It is a resource and tourist province which has little or no industry to protect, and could do very well on its own in the free trade world which is emerging.

I do tell British Columbians that, if they go, they should take Alberta with them. This shocks them until I explain that, in my own cynical and factious mind, it is not for Alberta's oil and gas, but for intelligent voters, of which British Columbia is desperately short.

The province which would have the greatest incentive to join the United States would be Ontario. It might have to do so in order to protect its massive auto industry, which is the industrial backbone of the province. I do not articulate these possibilities out of any sense of pleasure or to provoke. Rather, I think these are very real possibilities.

And, by the way, if Canada or the ROC does start to disintegrate because of Quebec, that province, or by then country, could also find itself falling into the United States, albeit very reluctantly. If that should happen, I want to be there when Quebec goes down to Washington to talk about bilingualism. If Quebec gets anywhere on this subject, the Americans are likely to tell them to speak Spanish.

It could be sobering for Quebec to hear about the ROC's terms if Québécois decide to go it alone, and it should be equally sobering for the ROC to contemplate its fate without Quebec. My faint hope is that these twin sobrieties could lead both sides to come to their senses before it is too late.

Otherwise, we may as well admit that we are on a mutual suicide course. Quebec may well suffer more than most of the ROC, but we will all pay dearly for the break-up of the greatest country the world has ever known. It is hard to believe we would knowingly do this to ourselves; but stranger things have happened, and current world trends are anything but encouraging.

The Liberal "Monopoly" in Ottawa

When I was an undergraduate student, I was taught that parliamentary government — indeed any democratic government — works best when there is an effective opposition. By that test, we are confronted by a hapless and hopeless situation on the national political scene, because we now have in power a government that cannot be defeated, no matter how many mistakes it makes. The nature and scope of the Liberals' victories in the 1997 and 2000 general elections made this abundantly clear.

The issue is not just the size of the Liberals' majority, but rather the fact that the opposition is so divided and fragmented that there is no viable alternative to turn to. The Bloc divided up Quebec with the Liberals, while Reform (now relabelled the Canadian Alliance) and the Tories split the right-wing vote west of the Ottawa River, and the Tories and NDP split the anti-liberal vote in Atlantic Canada, thereby allowing the Liberals to divide and conquer with little or no effort.

This situation means that the Liberals can do virtually anything they please, right or wrong, and get away with it without any fear of significant repercussions. The unbelievable and hypocritical circus they put us through over the GST bears out the fact that they can do whatever they want with almost complete impunity.

But let me not leave you with the impression that the Liberals have done nothing right since coming to power. They have made great progress on the fiscal front, and they have found their way back to their roots on free trade, and are doing a great job on that front. In the latter context, just thank whoever you want that they do not take their election promises seriously. Remember, these were the folks who were not going to sign NAFTA unless they got major concessions, none of which they secured.

But against these positives must be arrayed their totally misleading 1993 election campaign, and the arrogance and incompetence they have displayed on so many fronts since then. One only has to think of the Airbus debacle, the defence disgrace, the Toronto airport fiasco, or the Human Resources Development Canada scandal to realize that the Liberals know that they do not have to worry about any kind of accountability or responsibility.

So Canada's natural governing party may, by default, become its semi-permanent governing party. While this eliminates some instability and uncertainty about the future, it is hardly encouraging unless something as dramatic as a change in the leadership of the Liberal party takes place. Even I would have to vote Liberal if they got rid of the "little guy from Shawinigan" and put Paul Martin in his place. But do not hold your breath on this one, because this little guy would not move over to save his party, let alone his country.

However, the arrival of Stockwell Day on the scene as leader of the new Alliance Party could change the national and political stage dramatically. He brings a fresh, new, young face, is very articulate, and has a great TV image. Contrast that with the Cret — my only name for the Chicago Style patronage king who now leads our country — and you have the makings of a potential election upset if Day can use his position of Leader of the Opposition to demonstrate to more moderate Canadians that he is a viable candidate for Prime Minister. The results of the November 2000 election show he will have an uphill struggle, however.

On the negative side, Stock — as his friends like to call him — holds some pretty extreme views on some issues, and can be quite irresponsible at times. In addition, he will likely always end up with some candidates that will make his views look quite mainstream by comparison.

The Potential for Inter-generational Conflict

Another serious problem facing this country arises from the outlook of its younger generation. While I was fortunate enough to be born into the More Generation, today's youth now know that, absent some fundamental change, they are clearly part of the Less Generation.

Today's youth are paying more for their higher education, and yet they are getting less for it, at least in terms of their employability. Even when they find work — work which often underemploys them — they have little or no income or job security, compared to what my generation enjoyed in our prime years of life and work.

The range of reaction to this situation which I see among my students is immense. At one end of the spectrum, one of my male students alluded to the now-familiar adage that women have to work twice as hard to get half as far. He then added that he would have to work at least twice as hard as his father just to as well as his father and that he intended to do just that.

At a point part way along the spectrum, several students referred to the difference between standard of life and standard of living. They said they were quite prepared to settle for a lower standard of living as long as they could have a higher standard of life, especially in terms of less work and more leisure.

At the other end of the spectrum, there is rising anger and/or frustration among a few young people. These feelings could spread quickly, however, if, as I anticipate, young people find themselves working hard only to receive less than their parents are receiving in retirement by way of pension benefits.

American statistics reveal a massive transfer of public funding from the young, who have no lobby to speak of, to the elderly, who have one of the most powerful lobbies in the United States. This transfer has been in the form of reduced spending on education and increased spending on medicare and pensions. I do not think this transfer is anywhere near as dramatic in Canada, but it is still a potential imbalance with which we must come to grips. What compounds the unfairness involved in all of this is that our generation has set itself up for retirement, in part, by running up massive government deficits and debts, thereby mortgaging the future of our children and grandchildren.

Unless the economy performs remarkably well over the medium to long term, the younger generation may well insist on less public funding of the medicare and pensions which members of my generation are either looking forward to or are already receiving. I, for one, could not blame them for doing so. The priorities of my generation have led us to invest more in the past in the form of higher benefits for retirees, whereas today's young people would invest more in the future in the form of more education and opportunity for young people.

The Economic Outlook

It is now time to look at the more optimistic side of our future. Economically, this country's fortunes are looking up because it is becoming more competitive under the pressure of freer and freer international, though not domestic, trade.

Nothing makes me prouder than the several years of my life I devoted to fighting for the FTA with the United States. That agreement, plus the subsequent NAFTA and WTO agreements, have removed the artificial protection most of our industries enjoyed for over a century. By and large, Canadian industry has responded well to the resulting competitive challenge, so well that booming exports continue to be the leading growth sector in our economy.

The importance of becoming more competitive cannot be overstated. It is the key to virtually everything else. We cannot, for example, produce more high-paying, meaningful and secure jobs, grow our economy, or increase our standard of living unless we become more competitive. Enhanced competitiveness is also the key to generating the wherewithal to reduce our still massive government debts, to repair our deteriorating infrastructure, to restore our threatened environment, and to preserve a reasonably generous social security system.

Becoming more competitive is as much a public- as a private-sector challenge. In terms of private enterprise, we know our firms must become more efficient, innovative and productive, must treat the customers as kings, and must stress price, quality and service. Domestically based firms must find a market niche and then move abroad, while subsidiaries of foreign firms must win North American, if not world mandates, for goods or services they can produce more effectively than other affiliates of their parents.

Less attention is focused on the equally important challenge of getting our public policies right so that they help Canada become more competitive. Essentially, this requires that we put in place a framework of sane, sensible and sound public policies which allow the private sector to plan ahead with certainty and confidence.

One of the surest ways to move us in this direction is to insist on competitive assessments of everything our governments have done, and intend to do, in every area of public policy. With respect to the environment, for example, while there are many legitimate concerns about the effects of economic development on our environment, we should not just have environmental assessments, but rather combined competitive and environmental assessments, so that we are forced to weigh the competing and conflicting interests which are involved, and to make the appropriate choices and tradeoffs.

The Public Policy Agenda

Our biggest challenge on the public policy side remains creating a sound fiscal foundation. The Liberal government in Ottawa is slowly reducing the size of our national debt. However, a good part of the progress the federal government made on the fiscal front was made at the expense of the provincial governments, as it downloaded program costs to them while insisting, where it could, that they maintain existing high standards of service.

Now that our national fiscal position is improving, governments — especially the Liberals in Ottawa — are hearing conflicting views about what to do with their growing surpluses. Some voices are calling for debt repayment, others for tax relief and still others for the restoration and expansion of government programs ranging from health care to subsidies for athletes. What we must bear in mind, however, is that our current fiscal success is driven by an unprecedented North America-wide economic boom, and that our accumulated debt still represents a massive intergenerational transfer.

In the future, the biggest savings at both the federal and provincial levels of government are going to have to be derived from a more rational approach to all forms of social security. Three principles should underscore this rationalization process, the first being that no one in Canada should suffer through no fault of their own. We are too wealthy a society to take any other approach.

The second principle is that every able-bodied Canadian, in receipt of social assistance of any kind, should be obligated to be doing something either to improve their own prospects or that of their communities. Retraining and upgrading fall into the first category, while something like workfare falls into the latter category. I am aware that part of the costs of both these sets of approaches involves subsidized day care, something which has to be included in any package of proposals, to help people avoid the welfare trap in which so many of them are now enmeshed.

The third principle involves a clawback on all forms of social assistance, the amount of the clawback depending both on the individual's total income at the end of the year and on some sort of formula which ensures that the clawback does not entail such a disincentive to return to work that it is perverse in its effect.

Before leaving the fiscal front, I have to add a word or two about our present income tax system. I have always favoured a progressive income tax system based on the ability to pay principle. However, I am now prepared to contemplate just about any alternative to our current tax system, because it fails all three of the tests it should be able to pass. It is not efficient, but rather is an expensive boondoggle for government bureaucrats and tax accountants, consultants and lawyers.

Neither is it fair nor simple, since it is loaded with loopholes that only the wealthy can afford to pursue. The major consequence of all this is that the individuals who are the worst off are those who work for a straightforward salary or wage.

I'm so fed up with our burdensome, unfair and complicated income tax system that I am now more than willing to contemplate a simple flat tax with a generous enough exemption to ensure that those at the lower end of the income spectrum pay nothing. If we included all income under this tax, and made it revenue neutral, the rate would be somewhere around 25 per cent.

If such a tax system could be instituted, we might eliminate many of our present compliance problems as well as the aforementioned legions of government bureaucrats and tax accountants, consultants and lawyers. If these people ended up doing something productive — that is hardly what they are doing now — it would add significantly to our gross national product.

Another contentious issue arises from the need to rid our system of discriminatory employment practices. These are not only morally wrong, but economically wasteful, because they do not allow us to take maximum advantage of every individual's potential. But to ensure equal access and opportunity, which should be our objective, we need not, and should not, resort to affirmative action in the form of preferences or quotas. These things are merely reverse discrimination.

On the medicare scene, we are in an impossible situation, because there is no real limit to either the demand for, or supply of, health-care services in Canada. This results in an open-ended non-equilibrium situation which can easily run out of control. At the very least, we must take advantage of smart-card technology to stop the double doctoring, drugging and testing. This can be done both while protecting confidentiality and improving health care by avoiding the use of excessive and incompatible treatments and drugs.

More home-care and outpatient services must also be promoted, as well as the greater use of nurse-practitioners to take over some of the less demanding tasks now undertaken by highly paid doctors. To be more controversial, I should add that, with a rapidly aging population whose medical costs are sky-rocketing, we are going to be forced to give serious consideration to some form of voluntary euthanasia, which I favour for both economic and moral reasons.

Turning equally briefly to education, we have to introduce more choice and competition into the system in order to improve price, quality and service. The best way to do this — starting with our universities and then pushing it down through the entire system — is to finance education through income-based vouchers available at the post-secondary level to the best students applying on a provincial basis, based on their family's incomes.

One could go on and on, reviewing one socio-economic political challenge after another. In each case, all one has to do is think of the solution which is most cost effective and, therefore, most beneficial to Canada's competitiveness, allowing for any trade-offs which have to be made for environmental, social or other non-economic reasons.

Conclusion

Currently, Canada's prospects are looking better than they did even a short while ago, especially on the economic front. There do remain some serious non-economic obstacles, including the lack of mutual enlightened, self-interest on both sides of the Quebec question; the virtual monopoly the Liberals hold over political power in Ottawa; and the looming inter-generational crisis.

Reasons for optimism abound in both the private and public sectors of the economy. To start with the latter, real progress has been made on the fiscal side. It will still take many years to make a significant dent in some of their massive debts, but at last we are moving in the right direction. One can only hope and trust that we move fast enough to make some real progress on debt reduction before the next recession hits.

Most of our governments are also reducing their bureaucracies and moving towards more privatization and deregulation. All of this is to be commended, provided it does not lead to unwise sacrifice of our environmental, social and related standards.

As for the private sector, success stories abound almost across the land. Despite the dire predictions about the supposed decimation of our manufacturing industries because of free trade, many of these industries are booming. In autos and auto-parts, we are so far beyond the minimum levels of shared production which we are entitled to under the Auto Pact, as incorporated into both the FTA and NAFTA, that it is nothing less than staggering.

In the West, the chemical industry is growing apace with the oil and gas industries, and prairie farmers are doing extremely well. In many parts of the country we are achieving major new levels of performance and production in everything from entertainment to software. Wooden furniture manufacturing has even made a comeback in Ontario and Quebec.

Many factors help to explain these encouraging developments. Two of the most important are relatively low inflation and interest rates. Also very significant has been a low Canadian dollar, an advantage which will lessen if we continue making progress as we have been, progress which must inevitably be reflected in a higher exchange rate.

To get where we should be, there are two incompatible complexes we must reverse. The first is a still lingering and unwarranted inferiority complex about our ability to compete. Despite all the progress we have made competitively, many Canadians continue to feel that we cannot take on the Americans — because they are so good — or Mexico and other developing countries — because they are so bad in terms of their wage rates and labour standards. The fact is that we are doing well almost everywhere our entrepreneurs compete, and it is time Canadians recognized just how great we can be.

The second complex is reflected in an insupportable entitlement mentality which features benefits and rights as distinct from obligations and responsibilities. It's almost as if the only universal consensus which exists in this country is something to the effect that while it is time for governments to cut back and restrain themselves, it should not be in any way at my expense. Such selfish and short-sighted thinking may be receding, but not nearly fast enough.

The twentieth century was supposed to be Canada's century, but we blew it in the last 25 years. This century can still be ours if we get over the kinds of complexes I have just referred to, and put into effect the types of policies I have long advocated, and covered, ever so summarily, in this article.

The Quagmire of Industrial Policy

H.T. Wilson

The Chinese are reported to have a way of writing the word "crisis" by using two characters, one of which signifies "danger," the other "opportunity."

Louis Wirth

When you find yourself in a deep hole, it may be time to stop digging.

George Will

Our first duty is to become clearly and resolutely aware of what divides us. Then it will become possible to unite what can be united.

Daniel Johnson

AN APPROACH TO THE PROBLEM

The rise of the modern nation state, first in the advanced countries, and more recently throughout the world, provides a strong argument in support of the view that the "correct" direction of development is from the less to the more territorially, regionally and ethno-culturally inclusive unit of social organization. Nevertheless, there are many examples that challenge this view, not the least of which are those countries that came about as a consequence of colonialism in Africa and elsewhere.[1]

More important for the purpose of this article, however, is the break-up of the USSR, Yugoslavia and Czechoslovakia, and Quebec's desire for more autonomy. Even the existence of the European Union (EU), which obviously supports the conventional view, nevertheless provides evidence of the desire to resist integration. It is expressed in demands by heretofore suppressed or discouraged minorities within or across member states for recognition within the new transnational arrangements.[2]

These examples seriously challenge the view that equates progress with greater inclusiveness. They suggest that there are clear limits to size, scale and inclusiveness for any society desiring an industrial policy that is more than simply a passive endorsement of free trade and free markets. Failure to develop an industrial policy in the United States, for example, is not simply a consequence of conservatism with its bias towards free markets and free trade, or even of American institutional history and ideology. It is also due in large measure to the sheer size, scale and complexity of that nation.

Because Canada is so closely tied to American institutions, values and goals — even to the point of trying, since 1984, to systematically undermine its own economic and political-legal institutions in favour of miniaturized mirror-image American equivalents — it is very difficult to take a different tack from the United States in the matter of industrial policy.[3] Neither is Canadian economic independence helped by substantial American ownership and control of Canadian industries and businesses and adversarial federalism featuring what often amounts to no-win games between the provinces and the centre.

The North American Free Trade Agreement (NAFTA) adds yet another dimension to the problem, because American, and other foreign-owned, companies no longer need to locate in Canada to serve Canadian markets. Canadian companies are now persuaded to relocate either in the United States or (with their American cousins) in Mexico. This agreement will only serve to consolidate this line of development by encouraging even greater institutional imitation, while decreasing still further the amount of room we have in which to manoeuvre.

A DIFFERENT VISION OF CANADA

Instead of stubbornly trying to maintain the established arrangements with cosmetic or piecemeal modifications, we must undertake major structural changes. Such changes are, in fact, the sine qua non of economic renewal. Many "ordinary Canadians," in their support for the view that Quebec is a distinct society, in their recognition of the rights of the original peoples, and in their demand for a social charter that includes a real commitment to the goal of full employment and the right to a basic income, are indicating that they want such changes. But in order to achieve and reconcile constitutional, societal and economic goals, it will be necessary to embark on industrial policies that both proceed from, and are fitted to, the appropriate unit of socio-political organization.

Present structural impediments, proceeding in large part from the nature of Canada and its institutional development as a finance-capitalist, public-enterprise country, combined with emerging cultural and regional factors and the reality of NAFTA, the General Agreement on Tariffs and Trade (GATT) and the World Trade Organization (WTO), virtually guarantee that we shall **never** have a Canadian industrial policy as such.[4] The present national state level of inclusiveness is simply incapable of overcoming the combined impact, now and in the future, of the above factors. While the more inclusive (national) unit is becoming progressively less viable or concrete, the internal (provincial or regional) units — led by, but not confined to, Quebec — are becoming progressively more so.

Happily, this crisis is as much an opportunity as it is a danger for Canada and Canadians. Our very history and confederal character predispose us towards precisely the sort of solutions that are being demanded by increasing regional and provincial concreteness. We are fortunate indeed to have a federal and confederal history as a foundation for our continuing efforts to reconcile the realities of two founding peoples, multiculturalism and regionalism, within the desire for national existence and national purposes.

Because we have very sensibly insisted, since at least 1960, that Quebec's powers be couched in the language of federalism — that is, in terms that make them potentially available to all other provinces as well — it was possible, at least until the Meech Lake and Charlottetown debacles, for Quebec to gain powers formerly exercised (if at all) by the federal government without unduly irritating the other provinces. As some provinces or regions become increasingly concrete relative to the more inclusive whole, their very ability to deal with differences and conflicts that have become dysfunctional for the more inclusive unit depends upon this approach being taken up by other provinces or regions besides Quebec.

That this is, to some extent — and increasingly — an objective process is evident from the outcome of the 1997 and 2000 federal elections. Even in the face of an electoral system which is set up to facilitate brokerage between provincial and regional interests, the verdict was clear. Other provinces and regions are following Quebec's lead, becoming more concrete relative to the centre as the issues that divide them become no less, and often more, significant than those which unite them *as Canadians*.

This is a far more accurate reflection of the state of Confederation today, and underscores the fact that we can be *both* divided and united on key issues *and still remain Canadians*. In my view, this sentiment is just as strong among the large majority of supporters of the PQ and BQ as it is among those who supported the Reform Party and now support the Alliance in the Western provinces. What is called for, most believe, is *reconfederation*, not separation. This will become both more necessary and more feasible as the provinces and regions continue to adapt their industrial and business policies to the NAFTA and emerging Free Trade Agreement of the Americas.

If we focus our attention on Quebec, Ontario, the Atlantic provinces, the Western provinces and the recently created northern territory of Nunavut, we see that in every case, a regional or provincial approach has begun to manifest itself, not only as a vehicle for governmental coordination, but also to foster effective responses to emerging continental and global realities. The emerging capacity for inclusiveness in these jurisdictions offers us the best hope of holding back or, at the very least, slowing down the process by which functional differences and conflicts become dysfunctional, and are thereafter converted into structural contradictions that threaten to destroy the country. We can neither ignore these developments nor respond to them in a piecemeal fashion. The only way to preserve the nation is to transform it structurally.

While this certainly will not bring Canada to an end as a nation state in international law, it will effect transformations in its governance and political economy sufficiently to allow the emergent provinces and regions to abrogate NAFTA, and renegotiate their respective (and aggregate) relationship to the

WTO and its signatories.[5] It would meet Quebec's demands for something that is somewhere between sovereignty association and outright independence, allow for the emergence of the "regional nationalism" of both the Western and the Atlantic provinces, and give recognition to the demands of the original peoples.[6]

Provincial and regional institutions and arrangements are either already in place, or are emerging rapidly to take on the broader functions and activities that are required. Apart from Quebec, which has had a head start of 25 to 30 years over the rest of Canada, there are the more recent *Premier's Council Reports* in Ontario, which, with justification, treated that province as an economic entity in its own right 15 years ago.[7] The same can be said for the 20-year-old regional coordinations achieved by the Western provinces, and the more recent efforts presently emerging in the Atlantic provinces and among the original peoples.

Yet even while they seek out relations with other countries, these emerging jurisdictions will need to give priority to relations with one another, if they are to develop effective industrial policies.[8] Nothing makes NAFTA a more ridiculous document for Canada and Canadians than the fact that it was brought into force while the provinces and regions of Canada continue to have substantial barriers to interprovincial trade. Here also, present trends are encouraging, but far from complete.[9]

When looking at various provinces and regions as emerging concrete wholes within established, more inclusive wholes, it is necessary to recognize that their approaches to the reconciliation of differences and conflicts will take many different forms. There is no one "best way." The fact that geographic, social, cultural, ethnic, racial, historical-institutional, economic and political factors come together in diverse and often unpredictable ways only underscores the differences between provinces and regions. These differences can be expected to increase rather than decrease, whether or not these units become the dominant form of economic and political structure in Canada.

The always-present and thoroughly legitimate fear of being absorbed into the United States will no doubt motivate many Canadians to say that the argument put forth here will facilitate just such a process — indeed, that it will make it a foregone conclusion. My response to this parallels my suspicions with regard to the claim that progress in the social and political fields demands ever-greater territorial and demographic inclusiveness, and for many of the same reasons. The view that we must hold Canada together at any cost, and by any means short of force and violence, not only for reasons of loyalty and nostalgia, but also to prevent absorption by the United States, is thoroughly misguided.

In the first case — loyalty and nostalgia — we totally ignore the flexible and evolutionary nature of our economy and institutions when we imagine that Canada must either stay together in its present form or "fall apart." The metaphor of "falling apart" demonstrates little, if any, confidence in our history and capacities, and treats the present confederation as a static arrangement. This pessimistic assessment, which arises out of the tendency to regard institutions as nothing more than organizational forms, accounts for the present rigid and inflexible thinking of most of our current leaders, most of the time.[10]

The claim that the alleged "break-up" of Canada will facilitate, if not render inevitable, its absorption into the United States also ignores history and institutional development, but in a different sense. It can be, and has been, argued with great force that it is **economic and political centralization**, more than any other single factor, that has been responsible for Canada's failure to develop an independent economy in secondary manufacturing and resource extraction and refinement. Such centralization, even with a federal political system, has stifled regional economic development within and between provinces, by underwriting a centralized banking and financial system, tied formally and directly to the federal government in Ottawa.[11]

Indeed, the present metropolis-hinterland distinction exists precisely because the banking and financial system has preferred to back foreign inventors and entrepreneurs over Canadians. This probably would not have been possible had this system not had a direct pipeline to government through the Bank of Canada and the Department of Finance.[12] Our substantial level of metro-urbanization, relative to virtually any other nation,[13] has created a situation where the cities are progressively more detached from the rest of the country, even as they become focal points for the activities of foreign-owned and international businesses and financial organizations.

The point here is not to claim that this development has been a uniformly unfortunate one. I am concerned instead about the need to relate the implementation of affirmative industrial policies to the appropriate levels of social and political, as well as economic, organization required. And by "appropriate levels" I do not mean only provincial and regional jurisdictions. In response to those who believe that *any* devolution or decentralization in the direction of a more confederal Canada and away from central federalism will be regressive in its effects on public and social policy and standards, particularly for certain provinces and regions, I make the following additional proposal.

Complement what has been proposed above with the requirement that devolution to provinces and/or regions be accompanied by formal recognition of metro/urban areas as legal jurisdictions. They would then constitute a third jurisdiction, possessing exclusive as well as overlapping and shared responsibilities with the provinces and Ottawa, and would have the power independently to levy and collect taxes appropriate to these responsibilities. This would also serve to formalize already existing direct ties to Ottawa, which would continue to enforce minimum standards under any new division of responsibilities.

The idea that the places where over 80 per cent of Canadians reside should continue to function solely or mainly as "creatures" of their respective provinces is not only an anomaly, but an offence against common sense in the new supranational and global circumstances of the twenty-first century. This proposal should guarantee better representation of our large metro-urban majorities, while it acknowledges the close ties among these areas, the importance for them of non-traditional immigration to Canada and multiculturalism (like bilingualism) as official public and social policy. At the same time, it should increase the likelihood that those provincial and regional efforts at industrial policy still possible under the NAFTA and WTO will only be carried out with the support or acquiescence of the metro-urban areas affected.

CONCLUDING OBSERVATIONS

Instead of discussing specific industrial strategies or policies, I have confined myself to the task of addressing what I believe to be the issues that explain our inability to generate more affirmative industrial policies. To this end, I have been concerned with those basic realities that must be discussed and addressed not only as a prelude to specific recommendations, but in a continuous and on-going fashion.

Nevertheless, one point is clear enough. Movement along the lines I have suggested must address the present division of functions between the provinces and the centre as outlined in the British North America (BNA) Act and measure it against present-day realities and future goals. Since World War II, most of the significant growth in government and public-sector responsibilities has occurred in the provincial jurisdiction, which has led Ottawa to seek more shared jurisdictions and more "cooperative federalism."

Examples of this growth include education and training at all levels; health, medical care and hospitalization; social welfare and social administration; municipalities and metro-urban development; and the administration of justice and law enforcement generally. These developments, combined with the provincial, regional and metro-urban initiatives already cited or suggested, justify confidence that these emerging units of socio-political organization will be up to the tasks that will confront them in a more decentralized arrangement.

One major impediment to decentralization and reconfederation lies in the "convention" that has made it possible for the federal government to collect taxes for **both** jurisdictions since 1941. Quebec "opted out" of this arrangement in the 1960s, and the rest of the provinces should do the same thing.[14] It has caused serious problems, even forcing the provinces to go regularly, cap-in-hand, to Ottawa for **their own** revenues. The idea that centralizing tax collection is more efficient may be incontrovertible, but the price paid in terms of effectiveness is simply too high to allow this practice to continue. More significantly, my suggestions will reconcile the tax-collecting and debt-creating unit with the industrial policy unit to a far greater extent than has been true in the past, resulting in better synergy and institutional integration.

The collective social and economic preferences of each province, region or metro-urban area can never be fully implemented in a national system. It makes sense to study Quebec's post-1960 line of development, not only on this point, but on all others related to industrial policy that involve the constitutional division of powers. Far from treating Quebec as a pariah, we should be approaching it as an important object of study **and possible emulation**.

If we take the path I am advocating, the challenge would then lie in sustaining a residual confederal authority. Using the BNA Act as our point of departure, we would need to assess carefully the role that we wish Ottawa — or perhaps some other location of a future capital — to play. Areas that presently constitute a federal (or mainly federal) responsibility include many activities that would be absolutely essential for industrial policy making by the emerging provinces and regions. These include: banking and finance, currency, the role of the Bank of Canada (which presently forces the financial concerns of Toronto, Montreal and Ottawa on the entire country), the public debt, the

taxing power (as noted), and embassies and consulates (but not all trade lega-
tions, some of which are already provincial and regional).

Added to this are the many areas of shared jurisdiction that will have
to be renegotiated: labour, employment, immigration, customs, and energy and
resources. Note that some of these latter functions have already been taken on
by successive Quebec governments in an effort to gain (or regain) the social
and public powers that it believes are necessary for autonomy and development.
This process, perhaps begun initially for reasons of culture and language, at the
same time expressed Quebec's *economic* ambitions.

How ironic it would be if Quebec's developmental experience, consistently
reviled and belittled inside as well as outside that province, turned out to
be the very best chance for other provinces and regions to keep the Canadian
experience alive and viable in the global and international economy of the
twenty-first century!

NOTES

1. Patrick Marnham, *Fantastic Invasion: Dispatches from Contemporary Africa* (London: Jonathan Cape, 1980). This and related themes are discussed in H.T. Wilson,
   Tradition and Innovation (London: Routledge, 1984), chaps. 2 and 5–7.
2. James Laxer, *Inventing Europe: The Rise of a New World Power* (Toronto: Key
   Porter, 1991); H.T. Wilson, "The European Mind on the Eve of Full Economic
   Integration," *History of European Ideas* 13 (1992).
3. This process — supported and sustained by successive Mulroney and Campbell
   governments — is central to the line of argument and recommendations in H.T.
   Wilson, *Retreat from Governance* (Hull: Voyageur, 1989) and in Wilson, *No Ivory
   Tower* (Ottawa: Voyageur, 1999).
4. Several Science Council reports on American foreign ownership anticipated fully
   this difficulty in the late 1960s and early 1970s. See particularly: Report No. 15
   (Solandt), October 1971; Special Study No. 22 (Cordell), December 1971; and
   Special Study No. 23 (Bourgault), October 1972.
5. This could very readily be extended to include the view of the BNA Act as
   amended, along with the "entrenched" Charter of Rights, as a "constitution" above
   the enactments of legislatures, if this was desired. Our present American-style
   "Constitution" is supremely ill-fitted to a multi-ethnic, racial, linguistic and cultural
   country like Canada. Besides being symptomatic of our lack of confidence in our
   own institutions, its system of "entrenched rights" is a lightning rod, encouraging
   these groups to exaggerate their claims and demands, thereby creating more and
   more zero-sum games with significant consequences for the cost of governments,
   as well as political stability.
6. The dispute between the original peoples and Quebec has only been made to
   appear more serious than their concerns with the rest of Canada because of post-
   Meech and post-Charlottetown support in Quebec for special status, sovereignty
   association or outright independence, which would require more immediate settlement of territorial land claims etc. The present federal government's recent efforts
   are clearly a step in the right direction, but must not fail to address provincial and
   regional concerns as well as those of the original peoples.
7. Government of Ontario, *Premier's Council Reports*, beginning with volume 1 in
   1985. Note also that it is often as a response to the forced integration of discrete
   provincial and regional economies into a central structure that these latter

economies have resisted the process using internal tariffs and other barriers to interprovincial trade in the past.

8. While the "units" are usually larger in population, the process used in the European Union is not that dissimilar to the one I am recommending for Canada.

9. While some may argue that my recommendations will require, or lead to, more interprovincial trade barriers, the exact opposite is the case. Canadian history shows that it is **centralization**, not decentralization, which goes hand in hand with such barriers.

10. In *Retreat from Governance*, I tried to make this point by arguing that the essence of this retreat was the commitment of the Mulroney and Campbell governments to the wholesale destruction of legal, political, economic and financial institutions that are **of necessity** complementary to their U.S. equivalents, in the interest of preserving Canadian autonomy and independence. Note that it is these very Canadian institutions which can be expected to work **most** effectively as vehicles for implementing the more affirmative approach to industrial policy that my analysis supports. Also see H.T. Wilson, "Institutional Complementarity and Canadian Identity," *Canadian Review of American Studies*, 27(3) (1997), pp. 175–90.

11. Anthony Careless, *Initiative and Response: The Adaptation of Canadian Federalism to Regional Economic Development* (Montreal: McGill-Queens Press, 1977).

12. R.T. Naylor, *History of Canadian Business, 1867–1914*, 2 vols. (Toronto: Lorimer, 1975), and subsequent work.

13. See Stephen Hymer, "The Multinational Enterprise: Your Home is Our Home," *Canadian Dimension*, 8(6) (March-April 1972), pp. 29–35.

14. This is a matter of considerable moment that was hotly debated over a decade ago within the central agencies of the government of Ontario. On Quebec's continuing "special" arrangements following publication of the Constitutional Unity Committee (Beaudoin & Dobbie) recommendations, Kenneth McRoberts, *Misconceiving Canada: The Struggle for National Unity* (Toronto: Oxford University Press, 1997); and McRoberts, *Breaking the Impasse: English Canada and Quebec* (Toronto: Oxford University Press, 1997).

Index

A

aboriginal peoples
    Charlottetown Accord *244–245*
    Meech Lake agreement *244, 254*
    "right" to self-government *242–246*
abortion *240–242*
accountability frameworks *220–222*
assisted suicide *242*
Auto Pact, Canada–U.S. *116*

B

banks
    central bank *319*
    coercive tied selling *344*
    customer concerns *329–331, 334, 350, 354*
    holding companies *336–337, 353*
    leasing and insurance services *341–342*
    mergers *327–329, 330, 337–338*
    public accountability statements *344*
    reform proposals *343–344*
    rules on ownership *353*
    share of total financial assets *333*
    standard low-cost accounts *344*
    world's largest *328*
bilingualism *see* language policy
Bill 101 (Quebec language bill) *253*
Bretton Woods agreement *102–103, 106–108*
business cycle *41–42, 206–209, 210*

C

Caisse de dépôt et placement du Québec *79*
Canada Deposit Insurance Corporation (CDIC) *319*
Canada–U.S. Free Trade Agreement (FTA) *164*
    differences from NAFTA *167*
Canadian direct investment abroad *175*

Canadian financial services ombudsman *343*
Canadian identity *229*
Canadian International Development Agency (CIDA) *162*
Canadian Payments Association *340–341*
capital taxation *343*
Charlottetown Accord *244–245, 254–255*
Charter of Rights and Freedoms *237–238, 251*
    aboriginal peoples *244*
    women *239*
cities, increased powers needed *417*
Clarity Act *257*
commons or commodities *400–401*
communities *205–206*
competition policy *76–77*
competitiveness
    Attract Model *26–27*
    barriers to upgrading the economy *24–26*
    Canada's trade performance *11–16*
    capital-skill complementary (CSC) *28*
    concept *3–4*
    conclusions and implications *32–33*
    and economic growth *5–6*
    factor models *7–11*
    generalizable findings *29–32*
    important challenge *408–409*
    Krugman's view *4–5*
    Porter model *17, 19–24, 26*
    productivity assessment *16–17, 18, 19, 20*
    region state *28–29*
    technology districts *27–28*
concentration in Canadian industries *76–77, 78*
concentration of market power *193–194, 394–395*
concentration of wealth *72–75, 395, 396*
Confederation, regional or provincial approach *415–417*
conglomerates *73–74*

Constitution Act (1982) *250–251*
constitutional reform *249–258*
cooperative banks *343*
corporations in Canada *62–79*
    evolution of modern corporations *62–65*
    foreign investment *see* foreign
        investment in Canada
    key aspects *65–69*
credit unions *343*
crown corporations *77–79*

D

deficits and debts *53–56, 188–189, 212–215,*
    235
demographic trends *259–277*
    human resource implications *271–277*
    marketing implications *267–271*
    population projections *266–267*
    population pyramid *262–264*
    results of recent censuses *262–264*
    sources of demographic data *261–262*
Depression of the 1930s *231, 234*

E

E-government *216–217*
economic growth
    and competitiveness *5–6*
    neoclassical model *5–6*
    new growth theory *6*
    traditional theories *5*
education and the economy *369–374, 411*
    illiteracy *371–372*
    spending and performance *372–374*
employees, poor treatment of *293–294*
employment by sector *59, 60*
entrepreneurship *81–95*
    definitions *82*
    importance *82–87*
    and innovation *85–87*
    linked factors *87–90*
    policy choices *93–95*
    promotion by governments *90–93*
    statistical reporting on SMEs *344*
equalization payments *232–233*
equilibrium *37–38*
European Union (EU) *102, 122–130*
    Council of Ministers *122–123*
    Court of Justice *123*
    early growth and development *123–124*
    euro currency *128*
    European Commission *122*
    European Monetary Union (EMU) *125–*
    127
    European Parliament *123*
    problems *128–130*
    Single European Act *124*
    Treaty of Maastricht *124–125*
euthanasia *411*
exports, to Canada *157*

F

factor models *7–11*
Finance, Canadian Department of,
    proposed financial sector reforms *see*
    financial services sector reform
financial consumer agency proposed *342–343*
financial institutions *314–315*
    banks *see* banks
    four-pillar system *315–316*
    more players *338–340, 345–346*
    transformation of four pillars *316*
financial instruments *314*
financial services industry
    basic concepts *310*
    basic economic functions *308*
    central bank *319*
    competition *351*
    current environment *321*
    deposit insurance *319–320*
    financial intermediation *311–312*
    industry characteristics *310–311*
    insurance within insurance industry *320*
    market forces *355*
    new system of regulation *317–318*
    price formation *312–313*
    protection for securities investors *320*
    regulatory agencies *320*
    size *309*
    structure of the industry *315–318*
financial services sector reform *322–355*
    backlash from consumers *329–334*
    characteristics of financial sectors *324*
    consolidation *327–329, 330*
    consumer access *342–343*
    demand and supply *331–332*
    discrimination *349–350*
    Dobson's recommendations *351–354*
    Finance Department proposals *334–345*
    focus on the consumer *338–342, 350*
    foreign ownership *352*
    globalization and financial services *326*
    holding companies *336–337*
    implications of Finance Department
        proposals *345–351*
    long-term growth *350*
    merger review process *337–338, 352*
    ownership rules *335–336*
    policy objectives *323*
    political atmosphere *351–352*
    regulatory improvements *323, 344–345,*
    352–354
    repositioning *332–334*
    scale *346–349*
    technological innovation *325*
fiscal policy *53–56, 409–410*
foreign direct investment *168–175*
    Canada's foreign direct
        investment flows *173–175*
    and growth *172*

Multilateral Agreement on Investment
(MAI) *172–173*
theories *168–169*
and trade *171*
trends *169–170*
see also subsidiary companies, changes
foreign investment in Canada
foreign ownership today *69–72, 199–200*
National Policy *67–69*
Free Trade Zones *395–396*

G

General Agreement on Tariffs and
Trade (GATT) *103, 112–113, 158, 159–161*
Uruguay Round *158–159, 160–161*
global citizens' movement *390–392*
globalization
effect on national governments *178, 190,
217–218, 391*
and financial services sector *326*
global economy *394–395, 398–399*
global monoculture *395*
international cooperation needed *401–402*
government in Canada, changing role *211–217*
accountability frameworks *220–222*
E-government *216–217*
future directions *222–223*
globalization *217–218*
New Zealand model *218–220*
policy areas *209*
government decision-making *215–216, 223–228*
government intervention in economy *179, 230*
Japan *131–132, 138–140*
National Policy *66–69*
public economics *see* public economics
government policy, *see various topics*
(e.g. immigration; technology)
government spending *211–216*
see also deficits and debts
Gross National Product (GNP) *39–43*
Group of Eight (G8) *162*

H

Harper, Elijah *242, 243, 244, 254*
health care *410*
Heckscher-Ohlin model of trade *145–146*

I

illiteracy and economic effects *371–372*
immigration to Canada
figures *266–267*
policy *246–249*
industrial strategy
the 1990s *188–191*
Canada, 1867–1980! *186–188*
consultation processes *182–184*

essential features *180–182*
the global market place *178, 191–192*
moving into the 21st century *192–198*
new strategies required *179–180*
objections to *184–186*
strategies for the 21st century *198–200*
Industry Canada *375–376*
inequality *393, 395, 396*
inflation *49–51*
innovation
and entrepreneurship *85–87*
and industrial growth *360–362*
international competition *383–384*
insurers
consumer protection *320*
five largest *329*
intergenerational conflict, potential *407–408*
International Monetary Fund (IMF) *108–111*

J

Japan *130–140*
government intervention in
economy *131–132, 138–140*
political reform *137–138*
rebuilding of postwar economy *130–134*
recent economic developments *134–140*

K

Keynesian macroeconomic policy *44–45*
knowledge gap *395*
Korean War *131*
Kosovo conflict *105–106*
Krugman, Paul *4–5*

L

language policy *251–253*
Bill 101 (Quebec language bill) *253*
Leontief Paradox *148*
Lévesque, René *251*
Liberal "monopoly" in Ottawa *406–407*

M

Maastricht Treaty *124–125*
MacKay Task Force *331, 341, 344–345, 353*
macroeconomics
aggregates *35–36*
circular flow model *37*
distinguished from microeconomics *35*
equilibrium *37–38*
fiscal policy *53–56*
four sectors *36*
future *56–57*
injections and leakages *43–45*
main questions *34–35*
markets *37*
monetary policy *see* monetary policy
money: demand and supply *47–48*
multiplier *45, 46*

national accounts *39–43*
    paradox of thrift *45–46*
medicare *408, 410*
Meech Lake agreement *242, 244, 253–254*
mercantilism *144–145*
mergers, of banks *327–329, 330*
microeconomics *35*
monetary policy *48–53*
    exchange rate *51–53*
    and inflation *49–51*
    and the interest rate *48–49*
Morgentaler, Dr. Henry *240*
Mulroney, Brian *253*
multiculturalism *246–249*
Multilateral Agreement on Investment
    (MAI) *172–173, 391–392*
multinational enterprises
    trade theory *150–151*
    see also transnational corporations

N
national accounts *39–43*
National Citizens' Coalition *238*
National Policy *66–69, 230*
native peoples *see* aboriginal rights
"New National Policy" *231–232, 234–235*
New World Order *101–140*
    European Union *see* European Union
    (EU)
    international arrangements *101–122*
    Japan *see* Japan
New Zealand model *218–220*
North American Free Trade
    Agreement (NAFTA) *164–167, 414*
    differences from FTA *167*
    dispute resolution mechanism *166–167*
    labour mobility *166*
    liberalization of investment *167*
    rules of origin *166*
    tariff reduction *166*
North Atlantic Treaty Organization
    (NATO) *102, 103–106*
Nunavut *245, 246*

P
Parti Québécois *255–256*
population pyramid *262–264*
poverty *393*
"protected society" *233–236*
provincial autonomy *414–419*
public economics *206–209*
    externalities *207–208*
    failure of competition *207*
    incomplete markets *208*
    information failures *208–209*
    macroeconomic disequilibrium *209*
    public goods *207*
public sector *see* headings starting with
    "government"
public spending *see* deficits and debts

Q
Quebec *249–258, 415*
    1995 referendum *255*
    future in Canada *257–258*
    "regional nationalism" view *415, 418,*
    419
    separation risk *404–406*
Quiet Revolution *250*

R
race relations *248*
    see also multiculturalism
referendum 1995 (Quebec) *255*
refugee issue *248–249*
regional development programs *233*
"regional nationalism" view *414–419*
research consortia *376–378*
research and development (R & D) *363–*
    365, 369, 370
    multiplier effect *367*
Ricardian model of trade *145*
Rodriguez, Sue *242*

S
science advisory councils *376*
sectors in Canada's economy *58–61*
    service sector growth *59–61*
securities firms
    consumer protection *320*
    five largest *329*
SMEs *see* entrepreneurship
social concerns shown in poll *394*
social security system *233–236*
    cuts to *393*
    three principles *409*
    and World Trade Organization (WTO)
    397–398
"staple thesis" *187–188, 190, 198, 200*
    eclipsed by transnationals *194–198*
statistical reporting on SMEs *344*
Steering Group on Prosperity *191–192*
structural changes to Confederation
    suggested *414–419*
subsidiary companies, changes *194–195,*
    196–198
Supreme Court of Canada *238*
    aboriginal claims *244*
    abortion *240–241*
    and Charter of Rights and
    Freedoms *238*
    Quebec's right to independence *256–257*

T
tariffs *66–67, 68*
    see also National Policy
tax system *190, 232, 410, 418*
technological change theories of trade *146–*
    147

technology *357–385*
  Canada's weak position *358–359, 363–366, 384–385*
  Canadian organization and policy *362–366*
  commercialization *366–367, 368–369, 377*
  conclusions *383–385*
  and financial markets *379–380, 381*
  and government policy *367–369, 374–379*
  innovation and industrial growth *360–362*
  key challenges *380–383*
  role of education *369–374*
  see also Industry Canada; research consortia; science advisory councils
trade
  Canada's international trade *152–156*
  Canada's trade performance *11–16*
  foreign direct investment *see* foreign direct investment
  GATT *see* General Agreement on Tariffs and Trade (GATT)
  growth in world trade *152, 153*
  international agreements *see* trading blocs
  international institutions *156–162*
  toward a new international system *399–400*
  world trade flows *153*
  World Trade Organization (WTO) *158–162*
trade theory *144–152*
  economies of scale *147*
  factor price equalization *148–149*
  free-trade detectors *149*
  Heckscher-Ohlin model *145–146*
  Leontief Paradox *148*
  location theory and trade *147–148*
  mercantilism *144–145*
  Ricardian model *145*
  role of multinational enterprises *150–151*
  strategic trade theory *151–152*
  technological change *146–147*
trading blocs *162–168, 403, 408*
  Canada–U.S. Free Trade Agreement (FTA) *164*

Free Trade Area of the Americas (FTAA) *168*
North American Free Trade Agreement (NAFTA) *see* North American Free Trade Agreement (NAFTA)
transnational corporations
  citizen protest against *389–390*
  growth in power *390–391, 394–395*
  and national economic policies *194–198*
Trudeau, Pierre *250, 252*

U
unions *281–305*
  benefits of membership *294–301*
  in Canada *285–289*
  continuing need for *289–294*
  and the economy *301–304*
  future *282–285*
  influence in 20th century *282*
United Nations *117–122*
  creation *102*
  Human Development Report *398–399*
  International Criminal Court *119*
  military involvement *117–118, 120–121*
  Millennium Assembly *119–120*
  U.S. complaints *118*

V, W
Vietnam War *104*
wage stagnation *290–291*
welfare state *233–236*
women's rights *238–242*
workplace changes *291–293*
World Bank *109–110, 111–112*
World Trade Organization (WTO) *114–117, 158–162*
  and culture *398*
  and food *397*
  protest at Seattle (1999) *389–390, 396*
  and social security *397–398*
  and water *397*

About the Contributors

MAUDE BARLOW is the National Volunteer Chairperson of The Council of Canadians, a Director with the International Forum on Globalization and the best-selling author of 11 books. For more information on The Council: call 1-800-387-7177, or 613-233-2773; fax 613-233-6776; write to 502-151 Slater Street, Ottawa, ON. K1P 5H3; or visit the Web site: <http://www.canadians.org>.

DAVID BARROWS is an Adjunct Professor and Associate Director of the Master of Public Administration program at the Schulich School of Business at York University. He is also a vice-president of the Ginsberg Organization, an international consulting firm. For 20 years Professor Barrows was a senior executive in the Ontario Public Service. He has also served on a number of volunteer boards and has published widely in the fields of public policy and economics.

DONALD J.S. BREAN is Professor of Finance and Economics in the Faculty of Management, University of Toronto and an associate of The Centre for International Studies. Professor Brean has published extensively on international finance and investment, taxation, industrial organization and economic policy.

Professor Brean holds graduate degrees from the University of Toronto and The London School of Economics. He is a member of The International Panel of Tax Experts of the International Monetary Fund. He has advised numerous international agencies and governments, including the European Community, The United Nations Development Program, The World Bank, The IMF, USAID and, in Canada, the Department of Finance, the Department of Energy, Mines and Resources and the Treasury Board.

JOHN A. COTSOMITIS is an economist with the Ministry of Economic Development and Trade, Province of Ontario. He holds an MBA from McGill University and is a former research assistant with the Centre for Research in Technological and Industrial Development, University of Quebec at Montreal.

JOHN H.G. CRISPO is Professor of Political Economy at the Faculty of Management, University of Toronto. He completed his BCom at University of Toronto in 1956 and his PhD (Industrial Economics) at Massachusetts Institute of Technology in 1960. He has lectured in many institutions in Canada and abroad and has served on, and consulted for, governmental committees and organizations in the areas of labour relations and economic policy.

Author of many publications, including, most recently, *Can Canada Compete?* (Toronto: Hemlock Press, 1990), Dr. Crispo has also written articles appearing in numerous journals.

WENDY DOBSON is Director of the Institute for International Business, Joseph L. Rotman School of Management, University of Toronto; a former president of the C.D. Howe Institute; and former associate deputy minister of finance in Ottawa. She is co-author of *Financial Services Liberalization in the WTO*, published in 1998 by the Institute for International Economics in Washington, DC. She is also a director of a Canadian bank.

DAVID K. FOOT, Professor of Economics at the University of Toronto, is co-author of the best-selling book *Boom, Bust & Echo: How to Profit from the Coming Demographic Shift* (with Daniel Stoffman, Macfarlane Walter & Ross, 1996). This book reflects his current research interests, which lie in the numerous interrelationships between economics and demographics, and in the resulting implications for both private and public policies, especially in the Canadian context.

Following his undergraduate degree in Australia, Professor Foot completed his doctorate in economics from Harvard University. He has prepared research for and submissions to many provincial and federal government commissions and numerous consulting and conference assignments for both public and private organizations.

He is a two-time recipient (in 1983 and 1992) of the University of Toronto undergraduate teaching award, and in 1992 received one of the nationwide 3M Awards for Teaching Excellence administered by the Society for Teaching and Learning in Higher Education.

JAMES M. GILLIES is Professor Emeritus of Policy and Director of the Max Bell Business Government Studies Programme in the Schulich School of Business at York University. He established the Faculty of Administrative Studies (now the Schulich School of Business) at York University in 1965, where he served as Dean and Vice-President. In 1972, he was elected a Member of Parliament for the constituency of Don Valley in Toronto. In 1974, he was re-elected, but in 1978, he announced that he would not run again. In the election of 1979, he campaigned at the national level with Mr. Clark, and upon formation of the Clark government, Dr. Gillies was appointed senior policy adviser to the prime minister. In that capacity, he worked on the development of energy and economic policy and attended the Tokyo Summit as chief adviser to the prime minister. In July 1980 Dr. Gillies returned to York University.

Dr. Gillies is author of several books, including the national best-seller *Where Business Fails* and *Facing Reality: Consultation, Consensus and Making Economic Policy for the 21st Century*. Dr. Gillies has also written a column for *The Toronto Daily Star* and is currently Executive Editor of *Inside Guide: The Best in Business*, to which he also contributes a regular column. Dr. Gillies's most recent book is entitled *Power, Morality and Performance in the Modern Corporation: The Role of the Board of Directors.*

ED HOOVEN holds a PhD in Sociology and has taught at York University since 1975. He has written on topics as varied as global political economy and political correctness. He was a candidate for Toronto City Council in the 1997 municipal elections.

EDUARDO M.V. JASSON is currently a PhD candidate at York University's Schulich School of Business in Toronto, Canada. Born in Argentina, he has Industrial Engineer and Naval Engineer degrees from Instituto Technologico de Buenos Aires, Argentina. He also has an MBA degree from IDEA's Business School, Argentina, where he taught International Business Strategy and Strategic Management and Public Policy. In the private sector, he has served as Corporate Strategic Planning Manager at Group Moreno, an international agribusiness firm. His current academic research focuses on issues relating to leading edge innovation processes, strategic management development, and international business strategy.

GIL McGOWAN is Director of Communications for the Alberta Federation of Labour. The AFL is Alberta's largest labour organization, representing more than 117,000 unionized workers across the province. Gil is the author of several books on unions and the Alberta economy, including *Crumbs From the Table: A Re-evaluation of the So-called "Alberta Advantage"* (1997), and *Missing Out on the Boom: A Report Card on Jobs and Economic Security in Alberta* (1998). In addition to his work with the AFL, Gil is also communications coordinator for Friends of Medicare, the public interest group that recently led the fight against the Klein government's controversial private health care law, Bill 11.

CHARLES J. McMILLAN is Professor of International Business at the Schulich School of Business at York University, Toronto, Canada. He is the author of eight books and monographs, including *The Japanese Industrial System*, now available in English, Japanese, Malaysian and Russian editions. His monograph, *Building Blocks or Trade Blocs: NAFTA, Japan and the New World Order*, was published by the Canada–Japan Trade Council (Ottawa, 1994).

Active in public affairs, Dr. McMillan has served as Senior Policy Advisor to the prime minister of Canada, consultant to numerous national and international companies and agencies, and director on such bodies as the National Ballet School of Canada, Nova Scotia's Council of Applied Science and Technology, the Asia Pacific Foundation and the Canadian Children's Foundation. His report, *Standing Up to the Future: The Maritime Provinces in the 1990s*, has become the blueprint for economic cooperation and development in Atlantic Canada. In 1991, he produced the Economic Development Plan for the Republic of Kyrgyzstan, a former Soviet Republic in Central Asia, and serves as Founding Dean for the Bishkek International School of Management and Business. In 1993, he was appointed as Special Advisor to Goskominvest, the Kyrgyz State Commission on Foreign Investments and Economic Assistance.

In the private sector, his directorships include Chairman of the Midas Group and director of P.E.I. Trade Enterprises Inc., Nu-Stadia Inc. and

Yamaichi International (Canada) Limited, which is one of Japan's largest investment banks.

JOHN SAYWELL is University Professor and Professor of History at York University. A graduate of the University of British Columbia and Harvard in History and Government, he has taught at the University of Toronto, University of California at Berkeley and York University, where he has been since joining the university as Dean of Arts and Science in 1963. Author of many books and articles on history, politics and law, Professor Saywell also worked in economic development in Kenya for much of the 1970s, and spent two years in Japan attached to the Canadian embassy. He has wide experience in television as a host/narrator and as an author of documentaries and plays, and was Tokyo correspondent for CTV News.

JAMES (JIM) TIESSEN teaches international business at the Michael G. DeGroote School of Business, McMaster University, Hamilton Ontario. He has published research on small and medium enterprise (SME) internationalization, international joint ventures and Japanese business. He is now conducting work on how SMEs use the Internet to sell abroad. He studied at York (PhD in Administrative Studies), Guelph (M.Sc. Agricultural Economics) and Alberta (B.Sc.). Between degrees Jim lived in Japan and spent four years with a Japanese organization.

TOM WESSON is Assistant Professor of Strategic Management at the Schulich School of Business at York University. Professor Wesson received his Bachelor of Commerce from Queen's University and his MBA and PhD in Business Economics from Harvard University. His research focuses on issues of international business strategy and government policies towards business.

H.T. WILSON received his AB (Honours) in government from Tufts University in 1962, his MA in political science from Rutgers University in 1964 and his PhD in political science and constitutional law, also from Rutgers University, in 1968. He joined the Faculty of Administrative Studies (now Schulich School of Business) of York University, Toronto in 1967 and was cross-appointed to Osgoode Hall in 1969. His professional and scholarly interests are focused on critical social and political theory, the history of social, economic and political thought, public policy and administrative processes, higher education policy and scientific and technological innovation. He has taught at universities in the United Kingdom, Germany, the Netherlands, Sweden, Japan, Australia, Hong Kong and the United States. In addition to having published 12 books and monographs, and over 200 articles and essays, as well as having delivered 800 lectures, talks and addresses to various groups, he has been an advisor to a major political party and is, at present, a consultant in an area he has developed which he calls "political management," the title of one of his books.